TRINITY

A HISTORY OF THE WAKEFIELD RUGBY LEAGUE FOOTBALL CLUB 1872 - 2013

Mike Rylance

LEAGUE PUBLICATIONS LTD

League Publications Ltd
Wellington House
Briggate
Brighouse HD6 1DN
England

First published in Great Britain in 2013
by League Publications Ltd

www.totalrl.com

© Mike Rylance 2013

All rights reserved. No part of this book may be reproduced or transmitted in any form or by any means, electronic or mechanical, including photocopying, recording or by any information storage and retrieval system, without prior permission in writing from the publisher.

A CIP catalogue record for this book is available
from the British Library

ISBN: 978-1-901347-28-9

Designed and Typeset by League Publications Limited
Printed by Charlesworth Press, Wakefield

To the memory of Ron Rylance

CONTENTS

Preface	7
One – Cup-fighting Men: 1872-79	9
Two – A Glimpse of Professionalism: 1879-85	17
Three – A Time of Upheaval: 1885-92	27
Four – Towards the Split: 1892-95	39
Five – From Union to League: 1895-1905	45
Six – The Cup, Kiwis and Kangaroos: 1905-14	53
Seven – The Call to Arms: 1914-19	65
Eight – From Northern Union to Rugby League: 1919-27	69
Nine – Star Players but Scant Success: 1927-34	79
Ten – Cup-Winners in the Making: 1934-45	89
Eleven – Cup-winners once more: 1945-51	99
Twelve – A Time of Reconstruction: 1951-57	115
Thirteen – The Great Team Comes Together: 1957-59	125
Fourteen – The Challenge Cup Returns to Belle Vue: 1959-63	131
Fifteen – New Challenges: 1963-67	155
Sixteen – A Second Wave of Success: 1967-70	167
Seventeen – Towards the Centenary and beyond: 1970-75	181
Eighteen – Back to Wembley: 1975-80	195
Nineteen – A Second Descent into the Second Division: 1980-85	211
Twenty – Out of the Gloom: 1985-90	227
Twenty-one – Survival against the odds: 1990-95	241
Twenty-two – Into the Super League Era: 1995-98	257
Twenty-three – Big Ambitions: 1999-2003	267
Twenty-four – The Great Escape: 2004-07	281
Twenty-five – On the Brink: 2008-13	293
Afterword	305
Sources	306
Notes	306
Acknowledgements	308
Records	309

Preface

When the Wakefield Trinity team arrived back at Westgate Station on May 16, 1960 bearing the Rugby League Challenge Cup they had won by a record score two days earlier, Derek Turner and his men deepened the bond between the club and its public. Wakefield had never seen anything like it as the Cup winners returned to the cheers of a wildly enthusiastic crowd estimated at 40,000. Police linked arms to hold back the surge of supporters eager to catch sight of the players as they proceeded from the station to the Town Hall. The brass band, leading the way, trumpeted their arrival. Fans waved their flags, some climbing lamp-posts for a better view. Earlier the Chief Constable himself had walked the route of the procession to assess what safety measures should be taken. It was a time of unequalled excitement. Even the Queen, on her first visit to the Cup final, had been impressed, telling the chairman of the Rugby League Council that she thought rugby league was the best game she had seen on television.

Two more successful visits to Wembley in the next three years would confirm Trinity's reputation as cup-fighters and earn them a place in the history of rugby league. More than half a century later, the memory of the glorious sixties lives on in the minds of the team's older supporters, some of whom might not even follow the game any longer, but are proud to associate themselves with the achievements which put club and city in the national spotlight.

Those homecoming celebrations of May 1960 echoed the welcome which greeted the victorious Wakefield Trinity team of 1946 who lifted the Cup in the first post-war final. On that occasion, it was said that never in living memory had Wakefield seen such a spontaneous outpouring of enthusiasm, as the local heroes, carried on a red and blue decorated brewery wagon, followed the same route to the civic reception, cheered all the way by what seemed the entire population. They were heralded by the brass band, playing Handel's 'See the Conquering Hero Comes', greeted by the mayor, and toasted by dignitaries. Team captain Billy Stott called the day of the Cup final the greatest in his life. Club chairman Wilf Jackson said that the uproarious reception given by the townspeople of Wakefield was one of the most wonderful sights he had ever seen.

In pre-Wembley days, Trinity's Cup-winning team of 1909 returned in a decorated tramcar from Headingley, making their way first to the Alexandra Hotel, opposite their Belle Vue ground, where a formal reception was held, before touring the town in a charabanc, parading the trophy to the sound of the band playing Handel's famous oratorio. The tramcar which had brought the triumphant team back to Wakefield was festooned with bunting, union jacks and banners, one of which read 'It's 22 years sin' [since]'. It referred to the last time Wakefield Trinity had won the Yorkshire Challenge Cup in the era before the Northern Union broke away, and harked back to the times when, under Rugby Football Union rules, the club was practically expected to bring home honours.

That was the period when Trinity first earned their formidable reputation as a Cup team, a tradition that was revived in the immediate post-war period and above all in the 1960s. Between the 1877-78 season, when the Yorkshire Cup was first played for, and 1891, when they were finalists for the last time, Wakefield Trinity appeared in nine finals, winning four of them.

Trinity's first homecoming from their Yorkshire Cup victory, in 1879, set the pattern which would be followed for a century. Flags were put out, the bells of the Parish Church (now the Cathedral) were rung, and a great crowd of people rushed to Kirkgate station to greet the players who arrived back by special train from Halifax, where the final had been held. Led by the Parish Church Young Men's Association band, who struck up the tune that would later become familiar, the procession moved through the cheering throng towards the Woolpacks Hotel at the top of Westgate, where 'an excellent tea' had been prepared for them. In only six full seasons, Trinity had risen to become one of the top teams in Yorkshire, the strongest footballing county in England.

Rugby league in general and Wakefield Trinity in particular form part of the heritage of Wakefield and its surrounding area. The game and the club are also part of my personal inheritance. My mother's father, Joe Reyner, was, for some thirty years, secretary of Wakefield and District Amateur Rugby League. My father, Ron Rylance, was a member of that team which brought the Challenge Cup home in 1946 and left his mark on the club as a player and, later, as a committee member. It is to his memory that this book is dedicated.

Displaying the Challenge Cup they had won against Wigan, the players make their way from Westgate Station to a civic reception at the Town Hall, May 1946

One – Cup-fighting Men: 1872-79

What became Wakefield's greatest sporting institution, by a long way, owed its existence to the Young Men's Society of Holy Trinity Church, which was situated on George Street, between Kirkgate and Thornhill Gate, and was demolished in the 1950s. In the late Victorian era, churches often provided a range of educational activities at evening classes, including modern languages and sciences, as well as the opportunity to join sports teams. The Holy Trinity Young Men's Society had been active for six years when it was proposed to add a rugby football section to the already existing cricket and athletics clubs. It was set up in an era when the trend known as muscular Christianity was much in vogue, encouraging sport, and team sports in particular, as being important for physical and moral well-being. At the same time, rugby football had spread from Rugby School and other public schools which had taken it up. Former pupils of those establishments, returning to their home towns and cities, started up teams and though the earliest clubs, dating from the 1860s, tended to be socially exclusive, the sport soon became more widely popular. The Rugby Football Union, founded in 1871, was completely dominated by clubs from the south, but during the same decade an explosion of interest in the game resulted in teams being formed throughout Yorkshire, Lancashire and elsewhere. The majority of the 22 clubs which formed the Northern Union in 1895 were established during this period.

By the time the rugby section at Holy Trinity was formed, there was one other rugby club in the town, and that club was known simply as Wakefield, playing matches at Mount Pleasant, Eastmoor, which was also the home of Wakefield Cricket Club at the time. The Holy Trinity club, which quickly became known as Wakefield Trinity, is generally believed to have been established in February 1873, when their first full match was played. It is now clear that the club was actually formed before then, late in 1872, with John Henry Dixon, a local solicitor and churchwarden, a prime mover. Dixon had started the Young Men's Society as a means of keeping the sixteen and seventeen year olds interested in church activities. It was he also who took a warehouse behind the parsonage and converted it into a room for the Young Men's Society which later became the club room. [1]

There is ample evidence to show that the Trinity club came into being in November-December 1872. [2] A report of the Holy Trinity Young Men's Society annual meeting, in June, 1873, confirmed that 'during last winter session a football club was added under the auspices of the society…' [3] More precisely, at the annual distribution of prizes of the Society in November 1872, the chairman reported: 'The Society has held its athletic sports in each of the five years of its existence… A cricket club has flourished in the Society from its commencement… An effort is just now being made to establish a football club.'[4] In a newspaper article which appeared thirty years later, but which was based on information provided by four members from the first days of the club, including TO Bennett and JA Grace, it is stated that the football club branched from the Young Men's Society in December 1872. [5]

What may be regarded as the Trinity club's first match, which seems to have been previously overlooked, took place on Boxing Day, 1872. [6] At that stage the Young Men's Society was unable to field a complete 15-a-side team and had to rely on the opposition to make up the numbers. The opponents were Wakefield, who themselves had played their first match just three weeks earlier, losing to Leeds Grammar School on Woodhouse Moor.[7] The Trinity team lost to Wakefield by three goals and four touchdowns to none. [8]

The first match in which Trinity fielded a full side of their own club members took place on Saturday, 8 February 1873, against the Wakefield club again on their Mount Pleasant ground, off Stanley Road and Park Lodge Lane. It is this game from which the founding date of the club has previously been taken. Trinity lost by three touchdowns to one, which was made by Edmund Spink, with Bennett and Grace also showing up well. It might be more accurate to describe the result as a losing draw, since a touchdown was not a try, but a defensive action when a team touched down behind their own goal line. [9]

The two clubs met again six weeks later, on Saturday, 22 March 1873, once more on the Wakefield club's ground, watched by a large number of spectators. Trinity had clearly made progress, winning a closely contested game by one goal and two touchdowns to one goal and one touchdown, according to one account. However, in the absence of a referee, which was quite normal for the time, Wakefield disputed the score and walked off. Another published report gave a result in favour of Wakefield.

The Wakefield club was seen as socially superior to Trinity. Players of both clubs in 1873 were mainly in their late teens or early twenties. Trinity's team members included a number of clerks and skilled manual workers; a stonemason and a joiner among them. Several of Wakefield's players also worked as clerks but among them were the sons of a mill-owner, a newspaper proprietor, a clergyman, a coroner and a brewery owner. The son of the vicar of Holy Trinity, a Cambridge undergraduate, played not for his father's church side but for Wakefield.

Trinity have always been thought to have played their first matches at Heath Common, though there are no contemporary reports of matches having taken place there. In that first season of 1872-3, the only recorded games that Trinity took part in were against Wakefield at Mount Pleasant, though it is certain that members of the Young Men's Society played games among themselves on the common, as the account of the annual meeting confirms: 'The scene of practice was Heath Common, a place in every respect adapted for this healthful game.' [10]

Bennett and Grace confirmed that 'in the winter of 1872 the operations of the club were confined to Saturday afternoon practices on Heath Common. A year later a few matches were played there, the goal posts being proudly carried to the Common and affectionately taken care of by Arthur Hayley.' [11] Hayley lived at Beech Lawn in the village and it is likely that he and his team-mates played on land close to the King's Arms, where cricket, as well as knur and spell, also took place.

It is surprising, though, that practices were not held in the Ings, which was much closer to the church and where the Young Men's Society played cricket on a ground which they owned and held athletics meetings there, although the ground in the low-lying Ings may have become unsuitable in the winter months.

Before football, in one form or another, made its appearance, sport as we know it today hardly existed in autumn and winter. The few sporting activities available were horse-racing, running, pigeon- and sparrow-shooting and knur and spell, a game which involved tossing a small ball into the air and hitting it as far as possible with a flat-ended stick. Few people participated actively. The main attraction of these sports was as a vehicle for gambling. But for half of the year team sports were unheard of. No wonder then that rugby football, like association football elsewhere, began to arouse a good deal of interest among the citizens of Wakefield, as in other industrial towns and cities. It became a potent distraction from their workaday lives.

A century and a half earlier, Daniel Defoe, in his *Tour through the Whole Island of Great Britain*, described Wakefield as 'a clean, large, well-built town, very populous and very rich', its wealth based on the woollen clothing trade, much like its neighbours, Bradford, Leeds, Halifax and Huddersfield. By the time the Wakefield-born writer, George Gissing, wrote a thinly-veiled description of his birthplace in his novel, *A Life's Morning*, first published in 1888, the town had undergone considerable change.

Writing of a district named Banbrigg [clearly modelled on the Agbrigg-Belle Vue area], Gissing wrote: 'At no season, and under no advantage of sky, was Banbrigg a delectable abode. Though within easy reach of country which was not without rural aspects, it was marked too unmistakably with the squalor of a manufacturing district. Its existence impressed one as casual; it was a mere bit of Dunfield [Wakefield] got away from the main mass, and having brought its dirt with it. The stretch of road between it and the bridge by which the river was crossed into

Dunfield had in its long, hard ugliness something dispiriting. Though hedges bordered it here and there, they were stunted and grimed; though fields were seen on this side and on that, the grass had absorbed too much mill-smoke to exhibit wholesome verdure … The land was blighted by the curse of what we name – using a word as ugly as the thing it represents – industrialism.'

It may be that Gissing – whose siblings, incidentally, were all baptised at Holy Trinity – exaggerated the griminess to suit the purpose of his novel, one of themes of which is the opposition of North and South.

But in the classified news sections of the local papers, where Trinity's first reports appeared, the various items give an aperçu of the hardships of the period. Alongside the accounts of church meetings and horticultural societies sit stories of petty crime and drunkenness, both male and female, suicides, child cruelty and domestic arguments, all testimony to the difficult conditions in which many people lived.

Reports of Trinity's fixtures for the 1873-4 season are scant, but it is clear that by the end of January 1874 they were playing home matches in the middle of Wakefield. The ground was known as the Manor Field, off Vicarage Street and close to the Borough Market. The site is also described as 'in the fields, Teall Street' [12] and now lies, more or less, beneath the Trinity Walk shopping centre, whose name is more of a coincidence than an acknowledgement of the historical aspect of the place. But on March 7, 1874, several hundred spectators turned up for the match against Huddersfield, one of Yorkshire's senior teams.

The following season, the Wakefield club moved to their new ground at the nearby Wakefield Cricket Club, College Grove and played their first match there on October 31, 1874. From the start, both the Wakefield club and Wakefield Trinity had always played with a fifteen-man team, which was standard practice, although twenty had been the norm at the early stage of the game's development until officially reduced by the RFU in 1875. A team comprised nine forwards, two half backs, three three-quarters and a full back (usually known simply as a 'back'). The play consisted of scrummaging, dribbling and kicking, but virtually no passing. A goal – either a conversion of a try or a drop goal - was the all-important score. One goal was superior to any number of tries. Touchdowns are also sometimes recorded in early match reports but were not a synonym for a try, referring instead to when a team was forced to make the ball dead behind their own goal line. Referees were not yet a necessity and would not become so until 1885. The two captains would make decisions between them, with long disputes often interrupting the match if they could not agree. Later on, each team provided an umpire. By modern standards, the conditions in which matches were played seem chaotic. The future Trinity captain, Barron Kilner, gave an example: 'In those "dark ages" the laws of football were not as well known by some of the leading players as they ought to be. On October 26, 1877, we were playing Halifax at Wakefield. A few minutes before the end of a very hot match, the ball was forced across our line. Arthur Hayley was in the act of picking it up when one of the spectators – he must, I think, have come from Halifax – deliberately rushed up and kicked it from under his hands. It went into the hands of Jimmy Dodd [of Halifax], who claimed a try… We, of course, objected. It was the first and last occasion within my recollection on which a try was claimed from a spectator's kick.' [13]

By the end of their second full season of 1874-5, playing sixteen matches in all against various teams from Leeds and Bradford, as well as Halifax, Harrogate, Barnsley and Doncaster, Trinity had not lost a single match. They were dedicated too, these early players. The Boxing Day match at Halifax was played on a pitch reported as standing three feet deep in snow, but was 'keenly contested throughout'[14] . Such was the enthusiasm for the game that a second XV had also been raised. In a small cash note-book, the earliest known record of the club's activities, it was recorded: 'The interest taken in the club by the public of Wakefield is something extraordinary.'[15] No charge for admission to matches had yet been introduced, though a collection took place. With members' subscriptions, the cash balance at the end of the season amounted to 31 shillings. In the same newspaper article in which Bennett and Grace recalled the club's earliest days, it is noted that a photograph dated 1874 shows the players wearing jerseys with blue vertical

The earliest known photograph of a Wakefield Trinity team, wearing their original colours of black and blue hoops. The team members are believed to be: *Top row*: W Moody (at back); TB Waite (?), D Mackenzie, Rufus Ward, W Bell, G Powell. *Middle row*: A Hayley, W Baldwin, HB Pickersgill, I Redfearn, TS Whitehead, JW Atkinson, Ellis, TO Bennett, J Whitehead, J Milnes, JA Grace, Poppleton, F Gascoigne, Amos Shires, W Abell. *Bottom row*: J Verity, N Atkinson, EJ Spink, Fogg. The picture dates from 1875.

[sic] stripes, but since the design was a common one it was soon replaced with the famous red and blue bars. [16]

During the following season of 1875-6, the club played outside the county for the first time. Rochdale Hornets were their first Lancashire opponents and had the distinction of scoring the only goal against Trinity in three seasons. Just one match was lost and the club's funds were reported to be in a very flourishing state. The team had 'a strong forward team combined with a safe game by the backs', according to the Manchester-based *Athletic News*, which also gave an assessment of several individual players. 'H Hayley (back) is quite as good as anything we have in Lancashire. He is only young (seventeen, we believe), but possesses a great facility for drop kicking and keeps cool and self-possessed the whole of the game…. A Hayley, his brother, is almost as good … He is a fine drop kick[er], can tackle well, and does not lose his head when hard pressed. TO Bennett (the captain), three-quarter back, is an effective player and strong runner, whilst RA Ward, as half back, is a good runner, quick picker up of the ball and a thorough stayer …' [17]

At the start of the 1877-8 season, Trinity moved out of the centre of Wakefield to Belle Vue, an expanding suburb whose population increased tenfold in the 1870s as housing went up on land which had previously been open fields. Their new ground was situated on the other side of Doncaster Road to the present stadium, and was bounded by Elm Tree Street and Clarion Street. Close to the Alexandra Hotel, which was later used for changing, the pitch was described as adjoining Mr Hepworth's organ manufactory,[18] which, known as Fern Villa, was located at the angle of the two streets. This new ground was apparently known locally as Skinner's Fields, and was part of a short cut from Chantry bridge to Heath Common. [19]

The 1877-8 season was significant for other reasons. By now, numerous football clubs had sprung up in and around Wakefield. Some, like Trinity, were formed from a church, such as Wakefield Zion or Wakefield Unitarians. Some were works teams such as Calder Soap Works or RH Barker & Co, while others represented districts or villages, like Thornes or Westgate End. But there was no doubting the supremacy of Trinity. Leading players from the Wakefield club switched allegiance to their rivals, including Barron Kilner, who was to become a key figure in Trinity's future. Kilner, who had learned the game while working in London, was the head of a glass bottle manufacturing company, originally based at Thornhill Lees and famous for inventing Kilner jars.

The move by such players coincided with a new chapter in the history of the club, which, though already counting between sixty and seventy playing members,[20] started to attract new players from well beyond the Holy Trinity congregation. 'Perhaps the town club [Wakefield] may be considered to have rather more of the aristocratic element about it than its neighbour the Trinity,' noted *Athletic World* in a review of Yorkshire clubs, 'but the latter have certainly the finest lot of forwards of any club in the county of the broad acres.' [21]

By far the most momentous event of 1877 was the introduction of the Yorkshire Challenge Cup, whose importance in the history of rugby football and that of Wakefield Trinity was soon to unfold. It was in this competition that Trinity, so soon after their foundation, earned their enduring cup-fighting reputation. Trinity were one of sixteen teams invited to take part in the inaugural competition and beat Leeds St John's, the forerunner of the present Leeds club, on December 8 in the first-round tie at Belle Vue. Their second-round opponents, Halifax, had knocked out the Wakefield club in their first-round tie. Trinity and Halifax, the two favourites, met at Belle Vue, where the clash was watched by a crowd of three thousand people, described as the largest number ever seen at a similar gathering in Wakefield[22]. In the growing gloom – the Halifax team had arrived three-quarters of an hour late – the tight, exciting match ended in a narrow victory for Halifax, the eventual winners of the competition, by the only try of the game.

If they had not met Halifax in the second round, Trinity could easily have gone on to the final, but nevertheless it was a sign of their increasing prowess that the well-established Manchester club should come to Belle Vue to take part in a 'grand football match' played at the Easter weekend. Billed as the match of the season, featuring two of the North's strongest sides, it was watched by around 2,000 people and ended in a draw.

In the same season Harry Hayley became the first Trinity player to represent Yorkshire when he turned out against Middlesex on February 25, 1878. Hayley, a pupil-teacher at a local school who later played for the county at cricket, is believed to be the first player from a non-public school background to represent Yorkshire at rugby. His selection is an early indication of the rising importance of players not brought up on the game in the public schools, whose influence would begin to decline. Towards the end of the following season, Trinity's growing status was recognised when their ground was chosen to host a county match for the first time, Yorkshire meeting Middlesex there on March 30, 1879. County matches pre-date the creation of Trinity – Yorkshire first met Lancashire in 1870 – and it took five years for the club's best players to be recognised. But on this occasion, with Trinity men Barron Kilner and Harry Hayley in their ranks, as well as the Wakefield player CWL Fernandes, Yorkshire defeated their opponents, who fielded several international players.

An innovation brought about by the Yorkshire Cup, on entering its second season, was that the Trinity players 'had some practice with a view to the Challenge Cup'.[23] Specific training of this kind was unheard of. A practice match took place on the Thursday evening after work, so seriously did the club now take the competition, which had quickly caught the public imagination.

After defeating Bradford, Bradford Zingari and Leeds in the earlier rounds of the expanded competition of 1878-79, Trinity faced Halifax in the semi-final. Trinity were out for revenge for their defeat in the previous season's Cup campaign by opponents who had beaten Huddersfield, Dewsbury and Mirfield on their way to the 1879 semi-final. In view of the rivalry between the two semi-finalists, the Trinity club captain, Arthur Hayley, applied to the local magistrates for a police presence at the match. The magistrates were unanimous in agreeing that the policemen were required. The crowd numbered around seven thousand, four hundred of whom were accommodated in the grandstand, with supporters travelling by special train not only from Halifax, but also Leeds, Dewsbury and York.

The first Wakefield Trinity team to win a trophy: the Yorkshire Cup, 1879. *Back*: A Hirst, W Jackson, B Longbottom, TO Bennett, Bell (umpire), J Longbottom. *Middle*: B Kilner, W Ellis, H Pickersgill, A Hayley (capt), G Steele, H Hayley, JW Kilner, T Parry, E Bartram. *Seated*: J Leach (secretary), J Whitehead, CT Baldwin.

Urged on by shouts of 'Bravo, Trinity', the home side weathered Halifax's onslaught, which was led by a former Wakefield Trinity star player, the three-quarter back Rufus Ward, who, it was alleged, had been offered an inducement to join Halifax the year before. Trinity emerged as winners by eight touchdowns to one and went on to face Kirkstall in the final.

Halifax provided the venue to which ten thousand spectators from all over the county flocked on a snowy Saturday, 12 April 1879, to see Trinity play the first of their nine Yorkshire Cup finals in thirteen years. With outstanding play from brothers Arthur and Harry Hayley, Teddy Bartram and forwards George Steele and Barron Kilner, Wakefield carried off their first-ever trophy by two goals, kicked by Arthur Hayley, one try and six touchdowns to nil. Ugly scenes followed. The victory displeased some of the Halifax locals, mindful of the defeat Trinity had inflicted on their side in the semi-final. Ill-feeling between the two sets of supporters also existed on account of the transfer of Rufus Ward. CT Baldwin, the last to leave the field of play, was jostled and kicked. As the team omnibus was leaving the ground, 'a volley of stones broke the windows and it was feared the vehicle would be upset. It was, however, safely piloted through the crowd when another stone was thrown. Thomson [the Halifax captain] instantly jumped from the top of the bus, collared the assailant, gave him a good thrashing and handed him over to the police, whilst all the members of the Halifax club present did their best to protect the visitors.'[24] Barron Kilner, meanwhile, is said to have made his escape hidden under a blanket in the referee's horse-drawn trap.

Once back in Wakefield, however, the team were given a reception never seen before. The Trinity men proceeded through the town (Wakefield did not become a city until 1888), bearing the trophy decorated with white ribbons, to the sound of church bells and the cheers of the crowds, swollen with civic pride.

Two days later, on Easter Monday, Trinity were back in action, playing against the Manchester side, Birch, in a charity match in aid of Clayton Hospital. The game ended in a draw in Trinity's favour, but the greater significance lay in the fact that this match is generally believed to have been the first at their new ground on the other side of Doncaster Road, where they play to this day. Remarkably, local newspaper reports make no mention of the fact.[25] This game is also thought to be the first occasion that Trinity wore their now traditional colours of blue and red. Certainly the familiar blue jerseys with red band are worn in the team photograph taken outside Rishworth House (which stood on the site now occupied by County Hall) on the day of the match. Ernest Parker, a future club official, recalled that Trinity switched from black and blue horizontal stripes to navy blue with a scarlet band 'in their first season on the present ground, when they won the Yorkshire Cup for the first time.' [26]

There was no terracing around the Belle Vue pitch and the banking at the Doncaster Road end had not yet been put in place. Parker and his brother used to be given the job of hanging canvas on match days across the top end by St Catherine's Church and along the east side by the school, so that no one should see the match for free. [27]

What does transpire from the *Wakefield Express's* report is an indication of Trinity's style of play at the time. Like most other Yorkshire sides at least, the team's play was based on the strength of its nine forwards. After describing a passing movement – relatively rare at the time – involving three players, the reporter expresses the view that 'if Trinity would adopt the same tactics more frequently and systematically they would be almost invincible.' [28]

As rugby football became increasingly popular in Wakefield and throughout the county, junior clubs had sprung up in almost every area of town, but the Wakefield club went out of existence at the start of the 1879-80 season, having lasted just seven years. Two years before its demise, the club which was sometimes known as the 'aristocratic organisation' had lost some of its best players, including the Kilner brothers, to Trinity.

At this time also there was some experimentation with playing according to Association Football rules. A match against Hunslet, for example, was played in this manner, though it was condemned as a mistake. Hardly any association football was played in the Wakefield area. [29] Once Trinity had laid their hands on the Yorkshire Cup, only one sport mattered in and around Wakefield. As a sign of public affection and gratitude, the team were presented with gold medals before the start of the 1879-80 season. The medals were paid for by 181 local subscribers, were made by Perkin's Jewellers of Northgate and were distributed at a presentation evening at the Woolpacks Hotel. Team members were also given an illuminated memorial card in the blue and vermilion colours of the club. Echoing a familiar sentiment, the landlord of the Woolpacks, Henry Milsom, said that it was one of the proudest days in his life when he saw the Challenge Cup on his table. [30]

Two – A Glimpse of Professionalism: 1879-85

Only months after winning the Yorkshire Challenge Cup for the first time, Trinity found themselves on the brink of conflict with the County Committee. Trinity's three-quarter back Teddy Bartram, who had been recruited from Harrogate in the 1878-79 season and had been a key member of the Cup-winning side, had been left out of a county trial match even though it was generally agreed that his form warranted his inclusion. 'The non-selection of Bartram,' commented the *Wakefield and West Riding Herald* in a roundabout way, 'was not connected with his play, the merits of which were fully acknowledged, but was owing to a circumstance, which, being well known in Wakefield, had travelled as far as Leeds [HQ of the County Committee], and been the means of procuring this player's debarment.' [1] The 'circumstance' concerned the suspicion that Bartram was paid by the club in contravention of the public school ethos of amateurism which remained a cornerstone of the game, though not yet enshrined in the RFU laws. It was a major concern in Yorkshire rugby football, and was much talked about, though not directly in print.

'A certain well-known Yorkshire club has in its ranks a paid man,' reported the *Yorkshire Post*. 'Such a startling statement as this we can hardly give credence to, since it is so entirely opposed to the hitherto recognised notions of what has always been considered a purely amateur pastime.' [2]

Bartram, born in Leeds but brought up in the Knaresborough-Harrogate area, joined Trinity in November 1878 at the age of twenty. The club agreed to pay his rail fare from Harrogate. The three-quarter back had shown extraordinary versatility when he had played against Trinity and club officials set about persuading him to come to Wakefield. His team-mate Barron Kilner recalled: 'Trinity were playing Harrogate on the old ground at the back of the Alexandra Hotel… [Bartram] so impressed us with his wonderful resource and skill that we never lost sight of him and I think it was the year after that he was induced to play with Wakefield Trinity. At first he came backwards and forwards from Harrogate and the club paid his expenses but afterwards he commenced business and took up his abode in Wakefield.' [3] Though it went unrecorded, Bartram also appears to have received a loan from the club to set up in business once he had settled in Wakefield, where he stayed at the Woolpacks.

Trinity's agreement with Bartram, who also played cricket as a professional, had been prompted by the Yorkshire Cup competition. He had proved his value in Trinity's first successful campaign and the club were keen to retain him as they went in search of further trophies. That they were able to do so resulted from the gate money paid by the unprecedented crowds at cup-ties. There were not yet any laws regarding amateurism and professionalism and the club committee thought they were entitled to make terms with Bartram. But in response to the allegations, the Yorkshire Committee announced that no player who was 'not strictly an amateur' would be allowed to take part in Cup matches or any other match under the control of the County Committee. Bartram did eventually take part in a county trial, but the Trinity players selected for Yorkshire to face Durham were Barron Kilner, George Steele and Arthur Hayley. The whole matter was much debated at the time and long afterwards and 'has always been pointed at as the first sign of a tendency towards professionalism in rugby.' [4]

Bartram's place in history as the first rugby professional – though of course never admitted at the time - became clearer as a result of an agreement made during the 1880 close season. It is recorded in the club minutes for June 1st, 1880 'that the Assistant Secretary [i.e. Bartram] shall have a salary of £52 per annum.'[5] It was obvious that the role had been created for the star player, whose duties as 'assistant secretary' were not specified.

Looking back at the incident some twenty years later, Barron Kilner stated: 'Viewed in the light of more recent legislation, the case would have been taken as one of professionalism by the Rugby Union because the club advanced money to Bartram to buy his stock-in-trade. It was, however, innocently done. The Southern officials of the Rugby Union were always suspicious of Bartram's bona fides. There is little doubt that he would have had his England cap after the North v South match at Huddersfield in December 1881 but for this suspicion. On form he certainly ought to have received international honours.' [6] Unfortunately for Bartram, selection for Yorkshire, at least at first, and then England appeared not to be based entirely on ability. But there was no doubting Bartram's influence on the players around him. The man who would end his working days as a professional cricket coach at a public school gave useful advice to his team-mates. A decade later, *The Yorkshireman* reflected: 'The great want in the Trinity team is someone like Teddy Bartram – not particularly to play, but to train the young ideas how to shoot. Much of the past success of the club has been on account of Teddy spending so much of his time at the field during the week, and his hints to Fallas, Hamshaw, Hartley, Hutchinson and others were simply invaluable.'[7] Harry Hayley was an early beneficiary of one of Bartram's tips. In a clash with York, Trinity were awarded a penalty, Hayley tapped the ball with his foot instead of placing the ball for a goal kick, ran towards goal and drop-kicked the ball over the bar. It proved a match-winner but the RFU soon outlawed the practice. [8]

Teddy Bartram, a prolific points scorer and generally believed to be rugby's first professional player

Attendances continued to increase. The crowd for a match against Dewsbury, in late November 1879, was estimated at between eight and ten thousand, while the third round Cup tie against rivals Halifax attracted between twelve and fifteen thousand, just seven hundred of whom were accommodated in the grandstand. 'If anything were really needed to prove the popularity of the game of football, the scene presented at Belle Vue on Saturday would have sufficed to remove that last semblance of doubt,' reported the *Wakefield Express*. 'For fully an hour before 3.15 the highway to Belle Vue was crowded with pedestrians and also vehicles, all filled with expectant lovers of the game.' [9] Similarly, the fourth round tie at Dewsbury brought 15,000 to witness a close struggle, with players having members of the crowd as well their opponents to deal with: 'On one occasion, on Bartram bringing down [a Dewsbury player] near the onlookers, one of them ran out and attempted to strike him, Barron Kilner giving him a good cuff for his trouble.' [10] Trinity's one goal, scored in extra time, saw them through to the final the following Saturday against Heckmondwike at Cardigan Fields, Leeds. After Bartram dropped an early goal, the Cup-holders, captained by CT Baldwin, went on to retain the trophy without being seriously troubled, scoring five second-half tries and winning by three goals, six tries and seven touchdowns to one try and two touchdowns. Hutchinson set a record by scoring three tries. Once again the Trinity team were greeted on their return by a band which had travelled out to Newton Bar to meet their horse-drawn carriage before the players marched down Northgate on their way to the reception at the Woolpacks. It was a second highly successful season, crowned not only by the retention of the Cup but also by the selection of Barron Kilner as Wakefield Trinity's first international when he represented England against Ireland on January 30, 1880. Kilner, a powerful forward, was regarded as unstoppable close to the opponents' line and figured among Trinity's top try scorers.

Harry Hayley, the first Wakefield Trinity player to earn selection for Yorkshire, February 1878

Trinity now had so many playing members that it was decided to add a third team, which, when the second team was not in action, would play on the pitch which had now been marked out at the bottom end of the main field, at right angles to the first team pitch. At the time, the first team pitch sloped down towards the Agbrigg Road end. Later it would be built up and levelled and the remaining ground built on, displacing the field which had become the second and third team pitch.

For the prestigious match against Manchester, regarded as pre-eminent in the North of England, the Dewsbury captain and three-quarter back Alfred Newsome was drafted into the Trinity line-up, giving the club the best two three-quarters, with Teddy Bartram, in the county. Manchester, who were often in the habit of taking guest players from the best Lancashire clubs, could hardly complain even though, for the first time ever, they ended up losing to a Yorkshire team in a match described as probably the best exhibition of rugby that ever took place in Wakefield. The victory brought Trinity even greater stature, with the *Wakefield Express* suggesting, 'No achievement in the past has added such lustre to the renown of the club as the success [in that match].' [11]

Barron Kilner, who became Wakefield Trinity's first international when selected for England against Ireland in January 1880

But in the more run-of-the-mill matches, Trinity found it hard to sustain their best form. With as many as four players on county duty at any one time – the Hayley brothers, the Kilner brothers, Bartram, Herbert Hutchinson, George Steele and Bill Ellis among them – and with some players crying off from away games, the club had already lost four matches by early December, more than in any season of its existence. Though the *Leeds Mercury* reported that, without any doubt, Trinity and Halifax were the two outstanding sides in Yorkshire, some complacency had crept into the team and warnings were delivered in the local press that players ought to be training for the forthcoming Cup ties.

When the Cup matches got under way in March, football took on a different perspective. After knocking out underdogs Horbury, now led by Rufus Ward against his former club, Trinity went through to the final for the third year in a row, meeting Dewsbury at Cardigan Fields, Leeds, where a crowd of some ten thousand spectators assembled. For those unable to attend, news of the progress of the match was relayed by carrier pigeon and telegraph. Led by Barron Kilner in the absence of Baldwin, who was ill, Trinity had the upper hand for much of the match, and even more so when one of the Dewsbury forwards left the field injured, but they had the misfortune to have four tries disallowed. Towards the end of the game, Alfred Newsome, the Dewsbury player who had guested with Trinity against Manchester, fielded a wild kick from a Wakefield forward and dropped a goal which hit the post before going over. It was enough to decide the match and cause Trinity to suffer their first Cup final defeat. In his post-match speech, Kilner, never one to hide his feelings, spoke of Dewsbury's luck. [12] The 1880-81 season was the least successful in Trinity's short history, with eight out of twenty-eight matches lost and no fewer than forty players called up into the first team.

Rugby football had truly gripped the imagination of the people of Wakefield, who not only watched Trinity in their thousands but played in any number of teams. In the immediate vicinity, football clubs existed in almost every village or district - at Westgate End, New Scarborough, Eastmoor, Stanley, Flushdyke, Flanshaw, Alverthorpe, Thornes, Belle Vue, Horbury, Ossett, Middlestown and Kirkhamgate. There were the church teams of St John's, St Michael's, the Parish Church and St Austin's; works teams such as Portobello Mills; and at schoolboy level Wakefield Grammar School, whose earliest recorded match dated from November 1874.

Footballs and other equipment were advertised in the local papers and in an early example of player endorsement, one brand of football was recommended by Trinity's Teddy Bartram, who, in both club and county matches had earned the reputation as unquestionably the best three-quarter back in Yorkshire. Back in favour with the selectors, Bartram played for the North against the South at Fartown – an England trial – scored a try and kicked the only goal of the match. In that match, which took place in December 1881, it is widely accepted that Bartram became the first three-quarter to receive a pass from a half back, who was JH Payne of Lancashire. The following month the Trinity star kicked the match-winning conversion for the North against Wales at Newport.

In a preamble to a report on the match between Wakefield Trinity and Rochdale Hornets in January 1882, a reporter looked back to when the two clubs met 'six or seven seasons ago in the Manor Field, close to the Borough Market. In those days few clubs in the North of England had a greater name than the Rochdale Hornets and in arranging matches with them the Trinity executive thought they were taking a step in the right direction…' In the intervening period, the writer boasted, Trinity 'has prospered to a surprising extent; it has multiplied both its strength and riches, being not far off the best club in the North of England.' [13]

In the same month, Trinity set off on a tour arranged by Barron Kilner. They travelled to Ireland, where they played in Dublin and Belfast and received very favourable comment on the standard of their play. Not only was this Trinity's first tour, but it was believed to be the first 'overseas' tour undertaken by any football club. [14] Only a week earlier, the club's annual ball had taken place on the Friday evening, even if 'a night's enjoyment of this kind is not calculated to develop the abilities of a football player who has to appear on the field the day following.' [15] These were happy times for the Wakefield Trinity football player.

During that 1881-82 season, representatives of the Yorkshire Committee made recommendations to the Rugby Union concerning foul play and offside, which were becoming increasingly common in the North. The Southern clubs, however, backed by the Lancashire Committee, did not regard the matter as a serious problem and rejected the proposal. That rejection only increased the dissatisfaction among Yorkshire clubs at the way the game was being directed in London. The selection of the national team was another case in point. Despite the success of the Yorkshire side, not one player from the county was picked for England.

The most obvious exclusion was Teddy Bartram, who had been outstanding for Yorkshire and the North, but who did not fit in with the establishment's ideas about what a rugby footballer should be. 'The [England] selection is little short of an insult to Yorkshire,' railed one report. [16] The first hint of a North-South divide appeared with the suggestion, 'that the Northerners should, in the event of their ideas not being adopted, form a legislative body of their own.' [17]

In the Yorkshire Cup of 1882, Trinity progressed in their usual fashion to their fourth final in a row. They wore new, lighter-coloured jerseys for their third round tie against Salterhebble, in which they also adopted a new, more open style of play: 'We have been accustomed at times to see the half backs pass to Bartram, and a forward occasionally, when he has seen no possibility of getting away, has passed to someone behind him, but nothing more. On Saturday last the players all seemed to have made their minds up to play a fast passing game and the result was that tries were obtained which never otherwise would have been got.' [18] The final, played at Cardigan Fields, turned out to be an all-Wakefield affair as Trinity met Thornes, then a separate village within the borough. It also became one of the biggest upsets in Cup history, on this April Fool's Day, as little Thornes, a second level club, defeated the mighty Trinity, the overwhelming favourites. It was a classic case of over-confidence on the part of Trinity. That was epitomised by new captain Barron Kilner's arrogant pre-match question, 'Who, where, what and which is Thornes?' But Thornes had been practising and training for weeks in preparation for their Cup run, whereas Trinity by comparison looked out of condition. They were outplayed in the forwards, so often their strength, while Thornes backs Harry Wigglesworth, scorer of the only goal, and Harry Dawson were key figures. On arrival back in Wakefield, the winning team progressed along Kirkgate, stopping off at the now demolished Manor House Inn, before moving along Thornes Lane, via the Admiral Duncan Inn and finishing up at the Queen's Arms. At their own, more muted post-match dinner at the Woolpacks, Trinity consoled themselves with, as one speaker put it, 'having done wonders for the town of Wakefield' and the fact that 'the greatest thing in Wakefield was the Trinity Football Club'. [19]

The following week, Teddy Bartram showed his all-round sporting ability by playing lacrosse – a game which had been played earlier at Belle Vue as a demonstration – for the North against the South. Bartram also ended the season as Trinity's top goal kicker with 33 goals and leading try scorer with eleven. He was now acknowledged as 'the champion drop kick[er] in the country'.[20] His excellent form continued in the 1882-83 season when, playing for Yorkshire against Northumberland, he dropped two goals and scored a try in a performance which 'almost outshone all his previous achievements'.[21]

At county level there was creeping dissatisfaction with a number of issues, chief among which was the lack of representation of certain clubs at Committee level, particularly those which were not so long established. Those clubs which were entitled to be represented were Bradford, Dewsbury, Halifax, Huddersfield, Leeds St John's, Wakefield Trinity, York and the Yorkshire Wanderers. The stranglehold of the older – and in some cases socially superior clubs – was felt at both county and national level. 'Not only in Yorkshire does there want a sweeping reform but in the Rugby Union itself and almost all its connections,' declared the *Wakefield Express*.[22] In county matches, however, Yorkshire went from strength to strength. Though at first there was no room for any member of the champion club, Thornes, the omission was rectified when Harry Wigglesworth, 'the surest place-kicker in the county', was selected in February. The number and quality of clubs had risen dramatically. But in Lancashire, who were easily beaten by their white rose rivals, despite winning eight out of nine matches up to 1881, rugby football was not what it was, and even seemed to be on the wane.

At the beginning of the next season's Yorkshire Cup campaign in March 1883, it was noted: '[Since the institution of the Cup] the sport has gained much more favour; and the most important result of all … is that it has raised our county to be indisputably the champion county in England. As proven in the present season, Yorkshire can turn out the best county fifteen in the country and there are also more clubs, more playing members and more spectators … than in any other county in England.'[23]

The Cup semi-finals featured four teams who had all previously won the trophy – Dewsbury, Halifax, Thornes and Trinity. In a replay of the 1882 final, Trinity met Thornes in a very keenly contested match at Halifax. Captained by their county forward, George Steele, who had taken over from the retired Barron Kilner, Trinity knocked their local rivals out, though Thornes tried to raise doubts about the eligibility of Wakefield's Bill Ellis. There was even greater controversy in the other semi-final. Dewsbury beat Halifax at Belle Vue, but Halifax then claimed that one of the Dewsbury players, the forward and future Trinity captain Hampton Jones, was ineligible. Dewsbury then objected to a Halifax player on the same grounds, but too late. The two teams agreed to a replay, but the matter caused a great furore, particularly in Dewsbury. Two of their star players, Mark and Alfred Newsome, refused to appear in the replayed semi-final, which Halifax won.

The final saw Trinity appearing for the fifth year in a row during the six years that the competition had existed. Training intensively for three weeks up to the final, the Wakefield team showed superior form to their Halifax opponents and carried off the trophy for the third time, winning by one goal, two tries and eleven 'minor points' to nil. The Cup was once more filled with champagne at the Woolpacks. During one of the several speeches at the reception, former captain Barron Kilner recounted that Rowland Hill, the Rugby Union's secretary who had come up from London to referee the final, had told him that the Trinity club were second to no other in England.

Though gate receipts from the semi-finals and finals of the Yorkshire Cup were given to charity – in Trinity's case usually to Clayton Hospital – money from other matches was flowing in. Trinity's tour of Ireland, for example, was funded by admission charges at Belle Vue. As a means of coping with the crowds, turnstiles were first installed at the start of the 1883-84 season and were first used for the visit of Batley on September 15. But the strict amateurism imposed by the County Committee, following the lead set by the Rugby Football Union, meant that a clash of interests would soon arise. At the end of the 1882-83 season, the County Committee announced a resolution that, 'having heard that certain football competitions are being held in which money prizes are given, [we] wish it to be distinctly understood among Yorkshire clubs that they will be disqualified from the Yorkshire Challenge Cup if they take part in any of the above-mentioned contests.' Meanwhile, during the close season, Teddy Bartram and Harry Hayley would play cricket as professionals without hindrance.

By the start of the 1883-84 season, the rugby teams playing in and around Wakefield were many. On a typical Saturday, 36 matches were recorded in the *Wakefield Express*: 'Each succeeding Saturday points conclusively at Wakefield as being the centre of Yorkshire football.' [24] The Manor Field, where Trinity had played in their early days, was now being used by St Austin's.

Association football was virtually unknown, though an exhibition match between Blackburn Olympic and Darwen took place at Dewsbury, while the following week Trinity and Dewsbury played a demonstration game of rugby at Blackburn, won by Trinity in front of around 3,000 spectators in poor weather. Many of the clubs which would become regular opponents after the Northern breakaway of 1895 were by now on Trinity's fixture list. Barrow made their first visit in September and Salford provided the opposition two weeks later, both matches providing Trinity with easy wins. At Salford, Teddy Bartram was again the outstanding player, dropping three goals from the field of play and converting three place kicks from three attempts, as a result of which 'the large concourse of spectators gave Bartram such a cheer as could not have been beaten had the match been witnessed by a large gathering at Wakefield… E Beswick, the international, confessed that Bartram's exhibition was one of the finest ever shown on a football field.' [25] Bartram was not alone. After Trinity comprehensively beat Huddersfield, it was noted that three-quarter back WE 'Ted' Hartley, who was to end the season with 21 tries, was showing a turn of pace not seen since the days of Rufus Ward. Hartley's achievement was hailed as a club record, although Barron Kilner was reputed to have scored 26 in a season, but, given that individual players rarely broke into double figures – and forwards even more rarely – Kilner's claim appears to be without foundation.

Against Midland Counties, four backs from Wakefield – Bartram, Herbert Fallas, Herbert Hutchinson and Harry Wigglesworth (Thornes) – and one forward, George Jubb, were named in the Yorkshire side, with Hutchinson scoring a spectacular try which involved Bartram and Wigglesworth twice, while Bartram kicked three goals and scored two tries. In the great annual contest between Yorkshire and Lancashire, won by Yorkshire, Bartram was again in outstanding form, scoring the first try, making another and goaling both. It was reported of Bartram that 'he has beaten far and away all-comers as a skilful, reliable and consistent player. For four seasons now he has been ripe for [international] honours but they have been withheld and still there is no depreciation [in the quality of his play]: in fact this season he promises to surpass all his previous achievements and has this year scored six tries for his county … On Saturday he was once more the hero of this great match of the North.' [26] But in the North v South trial match, Bartram was not at his best in a game previewed as a contest between two styles: a forward-based dribbling style (North) versus the more open passing style (South). Trinity's half back Herbert Hutchinson was the North's best player in defeat. In the County matches, nine Trinity players represented Yorkshire: Bartram, Fallas, Hutchinson, Jubb, Harry Dawson, Harper Hamshaw, Joe Latham, George Steele and Herbert Ward.

During this 1883-84 season, attendances reached new heights. In January, Trinity played Bradford at Park Avenue in front of 15,000 spectators, believed to be a record crowd for a rugby match. A special train ran from Kirkgate station, with extra carriages added when it reached Westgate. Trinity's winning display was inspired by Hutchinson and Harry Dawson, newly recruited from Thornes. But it was Trinity's Herbert Fallas and Thornes' captain Harry Wigglesworth who gained selection for England against Ireland, which also raised the question again of why Bartram had been overlooked. One observer suggested that 'there is a clique who are determined that Bartram shall not have conferred on him the highest honour that a football player can aspire to – the international cap. That Bartram was ripe for this honour two years ago was almost universally admitted; and if there be some objection to him respecting an office he holds in connection with his club [as a paid assistant secretary], where is the consistency of the RU in selecting him year after year for the North v South contest … and leaving him out in the cold again last week, when they had to obtain the services of two such young players as Wigglesworth and Fallas?' [27] Bartram himself was clearly in despair at ever being selected for England and declined to play for the Yorkshire side which would end the season undefeated in inter-county matches for the third year in a row.

Herbert Fallas was one of a new breed of footballer who was able to take advantage of his fame, placing an advertisement in the local paper to announce that he had started business as an accountant in Barstow Square. Another well-known celebrity, Harry Hayley, also set up as a cricket and football outfitter in Bread Street, selling jerseys, footballs and other sports equipment.

As the game became more and more popular and greater emphasis was placed on the result of matches, negative play became more common. Salford was one team heavily criticised for their defensive tactics when they visited Belle Vue in February 1884. 'It is perfectly legal for any team to adopt what defensive measures they please,' wrote one reporter, 'but as football is regarded as a manly sport, those who exhibit such unmanliness as to be afraid of standing their ground for fear of a point being scored against them are unworthy to be classed amongst the exponents of our national winter pastime. Police had to intervene to stop spectators getting at the Salford full back, who often kicked dead or touched down when no one was near him.' [28]

This was also the year when the Yorkshire Challenge Cup was opened up to a wider range of clubs. The popularity of the competition was shown not only by the large crowds which it drew, but also by the lesser competitions which also sprang up. In Wakefield the minor clubs and second teams were invited to compete for a new trophy offered by the *Wakefield Express*, with silver medals for the winners.

In the first round of the older competition, no fewer than twenty-eight matches took place, but the favourites were again the previous holders – Trinity, Halifax, Dewsbury and Thornes – plus Bradford. The draw pitted Trinity against Dewsbury at Crown Flatt, where, watched by a 12,000 crowd, the visitors went through. But surprises were in store in the second round, when Trinity were knocked out by Heckmondwike – ending a run of five successive appearances in the final - and Thornes lost to Salterhebble. Trinity's shock defeat was their only loss to a Yorkshire club so far that season. They had their revenge a fortnight later at Belle Vue, winning easily in a regular match, but their pride was already dented. Heckmondwike, who had long been in training for the Cup, took full advantage of the very heavy conditions produced by a downpour on that day. Trinity could still have won if Bartram had managed to convert Hartley's late try, but, controversially, the Heckmondwike forwards, charging at the kicker, 'were close on the ball when Bartram kicked, after being frequently put back behind the line.' [29] The remaining past holder of the Cup, Halifax, went out in the next round in equally sensational circumstances, losing to Castleford, then a very junior club. It was dubbed 'the most singular season in the history of modern football' [30], as none of the four semi-finalists (Batley, Bradford, Castleford and Hull) had ever reached that stage before, with Bradford eventually beating Hull in the final.

There was controversy off the field as well. Rumours had abounded that the Trinity club rooms on George Street were being used for 'extensive gambling'. Since that reflected badly on the church, the football club was given notice to quit unless the gambling stopped. Following a members' meeting it was decided to do away with the card playing and remain in situ, though the motion was only carried by 35 votes to 26. Later in the year, in time for the start of the 1884-85 season, the club's dressing rooms were moved to the Crown Hotel, at the bottom of Kirkgate, where the veteran forward George Steele had taken over as landlord. It was common practice for football clubs to have their dressing rooms in pubs, where the licensee might well be a player or former player. Trinity's activities were not just limited to the football field. In addition to the annual dinner and presentations, the annual ball became a big event, with notable guests. The January 1885 version, held on a Wednesday, took place at the Corn Exchange at the top of Westgate and went on until four in the morning.

The new season began with an unexpected defeat for Trinity and a reflection on the football calendar, now overlapping with cricket. 'Saturday last [September 20, 1884] was just one week too early for football matches. The splendid weather offered conclusive evidence: whilst a large number of exponents of the summer pastime finished their season with a charmingly suitable day, the king of winter sport strode out in weather not at all fitted for a game one of the beauties of which is that it provides outdoor recreation and amusement during the very coldest season of our climate. The weather was so warm on Saturday that the usual period of a football match – eighty minutes – had to be considerably curtailed, in many cases to an hour.' [31]

Following their Irish adventure of the previous season, Trinity embarked on a Welsh tour in early October, setting off for Cardiff on a ten-hour train journey from Kirkgate station, an unusually enterprising venture for a Yorkshire club. They returned with three wins out of three, beating Cardiff, Newport and Swansea, all within four days. The outstanding players were Bartram, whose kicking won the first match, Hartley, with a turn of speed which ensured victory in the second, and the forward Shires, whose charge led to a winning try in the third. Swansea, however, would have their revenge when they visited Belle Vue in December.

What would now be recognised as a fundamental pattern of play was evolving as teams placed increasing value on passing the ball. It was noted that the 'slow, old-fashioned style … is becoming almost extinct at meetings of clubs of the first rank', giving way to a more varied style involving 'running, dodging, dribbling, kicking and passing'.[32] Particularly the passing between half back and three-quarters was developing with each season. 'Some people have set their faces against persistently throwing [i.e. passing] the ball back, but the ground gained by Bartram which a half back could not possibly have gained warrants the continuous "feeding" of such three-quarters as we now have – except, of course, in the home quarter of the ground. When a half back gets the leather behind a pretty close scrimmage it is six to one against him making headway himself, whilst the odds are reversed if the leather is smartly chucked into the hands of the three-quarters.' [33]

Still the application of the rules of the game could prove problematical, with unexpected results. Two weeks before Christmas, Trinity played Bradford at Horton Park in front of 20,000 spectators, 12,000 of whom had bought tickets in advance. When Bradford appeared to score a last-minute try, the referee, unsighted, could not give a decision; nor could the umpires, nominated by each side, agree. Trinity thought they had secured a draw, which was reported as such in the *Yorkshire Post*, but the referee later sent a telegram to that newspaper saying that Bradford had indeed scored a try and had therefore won. A week later, the Bradford club, angry at Trinity's apparent failure to accept the referee's decision, refused to play the return match at Belle Vue. The matter was finally settled several weeks later at a hearing of the RFU, who decided in favour of Bradford, although the decision appeared to have been accepted less than graciously in Wakefield. 'Trinity can well afford to let Bradford increase their number of victories over them from one to two, as against twelve victories against Bradford on the side of Trinity,' wrote one pundit. [34] Bradford eventually agreed to play the return game in March, but then postponed their commitment until late April.

In county matches, Trinity often had four representatives on duty. In the match against Durham, Herbert Fallas was the match-winner and the best three-quarter on view, although the match against Lancashire was lost – surprisingly, considering that 'in the great majority of inter-club matches the Lancastrians invariably come off worst and the Association game has recently made such strides in Lancashire that even many of their critics did not imagine that they would be able to hold their own with Yorkshire.' [35]

When the 1885 Yorkshire Cup competition got under way in March, the number of teams had increased to sixty-four, a four-fold increase on the number who had contested the inaugural version seven years earlier. Most teams now trained specifically for the Cup matches, the play had became more 'scientific', or tactical, and the large gate receipts had provided a boon for charitable organisations. In the first round Trinity met their former victors, Thornes, whose tackling was described as 'rough and unmerciful in the extreme'. Trinity won through but Thornes had the consolation of the largest gate in Wakefield that season.

After beating Cleckheaton and then Leeds Parish Church by the biggest score of the round, Trinity travelled to Crown Flatt to face Dewsbury, who had been beaten by the Halifax Free Wanderers in the previous round, but the match was ordered to be replayed following a dispute. Dewsbury won the replay and faced Trinity in a fourth-round match which began in a snowstorm. The Crown Flatt side were leading by a try and four minor points to nil when Trinity's Jim Tattersall went over for a late try. If Bartram could convert successfully from a straightforward position, victory would be Trinity's. But as Herbert Hutchinson was about to place the ball for his team-mate, Dewsbury players ran out from behind the goal-line and knocked the ball from his grasp, preventing Bartram from taking the kick. Trinity protested that Dewsbury had charged unfairly at the attempt at goal, just as Heckmondwike had done when Trinity were knocked out the year before. When the County Committee later upheld the result, Trinity's representative Arthur Hayley would have resigned if the Committee had not called a meeting of referees to discuss amending the rule. By the start of the next season, referees were given new powers to penalise, among other things, illegal charging at attempts at goal.

The great attraction of the Cup had prompted familiar tales of payment made to players for loss of work time caused by training. The County Committee declared these payments illegal and threatened to deal severely with any club found guilty of the offence. But broken time payments had been made for a while, as shown indirectly by the record of a Wakefield Trinity meeting almost four years earlier, on 28 November 1881. Players would be reimbursed for loss of earnings as a result of leaving work on Saturday mornings for away matches. For most people the working week had been reduced from six days to five and a half, with a clocking-off time of one o' clock on Saturdays. But the club stipulated 'no broken time be paid to any player in the first team when the train leaves Wakefield at 1 o' clock or after.' However the club cut back altogether the following month, when, as the minutes for 19 December 1881 recorded, a decision was taken that 'for the remainder of the football season 1881-2 no money be paid out of the funds of the Club to any member on account of "broken time" and that a notice be posted in the Rooms to this effect.' [36] The decision came at a time when the sport's governing body was hardening its position on amateurism and what had previously been regarded – at least by the clubs – as legitimate expenses was now being held up as an infringement of the amateur ethic.

Three – A Time of Upheaval: 1885-92

As the 1885-86 season approached, one observer wrote: 'We cannot but feel, on entering upon another football season, how highly favoured we in England are in having such sports as we have for the seasons, and how thankful we ought to feel that the dull routine of ordinary toil is through the whole year greatly relieved of its monotony by the interest which is created by the varied and manly games indulged in by the youth of the land.' What he wrote, despite the typically florid Victorian style, was true for an increasing number of people.

Embarking on their thirteenth full season, Wakefield Trinity had made changes which showed the continuing progress of the club. They were now using the Ings Field as a practice ground, since it was nearer than Belle Vue to their club rooms, which had transferred to nearby Holly Lodge, situated in Lord Rodney Yard, between George Street and Little Westgate. It was a development ahead of its time, as a gymnasium was erected nearby and showers installed.

Competition between clubs over the recruitment of players gained momentum. Trinity, for example, thought that a certain Horbury player had agreed to join them only to find that he had gone instead to Yorkshire Cup-holders Batley, 'who had evidently some strong and tempting boon to offer of some kind to entice him over at the eleventh hour.'

At a lower level, the game of rugby football incited passion which sometimes spilled over into excessive aggression. The Middlestown club wrote to the *Wakefield Express* to state their disgust at the 'filthy language' and bad behaviour of players and officials of the Stanley club: 'They said they were determined either to win or kill. Our team was very glad to get away without any broken bones.' Another local side, Alverthorpe St Paul's, found it necessary to complain about the 'mismanagement' of the Sandal Church club, who showed their visitors to a hedge bottom to change and provided no washing facilities. In addition the language of some the Sandal players was said to be 'very un-Churchlike'.

In the Yorkshire Cup, Trinity were bundled out by Halifax in the outstanding tie of the first round. Around 10,000 spectators made their way to Halifax's Hanson Lane ground, but the pitch was barely playable, being covered in frost as well as snow in parts. It was only after the captains had tossed for ends, however, that Wakefield skipper Bartram objected to the match going ahead. The referee overruled the objection, saying that he should have made his plea before the toss. Once the match had started, Bartram made it plain by his behaviour that he would rather have been elsewhere, showing a lack of concern and leadership. His demeanour caused such outrage among spectators and officials that he was dropped for the next match and was not expected to return to resume what had so far been a brilliant career.

Halifax went on to beat Bradford in the final amid talk of abolishing the competition, which gave rise to more controversy than the Committee would care to handle. Public enthusiasm for the competition was undimmed and the revenue from it benefited charitable institutions, as well as clubs big and small. Cup-winners Halifax, for example, profited from 'huge takings', which were important as they moved to a new ground, while the junior clubs which were drawn against the big clubs would see their financial situation changed overnight. Trinity would miss out on the Cup windfall for another season, although it was reported that 'the days of financial perplexities for a first-rate club are about past.' By Trinity's standards it had not been the best of seasons, but the side was still capable of beating the some of the best in Yorkshire and Lancashire, as well as Cambridge University twice.

It is clear from the report delivered at the annual general meeting that the club had moved a long way from its beginnings as a young men's society. The secretary, Mr Parry, gave the usual full account of the playing season – won 23, lost 7, drawn 3 – with the second team winning the Wakefield Express Challenge Cup and the third team also winning a majority of matches. Equally important was the report of the financial situation of the club and in particular the gate receipts, which had been affected both by the early defeat in the Yorkshire Cup and the unusually bad weather leading to cancellation of some of the most attractive fixtures, but the club was still substantially in profit, even allowing for improvements made to the football ground.

By contrast the Thornes club, the second most important in the Wakefield area, showed receipts for the season of £161, compared to Trinity's receipts of £1,017. At their own AGM, Thornes officials lamented their exit from the Yorkshire Cup, like Trinity, at the first round stage. The Thornes chairman took it upon himself to discuss the question of professionalism, which was 'calculated to be the downfall of any good club.' He was reported as saying that there was no fear of its progress as the County Committee had determined to put it down. 'They had had professionalism in their midst to a considerable extent, and neighbouring clubs had indulged in it, for to his mind a man who received any remuneration for his services, no matter in what manner, was a professional… Importation was the chief cause of professionalism, and piracy, too, which was an evil they had had to deplore very considerably, as some clubs at present were playing members formerly belonging to Thornes.'

The theme was one which had become, if not an obsession, at least a constant topic in many clubs. They had seen what was happening in soccer's professional world and were concerned that the financial problems suffered in that code would be repeated in rugby. As the 1886-87 season was about to begin, one writer made the observation, on considering what appeared to be the ever-lengthening rugby season, that 'the Associationists are the principal offenders in this respect, and as one bad step leads to another, so the engagement of professionals has necessitated the playing of more matches to bring in additional gate money to meet the increased expenditure. But as long as the Rugby game remains free from the professional element, there need perhaps be no fears for its general prosperity.'

As if to confirm these common ideas, the RFU formally declared professionalism illegal, with a professional being defined as any player who received money for his services, either actual or prospective; compensation for loss of time; training at a club's expense; employment in return for services; or money disbursed by the player in excess of actual travel and accommodation. In order to enforce this definition, the RFU gave itself the power to suspend, for as long as it thought fit, players or indeed clubs who had contravened these rules. At the meeting at which all of this was passed, on October 4, 1886, the Welsh clubs did in fact suggest that men should be compensated for loss of time, but were told, in what would become a familiar refrain, that if working men wanted to play rugby football, they must pay for it. Some of the Yorkshire clubs were known to be of a similar mind to the Welsh, but did not declare it.

The *Wakefield Express* put forward a representative view: 'Many clubs which are in possession of well-lined coffers have to thank solely the efforts of the working men players for this, and it is most unfair to say that, just because a working man player cannot afford to lose time when his club is going on a long journey, he shall not be compensated from the source he has had so much to do with replenishing, simply because the more well-to-do can afford to do without the compensation… To call a man a professional who works all the week and receives perhaps two or three shillings now and again when he has broken time is a fallacy. The question of "reasonable" expenses must also be cautiously handled. If some people's ideas on this matter went for much, many gentlemen cricketers, including no less a person than WG Grace, would have to be dubbed professionals… The working man player is as entitled to his consideration as are the high-minded authorities to their champagne lunches and the like.'

Two months later, the *Wakefield Express* was predicting a schism if the RFU carried out its rules on professionalism to the letter, at the same foreseeing disastrous consequences if a professional element were introduced, as had happened in association football in Lancashire. The insolvency of Blackburn Olympic FC was testimony to the so-called 'evils of professionalism', which, it was said, would be certain to beset rugby if payment to players were introduced. 'We are not in favour of the paying system, either under the head of expenses or anything else,' declared the *Express*. 'But we do think that working men players, of whom most of our best teams are almost entirely composed, should enjoy some of the luxuries and advantages which a club with well-lined coffers could comfortably afford, and we again protest against the officialism of snobbery which asserts that, if working men want to play football they must pay for it. Where possible, working men's connections with football clubs should be (and are in most cases) surrounded by every comfort and convenience, and it should not cost a working man player a penny, either in outfit, travelling, loss of time, or anything.' The RFU, meanwhile, had drawn up a further rule to insist that every club must send to headquarters a properly audited account showing all receipts and payments made.

Much less controversial was the recommendation to introduce a points-scoring system, making a goal worth three points and a try one. When a goal was kicked from a try, only the goal (i.e. three points) would be counted. The system had not yet been brought in to force when Trinity made their first visit to Wigan on September 18, when the home side won by a goal to three tries. Under the new scoring system, the match would have been drawn.

Trinity's County back, Harper Oliver Hamshaw. The 2011 jersey design was based on this photograph from the 1880s. (Collection Wakefield Museums)

Trinity's team looked almost as strong as it had ever been. The County backs, Herbert Hutchinson, Harry Dawson, Herbert Fallas and Harper Hamshaw, were playing behind a young pack strengthened by more experienced forwards like George Steele, Joe Latham and Paul Booth, not to mention Herbert Ward, described as being able to handle the ball like any back while being 'a scrimmager of the first water'. It was reported, however, that Teddy Bartram, following the Cup-tie controversy of the previous season, would not be turning out for Trinity again. But though the star three-quarter back appeared for Thornes, then a week later for St Austin's, by the end of October he was back in Trinity's ranks. Full back Hamshaw was being tipped for international honours, but Trinity missed out on signing nineteen year-old prodigy Dicky Lockwood, who, born in Crigglestone but playing for Dewsbury, had just made his debut for England and would become the most famous player of his generation.

In mid-season Trinity travelled south, playing the Midlands outfit Moseley and then London United Hospitals, winning both matches and maintaining their record of never having been defeated on tour. It was not just Cup-ties which attracted fans in number. At the end of January, Dewsbury's clash with Trinity brought an 8,000 crowd to Crown Flatt, paying a record £137, the biggest ever gate for an ordinary match, though still some way behind the previous best of £333 when the two sides met in the first round of the Cup in 1884, and when admission prices were doubled. In the 1887 Cup rounds, Trinity bounced back to their usual form, defeating Doncaster, Pudsey and Normanton before meeting Batley in the fourth round. The two rivals drew the tie, watched by 13,000 spectators. In the replay at Belle Vue, Trinity went through to the semi-final, taking record receipts of £220. After disposing of Ossett in the semi, Trinity met Leeds St John's at Halifax in their sixth final of the Cup's ten years' existence. Only Halifax, with three appearances, and Bradford, two, came anywhere near that record. As the match unfolded, the superiority of the Trinity backs - Hamshaw, Fred Ash, Fallas, Bartram, Dawson and Hutchinson - told its own tale. Half back Herbert Hutchinson kicked both goals as Trinity triumphed by two goals and two minor points to two minor points. The trophy returned to Wakefield for the fourth time without a goal or a try being scored against them in the whole competition. Almost as pleasing was the announcement by the secretary, Mr Parry, that the club's balance sheet, showing a surplus of £400, was the healthiest yet.

Trinity's second match of the new 1887-88 season was billed as the Cup final replay, since the opponents were Leeds St John's. Played at Leeds and watched by a crowd of around 7,000, the match was won by Trinity but crowd trouble erupted at the end of the game, when the Trinity players became the focus for 'a pack of undeniable ruffians, whose attentions were far more forcible than polite. By mounting the bus which was to convey them to the Green Dragon, the visitors obligingly put themselves into the position of targets during a bombardment in which stones etc were freely used by a heterogeneous mass of cads, for whom no name is bad enough. Booth received a nasty shock on the head from a large boulder and Ross was hit in the face with an old boot and mud was thrown about in all directions. It has been the custom for Leeds to plume itself with the idea that it is the centre of the football world, that Leeds clubs invariably play a gentlemanly game, that Leeds spectators are second to none in their treatment of visiting teams… From sheer decency the less such utter bosh is indulged in hereafter the better,' fumed the *Wakefield Express*.

Bad feeling between Yorkshire clubs was also evident when, in December, Trinity were at home to Bradford, the club who had declined to return the fixture two seasons ago and had also withdrawn from the Yorkshire Cup the previous year. A Bradford newspaper, commenting on the match which Trinity won, spoke of the 'tricky, dishonest and unscrupulous game of the Wakefield Trinity club' and its 'pugilistic offsidism [sic]'. There were early rumblings of dissension too between Yorkshire and the RFU, with demand for home rule from some parts of the county. It was felt that the RFU, with its headquarters in London, was ignoring the wishes of Yorkshire, 'the very heart and core of rugby football'. Yorkshire clubs, feeling under-represented, had requested that they should be allowed three members on the governing body, rather than the current two, but the request was dismissed. Despite an inconsistent first half of the season, Trinity had four players in the County side which beat Ulster: Johnny Fotherby (back) and forwards Fred Lowrie, Paul Booth and Jack Gomersall.

Feelings between Trinity and Bradford were still running high. Just before the match between the two rivals at Park Avenue, the Wakefield forward Joe Latham received a communication from one of the Bradford forwards, who threatened that if Latham continued to play the offside game, he (the Bradford player) would not be responsible for his actions. When Latham read the threat, 'a broad smile overspread his countenance.' The match was played in falling snow before a five-figure crowd who had come to watch the clash between Yorkshire rugby's most successful club and its wealthiest. In the end Trinity succeeded in doing the double over their rivals, but not without the Bradford press complaining of 'roughism [sic] on the field'. Soon after, Bradford cancelled their fixtures with Trinity for the following season, referring to the 'bitterness infused into the meetings between the two clubs recently.' Trinity, through secretary Parry, were quick to respond, stating that the cancellation was not 'in the interests of rugby football', as Bradford had claimed, 'but solely as an ebullition of temper, the foundation of which may probably be traced to their numerous defeats by the Trinity club.' Parry produced as evidence a letter from a Leeds official, who, speaking of the match at Belle Vue, noted: 'Bradford were beaten that day by the same tactics with which Wakefield Trinity have over and over again vanquished their opponents – they were out-manoeuvred. The Trinity team played towards their weak points and seized the openings given with telling effect.'

In the Yorkshire Challenge Cup, Trinity knocked out Dewsbury Clarence, Woodhouse, Goole and Leeds Parish Church, before meeting Leeds St John's in the semi-final at Crown Flatt. In another replay of the previous year's final, no tries or goals were scored, but Trinity went through to their seventh final by thirteen minor points to nil, and now faced Halifax at Cardigan Fields, Leeds. Herbert Hutchinson played in the same jersey, now rather faded, which he had worn in his previous five finals dating back to 1880, but it brought him no luck. He and his half back partner Harry Dawson both suffered cuts to the head, Dawson eventually retiring. Trinity failed to make the most of their chances and a 15,000 crowd saw them go down by two tries to one. By their own high standards, Trinity's season had not been one of their best, with ten matches lost out of 37, though most of the defeats had been suffered when the side was not at full strength. The team was rebuilding as some of the stars of past years retired from the game. Harper Hamshaw and Herbert Ward were the latest to announce that they were ending their playing careers, with Joe Latham taking over as captain.

The problems associated with replacing key men seemed set to continue into the 1888-89 season, but when they made a brief tour in the autumn, travelling to Swinton, then Hawick and Kendal, Trinity maintained their unbeaten touring record. Following the away defeat at Halifax, the *Wakefield Express* reporter reflected: 'The players have no shining light, no one on whom to depend particularly for any special effort; they are a good all-round lot ... but would be all the better for some specialist at three-quarter back.' With Bartram now gone, and Hartley, Dawson and Hamshaw also departed, Trinity's traditional thrust had been reduced. It was also lamented that, with Bartram's leaving, no one was able to teach the younger players how to kick. 'It is a fact that ... Fallas was the finest punter in his day because he owed most of his prowess to Bartram's teaching; it has also been claimed that Hutchinson's proficiency in place-kicking emanated from the same source.' Bartram had been the only Trinity player to take part in each of Trinity's six Yorkshire Cup finals from 1879 to 1887, winning four. Without him, they did not win the competition again.

Trinity played host to the first ever overseas touring side to this country when, on Wednesday, October 31, 1888, they faced the New Zealand Maoris, who, up to that point, had won five and lost five of their matches. Trinity scored the only try of the match, with county forward Fred Lowrie their best player, but it was said of the Maoris that 'they never seem tired and can run like racehorses.' JH Jones, who had represented Lancashire and Cheshire before moving to Wakefield, and Lowrie were later selected in the North team which defeated the South, Lowrie going on to represent England against the New Zealanders.

Though they had lost some of their star players, Trinity had been defeated in only one match out of 22 played by the mid-point of the season. Despite that record, crowds at Belle Vue had been on the decline. The *Wakefield Express* gave the explanation that there were now so many clubs in the area, all with their own members and loyal supporters, whereas in the past people would travel from miles around to watch the famous Trinity. Population also came into it. Wakefield at this time had 30,000 inhabitants, compared to Hull with 123,000, Bradford with 147,000 and Leeds with 260,000. It was also suggested that Trinity were now less attractive to watch. Their forward-based play had proved very effective in winning matches but had not provided the spectacle the Trinity fans were used to. The tactics were understandable since the team's strength lay in the pack rather than the backs, but there was an evident sense of frustration in the cry: 'Let the ball go loose!'

The team must have taken note, for in the first round of the Yorkshire Cup at Kirkstall, Trinity's easy victory was not only 'machine-like', but was founded on 'wonderful passing' as well as a strong defence. But the lack of real ability in the backs led the Trinity committee to enquire about the possibility of re-engaging Teddy Bartram. Barron Kilner questioned the County Committee about Bartram's status, but was told that Bartram was without doubt a professional and therefore could not play. The Committee arrived at their verdict because in the previous season the Trinity star had received money from the club towards his testimonial. To an outsider it must have seemed nonsensical and at best arbitrary. Dewsbury's Dicky Lockwood, by contrast, was not regarded as a professional because his testimonial fund was provided wholly by the public.

Earlier in the season, Leeds St John's had been suspended for professionalism for having provided employment

Wakefield Trinity appeared in nine Yorkshire Cup finals, winning four. This picture is thought to have been taken following their 1883 victory. (Collection Wakefield Libraries)

for a former member of the Kirkstall club. As might be expected, there was no expression of sympathy from the *Wakefield Express*, which continued to trumpet Trinity's success at the expense of the Leeds clubs. The rivalry extended beyond football, as there was talk of Leeds superseding Wakefield as the administrative headquarters of the West Riding, alluded to in an *Express* article. 'Leeds rugby football clubs have suffered heavily this season at the hands of Wakefield Trinity, and in whatever else they may claim supremacy, at football, Wakefield stands pre-eminent. They may lay claim to our new County Councillors making Leeds their headquarters – and get that. They may talk about, and organise, a Leeds Football and Athletic Club to raise a stronger fifteen than they have lately had – and get that. Nay, they may, and no doubt will, again play for the Yorkshire Cup – and get that, but, until a different race of football players are either born in, or imported into, our neighbouring town they will never play Wakefield Trinity – as at present constituted – even a decent game, and get that. It has been said … that the Yorkshire Challenge Cup was made for Leeds, and they can't win it.'

Bradford was the other great rival. Trinity's new style of play, involving much more passing of the ball and support of the player in possession, had brought success, as revealed by the victory in the third round of the Yorkshire Cup at the Bradford club, Manningham. 'Hitherto the mere mention of the Wakefield Trinity club to the average Bradfordian has had the same effect as a red rag to a bull, and the just claims Trinity advanced of being able to beat anything Bradford way, [was] met by a sneer and the retort that "you can win, but you'll never play football"… Never, said some prominent Manningham officials, have Trinity played such a fine game on Valley Parade … as they did on Saturday, and we had no idea they could do the scientific part of football so well.' Freddy Hulme, who had taken over the goal-kicking duties, converted six out of seven tries in Trinity's comfortable victory. In the fourth round, Trinity beat Dewsbury with equal ease in front of 10,000 spectators, providing one of the biggest gates ever at Belle Vue.

But in the semi-final disaster struck. Trinity, expected to progress easily to another final, were sensationally knocked out by Liversedge, regarded by some as a third-rate village club, but who nevertheless scored a goal to Trinity's try. All had not been well in the Trinity team. It came to light too late that the forward Fred Ross and the half back Ralph Dunn had been drinking heavily on the Friday night and into the early hours of Saturday. They had been unwell when turning out to play on the Saturday, though they did not tell any other member of the team. It was alleged that certain persons who had bet on Trinity to lose had plied the two with alcohol. The following Monday, at a Trinity committee meeting, Ross and Dunn were expelled from the club. For that reason they did not appear in the team photo taken at the end of the season.

The matter did not end there. Further allegations had it that other players had been drinking on that Friday and that one player and a prominent supporter had won large amounts of money from Trinity's loss. An official club enquiry, conducted by two vice-presidents, found, some six weeks later, that no other players had been involved in drinking before the match, nor was there any 'general unsteadiness' in the club. It was also stated that no members of the team were involved in gambling – rumours of this nature were rife in the game - though one member of the committee was 'not entirely free of the charge'.

In other respects the 1888-89 season had been very successful, with only three matches lost, including the Cup defeat, out of forty played. Despite that, attendances were again down, while expenditure exceeded income by £65. The president, ME Sanderson JP, the Tory MP for Wakefield, urged prudence in the handling of the club's finances, which now turned over some £1,200 per annum. He suggested that, if they acted wisely, the club might be in a position to buy the Belle Vue ground and add to it as appropriate for the benefit of spectators and players.

The discussion turned to a proposal which had been made among some of the major clubs in Yorkshire, with a first meeting having taken place at Wakefield in May, 1889. During the close season it was put forward that a league should be formed which would be made up of the leading clubs in the county who would play matches against each other home and away for the championship. Wakefield Trinity, believing that such a move would improve the game, decided unanimously to join the projected league, provided that seven other leading clubs also signed up. Sanderson was in favour of the project, thinking that it would increase funds and would be beneficial to all the clubs concerned. Though Barron Kilner disagreed on the grounds that such a league would be unconstitutional, the president countered that it would be 'rather harsh that the Rugby Union should try to prevent a number of Yorkshire clubs forming a league amongst themselves for the promotion of sport.'

The heavy-handedness of the Rugby Union in enforcing its rules on professionalism would inevitably make clubs think more fundamentally about their future. After Leeds St John's, Heckmondwike would also feel the Committee's wrath, and were suspended sine die for professionalism. Trinity found themselves in the dock too. The case of the alleged professional Teddy Bartram was about to reach its climax. In March, the Trinity committee had asked the Yorkshire governing body whether Bartram was eligible to play and had seen their request refused. However, at the end of the season, Bartram had again turned out in Trinity's colours in a match at Huddersfield. In a long meeting of the County Committee, presided by Mark Newsome, the former Dewsbury player, questions were put to Trinity's new secretary, Charles Berry, who stated that the club had not contributed towards Bartram's testimonial fund, as far as he was aware, but that the player had received loans from the club. Barron Kilner gave evidence that, on behalf of the Trinity committee, he had proposed to Bartram that the club would contribute £50 towards his testimonial if he then retired, or he could have nothing and continue to play. Bartram had said that he would retire. But neither Berry nor Kilner was in a position to say whether the money had actually been paid and so the County Committee called another meeting at which the former secretary, Mr Parry, and Teddy Bartram were required to attend, and all minute books, cash books, bank books and balance sheets from October 1886 onwards had also to be presented.

At the following meeting, at the Queen's Hotel, Leeds, and where Bartram's ex-team-mates Herbert Hutchinson and Herbert Fallas were also present, it was stated that in December 1887 the club had agreed to contribute £50 to

Bartram's fund in lieu of a testimonial match, which the Rugby Union had said could not be played. How the money was actually paid was the subject of protracted questioning, with the chairman, Rev. Frank Marshall, believing that what had originally been loans by the club to Bartram were converted into a donation. Herbert Fallas pleaded that the club had done no worse than other clubs and that Bartram had not played for some time. But after almost four hours, the enquiry concluded with the verdict that Bartram had received at least £50 from the club, that he had subsequently appeared for the club and that he must therefore be declared a professional. The Trinity club was suspended until October 31 and Bartram became the first player to receive a life ban for professionalism.

The matter became a big talking point in rugby circles and there were many – and not just in Wakefield – who believed that Trinity's suspension was excessive punishment. Few were the clubs who did not wonder if they would be next to be investigated. The Committee was turning the screw, with players and clubs coming under the closest scrutiny. Individual players were cross-examined by members of the Yorkshire Committee when summoned to their meetings, with questions asked about details of players' working lives which would appear intrusive and intolerable today. Such meetings had the air of a court-martial, with sentences handed down to so-called professionals as if they had acted in criminal fashion. The RFU, meanwhile, had just pronounced that players found to be professional with a certain club would never be allowed to play for that club again. Midway through the season, Dewsbury and their star player Dicky Lockwood, Leeds Parish Church and Holbeck would all be investigated by the County Committee, with Leeds Parish Church receiving a suspension for having 'made presents' to players.

As Trinity prepared to start their season – late, because of their suspension – it was noted that the club must endeavour to keep its house in best order so as to avoid the County Committee coming down on it again. 'It was said they had waited long for the opportunity the Bartram incident gave them,' reported the *Wakefield Express*, 'and dealt out the punishment quite irrespective of the nature of the offence, and members of that same clique, who devoutly wish Wakefield may be put out of the Cup contest even now, are on the look-out for any other slip...' The Committee's high-handed treatment of the Bartram case was seen as antagonistic and their attitude was beginning to drive a wedge between itself and clubs such as Trinity. It was suggested, later on, that no Wakefield Trinity players be proposed for county selection in the present season, which simply provoked the response that 'if they can do without Trinity, Trinity can do without them.'

When Trinity eventually took to the field, 6,000 fans turned out to watch them face Castleford – a sizeable crowd for an ordinary fixture. Herbert Fallas had taken over as captain, and Ralph Dunn, who had been expelled over the Cup semi-final debacle, made his return, while local clubs Thornes, Horbury and Ossett, continued to provide a number of players. Other teams had been playing for almost two months and, in Trinity's enforced absence, had had the field to themselves. A leading Bradford official was heard to declare, at one of their matches, that his club could 'lick creation', to which a spectator retorted: 'Hod thy noise. Wakefield start laikin' today.'

A *Wakefield Express* writer wondered how it was that Wakefield had become so eminent in the rugby world: 'We have no large population from which to pick and choose our men; we have no great wealth; we boast of no social height to which players may be raised; we are not specially favourites with the County and Rugby Union officials; we have served time; and we lack many things some clubs are favoured with. Yet we do boast of good footballers; we do say that we are good enough for all comers at the Rugby game...' It was probably also true that, in addition to the individual talent in the team, Trinity's success since their earliest days was based on team spirit, enhanced by regular training sessions and team meetings – something which was not the norm at that time. The team always used to meet on Friday evenings before Saturday's match to talk about how to improve on the previous weekend's performance and to formulate tactics. [1]

Trinity also had the advantage of having two pitches next to each other, which meant that second or third team matches could be played alongside, and also that the first team could switch to the lower field if the main ground, with which it formed a T shape, was unplayable, as occasionally happened. On the regular first team pitch a demonstration match of association football was played in January 1890 between a Wakefield team and one from Huddersfield. The former Trinity player Harry Hayley even took part, but the match passed almost unremarked. 'From a spectatorial point of view,' said the *Wakefield Express*, 'the association match did not seem worth the candle, that is, judging by the very meagre crowd.'

During the same month, changes to the club committee were voted in. Until then the committee members had been players or recently retired players, with only the president and secretary non-players. Now three non-playing members were to join the committee and the club was to have an honorary treasurer for the first time, those duties having previously been carried out by the secretary.

Trinity went on their now customary tour, but suffered their first-ever tour defeat at Swinton, before crossing to Ireland, where they beat Dublin University but recorded another reverse, at the hands of Bective Rangers. It was not the best preparation for the Cup, but, to show how seriously they took the competition, they played two practice matches and got down to some serious training. It paid off, because they sailed through to their ninth semi-final, beating Wortley, Elland and Batley before coming up against rivals Bradford on the ground of Leeds Parish Church at Crown Point. Bradford's standing in the game was undisputed: the richest club in the North, they had several county and international players in their ranks. The history of tensions between the two clubs also ensured a keen interest in the tie. Trinity's preparation for important matches left nothing to chance. '… The mode of the game is considered, the faults of last week spoken of in no uncertain tones, the how and why should certain things take place during a coming game, and what to do and when to do it got thoroughly drilled, first into each individual, then into them as a combination by actual practice two or three evenings a week,' commented *The Yorkshireman*.[2] Latham's try and Stafford's conversion gave Trinity the lead which they cherished throughout the second half. The energy and determination of their forwards saw to that, Trinity using their familiar tactic of detaching their wing-forwards to harass the Bradford half backs and go through to their eighth Yorkshire Cup final appearance. It was commented that Trinity would almost rather beat Bradford than win the Cup, but it seemed as if they had reached their peak too soon. The 1890 final tie between Trinity and Huddersfield drew a record crowd estimated at 25,000 to Halifax. It ended in a first victory for Huddersfield, who scored the only goal of the match, while this time Trinity came in for criticism for playing a game too dominated by the forwards.

Though the club was still in good financial shape, the suspension had inevitably meant that gate receipts had declined, since almost two months' play had been lost. To add to its expenses, the club had also had its £50 deposit confiscated by the County Committee when appealing against the suspension. The end of season also marked the retirement of Herbert Fallas, who had played over 340 matches for Trinity.

The captaincy for the 1890-91 season was taken on by the forward J Hampton Jones and among other changes a new grandstand was to be erected on the popular threepenny side, while the teams would use the Alexandra Hotel opposite the ground as changing rooms, saving on transport expenses from the Crown at the bottom of Kirkgate. At the same time as Trinity were showing further signs of progress, their neighbours and old Cup adversaries Thornes were in a desperate situation. Their attendances had dwindled along with the quality of their play. In one early season match against Outwood, for example, Thornes could only raise twelve players for a game which kicked off over an hour late. It was reported that some of their team turned out in their ordinary (and dirty) working clothes and had been drinking. An amalgamation with Trinity was proposed, with Trinity taking over the club's players, fixtures and liabilities. To clear Thornes' relatively small debts was not an obstacle to the takeover, but it was felt that, because membership of the Thornes club cost much less than at Trinity, the Trinity members would object to Thornes members joining them for, in effect, a much lower fee.

Trinity were not without their own problems. Their season began weakly with unaccustomed defeats. The team was in need of strengthening. Rumours circulated that the famous names of Albert and Walter Goldthorpe of Hunslet were set to join the club, but negotiations broke down, the *Wakefield Express* reporting that 'outsiders [who] wish to play with Wakefield will have to go about joining the club in the ordinary way.' But Harry Wigglesworth, who had been capped for England when playing with Thornes, was rumoured to be making a comeback and would turn out for Trinity in the three-quarter line after having been suspended as a referee during the close season. There was controversy too in the formation of the team. The Rugby Union had recently ruled that the forward positions known as 'end men', or 'wings' should disappear and become integrated into the centre of the nine-man pack, as it was at the time, although the majority of clubs in Yorkshire had not yet taken much notice of the RU's ruling. At Trinity, the two forwards who had long occupied these positions, Joe Latham and Herbert Whiteley, were two of the club's finest and had made a large contribution to the club's success. The new captain, Hampton Jones, had insisted on following the RFU's instruction despite changing the formula which had been so profitable to Trinity. The team also came in for criticism for the lack of attacking ideas and absence of passing in the forwards. Despite the difficulties, Jim Bedford and Billy Binks were selected for Yorkshire to play Surrey at Belle Vue. As the team began to pick up form, Leeds were defeated at their new Headingley ground, but Bradford were victorious at Belle Vue in circumstances which did nothing to improve feelings between the two clubs, the rift having only just been repaired. Trinity's captain, Jones, disputed a Bradford try, claiming that a Bradford player had obstructed the Wakefield full back. The referee dismissed the Wakefield captain, who refused to leave, at which the referee ended the match. Jones was suspended for two weeks. The *Wakefield Express* offered the opinion that 'Jones must consider himself lucky in getting off so easily, no matter how small his offence, for those who come in contact with the judicial side of the "Rugby Police" invariably suffer, and have a difficulty in getting their side of the question seen there.'

When Trinity lost the return match at Bradford by the biggest margin of the season – three goals – questions were asked about the team and its training, or lack of it. It was accepted that Trinity did not possess the quality of backs which they had once had, but their forwards were now regarded as too slow. Unlike some of their predecessors, the side was not practising together regularly, largely because certain players would have too far to travel. Comments appearing in the *Wakefield Express* suggested that it would be better to promote A-team players because 'home made 'uns' had more interest in fighting for their own than 'foreign bred 'uns' – 'foreign' meaning no more than that they came from another town. It was a comment that would be heard many times over during Trinity's history.

As teams considered their chances in the Cup, Trinity could hardly look forward with any confidence, for their record in regular matches was a sorry one: nine wins, three draws and sixteen defeats. But in the first round, played on March 7 1891, they put on a good performance at Sowerby, scoring two goals – their first, incredibly, since October. Trinity's ex-forward Fred Lowrie said that his present club Batley would run rings around Trinity in the second round but he spoke too soon. Batley were favourites, but it was Trinity who went through to the third round. There they entertained Holbeck in a very rough, scrappy game, after which Bedford was suspended for two weeks for striking, despite pleading provocation. Though their play was not sparkling, Trinity went on to defeat Wortley away before coming up against Cup-holders Huddersfield in the semi-final. Underdogs for once, Trinity pulled off one of their typical cup-fighting efforts to inflict a decisive defeat on their opponents and march on to their fourth final in five years and their ninth since the start of the competition. Their opponents, Pontefract, appearing for the first time, had caused a sensation by beating Manningham in the third round. They were not overawed by the occasion, which took place at Headingley in front of 15,200 spectators, and outplayed Trinity up front to take the Cup by one goal and a try to one goal.

With more matches lost than won, the playing record of 1890-91 had arguably been Trinity's worst ever. The club's bank balance had again dwindled, mainly as a result of improvements to the ground, including the building of the new grandstand and repairs to the old stand. For the first time in several years, the club had not been in a position to finance a tour. Consideration had been given to amalgamation with Wakefield Cricket Club, but the idea attracted little support. Among many other matters raised at the AGM, the president, Mr Sanderson, expressed the view that working men who had to take time off work to play important matches should have their wages paid, an idea that was gaining ground. The *Wakefield Express* repeated that it expected that a league would be formed from Yorkshire clubs and play championship matches, with payment for broken time also being put forward, which would act as a safeguard against 'real' professionalism. A commonly-held view was that since rugby was by now largely a working man's game, it was unreasonable to expect a man to lose money by taking time off work.

At the start of the 1891-92 season it was reported: 'The club is not rich enough to pay men or offer them special inducements and may suffer through that...' The club was starting to lose players that only recently it would have had no difficulty in retaining. After a string of five defeats in the early season, people started to wonder whether Trinity might go the same way as Thornes, resulting from a failure to nurture the second and third teams. It was significant that players who might once have clamoured to join Trinity were now leaving for other clubs. Players expected to go on tour once a season at the club's expense and the lack of such an arrangement during the previous year had proved a great disincentive. The committee took note, organising matches in February at Cardiff, Pontypridd, Penarth and Gloucester, and though only the match against Pontypridd was won, two others were lost by very narrow margins. But by the time the Yorkshire Cup matches came around, Trinity showed their usual form, defeating Kirkstall St Stephen's easily, the underrated Ossett narrowly, Buttershaw and then, in the quarter-final, Dicky Lockwood's Heckmondwike, which the England star had joined from Dewsbury. Heckmondwike, on their own ground, had started as favourites but Trinity, with their usual gritty performance, earned their place in the semi-final by a try to nil, now scored as 2-0 according to the recently introduced system, by which a goal counted as three points and a try two. Trinity were unfortunate not to make yet another final, losing 2-0 to Leeds at Bradford in front of 15,000 fans – a record for a semi-final.

Earlier, Trinity had again been in trouble with the County Committee, when Herbert Whiteley was suspended for six weeks for rough play and Paul Booth for the same period after being reported by Rev. Marshall for kicking an opponent, who, however, had stated that he did not think Booth's action had been intentional. Trinity were also censured for failing to provide a referee for the match against Bradford – a mistake on the part of the secretary – and had to answer a charge of professionalism brought by Outwood Church FC, who claimed that one of their players had received a broken-time payment to play for Trinity, which the club denied and the case was rejected. However, at a later meeting of the County Committee, Mark Newsome, the chairman, remarked with regard to the suspension of the two Trinity players that the Committee's inconsistency was 'assuming serious proportions', which was another reason why the proposal for a new league was gaining ground.

Four – Towards the Split: 1892-95

Three years after the meeting at Wakefield, where a league of top clubs had been proposed, a new ten-team championship came into being. The Yorkshire Senior Competition, as it was called, was intended to increase public interest – its proponents were well aware of the threat of association football - and raise the skill levels on the field of play. It had its detractors, including the secretary to the Yorkshire Union, JA Miller, who called it a selfish project, but by the start of the season a compromise was reached with the County Committee. The competition was to be managed by the ten clubs, forming a sub-committee of the Yorkshire Union and playing according to RFU rules. A championship table, with a format taken from association football, was to be drawn up for the first time, with two points awarded for a win and one for a draw, a formula which exists to this day. The clubs which took part were Batley, Bradford, Brighouse Rangers, Dewsbury, Halifax, Huddersfield, Hunslet, Liversedge, Manningham and Wakefield Trinity. Leeds, who had been part of the original scheme, withdrew. At the same time, a new points scoring system was introduced by the RFU and was applied across the game. Five points were awarded for a converted try (goal), four points for a drop goal, three for a penalty goal and two for a try.

Trinity's 1892-93 season began with three non-league fixtures before the Yorkshire Senior Competition got under way. But despite wins over Heckmondwike and Holbeck, the lack of a goal-kicker was proving a handicap, as was the refusal to play open football. There was also concern about having to give up the Belle Vue ground, which the club leased and which was soon to be required for building. A field behind Stoneleigh Terrace, on the same side of Doncaster Road as Trinity's first Belle Vue ground, was suggested as an alternative, while the question of amalgamation with Wakefield Cricket Club at their College Grove ground was once more raised. Though the idea had been earlier rejected, the example of Leeds and other clubs in forming a Football, Cricket and Athletic Club appeared attractive to some. In the meantime, traps would no longer be allowed into the ground as their owners were profiting at the club's expense, taking money from people who wanted a better view of the game.

In their opening fixture of the Yorkshire Senior Competition, on October 8, 1892, Trinity lost at home to Bradford. Despite Bradford's reputation as one of rugby football's richest and most powerful clubs, Trinity had won fifteen of the 27 meetings between the two clubs since 1874, with five drawn. But on this occasion they suffered a narrow defeat which was a harbinger of the season. Their home win over Dewsbury two weeks later was to be their sole victory in the new league, which was eventually won by Bradford. 'What are we coming to?' asked the *Wakefield Express* following an ignominious home defeat by Liversedge by 22-2. Two weeks and two defeats later the opinion crystallised: 'Wakefield Trinity are in a worse condition than ever we have known them before.'

At such an important time, the club was in a state of upheaval. Players were coming and going: many of the older, reliable players had left and had not been adequately replaced. There was dissension within the committee, leading to the resignation of the secretary, Hampton Jones, who was succeeded by James Henry Fallas. In an effort to arrest the slide, it was announced, in January, that the team was to go into strict training. After a narrow defeat in the return fixture at Bradford, whose victories in the 28 matches played between the two clubs now swelled to eight, the *Bradford Observer* stated Trinity's dilemma as it saw it: 'Wakefield have long held a monopoly of a particular style of game, which is purely preventive. There was a thorough understanding between the men who formerly played for Trinity. New names have started new ideas at Wakefield and the club is between two stools. There is not enough talent to play on modern lines successfully, whilst the old strength is getting rather too old to carry on the well-known but unpopular Trinity game. That, we believe, is the position in the Wakefield camp today and much as we deplore the downfall of the whilom Cup-tie cracks, we must say that they have brought it on themselves by refusing to introduce necessary reforms long ago. Perhaps we shall yet live to see Wakefield come to the front by means of good, scientific football.'

Trinity were bottom of the new league and, to make matters worse, half the players failed to turn up for the away match against Batley and had to be replaced with second-teamers at the last minute. Three had excuses but the action of the others was taken as a strike. The very idea would have been unthinkable a decade earlier, but the protest took place against a background of industrial conflict, typified locally by the very serious strike by Featherstone miners in the same year. The working man had begun to flex his political as well as sporting muscle. In the Trinity players' case, the protest was part of an ongoing dispute between players and committee over team selection, the bone of contention this time being the omission from the team of the popular forward Joss Dawson, who had proved his value to the side both on and off the field. The committee took the decision to expel four players who had not turned up for the Batley match, plus the three Dawson brothers, Harry, a Cup-winning former captain who strenuously denied involvement in the matter, Dick and Joss, who was at the centre of the storm. Paul Booth, who was also implicated, was stripped of the vice-captaincy.

At the end of the inaugural Senior Competition in March, Trinity, one of the four principal clubs which had instigated the new league, had managed only one win and one draw out of eighteen matches played. The *Athletic News* commented: 'Not to have won a single first-class match for six months is Trinity's experience and for a club with such a record it seems unique in the history of football. Trinity should now win the Yorkshire Cup to make their circle of eccentricity complete.'

But in the Cup, Trinity only got as far as the second round, where they lost at home to Halifax by 29-6. 'What a terrible licking!' remarked the *Wakefield Express*. 'This must be the worst season the city men have ever experienced. It has witnessed an almost complete change in the composition of the fifteen. It has seen the expulsion of some of its old players for breaches of discipline – an occurrence almost without precedent: in fact it has been a year of retrogression.' In the third round, Alverthorpe, surprise victors at Dewsbury in the first round, carried the Wakefield flag and even wore Trinity's colours in their 7-0 defeat by Bradford.

As the secretary, JH Fallas, declared, the season could only be considered disastrous. Though the club got off to a poor start, 'we were looking forward to brighter times,' said Fallas, 'when some matter of difference arose between five of our most prominent players and our late secretary, which have never been satisfactorily explained, causing them to withdraw their services.' After twenty years' existence, Trinity's playing record was easily their worst ever, with only five matches won and two drawn out of thirty-four played in all competitions.

It was ironic that Trinity had saved their poorest ever performance for the opening season of the Yorkshire Senior Competition, of which the club had been one of the pioneers. At the dinner following the presentation of the trophy to winners Bradford, the Yorkshire County Committee secretary, JA Miller, again had something to say about the question of broken-time payments – a matter which had clear implications for Trinity. Miller stated that he considered it an 'injustice' not to recompense men for working time lost. Two years earlier a motion in favour of the principle of broken-time payments, put forward at a Yorkshire Union meeting, had been narrowly carried, but Miller had believed it better to 'allow opinion to develop' before pursuing the resolution. He now firmly believed that there was a change in public opinion towards bona fide payments and intended raising the matter again, first among the Yorkshire Union members and then at the Rugby Football Union in London.

At the RFU meeting in September, Yorkshire's proposal, supported by Lancashire, met stiff opposition from Southern clubs, as expected. Yorkshire were also betrayed from within, with Rev. Marshall stirring the mood against the proposal and earning himself the description of 'political mountebank' from Wakefield delegate JH Fallas. However much the Northern clubs put forward the moral argument in favour of broken-time payments,

The Wakefield Trinity team, around 1892 (Collection Wakefield Museums)

there remained among them the fear of professionalism, which was foreseen as 'a terrible blow for such as Wakefield Trinity, Pontefract, Castleford and Alverthorpe,' while clubs such as Bradford and Halifax 'would always have their own way because they would be able by paying big prices to get the best players.' But at Trinity's AGM in June of the following year, Herbert Hutchinson, the club's representative to the Yorkshire Rugby Union, stated that he thought that the RFU made one of their biggest mistakes ever when refusing to support the resolution in favour of broken-time payments. A similar view was articulated in the *Yorkshire Post*: 'It is unfortunate that sportsmen of the south are inexperienced in the difficulties under which football is conducted in the north. The latter has long ago outstripped the south in the number and capacity of its clubs and players, and we are convinced that the future support and progress of rugby in England must be looked for more in Lancashire and Yorkshire than in all the other parts of the country put together. […] The leading clubs of the north are unanimously in favour of the concession which the Yorkshire Union proposed. To ignore an expression of opinion from such a body of clubs is unwise, and, viewed as a matter of tactics, a mistake.' [1]

The new season of 1893-94 began with Trinity being led by a 21-year old captain, Orlando Watson from East Ardsley. His appointment was meant to signal an era of reconstruction, with a fresh group of players, as the club attempted to recover from the previous season which had proved so catastrophic. Trinity badly needed to adopt a more open style of play, with more opportunities being given to the backs, and there was evidence of greater emphasis on the passing game, as they chose to adopt the four three-quarter system, as clubs such as Manningham and Liversedge had already done. In fact the first time four three-quarter backs were used was in the victory in mid-October over Huddersfield, who soon afterwards would be suspended by the RFU for offering inducements to players, having been denounced by a member of their own committee, the anti-professionalism crusader, Rev. Marshall. In the match before that, Trinity had fallen to their old rivals Bradford, the first winners of the competition, who themselves had lost their first six matches. The *Leeds Mercury* commented that Trinity were 'merely a shadow of the once powerful side which helped so greatly to spread the fame of Yorkshire football. But Trinity of old were such a thorn in the side of Bradford when the latter were at the zenith of their fame that one can well understand how the defeat of the famous "blue and red" brigade at Park Avenue must ever be regarded with a considerable degree of satisfaction.' [2] When Trinity lost the return fixture, they might have taken comfort in the fact that their side was composed of Wakefield players, 'trained on home soil', while Bradford's, it was pointed out, was made up 'chiefly of importations not merely from other towns, but from other countries.'

Regardless of Trinity's performances, rugby football remained the sole winter sport of interest to the Wakefield public. Soccer came nowhere. It was pointed out, following the 1895 Cup final involving Aston Villa and West Bromwich Albion, which drew somewhere between forty and fifty thousand spectators, that 'the Association code does not seem to catch on in Wakefield as it has done in other West Riding towns. After three years of fitful existence, we hear little of the city club now … We are afraid it is all through an apathetic public.'

Though discussions with Wakefield Cricket Club concerning amalgamation and ground-sharing had come to nothing, similar negotiations now took place with the successful Wakefield Athletics Club. For Trinity it was a double priority: first, because they would soon have to give up the lease on the present ground; and second, because their facilities compared unfavourably with the other major clubs, Bradford, Halifax, Huddersfield and Leeds.

Trinity's performances in the Senior Competition were mixed and included a period of seven matches where they failed to score. Orlando Watson got injured and gave up the captaincy and Jack Anderton, who originated from Wigan, took over. Two late season victories over Huddersfield and Halifax resulted in Trinity improving on their first season's record, but not by much as they finished ninth out of the twelve clubs.

In the Yorkshire Cup, Trinity went through to the third round after beating Morley and Alverthorpe but progressed no further as Bramley produced a last-minute drop goal to create a shock result. Halifax went on to take T'Owd Tin Pot by defeating Castleford by a record 38-6 score at Headingley before 17,000 spectators. Halifax also claimed a record by having won the Cup five times, compared to Trinity's four. Trinity had appeared in a record nine finals, as opposed to Halifax's six. No other club had won the Cup more than once.

For the 1894-95 season, Osbert Mackie, the son of wealthy corn merchant Colonel Mackie of Heath, and a playing member only since the previous March, was made captain. The early season progress, however, followed what was becoming a familiar pattern, with little for fans to rejoice about. In an interview, Mackie, who was soon to play for Cambridge University, stated that he thought professionalism was coming, but that it would be Trinity's 'absolute ruin', because the club would not be able to afford to pay players and if they did have good local players in their ranks they would soon be snapped up by richer clubs such as Bradford and Halifax. Mackie believed that the game would be dominated by three or four clubs 'and the rest nowhere'.

A showdown with the Rugby Union was approaching. In Lancashire, Leigh were suspended for two months and Salford for a year, the latter for offering 'pecuniary inducement' to a player. Broughton, Rochdale, Swinton, Tyldesley and Wigan were all due to face charges. If those clubs were all to be suspended, the Lancashire Club Championship, a parallel contest to Yorkshire's, would lose all but three of its ten clubs, hastening the revolution. An alliance under the name of the Northern League of Professional Clubs was already being hatched.

In November, Wigan found themselves suspended until February. At the same time, at a meeting at Huddersfield of Yorkshire and Lancashire clubs, the Rugby Union's stance on professionalism was discussed. In that light, the clubs agreed on forming an alliance though none was keen to embrace professionalism as such. Payment for broken time seemed to be the solution, but was not confirmed.

At a special meeting of the RFU in London in December, Trinity representative Herbert Fallas expressed the division of views on this vexed question of professionalism. 'It is said that Yorkshiremen are in favour of professionalism, either veiled or open,' he said. 'I am prepared to bow down and worship at the shrine of the Southern amateur, but I represent a working-class district where very different conditions prevail. I quite agree that a man should not make money out of playing football, but equally he should not lose money by it. To the Southern amateur "broken time" is an outside name, but to the Yorkshire workman it is a very real thing.' By January a northern rugby league was proposed and was starting to take shape.

Back in Wakefield, the ground-sharing proposal with the Athletics Club had fallen through. The two clubs were unable to agree on the site. The ground formerly used by the Thornes club, situated off Denby Dale Road, at the back of Cradock and Co rope works, was regarded as unsuitable because it was based on clay soil and would need laying out. To purchase Belle Vue would cost £1,000 more and though the ground was laid out it had the disadvantage of being less convenient and the making of a new street there could prove problematical. However the owners of Belle Vue were willing to subscribe £1,300 towards the required capital, while the lower field could eventually be sold off.

To buy Belle Vue was a bold move in difficult times. Despite Trinity's illustrious history, their showing in the Yorkshire Senior Competition since its inception had revealed the club to be at its lowest point in terms of playing record. With an expanded Northern competition now in the pipeline, it was a question of whether Trinity would still be able to compete at the highest level. Apart from an early season victory over Otley, they did not win a single match until beating Hull in March. 'Of all the clubs that one does not care to see Wakefield beaten by, that club is Leeds,' stated the *Wakefield Express*, echoing public opinion, but Leeds did indeed win, by 17-0 and at Belle Vue. As so often happened, Trinity hit their best form in time for the Cup, first beating Bradford and the current champions, Manningham, in the league, before causing a few surprises in the knock-out competition. In the second round they beat Liversedge, the Senior Competition leaders, 20-0 away, taking 2,300 travelling spectators with them and went on to beat Dewsbury before facing Morley away. As had sometimes happened in the past, Trinity came unstuck against a side they should have beaten. Morley, the leaders of the second division, were, however, undefeated all season and maintained their record by knocking Trinity out of the Cup by 15-0.

The two clubs could have had to face each other again, this time in a play-off to decide whether Trinity, the bottom club, should remain in the Senior Competition or whether Morley, as Second Competition winners, should take their place. The question led to a crisis in Yorkshire rugby football, with the Yorkshire Union and the Senior Competition squaring up to each other. The play-off would have gone ahead if the Yorkshire Union resolution had been accepted. But it was not, the Senior clubs reserving their right – as originally granted by the Yorkshire Union – to decide who should constitute the competition. The Yorkshire Union's next step was to withdraw that right, to which the twelve Senior clubs responded by withdrawing their membership of the County organisation. But the Senior clubs still came under the jurisdiction of the English Rugby Union, which, they believed, would aim eventually to bring the renegade clubs to heel. It was therefore suggested, among the twelve, that they break off relations with the RFU and take steps to form a Northern Union, 'to be composed of all clubs willing to throw in their lot with such a new organisation, and thus obtain freedom from the domination of the Southerners, which has been irksome enough in the past.'

During this month of August 1895, everything came to a head. The Senior clubs' stance hardened when the RFU brought out even more stringent rules on professionalism. The governing body's position was based on the belief that football was to be played solely for 'the honour and pleasure' of it. They therefore declared illegal any kind of material benefit derived from playing. The RFU categorically forbade compensation for loss of working time, nor were players allowed to do any work for the club or its ground for which expenses might be received. Players were not allowed to play in benefit matches either. The punishment for transgressing any of these rules was expulsion from all English clubs, which also applied to any player refusing to give evidence to investigations into professionalism.

Even within the Senior clubs who were heading towards a new alliance there was some division of opinion. Barron Kilner, for example, blamed the newspapers for stirring up the controversy and believed that the Senior clubs should not have broken off relations with the Yorkshire Union. He still hoped that connections between the two bodies could be repaired.

But the mood was against reconciliation. Meeting followed meeting, in Leeds and in Manchester, until finally the definitive break was made. On Thursday, 29 August, at the historic assembly at the George Hotel, Huddersfield, the Yorkshire and Lancashire clubs signed up to the new body, the Northern Union, which was to be run on amateur lines but with allowance of payment for bona fide broken time. The clubs represented were Brighouse, Oldham, Halifax, Leeds, Bradford, Hull, Huddersfield, Hunslet, Wakefield Trinity, Widnes, Broughton Rangers, Batley, St Helens, Leigh, Warrington, Tyldesley, Manningham, Rochdale Hornets, Liversedge, Wigan and Dewsbury. Stockport, who were not represented at the meeting, were also admitted, but Dewsbury, initially undecided, withdrew the following week, to be replaced by Runcorn.

Five – From Union to League: 1895-1905

This was rugby league's defining moment. The decision to break away from the Rugby Union and to establish the self-governing Northern Union resulted in a 22-team championship, spread across Yorkshire, Lancashire and Cheshire, in which each club would play every other, home and away, in a lengthy season of 42 fixtures. It was a long way, though, from being a professional competition. The principle of broken time – over which the northern clubs and the RFU had wrangled for so long – was put into effect with six shillings fixed as the set payment to a player who had to take time off work to play. But that was enough to professionalise Northern Union players in the eyes of the RFU, a number of whose own clubs also continued to pay their players in complete contravention of the RFU's own regulations.

The Northern Union's momentous resolution gave rise to a century of cold-shouldering at best, outright hostility at worst. A week before the revolutionary season kicked off, the older organisation informed the new that there could be no matches played between the two bodies and their member clubs. The breach was never to be mended – at least while ever rugby union remained an 'amateur' sport.

The rules of the game which would eventually become known as rugby league remained, however, essentially the same as those administered by the RFU. But within a few days of the first matches being played, it was already being suggested at a Northern Union meeting that, in order to make the game as attractive as possible and in order to give the backs the chance to produce fast, open play, the number of players per team should be reduced from fifteen to thirteen. It was also suggested that line-outs be abolished, since the usual result was a scrum. Both points, proposed at a further meeting in December, and seconded by Wakefield Trinity's delegate Herbert Hutchinson, were rejected, but the line-out disappeared within two years and teams were eventually reduced to thirteen players in 1906. But mindful of their duty towards a paying public, the NU instituted a system of fines on clubs which kicked off late, which had been a common occurrence in pre-NU days.

The first round of matches took place on Saturday, September 7, with Wakefield Trinity away at Bradford, where they lost 11-0. After also losing 10-0 at Huddersfield, it was not until the third match of the season, at home to Wigan, that Trinity recorded their first Northern Union victory, winning 13-9. Trinity's first try-scorer was the international forward Bill Walton, with Harry Morgan and Joe Allchurch claiming the others and AE Moorhouse converting twice. Their captain in this first season was George Thresh. Match receipts amounted to £39 twelve shillings and threepence.

Trinity took longer to adjust to life in the Northern Union than many had expected. With other clubs recruiting to bolster their sides, Wakefield looked to sign the former international winger Dicky Lockwood. Though born at Crigglestone, Lockwood had made his reputation first at Dewsbury and then at Heckmondwike. He was capped for England at 19 and later became captain – a remarkable achievement for a working-class player. He had acquired a reputation for his speed, ferocious defence, tactical awareness and kicking, although when he arrived at Belle Vue, it took some time for him to regain match fitness. Lockwood made his debut on October 19, 1895 at Warrington but it was not until a month later that Trinity won their first away match – at Widnes. That victory prompted a Manchester newspaper to comment on the signings from Wales that Trinity had made. 'It is a happy augury for Wakefield Trinity,' went the report, 'that directly they turn their attention to local talent and leave men with a flavour of leek in their constitution and an imagined reputation behind them alone, their fortunes should change. The Wakefield Committee have been severely criticised for their hankering after strange [foreign] talent and last week they looked to their second team. The result was a creditable win…'

Regardless of team selection, by the turn of the year Trinity were bottom of the league, with only four matches won out of nineteen played, and last in the Yorkshire championship, which was based on matches played against other clubs in the county. They rallied and won four in a row, but this first season proved full of event, some of it unwanted. At the end of March the Belle Vue ground was suspended from use for three weeks following crowd disturbance. As the final whistle blew at the match against Halifax, a number of spectators, incensed at some of the referee's decisions which they believed had cost Wakefield the match, climbed over the railings surrounding the pitch and assaulted the official, as well as members of the Trinity committee who were ushering him from the field. Angry not only because they held the referee responsible for their side's loss but also because of the money that had been lost in bets, the mob set upon and injured the official. In an attempt to forestall any further crowd disturbance, posters were put up at Belle Vue, and at other grounds, reminding spectators of the need for good behaviour.

As the first season drew to a close, a number of local clubs resigned their membership of the Yorkshire RU to join the Northern Union. Among them was Horbury, followed by Heckmondwike, Eastmoor and Castleford, who had just won for the first time the old Yorkshire Challenge Cup, a competition now much reduced in quality. Castleford, it was alleged, had spent more money on their team than any Northern Union club. The attack was made by an official at the presentation of medals to Trinity's A team, who had won their competition. Those called upon to speak reflected on this first season. Committee member Herbert Fallas refuted a suggestion that NU clubs were bankrupt, maintaining that Trinity 'had never been in more flourishing condition and had taken more money at the gates than they had ever taken in their best days [of RU].' The chairman of Brighouse and the Northern Union president, HH Waller, head of a textiles firm and former pupil of Silcoates School, restated the case for the new organisation. 'It was an anomaly,' he said, 'to ask working men to break their work and risk the danger of being dismissed without payment for broken time. It is a misnomer to call such a man a professional but I believe the public will soon have their eyes opened and will find that the Northern Union are working on lines of honesty and straightforwardness while those who profess to be amateurs are professionals. I hope that something will be done in the future whereby we might again be united and the Southerners acknowledge they were in the wrong.'

Not just 'the Southerners' but others elsewhere who clung to rugby's status quo were a long way from recognising any wrongdoing on their part. Quite the opposite. They in turn were quick to condemn what they saw as a rebel organisation tainted from the outset by mercenary instincts, while the older body upheld the purer sporting ethos. Commenting on the state of the Rugby Union in 1897, former RFU president Arthur Budd wrote: 'Though we are fewer in numbers than we were, I think we can congratulate ourselves that we are in a very much healthier condition, and that in purifying our ranks we have now the assistance of the Northern Union, who have proved themselves to be a most admirable drainage pipe.'[1] Thus began the hundred-year conflict between those who held to the ideals of the Rugby Union and, on the other hand, the Northern Union men whom they reviled.

There was no denying the popular success of the Northern Union's inaugural season, during which most clubs increased their takings and made a profit, including Wakefield Trinity, despite finishing nineteenth out of the 22 teams. Only Huddersfield, Broughton Rangers and Rochdale were placed below Trinity in the league, which was won by Manningham. But after the first season, the single-division structure embracing Yorkshire, Lancashire and Cheshire clubs was abandoned in favour of two county leagues, the Yorkshire Senior Competition and its Lancashire counterpart. It was felt that the time and distances involved in travelling to 21 away matches in the season was prohibitive. In the case of the Yorkshire competition, five new clubs – Castleford, Bramley, Holbeck, Heckmondwike and Leeds Parish Church – joined the eleven pioneer clubs for the 1896-97 season.

At Wakefield, the decision to join the Northern Union the year before had been almost unanimous. But there was one notable exception. Barron Kilner, a past president of the Yorkshire Rugby Union, stuck to his amateur principles. In a speech at the dinner which followed the Yorkshire v Westmorland Rugby Union match at Morley,

The reconstituted Belle Vue ground originally had a cycle track. The West Stand, shown here around 1900 but demolished in the 1980s, originally had seating down to ground level, before the cycle track was replaced by a sunken paddock.

the former Trinity captain said that he was proud of being a Yorkshire sportsman and an amateur. In his opinion, if rugby football was not played as a recreation and a sport it was not worth playing at all. When a man was paid for playing the game he was paid to win and it became a question of win, tie or wrangle. The Yorkshire Rugby Union team had to uphold the prestige, honour and integrity of their county, he declared. Let them stick to the Rugby Union and to honest amateurism and Yorkshire would succeed, let the Northern Union do what it would. To the longest day of his life he would wish success to the Yorkshire Union and prosperity to the cause of amateur football.

Kilner's remarks caused great displeasure at Trinity. Letters between the two parties went back and forth, with Kilner claiming to have been misreported and the club demanding that he contradict his comments or face expulsion. In January-February 1897, Kilner was in fact expelled from the club by unanimous agreement and his name struck off the list of vice-presidents in a move which brought a sad end to the club's connection with one of its early driving forces.

Kilner was, in any case, flying in the face of public opinion as the NU inexorably gained ground over its rival. The Northern Union Challenge Cup, first played for in 1897, completely overshadowed the old Yorkshire Cup. Trinity's first Challenge Cup match, against Leigh, ended in a 0-0 draw but the replay was won 13-4, with E Evans, Dicky Lockwood and Joe Breakwell scoring tries and Lockwood adding two conversions. Matches were played on consecutive weekends and a week later Trinity were knocked out by Brighouse Rangers, who won 11-4. In the first final, Batley defeated St Helens 10-3. The following year's final, again played at Headingley was watched by almost 28,000 spectators – double the previous attendance and a record for a club rugby match in England. By contrast the Yorkshire (Rugby Union) Cup, which had been responsible for the huge rise in popularity of rugby from its creation in 1877 and which had eventually attracted an entry of 132 clubs, could muster just eleven participating sides by 1901. [2]

When the Ossett club debated, in the close season of 1899, whether to switch allegiance to the Northern Union, the arguments in favour were overwhelming. Under the Northern Union they would have better fixtures and cup-ties, since in particular the RU cup-ties 'had not paid their way'. Most important, they would find it hard to raise a team if they stayed with the Rugby Union as 'all Rugby players were joining the Northern Union'. Many other clubs had already trodden a similar path, so that, before the turn of the century, the Yorkshire Union had lost an overwhelming majority of its clubs to the Northern Union and was in a state of virtual collapse.

County matches between Yorkshire, Lancashire and Cheshire were also instituted in 1896 and proved a popular success. Bill Walton, Dicky Lockwood and Jimmy Metcalfe were Trinity's earliest representatives. The match between Yorkshire and Lancashire, played at Bradford in November 1897, drew 14,000 spectators. By contrast, the equivalent Rugby Union match, played at Dewsbury, attracted a crowd of just 2,000. In a post-match speech at Bradford, NU president HH Waller said that he believed that if the Northern Union had not been formed, rugby would have been entirely replaced in Yorkshire by association football. Certainly soccer was on the rise, though it held few attractions for the Wakefield public. A Wakefield association team was in existence at this time, as at Altofts, Normanton, Ossett and Oulton, but by January 1898 the club bearing the city's name said it could no longer carry on and resigned from the West Yorkshire league.

During this period from the 1896-7 season to 1898-99, Trinity regularly found themselves in mid-table in the Yorkshire Senior Competition. As the club became more professional in a general sense, thoughts turned to renovating the ground, which had long been a topic of discussion but which now began to take shape. At the start of the 1896-97 season, plans were made to create the Wakefield Trinity Athletic Company, a limited company separate from the football club, which remained a members' club. Shares were issued to enable the purchase of the ground, which consisted of the main field and the lower field at right-angles to it. A new stand and dressing-rooms were also envisaged, as well as moving the club's headquarters from Holly Lodge to Belle Vue. Two years later the work was done. The revamped ground was formally opened on September 24, 1898 by Viscount Milton, MP for Wakefield, and was described as one of the prettiest enclosures in Yorkshire. At a cost of £8,000, terracing was provided on all sides, enclosed by iron railings, so that the ground could easily accommodate 15,000 spectators. A cycling track with banked ends was created around the playing area, which had been completely levelled by building up the slope at the Agbrigg Road end. The second field, part of a piece of land known at one time as Heathfield, was sold off for housing development, forming Trinity Street and part of St Catherine's Street. The club rooms at Holly Lodge were retained and refurbished for the benefit of the six hundred members. On the day of the opening of the reconstituted ground, the old Yorkshire Cup rivals Halifax were the visitors, but the match was a disappointment, Trinity losing 13-0 in front of 5,940 spectators, including numerous dignitaries.

The 1897-98 season began with line-outs abolished and the value of all goals set at two points (a drop goal had previously been worth four), since a try (three points) was rightly considered harder to get than a goal. Between the end of that season and the start of the next, the broken-time principle had given way to open professionalism. The payment of six shillings per man for working time lost had been replaced by remuneration according to market forces and the Northern Union had had to recognise the fact just three years after the breakaway. The rules which the Northern Union framed on payments to players began with the words 'Professionalism is legal' – a conscious contradiction of the Rugby Union's opening rule which stated the opposite. But anxious to avoid a free-for-all which might lead to the spectre of full professionalism, the Northern Union added stipulations which stated, for example, that all players must be in bona fide employment, which did not include jobs such as 'billiard markers, waiters in licensed houses or any employment in connection with a club.'

The 1903-04 team with the second division trophy. *Back row*: W Mitchell, R Jaques, H Parker, H Wood, J Webster, H Price, G Brunton (trainer). *Middle row* (players only): R McPhail, CW Cox, AK Crosland, J Walton, H Beaumont. *Seated*: JH Fallas (secretary), JB Cooke (chairman), W Royston (treasurer), D Holmes, EW Bennett, W Malkin (capt), J Metcalfe, J Edwards, H Senior (trainer). *Front*: TH Newbould, T Dixon, W Hale

Wakefield Trinity looked optimistically towards the new century, installed full back Jimmy Metcalfe as captain, and got off to a good start. Cumberland-born Metcalfe had been signed in 1897 from Featherstone, had represented Yorkshire in both codes and became the first Trinity player to kick a hundred goals in a season, which he achieved in 1901-2 and again in 1908-9.

Trinity took five points out of six over the 1899 Christmas period, beating Bramley on the Saturday, Hull two days later on Christmas Day and then drew at Castleford on Boxing Day. They ended the season in fourth place, their highest position since the start of the Northern Union, without losing a home match, and reached the fourth round of the Challenge Cup. But though it had been Trinity's most successful season in the Northern Union, the club president, Dr WA Statter, reported a deficit. More money had been taken through the gates than ever before - £836 as against £691 the previous season – but the outgoings had risen. 'The expenses have been very heavy owing to the new mode of paying players for their services, which rendered them really professionals,' said Dr Statter. Players' and attendants' wages had cost the club £601, not counting travel and hotel expenses. The club was still solvent, but could not afford another season like the one just past.

As the 1900-01 season approached, the great Dicky Lockwood, now in the latter stages of his career, was allowed to return to his first club, Dewsbury, but no new stars were announced. It was said that the club was unable to recruit players who were better than those already there. There was also the matter of competing with other clubs for the services of top players and the possible payment of a transfer fee, a practice which had sprung up recently. It was noted ruefully: '"For the love of the game" now seems to be a secondary consideration with Northern Union footballers and the first thing most of them think about is the amount of money they are going to be paid for their services.' By the middle of the season, Trinity were in fourth place in the competition but slipped back to ninth by the end. They were edged out of the Challenge Cup in the third round by league leaders Bradford, who won 5-4, but Trinity had the compensation of seeing 20,195 paying spectators, plus about 700 members, flock to Belle Vue to set a ground record. Receipts totalled £675, which was almost as much as had been taken in the whole of the 1898-99 season.

If Wakefield had retained their fourth place in the Yorkshire Senior Competition, they might have been better placed to withstand the shock which followed in the close season. At the instigation of Halifax, the twelve leading clubs from both sides of the Pennines banded together to form an elite league, purportedly to encourage a higher standard of play in the face of the ever-increasing threat from soccer. The matter was a hot topic at Trinity's annual meeting. Herbert Hutchinson, now president of the Northern Union, took the chair and reminded members of the inaugural 1895-96 season, when matches were played between Yorkshire and Lancashire clubs. The expenses were greater and receipts less, he recalled, because supporters tended not to travel far to watch matches. Hutchinson called the proposal unconstitutional, unjustifiable and unnecessary and he would do his best to thwart it. But his words were in vain. The new league – in effect a super league 95 years before Super League - was created and Trinity were left out. There was much ill feeling between the two camps and the

The programme for the match against Bradford, September 16, 1905

remaining Yorkshire Senior Competition clubs, like their counterparts in Lancashire, had no option but to carry on at that level, without their top clubs.

By the turn of the century, rugby union in Yorkshire and Lancashire had become very much a minority sport, confined to a handful of clubs. The famous Yorkshire Cup was contested by just a dozen clubs in the 1901-02 season. But still there were individuals in Wakefield who hankered after the old-style game. A month after the formation of the elite Northern Rugby League, a meeting was held with the aim of establishing a new club which would take the name of Wakefield Rugby Club – more than twenty years after the demise of the first – and would be based entirely on amateur principles. It is instructive to note the calibre of individuals who claimed to be in favour of the new club: Barron Kilner, the Bishop of Wakefield, Lord St Oswald and Arthur Hartley, of Castleford, president of the Rugby Union. It was envisaged that membership would encompass, among others, old boys of Wakefield Grammar School, who, it was maintained, had nowhere in the city to play – although at one period Wakefield Trinity had three Old Savilians – the two Kingswells and Willie Malkin - in their three-quarter line. The chairman of the meeting said that he thought it a particularly favourable opportunity to form a club as there had been a split in the Northern Union.

Other local rugby clubs, such as Alverthorpe, Eastmoor, Ossett and Outwood Church, were all playing under the auspices of the Northern Union in the Yorkshire Second Competition. Trinity began the 1901-02 season in the Yorkshire Senior Competition, which had been, with its Lancashire equivalent, the NU's top tier. Since the creation of the Northern Rugby League, however, the YSC was clearly an inferior division. Some of Trinity's players were targeted by the top clubs. Welsh winger Horace Price signed for Salford and forward Fred Smailes went to Bradford, though star full back Jimmy Metcalfe, despite interest from Oldham and elsewhere, chose to stay put. By November, the impact of playing at this level was clearly felt. It was reported: 'Never in the whole of Wakefield Trinity's history, we should think, have they been so badly supported by the public… If the gates do not considerably increase the club will be placed in a very serious position.' Though certain other clubs actually increased their attendances, Wakefield's followers, used to the achievements of the past, seemed to become disaffected. 'No doubt the formation of the Northern League … has had something to do with the lack of support,' it was suggested. Those feelings were confirmed at the end of a highly unsatisfactory season, described by secretary James Henry Fallas as 'the most anxious, disastrous and disappointing in the club's history'. It was now clear that Trinity should have put themselves forward for inclusion in the Northern League, since supporters' interest in the Yorkshire Senior Competition had waned to the point where another season of this fare was unthinkable from a playing and financial point of view. 'That the Trinity Football Club cannot continue to exist under present circumstances is conclusively proved by the balance sheet,' added Fallas at the AGM. The club treasurer TO Bennett recorded that gate receipts had amounted to only £530 as against £1,387 the previous season and though players' wages had been slashed the club was in a difficult position. The president, Dr Statter, saying that it had been a mistake not to join the Northern League, announced that Trinity had decided to join the newly-created second division of the Northern League, admitting that it would be a novel experience for Wakefield to be consigned to secondary status, but it was to be seen as a means to an end, which was to get into the first division.

Herbert Hutchinson, who had served the club so well as a player and an official, was not present at the meeting but tendered his resignation. His contribution to the club was recognised, but it was also said that his speech at the previous year's AGM, arguing for staying out of the Northern League, had led to Trinity's present dire situation.

As they began the 1902-3 season in the 18-team second division of the Northern League, Trinity found themselves lining up alongside Castleford and Normanton as well as Holbeck, Leeds and Manningham. But they would also have to travel farther afield, to the likes of Lancaster, Millom, Birkenhead, Morecambe and South Shields. Some of those clubs did not last, as the early years of the Northern Union saw many clubs attach themselves to the new organisation only to disappear a few seasons later. Locally, the Eastmoor club, founded in 1891, folded in the summer of 1902, suffering from a lack of support and the unavoidable expense of running a semi-professional organisation. On the other hand, Trinity actively promoted another layer of competition - at the workplace. The Inter-Workshops Competition catered for colliery teams at Ryhill Main, Parkhill, Manor, Lofthouse and Woolley and major manufacturers G Cradock & Co, Calder Mills, Calder Vale Boiler Works, Calder Soap Works, J Rhodes & Sons, Bradley & Craven and E Green & Sons, later to be joined by others.

Trinity's team, which included county winger Ernest Bennett, son of TO Bennett, was significantly strengthened when the Castleford and Yorkshire rugby union scrum-half, Tommy Newbould, was signed and made his debut on November 22, 1902, playing 'a grand game'. It was not long before he was being described as the finest half back Wakefield had seen for many seasons.

In this first season in the Northern League second division, Trinity finished seventh. Gate receipts were up, though a small loss was made on the season, since travelling expenses increased, but treasurer TO Bennett thought that the club had every reason to congratulate themselves. By the November of the following season, Trinity were top of the second division. An early Cup exit – at the hands of Runcorn in a replayed preliminary round tie – proved a blessing in disguise, allowing Trinity to concentrate on winning the second division, which they duly achieved, and with it promotion to the first. During that 1903-4 season, Trinity played 32 matches, scoring 387 points and conceding only 57. When the second division trophy was presented to the captain, Willie Malkin, a barren period of 17 years without a cup came to an end.

Trinity marked their return to top-flight competition, after a two-year absence, with a shock 6-2 win at Broughton Rangers, who had ended the previous season in third place. The match-winner was full back Jimmy Metcalfe, who kicked Trinity's three goals and played a fine all-round game. Crowds were on the up: 7,000 spectators watched the home defeat by Leeds and a similar number saw Trinity beat Widnes in the first round of the Cup. Over 12,000 fans witnessed their second round Cup tie at Fartown, with 10,853 paying spectators watching them beat second division Huddersfield in the replay at Belle Vue. Trinity were knocked out by Broughton Rangers in the next round but improved in the league, following a string of defeats, to finish in fourteenth place in the 18-team table.

The return to the top level of competition had put Trinity's finances back on a sounder footing, with accrued debts nearly cleared. The future did not look so bright, however, for the clubs which remained in the second division, as Trinity chairman JB Cooke pointed out. He was not alone in thinking that unless new measures were taken, a number of second division clubs would come to grief.

Six – The Cup, Kiwis and Kangaroos: 1905-14

After ten years of the Northern Union semi-professional era, players were ever mindful of their value, at least in their own judgement. Four first-teamers, including the previous season's captain, Willie Malkin, were holding out for a fee before signing on for the 1905-06 season. Their claim fell on deaf ears as the committee, believing that Trinity players were already well catered for, refused to meet their demands. Within two weeks the players' action ended and they were back in the team. The NU had also decided to abolish the employment clause by which a player had to be in work in order to play on the Saturday. Tommy Newbould, the new season's captain, had previously fallen foul of this rule when he found himself out of work for a few days and could not be selected.

Two divisions had been abandoned in favour of one combined league, in which positions were calculated by percentage of wins. By Christmas, when all three matches over the festive period were won, Trinity were in mid-table, the 21 year old forward Arthur Kenealy Crosland (known as 'Nealy') was selected to play for Yorkshire and an important signing was made in the shape of Herbert Kershaw, who had been playing for Wakefield Rugby Union club. But following the Cup defeat by Bradford, it was noted: 'In days of old, when each club played men from their own immediate neighbourhood, the Trinitarians had no difficulty in obtaining victories, but the paid player has changed all this and the introduction of professionalism – which permits club officials to pay exorbitant prices for players from all parts of the country – has resulted in Wakefield being far less powerful than they were in the days of unrecognised professionalism, and since the formation of the Northern Union they have had to play second fiddle to their more wealthy Bradford friends.' Trinity ended the 1905-06 season in 16th place out of 31, with an average of 46.87. At the AGM it was reported that there had been a 'wave of depression' among Yorkshire clubs, all of whose gate receipts had declined.

It was in the close season of 1906 that dramatic changes in the Northern Union took place, leading to the game we know today. The idea of reducing the number of players from fifteen to thirteen had been suggested in the earliest days of the breakaway movement and even before the split. In May 1906, Warrington and Leigh put forward the proposal again and this time it was accepted. The reduction in the number of forwards was expected to make the game faster, while the alteration in the rule concerning the release of the ball after the tackle was intended to cut down the number of scrums, regarded as a blight which was putting spectators off the game.

The NU leaders had become increasingly aware of the need to make the game more appealing to the public, who were finding soccer more to their taste. The round ball game was easy to follow and had a national dimension. Soccer's success was not lost on club officials. In 1903 Manningham, inaugural champions in 1895-6, went over to the Football League and became Bradford City. The following year, second division club Holbeck disbanded and in their place came Leeds City AFC, the forerunner of Leeds United. In 1907, Bradford, Trinity's great rivals from pre-NU days, First Division champions in 1904, Challenge Cup winners in 1906 and Yorkshire Cup winners in 1907, expressed their dissatisfaction with the NU and made it be known that they favoured a return to Rugby Union rules. That was both undesirable and impossible and eventually the rugby club gave way to a new organisation based at the same ground - Bradford Park Avenue association football club - although the formation of Bradford Northern that same year maintained the city's presence in the NU. Some committee members at certain clubs longed for the simpler, amateur lines of union club rugby. One of those, remarkably, was Trinity's former captain and NU president, Herbert Hutchinson, who left the club and later joined Headingley RU.

But the start of the 1906-7 season, with the new rules in force, saw an immediate improvement in the quality of play and more tries being scored than ever before. The game was more open and put greater emphasis on handling skills. It drew favourable comments from all quarters.

Wakefield Trinity expected, like other clubs, to capitalise on this more attractive game. With the demise of both the Normanton and Castleford clubs, it was also supposed that gate receipts at Belle Vue would increase. The foundations of a successful side were being laid, with the emphasis as usual on local talent. In the Challenge Cup, Trinity went out in the third round to Oldham after defeating Workington and Dewsbury in the previous ties, both of which were replayed. Despite the pre-season optimism, Trinity finished in sixteenth position – exactly the same as in the previous year, though there were five fewer clubs. For the first time a top four play-off was introduced in which Halifax beat Oldham in the championship final. Trinity made a loss of £58 on the season but better times were not long off, not just in Wakefield but for the Northern Union game as a whole.

Discontent with fixture lists, both in the old two-division system and the recently-tried one division in which positions were based on percentages, was resolved by retaining the single league, but percentages would be replaced by what would become the standard arrangement of two points a win, one point a draw. All the Yorkshire clubs would play one another, plus four Lancashire clubs; and vice versa for the Lancashire clubs. The NU was also seeking to extend its boundaries, both within Britain and internationally. Two Welsh clubs, Merthyr Tydfil and Ebbw Vale joined the league, while the Northern Union's first ever international matches took place when the newly professional New Zealanders toured the country as well as playing the first match under Northern Union rules in London.

At Belle Vue, there was the usual wrangling with a minority of players over playing terms. Ernest Bennett expressed his dissatisfaction by claiming to have signed for Wakefield City association football club, who drew a relatively modest 300 crowd for their first match, also played at Belle Vue. The winger soon returned to the fold.

Trinity became the first club to entertain Merthyr Tydfil, whom they beat 35-8, before meeting the previously undefeated New Zealanders on October 23. The first tourists under NU rules, the New Zealanders were still known as the All Blacks, just like the 1905 tourists who played under the auspices of the RFU. The New Zealanders started as favourites, but what ensued was described as 'a magnificent struggle' which ended in a 5-all draw in front of a 5-6,000 crowd on a Wednesday afternoon. Metcalfe opened the scoring with a penalty goal for obstruction before Billy Lynch crossed the All Blacks' line just before half-time, giving the hosts a 5-0 lead. The famous Dally Messenger kicked a penalty when Trinity were sanctioned for foot-up in a scrum and the visitors drew level when Rowe went over for a disputed try. Jimmy Metcalfe was Trinity's outstanding player and in recognition of his performance he was allowed to keep the match ball.

Just as the rule changes had ushered in the potential for a more attractive style of play, so the New Zealanders – soon to acquire the nickname Kiwis - added a new, international dimension to the Northern Union which was of vital significance for the future. The game stood on the verge of a breakthrough. That optimism was mirrored at Wakefield Trinity, who were about to enter their first period of success since the 1895 split. Although Trinity's half backs Harry Slater and Tommy Newbould were criticised in mid-season for their excessive kicking and for 'indulging in a style of play now considered out of date [and] neither useful nor entertaining', by the end of the season the team was being congratulated on its attractive play.

Though Trinity lost at Hull in the third round of the Challenge Cup, they finished the 1907-8 campaign in eighth place in a league of 27 clubs, their highest in a one-division system and an augury of things to come. Belle Vue also hosted the replayed Championship final between Hunslet and Oldham, which was watched by 14,000 spectators and was won by Hunslet, who famously made the first clean sweep of all four cups.

By the end of the season, takings had almost doubled, existing debts had been paid off and a surplus of £367 was banked, which was unusual in itself. For fifteen years between 1889 and 1904 the club had had no cash reserves.

The 1907-08 team, who finished the season in eighth place out of 27. *Back row*: G Taylor, Joe Taylor, J Riley, J Auton, AK Crosland, W Lynch, H Beaumont, H Newton (trainer), WW Wade (sec). *Front row*: WG Simpson, H Kershaw, H Booth, H Slater (capt), J Metcalfe, S Parkes, E Sidwell.

The chairman, JB Cooke, who himself had had the distinction of being chairman of the NU Council the previous year, put the success down to the team's more entertaining and open style of play. During the past season Trinity had, he maintained, given the finest exhibition of football he had ever witnessed.

One of the results was an unprecedented clamour for members' tickets at the start of the 1908-9 season, which began with five straight wins. A crowd of 8,000 turned up for the fifth of those victories, against Batley, followed by 12,000 for the visit of Huddersfield in the first round of the Yorkshire Cup, which had been revived three years earlier. Interestingly, Wakefield Balne Lane, one of the very few clubs in the area playing under Rugby Union rules, had to fill half their side on that day with newcomers who had never played before, because several senior players had cried off and gone to watch Trinity instead. Though Trinity lost, they kept up their unbeaten record in the league, winning at new club Aberdare – one of six Welsh clubs in the expanded NU - after a journey involving an overnight stay at Hereford, which they reached by train via Huddersfield, arriving at their final destination at midday on the Saturday.

Increasingly Belle Vue was being used to stage big matches. The final of the Yorkshire Cup drew 13,000 spectators to Trinity's ground to watch Halifax defeat Hunslet 9-5. The week before, the touring Australian Rugby Union team, the Wallabies, met Yorkshire at Belle Vue, winning 24-0 in front of around 4,000 onlookers. But, at the same time, important international developments in the Northern Union saw the Kangaroos tour England. The Australians played at Wakefield on Saturday, December 19 and were watched by around 5,000 spectators – a crowd which would have been bigger if the tourists had not insisted, as at all their matches, on a one shilling admission – twice the usual amount. The star of the Australian side was none other than Dally Messenger, who had fulfilled the same role for the New Zealanders a year earlier. '[Messenger] proved himself a great artiste and it was delightful to witness this man of brains varying his tactics and trying every move on the board and never for one moment relaxing his efforts,' it was reported. But not even he could prevent Trinity from triumphing 20-13. Tommy 'Trapper' Newbould inspired the victory, scoring the opening try with a tricky individual effort, before sealing the win in the second half when he darted over from a scrum and Metcalfe added his fourth conversion. During the whole tour, which lasted 45 matches and ended in March, Wakefield were one of only three clubs to score more than twenty points against the tourists.

Over the Christmas period Trinity won all their three matches to maintain their position among the top sides, and although a string of defeats in January would see them slip from fourth to tenth, they later climbed back to finish the season in sixth place. The festive period also saw famous names from the past back in action in a charity match in aid of the Children's Boot Fund. The Police took on the Old Trinitarians, who, with the likes of Harry Dawson and Dicky Lockwood in their ranks, won easily. A feature of this match was that the constabulary turned out wearing Trinity's old colours of black and blue jerseys and white shorts.

Trinity made up for their slip in the league by reaching the fourth round of the Challenge Cup, beating Bradford 13-3 and then Leigh 9-3, both away from home. In the third round they dominated Albert Goldthorpe's Hunslet, the winners of all four cups the previous season. It was at this time that the nickname 'Dreadnoughts' first appeared, in print at least: it was an allusion to the new type of battleship, heavily armed and famed for its speed. Trinity earned the comparison as, in front of 16,000 spectators at Belle Vue, they beat Hunslet 19-0 and went on to meet Wigan in the semi-final at Broughton. Wigan were riding high at the top of the league and were regarded as the finest as well as the costliest outfit in the Northern Union. Both clubs had league fixtures on Good Friday, the day before the cup-tie. Wigan put out a reserve side against St Helens, losing 8-5, and were eventually fined £25 as a result. Trinity faced Salford and put their full side out, though their minds were obviously elsewhere as they went down 53-0 with forward Joe Taylor suffering broken fingers.

Before the semi-final, Wigan's Lance Todd (in whose name the trophy for the Cup Final man of the match was later awarded) said to Trinity's Harry Slater and Jimmy Metcalfe in the dressing-room that he was sorry that Wakefield could not put out their strongest side but hoped that they would give Wigan a good game. Hot favourites Wigan got what they had asked for. Newbould scored a clever solo try and Metcalfe, of whom it was said that he never played better, dropped a goal from near touch to give a 5-2 half-time lead. Trinity kept up the pressure in the second half, when Slater bluffed the opposition and put Bennett in for a try, Metcalfe converting. Dave Holmes dropped a goal and Trinity were through to the final by 14-2. It was a fine exhibition of cup-tie football, characterised by the smartness of the backs, among whom Metcalfe was outstanding, and the fierce tackling of the forwards. Had it not been for Trinity's performance, Wigan might well have gone on to emulate Hunslet's feat by winning all four cups, but they had to content themselves with three. Lance Todd was the first to congratulate Trinity on their victory.

Wakefield Trinity played their first Northern Union Challenge Cup final when they faced Hull at Headingley on April 24, 1909. The crowd of 23,587 fell well short of the record of 32,860 set at the same ground when Halifax beat Salford six years earlier, but such was the interest in the Hull-Trinity clash that around 5,000 fans, after breaking down one of the gates, got in without contributing to the receipts of £1,489. The previous season's beaten finalists, Hull were full of confidence and, in an unusual take on match preparation, had an early lunch before being packed off to bed for a couple of hours. 'Probably,' commented the *Wakefield Express* sarcastically, 'the Hull committee tucked them in and sang them to sleep.' Hull's display never rose above the somnolent as Wakefield took an early initiative, dominating the forward battle. Once again it was the wily Tommy Newbould who set the tone, taking the ball from a scrum, dummying and crashing through to touch down after only five minutes' play. Captain Harry Slater, who had a fine game, threw out a long pass for Ezra Sidwell to send Ernest Bennett over and by half-time Trinity were leading 6-0. Despite Hull's best efforts after the break, Trinity made light of the wet conditions and went further ahead when AK Crosland charged through a gap for Metcalfe to goal. Winger Bennett crossed for his second try, with Billy Simpson finishing off a Newbould cross-kick to score Trinity's fifth try in their 17-0 victory. The *Wakefield Express* called it 'a glorious triumph for local talent and a lesson to those clubs who prefer to scour

The first Trinity team to win the Northern Union Challenge Cup, 1909. *Back row*: J Taylor, EW Bennett, W Lynch, P Unsworth, JB Cooke (chairman), AK Crosland, H Beaumont, J Walton, G Taylor. *Middle row*: E Parker (sec), H Kershaw, J Metcalfe, H Slater (capt), J Auton, S Parkes. *Front*: D Holmes, WG Simpson, TH Newbould, E Sidwell

the country for players instead of encouraging men in their midst.' The *Hull Daily Mail* commented: 'Hull were completely overplayed by a team imbued with wholeheartedness, local enthusiasm and pluck. Local enthusiasm is a grand tonic for the winning of a cup final. Its application has often a wonderful effect in demoralising the opposition, a fact which no one present at Headingley will doubt.' It was a fair point, since the only player in Trinity's team who came from outside the Wakefield area was Jimmy Auton from Hartlepool.

Bearing the Cup, Trinity made their triumphal return in an illuminated tramcar, decorated with banners hailing 'T'Dreadnowts' and 'T'Owd Brigade', as they were also known in reference to their status as Wakefield's senior rugby club. Another banner proclaimed 'It's 22 year sin", recalling Trinity's last Cup victory, which had of course taken place under Rugby Union rules. As the team passed through Lofthouse, the Rutland Mills Band were once again there to lead the parade into Wakefield, playing the familiar 'See the Conquering Hero Comes'. After riding through the Bull Ring, the procession carried on to the Alexandra Hotel opposite the Belle Vue ground, where they had a celebratory dinner and then returned into the city centre where the many thousands of fans cheered them until late.

Two more pieces of club history were written during the season. On April 5, 1909, Trinity established a club record score of 67 points against Bramley in a match in which Jimmy Metcalfe kicked eleven goals out of fifteen attempts, an individual record which would remain unbeaten for 58 years. Billy Simpson scored four tries in the same match, with Joe Taylor and Ernest Bennett both scoring three. Bennett ended the campaign as Trinity's leading try-scorer – the eighth consecutive season that he had achieved the feat.

It was no surprise that the club should post a significant profit of £548, despite an increase in players' wages and expenses. No wonder either that Harry Slater should be re-elected captain, or that a record 1,400 members' tickets would be sold before the start of the next season.

A month into the new season of 1909-10, the club was top of the league. A new centre, Tommy Poynton, originally from Castleford, showed his promise by scoring four tries in the 25-0 defeat of Leeds and ended the season with a club record of 24 tries, beating Bennett's haul of 23 of the previous season and 1903-4. Belle Vue was selected as the venue for the England-Wales match in December, when Tommy Newbould was a star performer, scoring a try and having a hand in two others in England's 19-13 win. Newbould and Herbert Kershaw were selected for the first tour of Australia, with Joe Taylor and AK Crosland also having taken part in the tour trial. Though Trinity went out of the Cup in the second round replay at home to Hunslet, they ended the season as Yorkshire champions and fourth in the league. They lost their Championship semi-final play-off against Oldham by 12-6, but for their achievement in the league the players were given a £100 bonus to divide among themselves. The club could afford it. After another successful season, there was a balance in the bank of £779. It was Leeds who lifted the Challenge Cup and at the celebration dinner at the Victoria Hotel in that city, the main speaker, JB Cooke, Trinity's representative on the Northern Union management committee, reflected the optimism in the game. Clubs were stronger than ever, he maintained, but, echoing other speakers on similar occasions, he still appeared to regret the split of fifteen years earlier. He was applauded when he questioned why the professional and the amateur could not play side by side in rugby football as they could in any other sport. 'No one,' he suggested, referring to Yorkshire cricket, 'thought the worse of Lord Hawke because he played side by side with George Hirst.'

'Trapper' Newbould had the distinction of playing in the first ever test match in Australia, partnering Wigan's Johnny Thomas at half back in the 27-20 victory in Sydney. Herbert Kershaw, who had joined Trinity as a half back before converting to the back row of the forwards, made a big name for himself on the tour and was selected for the second test, in Brisbane, scoring a try as Great Britain retained the Ashes with the 22-17 win.

County winger Ernest Bennett, Trinity's top try scorer in every season from 1901 to 1909. He was the son of one of the club's founder members, Thomas Oliver Bennett.

The first Midlands club to join the Northern Union, Coventry, made their first appearance in the 1910-11 season, taking the place of the Welsh club Treherbert. Numerous Welsh players now figured in the game, and not just at the Welsh clubs. New Zealanders and, later, Australians were also recruited, but Trinity maintained their policy of encouraging local players – 'one of the few clubs who favour this kind of thing,' noted the *Wakefield Express*. The strategy paid dividends, to judge by Trinity's position in the league. They did not lose a match until mid-November, centre Billy Lynch and Kershaw were selected for the county, and on December 3, Wakefield faced Huddersfield in the Yorkshire Cup final. It was twenty years since the two teams last met in the final of the competition under the old regime, when Huddersfield won by one goal to nil. Now, Trinity were undefeated in the Yorkshire league; Huddersfield were the Cup-holders. In front of 19,000 spectators at Headingley, Jimmy Metcalfe opened the scoring for Trinity with a beautifully judged penalty from near touch. The only try of the first half came when the Wakefield forwards held the ball in a scrum close to the Huddersfield line for George Taylor to touch down. Leading 5-0 at half-time, Trinity went further ahead in the second period when winger Billy Simpson raced in from Lynch's pass. Pinned back by Wakefield's voracious forwards and Newbould's astute kicking, Huddersfield scored a solitary penalty goal from Wrigley and went down by 8-2. Huddersfield's galaxy of players assembled from various parts of

The earliest known action picture of Wakefield Trinity at Belle Vue, taken at a match against Wigan around 1910. The malt kilns on the east side of the ground are visible in the background. (Collection Wakefield Museums)

the rugby-playing world, met their match in a Wakefield team well led by Jimmy Auton, captaining the side in the absence of the injured Harry Slater.

Trinity's re-acquaintance with the County trophy was evoked in the *Yorkshire Post*: 'The Yorkshire Northern Union Cup has gone to the descendants of a club whose cup-tie performances thirty years or so ago had much to do with firing the zeal for Rugby football throughout the White Rose county. Doubtless there were many present at Headingley on Saturday who, like the writer, were able to recall final cup-ties ranging from Halifax in 1879 to Headingley in 1891 – Wakefield Trinity's first and last appearances in the finals for the Yorkshire Challenge Cup… And they must have been reminded of the old Wakefield forward grit by what they saw in this fight for the new professional trophy. Eliminate the memory of the wing forward play of Latham and Whiteley, and there were the old characteristics of hard keen packing, quick rushing footwork, playing on to the ball, or on to the man with the ball, from first to last. These tactics won cup-ties for the Trinitarians of old… The deeds of Bartram, of Hutchinson, of the Kilners, Hayleys, Fallases and Dawsons, are they not jealously guarded in the affections of the old brigade and their contemporaries?' [1]

At the end of the year 1910, Trinity were still top of the league, and people were asking if this was the finest team the club had ever had. Though Slater and Newbould were greatly influential and Kershaw had also been good enough to tour Australia and New Zealand, this was a side with none of the stars boasted by other top clubs but which excelled through teamwork and a well-tuned understanding between all its members. Particularly when faced with the toughest opposition, Trinity were capable of thrilling play regardless of the conditions; as one observer put it: 'that style of football which the Northern Union legislators had in mind when they revised the rules.' By contrast, the former Trinity honorary secretary, Tom Parry, wrote from his London home to say that he had been invited to see the first game of American football ever played in England, at Crystal Palace. 'It is poor stuff,' he commented, 'even when compared to English Rugby [Union] … and in comparison to the sparkling Northern Union game it is absolutely gloomy.'

Going into the New Year of 1911, Trinity continued to head the Northern Union league and the Yorkshire league and remained undefeated at Belle Vue. It was a fine achievement, as the *Yorkshire Observer* made clear: 'Compared with the income of such clubs as Oldham, Wigan, Huddersfield, Halifax and Hull, the money which the Belle Vue directors have to handle … must be a very limited quantity but for the past three years they have provided football second to none in the Northern Union.'

The reserve team, which topped the Dewsbury, Wakefield and District League and won the Yorkshire Combination two years in a row, played an important role in providing a supply of young players to the first team. The other outfits in that competition were Hemsworth Colliery, Purston White Horse, Dewsbury Reserves, Featherstone Rovers, Knottingley, Normanton, Pontefract Victoria, Normanton St John's, Outwood Church and Netherton United. Below that level, junior sides playing in the Wakefield and District Intermediate League included Normanton, North Featherstone, Primrose Hill, Streethouse Red Rose, Sandal & Belle Vue, Lofthouse Gate, Wakefield Shamrocks, Knottingley, South Hiendley, Thornes United, Eastmoor, Purston and Balne Lane. A few months later Wakefield St Mark's followed Balne Lane's example and switched their allegiance to the Northern Union.

The latter part of the season was less successful, but Trinity still finished in third place – their highest ever position - which was good enough to retain the Yorkshire League title to go with the Yorkshire Cup they had lifted earlier. They went out of the Challenge Cup in the second round at the hands of Oldham and would meet a similar fate in the top four play-off for the Championship. For the second year running, Trinity were knocked out in the semi-final by Oldham (15-12), who went on to become champions by defeating Wigan, the third time in a row that these two teams would face each other at the final stage. It was also Oldham's fifth successive Championship final – a feat which would be equalled by Wigan two years later. While Trinity could not match the achievements of these two clubs, they could be satisfied with the progress they had made, as well as a healthy £300 profit on the season. The 1910-11 season also represented a personal triumph for winger Billy Simpson, whose 34 tries established a new club record which beat the previous best by ten and would endure almost half a century.

The 1911-12 campaign began with Jimmy Auton succeeding Harry Slater as captain and with Tommy Poynton and Herbert Kershaw selected for Yorkshire against the Australians, who were undertaking their second tour. Kershaw went on to represent England against the Kangaroos at Fulham the following month. But despite the international experience in the side, Trinity lost to the Australians, who had beaten Great Britain in the first test. Trinity took a 10-8 lead towards the end of the first half, after good work from Poynton had produced a try for Bennett, and in characteristic fashion Newbould had fooled the opposition to score a try converted by Smith, who also added a penalty. But the second period belonged to the tourists, whose forwards in particular showed superior strength and speed and laid the foundations for a 24-10 victory. Poynton earned praise for his performance, as did Newbould, who was compared favourably to the great half back and Australian captain, Chris McKivat.

The fast and elusive Poynton was selected to partner Harold Wagstaff in the centre in the England side which beat Australia 5-3 at Nottingham – another venue chosen to advertise the Northern Union's attractions. But the small 3,000 crowd led to some regretting the fact that big matches were being taken to untried areas 'because people will not pay for something they do not understand.' But although a crowd of 20,000 witnessed the Yorkshire Cup final at Belle Vue, where Huddersfield beat Hull KR 22-10, a paltry attendance of 2,000 was recorded as Trinity lost at home to Leeds three weeks later in one of several surprisingly poor displays.

The sudden decline in form coincided with a dip in the influence of Harry Slater on the team as well as the unusual complaint that players coming through from the reserve side were not good enough. Three weak performances over Christmas culminated in a 62-5 thrashing at Fartown, where the Huddersfield players earned bonus money for every point scored. Though Trinity had a weakened side out, that display and others were 'the talk and surprise of football people throughout the Northern Union area.' The troubles continued when Newbould and Kershaw were in dispute with the club and were dropped. The differences were quickly mended and both returned for the first round Challenge Cup win over Leeds, watched by the weekend's biggest crowd of 14,000 – quite a turnaround from two months before. After beating Keighley in the second round, Trinity knocked out Warrington by 10-5 in a replay after drawing 3-3 away, but Oldham were once more to provide Wakefield's downfall by winning 17-0 in the semi-final at Broughton. Trinity's performance was described as 'a shocking display', but in the league, despite their inconsistent form, they finished a creditable sixth in the fortieth year of their existence.

The early part of the 1912-13 season proved no different from the second half of the preceding campaign, the Cup run apart. Once again it was lamented that the reserve team did not provide the first team with players of quality and that some of those players brought in from local clubs did not come up to the mark. Wakefield's policy of fostering local talent was therefore once more under scrutiny. Comparisons were made with wealthier clubs who signed Australians, New Zealanders and other stars. Even if Trinity could afford them, there would be potential for upset within the team, it was pointed out. These players commanded their own rates of pay, whereas in the Trinity camp all were paid the same: a maximum of thirty shillings (£1.50) a match. The arguments for and against imported players would echo down the twentieth century and beyond. One side of the debate was put forward by the *Wakefield Express*, which proposed: 'Surely it is about time the Northern Committee put an end to the importation of Colonials who, after being boomed for all they are worth, very readily accept the fabulous sums offered to them by wealthy clubs in this country. It is a very serious business and is doing considerable harm to Northern Union football. With preference given by some clubs to these ready-made footballers from across the water, the result is that very little encouragement is given to local youths to go in for rugby football.' Not that Trinity had the means to indulge as other big-spending clubs like Huddersfield and Wigan could. Crowd figures were generally below what the top clubs could expect, as was made obvious when under 4,000 arrived at Belle Vue for the visit of Hull in early October sunshine. Supporters would not take the trouble to travel to Belle Vue if the team was not winning or if the standard of play was inferior to what other teams could provide.

But the return to form of Newbould and Slater forced dismal thoughts aside as Trinity moved into the top four by December and the stand-off and captain was recalled to the Yorkshire side which beat Cumberland 19-5. Slater had the pleasure of seeing his team go second by the end of the year after defeating glamorous Wigan 19-6 at Belle Vue. Still it was proving hard to attract consistently high crowds, the Wigan match producing fewer than 7,000 spectators, though the visit of undefeated Huddersfield on Boxing Day brought a crowd of 17,800, paying £466 – a consolation for Trinity's first home defeat of the season.

Slater's career was soon to be ended by damage to his knee; Newbould suffered a similar injury and with that Trinity's league form dipped. They ended the season in eighth place (in fact equal sixth on percentage) and appeared in another Challenge Cup semi-final after defeating York 7-3 in the third round, watched by 7,000 spectators. In contrast, the Wigan versus Huddersfield tie drew a record crowd of 33,000. The victors, Huddersfield, met a depleted Trinity side lacking the two half backs, as well as Bennett, Kershaw, Walton and Burton and had no difficulty in progressing to the final, winning 35-2 before beating Warrington to take the trophy. The Fartown side also beat Wigan 29-2 in the championship final at Belle Vue, where a 17,000 crowd yielded record receipts for a league final of £916.

Trinity's team was in need of new talent. One of the most significant signings in the club's history was made in March 1913 when 18-year old Jonathan Parkin, of Sharlston, was recruited. Making his first-team debut in the 7-6 win at Bradford on April 19 of that year, Parkin, it was reported, 'gave a very promising display and went about his play with the air of a veteran. He seems to possess all the attributes of a good half back.'

The Trinity team which reached the final of the Challenge Cup in 1914, when they were defeated by Hull. *Back row*: E Parker (hon. treasurer), J Abbott, JJ Mills, T Dixon, AK Crosland, T Poynton, T Newbould, G Bolton. *Front row*: J Parkin, W Lynch, E Parkin, A Burton, H Kershaw, WL Beattie, B Johnson, L Land

Taking over from Harry Slater, Herbert Kershaw was elected as the side's leader for the 1913-14 campaign. Tommy Poynton was selected for Yorkshire v Cumberland and despite the club's modest showing in the league, no fewer than four players represented the county against Lancashire in December. Poynton was named captain, Billy Lynch and Arthur Burton also played, as did Nealy Crosland, a replacement for another Trinity player, George Taylor, who had been suspended. In addition, Trinity's Scottish forward, William Beattie, was earning a solid reputation for himself and was tipped as a possible tourist to Australia. But Trinity's form was inconsistent, with an unusual reason for one defeat – at Broughton – in which the players were described as lifeless and off colour. The players had travelled by train, the *Wakefield Express* reported, and in their overcrowded carriage, many of the passengers were smoking, which was held to have had a detrimental effect, particularly on those 'not in the habit of inhaling smoke.' Professional arrangements for matches were still a long way off, as another incident illustrates. For the match at Keighley, it was decided as late as the Friday evening before Saturday's match to advise players by post not to travel by train but by tramcar as far as Leeds. One of the players did not receive the instructions and another unaccountably failed to turn up, with the result that only thirteen of the fifteen players due to travel reached Lawkholme Lane, where Poynton and Newbould announced they were not well enough to play. Trinity took to the field with eleven men, just four of them forwards, and played in a storm in the second half, causing the referee, on appeal by the captains, to cut the second half short by ten minutes, Trinity copping a 19-5 beating.

Despite their worst showing in the league for seven years – they were to end the season in seventeenth place out of 25 – Trinity had centre Poynton and forward Beattie selected for the trial match for the Australasian tour. A month later, Poynton was surprisingly left out but Beattie was invited to join the tour party though he declined for business reasons. Trinity's league form may have been disappointing, but once more they reserved their best efforts for the Challenge Cup. After beating Swinton in the first round, Newbould's drop goal being the only score of the game,

Trinity met Leeds at Belle Vue in front of 12,000 spectators. Trailing 6-0 and down to twelve men after Newbould had been dismissed for striking, Wakefield fought back magnificently to win 9-8 and beat Leeds for the third time that season. A similar-sized crowd was present for the third round encounter against high-flying Wigan, second in the league. Trinity's terrier-like tactics, with the forwards leading the way, put Wigan off their game. Nealy Crosland scattered four defenders to score a converted try, Leonard Land booted a fine drop goal and Beattie, as in the previous round, kicked a long-range goal from near the middle of the field, which saw Trinity home by 9-6. Their third Cup semi-final in a row took Trinity to Rochdale, where they played out a 3-all draw with Broughton Rangers before winning the replay 5-0 at a wind- and rain-swept Fartown in another forward-dominated tussle. In the other semi, Hull overcame favourites Huddersfield 11-3 to set up the second Cup final clash with Trinity in five years.

Hull, twelve places above Trinity in the league, were overwhelming favourites to lift the trophy at the fourth attempt. It was widely regarded as Hull's best team yet, with their record signing, the Kinsley-born Billy Batten – reported to be on the huge fee of £14 a match – the star player. In contrast, Wakefield's improvised back division had youngsters Jonathan Parkin and Bill Millican pairing up for the first time at half back. But at Halifax on Saturday, 18 April, 1914, with 19,000 present, Trinity came close to upsetting the odds. Neither side scored in the first half, but Wakefield were dealt a huge blow when their captain Herbert Kershaw was dismissed on the intervention of a touch judge five minutes into the second half. Trinity's magnificent defence, with the five-man pack never allowing their opponents to get on top, kept Hull at bay until the 73rd minute when the black and whites scored through winger Jack Harrison, whose name was destined to be known throughout the game for being posthumously awarded the Victoria Cross after being killed in action in 1917. On Hull's other flank AJ Francis went in for a second try, giving a 6-0 victory. Trinity's forwards once more played courageously, but though the defence behind the scrum was equally tough, the backs made little capital of what few opportunities they had. The exception was Poynton, who fielded and defended brilliantly, particularly against Batten, and tried all he knew, including an inch-perfect kick for winger Ben Johnson, which should have brought an early try that might have altered the complexion of the contest.

The Cup final defeat and the mediocre performance in the league opened up the familiar debate about the committee's recruitment policy. There was criticism too of the team's unadventurous style of play, leading to a total of 53 tries being scored in the season, as opposed to the previous 83. A rather facile comparison was made with Huddersfield, who posted a record profit of £2,300 (Trinity made a small loss) and significantly, it was thought, played attractive football. Club president JB Cooke, responding to criticism at the AGM, pointed out that Wakefield did not have such a big population to draw on as Huddersfield and made clear the difficulty of signing good players. 'If we can live [with the top teams],' he said, 'I shall be satisfied. I think it would be better for all clubs if they paid more attention to local players instead of devoting their attention to men such a long distance from home.' In reply to a remark that other clubs were signing top players, he replied, 'It is the power of the purse.'

In spite of the expensively assembled teams of their rivals, Trinity had one of their most successful eras between 1909 and 1914. They won the Challenge Cup once, were runners-up on another occasion and appeared in three consecutive semi-finals. In the league they contested the top four play-offs twice and won the Yorkshire League twice as well as lifting the Yorkshire Cup. In view of the club's limited financial resources, their record over those five years represented a considerable achievement.

Seven – The Call to Arms: 1914-19

In the summer of 1914 all changed. In August, Britain declared war on Germany. Men of serviceable age would be asked to enlist in the fight, which forced sporting bodies to question whether they should continue to organise competitions. Barron Kilner acted as a mouthpiece for the Yorkshire Rugby Union when he expressed the view that all matches should be cancelled for the season. 'Those who can play football would be better engaged in defending their country,' he opined. The YRU agreed and passed a resolution recommending that all football in the county be stopped for the duration of the war and that players should join up. The Football Association, however, thought that complete cancellation of fixtures would be 'mischievous rather than beneficial' and simply urged clubs with professional players to give all assistance in releasing those who wished to join up. The Northern Union went one step further, declaring that matches should not be stopped. Wakefield's representative, JB Cooke, stated: 'It seems to me far better that the ordinary course should be followed rather than the programme abandoned, more especially because of the effect on the public at large… So long as amusement and recreation are kept within reasonable bounds I think it is far better for the country that they be continued… The fact that so many have already volunteered for service is some evidence that the great bulk of players are prepared to do their duty and if others are required they will be in far better trim when wanted if they continue playing the game than if they cease to do so.'

That view was endorsed from the pulpit by Rev. Frank Chambers of Dewsbury, who, when not delivering sermons, could be seen running the line and later refereeing Northern Union matches. At a special service for footballers at the Zion Church in Wakefield, he commented on Wakefield's justifiable pride in having a team made up mainly of local players before going on to give his views on whether football should be continued. He was glad that matches were going ahead, he said. 'I have never yet known a game of football make a man incapable of serving his country as a citizen or a soldier and quite apart from a national safety valve, which is needed right now, it is the finest asset for keeping patriotism alive.'

Among the Wakefield players who enlisted was the goal-kicking forward, William Beattie, whose role as team captain was taken over by Tommy Poynton. Belle Vue became a recruiting ground for the King's Own Yorkshire Light Infantry, whose officers first appeared when Beattie and fellow-soldier Ernest Parkin (the forward) returned to the side when granted leave. Harry Rafter also joined the KOYLI, serving at Ypres and on the Western Front. Lance-corporal Beattie later gained a commission as second lieutenant in the 10th Border Regiment.

Attendances at matches throughout the Northern Union fell by up to 50 per cent compared to the previous season, forcing the committee of the NRL to recommend a 25 per cent cut in players' wages. It was not a popular move among players, with several clubs suffering strikes. Trinity players withheld their services briefly but on their return the committee found that the gate receipts were insufficient to pay their wages, which meant that the reserve fund had to be called upon. Though the takings for the match on Boxing Day against Huddersfield – who went on to win all four cups, including the championship title at Belle Vue – were substantial at £136, the average was considerably lower. The visit of Bradford in February, albeit in sleet and wind, produced just £4 from around 200 hardy souls. The following month it was noted that, as at other clubs, 'the war and the weather have played havoc with attendances at Belle Vue … There has been a big loss on the year's working and the players are the only persons who have not any cause to grumble.'

Perhaps surprisingly, there appears to have been a decline in the standard of behaviour on the field during the war period, with numerous examples of players being sent off. Rough play was far from confined to Trinity, but as early as October 1914, it was reported: 'The sending-off of [George] Taylor makes the third Trinitarian to receive marching orders in the last four matches and such conduct will undoubtedly gain a very unenviable reputation for the team. If players feel in such fighting trim, there is a place at present where their services would be more acceptable than on a field of sport!' In a particularly bad-tempered game at Batley towards the end of the season, no fewer than three Trinity players were dismissed. For the last match of the season at Hull, Trinity, who were to finish tenth, struggled to raise a team: not so much because of suspensions but because their playing strength had been depleted by enlistments, which, as early as December, had caused the reserve team to be withdrawn from competition.

Towards the end of the 1914-15 season, it was calculated that some 1,500 Northern Union players had joined up. That may or may not have been a contributory factor to the decision to stop all competitive and professional football until the end of the war, though friendlies and under-18 fixtures would be allowed. In proposing the move, NU president JH Smith of Widnes asked, 'Is there a single person present who can honestly say that he got any satisfaction at all out of football last season? There may have been some distraction from the national trouble, but there certainly was no genuine pleasure or excitement to be obtained from it.' Wakefield's JB Cooke, seconding the proposal, said that when in August last they considered the question of carrying on, there was hardly a man among them who thought the war would continue very long, but now they realised the position in which the country was really placed. 'After ten months of hard fighting, with dreadful losses to the country in money and lives, we realise what the great game going on in France really means. As a sporting body we cannot understand how any man could fail to put the interests of his country before his sport and therefore we cannot offer any inducement to any player to stop at home when his country claims his services elsewhere.'

What would have been the 1915-16 season was therefore almost entirely blank as far as Trinity were concerned, but while Widnes also followed the recommendation of their Northern Union leader, Warrington were the only other club to suspend their activities for the season. In October, Tommy Newbould raised a Wakefield Trinity team to play at York, but his effort was slapped down by the Trinity committee, who stated that this team was a scratch side put together 'without either the knowledge or consent of the committee.' Several Trinity players guested with Dewsbury, however. Among them were Tommy Poynton, Jonty Parkin, Nealy Crosland, Herbert Kershaw and Jack Wild. It was no wonder that, with players such as these added to their side, Dewsbury became unofficial champions and again the following season.

At the same time, Trinity's first casualties of the war were announced. Sergeant Herbert Finnigan, a threequarter formerly of Outwood Church, serving with the King's Own Yorkshire Light Infantry, died of gas poisoning on the Sunday before Christmas. Winger Ben Johnson, a sapper with the Royal Engineers, lost a foot in a dock accident.

In August 1916 it was announced that Trinity, in common with other Northern Union clubs, would resume playing. The apparent volte-face was explained by the fact that conscription had now been introduced, so that football could only be played or watched by those who had been exempted from military service for one reason or another or those who worked on munitions. The Trinity committee made it clear that if enlistment had still been voluntary they would not have allowed football to be played again. However they were forced to rethink when the club's finances were severely tested by a combination of poor attendances, caused partly by bad weather, and the increased cost of rail travel to away matches. In mid-season the committee took the decision to discontinue playing again in order to avoid further losses, having already incurred a £74 deficit. The members' club at Holly Lodge, which had been losing money for some time through lack of support, was closed and the furniture sold off. It was the committee's intention not to restart playing until the war was over. But there were other financial implications. The lack of income from matches put the Wakefield Trinity Athletic Company in a 'serious and critical position'. The mortgage debt of £3,250 on the ground needed to be serviced, resulting in the club making an appeal in December 1917 so that the interest could be paid.

The casualties of war continued to pile up, with the photographs of the killed or wounded amounting to as many as twenty each week on the front page of the *Wakefield Express*. The Trinity team, like other clubs and associations, sustained significant losses. In January 1917, William Beattie, the club captain who had been invited to tour Australia in 1914, and who had become a lieutenant in the Border Regiment, was killed in action on the Western Front. Aged 26, he had originally arrived in Wakefield from Dumfries in 1911 and worked for the Prudential Assurance Company. He had seen action in the Dardanelles and recovered from serious illness in hospital in Alexandria before returning to action in France. The player who succeeded Beattie as club captain when he went off to war, Tommy Poynton, was himself seriously injured in September of the same year. The Yorkshire county centre, a gunner in the Royal Garrison Artillery, had spent over a year in France when he was wounded. Acting as a signaller, he suffered injury to several parts of the body when a shell exploded near him, killing one man and wounding two others. Though he recovered in hospital, he would not play rugby again. In addition to Beattie, Poynton, Johnson and Finnigan, six other Trinity players – Arthur Cockroft, Ogley, Oakley, Billy Parkes, R Ward and B Ward – were either killed or prevented by injury from playing again. Corporal Fred Howe, who had played for Trinity as a forward a decade earlier, died from gas poisoning after having served with the KOYLI for over four years. Cockcroft, who showed great promise as a centre, had been signed at the same time as Jonathan Parkin. Trinity officials had gone specifically to watch him play for Knottingley against Parkin's North Featherstone, and since Parkin also made a big impression, both players were signed for £5 each.

In one sense the war had brought the two rugby codes closer together. The Rugby Union had relaxed its rules banning its own men from playing against or alongside Northern Union players, whether the latter were professionals or not. Northern Union stars such as Huddersfield's Harold Wagstaff and Douglas Clark featured prominently in Forces sides, which of course played under RFU rules. At the ending of hostilities, in November 1918, a charity match took place in Leeds, in which the Yorkshire Rugby Union side faced the Northern Command team. During the speeches which followed the post-match dinner, Barron Kilner repeated the oft-made point that amateurs and professionals played together in cricket, just as they had done at rugby during the war. He suggested that the Rugby Union and Northern Union might find a way to allowing the same to happen in peace-time. Talk of a rapprochement was in the air, with another Wakefield man, JB Cooke, speaking of the common bond of rugby. He proposed further charity matches in which the Northern Union might meet the Rugby Union, adding that 'if the two unions could not unite in the interests of the game, they might at least do so in the cause of humanity.' A less optimistic though ultimately more realistic view was proposed by the Yorkshire Rugby Union secretary JA Miller, who said that 'it was to be regretted that there were two Unions, but they differed in fundamentals and it was quite hopeless to expect that the Rugby Union would relax the principles of amateurism upon which their body was founded.'

Naturally the two bodies went their separate ways, with the Northern Union announcing the resumption of official matches on January 18, 1919, when fixtures were organised on a county basis. War-time restrictions such as payment to players were lifted from February 22, although it was well known that some clubs had continued to pay their players in wartime. A month before that date, the *Wakefield Express* reported: 'During Trinity's idleness [suspension of matches], seven of their prominent players have been assisting the Dewsbury club and three or four of them, for monetary reasons, do not relish the idea of returning to the Old Brigade. The Trinity committee, however, are determined to take a firm stand and if the players on their register stupidly decline to play for them they can rest assured they will not play for Dewsbury.'

There was some upheaval at the start of official fixtures with the pool of players having been diminished by the war. It was even more confusing when, before the first match, four players – Land, J Parkin, Dixon and Wild - cried off, so that reserves had to be brought in at the last moment. As the *Express* noted: 'They did their best but it was not to be expected that they could adequately fill the places of men who had been playing regularly throughout Wakefield's patriotic suspension of operations.' George Taylor, on leave from serving with the Coldstream Guards and attending the match as a spectator, was pressed into action, as was Edgar Woolley, who had just returned from a spell with the army of occupation in Cologne, and John Todd, a seaman on HMS Resolution. Crosland, Kershaw and Burton, who had been playing with Dewsbury, duly left Crown Flatt for Belle Vue. For at least part of this reconstituted season, Trinity had been obliged to wear black jerseys – not for any symbolic reason but because their traditional red and blue could not be replaced until the sports outfitter, Harry Hayley, the Trinity star from the early days, managed to procure a set. A series of withdrawals and injuries led to disappointing form and Trinity finished eighth out of the eleven teams competing in the Yorkshire League, although they reached the semi-final of the Yorkshire Cup, in which, ironically, they were beaten 3-2 by Dewsbury.

Despite the curtailed season and their indifferent form, Trinity made a much-needed profit of over £500, which also silenced those critics who had censured the club for not playing during the war. It contrasted with the substantial loss made by continuing to play during the first year of the war, as also happened when they began playing again in 1916-17 but abandoned fixtures in mid-season. These points were made by president JB Cooke at the 1919 AGM, when he claimed that it had been evident that the people of Wakefield had no appetite for 'serious football' while the Great War was on. But supporters of the club had twice responded to the appeal for funds during that time, producing first £100 and then £88. Referring to the mediocre performance of the team in the season just past, he stressed the difficulty of finding new players, because no local clubs had played since the start of hostilities. In terms of the ground, the small stand [on the east side] had had to be demolished because it was unsafe although replacing it was out of the question at the moment. The ground now 'practically belonged to the club', who held 2,000 of the 3,700 shares. Members approved a proposal to commemorate the club's war dead by providing a memorial in the form of a flagstaff and flag.

Eight – From Northern Union to Rugby League: 1919-27

The first full season since 1915 began on August 23, 1919 with a sense of optimism in the Trinity ranks. Jonathan Parkin was elected captain and several promising younger players emerged, among them Charlie Pollard and Archie Siswick. Parkin, together with the veteran but still fearsome forward AK Crosland, was selected for Yorkshire.

Of Pollard it was said, following a defeat at Hull in mid-October, that he was 'by far the best man on the Wakefield side and his clever play under difficulties was often applauded by the Hull crowd. His kicking was marked by precision and power and in defensive work he was never found wanting.' Pollard had had an eventful war. A member of the Belle Vue Intermediate team in the 1913-14 season, he joined up when only just 17 years old, after giving his age as 19. With the Royal Field Artillery he was gassed at Ypres and was invalided home. Sufficiently recovered, he returned to the front in Gallipoli, Egypt and Mesopotamia before finally being demobbed in 1919 after four years' service.

'Never since the formation of the Northern Union,' the *Wakefield Express* claimed, 'have Wakefield Trinity possessed such promising young players as they do at present and the committee are to be congratulated on their policy of having a reserve team composed wholly of promising young players ... and not, as in years gone by, of men who had done service with the first thirteen.' But it was not long before the optimism proved premature and the same reporter was forced to admit: 'You cannot put old heads on young shoulders. There are no backs with ripe experience in the team.'

That accounted for some unexpected failures, but Trinity saved their best for the cup matches. Although losing 15-5 to Huddersfield at Fartown in the semi-final of the Yorkshire Cup, Trinity became embroiled in an enthralling series of matches against St Helens in the first round of the Challenge Cup. After a 2-2 draw on the Saturday at Knowsley Road, the teams met again at Belle Vue on the Wednesday, when, remarkably, another 2-2 draw ensued in front of 14,000 spectators. A second replay took place at Leeds on the Friday, when Trinity eventually won 12-3 and which brought the total receipts for the three matches to over £1,500. The very next day Trinity once more faced mighty Huddersfield, this time at Belle Vue, where a 21,000 crowd paid £1,162 to see the second round tie. The winners of the Cup the last time the competition was held, in 1915, Huddersfield trailed 2-0 thanks to a Charlie Pollard penalty goal. With Crosland the only survivor from the 1909 Cup-winning side, but strong as ever as the cornerstone of the pack, and with Pollard giving the finest exhibition of full back play seen on the ground for many years, Trinity battled against the effects of the past week. But their hopes of a sensational victory disappeared when, with four minutes left, Huddersfield's great centre Harold Wagstaff made an opening for top-scoring winger Albert Rosenfeld. Though there were doubts about whether the Australian had grounded the ball properly, Rosenfeld's effort proved the matchwinner and the Fartown side went through to the third round by 3-2 and from there to retain the Cup against Wigan. But the match had been a classic and for a long time was remembered as the best ever at Belle Vue.[1]

By contrast a series of poor performances at the end of the season, including a heavy 64-0 defeat at Rochdale, partly explained by numerous injuries, saw Trinity fall to eighteenth place. A word of caution was being sounded in some parts, with Trinity being advised to watch out for competition from the other football codes, in the form of Wakefield Rugby Union, who had won the Yorkshire Cup that year, and the newly-reformed Wakefield City Association Football Club, playing at Thornes Lane in the Yorkshire League, and who were attracting interest by playing exhibition matches against such sides as Manchester City and initially at least producing crowds estimated at three to four thousand.

Like other Northern Union clubs, though, Trinity experienced a post-war boom in attendances, which only served to emphasise their predominance among the city's sports clubs. At the 1920 AGM, record receipts of over £5,000 were announced and a profit of over £2,000. With a substantial bank balance, Trinity were able to make progress in several areas. For the first time the club appointed a full-time secretary-manager, a post taken up by JA Quinn, with an office in Tammy Hall Street. It was he who introduced the twopenny Wakefield Trinity Gazette, a forerunner of the modern match programme with team lists and other information, which made its first appearance on October 30, 1920. A supporters' club was formed in February 1923, following a meeting at the Grey Horse, Kirkgate.

With substantial funds behind them, the Wakefield committee started to dip into the transfer market. They did not set their sights on overseas players, as the bigger clubs did, or on British-born stars but tended to settle instead for experienced, lower-ranking players. Over the next couple of years players were bought in for relatively modest sums from clubs such as Rochdale, Swinton, Leeds and Dewsbury, albeit with limited success. In its search to rebuild the side in the post-Great War era, the club continued to give trials to players from the reserve or intermediate sides. But that necessarily involved a good deal of experimentation in team selection. Even young players such as Charlie Pollard, Archie Siswick, Clifford Pepper and Tommy Pickup, who were expected to provide the backbone of the team of the future, were constantly required to change position. An unsettled side produced some below-par performances, especially in the absence of Jonty Parkin, who did not return to the Trinity side until mid-November following his role in the tour to Australia and New Zealand.

Full back Charlie Pollard, Trinity's leading goal kicker throughout the 1920s and a Great Britain tourist to Australia and New Zealand in 1924

Parkin played in two of the three tests in Australia and all three in New Zealand, scoring a hat-trick in the first at Auckland. Three years later, when addressing a meeting of the newly formed Trinity Supporters' Club, RFL secretary John Wilson recalled Parkin's performance in Auckland. 'I never saw a better display of half back play than the one Parkin gave that day,' he said. 'In the first few minutes of the game ... Parkin went round the blind side of the scrimmage and went through practically the whole side. He had Jim Bacon [of Leeds] on the wing with him and by selling the dummy on many occasions he beat the defence and scored a try by the posts.' It was no surprise that on his return to action with Trinity, Parkin was described as being in a class of his own.

The season of 1920-21, in which Trinity could not improve on their previous position, was unremarkable except for two vastly different matches. One, on January 15 at Hull, ended in the highest score ever recorded, at the time, against Trinity, who, with an inexperienced side lacking Parkin, Pollard and Kershaw, were dealt a 69-11 thrashing. Despite other unsatisfactory performances, the first round Challenge Cup tie held the promise of better things. Drawn for the second year running at home against the powerful Huddersfield side, Trinity typically saved one of their better displays for this competition. Hours before kick-off, charabancs and vehicles of all descriptions streamed through Wakefield towards Belle Vue. Thousands of supporters made their way on foot over the Calder bridge and along Doncaster Road. It was, said the *Wakefield Express*, 'the most remarkable sight one has ever seen in the "Merrie Citie".' Though Huddersfield again won, by the narrow score of 8-4, the attendance was a record at 30,676, with receipts of £1,752.

Those takings contributed to the record income of £6,862 for the season. Despite the club's relatively lowly position and a players' wage bill that was fifty per cent higher than previously known, membership had increased and there

The Wakefield team of 1920-21, captained by Jonathan Parkin. *Back row*: J Wild, A Armstrong, H Kershaw, JW Todd, AK Crosland, J Barraclough, H Rafter, CA Pollard. *Front row*: J Paterson, T Pickup, J Parkin, A Siswick, C Pepper

was a profit on the season of £797. With the finances in a healthy state, the club looked to secure the ground. There were two mortgages, one of £2,000 and another of £1,250. The lesser of the two was held by Messrs Fernandes & Co, who, on the intervention of the club's former president, JB Cooke, accepted £850 to pay it off. It was hoped that the other mortgage would be paid off by the end of the season, so that the ground would then practically belong to the club. Though not yet in a position to build a new stand, the club made other improvements during the summer of 1921, with the church end being banked up to cater for more spectators. Among the signings, the one which created the biggest stir was that of 35-year old Albert Rosenfeld from Huddersfield. The Australian winger, who had run in no fewer than eight tries in the 62-5 rout of Trinity ten years earlier, as well as scoring the winning try in Trinity's Cup defeat in 1920, had been at Fartown since making an impact on the Australian tour of 1908-9. Creating a record which still stands today, Rosenfeld scored a record 80 tries in the 1913-14 season, beating his own previous best of 78. In Trinity's ranks he scored the first try at Hull KR's new Craven Park ground on September 2, 1922.

The 1921-22 season saw the third tour by the Australians, the first in ten years. Jonathan Parkin, after playing for Great Britain in the first test, led Trinity in their match at Belle Vue against the tourists, creating the opening for Pickup's early try before the Australians, with the great wingman Harold Horder and loose forward Frank Burge in top form, cut loose to win 29-3. Only Parkin and Pollard were a match for their opponents.

After captaining Yorkshire, Parkin was invited to lead Great Britain in the second test, which was lost 16-2 at the Boulevard. Two weeks later the Wakefield half back captained Yorkshire to a 30-12 win over Cumberland, scoring a record five tries and kicking two goals. The following month, Parkin was again at half back in the Yorkshire side which met Australia at Belle Vue, losing 24-8.

Trinity went out of the Challenge Cup in the first round at Wigan and in the league rallied from fourth from bottom to seventeenth. But for Parkin, captaining both county and country, the season had been a personal triumph. He was granted the match against Leeds as his benefit – a plum fixture, which, together with other fund-raising, made for the Trinity skipper the sum of £649, an enormous amount in those days, when the working man earned on average around £3 a week. As the *Wakefield Express* pointed out, it was quite a contrast to some of the benefits

71

that other prominent Trinity players had received. The previous year Kershaw and Taylor shared a benefit match, while at the end of the season Trinity played a friendly against the county side in aid of Poynton, Burton and Lynch, who had all retired, and Crosland, who was still playing after two decades but was also soon to retire after making a club record 533 appearances. Born at Lord Rodney Yard, close by the original Holly Lodge club rooms, Crosland, a cab driver by trade, had the equally remarkable record of having represented Yorkshire over fourteen seasons. In November 1922 the Leeds match was also reserved as a benefit, but for three players – Ernest Parkin, who had just been selected for Yorkshire, Harry Rafter and Jack Wild. Gate receipts of £383, plus a collection, was divided between the three men, realising the sum of £167 each.

An important change was made for the start of the 1922-23 season. The title of Northern Union, with all its implications, was dropped at the instigation of the touring Australians and henceforth the name of Rugby Football League was adopted to describe the governing body and the game it managed.

Parkin was once more elected club captain, but there were some who were dissatisfied with his unavailability for certain matches, which was interpreted as picking and choosing when he felt like playing, at least according to a letter-writer to the *Wakefield Express* who called himself 'One desirous of getting shut'. In a special meeting called by the committee, Parkin explained his unavailability and produced medical testimony concerning an injury, which the board fully accepted. He also assured the committee 'that he had the interests of the club at heart and that it was his desire to continue to serve the club faithfully.' The Trinity captain's riposte to the anonymous supporter showed as much wit, in a letter to the *Express*, as he did on the field:

'At no time during my playing career with Wakefield Trinity have I ever received a farthing more remuneration than the other members of the team. I do not claim to be a better player than anyone else but I do claim, without blowing my own trumpet, that no other players holding the same honours as myself and playing Northern Union football could say the same. Surely this proves my loyalty to Wakefield Trinity. With regard to the writer's remark advising the committee to sell me and with the proceeds to erect a stand, I should be glad to give £50 towards the building of the stand if the committee will reserve the stand's use for men like "One who is desirous of getting shut" and all others who have not the decency to put their names to anything scurrilous they have to say. An ideal spot, in my opinion, for the erection of the stand for such supporters would be in the Cattle Market. Yours, etc, Jonathan Parkin, Griffin Hotel, Wakefield.'

Parkin was soon proving his value again, if proof were really needed. In the match against Rochdale in early October, it was noted: 'Once again, Jonathan Parkin, the greatest of all half backs, was in his glory: he appeared to be uncanny and the Rochdale men were absolutely unable to cope with him. He was able to oblige with that brilliant individualism for which he is famous… Not only was he clever in attack but he was equally clever in defence.'

The Great Britain captain continued to achieve representative honours, but since signing for Wakefield in 1913 he had won no trophies. An opportunity presented itself in the Yorkshire Cup campaign of 1922, when, in the first round, Trinity won at Hunslet after having three men sent off. In the second round, they beat Dewsbury 6-2 before meeting York in the semi-final at Belle Vue, watched by a crowd of 17,000. But Trinity's hopes were dashed when York sprang a surprise by winning the semi and going on to beat Batley in the final.

The optimism of the immediate post-war era turned to disillusion as Trinity continued to occupy a place in the lower half of the league table, their best position coming in 1922-23 when they ended the season in thirteenth spot out of 27 clubs. The committee came in for some criticism for buying in second-rate players from other clubs many of whom failed even to stay in the first team, or for recruiting locally without sufficient discrimination. Another letter to the *Wakefield Express* echoed supporters' disappointments: 'Cast-off players and striplings from

Intermediate teams are not much good,' wrote someone under the pseudonym of Modernist, from Netherton. 'There is a big demand by the sporting population in the area served by Trinity for high-class Rugby football and if Wakefield Trinity would supply this demand the "gates" at Belle Vue would repay all the money wisely spent on first-class players. Wakefield is surrounded by thickly-populated districts whose people long for up-to-date Rugby football and with buses now running into the city football enthusiasts would flock to Belle Vue if they could be assured of witnessing good football. But with the present class of play they will neither go to the trouble of leaving their village nor pay the price.'

The Challenge Cup brought no glory either, apart from a club record-equalling score of 67-13, including seventeen tries, over Cumberland amateur club Hensingham, who had agreed to switch the tie to Belle Vue. Trinity went out in the following round at Salford but the club had the honour of staging the final for the first and only time when on Saturday April 28, 1923 Hull met Leeds. In readiness for the huge crowd, expected possibly to exceed the previous year's record of 32,596 at Headingley, the banking was improved and extended and new crush barriers put up. In the event, Leeds's 28-3 triumph was seen by a crowd officially given as 29,335 (29,413 according to other reports) – just short of the figure for Trinity's first round clash with Huddersfield two years earlier.

At the end of the season, club secretary J Quinn, delivering the annual report, was in almost apologetic mood. 'In years gone by,' he said, 'Wakefield were always able to pride themselves on the sterling qualities of their forwards and not much difficulty was experienced in getting a formidable front line [pack]… Unfortunately in this district there has been an obvious scarcity of well-built and intelligent young fellows suitable for a first-class team… Nearly twenty men have been tried in the forward department.' At the same time, fifth-placed Wigan, in proposing that the RFL ban on overseas players be lifted, claimed a similar difficulty in recruiting local talent of suitable calibre. After the boom of the immediate post-war era, a fall in gate receipts resulted in a £558 loss on the 1922-23 season.

Wakefield's outstanding players were of course club captain Jonty Parkin, selected again for England and Yorkshire, and Charlie Pollard, who, playing for the county against Cumberland, scored a try and kicked six goals in the 51-12 win. In the forwards, Jack Wild was playing as well as ever after twelve years, but the lack of a settled side resulted in some unpredictable performances throughout the 1923-24 season. In November, for example, Trinity lost at bottom club Bradford, giving them their first win of the season, and then the following week beat Leeds, the league leaders, at Headingley. But during the course of the season, at least one young forward gave notice of a successful career to come. Charlie Glossop stood out as an attacking forward of some promise, showing intelligence and speed off the mark.

Unusually, Trinity reached the third round of the Challenge Cup, winning first at St Helens Recreation, the second club of that town, and then at Leeds with a fine display master-minded inevitably by Parkin. In the next round, drawn away from home again, they once more fell foul of Oldham, losing 24-10 in front of 20,000 fans, though they could at least console themselves with having made about £800 from the shared gate receipts of the three cup-ties. Trinity's erratic form continued over the Easter period. On the Good Friday of 1924, they lost to Dewsbury, who would finish the season one place above them in the league; on the Saturday they registered their first win over Huddersfield for fourteen years, causing the Fartown side to miss out on a top four spot; and on Easter Monday they lost to Featherstone, fifth from bottom, for the third time that season. Parkin and Pollard, who were on tour, were missing from the team, who counted as many as seven non-local players in their ranks. Trinity's signings had failed to prevent them from slumping to their lowest league position of nineteenth, which equalled their worst performance in a single division since the inaugural 1895-96 season. Though making a profit of £479, the committee were forced to admit that it had again been hard to find talented young players who could adapt to the requirements of top-level rugby league. But if it was any consolation, the supposed threat from association football failed to materialise, in Wakefield at least. The Wakefield City AFC, after operating in the Yorkshire League for four seasons, had failed to capture the imagination of the public, who, if they wanted to watch soccer, turned to Leeds, Huddersfield or Barnsley. The club's total gate receipts for the season amounted to a mere £210, less than Trinity would expect to take from a single match. Looking to the future, the Trinity committee decided to build a stand to provide covered accommodation along the east side opposite the existing stand, which itself would be provided with seating. The new stand – or more accurately covered terrace - was opened towards the start of the 1924-25 season on September 27 at an estimated cost of £3,200. Running the length of the pitch, it had a capacity of 8,550 places, of which 5,800 were under cover.

From Australia, Great Britain skipper Jonty Parkin, writing to a friend back in his home village of Sharlston, said that he wanted to win all three tests and set up a new record. 'I not only want to break the record for my own sake but to uphold the traditions of my native village.' In the first test, Parkin scored two tries and made another in the 22-3 triumph, while in the second his solo effort, kicking ahead and touching down for Great Britain's only try seven minutes from the end, with Jim Sullivan's conversion, produced the 5-3 win and brought home the Ashes. Despite a 21-11 defeat in the third test, Parkin was again in fine form, dominating his opposite number and scoring another try to equal Wigan half back Johnny Thomas's 1908-9 record of scoring a try in all three tests.

Trinity and Great Britain captain Jonathan Parkin, who toured Australia and New Zealand in 1920, 1924 and 1928

Parkin's Wakefield team-mate Pollard was not chosen for the test matches, but one of his legendary exploits created an unofficial record in a touring party which included the great goal-kicker Jim Sullivan. In a kicking practice at Sydney Cricket Ground, Pollard was said to have kicked a 75 yard goal on two occasions, using a run-up of about twenty yards. The Trinity full back or centre is reported to have booted the ball high between the uprights so that it landed fully fifteen yards beyond the posts – an astonishing distance of around 90 yards.

During the 1924 close season, Trinity made a major signing in bringing Billy Batten from Hull to Belle Vue at a fee of £350, beating several other prominent clubs to his signature. A native of Kinsley, he was, at nearly 36, approaching the end of his career but was still regarded as one of the finest centres in the game. With Harold Wagstaff, Batten formed one of the greatest ever centre partnerships in the Great Britain team, and his prowess was borne out not only by his record £600 transfer from Hunslet to Hull in 1913 but also by the fact that he was believed to be the highest paid footballer in either the rugby or soccer code.

Batten brought changes with him. Jonty Parkin had maintained that he personally had never been paid more than any other Wakefield player. That was true, since club records show that, up to the 1924-25 season, all players were paid £3 and ten shillings for a win and £2 for a loss. But when Batten and Parkin arrived back from the tour, Batten was paid £5 per match regardless of the result, later increased to £6, the same as Parkin had begun to receive, while the rest remained on the same terms as before.

Whether it was because of the acquisition of Batten or not, crowds were flocking back to Belle Vue. For a league match against York, third from bottom, 10,000 turned up. The following week, 14,000 witnessed the Yorkshire Cup first round clash with Hull, once more causing serious congestion on the medieval Calder bridge. That was one of ten wins in a row up to the end of November. Trinity were also playing more attractive football than ever, to which Batten made a contribution with his powerful and intelligent play in both attack and defence, fulfilling a role which had been to some extent neglected. In the forwards, the promising duo of Bill Horton and Charlie Glossop added dash. In the second round of the Yorkshire Cup at Keighley, it was Horton who scored the winning try, outpacing

The Yorkshire Cup winners 1924: *Middle row* (*players only*): R White, L Abrahams, W Blower, C Glossop, W Horton, A Siswick. *Seated*: A Bonner (chairman) P Reid, C Pollard, J Parkin (capt), W Batten, E Thomas. *In front*: W Jubb, T Pickup

the cover defence over 50 yards from Parkin's pass. Trinity were deprived of the services of Parkin, Batten and Siswick when they were selected for Yorkshire, though Parkin in particular proved his inestimable worth in the semi-final at Headingley, watched by 27,000 spectators. In the tenth minute the Trinity captain dummied his way over the Leeds line direct from a scrum, Pollard converting. Despite having Tommy Pickup sent off in the second half, Trinity's defence held firm, Leeds managing only two penalty goals in reply.

From that 5-4 semi-final win Trinity travelled to Headingley again a fortnight later to meet Batley in the final. In front of 25,546 spectators, Batley took an early lead and led 8-5 at half-time, Trinity's points coming when Parkin backed up a Glossop break, touched down and kicked the goal himself. After the break, Pollard kicked a fine 45-yard penalty and then landed another magnificent effort from the touchline to put Trinity ahead at 9-8. With the forwards doing sterling work and Parkin outwitting the opposition around the scrum, Trinity held on to claim the Yorkshire Cup for the first time in fourteen years. Batten, about whom it was said that success followed him around like a shadow,[2] had now won a Yorkshire Cup winner's medal with each of his three clubs. Parkin, for all his illustrious career, had only this one medal to show for it. It would be more than twenty years before Trinity landed another trophy.

After Rosenfeld, now retired, and Batten, Trinity signed another illustrious player at the end of his career. In January, Johnny Rogers, Jonty Parkin's former international half-back partner, was signed from Huddersfield for £300 and was the man of the match in the 19-0 victory over his old team. He became the third member of the team to receive a special rate of pay, earning £5 per match.

Trinity's Challenge Cup run was a brief one. After beating Salford in the first round, they travelled to Keighley, where they came unstuck by three points to nil. But the whole city was affected when Belle Vue staged the semi-final between Hull KR and Leeds. The 25,000 spectators who arrived in Wakefield for the match once more caused severe congestion on Calder bridge. Since at the time there was only one narrow bridge over the river, motor vehicles had to be re-routed away from Doncaster Road at the end of the match to rejoin the bridge after pedestrians, who shuffled across a dozen or more abreast, had had the chance to get away first.

Trinity may have had a poor Challenge Cup campaign and ended the season in fourteenth place in the league, but the club made a record profit of £1,280. The new covered terrace had brought in more spectators, while the mortgage on the ground was now paid off. In giving his report at the end of the season, the club president, Councillor Arthur Bonner stated, to loud applause, that he was in the happy position to say that so long as the Trinity Football Club was in existence, rugby league football would be played at Belle Vue. Cr Bonner, on being re-elected president, said that it was a high honour to occupy a position which was second only to that of Chief Magistrate – which testified to the civic importance, not to mention the probity, of the position.

Left: Trinity and Yorkshire centre Archie Siswick.
Right: Centre Billy Batten, who joined Trinity from Hull in 1924, and, like Jonty Parkin, was elected as one of the first members of the Rugby League Hall of Fame.

In the early part of the 1925-26 season, Trinity's main objective was to retain the Yorkshire Cup. But they went only as far as the second round, when, despite the home tie, they were once more undone by Featherstone Rovers, who thus recorded their tenth victory over Trinity in twelve matches since joining the Northern Union in 1921. Belle Vue did, however, host the final, in which Dewsbury beat Huddersfield in front of a 13,000 crowd, many people having been put off by the frost which threatened the match. But a statement made by the Dewsbury president after his side's victory made an interesting contrast between Trinity's financial state and that of other clubs. It was no secret, said the Dewsbury official, that his club had been on the verge of bankruptcy for several years. Halifax too, it was later revealed, were in financial difficulties after spending £2,671 on transfer fees the previous season and £1,200 in the present season. Yet huge crowds flocked to the big games.

After a stuttering start to the season, Trinity put together seven wins in a row, inspired as ever by Jonty Parkin. It was often noted that the great half back stood head and shoulders above any other player on the field but of course there were other talented players around him, despite obvious weaknesses in certain positions. Bill Horton was making a name for himself as a dangerous back-row forward and scored three tries against Rochdale in a match in April. On the horizon was Ernest Pollard, brother of Charlie, and already catching the eye as a 15 year old in the Trinity Supporters' Club under-16 team.

Though Trinity finished eighth, their highest position for thirteen years, they made a shock exit from the Challenge Cup, in Parkin's absence, at the hands of Wigan Highfield, who, in only their fourth season, went on to cause further upsets, accounting for both Huddersfield and Leeds.

At the end of the year it was commented, as it could have been for many a previous year: 'It is a remarkable thing that our players have invariably given their best displays when opposed to teams of high repute and in support of this one need only mention the great game at Wigan, where the home team were unable to score a solitary try, and the match at Belle Vue, where our players gained a brilliant victory.' In contrast with Halifax, for example, Wakefield

The Trinity team of 1926-27, who reached the semi-final of the Challenge Cup. *Back row*: W Howell, L Higson, C Glossop, W Horton, CA Pollard, R White. *Front row*: T Coles, R Ward, J Pearce, T Pickup, J Parkin (capt), A Siswick, E Bateson

had spent £490 on transfer fees in that season, and £1,251 the year before. Though players' wages, including the second team, had risen to £2,992, the club still managed a profit of £711, some of which went to paying off the loan on the new covered terrace. It was said that only four clubs were in a sounder financial position than Wakefield Trinity.

During the 1926 close season, Trinity made a relatively rare foray into South Wales to sign the second rower DJ Maidment from Ebbw Vale. There were four other Welshmen on the register, mainly signed from other rugby league clubs - E Thomas, Johnny Rogers, Bernard Gould and Thomas Coles – and two Scots, Peter Reid and R Naylor. The remaining non-local players were Bob White and J Hesketh from Wigan, Joe Kendall from Aspatria and Ted Bateson, who had played professional soccer with Blackburn Rovers and cricket with Lancashire Second XI, from Skipton Rugby Union. The 42-man playing register thus counted eleven players from outside Wakefield and district.

Rugby league was still by a very long way the major winter sport of Wakefield and district. In their own AGM, Wakefield City AFC, who had once harboured big ambitions, recorded income of £261 for the whole season, with a total of just £94 from gate receipts. The club struggled on but failed to start the 1928-9 season, though a number of local amateur clubs played soccer in Wakefield and the surrounding area.

On the 25th anniversary of the re-founding of Wakefield Rugby Union Club, the honorary secretary, reviewing the previous quarter of a decade, stated: 'At the time of the great split of 1894-5 and during a number of succeeding years when practically all Rugger enthusiasts had gone over to professionalism [sic], there appeared to be little likelihood of representative amateur Rugby football ever again being played in our city … In 1901 the Wakefield Rugby FC was inaugurated … the playing pitch being the old Thornes ground. At this period the amateur game in our county was at its lowest ebb. Its former glory had entirely departed, there being only ten affiliated clubs. Season 1901-2 saw the commencement of a great revival … with three amateur clubs, Balne Lane (founded 1900-1),

St Mark's and our own club being run in the city. Unfortunately after a few successful years the first two clubs had to be disbanded and we were left the only representatives of the game in the city.'

Trinity supporters were forced to endure another mediocre start to the season. By mid-October 1926, their team had lost six matches but had reached the semi-final of the Yorkshire Cup by beating Hull 15-5 at Belle Vue to set up a final tie against Huddersfield at Headingley. The Fartown side had fallen from their previous lofty position to occupy nineteenth place in the League. Trinity were faring even worse at twenty-third in a competition which had expanded to twenty-nine clubs with the arrival of Castleford and Pontypridd. Fog caused a postponement of the final from the Saturday to the Wednesday, with a consequently reduced attendance. In the end Trinity were beaten for possession, though new winger Bateson showed an impressive turn of speed in eluding two defenders to score his side's sole try. Huddersfield were victorious for the seventh time, winning 10-3.

Jonty Parkin twice captained England against the New Zealanders, who had embarked on their second tour. The Trinity captain, along with Batten and Horton, was selected for Yorkshire to play against Cumberland and Lancashire, although Batten was unable to play in the second match, held at Belle Vue, and his team-mate Pickup took his place.

Trinity met the New Zealanders, still known like their rugby union counterparts as the All Blacks, at Belle Vue on December 28, 1926 in what turned out to be a very attractive game. Though Wakefield's team was without five regulars, they turned in a pleasing performance under the direction of the masterly Parkin, before losing the high-scoring match by 29-24, Pollard kicking six goals to keep Trinity in contention.

On New Year's Day 1927 Trinity posted their first away win of the season by inflicting Wigan's first defeat of the campaign at Central Park. It was Charlie Pollard who sealed the victory when, with Trinity trailing 6-5, he refused to be outdone by Wigan's Jim Sullivan and kicked a huge penalty goal from the half-way line.

Two weeks later Billy Batten was on his way to newcomers Castleford. He had still been good enough to represent Yorkshire earlier in the season, stretching his county career to a remarkable eighteen years. At the same time and despite serious interest from other clubs, Trinity signed the young prodigy Ernest Pollard, at sixteen and a half some twenty years younger than Batten. Coincidentally, Pollard would make his debut playing opposite Batten in the match against Castleford, which Trinity won 17-14. Charlie's younger brother was described as 'not yet seventeen but old enough and clever enough to be included in first-class company.'

In the Challenge Cup Trinity profited from a series of home draws, gaining revenge over Wigan Highfield in winning 13-5, before going on to knock out Halifax 7-2 and then Batley 10-6. In the semi-final, Trinity faced renowned cup-fighters Oldham at Wigan. There were no heroics at Central Park this time as Trinity went down by 7-3, after leading 3-0 at half-time thanks to a Bateson try from Siswick's interception. In their fourth successive final, Oldham easily accounted for Swinton to take the Challenge Cup for the third time. For Trinity, a disappointing pattern followed. Throughout the next decade Trinity's inability to reach the final of the Challenge Cup was matched by regular defeats in the final of the Yorkshire Cup.

Nine – Star Players but Scant Success: 1927-34

Through the 1920s and into the following decade, Trinity rarely rose above the middle of the league table and, though there were several near misses, they had just one trophy to show for their efforts – the Yorkshire Cup which had been won in the 1924-25 season. Yet the club continued to produce some fine individuals. Apart from the inimitable Parkin, one of the greatest in the game's history, Knottingley-born back row forward Bill Horton built an impressive international reputation. Charlie Pollard and younger brother Ernest, both prolific points scorers who toured Australia, were mainstays of the back division and winger Stan Smith proved one of the best ever in his position and also toured Australia with Great Britain.

At the end of the 1926-7 season, Trinity occupied fifteenth position in the league, with Charlie Pollard having played in all but one of the 46 matches in his benefit year, which yielded £463, regarded as a 'magnificent' amount in view of the continuing industrial depression, which contributed to a £76 loss for the club. Pollard's rock-solid defence at full back inspired confidence throughout the team. According to JC Lindley, 'sometimes he would suggest to his captain Parkin that a certain opponent who was causing some trouble should be allowed to "come through" and be met by one of his bone-shaking tackles. After he had dealt with them, more often than not Charlie would claim that they "never came again".'

Pollard's prodigious goal-kicking was a feature at the start of the following season too. Against Keighley, in the first match of the 1927-8 season, he landed a penalty goal from five yards inside his own half. His younger brother Ernest was making progress and, on his first appearance in Lancashire, had a hand in all Trinity's three tries at Oldham. Though the two teams did not play each other every season, it was Trinity's first win there since the start of the Northern Union.

Another future star, Stanley Smith from Fitzwilliam, a nephew of Billy Batten who had come through the Supporters' Club ranks, made an early, very favourable showing. The recently signed Welshman, Dai Maidment, scored three times in the win over Warrington and was described as the best man on the field. Parkin and Horton again won Yorkshire caps as Trinity maintained their fine form to head the league table in the run-up to Christmas 1927. Unfortunately attendances fell away for ordinary league matches, so that only around 5,000 saw them do the double over Oldham in December. One of the reasons given was that, in the harsh economic climate, supporters who lived in outlying districts – and there were many - could not afford the transport to the ground as well as the shilling admission.

Since they had gone out of both the Yorkshire Cup and Challenge Cup at the first round stage, Trinity had no distractions from their league campaign. But a sensational 13-7 win over Swinton, who had regained the league leadership, was followed by a drop in form which resulted in a series of five successive defeats in March-April. Tenth place was scant reward for Trinity's fine performances in the autumn. The financial situation was equally disappointing. A loss of £679 could be partly explained by Archie Siswick's exceptional benefit of £544, much of which came from the Leeds match receipts, and a decrease in cup-tie takings of around £1,500. Among the individual highlights, Ted Bateson's six tries against Castleford – a club record - took his total for the season to 28, which had been bettered only by Billy Simpson's haul of 34 in 1910-11.

Jonty Parkin, who was to embark on a record third tour of Australia, had the honour of captaining the tourists for a second time. Owing to injury, Parkin played only one test in Australia and one in New Zealand, but his reputation was already sealed. Bill Horton, who played loose forward in all six tests and made a big impact himself, spoke of his skipper's 'god-like' status in Australia. 'Everybody wanted to see Jonty in harness,' Horton said. 'Although he played in only a few matches, he showed himself to be still a great player. He was really the player-coach. His experience gained in his two previous visits was invaluable, his wonderful knowledge of the game and the advice he gave to the players had a great deal to do with the success of our team and the winning of the Ashes.' Horton too came in for special praise from none other than former half back great Duncan Thompson, who declared, after the third test, that Horton's work was one of the finest exhibitions of loose forward play he had ever seen. The tour of Australia, New Zealand and Canada (where an exhibition match was played) produced record profits of over £10,000, with each player receiving £136 – about as much as a miner would earn in a year.

On their return, Parkin and Horton were picked as usual to play for Yorkshire and then England against Wales. But despite having two leading international players in their ranks, Trinity again performed erratically in the league. In the first round of the Yorkshire Cup, Trinity drew with Hunslet at Belle Vue but went on to win the replay 20-11 at Parkside, scoring six tries to three. In the second round, following a controversial refereeing decision to disallow what looked like a valid Parkin try when Trinity were 7-6 ahead, the course of the game went the way of Leeds, who won through 24-7. Leeds and Featherstone reached the final, which, after much debate, was staged at Belle Vue. In heavy rain and wind a crowd of just under 13,000 saw Leeds take the trophy.

In addition to finals such as these, the Belle Vue ground was also used for amateur finals, as well as the occasional rugby union match, as when the Yorkshire County side took on the Old Savilians (Wakefield Grammar School Old Boys) in a match in aid of the Grammar School Library funds. It was believed to be the first time that a full Rugby Union county side had appeared in Wakefield since the 1895 split. Appropriately the match was refereed by the vicar of Holy Trinity.

On November 10, 1928, Trinity registered their highest score when routing Bradford Northern by 68-7 at Belle Vue. A triallist, later revealed to be winger Stephen Ray from Bath, scored five tries and was signed up, though Bateson and the promising youngster Stan Smith were the team's first-choice wingers. It was said of one of Smith's displays, against Bramley: 'The best effort seen for a very long time was the solo contribution by Smith. He took the ball near his own 25 and with practically all the Bramley team in front of him he eluded first one man and then another. During his whole progress opponents were in his way but he dodged them cleverly and ended up by scoring a brilliant try.' It was a logical choice when the young winger was included, along with Parkin and Horton, in the county side to face Cumberland.

Trinity went out of the Challenge Cup at the first hurdle, losing 11-5 at Hull and therefore abandoning all hope of appearing in the first final to be played at Wembley. The decision to take the event to the capital was another milestone in the making of the game and created much excitement and anticipation among people who often had not been outside their own county. In practically every rugby league town with a railway station, excursions were advertised. From Wakefield the return journey cost £1, setting off at 6 a.m. and coming back from King's Cross at 12.20 a.m., and included breakfast and supper on the train. Optional excursions were offered in the morning to the West End, Richmond, Hampton Court and Kew; a chance to take a 'meat tea' at Lyons Corner House; and an evening trip through Chinatown and the East End, which thrillingly promised a visit to the Underworld.

Both Cup finalists, Dewsbury and Wigan, went down to defeats at Trinity's hands over the Easter period. In typically unpredictable fashion, Trinity beat league leaders Wigan 14-2 at Belle Vue as they strung three wins together to lift themselves out of the bottom half of the table. Only a week later they would lose at home to mid-table side Wigan Highfield, at which point an exasperated *Wakefield Express* reporter noted: 'Wakefield Trinity's inconsistency is positively appalling.'

The final position of seventeenth – their worst for five years – had caused both supporters and committee some concern. Secretary JA Quinn reported: 'It has been a very anxious time for those having the responsibility of the management of the club, who cannot be accused of want of patience with regard to several players, whose erratic play has been a source of perplexity to those who have had to select the team week by week… It has been absolutely impossible to get hold of first-class players, who have been scarcer than they have ever been since the formation of the Northern Union – a fact which this season has been the experience of most clubs in the Rugby League.' Total receipts from league games were down by nearly £1,300. The President, Cr Bonner, put it succinctly. He regretted that the report and balance-sheet were not brighter but put that down to two things: bad play and bad trade.

There was none of that when Trinity faced the Australian touring team towards the start of the 1929-30 season. The Australians had won all six of their previous matches, including one against Lancashire, and had scored an average of thirty points a match, producing free-flowing football in doing so. But Trinity's captain Jonathan Parkin had long experience of playing against the Australians and masterminded a sensational performance which left the visitors with no room to display their spectacular brand of football. Charlie Pollard was in great form with his kicking, landing two penalties and, unusually, a drop goal in reply to Australian winger Finch's unconverted try. Parkin was seen at his irrepressible best when the tourists got the ball from the scrum but the Trinity skipper snapped up his opposing scrum-half's pass, went past the full back and planted the ball over the line, Pollard converting to put Trinity into an 11-3 half-time lead. Trinity maintained their grip on the game throughout the second half, in which winger Ray scored the only try, giving a brilliant victory by 14-3, watched by a 10,000 crowd. Just a week later in the first test, the Australians recorded a 31-8 win over a Great Britain side from which Parkin had withdrawn with a back problem. In November at Belle Vue, the Aussies went on to beat a Yorkshire county side, also lacking Parkin, by 25-12.

International winger Stan Smith, who left Trinity for Leeds in 1930 and toured Australia and New Zealand in 1932

If Trinity's display against the Australians showed what heights they could reach, it was all the more surprising that they should also plumb the depths when beaten by clearly inferior sides. Stan Smith became the latest Trinity player to win his international cap when selected to play against Australia and joined a group of Wakefield players who had already won representative honours: Parkin, Horton, Charlie Pollard, who toured Australia but did not play in a test match, Charlie Glossop, who played for England against Other Nationalities, and Dai Maidment and Stephen Ray, who both represented Wales. Ernest Pollard was poised to make his test debut. Front rower Len Higson was the most recent Trinity player to earn his county cap. With stars like these, it is surprising that Trinity did not achieve more, even in an era of many great teams. It must have been particularly frustrating for the great Jonathan Parkin not to have been better rewarded at club level than to win the Yorkshire Cup just once during his career. The half back announced his international retirement after captaining Great Britain in the third, and scoreless, test against Australia at Swinton on January 4, 1930. When handed the captaincy for the final time, it was said of him: 'It is a great compliment to a man who has been playing in first-class football since 1913, and he will have to be regarded as one of the finest exponents of the game since the introduction of professional Rugby football. Not only has he been a great asset to the Rugby League but for many years he has been the shining light for Wakefield Trinity … Wherever he goes he has to pay the penalty for his greatness and one cannot expect him to remain in harness much longer.'

As Trinity limped along in mid-table, officials became concerned at a 'very big' decrease in gates, partly due to some bad weather and also to the difficult economic situation. With the prospect of a considerable loss looming, the committee took the decision to sell winger Stanley Smith for the record transfer fee of £1,075. Already an international at 19, Smith became the first big-name player to be transferred to Leeds, a route which would become a familiar one to Trinity players in the coming years. An exceptionally fast, side-stepping winger who was also very sound in defence, Smith appeared as a Leeds player in the hurriedly arranged fourth and deciding test and scored the only try, the match-winner.

Horton replaced Parkin as Yorkshire skipper in the win over Cumberland, while Len Higson and Ernest Pollard were chosen for the county against Glamorgan and Monmouthshire, for which Ray was selected but had to withdraw. The winger sustained a broken fibula in the drawn first round Challenge Cup tie at Swinton, but remarkably carried on playing. In the replay at Belle Vue, watched by 14,000 – which did something to boost the club's finances – Trinity went out 7-2 and Horton, after suffering cracked ribs, also cried off from the county match.

At the season's end, Belle Vue hosted the Championship final for a fourth time, which produced a record crowd of 30,350 when Huddersfield met Leeds for the second year in a row. Once again the route to and from Belle Vue was the scene of much congestion as trams, buses, cars and motorbikes with sidecars came to a standstill on Ings Road and moved at a snail's pace over Chantry bridge. The match ended in a 2-2 draw and was replayed at Halifax.

With a small commission on the final and especially with the transfer fee from Leeds for Stan Smith, Trinity made a decent profit, in the circumstances, of £608 on the season. But Trinity's league position of seventeenth satisfied no one. The committee cursed their fate that so many matches were lost by the narrowest of margins and that key players, including Parkin, Ernest Pollard, Horton and Ray had been unavailable for lengthy periods. Nine matches had been lost by fewer than four points, the officials maintained; and if Trinity had won just two more matches, they would have been five places higher. But this 'what if?' attitude cut no ice with some fans, who blamed the poor showing on the committee's too cautious approach to signing players. Economy was all very well, but it didn't win matches.

The previous decade bore the stamp of Jonathan Parkin, but by the 1930-31 season Parkin had gone. He had refused to re-sign at the start of the season, when the committee, in order to quell some dissatisfaction in the team, reintroduced a flat rate of payment for all players. For six years, the captain had received considerably higher wages than other players and was aggrieved to see the preferential treatment end. The matter was discussed between committee and player at a Wednesday evening meeting, when he was placed on the transfer list at the modest fee of £100 in recognition of the valuable service he had given over a long period. The next day, in a unique move, Parkin handed over a cheque for £100 to the secretary in order to buy his own transfer. Within a short time he was on Hull KR's books.

To add spice to the situation, Trinity and Hull KR met three weeks later in the first round of the Yorkshire Cup at Belle Vue. There was no triumphant return to the scene of former glories. Parkin, playing behind a beaten set of forwards, was kept under close control by his ex-team-mates, who won 14-0. Ernest Pollard was a key figure in the victory, as he was, along with Bill Horton, in the Yorkshire side which beat Lancashire at Belle Vue for the first time in seven years. Trinity went on to knock Batley out in the second round before losing 9-5 in the semi-final at Fartown, handicapped by the absence of new captain Charlie Pollard, who had been in top goal-kicking form. Trinity were again without Pollard when knocked out of the Challenge Cup in the first round by Hunslet at Parkside, but the skipper was responsible for one of the few highlights of the 1930-31 season when he equalled Jimmy Metcalfe's goal-kicking record of 1908. Pollard landed eleven attempts out of twelve in Trinity's 46-10 home win over Castleford on April 11, 1931.

The secretary's report at the end of the season held little comfort for fans who had again seen their team finish in mid-table. It was one of the most difficult seasons the club had ever had, the secretary recorded. Not that Trinity were alone. Most clubs 'found it impossible to make ends meet', with Trinity's financial position described as 'unenviable'. The loss on the season amounted to £1,187 - almost twice as big as any previous loss. Gates from league matches had yielded only £2,224, compared to £3,050 the year before and the average for the past ten years of £4,170.

Once more a combination of bad weather and the economic depression were held responsible for the deficit, though the covered terrace – for which an extra admission charge was made – proved a valuable asset. As for performances on the field, the team again confounded everyone by losing matches they should have won but beating Swinton, Leeds and Wigan – three of the four play-off finalists. Secretary Quinn, whose last report this was – he resigned, claiming that his position was continually undermined by certain members of the committee – admitted the club's frustration at not being able to sign suitable young local players. 'The committee have done all they can to encourage young local talent,' he stated, 'but they continue to be handicapped by the fact that there are young fellows with an exaggerated opinion of their capabilities who … demand sums which are out of all reason despite the fact that the committee think that they pay their players well for their services.'

Ernest Pollard, the brother of Charlie, and Bill Horton on board ship en route for Australia and New Zealand, 1932

The worrying financial situation was uppermost in the committee's minds when they accepted Leeds's offer for Charlie Glossop, who was transferred for £435 at the start of the 1931-32 season. Among others, Dai Maidment was now at Barrow and centre or half back Davies at Keighley. But in spite of the committee's insistence that it was difficult to find good local talent, one very promising centre, Gilbert Robinson, an Eastmoor product, made his mark with a brilliant solo try over half the length of the field against Salford. On the other hand, Charlie Pollard had begun the season with one of his speciality penalty goals from five yards inside his own half in the Lazenby Cup match against Dewsbury. But he played his farewell match, also against Dewsbury, on Boxing Day. The popular captain, who stayed at the club as player-coach of the reserves, contributed six goals to Trinity's 30-7 victory. It coincided with a good run which included a 22-7 defeat of league leaders Leeds at Headingley as Trinity moved up to fourth place. Ernest Pollard, taking over where his older brother left off, scored a club record 24 points with nine goals and two tries in the 51-5 win over Bramley. Pollard and Horton, with Robinson as travelling reserve, were picked for England against Wales before all three went on tour to Australia and New Zealand, Horton making the trip for a second time.

Though failing in the Yorkshire Cup, being knocked out by Hull KR in the first round, Trinity put some good performances together later in the Challenge Cup. Ex-Huddersfield winger Freddie Smart, who scored 30 tries that season, touched down four times in the 26-8 first round defeat of Bradford. Warrington fell 15-2 in the second round, where half backs Joe Pearce and Sam Herbert made an effective pairing, and at Crown Flatt Trinity triumphed 14-7 over Dewsbury. In the semi-final at Rochdale, Trinity faced Swinton, three places above them in the league and with four tourists in their side. Trinity led by two Ernest Pollard penalty goals to nil at half-time and were dominating the game despite not making best use of their chances. Swinton grasped the one clear-cut opportunity that came their way and went through by 7-4 only to lose to Leeds in the final.

Trinity's challenge for a top four place, which had looked so convincing, faded to tenth. All appeared to be going well until a point was dropped at Bradford, followed by a major disappointment of defeat at Castleford, where the three Great Britain players announced themselves unavailable. A season which promised so much delivered little, apart from a very welcome profit of £1,319, made possible by an increase in gate receipts and the fee for Glossop. Unlike the season before, the committee now felt confident enough to announce that a new stand was to be built with accommodation for 900 spectators.

In Australia, Ernest Pollard made his first appearance for Great Britain and Bill Horton his eighth in the opening test in front of a record 70,000 crowd at Sydney Cricket Ground. Pollard, usually a centre with Trinity, played at stand-off in what was regarded at the time as Great Britain's best-ever touring team, who claimed a narrow 8-6 win in a hugely demanding match. Pollard and ex-Trinity winger Stanley Smith were the only British try-scorers in the ensuing 'Battle of Brisbane', a match which turned out even rougher than the first and ended in a British defeat. Only Bill Horton kept the Wakefield flag flying in the decider, in which Smith's rare achievement of a hat-trick brought home the Ashes. Smith was a try-scorer in all three tests in New Zealand, Horton also touching down in the second. As for Gilbert Robinson, the centre broke a bone in his wrist, which very much limited his appearances on tour.

Wakefield's three Great Britain tourists of 1932: centre or stand-off Ernest Pollard, back rower Bill Horton and centre Gilbert Robinson

As the tourists returned, the Trinity committee decided that players who represented their country or county at rugby league should receive extra match payments. The new measure did not therefore apply to new signing Gordon Bonner, the president's son, who had learned his rugby at Wakefield Grammar School and was playing for Bradford RUFC when selected for the British Rugby Union tour of Australasia in 1930.

Trinity reached the final of the Yorkshire Cup in that 1932-33 season, after beating Halifax 16-11 in the semi at Belle Vue. In their first appearance in the final for six years, they met a Leeds side featuring Charlie Glossop and Stan Smith at Huddersfield. At that moment, Trinity were third from bottom in the league table, Leeds eleventh from top. The underdogs put up fine defence but had less to offer in attack and went down by eight points to nil.

The redeveloped west stand, with sunken paddock in front, was officially opened on Saturday, October 29, 1932 by Walter Popplewell, chairman of the Rugby League, before Yorkshire met Lancashire. Trinity had three men on duty – Ernest Pollard, front rower Len Higson and the young back rower GH 'Mick' Exley – as the home county triumphed 30-3. The same trio were subsequently selected for England against Wales.

Trinity's indifferent league form improved towards the end of the season with a run of seven matches without defeat to allow a finish in nineteenth place, which was still nine places below the previous season's performance and the worst since 1924. It was hardly compensated for by progress in the Challenge Cup. A 6-5 win at Broughton Rangers was followed by a 9-4 defeat at home to Hull. Wakefield's only remaining interest in the Cup lay in the staging of the semi-final at Belle Vue, which had been the venue for the replayed Leeds-Halifax semi the year before. In the 1933 version Leeds and Huddersfield were expected to attract a big crowd and so they did. A record attendance of 36,359 at Belle Vue beat the previous best of 32,095 for the 1930 Championship final and Huddersfield rattled up a record semi-final score of 30-8. Special motor traffic routes were enforced and parking areas were provided behind the Alexandra Hotel on Doncaster Road and opposite the Duke of York Hotel on Agbrigg Road. Fortunately the newly-built bridge over the Calder relieved the congestion which had been a problem at previous big matches.

Wakefield Trinity team, 25 January 1930: *Back row*: E Pollard, S Ray, C Glossop, L Higson, W Moss, J Metcalfe, T Davies. *Front row*: J Pearce, E Bateson, W Horton, CA Pollard, H Field, R White

Despite the loss of centre Gilbert Robinson, who was transferred for £600 to Barrow, where he was also promised a job, the 1933-34 season began brightly. Trinity had no fewer than four players – Higson, Horton, Exley and Pollard - in the Yorkshire side which lost 13-0 to the Australians. In particular Horton, who was everywhere on the field, had another outstanding match against the Aussies, whom he would help beat in the first test at Belle Vue, Manchester. On September 20, Trinity became the first team to visit newly-formed London Highfield (formerly Wigan Highfield and the capital's first professional rugby league club), playing under floodlights at the White City Stadium before a 5,000 crowd. Trinity won 9-8 and did the double a week later over the short-lived London club. Eric Batten, son of Billy, made his debut on the wing in the win over Bradford – Trinity's seventh victory in eight games, which put them second to Salford in the league. After a quick exit from the Yorkshire Cup in the first round at Halifax, Trinity made a creditable performance against virtually the full Australian test team. The forwards, ably led by Horton, put up strong resistance in the 17-6 defeat, Bonner's two drop goals and a Thompson penalty accounting for Trinity's points.

The absence of Ernest Pollard, who had broken a fibula, and the thinness of the reserves started to tell. Six consecutive defeats had an effect not only on Trinity's league position but also on gates. Only 2,500 showed up for the match against Hunslet in mid-December. It was suggested once again that, in difficult economic times, many people could not afford the minimum one shilling admission.

The committee's recruitment policy once more came under fire when the *Wakefield Express* questioned the value of many of the players signed from other clubs. 'Since the beginning of professional Rugby football,' it argued, 'Wakefield Trinity have spent a considerable amount of money on players from other clubs but with two or three exceptions they have been no better or as good as the men obtained from their own district. Knowing this, it makes one regret that more encouragement is not given to the juniors, who, if properly tutored, would develop into first-class players. This applies throughout the league and money spent on junior football would, we are sure, produce good results.'

Wakefield Trinity team, August 1933: *Back row*: H Farrar, L Higson, H Wilkinson, GH Exley, G Robinson, J Hobson, WG Bonner, W Horton. *Front row*: E Pollard, E Thompson, S Herbert, H Field, J Pearce

These sentiments were echoed by a letter from a supporter, who wrote: 'It is all moonshine to say that good footballers cannot be found in Wakefield and district, and past experience proves that clever footballers, equal to any in the land, have been produced in this area, but the fact of the matter is that lads and young men who show promise do not receive proper encouragement, and it is ridiculous to place young and inexperienced players in a first team when they are not receiving proper tuition. I was present at Belle Vue on Saturday and enjoyed the game but there was an appalling weakness at centre three-quarter and the irony of it all was that the two men who filled this important position had been purchased from elsewhere. We must have men in our district who could have done better than they did.'

'Tuition', or coaching, was an issue of the moment. Another writer to the *Express* put it thus: 'When is the Wakefield Trinity club going to appoint a coach for their young players? … It must be apparent to all supporters that one is needed, the play of the young backs being very crude … It is the duty of the Committee to see that the players are taught the finer arts of the game and how to put them to effect. It is also their duty to spread knowledge of the game to juniors, intermediates and even schoolboys throughout the district, for the junior of today is the star of tomorrow. There is no need to go to the other end of the country for players. They are always with us, but want developing…' The editor replied that Joe Jones, the former Wales, Leeds and Trinity centre three-quarter, was the coach for the reserve team.

The same question was raised at the half-yearly meeting, when president Bonner replied that players trained on two nights a week under the supervision of the secretary-manager and two members of the committee, though there was no first-team coach as such. A member countered that there must be 'something queer' if Joe Jones was coaching the second team but there was no coach or player-coach for the first team. The president answered that the second team were 'mostly young boys' and needed coaching, whereas, he pointed out, the first team did win fifteen matches out of nineteen without a coach.

One young local player, however, was to prove the value of recruiting from the Wakefield district, with or without coaching, when he made his debut on March 3 in the 17-0 home defeat of Keighley. Seventeen year old Herbert Goodfellow from Sharlston, son of Fred Goodfellow, the former Holbeck, Dewsbury and Hull centre, scored two tries and made another for Mick Exley. 'This match will always be remembered for the successful debut of the youthful scrummage half back from Sharlston,' it was recorded. 'There is no doubt whatever that Goodfellow knows what is expected from a player who is the pivot of the team and there was intelligence in all his movements. A quick-thinking lad, he worked the blind side with the ability of a veteran.'

As Trinity slipped alarmingly down the table, the gloom was lightened by the play of some individuals, mainly forwards, including the hooker, Harry Field, of whom the *Leeds Mercury* said, following a generally poor offering by Trinity at Headingley: '[He] is a pocket Hercules. He is a smallish man for a forward but has great strength, never stops trying and does more work in the open than nine out of ten hookers. He gave a remarkable display and on this form we shall hear a lot more about him.' The hooker had only become a specialist role in the previous decade and Field made it his own, going on to represent Great Britain in Australia in 1936 after signing for York.

The 1933-34 season ended with Trinity in 22nd position, their lowest-ever placing. They had been knocked out of the Challenge Cup in the first round at Belle Vue by Wigan, the only compensation being the 16,000 crowd – far higher than some of the meagre attendances which had been recorded. Belle Vue was still proving attractive as a venue for major matches. The Cup semi-final between Hunslet and Huddersfield – the fifth year in a row that Wakefield had staged a big match - drew 27,448 spectators. The secretary's end-of-season report had a familiar ring to it, though it was certainly true that Ernest Pollard's injury in September, which kept him out for the rest of the season, was a serious handicap to the team. The committee, reporting a £247 deficit, once more bemoaned the fact that matches had been lost which should have been won comfortably. Trinity's placing in the league table would have been much higher if championship points had not been squandered against lowly placed sides. As at the half-yearly meeting, the question of employing a coach was considered but no action was taken.

Ten – Cup-winners in the Making: 1934-45

As Trinity sought to improve on their performance of the 1933-34 season, they were assisted by the return to action of Ernest Pollard, who also captained a Yorkshire selection which played Jean Galia's pioneering Villeneuve team at Keighley. Bill Horton had had the distinction of becoming the first Wakefield Trinity player to play in France when representing the England team which faced Australia in Paris on December 31, 1933, in the exhibition match that provided the launching pad for rugby league in that country.

As so often happened, Trinity saved some of their best form for the Yorkshire Cup. After beating Batley and Hull KR, they won 10-0 at Castleford in the semi-final, where Bill Horton was an inspiring captain. 'What a big difference the presence of Horton makes to the team,' the *Wakefield Express* reported. 'The forwards are never the same when he is not there to lead and encourage them. He is still a great forward, one of the greatest Trinity have ever had.' Between the semi-final and the final, Horton and Exley represented Yorkshire against Cumberland, with loose forward Rowan, a recent signing from Bramley, as travelling reserve.

The 1934 Yorkshire Cup final between Trinity, twenty-first in the league table, and Leeds, sixth, was a remarkable affair. The two teams met at a rain-lashed Crown Flatt on October 27, when the match ended in a 5-5 draw. Burrows touched down for Trinity from his half back partner Pickard's break and Pollard goaled. For Leeds, second rower Jubb scored a late try, to which Brough added a difficult goal to draw the match.

The replay took place the following Wednesday at Fartown, where neither side managed to cross the other's line. Pollard kicked a penalty goal for Trinity just before half-time and the score remained at 2-0 until well into the second half. Trinity were forced to drop out from their own line but Bonner's kick was caught by Leeds half back Ralph, who dropped a goal to secure a 2-2 draw. It was a tribute to Trinity's fighting spirit that for 160 minutes they succeeded in preventing Leeds's expensively assembled back division from crossing their line. The two performances also made nonsense of the two sides' league placing.

The final went therefore to an unprecedented second replay, staged at Parkside, Hunslet the following Saturday. Trinity's former international winger, Stan Smith, playing alongside another ex-Wakefield man, Len Higson, proved the difference between the two teams. On this third occasion, Leeds's backs finally got the upper hand and Smith proved what a dangerous finisher he was by scoring all his side's three tries in their 13-0 victory.

No trophies were involved but Trinity got some revenge on Christmas Day at Belle Vue by winning 13-6 against their rivals, who had not been beaten that season by a Yorkshire club and topped the league table.

Higson had been transferred after Leeds had made an offer too good to refuse and the fee was put towards relieving Trinity's overdraft. And so the front-rower followed Stan Smith and Charlie Glossop on the road to Headingley. He would not be the last.

After Bill Horton, Mick Exley became the second Trinity player to assist in rugby league's expansion in France when he travelled to Lyon, Grenoble and Roanne as part of an English Rugby League select team in January 1935. Joe Pearce, the former Trinity player who had signed for Keighley, went to Roanne as player-coach. The amateur game also played its part in fostering relations with the fledgling French league. At Belle Vue, Eastmoor WMC, one of the top amateur sides, provided the opposition for a French student team who were on a short self-financed tour in April 1936. The Parisian students had taken up the game immediately after seeing the England-Australia exhibition match in the French capital and were keen to learn more. Despite the heavy conditions, the emphasis was on open football. It was reported that 'there were some delightful bouts of passing and at times nearly the whole

French team handled in an endeavour to force an attacking position. The visiting players fielded the ball at all kinds of angles and managed to pass the ball in most difficult smothered situations that won the admiration of the crowd.' After the match a reception at Eastmoor WMC featured a comedian and singers in what for the Parisians must have proved a valuable insight into English culture. Two years later, in April 1938, Exley, Wilkinson and Goodfellow were members of a British Rugby League XIII which made a short tour of France, playing in Pau, Bordeaux, Lyon and Toulouse.

In the Challenge Cup, Trinity beat St Helens Recs in the first round at Belle Vue, winning 23-8. New recruit Bob Appleyard, in only his fourth game since signing from Morley RU, scored two fine tries on the wing. The drawing power of the Cup was demonstrated by the 15,000 crowd which saw the second round clash with Keighley – an attendance at least three times greater than could have been expected for a league match. Keighley, fifth in the league at the time, were knocked out by 18-6. But that was as far as Trinity would get, defeated 7-0 in the third round by Hull, again at Belle Vue and in front of 19,000 fans.

Despite another mediocre season in terms of league placing – Trinity ended in sixteenth place – a profit of just under £300 was announced. In those days of generally low-scoring matches, Trinity's record of having lost six matches by a total of just eight points showed how finely balanced those matches were. Surprisingly, they had also scored more points than three of the top four clubs, while only seven clubs had a better defensive record. Whether it was a matter of bowing to members' demands or an attempt to turn narrow losses into victories, the committee finally agreed to make Joe Jones the first team coach, with Jimmy McGee succeeding him as second team coach. The duties of the coach, however, were different from those of his modern-day counterpart. His first responsibility was the physical fitness of the players and though tactics were generally discussed at the training session before the match, the notion of the game plan was a long way off.

The 1935-36 season did not get off to the best start. Knocked out of the Yorkshire Cup in the first round at York, Trinity suffered from having three half backs – Pickard, Burrows and Goodfellow – all injured at the same time. But still Trinity had outstanding players in their ranks. Mick Exley, a product of St Catherine's School, and Harry Field were selected for the tour trial, with Appleyard and Wilkinson as reserves. Field, who had by that time been transferred at his own request to York, was picked for the Australian tour, along with Exley, though there was some surprise that Bill Horton did not make his third trip.

Once more Trinity improved their form in the Challenge Cup. In February, with only one away win to their account during the whole season, they travelled to high-flying Swinton and won 9-2. Horton and Exley, as fine a second row pair as Trinity have ever had, were outstanding against arguably the best set of forwards in the league. The recently-opened Odsal Stadium, at whose dimensions many of the Trinity supporters were aghast, provided the venue for the second round tie. Watched by 24,000 spectators, the match was heading for a scoreless draw until, with less than ten minutes remaining, Pollard seized the opportunity to kick ahead from a spilled Bradford pass and touch down for a 3-0 victory. But Pollard was injured for the next round at Huddersfield and his absence was significant. Trinity went out of the Cup, losing 12-0. But they made amends, of sorts. The following Wednesday they inflicted the heaviest defeat of the season on Leeds, who appeared to have one eye on their forthcoming Cup semi-final. Without Horton, Pollard and five others, Trinity triumphed 22-5.

Leeds returned to Belle Vue ten days later, on March 21, 1936, for the Cup semi-final against Huddersfield. The match produced the all-time attendance record at Belle Vue, where 37,906 spectators paid £2,456 to watch Leeds go through to the final by 10-5. The previous highest crowd was 36,359 when the same teams met at the same stage three years earlier.

Trinity's position of 22nd in the league equalled their worst ever performance of two years earlier. This time, along with St Helens, they found themselves sandwiched between the two new London teams, Acton & Willesden

Belle Vue, March 21, 1936. The Challenge Cup semi-final between Huddersfield and Leeds attracted a ground record attendance of 37,906.

and Streatham & Mitcham. The club made a loss of £92, though Ernest Pollard's benefit raised £270. Once again the committee reported problems in finding the right calibre of player. 'Ever since the inception of the club,' it was reported at the AGM, 'there has been no difficulty in obtaining the services of sterling forwards from our own area and during the past season our forwards were equal – sometimes superior – to the teams which defeated us. This compliment cannot be paid, however, to most of the men who have constituted the back department ... Even if men of outstanding ability were in the market Trinity cannot compete with those clubs who seem to have plenty of money at their disposal. There is another important matter. When players from a distance have been obtained we have been faced with the employment problem and the committee cannot be expected to be going on forever putting men on what is known as the ground staff and paying money they cannot afford.' Five men, all from well outside the local area, were employed in this way.

During the close season, Trinity's international centre or stand-off Ernest Pollard, who had set the club points scoring record of 207 in 1934-5, was placed on the transfer list at his own request and was soon signed by Leeds for £825, but immediately afterwards Trinity brought centre Johnny Malpass from Featherstone for £425. Eric Batten was also transfer-listed and was bought by Hunslet, his father's first professional club, for £400. Batten, a future international, was to appear in eight Challenge Cup finals with Leeds and Bradford. Nat Pickard and Gordon Bonner were both signed by the new club at Newcastle.

Two young players put in outstanding displays in the excellent Yorkshire Cup win at Huddersfield. Alf Watson, still only 18, impressed everyone and was thought capable of developing into one of the best loose forwards in the league, while it was said of Herbert Goodfellow that no player on the Huddersfield side was his equal as he

91

played a cool and crafty game. After beating the Fartown side again in the league, Trinity moved into fourth place and maintained their progress in the Yorkshire Cup by dismantling Bramley's hopes in the second round. The semi-final was notable not only for Trinity's 11-6 defeat of Hunslet at Belle Vue but also for the debut of full back Bob Oliver, not yet seventeen, who took over the goal-kicking duties and made some copy-book tackles. But Trinity's youthfulness in the backs was given a severe testing in the final at Headingley on October 17. Trinity had won the trophy twice, in 1910 and 1924. Their opponents, York, had also twice lifted the Yorkshire Cup, in 1922 and 1933 and were appearing in their second consecutive final. At half-time Trinity were 2-0 ahead from an Oliver penalty, though he would miss three more. York scored the only try of the match from a Wakefield dropped pass, which, with the conversion, a penalty goal and a dropped goal, gave them victory by 9-2. Trinity captain Bill Horton once more failed to get his hands on the trophy. Now nearing the end of his playing days, Horton, like Jonty Parkin, had only one Yorkshire Cup medal to show for a career which has perhaps been under-valued. The second rower earned more County caps than any other Trinity player and his ten appearances for Great Britain was a record for a Yorkshire forward in tests against Australia until he was overtaken some seventy years later by Stuart Fielden and Jamie Peacock. Only four others played more matches for Trinity.

International back row forward GH 'Mick' Exley, Trinity's only representative on Great Britain's 1936 tour

Trinity brought more experience into the backs when they signed full back Billy Teall from Broughton Rangers. The former Hull player made his first appearance at York, Trinity winning 23-10. Trinity played a much more open and constructive game than they had done in the final and, had they adopted the same tactics then, they would surely have won against a York side which had now dropped to fourth from bottom in the table.

The ups and downs of a league season almost inevitably included matches where the weather played a determining factor. One such game was played in December at Odsal, where it was said that Trinity covered themselves more with mud than glory. Much of the ground was a quagmire, making it impossible to play open or accurate football. To make matters worse, two of Bradford's best were the two former Wakefield forwards, Len Higson (since transferred from Leeds) and Sandy Orford.

One of Trinity's unsung heroes, the veteran forward Hobson, a hard-working scrummager who rarely missed a game, decided to retire because of the demands of his work. Welsh winger Freddy Smart joined the band of Trinity men who helped to spread the game in France when he toured with a Rugby League XIII which played matches in Paris, Bordeaux, Lyon and Bayonne in February 1937.

In the first round of the Challenge Cup, Trinity upset all the odds by beating Leeds, the league's most expensive side which again included three Wakefield men in Pollard, Smith and Jubb. Trinity winger JC Milner kicked the only successful penalty of the match – Leeds had three attempts, Wakefield two – and despite the visitors having the majority of possession, Trinity went through 2 0. Another stern test awaited at Thrum Hall in the next round. Long-striding loose forward Watson went over from Horton's pass for the game's only try, converted by Milner, to which Halifax could only muster two George Nepia penalties. For the third round tie at home to Warrington, snow had to be shifted from the pitch before the match could be played. The crowd of 22,075 included Lord Harewood and the Mayor, though Trinity captain Bill Horton was absent. Mick Exley willingly took on the role of leader, Billy Teall gave a masterly display at full back and young Watson had another memorable day. The loose forward made a

92

break deep inside his own half and Johnny Malpass was twice involved as Sam Herbert finally touched down from a movement covering three-quarters the length of the field. Milner converted and Trinity progressed to the semi-final by five points to nil. After beating Leeds and Warrington, who would finish in the top four, as well as Halifax away, Trinity were in confident mood as they approached the semi-final against Keighley, whom they had twice beaten in the league. A record crowd of 39,998 at Headingley saw Trinity fail to play the kind of constructive play which would surely have seen them through to their first Wembley final. Instead they had three failed drop goal attempts, though Milner forced his way over but was judged to have hit the corner flag. Trinity were virtually down to twelve men after Teall was lamed but remained on the field and Keighley's defence held out for a 0-0 draw.

In the replay at Fartown, Keighley led 2-0 from a penalty goal at half-time and then went further ahead when Herbert's kick was charged down by Bevan who scored the first try against Trinity in the whole competition. Carter replied for Wakefield but Teall's conversion attempt went just wide and Keighley went forward to their only Challenge Cup final by 5-3.

Towards the end of the season Trinity did the double over newcomers Newcastle, who were captained from loose forward by the former Wakefield full back Bonner. Though the north-east innovation was to last another season, one of the two new London clubs, Streatham & Mitcham, dropped out at the end of March, while Acton & Willesden had not even started their second season.

Trinity finished with a flourish, beating Castleford in the last match to finish eighth – their highest placing for a decade. The attendances at league matches during the season averaged out at 4,400, including members, and the announcement of an £814 profit on the season went down well. In the view of the committee and many others, it had been, despite the disappointments in the Yorkshire Cup and Challenge Cup, one of Trinity's best seasons for years.

In yet another closely-fought cup-tie, Trinity drew their Yorkshire Cup first round match with Halifax at the start of the 1937-38 season. Both sides had scored two penalty goals at Belle Vue before Halifax won the replay by a single point, winning 7-6 at Thrum Hall. As the Australians arrived in England, Trinity's match against the tourists was eagerly anticipated. The Aussies dominated the scoring from the start, scoring two converted tries to Whitworth's touchdown for a 10-3 half-time lead. After the two sides had traded penalties, Watson finished a sweeping move and, with the outstanding Teall converting, Trinity were within two points of their opponents, but Aussie stand-off Reardon scored the matchwinner with three minutes left to give a 17-10 scoreline.

Whitworth, playing on the wing, also had the pleasure of scoring four tries in the 43-0 win over Bramley, a match in which Mick Exley, Trinity's captain, also touched down three times. Goal-kicking had become a problem but was solved by the arrival of hooker Sam Lee from Swinton, who landed six in the 33-2 defeat of Hull KR. The same match saw the comeback of Bill Horton, now living in the West Country but keen to pull his football boots on again.

Belle Vue once more provided the setting for a big game involving Leeds and Huddersfield when the two teams met in the final of the Yorkshire Cup. By this stage Huddersfield had won the trophy eight times and Leeds would increase their total to seven. But there was no repetition of the record crowd of eighteen months earlier as rain and gales played their part in reducing the attendance to 21,814.

In the new year of 1938, Trinity signed Leeds's 19-year old half back Johnny Jones, who was immediately selected as a reserve for the England team to meet Wales and later for Yorkshire. In a move which initially pleased neither set of fans, 20-year old loose forward Alf Watson went to Headingley in exchange plus a cash adjustment in Trinity's favour. Watson, who was from Portobello and had begun playing rugby league at Manygates School, was selected for England in the same year. Into Wakefield's back row came Len Bratley, who set two club records for a forward by scoring fifteen tries in the season, including five in one match – the 34-12 defeat of Huddersfield. Twenty-year old Bratley, who was born and lived at Newton Hill, had played for York before signing for Wakefield.

In the Challenge Cup, Trinity beat Cup-holders Widnes 7-3 at Belle Vue but lost to Swinton 7-3 away in the second round. Tenth place in the league - Wigan claimed ninth on points difference – was seen as satisfactory, given the large number of injuries, but the gates were described by the committee as 'very disappointing and discouraging, and totally inadequate to carry on the club successfully.'

With Bill Horton no longer on Trinity's playing register, Mick Exley continued as captain and set a fine example. In the 23-5 defeat of Huddersfield in late September he scored two tries and was described as irrepressible, the inspiration of his side, while his fearless tackling was always a feature of his play. Exley was one of four Trinity players in the Yorkshire side to face Cumberland, along with Herbert Goodfellow, Harry Wilkinson and Bob Appleyard. The Trinity captain was also in the England side which faced the French in February at St Helens. That match saw France earn their first international victory on English soil.

In the Yorkshire Cup, following a first round bye, Trinity beat Halifax 14-8 at Thrum Hall but lost the semi-final 6-2 at Huddersfield in freak weather of rain and 'hurricane force' wind. But in the league the team were playing consistently well and recorded two big wins in an era when high scores were not common. In the first, they scored thirteen tries to beat Dewsbury 55-9 and two weeks later defeated York 56-4. In this match Goodfellow, it was reported, 'was the pivot of his side and by his quickness and intelligence the whole passing machinery was often set into smooth motion. He received able assistance from Jones but the man with whom he seemed to co-operate the most was Bratley, who looks like developing into one of the finest forwards in the League.' An example of that combination came, among others, in the defeat of Hull at Belle Vue, when, from just over half-way, 'Goodfellow got the ball, eluded two would-be tacklers and went away with a fine side-step. Bratley was as usual in close attendance and with that perfect understanding which has been a pleasing feature of the play of those two men throughout the season, Goodfellow gave a perfect pass to his loose forward, who, having a clear field, ran away to place the ball over the line.'

By mid-November Trinity were in second place, with a better attacking record than any other club. The forwards were among the best packs in the league – and were improved further when Sandy Orford, a product of Trinity Supporters' Club, signed from Bradford - but it was clear that Goodfellow lacked support in the backs and in the centres in particular. When the Challenge Cup ties came around, Trinity experienced yet another drawn game at Broughton Rangers, pushing the number of replays they had been involved in since the start of the competition into double figures. After beating the Manchester side 21-10, Trinity went on to defeat Warrington 7-2 and then came up against Halifax in the third round. The tie prompted former Trinity honorary secretary Ernest Parker to recall the time, sixty years earlier and under Rugby Union rules, when Trinity met Halifax on April 5, 1879 in the semi-final of the old Yorkshire Cup and went on to win the trophy for the first time. Thirty years after that Trinity lifted the Challenge Cup for the first time, raising the question of whether, another thirty years on, they would take the trophy again. Watched by almost 25,000 fans at Belle Vue, Trinity and Halifax fought out a 5-5 draw before the Thrum Hall side put an end to Trinity's hopes by winning 15-12 in the replay, despite outstanding performances by Trinity's back row of Exley, Orford and Bratley.

Trinity also started to lose their grip in the league, slipping eventually to eleventh. Sam Lee became the first Trinity player to kick a hundred goals in a season, his total of 111 coming second only to Jim Sullivan's haul of 122 for Wigan. Herbert Goodfellow figured in the try-scoring list with twenty, followed by Len Bratley with seventeen. The cup-ties had made a difference to the club's finances, which were improved by the £759 profit.

But in September 1939 rugby league, along with other aspects of everyday life, became subject to the threat of war. Trinity's first home match of the season, on September 2, was poorly attended as a result of the international crisis. The following week the Government called a halt to any organised sport likely to attract crowds. The league was disrupted, as was the tour by New Zealand, who had been in England only a week, during which time they managed to play St Helens before being urged to return home as soon as possible, for which they incurred a loss of five to six thousand pounds. Two weeks later, it was permitted to play matches on a friendly basis and a wartime Emergency League was established, split into a Lancashire section and a Yorkshire section.

Trinity's first match under this system took place at Belle Vue against Hunslet and drew a crowd of 3,360. But although some notable young players were to make their debut in the wartime league, including Len Marson, there was a good deal of coming and going of players. Some, like Johnny Jones or Len Bratley or Johnny Malpass, were called up. Those who remained were allowed to make guest appearances for other clubs, particularly those nearest to their homes, and on a match-by-match basis. Hull KR, for example, used Teall and Eddom for one match; a fortnight later Whitworth, who had played for Trinity the previous week, turned out for the Robins against Trinity the next weekend.

An exceptionally severe winter intervened, forcing the cancellation of sporting fixtures until March. Team selection proceeded on an improvised basis as players moved back and forth between teams. High scores became more common, particularly towards the end of this stop-start season. Huddersfield beat Trinity 38-17 at Fartown, only for Trinity to turn the tables by defeating the claret and golds 34-18 at Belle Vue – a match in which the ex-Wakefield winger Eric Batten, now with Hunslet, rejoined his former club to score four tries. The league season ended with Bradford topping the Yorkshire League and meeting Swinton, the Lancashire leaders in the grand final, won on aggregate by Bradford. Trinity came eighth on points difference from Leeds.

The 1939-40 season was not over yet. For the first time ever, matches continued into June with the Yorkshire Cup competition, which normally took place between September and November. Trinity's first round opponents, Bramley, scratched, being unable to raise a team; Hull were defeated 27-3 at Belle Vue in the second round; and in the semi-final Trinity knocked out Hull KR 8-7 in a replay after a 5-5 draw at Craven Park. Trinity met Featherstone in the final at Bradford and, as they had done in their early days in the league, the Rovers once more showed they could be Trinity's bogey side. Turner scored a try for Trinity and Teall a conversion and two penalties, but Featherstone took their first trophy by 12-9.

The same league arrangement carried on into the 1940-41 season, when Trinity were again joined by Whitworth and Milner as well as Ness, all from Hull KR, who were not operating. But it was a blow to Trinity that their captain Mick Exley announced his retirement. Originally from the Trinity Supporters' Club side, he had signed for Trinity in 1928 at the age of sixteen. But no sooner had Exley said his farewell than another great local product, Harry Murphy, made his first impact. In the second match at Dewsbury, he played outstandingly well, being described as 'a young forward whose earlier promise has materialised.'

With players arriving on loan and then leaving again, and others returning on leave from the Services, teams were rarely the same from one week to the next. In Trinity's team to face Featherstone in December, three ex-Rovers – full back Pollitt, winger Reg Jenkinson and hooker Vic Darlison (on loan from Wigan) played against their recent team-mates. In April three Warrington players – Les Jones, H Jones and De Lloyd – arrived at Belle Vue and assisted in Trinity's Challenge Cup run. All of this gave the war-time competition a quite different aspect from the regular championship and it was reflected in the crowd figures. Following a disappointing 3,000 crowd when Trinity played at Headingley, an even smaller gate was recorded at Belle Vue for the match against Bradford. 'Attendance figures in these times are perhaps not so important as in pre-war times,' commented the *Wakefield Express*, 'but an attendance of 2,000, with receipts of £86, to see the League leaders and Wakefield Trinity in opposition might be interpreted as a commentary on war-time football and the appeal it makes.' In the circumstances, and given that not all clubs took part, honours won in war-time could not have the same value as in peace-time competition.

Trinity went out of the Yorkshire Cup in the second round at Bradford but fared better in the Challenge Cup. After beating Keighley 25-0, they went on, with the Warrington trio in the side, to beat Wigan 22-0. In the third round, with on-loan winger Jenkinson scoring three tries, Trinity also defeated Batley 22-0. The semi-final, however, played over two legs, was lost on aggregate to Halifax, who were in turn defeated by Leeds in the final at Odsal. Relatively low attendances, as experienced by most clubs, led to a substantial loss on the 1940-41 season of £583, even though players' wages were much reduced.

The Lazenby Cup match, the opener to the season, contested by Wakefield and Dewsbury, showed the value of the recruitment at Crown Flatt. The great Jim Sullivan, made captain by Dewsbury, brought off a try-saving tackle on Trinity's Jenkinson to save the match at 15-13. But Trinity continued to foster local talent during this period, the Lazenby Cup match also seeing the debut of 17-year old stand-off Ron Rylance, who, during the wartime period, would also make guest appearances for Dewsbury (against Wakefield), Castleford and Leeds, as well as featuring in the Rugby League seven-a-side team which won a twelve-team rugby union competition at Headingley in May 1943, and again in 1944 and 1945.

As the third war-time season began, the two county leagues came back together to form a single competition consisting of seventeen clubs only. The league table was decided on a percentage basis, as it had been before the 1930-31 season. Trinity ended the 1941-42 campaign in eleventh place, having gone out of the Challenge Cup at the hands of Leeds in the second round, just as they had been knocked out of the Yorkshire Cup in November by Halifax.

At the AGM in July, secretary-manager John Tom Wood stated that Trinity 'shared credit with other clubs who had done their utmost to keep alive the rugby league game and they had the satisfaction of knowing that their efforts had met with some success. It had been a great struggle but well worth it and they had been able to provide recreation for a large number of people.' AA Bonner, JP, who had been president since 1924, resigned due to pressure of work and was succeeded by Cr J Bullock. Like his predecessor JB Cooke, Bonner was made a life member. In his report he said that during the three years of war Trinity had lost £1,100 but the club's financial position was 'sound and good'. In his final address he said that he had tried to make Trinity a civic institution – a club for the city and not just for profit-making.

Trinity were among the even fewer clubs which competed in the 1942-43 season. Of the fourteen teams only three came from Lancashire – Wigan, Oldham and St Helens. Trinity went out of the Yorkshire Cup at the first hurdle, losing to Batley over two legs and faring only a little better in the Challenge Cup, in which they were beaten in the second round by Leeds after defeating Featherstone in the first. Harry Wilkinson had the honour of being selected for England against Wales but it was an otherwise fairly undistinguished campaign, with Trinity in mid-table.

Though the 1943-44 season began with a loss at Leeds, Trinity performed well during much of the rest of the season. Winger Jack Perry, an Altofts lad from the Wheldale Colliery team, made his debut at Headingley after signing for £100. Experienced centre Jim Croston arrived on loan from Castleford, who had given up the competition in 1942. Following the 15-6 defeat of Halifax in late September, it was reported: 'People who saw [the match] were regaled with rugby league football containing a high percentage of pre-war flavouring.' The comment reflected Trinity's progress but also the fact that war-time football, as can be imagined, did not generally come up to the standard of the peace-time game, but it was being played in difficult conditions. Jack Perry recalled his own circumstances.

'When I first started work at the mine at Altofts,' he said, 'I worked at the pit top, separating the coal from the stone by hand. After a year or so, I went into the fitting shop and did engineering work. Normally I started at seven in the morning and finished at four, but in war-time we worked from seven in the morning till seven at night, often seven days a week, making shafts for torpedo boats. On Saturdays I got up at five, ran across three or four fields to get to work and started at six. I asked to finish early at twelve to play in the afternoon. But I never felt tired. I was only nineteen.'

Despite their performances in the league, Trinity's progress in the Yorkshire Cup once again went no further than the first round. But by December they had not lost a single league match since the opening weekend.

The unbeaten sequence in the league extended into mid-February, by which stage seventeen wins had been clocked up. 'The team is of a vintage that has both punch and sparkle and will certainly go down in history as one of the best sides ever to represent Trinity,' said the *Wakefield Express*. If Goodfellow was the hub of the team, he was well supported by mainstays of the side such as full back Billy Teall and guest centre Jim Croston, who was to join Trinity on a permanent basis at the end of the war; and in the forwards Harry Wilkinson and Sandy Orford. A rich crop of young local talent was also making its way, including Dennis Baddeley, Jack Perry and Ron Rylance among the backs and Harry Murphy and Kinsley-born Len Marson in the forwards. It was in the immediate post-war era that this team, with a few additions, including those who were returning from service, would really make its mark. Perhaps the biggest threat to Trinity's long winning run came with the visit of Wigan, in second place behind Trinity in the league and who had a twelve-match unbeaten run of their own to defend. A ten thousand-strong crowd, unusually high for the time, piled into Belle Vue to see Trinity overcome the men in cherry and white by two Rylance penalty goals to nil. In recognition of the quality of their play, Croston, Orford and Wilkinson were selected to play for England against Wales, though Croston withdrew injured. Trinity were finally defeated, for the first time in over five months, at Odsal, where Bradford triumphed 6-0. But that did not stop Trinity from doing the double over Wigan two weeks later and inflicting their first home defeat of the season.

Odsal was proving to be Trinity's bogey ground. Bradford beat Trinity 15-2 there in the first leg of the first round of the Challenge Cup and though Trinity won the return leg 7-5, Bradford went on to eventually defeat Wigan in the final. Trinity's unbeaten home record remained intact until the very last match of the season, when Dewsbury came away with the spoils. Nevertheless, Trinity finished top of the sixteen-team league with nineteen wins from twenty-two games, but in the semi-final of the championship play-offs, and without Croston and Murphy, they again went down at home to Dewsbury, losing by 11-5.

With Mick Exley as trainer-coach, Trinity started the new season of 1944-45 with confidence. But like in the previous campaign, they were bundled out of the Yorkshire Cup at the first stage by Halifax. The bad weather put paid to matches for a month up to February, after which Trinity began to move up the league table, but without the same level of success as the previous year. Harry Wilkinson was again selected for England against Wales, a match for which Wigan supplied no fewer than six players. The men from Central Park were outplayed in the league by Trinity's homegrown side, losing 26-5. That match pointed to the growing promise of Trinity's team.

'There was speed, skill and a finesse about Trinity's work that was a real tonic for their supporters,' it was said in the *Wakefield Express*. 'Goodfellow produced form in keeping with his big reputation as a scrum half and Rylance, always with an eye for an opening, was an excellent connecting link with the threequarters. Especially was his quickness off the mark of great value. There was a splendid understanding between the half backs and Murphy collaborated on many occasions to make up a powerful trio on the fringe of the scrums. Copley made splendid use of his physical endowments and Perry, short in stature, has the heart of a lion backed by considerable talent. It is a long time since Trinity had the speed there is in their ranks at the moment.' In addition, Billy Stott led the list of points scorers in this wartime emergency league.

Trinity made sure of a top four play-off spot after winning away at Castleford – themselves top four contenders – and Featherstone in the last two weeks of the season. But just as they had gone out of the Challenge Cup once more at the hands of Bradford on aggregate, so Trinity were not at their best against Halifax in the Championship semi-final and lost 17-11. When the war came to an end later in the year, however, and rugby league returned to a more regular competition, Wakefield's promise began to unfold.

Eleven – Cup-winners once more: 1945-51

As the war drew to a close, the Rugby Football League acted quickly to restore peacetime normality. An almost full complement of clubs lined up to contest the 1945-46 season, the exception being Leigh, who had ground problems and were replaced by Workington. During the six years of abbreviated, and in some ways abnormal competition, many clubs had taken on guest players. Wakefield, by and large, ignored that policy and managed to build up a team of young players from the city and surrounding area. In addition, players such as Johnny Malpass and Len Bratley arrived back from the forces to don Trinity's colours again, which, for this season, consisted of red and light blue hoops. Two players did not return: Private W Ball and Private H Holt had both been killed on active service.

Jim Croston, one of the few regular guest players, joined Trinity permanently from Castleford, though initially as team manager rather than as a player. But in an appeal to the Wakefield public, the committee made it clear that the club needed gate receipts of around £300 – meaning an average attendance of roughly 5,000 - to carry on successfully.

What set all of Wakefield talking, at the start of this first post-war season – and for many a season after – was an astounding performance on Wednesday evening, September 12, when Trinity delivered a historic thrashing to rivals Leeds. At a time well before high scoring became commonplace, Trinity's 71-0 rout of a Leeds side, depleted though it was, struck the rugby league public as nothing short of sensational. The seventeen tries and ten goals which the Headingley side conceded far surpassed their previous heaviest defeat of 46-4, inflicted by Halifax in 1908. It exceeded Trinity's earlier best effort of 68-7 against Bradford in 1928-29. At half-time Trinity had run up 22 points but nothing could have prepared Leeds for the onslaught which was to follow. Unstoppable, Goodfellow and his troops tore through the Leeds defence almost at will. Baddeley scored four tries, Malpass three, Allinson and Bratley two each, Flowers, Goodfellow and Perry adding the others, Teall scoring a try and a goal. Rylance, with two tries and nine goals, ended by equalling Ernest Pollard's club record of 24 points, set in 1932.

Soon Trinity were heading the league. One of their finest displays came at Fartown in the second leg of the first round of the Yorkshire Cup. Trinity had already won the home leg 20-5 and might have been expected simply to maintain their advantage. Far from it – they outplayed Huddersfield and showed a confidence in their own ability which they had not revealed at Fartown for many years. The scrum-base triangle exposed Huddersfield's weaknesses. 'Goodfellow, after one of his celebrated hand-offs, opened the Huddersfield ranks and sent an inside pass to Bratley, who planted the ball over the line,' reported the *Wakefield Express*. Rylance scored four tries, from varying distances. For example: 'Stott supplied Rylance with a clean pass which the stand-off utilised to the best advantage – a lightning flash and he was under the posts.' The *Express* went on: 'The two halves played a storming game and demonstrated most convincingly the high dividend that can be paid when there is speed and precision immediately behind the scrummage.' No less a figure than Harry Lodge, of Huddersfield, the highly respected rugby league writer of the pre-war era, wrote to Trinity's former president, Arthur Bonner, to praise what he had seen. 'This game gave me one of the greatest treats in the magnificent display by the best all-round Wakefield team I can remember over many years,' Lodge wrote. 'It was not that Huddersfield were weak ... It reminded me of the old days when our Fartown attack bewildered defences.'

In the second round, Hull were easily accounted for and Leeds succumbed to an attack led by the Bratley-Goodfellow-Rylance trio. By contrast the final against Bradford at Halifax proved a major disappointment. Trinity's free-flowing creativity, responsible for eight consecutive wins, was muffled by Bradford's stout defence in poor conditions.

Trinity secretary John Tom Wood, scrum half Herbert Goodfellow, stand off Ron Rylance and centre Jim Croston at Belle Vue at the opening of the 1945-46 season

Leading by a Stott penalty goal to nil, Trinity emerged for the second half unprepared for what was to happen next. The referee blew his whistle to restart play, but Trinity appeared unready. Bradford scrum-half Donald Ward kicked off into the centre of the field, where neither Jones nor Teall could gather the skidding ball. Bradford prop Frank Whitcombe was there to seize his chance and head to the posts for the only try of the match, goaled by George Carmichael. Trinity failed by 5-2 to take the Cup for the first time in 21 years.

By Christmas, Trinity, with 373 points for and 97 against, were second in the league to Wigan, who had played more games. Five Wakefield players – Baddeley, Goodfellow, Rylance, Bratley and Wilkinson - represented Yorkshire in the narrow 17-16 defeat by Lancashire at Swinton, Bratley scoring a try and Rylance a try and two goals. Bratley was picked for England against Wales, while Rylance, who rattled up a hundred points before Christmas, and Goodfellow were named as reserves. Former international Mick Exley, who had only played one match since 1940, decided to come out of retirement to add his strength to Trinity's forward pack. As the Great Britain tour to Australia was being planned, Trinity's county representatives, minus Goodfellow, took part in trial matches, together with Marson and Murphy. When the touring team was announced in March, there was surprise in Wakefield and elsewhere that Trinity, second in the league and one of the favourites for the Challenge Cup, had just a single representative in Harry Murphy.

At the end of January, winger Ron Copley, who had already scored 20 tries, signed for Castleford in a deal which involved Jim Croston. The former Castleford international centre, who was acting as Trinity's team manager, would now be permitted to play for Trinity, as he had done during the war years.

Trinity faced Huddersfield in the first round of the Challenge Cup and maintained their excellent record over the

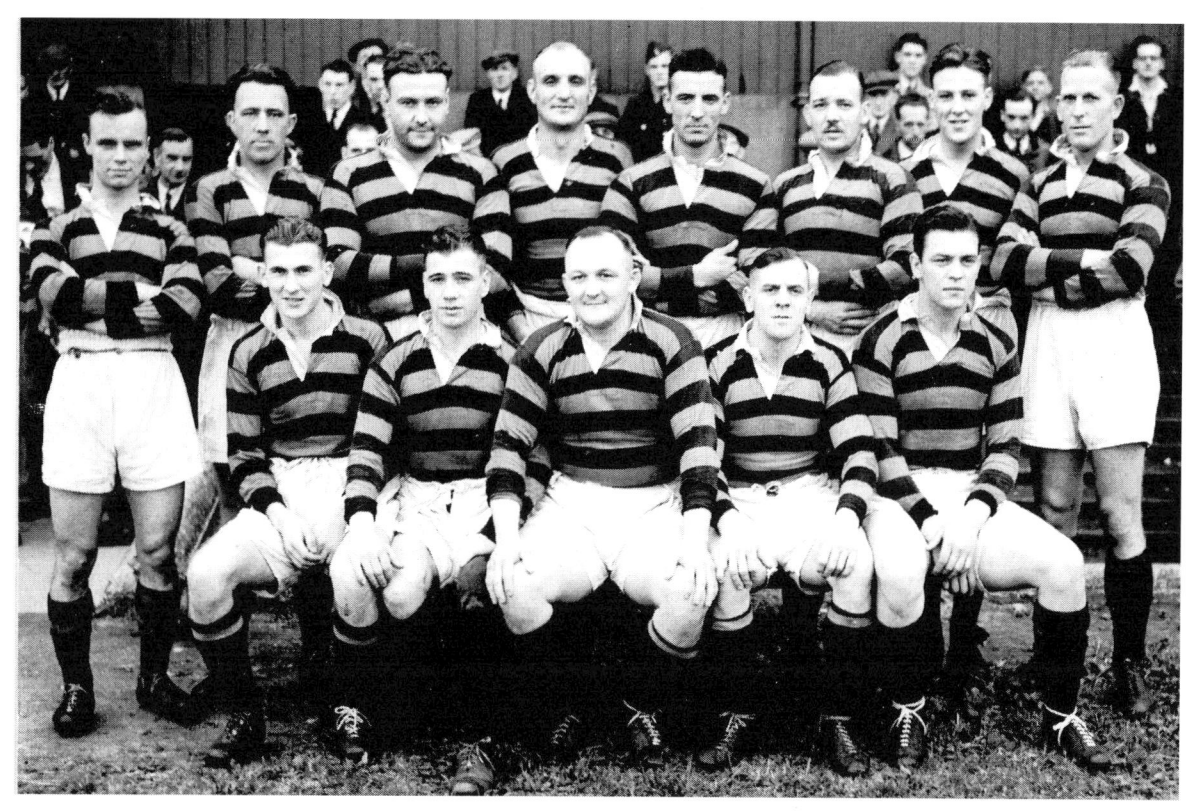

The Trinity team which beat Leeds by a record 71-0 score, September 12, 1945: *Back row*: J Perry, J Malpass, A Flowers, L Bratley, D Baddeley, W Allinson, F Townsend, W Teall. *Front row*: R Rylance, N Kielty, H Wilkinson, H Goodfellow, H Murphy

Cup-holders, winning 14-3 in the first leg at Fartown and 5-2 in the second at Belle Vue, thus making it five wins out of five over the men in claret and gold. The timing of the second round meant that Trinity had to forgo a short tour to France but they settled for beating Halifax 10-0 at Belle Vue in front of 21,000 fans. They left it late, scoring their first points through Baddeley after 70 minutes and then through former Keighley and Wigan winger Caldwell minutes later, both tries goaled by Stott. Between the second and third rounds, Trinity stumbled, incurring their heaviest defeat of the season, by 20-5, at Headingley, which was all the more surprising given that Wakefield were second in the table and Leeds fourth from bottom. They were back on track to defeat Workington 14-4 at home, although, apart from reaching the semi-final, there was no great kudos attached to the victory since their opponents had famously lost in the first leg of the first round at Sharlston.

The semi-final against Hunslet at Headingley attracted a crowd of 33,000, producing receipts of £4,993 – a record for Leeds at either code of football. Trinity led 2-0 from Billy Stott's superb touchline penalty goal, but Hunslet went ahead with a blind side try from Williamson. The match-winner came when winger Dennis Baddeley went over direct from a scrum, Stott converted from near touch and Trinity were on their way to their first Wembley final by 7-3.

An injury crisis in April, added to Murphy's departure with the touring team to Australia, resulted in three away defeats and a slide down the table to fifth. But a sparkling 37-10 win over second-placed Bradford and Bratley's hat-trick in the 22-5 defeat of St Helens – taking his total to ten in four games over the Easter period - restored Trinity's confidence and position in the top four. In the week before Wembley, Trinity beat Hunslet to consolidate their play-off spot. On the Monday, they suffered their first home defeat of the season, at the hands of Featherstone.

Wembley 1946: The Wakefield team is presented to Prime Minister Clement Attlee. *From left*: Mick Exley, Jim Higgins, Len Marson (shaking hands), Harry Wilkinson, Herbert Goodfellow, Johnny Jones

Straight after, the Trinity selection committee got to work on the team to face Wigan in the final. They settled for experience with Jones selected at stand-off and Stott and Croston in the centre. Wingers Perry and Caldwell were left out, with Rylance taking the right wing position – where he had hardly ever played before – to give cover both for Jones, about whose fitness there were doubts, and for goal-kicking. With Murphy on his way to Australia, it was an easier task to pick the forwards. Trinity's second rower was accompanied on tour by Wigan's Martin Ryan, Ted Ward, Ken Gee and Joe Egan, which put the men in cherry and white at an obvious disadvantage.

In the first post-war Challenge Cup final, it was Wigan who settled to their task better. Stott had missed an early penalty before Wigan forward Jack Blan, in only the sixth minute of play, seized on a loose ball and went over for the opening try, Brian Nordgren missing the conversion. Wigan's powerful New Zealand winger made amends for his miss by running in his side's second try, again unconverted, and Trinity trailed 6-0 after less than 20 minutes. In a game in which several goal attempts were unsuccessful in the swirling Wembley wind, Stott again failed with a penalty attempt but opened Trinity's account by taking Rylance's return pass and crashing through the Wigan defence for a stirring try which, however, he could not convert. After Goodfellow and Bratley threatened to break through, Stott kicked a penalty, and by half-time Trinity had narrowed the deficit to one point.

But the second half did not begin auspiciously for Wakefield. Though the forwards got the majority of the ball from the scrums, stand-off Jones, injured early on, was subdued and then when Stott fumbled Exley's pass, Wigan's Stan Jolley sprinted away for his side's third unconverted try, Nordgren again missing the goal attempt and then a penalty. Again Trinity came back when Goodfellow went clean away from a scrum for Stott to touch down for a second time at the corner, again too far out for him to convert. At 9-8, Trinity had once more closed the gap, but

The 1946 Challenge Cup final: Trinity's Ron Rylance looks to evade Wigan's Stan Jolley, with Harry Wilkinson and Herbert Goodfellow looking on

The famous picture of Billy Stott's goal which won the Challenge Cup 13-12 against Wigan

though Nordgren was having no success with his goal-kicking, he made no mistake when full back Jack Cunliffe broke and handed on for the winger to score his second try, albeit unconverted. Trinity trailed by four points with less than a quarter of an hour remaining in a situation of mounting tension. From Teall's touch-finding kick, Wakefield got the ball from the scrum and Howes opened up a gap for Wigan-born Croston to go over the line, taking a defender with him. Trinity's third try reduced the arrears once more to a single point, but Stott could not add the conversion.

With a minute and a half remaining, Wigan were penalised for obstruction just inside their own 25, presenting

Trinity parade the Cup. *From left*: Johnny Jones, Ron Rylance, Len Marson, Harry Wilkinson, Billy Teall, Jim Higgins, Billy Stott, Mick Exley, Jim Croston, Len Bratley, Herbert Goodfellow, Derek Howes.

Wakefield with the chance to take the lead for the first time in the match. It had not been a good day for goal-kickers. Nordgren had missed all five shots and Stott had so far kicked just one goal from six attempts. But the Trinity captain kept faith with his own ability and placed the ball. 'The eyes of those on the main stand shifted uneasily between Stott and the clock, the minute hand of which moved slowly, aye, mockingly it seemed, forward! The critical moment arrived and with deliberation and coolness Stott's left foot swung behind the ball. "Yes, yes, it is, it is – a goal!" What a roar went up from all sides of the huge bowl as the linesman's flag shot up!' One minute remained to play. Trinity led 13-12. Remarkably Wigan were given a slim chance to regain their ascendancy when Nordgren took a penalty kick from inside his own half. For the sixth time he fluffed the attempt as the ball dropped short, Goodfellow gathered and, for the first time in 37 years, Trinity landed the Cup, presented to them by Prime Minister Clement Attlee. Trinity's forwards had battled tirelessly throughout; behind them Goodfellow had worked all his craft, but it was captain Stott, the £90 bargain buy from Oldham, who won the first ever Lance Todd trophy for his two tries and two goals, receiving six of the eleven votes cast.

When Trinity arrived back at Westgate Station at around six o' clock on the Monday evening, they were greeted by scenes of spontaneous enthusiasm not witnessed in living memory. Tens of thousands of cheering people lined the streets from the station to the Town Hall – 'one solid mass of wildly excited citizens' – where the civic reception was to take place. As in the old pre-1895 Yorkshire Cup winning days, a brass band was there to play 'See the Conquering Hero Comes', to whose strains the players mounted a red and blue festooned brewer's lorry to transport them through the middle of the city. It seemed as if the whole population had turned out, thronging the pavements and spilling out on to the road. After arriving at the Town Hall, the players forced their way through the crowd before reappearing, to a tremendous ovation, on the balcony with the Cup. It was one of the most wonderful sights he had seen in his life, said Trinity chairman Wilf Jackson at the civic banquet. Billy Stott said it was the greatest moment in his life and the team were the greatest lads he had ever played with.

Wakefield Trinity, Challenge Cup winners 1946: *Back row*: J McGee (kit), F Banham, H Blackburn, J Breakwell, SH Hadfield, E Gibson, F West, S Phillips, O Stansfield (all committee), JT Wood (sec), OS Best (masseur). *Middle row*: L Bratley, D Baddeley, H Wilkinson, J Bullock (president), W Stott (capt), WL Jackson (chairman), W Teall, GH Exley, L Marson. *Front row*: WJD Howes, AJ Croston, J Jones, H Goodfellow, R Rylance, J Higgins

Bearing the Cup, the team parades up Wood Street

The Trinity team which won the Yorkshire Cup at Headingley, 2 November 1946 by beating Hull 10-0. *Back row*: GH Exley, H Murphy, J Higgins, L Bratley, L Marson, W Teall, H Wilkinson. *Front row*: J Croston, D Baddeley, A Fletcher, J Perry, R Rylance, J Jones

With the Challenge Cup and the Yorkshire League already in the bag, Trinity sought a third trophy in the Championship. After finishing behind Wigan and Huddersfield, they travelled to Fartown for the semi-final play-off where a ground record of 32,573 was set. Without Stott, Croston and Jones, Trinity lacked penetration in the centre. Huddersfield went 8-0 up but Wakefield could only manage a single try through Arthur Fletcher and it was the claret and golds who went on to face Wigan in front of over 67,000 fans at Maine Road, Manchester.

At the end of the season, 33-year old Stott, originally from Featherstone, announced his retirement from playing and his acceptance of the post of trainer-coach of one of his former teams, Belle Vue Rangers (formerly Broughton Rangers). Back-rower Harry Murphy, on his return from Australia, reported that he had received an offer from Balmain, which he had decided not to accept.

The first post-war season had been a huge success – not just in playing terms but financially as well. Gate receipts from league matches more than quadrupled while takings from cup games increased almost sevenfold. Herbert Goodfellow, who had joined the club in 1934, was the beneficiary of a testimonial which raised £779.

At the start of the 1946-7 season, half back Stan Kielty and back-rower Alan Flowers both went to Halifax, while winger Harold Caldwell, who resented having been left out of the Cup final side, was sold to Leeds for £625, the same sum as he had cost to sign from Keighley. The team was disrupted by injuries thoughout the first half of the season, with Goodfellow suffering a long-lasting knee injury. In the pre-season Lazenby Cup match against Dewsbury, Rylance broke his breastbone in scoring the opening try but added the conversion before leaving the field.

All of that proved hardly significant compared with a tragic event which occurred in late September at Featherstone. Trinity's 21-year old centre, Frank Townsend, who had made his breakthrough into the first team the previous season, was dazed in a heavy tackle. He died in Pontefract Infirmary hours later. The inquest showed that Townsend, an assistant colliery surveyor who lived at Robin Hood, had died of brain injuries, but no blame was laid on any player in the match, which had been played in an excellent spirit.

In the Yorkshire Cup, Trinity beat Keighley on aggregate after losing the first leg. Castleford were beaten 11-2 in the second round and Hunslet went down at Belle Vue by 7-4, watched by 21,000, to put Trinity through to the final for the second year in a row. In their seventh Yorkshire Cup final since they last won the trophy in 1924, Trinity faced Hull at Headingley, and, watched by a crowd of 29,000, neither side had scored by half-time. Fletcher was first to cross early in the second period, Perry goaling. But, in his unaccustomed position of scrum-half, Fletcher was injured while touching down and had to leave the field. With only twelve men for most of the second half, Trinity not only resisted but added a second try. The Hull defence was foxed when Croston made a try scored by Rylance, Perry again converting and Trinity

A cartoonist's impression of the 1946 Yorkshire Cup final

took the County Cup for the first time since 1924, winning 10-0. It was their third trophy of 1946.

Stott, who had retired at the end of the previous season, played in a testimonial match against Featherstone and was presented with the sum of one hundred guineas. At the same time he announced that he had given up his post in Manchester, had taken over as manager of the Scarboro Arms and was available once more as a player. With Goodfellow still out of action, the 22-year old ex-Maesteg rugby union scrum-half Billy Banks was signed from Leeds. Towards the end of the season, Arthur Gray, the 26-year old Otley, Yorkshire and England rugby union full back was signed for an undisclosed fee but struggled to find a place in the team.

At the home match against Wigan in January 1947, all six rugby league trophies – three in the possession of Trinity, three belonging to Wigan – were put on show in front of the main stand. Trinity's Rugby League Challenge Cup, Yorkshire Cup and Yorkshire League trophy stood alongside Wigan's Rugby League Championship trophy, Lancashire Cup and Lancashire League trophy. To show that the two sides were still equal to each other, Trinity won the match 8-7 to avenge their New Year's Day defeat.

In the 1947 Challenge Cup, Trinity drew the first leg of the first round 3-3 at Leigh, with Jack Booth, who had just come into the first team, playing second row and proving the most effective of Trinity's forwards. The return leg, won 5-0, saw the return of the Goodfellow-Rylance half-back partnership, the scrum-half having recovered from a cartilage operation followed by a serious illness. Winger Albany Longley was also making a name for himself after signing from Featherstone for £700. All three played a big part in Trinity's second round success against Widnes, who were beaten 8-5 at Belle Vue: Rylance, 'with his quick perception of an opening, took a chance. The moment he received the pass [from Goodfellow] he was away like a flash on a run down the middle; a delightful side-step and a timely pass to Wilkinson opened Trinity's account.' Perry scored Trinity's other try 'with a sparkling sprint' after Longley had snapped up a loose Widnes pass. Liverpool Stanley, who had made their first appearance in the league in the previous season, were Trinity's next victims, going down 15-0, with Banks and Fletcher both showing their value: 'Banks, with a perfect service, got Rylance away and he worked a captivating scissors move with Stott before transferring to Fletcher, who put Longley in possession. The resolute running of the wingman achieved the desired result.' And then 'Fletcher, fast becoming an artist at selling the dummy, sold a beauty, swerved to avoid another would-be tackler and that was all that was required.'

The Cup semi-final pitted Trinity against Leeds in rugby league's first-ever all-ticket match, played at Fartown. The crowd of 35,136 was Huddersfield's biggest ever, the gate of £6,350 was a record for rugby league in Yorkshire, and it was said that the tickets could have been sold twice over. The first half of the game was played at a hectic pace, with Leeds scoring the only try of the first period against the run of play. After the break, Baddeley was in a scoring position and could easily have opened Trinity's account had it not been for the intervention of a touch judge, on whose advice the referee blew for obstruction by Leeds and gave Wakefield a penalty, which produced nothing. That was the turning point, after which Trinity folded and lost 21-0.

In Leeds's ranks that day was the former Trinity back row forward Alf Watson, who had made a remarkable recovery from the deprivations of having been a prisoner of war. Watson had been captured by the Germans in the retreat to Dunkirk in 1940 and spent the rest of the war in a camp. In 1945, as the Russians advanced from the east, Watson took part in a forced march over some 500 miles from what is now Poland towards the west of Germany. Over a period of four months, the party trudged through snow and ice, eating what food they could find and often suffering the effects of dysentery. Watson, who suffered badly swollen ankles, lost four stone.

As for the Wakefield team, questions were inevitably asked about whether some were now past their best. Certainly the likes of Teall, Stott, Wilkinson and Exley, all in their mid-thirties, were at the veteran stage and Exley announced his retirement immediately after the semi-final.

Trinity could not emulate the previous season's success in the league, finishing tenth, but made a substantial profit of £1,306, while the benefit for prop Harry Wilkinson, who was to establish a never-to-be-beaten club record of 618 appearances over twenty seasons, produced £1,117. The question of whether to convert Wakefield Trinity Football Club from a members' club to a limited company – which had been raised on previous occasions – was put forward, with the idea of raising capital from share subscriptions. But when the matter was put to members at the annual general meeting, it was resoundingly rejected by 438 votes to 159.

As the new season of 1947-48 approached, 23-year old Ron Rylance was made captain, a role he also assumed in the Yorkshire county side. Johnny Malpass was appointed player-coach and Trinity made their first direct signing from Australia. (Albert Rosenfeld, Trinity's first Australian, had arrived at the end of his career from Huddersfield.) Just as the five-year ban on recruiting Australian players was about to come into effect, Trinity captured Welsh-born Dennis Boocker, described as 'the best centre threequarter in Australia today'. Boocker, from the Wyalong club, eventually arrived at Westgate Station after travelling from Australia by flying-boat to Poole and made his debut a week later in the 15-8 home win over Salford.

Trinity already had plenty of options available in the backs, though Stott, having retired once, and Teall were now at the end of their careers. There was competition particularly at half back, where Rylance and Goodfellow remained the first-choice pair, but scrum-half Banks was first team quality in his own right, while stand-off Fletcher, who also operated at centre, gained county recognition. Rylance was selected at stand-off for England against Wales and again to face France, but had to withdraw from the match against the French as a result of a groin injury sustained while playing for Yorkshire against Cumberland. Fletcher, Perry, Marson and Booth, the latter a local product who had first turned professional with Leeds, all represented Yorkshire against Lancashire, while another significant addition was made from Trinity Supporters' Club, when 16-year old centre Frank Mortimer was signed.

In the Yorkshire Cup first round against Hull KR, Goodfellow 'weaved his way through the opposition and with unfailing regularity Bratley was there to take a reverse pass and share in a trick the Rovers fell for repeatedly.' Trinity eliminated the Robins 30-14 on aggregate and went on to defeat Hull 23-14 before beating Huddersfield 18-15 in the semi-final, the quality of which was described as breathtaking.

In their third consecutive County Cup final, Trinity met Leeds at Fartown, watched by 24,334 spectators. Despite Trinity's dominance, they led by only a Stott penalty goal until, early in the second half, Goodfellow took Marson's pass to go under the posts, Stott converting. But Leeds came back strongly with a penalty from Whitehead and a converted try scored by Williams to finish a sweeping move over 70 yards. The score remained at 7-7 and the replay was staged at Odsal on the Wednesday.

As a result of an injury to Stott, it was decided to move Jenkinson into the centre, with Rylance, who had withdrawn from the England side to play France a week earlier, coming into the side on the wing. At this stage in the season Leeds were fourth in the league table, Wakefield ten places below them, but it was Trinity who, as in the first match, went 2-0 ahead, this time through a Perry penalty. Leeds's excellent cover defence prevented Trinity from taking a bigger lead. Cook equalised for Leeds shortly after the interval, but then Trinity prop Wilkinson charged through for an unconverted try. Bratley picked up a Leeds dropped ball and touched down to give an 8-2 lead. Leeds hit back and only a fine last-ditch tackle by Perry, racing in off the wing, stopped Williams from scoring, though Flanagan capitalised on a Trinity error to go over, Whitehead goaling. Trinity led by a single point and came under immense pressure from Leeds's attack, but they held out to retain the trophy by 8-7. 'The brunt of the battle was borne by the forwards; none emerged with more credit than veteran Harry Wilkinson, Murphy, Booth and Bratley.' Behind the pack, the Trinity supporters were forced to admit: 'There's only one Goodfellow.'

But that did not stop the Trinity scrum-half from putting in a transfer request – subsequently withdrawn – resulting from the behaviour of a section of Wakefield supporters towards him at the Fartown final. His value to the side was illustrated by his performance the following week in a league match against Bramley, when it was reported that 'Goodfellow went through the opposition just when and how he liked… The simplicity with which he appeared to glide through the hands of would-be tacklers often denied him, as on many other occasions, the credit that was rightly his.'

In December Trinity faced the New Zealand touring team and, for once, were outplayed. The tourists had guile and speed in abundance and won by the impressive score of 30-3. Trinity's lone try, scored by Bratley, was, however, out of the top drawer, coming, as so often, from Goodfellow's break from the scrum and an inside pass. Immediately after the match, the tour manager and president of the New Zealand Rugby League, Mr Redwood, went into the home dressing-room to congratulate Goodfellow on his display. The New Zealanders had not met the Trinity half back's equal on the tour, he said. Yet in spite of that commendation, among others, Goodfellow was not to receive the international recognition his form deserved.

In the first round of the Challenge Cup, played as usual over two legs to maximise income, Trinity had a straightforward 13-2 win at Salford. But in the return leg at Belle Vue, the home side were in unusually lethargic mood and were losing 15-4 at the end of 80 minutes, making an aggregate of 17-all. In fact Trinity only managed to level the scores when Perry kicked a crucial penalty goal just 50 seconds from the whistle. Extra time was played and only then did Trinity strike something resembling their usual form, adding four tries and two goals to nil to go through with an aggregate score of 33-17. In Marson's absence, Trinity had difficulty in getting the ball from the scrums. In the first half, Salford heeled the ball fourteen times to Trinity's four. A reporter was reminded of what a former well-known scrum-half said in a similarly impoverished situation. 'Yer knaw,' he said, 'I like t'ball to be laikin' wi'; not ter hev it ter seek.'

In the second round, against Bradford at Belle Vue, watched by 27,330 fans - a post-war record for the ground - it was Perry to the rescue again. This time, Trinity had almost three times more possession than their opponents,

Wakefield and Wigan, who between them had won all six cups, show off the trophies before the league match between the two teams at Belle Vue, January 4, 1947. The Trinity players are (*at back*): Dennis Baddeley, Jim Higgins, Mick Exley, Albany Longley, Len Marson, Jack Booth, Derek Howes, Len Bratley; (*at front*) Ken Brooks, Billy Banks, Jack Perry, Billy Stott, Harry Wilkinson (*capt*), Billy Teall

'Marson heeling the ball with such regularity it was as if it was tied to his bootlaces.' But it took a last-minute try from Perry, who sprinted over from thirty yards, to earn a 3-3 draw. In the replay at Odsal, with a huge crowd of 44,132, a record for any match other than a semi-final, final or test match, Marson again won the scrums, getting the ball 43 times to Bradford's 15. But Bradford's defence was resolute and a 9-2 win saw them on their way to Wembley for the second year in a row.

The following week, Trinity put their Cup disappointment behind them and gave a fine display in a 13-6 league win over Huddersfield. It was Boocker's best performance since arriving and the fact that he faced three fellow-Aussies in full back Johnny Hunter, centre Pat Devery and, above all, winger Lionel Cooper no doubt had much to do with it. After Cooper had scored a 45-yard try, bumping off two or three defenders as he went, Boocker produced what was labelled a masterpiece. From the same distance the winger confused the defence with his weaving run before side-stepping Hunter to plant the ball over the line. To cap the performance, he hauled Cooper down to save a certain try after dashing across from the opposite wing.

Three wins out of four over Easter, including a 33-0 victory over Widnes, boosted Trinity's league placing to an eventual tenth. But that great servant of the club, Billy Teall, announced his retirement at the end of the season, aged almost 36, and left a void waiting to be filled. The ex-England RU full back Arthur Gray had played only a handful of games since signing and the selection committee once more called on Rylance to switch to the number one jersey. His performance against Widnes inspired confidence: 'His safe fielding of the ball, ability to kick with either foot and readiness to link up with the three-quarters in attack made his display one of the best of the aggressive types of full-back play seen at Belle Vue this season.' But his favoured position was stand-off and his value there was shown yet again in the 35-0 win over Featherstone, when he and Goodfellow cut the Rovers' defence to ribbons.

Billy Banks appeared the most dissatisfied, vowing never to play for the club again after being continually overlooked in favour of Goodfellow. The Welshman, who had cost £500 from Leeds, was transferred to Huddersfield in the close season for £1,850, helping to turn a loss on the season into a slight profit. Teall and Bratley, in their joint

Trinity captain Ron Rylance receives the Yorkshire Cup following the 8-7 victory over Leeds in the replayed final at Odsal, November 5, 1947.

benefit year, received £483 each and there was recognition too for club chairman Wilf Jackson, who was elected a life member of the Yorkshire County Committee after serving for 21 years, following in a distinguished line of club officials including JB Cooke and AA Bonner who had also done long duty with the governing bodies. On the playing front, further honours came early in the 1948-49 season, when Harry Murphy was selected for England and Derek Howes, who had been persuaded to take up rugby league by Billy Teall when the pair faced each other in a National Fire Services match, lined up in opposition for Wales.

In the first round of the Yorkshire Cup, Trinity beat Hull KR 24-19 over the two legs and the following week faced the Australian touring side. The Aussies lived up to their reputation for speed, direct running and support play, but Trinity ran them close, losing by only 26-19. Trinity stand-off Arthur Fletcher scored two tries, described as 'masterly'. Featherstone were beaten 19-5 in the second round of the County Cup, but Trinity, who had figured in every Yorkshire Cup final since the war, were robbed of a fourth appearance in a row when they were unfortunate to lose 6-5 to Castleford's last-minute penalty goal in the semi-final.

To strengthen Trinity's options in the centre, 21-year old John Leighton Davies was signed for £800 from Neath RU club and made his debut in the home defeat by Gus Risman's Workington. A schoolboy international, Davies had also played at senior level for Glamorgan. Goal-kicking winger Jack Perry was transferred to Batley, who paid a club record fee of over £1,000. But for a team occupying a mid-table position, Trinity still had three players on view – Fletcher, Marson and Murphy – in Yorkshire's first ever defeat of the Australians, while Boocker represented Wales against the tourists.

At the turn of the year, the committee received the unwelcome news that Ron Rylance, currently playing at centre, but also having been used at full back and wing, would put in a transfer request unless he was able to revert to stand-off in order to further his international claims. But Trinity also had county stand-off Arthur Fletcher in contention for the same position. The *Wakefield Express* claimed to have received 'an avalanche' of mail regarding the development. Meanwhile Rylance continued in the centre, playing very well. 'Without doubt the outstanding feature of the holiday games has been the brilliant centre play of Rylance, the club's international stand-off,' said the *Express*. 'With Davies, he has added punch to the middle.' At Castleford, he was 'in irresistible form. The try he scored bore the stamp of class in every step he took.' Against Leeds, Rylance 'again revealed football artistry of a high degree and with the powerful running of Davies Trinity's centre play was one of the bright features of the match.' The dispute was settled, with the stand-off revealing that he had also complained about the attitude of some of the spectators towards him. 'There will be plenty of support for the view that Trinity's most prolific points-gatherer has some grounds for complaint,' said the *Express*.

Two significant debut performances in the early part of 1949 were those of Des Foreman, the ex-Castleford and Leeds second rower, who scored a try over 50 yards, leaving his former team-mates from Wheldon Road in vain pursuit; and of local boy Don Froggett, appearing at Belle Vue for the first time in the 30-4 home win over Hull. Froggett's promising display was, however, overshadowed by more established stars. Herbert Goodfellow, who once again drew comparison with Jonathan Parkin, scored four solo tries, prompting the eulogy: 'The mesmeric power of Goodfellow in possession of the ball, had, seemingly, half the Hull team transfixed to the ground as he so often glided deceptively through their ranks.' Rylance, restored to the stand-off role, gave ample support. 'Equally brilliant was the display of Rylance. His lightning thrusts and skilful feints often had the defence running in the wrong direction… The dominance of the half-back pair was complete and behind them Davies and Froggett responded gallantly to the fine example set.'

Rylance and Murphy represented Yorkshire against Cumberland, and both were outstanding in Trinity's 24-7 victory at Headingley. 'While forwards Howes, Foreman and Murphy were continually in the limelight, the foundation of Wakefield's success was unquestionably at half back, where the Leeds Welsh international pair [Williams and Jenkins] were second best to the Wakefield men… Rylance repeatedly left Dicky Williams far behind and again the "trick triangle" was seen at work for [loose forward] Murphy, developing splendid understanding with the half backs, joined in the fun with considerable success.'

But Trinity's Challenge Cup campaign, after a total of 73 points were amassed in beating Liverpool Stanley home and away, foundered at Wigan. Owing to the heavy state of the Central Park pitch, the second round tie was postponed, though not long before kick-off, which infuriated Trinity fans. When the tie was played on the Wednesday, Trinity, lacking flu victim Goodfellow, seemed to have little heart for it and were beaten 37-2.

For the first time since the war, Trinity had nothing to show for their season. They finished twelfth in the table, though their attack was bettered only by Warrington, Wigan and Huddersfield. The most successful period in the club's history had come to an end. In the three preceding seasons, from 1945 to 1948, Trinity had won the Challenge Cup once, reached three Yorkshire Cup finals, winning twice, won the Yorkshire League once and had played a Championship semi-final. Only the period from 1908 to 1911 saw similar fortune, when Trinity first won the Challenge Cup and the Yorkshire Cup, took the Yorkshire League trophy twice and also featured in a Championship semi. But, in the midst of the post-war boom, the committee could be well satisfied with a healthy profit of £2,596 on the 1948-49 season.

The 1949-50 season did not begin auspiciously, with only one league win from five games. Featherstone were beaten in the first round of the Yorkshire Cup, however, and hooker Len Marson and 20-year old winger Johnny Duggan, a product of St Austin's School like Harry Murphy, were chosen to play for Yorkshire. Trinity went out of the Yorkshire Cup in the second round at the hands of Huddersfield, where they displayed typical cup-fighting commitment despite having Goodfellow sent off for an alleged trip. It was a spectacular match which 12-man

Trinity were unlucky to lose. 'Ignore the result as a basis for analysis of as exciting a match as anyone has a right to expect in a lifetime of watching football,' wrote no less an observer than the *Yorkshire Post's* Alfred Drewry, marvelling at Trinity's skill and courage which saw them fight back from 5-0 down to take the lead at 12-10 before finally succumbing by 20-12. 'It is the unflagging team spirit of Trinity for which this match will be remembered,' said Drewry.

The quality still present in the team's ranks was shown when Marson was selected to play for England against France, with Rylance as reserve, while Boocker and Howes earned caps for Wales against them.

As the new decade began, the big talking-point was a second transfer request from leading points scorer Ron Rylance, who, believing he had been unfairly treated by certain sections of the crowd and the press, was far from happy at Belle Vue. Within a week, Dewsbury, ahead of Warrington and Castleford, signed the international stand-off for a club record fee of £3,500. Trinity moved quickly to sign Welshman Glyn Meredith from Newbridge RU as cover for the stand-off position and though the lack of a reliable goal-kicker was to prove problematic, Harry Murphy initially took over with some success, equalling the club record of eleven goals in a match, kicked against the Cumberland amateur side Broughton Moor, who were defeated by Trinity's highest score of 73-3 in the first round, second leg of the Challenge Cup.

Rylance's Dewsbury were Trinity's second round opponents in a match which became notorious as the 'Battle of Belle Vue'. This Monday evening game attracted a 26,000 crowd, who witnessed a forward battle that ended in a 2-2 draw, three sendings-off, including Higgins and Murphy, and eight players injured. Though Rylance, who called it the dirtiest match he had ever played in, did indeed create the two best scoring chances, the game was reported as 'a travesty of rugby league'. In the replay at Crown Flatt, Trinity's strength in depth proved vital, 17-year old forward Don Robinson, who had signed from Kippax Juniors, making a promising debut, for one so young, in the 15-10 victory. A capacity all-ticket crowd of 37,114 filled Headingley to see the third round match, in which Trinity, depleted by the absence of the suspended Higgins and Murphy and the injured Howes, and though playing their third match in six days, held the lead for almost an hour. Both sides scored two tries, but it was Leeds's superior goal-kicking which saw them home by 14-8.

Trinity ended the season in fourteenth position, their lowest post-war placing, but had the pleasure of hosting, for the first time, a match against French opposition. A touring team composed of players from Bordeaux and Villeneuve were beaten 36-7 in front of 10,000 spectators. Harry Murphy was chosen to take in part in his second Australasian tour, though hooker Len Marson, it was generally agreed, was very unfortunate to miss out.

Murphy, whose benefit that season had raised just short of £900, kept a tour diary. Encounters with Arab peddlers in Port Said and the effects of inoculation against cholera and typhoid before the ship dropped anchor at Bombay were forgotten once the party arrived in Australia. The outstanding hospitality and abundance of food contrasted with the rationing left behind in England. As for the rugby league, Murphy had this to say about a match at Newcastle, Dennis Boocker's home town: 'The Newcastle boys play rough football and I now know why Dennis plays the ball as quickly as he does. We had the experience of being kicked off the ball before we had the chance of even putting our feet to it.' The frenzy of the Great Britain v Queensland match, which ended in a free-for-all, contrasted with the idyllic pleasures of collecting coconuts on a sub-tropical island which Murphy described as paradise. Murphy made his only test appearance at Brisbane in the Lions' 15-3 defeat, which led up to the decider at Sydney Cricket Ground. On a quagmire, in pouring rain, Australia won a gripping match 5-2 to win back the Ashes for the first time in thirty years. 'The spectators were mad with joy,' Murphy wrote. 'It was the greatest spectacle I have seen in a sports arena.'

Another international forward, Bill Hudson, who was born at Crofton and first played at Streethouse, but had played most of his football with Batley, was signed from Wigan in the close season to give a boost to the pack. Reg Hughes, recruited the previous season from Headingley RU, was laying a strong claim to the loose forward role but back-rower Des Foreman was transferred to Hull and long-serving centre Reg Jenkinson to York.

Meanwhile two former players showed the current team how it was done. Trinity had beaten York 66-6 on aggregate in the first round of the Yorkshire Cup. In the second, they came up against Jack Perry's Batley. Without a reliable goal-kicker, Trinity looked on helplessly as the nerveless Perry, with one of his late specials, landed a touchline conversion four minutes from the final whistle to see his side through by 10-8. In a league match at Dewsbury, which Trinity lost 17-8, it was noted: 'Meredith was overshadowed by Rylance, who, several times, sliced through Meredith's would-be tackles with a gay abandon that was disconcerting to Wakefield followers.'

After Banks and Rylance, who would eventually join forces at Huddersfield, the latest Trinity half back to put in a transfer request was Herbert Goodfellow, who had served Wakefield with such distinction for sixteen years, the last three of them as captain. Recently installed as the landlord of the Jacob's Well Tavern in Wakefield, Goodfellow was valued at £2,000, and, though he asked to be taken off the list six weeks later, he was eventually transferred to Oldham in February 1951. It was an inglorious end to an exceptional career at Belle Vue.

More heartening was the form of the redoubtable prop forward Jack Booth. After scoring a memorable try over half the length of the field against Hull KR, Booth put in some telling performances, such as against Castleford in late December. 'Booth was a shining light, his work from the front row being as good as that shown by any Trinity club player for a long time. It was of international standard. To him went the credit for Hughes' second half try. A piece of astute work it was on Booth's part that took him clear of the ruck and, after selling a dummy in the style of an expert, his massive form covered nearly half the length of the field (in similar style to that never-to-be-forgotten try against Hull KR at Belle Vue) before he handed over to Hughes, who had positioned himself creditably to take the pass which sent him, unopposed, over the line.'

Nevertheless the 1950-51 season was an inauspicious one. In the Challenge Cup, Trinity lost the first leg of the first round 16-10 at Salford but entertained high hopes of reversing the result at Belle Vue. Their performance was disastrous. Trinity, ninth in the league, lost 6-2 to Salford, then second from bottom. It was the first time in seventeen years that Trinity had suffered defeat in the first round at Belle Vue. A letter to the *Wakefield Express* from a supporter echoed the feelings of many when he wrote of the gradual decline of the club since winning the Cup in 1946. Complaining of unimaginative management of the team and insufficient training methods, he made the point that individually the players appeared the equals of most but collectively their standard was low.

The supporter had made a fair, if slightly exaggerated point. Of the 1946 Cup-winning side, Teall, Stott, Rylance, Croston, Jones, Wilkinson, Exley, Bratley and Goodfellow had all gone. Now under the leadership of Bill Hudson, the forwards had a blend of experience and youthful talent. Booth and Robinson had both caught the eye early in their careers. Robinson had just been chosen to play for England Under 21s against France and another future international, John 'Joby' Shaw, a 16 year-old hooker from Nostell Miners' Welfare, had been signed. Murphy, Marson and Howes were all internationals, Higgins was a highly experienced front rower and Hughes at loose forward was making a good impression. Though there were gaps, the backs were not without talent either. Stand-off Fletcher had county experience, Froggett was as tireless as he was consistent in the centre and, though his partner Davies was injured, Welsh international Boocker and Yorkshire winger Duggan were a dashing pair on the flanks, while Luckman was a dependable full back. Booth was chosen to play for a Great Britain XIII against Australasia, a team made up of Australians and New Zealanders playing in England, a match which formed part of the Festival of Britain celebrations. Hughes was selected as reserve for an Empire XIII against a Welsh XIII. Trinity's 1950-51 side was no longer the equal of Wigan – the league leaders – but once more, as in 1947 and 1948, its final league placing might well have been higher than tenth.

Twelve – A Time of Reconstruction: 1951-57

In the early fifties, Trinity started to rebuild the team which had been depleted by the departure of important players. But the reconstruction was made more difficult by the recently announced deficit of £1,530 on the 1950-51 season, as opposed to a profit of £470 the year before and almost £2,600 the year before that. As a result, chairman Frank Banham and committee member Stuart Hadfield were voted off at the AGM. Jim Croston took over as manager-coach from Harry Beverley, with Johnny Jones in charge of the second team and Johnny Malpass trainer. The playing terms for the 1951-52 season were £8 for an away win, £7 a home win and £4 a defeat. Still, the team got off to an ignominious start, beaten 10-3 by newcomers Doncaster. Trinity thus became the first team to be beaten by a side new to the league on their debut, though the Dons were to finish the season in eleventh place out of 31 clubs. Trinity fared better, though, against the league's other new club, Cardiff. The unrest among certain players continued as forwards Murphy, Howes and Hughes all asked for a move.

In the Yorkshire Cup, however, after knocking Hull out, Trinity beat Huddersfield 14-5 in the second round, young hooker Joby Shaw playing a key role. As if to show what they were capable of, Trinity pulled off a shock 18-17 win in the semi-final against Leeds at Headingley, where, after establishing an 18-7 lead early in the second period, they held on to go through to their fourth final since the war. Trinity's defence, severely tested in the last quarter of the match, was epitomised by a last-ditch tackle, four minutes from the end, by full back Les Hirst on rampaging forward Arthur Clues. Don Robinson in the forwards and Arthur Fletcher at half back were outstanding, while Frank Mortimer, the 20-year old centre making his debut, 'displayed the coolness of a veteran'. At Fartown in the final, before 25,495 spectators, Trinity were up against a Keighley side making their first peacetime appearance in a Yorkshire Cup final. In the Trinity side, only Boocker, Fletcher and Booth survived from the 1947 triumph.

Trinity established a 9-3 lead when Hughes went over from Fletcher's inside pass direct from a scrum, and Hirst, the former Wakefield RU player, converted and kicked two penalties. Robinson beat four defenders to dive over the

The 1951 New Zealand tourists played at Belle Vue on November 14, 1951 and beat Wakefield by 26-18 in front of a 9,800 crowd. Trinity (*back row, from left*): J Booth, WJD Howes, D Robinson, D Froggett, F West (chairman); (*middle row*) JT Wood (secretary), W Hudson, G Meredith, R Hughes, A Fletcher; (*front row*) F Mortimer, E Luckman, D Boocker, J Duggan, SJ Shaw.

line, Boocker posted a late try and Hirst added another goal to give Trinity the Cup by the score of 17-3.

Despite Trinity's familiar inconsistencies over the remainder of the campaign, there were some fine individual performances. Arthur Fletcher, playing in his now customary scrum-half position, received high praise for his performance in the 15-0 win over Warrington, 'giving a display the likes of which could only have been expected of a Parkin or Goodfellow… He scored the game's most sparkling try when with the grace of a ballerina he toed his way in rapid succession past the loose forward and full back.' Johnny Duggan, who was to emigrate to New Zealand at the end of the season, put in some promising displays too. Despite the side's moderate form over the Christmas period, the winger scored four tries against Castleford, three against Leeds and one against Hull KR.

On January 12, Trinity took part in the first televised league match, from Central Park, Wigan. To televise or not to televise was a hotly debated question, and only the first half of the match was shown. Trinity went on to lose 29-13.

Yorkshire and England centre Don Froggett, a mainstay of the Trinity side in the 1950s

Before the Challenge Cup got under way, ex-Wakefield winger Jack Perry proved once more Trinity's undoing as he converted his own try from the touchline, late in the game, to give Batley a 7-6 victory. In the first round of the Cup, Trinity beat holders Wigan 18-13 in the first leg at Belle Vue, with Les Hirst kicking five goals to ensure the win. But in the return leg at Central Park it was an altogether different story. With ex-Dewsbury stand-off Len Constance exploiting every opportunity, Trinity were outplayed by 40 points to 3. Hirst, at least temporarily, seemed to have solved Trinity's goal-kicking problems. Eight goals against Leeds saw him reach a total of 107 for the season, just short of Sammy Lee's record of 111 in 1938-39. Among the league's top scorers, Hirst finished fifth in the goal-kicking table. Don Robinson, surprisingly for a forward, also figured in the try-scoring list with 21.

Eddie Thomas, the 43-year old secretary of Keighley, was appointed to succeed John Tom Wood who was to retire after 21 years' service. Thomas, originally from Halifax, had played rugby union with Brighouse before turning to rugby league as a referee. Wood received a testimonial amounting to £640, which showed something of the esteem in which the secretary-manager (and masseur) was held. His successor, speaking of his decision to take up the post at Wakefield, said that the club was considered to have 'the soundest potential in the league.' Trinity should rank consistently among the top six clubs, he added, and he would do everything in his power to ensure it.

Among the comings and goings at the end of the 1951-52 season, Bill Hudson retired from the game. Stand-off Len Constance arrived from Wigan and Keith Holliday was signed as an 18-year old stand-off from Trinity Juniors. Among the backroom staff, another figure who would long be associated with the club, William 'Paddy' Armour, a native of Belfast and highly respected physiotherapist, was appointed as masseur.

Before the start of the 1952-53 season, chairman Frank West revealed that there had been moments during the previous campaign when there had been no harmony in the dressing-room, a fault which he attributed to the attitude of certain players. He now believed that the 'disruptive spirit' had gone. Nevertheless, when Trinity were beaten 38-26 on aggregate by Hull KR – who finished the season third from bottom - in the first round of the Yorkshire Cup, after being defeated 22-15 at Belle Vue, it was said that the team had hit 'rock bottom'. Their performance was described as their 'most inept display in a cup game since the war.' The following month, Trinity lost for a third time to the Robins, giving them their first league points of the season.

The remaining members of the team which enjoyed such great success immediately after the war left one by one.

Harry Murphy eventually departed for Keighley, after 23-year old second-rower Bob Kelly had moved in the opposite direction. Murphy had earned the right to be remembered as one of Trinity's greatest ever forwards. As his former team-mate Ron Rylance wrote in an obituary, 'His tackling was fearless, his handling accomplished and his speed exceptional. His attacking skill was outstanding, a reflection on his schooldays when he played centre threequarter. When the going was hard, Harry was better to play with than against. In my opinion he had no peer among all Trinity's great forwards of the past.' The hooker who set the standard by which all other Trinity number nines would be measured, Len Marson, who had announced his retirement eighteen months earlier, went to Hunslet. Jim Higgins, who had originally joined Trinity from an Oldham amateur club, returned across the Pennines the following year to join Liverpool City.

Trinity had not been allocated a match against the touring Australians but had arranged a midweek fixture by speaking directly to the tour management. Apart from giving the 6,000 spectators at Belle Vue the chance to watch some scintillating rugby league, Trinity might have wished they hadn't bothered. In the 58-8 hammering, Jack Booth was sent off, along with Roy Bull, and was suspended for four matches. None of the team from the recent test at Swinton played, but winger Noel Pidding's haul of 31 points from three tries and eleven goals created an individual record for a Kangaroo tour of Great Britain. Trinity's two tries both came from scrum-half Ronnie 'Curly' Evans.

International forward Don Robinson, who, in 1954, became Trinity's first Great Britain World Cup squad member before moving to Leeds two seasons later

On November 15, 1952, Trinity played under floodlights for the first time at Belle Vue. It was an impromptu affair, though, because as darkness fell in the match against Oldham, referee Railton asked for the training lights to be switched on a quarter of an hour from the end, and, with the use of a white ball (brown leather balls were standard), the game was able to be completed.

Trinity had been having a dismal season and it was no surprise that they should lose at home to Leeds on Boxing Day. The 27-9 defeat was witnessed by 12,000 spectators, the biggest crowd of the season so far. With talk of two divisions in the air, Trinity's performances made them likely candidates for the lower tier. But, unpredictable as ever, they went to Headingley ten days later and won 19-9. Don Froggett, the captain, 'gave a grand lead with some Billy Batten-style crash tackles, leaving folk wondering where he found his limitless energy.' Frank Mortimer scored a try and kicked five goals, while Ernest Luckman and forwards Tony Storey and Reg Hughes were also outstanding. But that display proved the exception to the rule. In the first round of the Challenge Cup, Trinity lost the first leg at home to Leeds by 33-9 before losing the second leg 32-9. Winger Eric Cooper, signed from Doncaster, made his debut in the first match, and from the same club came loose forward Arthur Street, brother of international Harry. Arthur Fletcher returned to the side after almost a year, following a knee operation, but Len Constance asked to be put on the transfer list after finding that the travel from his home in St Helens was affecting his form. Second rower Tony Storey, who was named in the shadow England side to face France, was listed at his own request at £3,000; Reg Hughes also asked for a transfer and was valued at £2,500; and Glyn Meredith was put up for sale at £1,000. Storey, brother of novelist and playwright David, was quickly signed by Bradford for a fee approaching the asking price, their highest ever for a forward. Meredith returned to Wales, while Hughes, after a spell on the sidelines, was eventually transferred to Halifax. In March Trinity suffered one of their heaviest ever defeats when they were routed 69-17 at St Helens – the highest score against a Trinity side since Hull racked up 69 points to 11 in the 1920-21 season.

The Trinity A team, which, under captain Jack Booth's guidance, won their competition trophy in 1954-55

A crowd estimated at only 700 for the visit of Doncaster at the end of March reflected the supporters' view of Trinity's uninspiring play. Their final league position of eighteenth was their worst showing since the 1935-36 season and a loss of £1,428 was made, in contrast to a profit of £459 the previous year. As was pointed out at the AGM, the only redeeming feature of this miserable season was the election of chairman Frank West as mayor, a unique distinction in holding both offices at the same time.

Not that the new season of 1953-54 began much better. New coach Bill Duffy resigned after less than two months, leaving Johnny Malpass in temporary charge. Derek Howes, the last member of the 1946 Cup-winning side still playing in Wakefield colours, was transferred to Featherstone for £600. There were some galling early defeats. In Leigh's 24-13 victory at Belle Vue, the performance of the visitors' international full back, Wakefield-born Jimmy Ledgard, was described as a 'superb exhibition … the best we have seen since pre-war days.' In the first round, first leg Yorkshire Cup defeat at the hands of Huddersfield, former Trinity half backs Ron Rylance and Billy Banks were among the tormentors responsible for the 47-9 defeat. Banks was later selected for Wales against France, while another ex-Wakefield half back, Stan Kielty, of Halifax, was chosen to play for England against Other Nationalities. But some significant junior signings were made at this period: Albert Firth, a 16-year old second-rower from the Stanley club; 17-year old Aubrey Holden, a County amateur stand-off from Heworth; 17-year old loose forward David Lamming from Wakefield Trinity Juniors; and Eric Lockwood, a 21-year old stand-off from Trinity Boys' Youth Club.

In November Trinity again fell at home to Leeds, who inflicted a 46-5 defeat described as 'one of the saddest experiences in Trinity's history'. In spite of all this, Don Froggett's talent and unquenchable enthusiasm stood out enough for him to be chosen for Yorkshire against Lancashire and then for the England team to face France at Odsal.

In the first round of the Challenge Cup, Trinity made a surprise exit. After winning the first leg 24-13 at home to Whitehaven, with Don Robinson scoring three tries and Don Froggett two, they travelled to the Recreation Ground, where they led 3-0. But Whitehaven, aided by John McKeown's goal-kicking, rallied to win 15-3 and go through to the second round by an aggregate score of 28-27.

For the first time, no Wakefield Trinity player was selected to go on tour to Australia. (In 1914 W L Beattie was chosen but declined to take part for business reasons.) Huddersfield's Wakefield-born forward Brian Briggs, a former Stanley Rangers player, did, however, make the trip.

Denis Boocker, in his last game for Trinity before sailing home to Australia, touched down twice against Doncaster, taking his tally for the season to 32, which, at the time, was the second-highest number of tries scored by a Wakefield player in a season. In more than 200 matches and with five appearances for Wales, Boocker had been one of Trinity's most popular players, scoring 127 tries, many of them with his famous 'swallow-dive' technique, and figuring fifth in the all-time list of the club's top try scorers.

At the end of the season Trinity had found themselves in an improved position of eleventh but had made a £1,120 loss and now had a bank overdraft standing at £4,163. Caretaker coach Johnny Malpass, who was to be retained for the following season, explained that 'the general standard had improved by seven places and that the team promised well but at times, unaccountably, failed when put to the test.' He referred to the regular failure to play for the full eighty minutes but also pointed out that Trinity had one of the youngest sides in the league. Don Robinson was 20, hooker Joby Shaw and props John Lindley and Wilf Adams were all 19, as was loose forward Colin Clifft, while another loose forward, Dave Lamming, and second row Albert Firth were just 17. Jack Booth, at 33, and Bob Kelly, at 24, were easily the oldest.

As the 1954-55 season got under way, with veteran Arthur Fletcher the new captain, no fewer than eight players were on the injured list, six of them recovering from injuries sustained the previous season. Among them, Joby Shaw had had a shoulder operation after suffering seven dislocations. The most serious was Don Froggett's. The hard-as-nails centre had sustained a fractured skull in a match against Leeds, but returned to action in time to be selected for Yorkshire against Cumberland, alongside Fletcher and Robinson, with young forwards Wilf Adams and Colin Clifft picked as reserves. Robinson later had the honour of being Trinity's sole representative in the Great Britain squad which won the inaugural World Cup in France.

Trinity's Yorkshire Cup campaign got as far as the second round. After defeating Dewsbury 30-16 at Belle Vue, Trinity lost at Leeds by 27-17. Full back Ernest Luckman, who had signed from Featherstone six years earlier, decided to retire from the game following a shoulder injury. Winger Stan Smith was signed from Trinity Juniors, as was 17-year old captain and scrum-half Ken Rollin. Once again Trinity failed to make an impression in the Challenge Cup. In the first round they faced Rochdale away and led 9-0 but lost momentum and were defeated 11-9.

The season was littered with below-par performances, one of the worst being the 48-14 trouncing at Headingley, 'a disgraceful exhibition', in which Trinity's tackling was described as 'shocking'. But they followed it up with perhaps their best display of the season by defeating Bradford at Belle Vue by 31-12 in front of a meagre 2,817 crowd. Peter Armstead and Ray Jaques formed a solid second row, while Don Robinson, at loose forward, was by far the best forward on the field. As some consolation for an unremarkable season and sixteenth position in the league, Trinity's A team won the Yorkshire Senior Competition Cup for the second time in the post-war period, beating Featherstone 13-12 at Belle Vue.

Once more Trinity made a loss of over £1,000 on the season, raising the bank overdraft to £5,000. Secretary Eddie Thomas said in his end-of-year report that a large proportion of the current season's loss was accounted for by the running of the A team, which cost £900. Overall the deficit, said Thomas, 'could be a challenge, or threat, to our continued existence.' He referred to the fact that the Belle Vue ground, with its 'splendid' playing area, stands and terraced accommodation, put the club in the top bracket, but attendances in general were what could be expected of a lower level club. Thomas also commented on the team's performances, referring to the 'hardly believable' injury situation, but also commenting that it was not the games which had been lost, but the manner in which they had been lost, which had strained, 'almost to breaking point, the loyalty of supporters.' He took the players to task, reminding them that, 'having accepted payment as professional footballers, they became paid entertainers of the public. Not only did they contract physical obligation to give of their best but, in addition, there was a moral responsibility for providing entertainment of value.'

On the committee, Wilf Jackson, a life member and chairman of the club from 1945 to 1956, stepped down after 31 years' service. His association with Wakefield Trinity went back over half a century when he first played for the club as a winger. David Armitage took over as chairman from Frank West, who did not put himself forward for re-election. There was another break with the past. The famous navy blue jersey with red band was to be replaced after some 75 years by a new design, which was all red with a broad blue band and thin blue band above. For the first six or seven years of Trinity's existence the club colours were blue and black horizontal hoops and for at least part of the 1945-6 season red and light blue hooped jerseys had been worn.

The season 1955-56 started promisingly enough with a 45-26 win over a depleted Hull side, Frank Mortimer kicking nine goals. In the first round of the Yorkshire Cup, Leeds were beaten 31-3 at Headingley, where scrum-half Ken Rollin made his first-team debut and an immediate impression. Just before half-time, feigning a pass to loose forward Robinson, Rollin found a way through to put the ball down under the posts in eye-catching style. Trinity's forwards, though beaten in the scrums, outplayed the opposition in the loose, with Robinson an inspiration. Mortimer, who landed eight goals, was described as immaculate at full back. In the second round, however, Cup-holders Halifax, who went on to retain the trophy, barred Trinity's progress with a 21-4 victory at Belle Vue, watched by an 11,000 crowd.

Two weeks later, Trinity lost 22-11 in a league match at Rochdale after leading 11-7 at half-time. No great disgrace, since the Hornets had won six of their seven matches to date and Wakefield only three from eight. But the frustration of those who followed unpredictable Trinity was explicit in the comments of the *Wakefield Express* reporter: 'True to tradition, Trinity performed their act of charity … Shades of the past stole across the scene and turned the match into what has now become a familiar trend – Trinity on top in the first half and then making an inglorious exit from the scene after the interval … similar to their unforgettable retreat on the same battlefield in the first round tie of the Rugby League Cup.' In an attempt to oversee team matters, Eddie Thomas's role at the club was altered to that of secretary-manager.

In October Trinity made one of their most significant signings ever. Goal-kicking centre Neil Fox, aged 16, was signed from Featherstone Rovers Juniors, although it had been widely expected that he would follow his brothers Peter and Don in joining Featherstone. It would not be long before the youngest of the Fox brothers would make an impact at first team level.

Among early-season highlights, Don Robinson, by now an established international, played for England against New Zealand. Winger Colin Bell scored one of the fastest hat-tricks ever as he crossed three times in six minutes in the 24-2 win over Hunslet. In November Trinity faced Warrington in a midweek match in London, one of an innovative series of televised games presented by ITV but not broadcast in the north. Trinity lost 33-9. The same teams had played 47 years earlier in an exhibition game staged at West Ham. Trinity won that match 11-6, with winger Billy Simpson scoring all his side's three tries.

Trinity's inconsistent present form continued to worry the committee and supporters alike. Following a miserable

The Yorkshire Cup-winning team of 1956-57: *Back row*: J McGee (kit), E Thomas (sec), D Froggett, F West, SH Hadfield, W Simpson, E Sugden, H Wilkinson (trainer). *Middle row*: C Bell, F Mortimer, K Holliday, DW Armitage (chairman), R Kelly (capt), L Pounder (vice-chairman), E Cooper, R Coverdale, P Armstead. *Front row*: J Malpass (coach), D Harrison, J Shaw, K Rollin, F Smith, F Haigh, L Chamberlain, W Armour (masseur)

home defeat at the hands of lowly Bramley, the committee, 'gravely concerned at the falling-off of form of certain players' held a 'fact-finding meeting'. Their conclusions were not revealed, but there was no immediate effect. Trinity lost 27-16 to the touring New Zealanders, though the match was described as 'sparkling'. Jack Booth, at the age of 36, made his first appearance of the season, but the star of the show was New Zealand winger Vern Bakalich, who scored three fine tries.

Injuries were fewer than in the previous season, but they were significant. Don Froggett, after a six-week absence, returned to action only to suffer a broken jaw. Don Robinson came back into the side following a two-month lay-off, but in January he was transfer-listed. The committee put a value on him of £3,500 and it was not long before clubs on both sides of the Pennines took an interest. The 23-year old international forward's eventual transfer was to take place in unusual circumstances. Eight minutes before kick-off in the home game against Leeds, who were poised to capture his signature, Robinson was told to stand down and forward Frank Haigh was made to take the number 12 jersey, with Bob Kelly taking over as captain. The transfer was completed after the game, in which Trinity beat Leeds at Belle Vue for the first time since the 1951-52 season, winning 20-10. Trinity agreed to accept £2,750 plus winger Fred Smith. Robinson's loss was a big blow, but the acquisition of 20-year old Smith, a former Stanley Rangers player and son of the ex-Trinity, Featherstone and York centre or wing of the same name, turned out to be a valuable one.

Robinson, who had first been spotted by Harry Wilkinson playing amateur rugby league at Kippax, and had been

121

a first team player since the age of 17, recalled his move to Leeds. 'Wakefield couldn't pay their overdraft and wanted to sell me. Then when I went to Leeds they wanted me back, but Leeds put a big fee on me. The difference between a good team like Leeds and others was that it was easy – I didn't break sweat. In my first match I scored a try, though it was only against York, and everybody was clapping.

'At Wakefield I remember that the jerseys would be stiff for training. You used to have to rub them. Once when we were a bit late, I pointed it out and I was told, "If you'd come at six o'clock you'd have got a clean one."'

In the Challenge Cup, Trinity survived the first round for the first time since 1950, beating Bramley 30-10 at Belle Vue and thus avenging the 12-8 league defeat earlier in the season. Centre Albert Mortimer, brother of full back Frank, scored three tries. Between the first and second rounds, however, Trinity went down at Halifax, losing 34-6 at Thrum Hall, their biggest margin of defeat of the season. They picked themselves up for the second round at Leigh, where, with Bob Kelly's strong leadership and with good work from half backs Keith Holliday and Ken Rollin, Trinity triumphed 11-5, winger Eric Cooper sealing the victory with a try two minutes from the end in a frenzied final spell. That win sparked something of a revival as Trinity beat Bradford, one of the contenders for the championship play-offs, winning 11-10 in front of 8,700 spectators, Belle Vue's biggest crowd of the season. That figure was easily surpassed in the excitement caused by the third round clash at Belle Vue, where Cup-holders Barrow formed the opposition. Watched by a crowd of 18,000, a high quality match ended in victory for the visitors by 14-10, with Trinity beaten 29-9 in the scrums.

The form of certain Trinity players had not gone unnoticed by the RFL's international selection panel, of which Wakefield committee man Joe Jones was a member. Team captain Bob Kelly was rewarded with a place in the Great Britain side to face France at Odsal, alongside ex-Trinity forward Don Robinson, while Keith Holliday, originally named in the shadow team, was also called up to play at stand-off. Later on, 21-year old loose forward Colin Clifft was chosen to play for England against France at Lyon. Towards the end of the season, and as Trinity looked more and more to local products, Neil Fox, Fred Smith and prop Mick Lumb all made their first-team debuts in the 9-5 defeat by Keighley. In the penultimate match of the season at Huddersfield, Fox, at full back, gave an indication of what was to come by kicking six goals from six attempts in the first half. It was Frank Mortimer, however, who ended the season as Trinity's top scorer, as he had done twice before, with 165 points.

Trinity finished the 1955-56 season in a slightly worse position than the season before. Their seventeenth place out of thirty clubs would have put them in the second division if the proposal to split the league into two divisions had not been rejected. Trinity had been, in fact, in favour of the two-division plan. The good news was that, reversing the trend of previous seasons, the club made a profit of £2,327, with gross gate receipts up by almost £7,000.

Trinity's ability to produce home-grown players was very much in evidence, as players came through from junior level via the A team to the first team. The A team, captained and nurtured by that great clubman, Jack Booth, and coached by Johnny Jones, showed its prowess by achieving a cup and league double. They retained the Yorkshire Senior Competition Cup by beating York 31-0 in the final and took the Championship title by defeating Halifax 17-4.

With Johnny Malpass continuing as trainer-coach, Trinity looked to improve on their previous season's form. For the second season running, they beat Leeds in the first round of the Yorkshire Cup, winning 36-15, with Frank Mortimer, who was also selected for Yorkshire against Cumberland, kicking nine goals from ten attempts. In the second round, with Les Chamberlain outstanding, Trinity knocked out Huddersfield 13-11 on a Monday evening at Belle Vue, and went on to meet Halifax, the Cup-holders for the past two seasons, on a Tuesday, also at home. Trinity were down to twelve men soon after half-time when Don Froggett was injured and had to leave the field, but they held out to win 14-13, Colin Bell scoring the try of the match from a Mortimer pass.

Trinity's record of twelve Yorkshire Cup final appearances since the creation of the competition in 1905 had been bettered only by Huddersfield. Their opponents, Hunslet, whom they met at Headingley in front of 31,000 spectators, had not won the trophy since their All Four Cups season of 1907-8. The Parkside club's record remained unchanged as Trinity registered their fourth victory since the war, winning 23-5. Against a heavier Hunslet pack and despite being beaten by a ratio of two to one in the scrums, Trinity seized all the chances that came their way. Loose forward Les Chamberlain, though sustaining a cut above his eye, was again in top form and wingers Fred Smith and Eric Cooper both touched down twice, Albert Mortimer scoring Trinity's other try and his brother Frank landing four goals.

As scrum-half Ronnie 'Curly' Evans was transferred to Castleford and loose forward Colin Clifft went to Halifax, Trinity signed 16-year old Morley Rugby Union winger Ken Hirst. Four other Yorkshire clubs had been chasing the signature of the former Hunslet Junior who had captained Yorkshire Schoolboys at both rugby league and soccer, had played for Yorkshire Schools at cricket and had competed in the English Schools Athletics Championships. Frank Mortimer was chosen to represent Great Britain against Australia in the first two tests and kicked three goals in each. In the second test, Oldham's Derek Turner, Wakefield-born and later to become such an important figure in Trinity's history, made his international debut at loose forward.

In a late addition to the tourists' itinerary, Trinity met the Australians in their final match in England. The 3,381 spectators who were able to get to the match on a Monday afternoon saw Trinity make a sensational start as young winger Ken Hirst, on his debut, raced in for a 60-yard try after just two minutes' play. Trinity never looked back. There was controversy when Aussie forward Norm Provan was sent off and then, immediately after, Joby Shaw for ungentlemanly conduct in approving the referee's decision, for which he was suspended for three matches. Ken Rollin, one of five teenagers in the side, scored Trinity's second try when the great Clive Churchill, of all people, dropped the ball near his own line. Scrum-half Johnny Bullock went over for the third, collecting the ball which came out on Australia's side of the scrum and 17-year old Neil Fox kicked four goals in the 17-12 victory, Trinity's third against the Australians, to go with those of 1908-9 and 1929-30.

The new year of 1957 began with excellent news announced at the half-yearly meeting. The club's financial situation, once highly problematic, had been dramatically turned to the good. Chairman David Armitage stated that, twelve months ago, the club had debts close to £8,000. Since then, with the team playing attractive football and winning more matches, attendances at league matches had increased from around 2,500 to 4,000, while the Yorkshire Cup ties averaged 14,000. Just as important, the development fund – to be used for signing players or for ground improvements - stood at around £7,000 thanks to the pools, or lottery, which had been set up in February. It was a highly significant step which had a considerable influence on the club's immediate future.

The team was on the brink of great achievements. The local talent on which Trinity had historically relied in the club's finest eras was once more coming together to make up a formidable side. The latest to sign was 18-year old hooker Geoff Oakes from Trinity Juniors. Neil Fox was already giving indications of his talent, and winger Fred Smith used his speed to good effect in scoring four tries in the first round Challenge Cup tie against York, which was won 37-15. In the second round, however, Trinity would learn not to underestimate the opposition. Blackpool, who had recently joined the league and whom Trinity had never met before, pulled off a shock victory at Belle Vue when they triumphed 11-9.

Trinity dipped into the transfer market and signed front rower Bob Coverdale from Hull. The World Cup player was made captain for the day on his return to the Boulevard, where his experience was an important factor in the 24-18 win against the reigning champions.

But once more it was the signing of local players which would make the greater impact in the long term. When Trinity signed 24-year old Don Metcalfe from Featherstone for £3,000, the club re-established a connection going back to the earliest days. Don Metcalfe's grandfather, Jimmy, was a key player in the 1909 Cup-winning side and his father, also named Jimmy, played at half back in the 1930s. Don's grandfather on his mother's side was the winger Ernest Bennett, the son of Thomas Oliver Bennett, a founder-member of the club. To extend the connection further, Don was also the nephew of international winger Stanley Smith, who left Wakefield for Leeds in 1929. Don himself, who was a member of Featherstone's 1952 Cup-winning side, lived a stone's throw from Belle Vue.

In terms of league placing, Trinity leapt nine places from the previous season to finish 1956-57 in eighth position. Frank Mortimer, with 112 goals, could have beaten Sam Lee's long-standing record if his tally had not included five from a friendly match with Warrington. In terms of consistent effort, prop Derek Harrison's record of having played 45 out of 46 matches was an impressive one. The A team continued to figure among the best in the league and, though losing in the Yorkshire Senior Competition final and the championship semi-final, they ended the season as league leaders. With the development fund producing £300 a week, the Committee was able to get work started on providing covered accommodation at the Agbrigg end of the ground, which was completed by the end of the year. During the close season, Arthur Fletcher, the remaining link with the great team of the immediate post-war era, retired, while threequarter Colin Bell also gave up the game to concentrate on his career as a doctor. Keith Holliday was named captain of a team which was on the verge of major honours.

Thirteen – The Great Team Comes Together: 1957-59

During the 1957 close season Les Pounder took over as chairman from David Armitage and announced the Committee's intentions of continuing 'to show the greatest interest in local talent … Certain positions need strengthening and we are prepared to go into the transfer market for ready-made players of top class only. We have no intention of cluttering up the books with players not up to the standard we have set out to achieve.'

In the early part of the new season Trinity had the unusual experience of recording a long unbeaten run. In the first round of the Yorkshire Cup, Halifax were edged out 19-16 after having a man sent off. Neil Fox was responsible for sixteen of Trinity's points. By September the only unbeaten team in the league was Wakefield. One of the more significant victories was Wigan, who were defeated 23-16 in a match in which Albert Firth scored two tries and Les Chamberlain shrugged off three or four tacklers to score the match-winner. In the second round of the Yorkshire Cup, however, Huddersfield's 13-10 victory halted Trinity's run of fourteen consecutive wins which stretched back to the previous season. But Trinity were top of the league and Metcalfe, Holliday and Rollin all gained county selection, though the latter pair missed the Yorkshire v Lancashire match because of flu. In the league, Trinity gained revenge for their County Cup defeat with a decisive 23-9 victory over Huddersfield, a match also notable for Ken Hirst's hat-trick on his first appearance of the season and Albert Firth's amazing breakaway try. It was not until mid-October that the unbeaten league run came to an end. It happened at Odsal, never a place where fortune shone on Trinity, Bradford winning 11-10. It was the first time Wakefield had lost in the league since April, since when they had registered eighteen matches without defeat.

Former captain Bob Kelly, the Irishman who had represented Great Britain as well as Other Nationalities, was put on the transfer list at his own request. Two weeks later Trinity suffered their first home defeat of the season at the hands of Leeds, a match in which the former Hunslet, Bradford and Halifax back-rower Ken Traill made his debut. Unfortunately Traill's arrival coincided with a run of six consecutive defeats, including a 52-5 trouncing at St Helens. Traill was forever to be associated with Trinity's future successes but after playing only seven matches, the former international loose forward, aged 31, was listed at £1,500, the same fee as had been paid to Halifax. New signings included front-rowers Sam Evans from Hull KR, in an exchange deal for Bob Coverdale plus £2,000; and Mal Kirk from Featherstone, both making their debut alongside new hooker David Wakefield. Two of the most important signings resulted in the arrival of Harold Poynton, a Wakefield City Schools product and a descendant of Trinity's pre-First World War centre Tommy Poynton; and Gerry Round, an 18-year old amateur international full back from Hebden Bridge and an engineering student at Leeds University. Former international second-rower Reg Parker was transferred from Barrow for £1,000 under an arrangement that was far from ideal. Parker agreed to drive from his home at Grange-over-Sands on the Saturday morning of each match and return afterwards. It didn't last long – he was signed by Blackpool later that year.

Parker, Poynton and Oakes all made their debuts in February 1958 against league leaders St Helens in a match which saw the opening of the south stand at the Agbrigg Road end. Though 12-2 down at half-time, Trinity 're-discovered their fighting spirit.' Poynton, brought in to cover for the injured Holliday, 'revealed pace, guile and all-round natural football ability in quantities that marked him as a player who, most certainly, will go far. Was there,' asked the *Wakefield Express*, 'a more polished exhibition of collaboration and amazing understanding for a strange [i.e. unaccustomed] pair as that between [scrum-half] Rollin and [stand-off] Poynton which led to the try by Fox?' Centre Don Metcalfe also scored a try 'of individual brilliance'. Controversy, however, surrounded Parker's signing.

Yorkshire League champions 1958-59: *Back row*: DW Armitage, Joe Jones, W Simpson, SH Hadfield, F West, R Rylance, S Milner, EW Sugden (all committee), E Thomas (sec). *Middle row*: W Armour (masseur), J Booth (staff), K Traill (player-coach), K Rollin, S Smith, F Smith, D Metcalfe, A Skene, J Lindley, D Harrison, H Poynton, J Malpass (trainer), Johnny Jones (asst coach). *Front row*: S Evans, A Firth, D Lamming, W Adams, J Bullock (president), K Holliday (capt), L Pounder (chairman), D Turner, G Oakes, D Vines, N Fox

When he turned out for Trinity in that match, his registration forms had not been received by the RFL. His signing also took Trinity over the limit of 50 players on the register at any one time. As a result the club was fined £50. Almost three decades later, Reg Parker, of Blackpool Borough, became chairman of the RFL Council.

In the Challenge Cup Trinity had an easy passage into the second round, beating Doncaster, then bottom of the league, by 29-0. But, as in the previous season, they failed at the second hurdle. At Belle Vue, Wigan, the eventual Cup-winners, were the victors by 11-5, Trinity's cause not helped by the fact that both Eric Cooper and Poynton, in separate incidents, suffered concussion when trying to tackle Billy Boston.

As the famous team of the sixties began to be pieced together, Gerry Round became the latest to make his debut. It was a rare highlight in an otherwise poor team performance in the 11-0 defeat at home to Hull KR. But there were changes in the air. The new-found confidence – and increased wealth of the club - was implicit in a statement made by chairman Les Pounder at the Supporters' Club annual dinner. 'The day has gone,' he said, 'when other clubs can come to Belle Vue and steal men we have produced, then come back a week or so afterwards with the same men and give us a thrashing.'

The season was also significant for the records broken by 18-year old Neil Fox. With a total of 30 points from six goals and six tries in the 48-13 win against Doncaster, he established a new club record, passing Ron Rylance's 24-point haul against Leeds in 1945 and Ernest Pollard's of 1932. His six tries equalled Ted Bateson's record, set in 1928. A week later, in the 61-12 defeat of Batley on Good Friday, the young centre broke his newly established record by amassing 31 points from eleven goals and three tries, his goal tally also equalling those of Jimmy Metcalfe, Charlie Pollard and Harry Murphy. The records continued to tumble. A week after the Batley match, in the 40-5 victory over Dewsbury, he broke the record for the number of goals in a season before rounding off the campaign with the highest-ever haul of 344 points. That total, made up of 32 tries and 124 goals, was reached in 37 matches.

At the end of the 1957-58 season, loose forward Ken Traill, who had at first been unsettled at the club, was appointed player-coach, although Workington Town coach Jim Brough, the former Leeds player, had originally

A Trinity team of 1958: *Back row*: G Round, F Smith, A Firth, S Evans, W Adams, F Mortimer, K Holliday. *Front row*: SJ Shaw, S Smith, K Traill, K Rollin, N Fox, L Chamberlain

been sounded out about a manager's role. Johnny Malpass stayed on as trainer.

At the AGM, former player Ron Rylance was voted on to the committee despite not being a member – the first person to be elected in such a way, though not in breach of club rules, which were consequently amended the following year. He was quickly installed on the slimmed-down selection committee, which also included chairman Les Pounder, vice-chairman Stuart Hadfield, Joe Jones and Ken Traill. Former chairman Frank West became president of the Yorkshire Rugby League, following distinguished predecessors Wilf Jackson and JB Cooke.

Improved playing terms were offered to the players. Against Yorkshire clubs, a home win was worth £10, an away win £11 and a defeat £6. Against Lancashire opposition, players were paid £12 home or away.

Notable among the early season wins of 1958-59 was the 33-13 victory over Leeds at Headingley in which Fred Smith scored three tries against his old club. In the first round of the Yorkshire Cup, a 10-10 draw with Hunslet at Belle Vue was followed by a 15-11 success at Parkside in a game featuring no fewer than 41 penalties. Ken Traill, on his original ground, was in inspiring form and played a part in all three Trinity tries. The Trinity player-coach was recalled to the Yorkshire team, replacing the injured Johnny Whiteley, and turned out alongside the debutant Neil Fox.

Trinity continued to make forays into the transfer market. The Welsh second-rower or prop Don Vines was signed from Oldham for a club record fee of £4,500. A deputation was sent to Whitehaven in an attempt to sign second-rower Dick Huddart, for whom a fee of £7,000 was reportedly discussed but the Cumbrian club refused to sell. As would soon become clear, St Helens had more success in persuading Whitehaven to part with their star forward.

In the second round of the Yorkshire Cup at Hull, a late Fox goal took Trinity through by 17-16 to a home semi-final against Batley, where a laborious performance resulted in a 21-13 win after Batley had seen their scrum-half carried off in the first minute. In their sixth County Cup final since the war, Trinity donned their new jerseys of white with red and blue band, which would become so familiar through the next decade and beyond. But initially at least the new kit brought no luck. In front of 26,927 spectators at Odsal, Trinity lost 24-20 to a Leeds side whose superiority was greater than the score suggested. Half back Jeff Stevenson and centre Lewis Jones were the pick of the Leeds side, though Trinity centre Don Metcalfe had the consolation of scoring three tries.

Joby Shaw, dropped after that defeat, was transfer-listed at £3,000 and was snapped up by Halifax, where he prospered. He was selected for Great Britain, playing in the 1960 World Cup and going on tour to Australia in 1962, but was to regret missing out on playing with Trinity at Wembley. Shaw was yet another player whose heart stayed closest to Belle Vue, later saying that the early days of his career, spent in Trinity's A team, were the happiest of his life. It was there that he began to disprove his father's view that he 'would never be able to lace Marson's boots.' He recalled what life in the front row was like in the fifties and sixties.

Before transferring to Thrum Hall, Shaw played against Halifax, who had the future Trinity star Jack Wilkinson at prop and Alvin Ackerley at hooker. 'Alvin was the best hooker for getting the ball. He didn't use the loose arm and didn't expect others to either. "Oh aye and who's going to make me?" I said. So Wilky got his head under my arm and lifted my shoulder out with his head. Paddy Armour came on and put it back in.

South African Alan Skene, who formed a classic centre partnership with Neil Fox and scored 35 tries in the 1959-60 season

'Joe Egan was player-coach at Leigh. I was beating Joe for the ball at Wakefield. Jack Booth was at number eight and the pack broke up. Joe Egan went for me. Jack said, "Nah then, Joe, he's only a lad." And Joe replied: "He's getting a man's wage, isn't he?"'

Don Froggett, the lion-hearted centre who spent all his career at Belle Vue, made his first appearance since the Yorkshire Cup semi-final of 1956-57, an absence of two years. In the other centre berth, Neil Fox continued his prolific scoring, contributing, for example, five tries and four goals in the 39-12 win over Workington, a match in which Les Chamberlain broke his leg in two places.

Like other top clubs such as St Helens and Leeds, Trinity began to test the South African market. They had obviously been impressed by winger Tom van Vollenhoven's six tries against them in the 52-5 defeat at St Helens a year earlier. The first to arrive was 28-year old forward Ivor Dorrington, billed as the 'Iron Man of South African rugby'. Trinity's agent, and Wigan's as well, the former Hunslet player Ron Colin, said: 'Everyone wants a Vince Karalius in their team. Well, here is a tougher South African version. This player is a must for rugby league.' It was a ridiculous claim that Dorrington could not hope to live up to. He made his debut in the fog-bound 23-10 win over Hunslet, the first match to be televised from Wakefield. Another Western Province player, centre or winger Jan

Lotriet, arrived soon after Dorrington. Trinity's third and most successful signing, 23-year old centre Alan Skene, a Springbok who had played against France and who was also wanted by Leeds, was recommended by Dorrington. The trio had reportedly cost the club a total of £7,000 in signing-on fees. Skene and Lotriet both made their debut in the Christmas Day win at Castleford, Lotriet scoring a try made for him by Fox.

Among a number of departures, Frank Mortimer, the club's second highest points scorer at the time, after Charlie Pollard, went to Keighley for £1,500 following a seven-year career at Wakefield. Another mainstay of the team in the first half of the decade, Don Froggett, who had battled his way back from injury after injury, was given a benefit in the match against Huddersfield and briefly returned to the side. It was said of him: 'Although he has no Rugby League Challenge Cup medal to show, and no League Championship medal ... Don Froggett will go down in history as one of the best clubmen Wakefield have ever had, both for his playing ability and his loyalty.'

Froggett had joined Trinity in 1948 while still in the Army. He had played in open-age teams from the age of fifteen. 'It was a hard upbringing in those colliery teams,' he said. Committee member David Armitage, Froggett's former teacher at nearby St Catherine's School, went to see him and first suggested having a run-out with the A team before chairman Wilf Jackson gave him £800 'out of his own pocket' to sign on. Froggett remembered how difficult it had been at Belle Vue in the early fifties. 'It was so easy playing with Yorkshire or England. You didn't have to chase about all the time. At Belle Vue each man had to do three men's work. It was very hard. Tackling became a feature of my game. In those days everybody had a better pack than Wakefield, then all the youngsters came through.

'The chairman used to come into the dressing-room before the kick-off and I remember him saying, "I hope you give a good account of yourselves, but it would be an embarrassment at the bank if you won." Then the Trinity Pools got things going financially.'

There had been much talk of Wakefield-born international loose forward Derek Turner being unsettled at Oldham and wanting to move to a club nearer his Ossett home. Oldham listed him at £10,000 and though Leeds and Halifax were also interested, within two days Turner became a Wakefield player in exchange for a club record £8,000 and therefore followed his former clubmate Don Vines, who had just been selected for Wales against France, to Belle Vue.

Turner was cup-tied and could play no part in Trinity's campaign, which had begun with an 18-2 first round victory over Swinton and which continued with a draw against Hull. Thanks to a late Fox drop goal, Trinity had managed a 4-4 draw at the Boulevard, and replayed at Belle Vue, where in a bruising encounter which ended in forwards John Lindley and Jim Drake being sent off, champions Hull defeated Trinity for the first time in five meetings that season, winning 16-10.

Fred Smith twice broke the Trinity record for the highest number of tries in a season. His 1959-60 total of 38 tries (equalled by David Smith in 1973-74) remains unbeaten, as does his record of seven tries in a match

Trinity were aiming for a top four place for the first time since the 1945-46 season, but surprise defeats against Bramley and Bradford proved a setback. In fact Trinity finished fifth – coach Ken Traill therefore missing out on a £100 bonus – but they had the consolation of posting the best defensive record in the league, representing a significant improvement. Towards the end of the season, winger John Etty became the third player to be signed from Oldham, costing just £500. Etty had previously spent ten seasons at Batley, where he had been captain, before establishing an Oldham post-war record of 43 tries in a season and was to prove that there was still plenty of rugby league left in him. Remarkably, of a handful of players who have won all six winners' medals (Challenge Cup, Championship, Lancashire Cup and League, Yorkshire Cup and League), three of them played for Wakefield and Oldham: Derek Turner, John Etty and Don Vines.

Vines was named in the Great Britain side which faced France, and Neil Fox as reserve. Keith Holliday, the club captain, who had made a successful transition to scrum-half, where his defensive strength was a great asset, notched up 42 matches. Fox amassed 370 points, another club record, and Fred Smith broke the club try-scoring record with 37, surpassing Billy Simpson's total of 34, set in 1910-11. Smith also scored a record seven tries in the defeat of Keighley, beating Ted Bateson's feat of six tries in a match thirty years earlier and Fox's of the year before. Trinity finished top of the Yorkshire League, becoming Yorkshire champions for the first time in thirteen years. They also recorded a profit of £2,419 on the season, despite laying out a record £22,744 in transfer fees; signing-on fees and travel expenses for the three South Africans; and payments to players. All of this was made possible by taking a total of £24,500 from the development fund. The question of extending and improving the old stand was raised at the AGM. Chairman Les Pounder said that the committee believed that the first priority was to get a 'really good team together, a team which is going to last a long time.' The success of that team would in turn produce the funds to develop the stand. He also mentioned that half the clubs in the league owed money to the RFL, but Trinity did not owe a penny to anyone.

Fourteen – The Challenge Cup Returns to Belle Vue: 1959-63

With the possible exception of Jonty Parkin, Wakefield Trinity never had a more inspiring captain than Derek Turner, who led the team from the start of the 1959-60 season, officially succeeding player-coach Ken Traill, though Keith Holliday had fulfilled the role for most of the preceding campaign. Turner's appointment was the obvious one. At the same time, Stuart Hadfield, who had been on the committee since 1944-45, though not continuously, was elected chairman and coach Traill was given an increased incentive: £200 was promised for a top four place.

The season began brightly with a 21-14 home win over Wigan in which the leadership qualities of Turner, who scored two tries, became immediately apparent. 'So far as it was possible for an individual to win a match on his own, Derek Turner did so. Inspiration to his colleagues did not just arise from crafty leadership,' the *Wakefield Express* reported. 'It came also from a shining personal example of "this is the way it should be done".' The half backs shone too. There was no Poynton, who was injured, but 'Holliday and Rollin were always masters of the situation behind the scrum. The former's cast iron defence and deceptive running with the ball … and Rollin's speed and evasive tactics were delightful to see.'

But gratifying as that victory was, Trinity had some way to go before being able to rival champions St Helens, who handed out a lesson with a 40-7 victory at Knowsley Road. Theirs was a side with no weak links, from Austin Rhodes at full back and Jan Prinsloo and Tom van Vollenhoven on the wings to Alex Murphy at scrum-half. A formidable pack included vastly experienced props Abe Terry and Alan Prescott and the best back three in the game, Dick Huddart, Brian Briggs and Vince Karalius. Had they won, the Trinity players would have received £25 per man as a special bonus. As it was they drew £6 losing pay.

Nor could Trinity count on success in the Yorkshire Cup. They were beaten 17-14 at Halifax. But good came of it when Trinity signed Halifax's 29-year old international prop Jack Wilkinson for what some took to be an exaggerated fee of £4,500. At the same time, Trinity declared their interest in St Helens's winger Frank Carlton and there was speculation that Saints' second row Brian Briggs, originally from Stanley, might join his home town club. Among the departures, Bob Kelly was given a free transfer to Batley in recognition of his seven years' service, John Lindley was transferred to St Helens for £2,000 and fellow prop Derek Harrison also went to Batley, who paid £800. Yet another front rower, Sam Evans, who had only been at the club for just over a year but had suffered a fractured leg during that time, returned to his native city of Hull.

Trinity had the pleasure of doing the double over Wigan, who had finished second in the league the previous season, when they won 27-19 at Central Park despite a lack of possession from the scrums. Wilkinson made his debut, but it was Albert Firth who stood out, while Turner and Vines were 'remorseless in their full-blooded efforts, both in attack and defence'. But Trinity had the tables turned on them when they were on the receiving end of a double by St Helens, who won 16-2 at Belle Vue.

Stand-off Tony Thomas, from Trinity Juniors, was signed, but there was no future at Belle Vue for two of the three South Africans. Ivor Dorrington and Jan Lotriet asked to be released from their contracts. Dorrington, who had arrived with a big reputation, had made twelve first-team appearances and Lotriet just three. Dorrington commented that he had found it hard to fit into rugby league after playing union for twelve years. 'Too old and too cold,' was how he put it. But at a farewell presentation organised by the Supporters' Club, Dorrington said he was 'deeply moved by the presence of all the players at this farewell gathering. In a well-worded little speech, he referred to the grand comradeship he had found at Belle Vue and deeply regretted not having made contact earlier in life.'

Neil Fox's form would not be long in gaining recognition from the international selectors. In Wakefield's 27-5 win over Huddersfield, it was noted: 'On a day when most of the team earned laurels, Fox stood out as a great personality. His physical power is well known to Wakefield followers. And if it wasn't so well known to Huddersfield's spectators, the way he buffeted his way through three defenders to send Skene away for a try afforded the home crowd an opportunity of passing judgement on the 20-year old's claim to a place in the Great Britain side.' The centre reached 1,000 points in the 44-9 win against Hull KR the following week and a fortnight later reached 1,000 points for his club in the 31-6 win over Huddersfield, a match in which 19-year old Malcolm Sampson made his debut in the second row, with namesake Trevor Sampson (no relation) in the front row. Full back Gerry Round was also beginning to make a reputation for himself. In that same match at Fartown, 'Round's fielding of the ball, a highly skilled task on such a day, was brilliant. And his smooth style in making an extra three-quarter was impressive to see.'

At the end of November, Trinity met the Australians for the tenth time in the club's history. A crowd of over 17,000 watched Trinity register their fourth victory over the Aussies, outplaying a side which included nine test players, including the likes of Harry Wells and Reg Gasnier in the centres and Rex Mossop, Elton Rasmussen and Brian Hambly in the back three of the forwards. There to see it were Trinity's former tourists to Australia, Tommy Newbould, Jonty Parkin, Bill Horton, Charlie and Ernest Pollard, Gilbert Robinson, Mick Exley and Harry Murphy. In a stirring game, Trinity were deserved winners by 20-10, a point which the Aussies were quick to acknowledge, saying they were beaten by the better team. Firth scored Trinity's first and last tries, with Fox and Vines running in the other two, Fox also kicking four goals.

Derek 'Rocky' Turner, a feared international back row forward and Trinity's most successful captain ever. His arrival in 1959 gave the team inspirational leadership in the club's most illustrious era.

In the test series, Derek Turner had been Trinity's sole representative in the first clash at Swinton, in which he was a try-scorer, but injury prevented him from taking further part in the series. For the second test at Headingley, Neil Fox, who had scored a record 23 points for Yorkshire against the Kangaroos two months earlier, was called up to make his Ashes debut, together with Don Vines. Fox scored a try and goal, while in the decider at Wigan, the 20-year old centre accounted for fifteen of Britain's eighteen points with a try and six goals, which effectively won the series. He was accompanied in the side by Jack Wilkinson, battling it out in the front row, and Gerry Round, who

The Trinity team line-up of 1960

had been called up after less than two years in the professional game to replace Eric Fraser at full back.

Yet another international in the making, Harold Poynton, had been linked with Leeds after Holliday and Rollin had claimed the half-back positions, but, against all precedent, stayed at Belle Vue. Trinity's run of ten consecutive league wins came to an end at Swinton, but a valuable 20-2 home win over Castleford on Christmas Day was followed up by a thumping 39-5 triumph at Headingley, where, despite the muddy conditions, Trinity produced some scintillating play which Leeds were almost powerless to halt.

Some of the old inconsistencies were being ironed out as Trinity took all-comers in their stride. Hull, who would finish the season in third place, were beaten 34-9. The quality of the side was now evident as next Oldham, who had ended the previous season in fourth, were defeated 14-8 at the Watersheddings, a match in which the Trinity forwards took much of the credit. Jack Wilkinson 'tore through [Oldham's] ranks with devastating effect.' Don Vines, on his first outing at his old club in Trinity's colours, 'left locals in no doubt at all as to the conspicuous gain Wakefield had made against Oldham's severe loss in parting with the virile Welshman.'

When the draw for the Challenge Cup was made, Trinity's task could not have been harder. They were to play at St Helens, who topped the table and who had twice beaten them decisively in the league, including that 40-7 victory at Knowsley Road. As a preview of the tie, three weeks before the event, the *Wakefield Express* sounded out various Trinity personalities. 'Our boys are very confident and fully expect to win,' said chairman Stuart Hadfield. 'It won't be for lack of trying if we don't win,' admitted a slightly less confident Fred Smith. 'I think we shall beat 'em,'

Daylight training in preparation for the Cup run. *From left*: Gerry Round, Neil Fox, Jack Wilkinson, Keith Holliday, Ken Hirst, Derek Turner, Don Metcalfe, Albert Firth, John Etty, Don Vines.

Neil Fox and Saints' Tom van Vollenhoven look on as John Etty evades Brian Briggs's tackle to score one of his two tries in the first round Challenge Cup tie at St Helens. The 15-10 victory against the league leaders marked the start of Trinity's Cup supremacy.

confided Keith Holliday, while coach Ken Traill was in equally upbeat mood, saying, 'It will be tough, but the boys will do it.' Derek Turner's confidence was as unshakeable as it was inspirational. 'We shall win all right,' he said.

How well-founded Turner's prediction proved. In an unforgettable, pulsating match, Trinity, playing with an assurance that deflated the home side, went 7-0 up after 22 minutes. John Etty, whose brief was to subdue Tom van Vollenhoven on the opposite wing, earned the plaudits for his attacking feats and went over following Fox's 'shattering burst' through the Saints' defence. But on the half-hour, with Saints having closed the gap to 7-5, disaster struck when Gerry Round and Harold Poynton clashed going to take a high kick and were laid out. Round suffered a double fracture of the jaw and Poynton a deep gash over his left eye that needed four stitches. Amazingly, both returned to the fray. As play swept across the field Etty was sent over for his second try, evading Briggs' tackle and squeezing over by the corner flag. Just after half-time, when Trinity led 10-5 and with Geoff Oakes dominating the scrums, Jack Wilkinson scored his first try for the club. Despite a converted try from Austin Rhodes, Trinity were clearer victors than the 15-10 score suggested, as most of the 29,371 spectators must have agreed. Led by the imposing Turner, Wakefield 'attacked with precise handling movements and thrilling individual thrusts … which had supporters going wild with excitement… Just as the winners' aggressive tactics robbed the home team of the initiative, so Trinity's defence crumbled most of the Saints' attacking moves.' Typical of his sportsmanship, Saints' captain Alan Prescott wrote to Ken Traill: 'On behalf of my team and myself may I say many thanks for the wonderful game you gave us last Saturday. Will you please convey to your boys all my best wishes for success in future rounds, and hope that this is your Wembley year.' Prescott's wishes were more than realised as with that match Trinity entered the most celebrated phase of their history.

Both Harold Poynton (left) and Malcolm Sampson (right) missed the 1960 Cup final through injury. Half back Ken Rollin signs Sampson's plaster cast as chairman Stuart Hadfield looks on.

In the second round, Trinity were again drawn away in Lancashire, this time at Widnes. Though the visitors created the best chances, Keith Holliday twice had tries disallowed before the match was decided by a single try in the second half. It took a blind-side burst by Holliday, direct from a scrum, to settle the issue as the scrum-half released Etty on a 30-yard sprint to the line. With a Fox penalty, Trinity won 5-2, after the forwards had once more put in a mighty stint. Turner and Vines 'kept up a non-stop barrage', and Wilkinson 'rattled those who had the misfortune to be in line to stop him.'

Between the second and third rounds, Turner, Fox and Wilkinson were all selected to play in the Great Britain team to play France in Toulouse in a match full of controversy and fluctuating fortunes. The scoreline favoured one side, then the other, and finally France emerged as 20-18 winners, but not before Turner had been sent off for his part in a huge brawl.

Trinity faced another tough away tie in the third round, in which they were pitted against Whitehaven, who were aiming for a top four spot in the league and, until the week before, had not lost in eleven matches. Trinity had played Whitehaven in only three seasons of the club's twelve-year history but were out to avenge the shock first-round defeat of six years earlier. In front of an all-ticket crowd of 18,619 – still a record for the Recreation Ground - Whitehaven's veteran full back John McKeown kept the home club in the game with precision goal-kicking. The first half was a particularly stormy affair, with no fewer than seven forwards spoken to by the referee. Trinity led by just 8-4 at the interval, thanks to tries from Fred Smith – a signature back pass from Poynton to Fox sparking the move - and Malcolm Sampson and a goal from Fox. It was Turner who, leading from the front as usual, swung the match decisively in Wakefield's favour. He crashed over the line to put Trinity 11-4 up before McKeown raised the tension with three penalties, reviving the home side's chances of an upset. But the Wakefield captain, through sheer strength and willpower, ploughed straight through the defence for his second try just before the hour, which, goaled by Fox from the touchline, effectively settled the issue. A late try from Skene, converted by Fox, gave a final score of 21-10.

Trinity had reached the semi-final for the first time since 1947 but a hard task lay ahead. Featherstone occupied third place in the league table, just behind Trinity and would provide stiff opposition, even though they were without four key players, including ex-Wakefield loose forward Colin Clifft. Trinity prepared themselves for the clash at Odsal by staying on the Thursday and Friday at Harrogate. A crowd of over 55,000 witnessed a typical cup semi-final. Wakefield could count themselves lucky to be 3-2 ahead at half-time, thanks to an Etty try from Turner's pass after Fox had made a powerful surge. In the second half, Skene went over to finish Sampson's break, well backed up by Poynton, before Etty crossed for his second - and fifth in the Cup run – after brushing off defenders on a strong run to the line. 'This was Etty's finest hour,' wrote Arthur Brooks in the *Sunday Pictorial*. With Fox landing just one of seven goal attempts, Trinity won 11-2 and sent Featherstone to their third successive semi-final defeat. Poynton and Sampson – the latter rated by Brooks as the best forward prospect in rugby league at that time - were the pick of the Wakefield side, while in defence Metcalfe, as in the previous round at Whitehaven, tackled fearlessly.

Featherstone had the consolation of beating Trinity in a league match at Belle Vue the week after, but that defeat did not prevent Wakefield from becoming Yorkshire League champions, which they sealed with a 28-5 victory over Bradford.

But in the run-up to the Wembley final against Hull, who had beaten Oldham in the other semi, Trinity had the misfortune to lose the services of two players. Blind-side prop Malcolm Sampson, still only twenty, was injured in a road accident and broke his wrist. Harold Poynton's shoulder injury, despite the best efforts of physio Paddy Armour, was not responding to treatment, ruling him out of the final.

It was Trinity's second Wembley final, their fourth Challenge Cup final in all. In three of them Hull formed the opposition: Trinity won in 1909 and lost in 1914. Hull, who were appearing in their second successive final, having lost to Wigan in 1959, also faced Trinity in the Championship semi-final in the week before the Cup final. In a game of few highlights, Trinity went through by 24-4.

Trinity were clear favourites to lift the Challenge Cup for the first time since 1946, facing an injury-hit Hull who had four forwards missing as well as their full back and goal-kicker. The Queen and Prince Philip looked on as, within three minutes of the kick-off, Trinity stand-off Ken Rollin, with a quick change of direction, made an electrifying burst from deep within his own half, kicked past the full back and picked up to claim the opening try, Neil Fox having begun the scoring with a penalty. Hull struck back when centre Stan Cowan crossed direct from a scrum and ex-Trinity prop Sam Evans converted to level the scores. Fox put Trinity ahead again with a penalty on the quarter-hour, the last score of an error-strewn first half.

The second period was an entirely different matter. Hull, sparked by hooker Tommy Harris, had their moments but Trinity cut loose, following Ken Traill's half-time instructions. 'Traill told the forwards they'd done enough work and should give the ball to the backs,' recalled John Etty. Don Vines, Rollin and Alan Skene were all involved as Fox went on a diagonal run to the line. Skene, not to be outdone by Rollin's first-half effort, picked up a pass on the half-volley near his own 25, swept through the defence and eluded the full back to score a sparkling solo try. In the last quarter of the match Trinity unleashed all their attacking strength to run in five more tries, all improved by Fox. With Lance Todd trophy winner Harris off the field concussed and partially blinded, Turner broke from inside his own 25 and sent Keith Holliday to the line. Four minutes later the Trinity captain took Wilkinson's pass to release Skene for his second try. In another thrilling passage of play, Gerry Round collected a loose ball ten yards

Neil Fox beats the Hull cover defence to score one of his two tries. Fox's twenty points in the match established a Cup final record.

A view of the Trinity bench in front of the Royal Box, Wembley 1960. *From left*: Paddy Armour, Eddie Thomas, Harold Poynton, Ken Traill, Jack Booth. *In front*: Don Metcalfe, Dave Lamming

The victorious Wakefield team. *From left*: Geoff Oakes, Les Chamberlain, Keith Holliday, Albert Firth, John Etty, Jack Wilkinson, Derek Turner, Don Vines, Neil Fox, Fred Smith, Ken Traill. *In front*: Alan Skene, Ken Rollin

from his own line, beat off two tacklers and set off down the touchline as far as half-way, where the supporting Fox took over and finished behind the posts to score Trinity's fourth long-range try, confounding the critics who questioned his pace. The scoring spree continued almost to the final whistle as Fred Smith jinked through and sprinted to the line to equal his own club try-scoring record, before Holliday again glided past the overworked Hull defence for the eighth try.

In a spectacular final, Trinity's 38 points to 5 created a new highest score which stood for 39 years, while Neil Fox claimed a still unbeaten individual points-scoring record with twenty.

When the team returned to Wakefield on the Monday evening, the streets were thronging with supporters from Westgate Station to the Town Hall. Wakefield had never seen anything like it, they said, not even in 1946. 'When the train drew in at the station, a roar went up which could be heard at the Town Hall,' the *Wakefield Express* reported. A decorated brewery wagon with the team aboard, preceded by the Nostell Colliery band, made its way up Wood Street to the civic reception. At the Town Hall, the police linked arms to hold back the press of supporters eager to see the players appear on the balcony and hold the Cup aloft. 'Rocky' Turner, never one to exaggerate, told the crowd, 'We have a good team spirit, a good coach, a good committee and some very good supporters.'

The league and cup double was within Trinity's reach. At Odsal the following Saturday, in front of 82,087 spectators - more than at Wembley - the Cup-winners clashed with Wigan, who had finished fourth in the league, eight points adrift of second-placed Wakefield, who had already beaten their opponents twice. Trinity made a fine start as Fred

Smith touched down after only three minutes to establish a new club try-scoring record of 38. But disaster struck when Neil Fox was injured ten minutes later and spent the rest of the game as a passenger on the wing. Wigan did not cross Trinity's line until just before half-time but the second half was one-sided, with Billy Boston and Eric Ashton both ending up with two tries and Fred Griffiths kicking six goals in the 27-3 upset. For the first time in over two years, Fox had not managed to score, although he still finished the season as the league's leading points scorer, as he would also do in 1961-62 and 1963-64. Alan Skene's 35 tries in the season showed how fruitful was the right-side pairing with Fred Smith, the only try-scorer in the club's history who was above the South African, until David Smith equalled his namesake's record.

At the end of the season, Brian Briggs, the former York and Huddersfield international second rower, became the latest player after Derek Turner and Fred Smith to return to his native city when he signed from St Helens for £5,000. Briggs made his first appearance in the first match of the 1960-61 season when Trinity defeated Swinton 17-7. After eight years at Wakefield, barrel-chested prop Wilf Adams went to Hunslet for a fee of £1,100. Full back Don Metcalfe, unsure of his future, applied, along with ex-Trinity players Don Froggett and Harry Murphy, for the position of coach at Hunslet but returned to Belle Vue a month later.

The 1959-60 season had been widely spoken of as the club's best-ever, although, in terms of honours, the 1945-46 team carried off the same two trophies – the Challenge Cup and the Yorkshire League. But Billy Stott's men had finished third in the league and went out of the play-offs in the semi-finals, whereas Turner's team came second – the club's highest ever position – and reached the Championship final. It was certainly true that the club had never spent so much money putting a side together. It was reckoned that the team had cost £33,000 to build, with 45 per cent of income going on players' wages. In spite of the huge expense, the club showed a profit on the season of £4,629 and had £11,000 in the bank. That had been made possible by the money produced by the pools, which, in five years, had yielded over £53,000. For the first time the club was generating significant revenue from a source other than the turnstiles. But also, as a result of the previous season's success, Trinity now had almost 3,000 members, believed to be the highest figure in the club's history. It was a time when it seemed that all of Wakefield, at every level of society, wanted to be associated with Trinity.

Naturally enough, there were high expectations of the 1960-61 season, but the campaign got off to a patchy start. In the defeat at Warrington, Keith Holliday suffered a double fracture of the jaw and Brian Briggs a cracked rib only a week after making his debut. In the first round of the Yorkshire Cup against Halifax at Belle Vue, the two sides battled through a thunderstorm, hail and driving rain. Fox, injured and hobbling along the wing as in the Championship final, scored the only points of the game after Ken Rollin sent him over the Halifax line. Fox, Fred Smith and Derek Turner were in the Yorkshire side beaten 21-20 by Lancashire at Belle Vue and Harold Poynton made his county debut against Cumberland, alongside those three, plus Jack Wilkinson. Turner and Wilkinson were selected in the World Cup team, with Fox and Geoff Oakes as reserves, while Paddy Armour was appointed team physio. Don Vines, who had been at the club less than a year, wanted to leave and was put on the transfer list. St Helens swiftly signed him at the asking price of £8,000, though he did not play in Saints' 18-5 defeat by Trinity at Knowsley Road.

In the second round of the Yorkshire Cup, Trinity beat Bramley 40-6 and then scraped home against Keighley in the semi-final. Unusually, the match was played under floodlights at Odsal in front of a disappointing crowd of 6,894. Trinity owed their success to the quick thinking of Les Chamberlain who, a yard from the line, played the ball forward to himself and plunged over, Fox converting for a 5-4 victory with two minutes to spare.

In the final at Headingley, attended by 17,000 spectators, Trinity were too good for Huddersfield despite not playing at their best. Two of Trinity's four tries came from interceptions, Fred Smith opening the scoring after seizing a stray pass. Fox followed up his own high kick and with the ball bouncing generously for him he strode away to claim the second try. Etty went over at the corner from Briggs's pass before Fox claimed his second, intercepting on the Huddersfield 25, and Trinity lifted the trophy for the seventh time, winning by 16-10.

On Boxing Day Trinity beat Leeds 14-9 at Headingley despite having five players missing. The crowd of over 30,000 saw half backs Poynton and Rollin set up the victory, with Metcalfe outstanding in defence at full back. The versatile Albert 'Budgie' Firth was selected on the wing and given the job of marking Leeds's top-scoring South African winger Wilf Rosenberg. Turner, who played in both internationals against France, once more led by example and scored a typically storming try, tearing through the opposition ranks.

Trinity were joint leaders with Leeds, but their form – not helped by injuries - was at times disappointing and had not yet reached the standard of the previous season. The committee, continuing in their search for new players, brought 20-year old second rower Eric Payne from Yorkshire Copper Works RU club to the club and were seriously interested in signing Wigan's international winger Mick Sullivan, but St Helens stepped in and paid £11,000 for his transfer. Instead Saints' South African winger Jan Prinsloo arrived at Wakefield for a new club record fee of £9,000, followed by stand-off or centre Roy Bell from Featherstone for £3,000.

South African winger Jan Prinsloo was signed from St Helens in 1961 for a club record fee of £9,000.

Trinity began their defence of the Challenge Cup with a not entirely convincing 11-3 home win over York. The second round brought together the Cup-holders and the current champions Wigan in one of those matches between the two teams which have become part of Belle Vue folklore. The eagerly anticipated tie was made all-ticket and limited to 26,000. Unfortunately the persistent rain made conditions difficult and the only points came, early in the first half, from a Fred Griffiths penalty goal, taken directly in front of the Trinity posts. Try as they might, Trinity could find no way through the Wigan defence. With Wigan's heavyweight forwards Barton, Collier and McTigue dominant, they kept possession for long periods and hung on in an increasingly tense final period to achieve a 2-0 passage into the next round.

Prinsloo made his debut in the 11-5 defeat by Hull three weeks earlier and with the new signing installed in the left wing position, where he formed a powerful partnership with Fox, the popular John Etty, at the age of 34, decided to retire. This gentlemanly player, who had played eight times for Yorkshire and had made such a telling contribution to Trinity's Cup run the year before, bowed out against Dewsbury, the club for which he had made his senior debut at the age of 17. Etty scored two tries in the 36-6 win, which saw Eric Payne and 18-year old loose forward David Blakeley make their debuts.

Chairman Stuart Hadfield headed off to South Africa, ostensibly in pursuit of the Springbok forward Doug Hopwood, whom Wigan were already chasing. Hadfield was reported to have said that he was prepared to offer between four and six thousand pounds for Hopwood's signature, return fares for him and his family, £20 per week playing terms, accommodation and a job. Back in England, president Frank West countered the suggestion that Hopwood could ever have been paid a higher wage than the rest of the team and thought Hadfield must have been misquoted. 'Differential payments at Wakefield stopped many years ago,' he said. 'Players are all paid alike.' However the main target was not Hopwood but a 25-year old centre or stand-off, a Springbok triallist who turned out to be Colin Greenwood.

The Trinity team following their Yorkshire Cup final victory over Leeds at Odsal, November 1961. *At back*: Eric Payne, Geoff Oakes, Neil Fox, Harold Poynton, Milan Kosanovic, Dave Lamming, Keith Holliday, Johnny Malpass. *In front*: Eddie Thomas, Harry Wilkinson, Ken Rollin, Alan Skene, Colin Greenwood, Gerry Round, Fred Smith, Derek Turner, Jack Wilkinson, Don Vines, Brian Briggs, Albert Firth, Ken Traill, Paddy Armour

Despite the quality of their team, Trinity continued to disappoint their supporters all too frequently. Hull KR recorded their biggest post-war victory over Trinity when they won 19-2 at Craven Park. Nevertheless, by April the team was still in contention for a top four play-off spot. A titanic struggle against fellow-contenders St Helens on a Monday evening at Belle Vue ended in a 4-2 win for Trinity. Former Saints winger Jan Prinsloo had two tries disallowed but Round made up for that by landing a match-winning penalty three minutes from full time. But despite a 10-2 win at Post Office Road in which Albert Firth and Prinsloo scored brilliant tries, a home reverse at the hands of the same opponents dented Trinity's hopes. It was followed up by a 17-13 defeat at Fartown, as a result of which Huddersfield became the only team to do the double over Wakefield that season. A bizarre match at Doncaster, which was won easily enough by 32-9, with Prinsloo scoring a hat-trick, ended in six players being sent off, four of them Trinity men. Briggs was sent off for fighting, Turner for 'talking back' to the referee, Wilkinson for 'talking out of turn' and Metcalfe, who had never been sent off in his nine-year career, for striking. Turner and Briggs were suspended for two matches and the others for one. But Turner was particularly incensed by the decision, claiming that as captain he had a right to ask the referee for clarification and, since he had only just returned from suspension, felt he was receiving undue attention from referees. Trinity's play-off aspirations finally came to grief with a 15-8 home defeat by Leeds in the last match of the season, which meant that they finished in seventh place in the league, much lower than had been hoped for at the start of the season.

On Sunday April 9, history had been made when the Belle Vue ground was used for the first time on the Sabbath, when a semi-final of the Wakefield and District Amateur Rugby League Open-Age Cup took place. In another historic move, Trinity backed a proposal for two divisions to operate from the 1962-3 season, with four teams to be promoted and four relegated.

The team's failure to go beyond the second round of the Challenge Cup and inability to reach the Championship play-offs resulted in a drop in profits, despite the the Yorkshire Cup success. The A team, which had won the Yorkshire Senior Competition and seen a good deal of winning pay, was also a source of greater expenditure. Profits were down by £2,600 on the previous season. A total of almost £22,000 was paid out of the development fund for transfer and signing-on fees, while transfer fees received amounted to £9,575. In his report on the season, secretary-manager Eddie Thomas stated that the sparkle of the 1959-60 season had been seen too rarely, despite the double over St Helens, home wins against Wigan and Warrington and away wins against Leeds and Hull. 'The incentives to our first team players have not yielded the hoped-for returns,' he said.

Hooker Milan Kosanovic, who was born in the former Yugoslavia and settled in Halifax after the war, was signed from Bradford, for whom he had played six seasons during which he had represented Yorkshire against Australia. Don Vines made a quick return from St Helens after just one season, at a fee slightly less than the selling price of £8,000. After settling his differences with the club, Ken Traill remained as first-team coach while also being involved in the promotion of the pools.

World record points scorer Neil Fox on his way to collecting three of the 22 (four tries, five goals) he registered in the 40-18 victory over Warrington in the first round of the Challenge Cup, February 10, 1962

Colin Greenwood made a try-scoring debut in the 18-12 win over York, though not all supporters were pleased with the spate of signings. 'Wakefield have too much money to throw around,' complained one supporter. 'Give your own lads a chance, like the ones who got you to Wembley.' Another thundered: 'It appears that the Trinity Football Club have money to burn. The players are paid too much …' The following week Trinity beat Bradford 73-5 in the first round of the Yorkshire Cup, a club record for the competition, easily beating the previous highest score of 43-4 against York in 1950. Trinity's highest league score and margin remained the 71-0 defeat of Leeds in September 1945. In the Bradford tie, Gerry Round equalled the club record of eleven goals in a match – and missed eight others. Among Trinity's seventeen tries, four were scored by Poynton and three by Skene.

Fox, Smith, Wilkinson, Turner and Firth were all selected in the county side, but to everyone's surprise Fox was dropped from the Trinity team, apparently for 'lack of form'. Supporters envisaged their prolific centre and undoubted matchwinner being transfer-listed and, unthinkably, being sold to rivals St Helens or Wigan. They were relieved when the unfortunate decision had no repercussions and Fox was quickly restored to the side.

Albert Firth had thoroughly deserved his county cap and the move from second row to cover for the long-term injured Malcolm Sampson at prop did not deter him. In the 29-15 victory over Hull it was noted: 'The forward of the afternoon was again Albert Firth. Even the testing blind-side prop position cannot tax his amazing energy enough to blow him down! On top of his work in the front row, he obliged with two tries that would have done credit to a back.' The first was a 30-yard dash to the line, the second an even more spectacular 70-yard sprint.

Trinity met Hull again the week after when the sides clashed in the second round of the Yorkshire Cup. It was a match which had an unexpected twist at the end. Trailing 7-6, Trinity snatched the lead four minutes from full time when Fox kicked a penalty. But that wasn't all. When Hull were awarded a penalty and the chance to grab victory, Bateson failed with the kick but Wakefield loose forward Dave Lamming gathered the ball and set off upfield, transferring to Smith in a move which ended with Skene going over near the posts and Fox converting for a 13-7 win.

In the league, champions Leeds were Trinity's next victims when they went down 21-4 at Belle Vue, but, despite Wakefield's excellent form, only Derek Turner was chosen to play in the Great Britain side to face New Zealand at Headingley. The three South Africans, Skene, Prinsloo and Greenwood, were, however, selected in a Rugby League XIII to play a France XIII in Paris. Apart from other considerations, former rugby union players had been chosen because the RFL wanted to experiment with a new play-the-ball which was very similar to a rule in force in the 15-a-side code.

In the semi-final of the Yorkshire Cup, Trinity brushed York aside, winning 24-4 with Turner and Firth scoring late tries from half-way, while Round gave another international class performance. In the 38-7 defeat of lowly Bradford, leading try-scorer Jan Prinsloo went over six times, three of them in a nine-minute spell just before the interval.

For the first time since the war, Trinity defeated the touring New Zealanders. Watched by 16,528 fans, the Kiwis were beaten 20-7, Trinity's tries coming from Fox, Prinsloo, Skene and Holliday, with Fox kicking three goals and Round one.

Not for the first time, chairman Stuart Hadfield had differences of opinion with other members of the committee, and specifically the selection committee. He resigned, saying that others – Messrs, Simpson, Pounder and Milner - were 'ganging up' on him. 'If the members will not take advice from the coach or myself there is no useful purpose in remaining on the committee,' he said, before returning the following week.

In the Yorkshire Cup final at Odsal, Trinity faced Leeds, who had beaten them in three out of four previous finals. Leeds were below strength and Trinity lacked the injured Prinsloo. The start of the match was delayed in extraordinary circumstances. Leeds had arrived without boots, which necessitated a dash back to Headingley under police escort. Whether or not the delay affected Leeds was impossible to say, but Wakefield, with Kosanovic winning twice as many scrums as his opposite number, won deservedly 19-9. Turner charged over from Vines's pass, Skene touched down from Poynton's well-judged kick and Smith took advantage of a poor clearance kick by Jones. Fox kicked five goals, most of them from near touch, as Trinity took the trophy for the second year running and the eighth time overall.

Towards the end of the year, with a 12-10 home win over St Helens, Trinity rattled up their seventeenth consecutive win. With only one defeat, they were second in the league to Wigan on points difference. In the 58-5 win over Dewsbury, Fox again equalled the club record of eleven goals and headed the list of goal-kickers. In the try-scorers list, Trinity had seven in the top thirty: Jan Prinsloo third, behind Billy Boston and Tom van Vollenhoven, Fred Smith fifth, Alan Skene ninth, Albert Firth seventeenth, Neil Fox twenty-first and Keith Holliday and Harold Poynton twenty-fourth equal.

In January 1962, Trinity established a new post-war record for a Yorkshire club by registering nineteen wins in a row and by the end of the month, with a 27-7 win over Keighley, they equalled Warrington's feat of twenty-one successive wins. Ken Hirst, in a rare first-team outing in the Keighley match, helped them do it by scoring four tries. By February the record was extended to twenty-two as Trinity ground out an 8-7 win at Halifax, Alan Skene scoring the match-winner two minutes from the end.

In the Challenge Cup, 19,330 fans saw no less a side than Warrington swept aside at Belle Vue as Trinity played 'glorious' football to win 40-18, posting ten tries to four, Neil Fox alone scoring four of them. The *Express*, looking to the forthcoming tour, said of the international centre: 'The Australians are certainly going to see a player fit to join the legendary figures of the past. Was there anything more attractive than Neil's strong, straight running and exhibition of strength as he either handed off or crashed his way through a bunch of opponents?' The reporter was equally enthusiastic about Fox's centre partner. 'And that other great artist, Alan Skene? Pace and skill in every step taken by his twinkling feet. Backed by body swerve and a most deceptive change of pace, he demonstrated quite plainly that he is one of the greatest exponents of the code. But in this game the entire Trinity side functioned like a mammoth, precise and powerful…'

Surprisingly, the run of victories came to an end at Batley, where a dull 0-0 draw ensued, so that Trinity's record now became a 24-match unbeaten sequence. League leaders Wigan were vanquished 14-11 by a side lacking Prinsloo, Kosanovic and Vines. A post-war record crowd of 27,614 witnessed Trinity take a 9-0 lead before losing it to trail 11-9 with six minutes left to play. The match-winning try came when Skene made a burst and passed to Smith, who lobbed the ball back inside for Fox to touch down and add the goal. Turner and Briggs came in for special praise for 'their energy in attack and their equally insatiable appetite for tackling.' Trinity's men received £30 winning pay, more than twice as much as the regular pay-packet for a home win.

Loose forward David Lamming, a constructive player who would have commanded a regular place in most first teams, but had to settle for covering for the back three, was the subject of a surprise enquiry by Featherstone and was transferred for the asking price of £4,000. The fee was welcomed in getting Trinity out of a freshly dug 'financial hole'.

Wakefield were due to play Wigan in the return fixture the following week, but because the Central Park side had six men in the Great Britain side to face France – Trinity had Fox and Round on duty - they were allowed to postpone the match. A fixture backlog loomed for Trinity, who had to rearrange five games from earlier in the season. Chairman Stuart Hadfield made an unprecedented offer to Wigan to consent to the original schedule. Regardless of what the RFL would have made of it, let alone Wakefield supporters, he proposed dropping three first-team players in order to equal the five Wigan would have unavailable. The offer was not accepted.

In the second round of the Challenge Cup, Trinity faced Blackpool for only the second time. On the only previous encounter, five years earlier, Blackpool had run up a shock 11-9 victory at the same stage of the Cup. But on their first visit to the St Anne's Road ground, Trinity made no slip-up as Fox, with two tries and five goals, scored all Wakefield's points in the 16-4 win.

The rearranged league match at Wigan took place on the Monday before the two teams were set to clash again in a third-round Cup tie at Belle Vue on the Saturday. Trinity's unprecedented 28-match winning run finally came to a halt at Central Park in front of 30,674 spectators, which was the highest attendance for any match up to that point in the season. Wigan rested Griffiths and Boston but Wakefield had only four first-team regulars on duty in the 28-9 defeat.

The Cup tie was a different matter altogether. The two sides were back almost to full strength, with Wigan paying Trinity the compliment of switching Billy Boston to centre to mark Neil Fox and Eric Ashton to stand-off to oppose Harold Poynton. The match was as tense as a cup tie between the league leaders and their second-placed challengers was expected to be, with the added interest that Trinity were out to avenge the 2-0 defeat suffered in the second round at the hands of Wigan only the year before. Belle Vue's post-war attendance record was broken again as 28,524 spectators watched the sides cancel each other out in a first half which ended 2-2. But soon after the restart Wigan captain Ashton dropped a most fortunate goal, the ball hitting an upright before bouncing off the cross bar into the in-goal. When Skene was off the field for a second time, having come in for some rough treatment, Holliday worked the blind-side with Briggs in support. The second rower passed to Smith, who dived over at the corner to give Trinity a 5-4 lead - and so the score remained for fully half an hour until the final whistle. Holliday gave a forceful display in attack and defence, Poynton eluded Ashton's attentions in a fine all-round performance,

Neil Fox, Brian Briggs, Harold Poynton and Alan Skene in the 12-6 defeat of Huddersfield in the Wembley final of 1962

Turner was determination personified, while Cumbrian forward Denis Williamson was 'as good as any forward on view' – high praise considering the calibre of both packs.

When the tour party to Australia was selected, Turner, who was named vice-captain, and Fox were seen as automatic choices. They were joined by Round, Poynton and Wilkinson, making Trinity's representation easily the highest ever. Chairman Hadfield had already been elected tour manager.

Wakefield were drawn to meet Featherstone in the Cup semi-final, as they had been two seasons earlier when Trinity went on to win the trophy. Both clubs wanted to play on a Saturday at Headingley, but the RFL ruled that they must play midweek at Odsal, which had a bigger capacity. A crowd of 43,637 turned up to see Trinity win a forward-dominated battle by 9-0. Turner was once more an inspiration, seconded by Briggs, and Hirst scored the only try of the match from Round's pass, Fox kicking three goals.

Three weeks later, as Trinity were approaching the end of a hectic schedule of rearranged matches, Featherstone were again the opponents in a league game. As both clubs had an eye on the play-offs – Featherstone were in third place – they fielded virtually two reserve teams, Trinity winning 17-9. The match was notable for the try-scoring debut of centre Ian Brooke. The two teams met again in the Championship semi-final, in which Featherstone were handicapped by the absence of five first-teamers, Trinity winning 13-8.

As the team for Wembley was announced, it was confirmed that Kosanovic, with an ankle sprain, and Vines, suffering from a thigh injury, would stand down, while Ken Hirst was preferred on the left wing to Prinsloo or Greenwood. The Cup final turned out to be a dull affair, in which Huddersfield did their best to close Wakefield down while knowing that they could not compete in an open style of football. What was most memorable in Trinity's 12-6 win was Fox's history-making three drop goals, one in the first half and the other two in the last quarter. Trinity's game was affected when Turner went off in the 17th minute, suffering concussion from Ramsden's hit, and was off the field for ten minutes. During the captain's absence there was a rare moment of exhilaration when Fox pushed off a defender and sent Hirst sprinting down the touchline. The winger somehow got the ball back to his centre, who, showing a fine turn of speed, outpaced the cover over more than 30 yards and touched down at the corner. Against the run of play, Huddersfield scrum-half Tommy Smales cut through for a try which brought the half-time score to 5-3. Fox broke the second half deadlock with his second drop goal before Briggs, who also stopped two possible try-scoring moves, provided the pass which set Hirst off on a 50-yard sprint to the line, beating two defenders and evading full back Dyson. Though Trinity always held the upper hand, Huddersfield refused to be shaken off and came back with a late try from Ramsden. Fox confirmed Trinity's superiority with a last-minute drop goal from in front of the posts and was awarded the Lance Todd trophy, with second rower Briggs second in the voting. For the second time in three years Trinity lifted the trophy and retained their record of having gone through the season undefeated by a Yorkshire club.

At the post-match banquet, held at Bailey's Hotel, the team's headquarters on Gloucester Road, Richard Harris and David Storey, star and author of *This Sporting Life*, the screen adaptation of Storey's novel, joined the players and officials. The filming, which had included crowd scenes from the third round tie against Wigan at Belle Vue, was about to resume at Wakefield's Mecca Ballroom and Dolphin pub. Wakefield born and educated, Storey had played professionally in the Leeds A team; his brother Tony had been on Trinity's books before signing for Bradford. The film was directed by Lindsay Anderson, who knew Wakefield from having put together a publicity film for the *Wakefield Express*. A detail which has since gone down in Trinity folklore was that Harris swapped his expensive sheepskin jacket (with a slight tear in the back), for Keith Holliday's Wembley jersey.

The Challenge Cup is lifted again after victory over Huddersfield. *At back*: Ken Traill, Fred Smith, Dennis Williamson, Brian Briggs, Neil Fox, Derek Turner, Jack Wilkinson, Keith Holliday (obscured), Gerry Round, Paddy Armour. *In front*: Harold Poynton, Albert Firth, Alan Skene, Ken Hirst, Geoff Oakes

Just as in 1960, the Monday evening welcome home took the form of a procession on a decorated brewery wagon, preceded by the Nostell Colliery Band. From the station they were once again cheered along Wood Street to the Town Hall for the civic reception, with players coming out on to the balcony to greet their supporters, who were numbered at 30,000.

Trinity now had a chance to win all four cups and to emulate the feat achieved by Hunslet (1907-08), Huddersfield (1914-15) and Swinton (1927-28). To do so they would once more have to beat Huddersfield, who had signally beaten league leaders Wigan at Central Park in the semi.

It turned out to be a dismal end to the season. In heavy rain and wind, Trinity failed to rise to the task and succumbed to a Huddersfield side eager for revenge for their Wembley defeat. Fartown's first try, however, should never have been. Skene shoved the ball back to Round, who was held by Ramsden and prevented from collecting it, giving winger Wicks the opportunity to pick up and score a try, superbly converted by Dyson. With Trinity scoring a fine converted try by Fox, after combining with Smith, Huddersfield led by just 7-5 at the interval. But, 'apart from the considerable promise of Fox, who used his strength most effectively on several occasions, Wakefield never looked like pulling the game round in the second half,' said the *Wakefield Express*. Huddersfield added a try by Tommy Smales and two goals from Dyson to win 14-5 in front of a 37,451 Odsal crowd, and thus deprive Wakefield of lifting all four cups as well as their record of having gone through the season unbeaten by a Yorkshire club. Fox, however, had the distinction of increasing his best-ever points total in a season to 456, making him easily the league's top points scorer.

The five Wakefield players selected to tour Australia and New Zealand in 1962. From left: Gerry Round, Jack Wilkinson, Neil Fox, Derek Turner and Harold Poynton.

Nevertheless, the season was widely regarded as the best in the club's history. In addition to their three cups, Trinity had finished the season on the same number of league points as leaders Wigan, only an inferior points difference putting them into second place. The congratulations were many. Among them were those from the Wakefield District Chamber of Trade, who in their Bulletin recognised the beneficial effects on the city: 'We congratulate them most heartily on all they have done, [for] we, as tradespeople, do well realise the fillip given to local trade by a successful football team.'

At the end of the season, Trinity accepted an offer to make a promotional tour of South Africa, where they played six exhibition matches. Thirteen Trinity players were augmented by Tom van Vollenhoven (St Helens), Wilf Rosenberg (Hull), Ted Brophy (Leigh) and Fred Griffiths (Wigan), with Alan Skene as captain. The party was accompanied by Eddie Thomas, Ken Traill and Paddy Armour. The first club side to tour the Republic, they won all their matches by big scores.

At the AGM, a question was raised about Trinity's performance in the Championship final and whether the fact that four players had been fined for a breach of club discipline at their Bridlington headquarters before the match had anything to do with the display on the field. President Frank West, chairing the meeting in the absence of Stuart Hadfield, who had left for Australia, replied that the players had done nothing wrong except to stay out late. Only one of the culprits had played in the final. From a financial point of view, it was announced that the club's assets – though profit and loss was not recorded - had swollen to over £30,000. A cheque for £5,000 had just been presented by the Supporters' Club to contribute towards the cost of the alterations being undertaken at St Catherine's School. In response to a question about ownership of the ground, it was again stated that it was the property of Wakefield Trinity Athletic Company Limited, of which the club owned 67 per cent of the shares.

In Australia, Fox and Round played in all three tests as Great Britain won the series 2-1. Only injury prevented Turner, a try scorer in the first but absent from the second, from joining them. Poynton made his debut in the second and was retained for the third, in which Turner was sent off for retaliation against prop Dud Beattie. For the New Zealand leg, Turner took over the captaincy from Eric Ashton, who returned home injured, and all five Trinity tourists, including Jack Wilkinson, plus ex-Wakefield hooker Joby Shaw, played in the second test, which was lost in the mud of Carlaw Park. Neil Fox, who kicked twelve goals in the three Australian tests, came back home with the enviable haul of 227 points in 21 appearances on tour.

Just before the start of the 1962-63 season, Bill Simpson became chairman, but within a month of his election died in hospital. He had served on the committee for three periods since 1950. With former chairman Stuart Hadfield still on tour, Ron Rylance became acting chairman.

Ken Traill was contracted as coach for a further three years, but despite the great success of the previous season, all did not go smoothly. Five players were still on the New Zealand leg of the tour when the season began, with Jack

Wilkinson and Don Metcalfe talking of retirement. Jan Prinsloo wanted to return to South Africa and Don Vines was not selected after missing training. Cumbrian forward Denis Williamson was in hospital with an infection picked up on tour in South Africa.

The biggest shock came when captain Derek Turner asked to be released in order to take up a player-coach role in Australia, where he had been promised £50 a week, a house and a good job in addition to the rugby league. At the same time, three other tourists, Neil Fox, Harold Poynton and Jack Wilkinson were in dispute with the club, claiming payment for the early season matches which they missed because they were in South Africa with the Great Britain tour party. But in view of the fact that each player who went on tour was given over £100 pocket money by the club, and because each player who went on the South African venture was paid £25, Trinity resisted their claim.

Just three signings were made, and all of them local. Roger Pearman, who had played union at school at QEGS, at college with Loughborough, and at club level with Sandal and Headingley, joined Trinity as a loose forward. Another back rower, 18-year old Bob Haigh, was signed from Trinity Juniors and 20-year old prop Ted Campbell made his debut in the 39-0 defeat of Doncaster.

This Sporting Life, based on Wakefield-born David Storey's novel of the same name, was filmed in Wakefield in 1962. In one of the scenes shot at Belle Vue, the film's leading actor, Richard Harris, runs the ball out of defence.

For the first time since 1904-5, the league was to be split into two divisions, though the early part of the season would begin with the sixteen Yorkshire clubs forming the Eastern Division and the Lancashire clubs making up the Western Division. Wakefield, having been in the top four of the previous season's Yorkshire League, were to play against the bottom four, home and away, before cross-county first and second divisions came into being.

Despite improved match fees of £14 a win, £10 a draw and £7 a defeat, whether home or away, Trinity did not have the start they had hoped for. Though they beat second division Batley, Prinsloo scoring three tries, they lost to Dewsbury with only six regular first-teamers in the side.

Symptomatic of the early-season malaise was the 34-9 defeat at Hunslet in the first round of the Yorkshire Cup. The holders lost Alan Skene with a dislocated shoulder after only eight minutes' play, but should have performed much better against a second division team. A defeat at Batley followed, but soon the key players were returning to the fold, Poynton and Turner among them. Smith, Fox and Briggs represented Yorkshire against Cumberland and Fox kicked five goals in the 22-8 victory over Lancashire at Belle Vue. Something approaching Trinity's better form came in the 45-11 defeat of lowly Bradford. 'A more impressive return could not have been wished for by either the crowd or 'Rocky' [Turner] himself. He was every inch an international with his tearaway, defence-splitting runs, a leader who inspired others by his own stirring example.'

Stuart Hadfield, who had taken over again as chairman, resolved to persuade Turner not to go to Australia.

This Sporting Life team photo: players, cast and crew. Harris stands in the middle, to the right of Turner. To the right of Harris is fellow actor Jack Watson and behind them Colin Blakeley; to the left is director Lindsay Anderson (with cap).

'Turner is irreplaceable at the moment and in the foreseeable future, both as a leader and for his greatness as a footballer,' said the *Wakefield Express*.

But two of Trinity's South Africans decided to leave. Alan Skene, whose litheness and pace had complemented Neil Fox's power so effectively, made his last appearance in the 16-3 win over Swinton in November. His three-year contract was up and the RFL bye-laws did not allow a second signing-on payment. Jan Prinsloo was also set on going home. The winger had played just 48 games for Trinity since signing from St Helens for a record fee of £9,000 eighteen months previously, during which time he had scored 45 tries – the highest strike rate of any Trinity player. According to the *Wakefield Express* 'the desire of Prinsloo to return to South Africa has been a talking point ever since he failed a fitness test for the Wembley final in May.' Prinsloo finally took the matter into his own hands in late December when he, his wife and two children suddenly left the country, their departure hastened by the death of his father-in-law and illness of his mother-in-law. In an interview given at the airport, Prinsloo said: 'There has been bad feeling on both sides since I received a groin injury last October. I have played only eight games out of sixteen this season because of this injury. I've tried to get away for six months but the club said I had a life-long contract. This is nonsense. I signed nothing when I joined them. I don't think the trouble I've had will stop me playing in South Africa.'

St Helens announced that they were keen to sign Harold Poynton, offering £7,000, then upping their bid to £8,000 for the stand-off, to which the club appeared to agree, though the player himself did not want to leave Wakefield. Whitehaven, meanwhile, were interested in signing Keith Holliday, who, not wanting to play centre again and unable to displace Ken Rollin at scrum-half, had played A-team football. Only the difficult financial situation, about to get worse with ground reconstruction work priced at between £12,000 and £14,000, made Trinity consider such offers. The *Wakefield Express* received many letters in full support of keeping the half-back pair, who had never sought to play elsewhere. But although that problem was soon resolved and with Fox and Turner back in the side after playing for Great Britain against France, the turmoil persisted. Second rower Albert Firth, who had also been used successfully at prop, was later transferred to York for £3,000.

By comparison with the previous season, the 1962-63 campaign proved disappointing and supporters raised numerous questions about the team, payments to players, why the club had financial difficulties and the lack of communication between the committee and the fans, with chairman Stuart Hadfield coming in for the major share of criticism. The *Wakefield Express* did not hold back, either, commenting on what it regarded as the unsatisfactory relations with the press: 'How different is the present attitude from that of all previous chairmen of the club without exception since the time of those immortals Mr JB Cooke and Mr Arthur Bonner.' There was further criticism of 'the predicament into which a fabulously wealthy sports organisation should land itself.'

At the half-yearly meeting the chairman answered some of those criticisms by saying that Trinity had had five players on tour and after returning home they had felt tired and had taken a while to recover their form. But Hadfield believed that supporters would soon see a different Trinity and was confident that they would secure a place in the top four.

Some of the Trinity players had been involved in the filming of *This Sporting Life*, which went on general release in mid-March. The director, Lindsay Anderson, and the author of the novel from which the film was adapted, David Storey, as well as players, officials and dignitaries, attended the Northern premiere in Leeds. Richard Harris was unable to attend but wrote a letter which was read out at the screening:

'Dear Dreadnoughts,
Please forgive me for not coming up to Leeds for the opening of "This Sporting Life", which I had been looking forward to so much. As Lindsay [Anderson] will explain, I am in the middle of rehearsal for "Diary of a Madman", in which, although I am suitably cast, I find that after the bashing I got in Belle Vue, I have difficulty in retaining my lines. As it is a two-hour show – and there is no one else in the cast to fill in for me (which I could always blame Rocky Turner for throwing me a bad pass) – in this I am on my own.
I hope you enjoy the picture which you and everybody else up North helped to make a success and to show the world where the blood and guts of England really lie.
On reflection, I personally feel some of the happiest moments of my career were spent on the field of Belle Vue – not to mention those late night sessions at Ken's [Traill] or Brian's [Briggs] and, of course, not forgetting Fred Smith's great try against Wigan, which he so kindly "lent me" for the picture.
When the play comes off I hope to travel up North to see you again – or better still to take a bath with you all at Wembley after your next victory.
So Keep Right On To The End Of The Road.
May God bless you all.
Richard.'

Harris had given one of his most powerful performances in the film, for which he was nominated for an Oscar and won a best actor award at the Cannes Film Festival. A former rugby union player in Ireland, he had appeared to enjoy his involvement in rugby league more than the character he portrayed. The rugby league public were intrigued by the attention which the film brought. It won great critical acclaim but it presented a bleak view of the game, accentuating its brutality and mercenariness.

For three months, between December 15 and March 9, freezing weather meant that Trinity would play no matches at all, which precipitated a huge fixture file-up. New signing Gert 'Oupa' Coetzer, who had arrived on trial from South Africa, must have wondered what he had let himself in for. The 23-year old former rugby union

Centre Ian Brooke eludes the defence in Trinity's 25-10 victory over Wigan in the 1963 Challenge Cup final

centre or winger had represented Orange Free State on more than forty occasions and had played rugby league with Johannesburg Celtic and Bloemfontein Aquilae, for whom he had played against Wakefield on their promotional tour of South Africa.

Because of the bad weather, Trinity's Cup campaign got off to a late start with a midweek match in difficult conditions at Odsal. By scoring five unconverted tries to one, Trinity went through to the next round by 15-3, but their second round performance did not give much cause for confidence. With both sides scoring two tries, Trinity were fortunate to scrape home against Liverpool City, another lowly club, winning 14-12 at Belle Vue.

In between rounds, Coetzer was beginning to make his mark, scoring three tries in the home defeat of Leeds. Even more significantly, Neil Fox reached 2,000 points for the club, scored in 233 matches. The game, though, had an unsavoury aspect. Leeds full back Ken Thornett felled Trinity's Ian Brooke with a head-high tackle as the young centre was heading for the line, but the Leeds man got away with a warning from the referee. Four minutes later, Thornett himself was being stretchered off. Despite the battering he received, Brooke gave another encouraging display. 'His work alongside the super centre play of Neil Fox must have led Trinity officials to realise they were watching a great prospect.' They must also have realised that they had an obvious replacement for Alan Skene.

For the third time Trinity faced second division opponents in the Cup when they travelled to York and came away with a 9-9 draw after being 9-0 down. An Albert Firth try and three goals from Vic Yorke put the home side ahead before a Fred Smith try and two goals by Fox brought Trinity to within two points of their opponents, but it was not until six minutes from full time that a Fox penalty levelled the scores. The replay at Belle Vue was not quite the formality some had expected. York went ahead 5-2 after a quarter of an hour, but Coetzer equalised with a try and then touched down a second time after breaking free of a tackle. On the hour, a Holliday try described as one of the best solo efforts of the season, in which the scrum half bluffed the opposition with a deceptive change of pace, set Trinity firmly on the way to a 25-11 win. Coetzer, to no one's surprise, was signed in a £4,500 deal.

In the semi-final at Swinton, Trinity faced Warrington, who had beaten them three weeks earlier by 5-0 at Wilderspool. As part of their preparation, Trinity made their base at Southport from Thursday onwards. The match turned out to be a typically low-scoring affair. In the eighth minute Neil Fox scored Wakefield's only try when he took a pass from Harold Poynton, beat two would-be tacklers, kicked ahead and won the race to the line. But in scoring the try, the centre was injured and required a pain-killing injection at half-time. In the remainder of the match, Milan Kosanovic's hooking deprived Warrington of the ball and the forwards, with Brian Briggs and David Blakeley well to the fore, took control as Trinity won 5-2.

In the final, Trinity met Wigan, who had put out Hull KR. It was to be Trinity's third final in four years and Wigan's fourth in six, but whereas Wigan had won in successive years in 1958 and 1959, Wakefield had never managed to retain the Cup. On the other hand, Trinity had not lost a Cup-tie since the third round in 1961, when they were beaten 2-0 by Wigan.

Wearing jerseys with a red and blue v for the first time, Trinity matched the favourites throughout the first half. Roger Pearman, who had only played six first team games, came into the side for the unfit Brian Briggs, Turner moving up to the second row, and Colin Greenwood took the right wing position in place of Fred Smith. Despite enterprising play from both sides, the opening half remained scoreless – Fox and Ashton had each failed with three penalty attempts – until two minutes from the interval. Turner made a telling break from his own half to take the ball deep into Wigan territory and several play-the-balls later Holliday, with a short burst, fed Sampson, who, in a strong all-round display, scored under the posts, Fox goaling for a 5-0 lead.

Though full back Dave Bolton had left the field after a Fox tackle, the brilliant play Wigan were famed for was glimpsed, a minute after the restart, in a movement which ended in a try by scrum-half Frank Pitchford. Midway through the half Gert Coetzer, who had made his Trinity debut only two months before, stepped inside one tackler and beat off another to go over at the corner, Fox goaling superbly from near touch. At 12-7, after Fox and Ashton had each landed penalties, the decisive moment came when Bolton, who had returned, had a pass intercepted by man of the match Harold Poynton and the stand-off raced over to open up a ten-point lead with ten minutes remaining. Carlton reduced the deficit with a try, but a more energetic Wakefield side finished with two more tries, as Coetzer took full advantage of a pass by Pearman and Brooke sprinted through from Holliday's short ball. The 25-10 victory was Trinity's finest of the three recent Cup final wins and Derek Turner was rewarded for his decision to stay with Trinity by becoming the first captain to lift the Cup three times at Wembley. As for Poynton's performance, Eddie Waring, writing in the *Sunday Mirror*, had this to say: 'Trinity's off-half smashed Wigan to dramatic and utter defeat in one of the finest Challenge Cup finals ever seen. He stepped in to score a brilliant try at exactly the right moment and his darting, jinking, non-stop display earned him the Lance Todd trophy.'

Harold Poynton, Lance Todd Trophy winner, Wembley 1963.

Gert Coetzer, the South African winger who joined Trinity in 1963, scored two tries in the Cup final and was on four occasions the club's top try scorer of the season

Neil Fox later reflected: 'Wigan were favourites and if they had scored after putting us under pressure for about thirty minutes I think they would have run away with the match. But luckily our defence held tight and we were first to score a try and from then on it was all Wakefield Trinity. That was our best win at Wembley, without a doubt. Everybody tackled, led from the front by Derek Turner.'

Trinity had become the first Yorkshire team to retain the trophy. Jack Wilkinson, who had twice been to Wembley with Halifax, became the first player to appear in five Challenge Cup finals, while Neil Fox's record haul of 39 points from three finals was to stand for 32 years.

The well-rehearsed homecoming arrangements on the Monday gave the Wakefield public – around 20,000 of them - another chance to greet their heroes. But there was much unfinished business, with eight matches to fit in before the end of the season. Among the better performances, Trinity again beat Wigan, this time by 21-13 at Central Park, and at Belle Vue by 21-8, before ending the season in fifth place.

During the four seasons from 1959-60 to 1962-63, Wakefield Trinity were rugby league's most successful club. It is not for nothing that the period is recognised as the most prestigious in Trinity's history. The Challenge Cup was won three times, the Yorkshire League three times, the Yorkshire Cup twice and the Championship final was reached twice. A table produced by JC Lindley, based on all matches in the league, cup and against touring sides, shows that, of the Rugby League's ten most successful teams in that period, Trinity come top ahead of (in order) St Helens, Wigan, Featherstone, Swinton, Leeds, Huddersfield, Warrington, Hull KR and Widnes.

Fifteen – New Challenges: 1963-67

As had happened on previous occasions in the club's history, players refused to sign on for the new 1963-64 season. They objected to the rates of pay being proposed: £20 for an away win, £16 for a home win, £10 for an away loss and £8 for a home loss. The committee were acting on restrictions imposed by the RFL, who were anxious to halt financial difficulties caused by a drop in attendances. The problem was common to all spectator sports; in rugby league, crowds had fallen by half in a decade. The Trinity players, believing they would lose money over the season, were demanding higher losing pay, but within a week they had all signed on.

The club declared a profit of £1,053 (including a £1,000 donation from the Supporters' Club), despite a £6,000 fall in gate receipts. The previous year's profit was £4,000, thanks again to the Supporters' Club having contributed £5,000. The Supporters' Club hoped to contribute the full £12,000 cost of the conversion of St Catherine's School into changing and refreshment rooms. In addition, the development fund, based on the pools, had crucially provided, over the eight years of its existence, £93,000 for the club.

The close season saw the departure of two much-respected Trinitarians. Johnny Malpass, after a 27-year long association with the club stretching back to pre-war days, was appointed coach at Featherstone, where he still lived. Johnny Jones, A-team coach and a member of the 1946 Cup-winning team, retired after 26 years at the club. Malpass's position as trainer was offered to Derek Turner, who had been promised a job on the training staff when he had been considering a move to Australia, but he declined the offer.

From Trinity Juniors, 19-year old centre Dave Sampson, brother of Malcolm, was signed, along with 19-year old forward Derek Plumstead. But forward Denis Williamson could not be lured back to Wakefield and returned to the Whitehaven club for less than £500, though he had cost £3,250 two seasons earlier.

As the 1963-64 season started, supporters were shocked to hear that 28-year old winger Fred Smith had been transfer listed at £4,000 at his own request; 34-year old Jack Wilkinson at £1,500; and young loose forward David Blakeley at £2,500. At the same time, 21-year old second rower Malcolm Storey was signed from Hull for a fee described as below the asking price of £5,000.

Not for the first time, Trinity's early season performances left something to be desired. The 33-7 defeat at Castleford was described as 'pitiful' and the 7-5 loss at Halifax came in a 'shockingly weary' match.

The first round of the Yorkshire Cup drew Trinity at Hunslet, as in the previous season, but the 9-4 victory was obtained at some expense. The injured Fox and Poynton did not play and among a number of players hurt during the game debutant Dave Sampson broke his collar bone after just ten minutes' play.

Keith Holliday, who in both the previous seasons had been voted Player of the Year, received a record benefit of £1,383, well deserved, as the *Wakefield Express's* John Allen wrote in the testimonial brochure. 'Now, in the days of plenty at Belle Vue, easily overlooked are those trying years of not so very long ago when Wakefield had to struggle for a bare existence. In that sad period, when handsome bonus payments were unknown, and playing terms were at their lowest ebb, Holliday was one of the rising stars who had come up from the juniors. It was a severe test of his loyalty to Trinity for him to remain at Belle Vue for he could easily have gone elsewhere to receive far better remuneration.'

Fox, Turner and Briggs figured in the Yorkshire team which beat the touring Australians 11-5, but Trinity's form was erratic. In an up-and-down period, a 14-7 win came at Featherstone even with Turner sent off, Poynton injured and newcomer Storey hobbling along with broken toes. Vines, Wilkinson and Briggs shored up the forwards and played a big part in the win. But the second round of the Yorkshire Cup provided another upset when Trinity, lacking the suspended Turner, were knocked out by Halifax, who inflicted a 12-4 defeat at Belle Vue. The loss was described as 'humiliating', and even more so since the visitors had two men sent off. The following Thursday evening, at training, chairman Hadfield spoke to the players, whose loss of form had caused some consternation. Vines was dropped after failing to attend the meeting when all had been instructed to do so and was later listed at his own request at £6,000. The Trinity chairman also had cause to criticise the international selectors for dropping Turner from the Great Britain team to meet Australia at Wembley. Hadfield reminded the selection panel of the Trinity captain's value in Australia. 'He led the forwards magnificently,' he said. 'I am quite certain the Australians will be delighted at his omission … because if there was anyone they were frightened of when we were in Australia it was Turner.' In the meantime Turner had applied for, and declined the vacant coaching position at Leeds, taking on instead the job of assistant coach at Belle Vue.

When Trinity met the Australians it was a stormy affair which ended in a 29-14 victory for the tourists, who prevented their hosts from scoring a single try, Wakefield's points coming from Fox's seven goals, a tally equalled by the Aussie centre Graeme Langlands. A crowd of over 15,000 saw the game erupt ten minutes from the end as players from both sides piled into each other, fists flying. Order was only restored on the intervention of half a dozen police officers. Aussie hooker Walsh was dismissed by the referee but refused at first to leave the field and only did so when persuaded by his team-mates.

The Yorkshire Cup final was held at Belle Vue for the first time since 1937, Halifax beating Featherstone 10-0, though the attendance of 13,238 was regarded as disappointing. Roy Bell was transferred to Castleford for £2,000 and Trinity immediately set about chasing another centre. First in their sights was St Helens' Brian McGinn, on offer for £3,000, and then their attention turned to Hull's Dick Gemmell, valued at £15,000. A deal was done when Trinity offered £8,000 plus forward Eric Payne, but the move faltered when Gemmell's wife refused the house in Wakefield which they had been offered. However Trinity made a good investment for the future by signing Leeds City Juniors full back or centre Geoff Wraith, aged 17.

Trinity's form brightened with a 32-8 victory in the traditional Boxing Day match at Headingley. The match was notable for the performance of young Bob Haigh in the forwards, of whom it was said: 'His forceful breaks and good handling, coupled with skilful positioning to afford the most effective support for a colleague in possession, set a fine example to much older colleagues.' Neil Fox, as prolific as ever, bagged four tries and four goals. Of him it was noted: 'In the centre Fox provided some of the afternoon's greatest sensations. The way this supposedly "slow" player several times left the "speed" man in the opposition trailing when in pursuit of his four tries … was sometimes as laughable as it was productive.' Alongside him, the performance of Dave Sampson in the centre was 'very sound,' and made fans wonder why, with Sampson and Ian Brooke to choose from, the committee persisted in chasing other centres such as McGinn and Gemmell. Trinity beat Leeds in the return match too, winning 24-2 at Belle Vue, Colin Greenwood scoring three tries and Sampson two. The search for a centre ended with the capture of 27-year old Willis Rushton from Bramley for £4,250. Rushton made a try-scoring debut, described as 'quietly impressive' in the 12-8 home defeat by Wigan.

When the Challenge Cup campaign began, Trinity had high hopes of pulling off a third successive victory. It was nine years since they had lost an away Challenge Cup tie, which boded well for their first round trip to Hunslet. They came away with their record intact but only a 4-4 draw, which forced a replay on the Wednesday at Belle Vue. Trinity's performance was unusually sluggish and was no match for Hunslet's gritty display, in which Gunney and Griffiths scored tries to lead the Parksiders to a 14-7 victory in front of 20,822 spectators. Trinity never got into the match and did not post their first try, scored by Geoff Oakes, until twelve minutes from the end.

The surprise defeat led to speculation that the club's glory days were over and that the team was now too old and

Trinity at Hunslet in the first round of the Yorkshire Cup, 1963. *Back row*: Geoff Oakes, Jack Wilkinson, Bob Haigh, Eric Payne, Dave Sampson, Keith Holliday, Gerry Round. *Front row*: Gert Coetzer, Don Vines, Derek Turner, Ian Brooke, Ken Hirst, Colin Greenwood

needed rebuilding. That did not happen immediately, but Milan Kosanovic was transferred to Featherstone for around £500 and Roger Pearman, already in Australia, where he had taken a teaching post, signed for Canterbury-Bankstown for £2,500. Colin Greenwood, nearing the end of his three-year contract, joined North Sydney. The popular utility player, who had represented Trinity in every back position except scrum half, captained the side from stand-off in the 35-8 win over Hull KR, his final game for Trinity. Reports were rife that Neil Fox was to become the third Trinity player to head down under. Parramatta had made enquiries but were finally put off by the £15,000 transfer fee which Trinity had demanded.

It made sensational news, as did Trinity's latest signing. Welsh sprinter Berwyn Jones, described as the fastest man in Europe, the holder of the British 100 metres record and a member of the 4 x 110 relay team which had broken the world record, signed on after two trial matches under the ironic pseudonym Walker. In the second trial match, Jones, who had played rugby union but not for three years, scored a try as Trinity hammered Doncaster 44-3, a match in which Trinity's other winger, Gert Coetzer, scored five. The Trinity committee had seen enough and offered the 24-year old a signing-on fee in the region of £6,000. Jones made his official debut in the 38-10 victory over Halifax when a 10,000 crowd producing the best receipts of the season went away disappointed to see the Welshman barely receive a pass. It was a different matter at Batley, where Jones scored two tries, one of them a 90-yard solo effort, while on the other wing Coetzer kept the public entertained with another five-try haul.

While Jones was making his way in rugby league, Don Metcalfe, in the wilderness since retiring two years before, made such a successful comeback that, at the age of 31, he was named Player of the Year. At the same age Trinity's most successful captain, Derek Turner, who had been operating at blindside prop, decided to retire, as did those

157

other great forwards, Jack Wilkinson and Brian Briggs, though Wilkinson re-emerged at a revived Bradford. The dilemma now confronting the club was outlined by secretary-manager Eddie Thomas at the annual general meeting. 'Our previous high reputation as a winning side has suffered not only by defeats but often by the quality of many of our performances,' he reported, referring particularly to the Yorkshire Cup defeat by Halifax and the first round Challenge Cup exit at the hands of Hunslet. It was, in fact, the first season without a trophy since 1957-58. 'Age retirements and transfers have made great inroads to the playing personnel who gave four seasons of glory,' Thomas went on. 'For the future a new-look Trinity must be created.' A decline in income from the pools had led to worsening finances, and a £1,000 cheque from the Supporters' Club was gratefully received.

Before the start of the 1964-65 season, 23-year old scrum-half Ray Owen, a member of Widnes's Cup-winning side just months earlier, was surprisingly released by the Chemics for £2,000 and was added to Trinity's squad. Among the changes in the rules for the new season, substitutes were to be allowed for the first time, but only up to half-time and for injured players, while the league reverted to a single division of thirty clubs after a two-year experiment with two divisions.

Trinity did not make the best start but scraped an 11-10 win at Dewsbury in the first round of the Yorkshire Cup thanks to a disputed penalty from which Neil Fox, the new captain, kicked the winning goal four minutes from the end. It was at least a marginally better performance than in the earlier league game against the same opposition when Dewsbury won at Belle Vue for the first time since 1946-47. In the second round a breathtaking 75-yard try from Jones and a fine effort from the half-way line from Fox helped Trinity to a 15-5 win at Featherstone. Two weeks later in the semi-final at Fartown, Trinity, denied possession from the scrums, put in a heroic defensive stint to overcome Huddersfield by 7-0. Jones saved two certain tries, Fox kicked a superb 50-yard penalty goal and Holliday, playing at loose forward, wrapped it up almost at the final whistle with a try under the posts, converted by Round in the absence of the injured Fox.

In between Fox equalled the club record of eleven goals for the third time and Jones scored a hat-trick of tries described as 'scintillating' as Trinity gave Keighley a 46-5 drubbing. But Jones was coming in for some harsh treatment from opposing teams, some of whom were ready to stop him at all costs, often when he used the tactic of kicking ahead and following up. After the winger had been obstructed three times in the same match against Featherstone, chairman Stuart Hadfield spoke out: 'It seems that teams realising the danger of Jones if he gets off and knowing that he is not just a sprinter are using every endeavour, illegal as well as fair, to stop him – knowing that it is likely only to be a penalty against them...'

Coach Ken Traill, who had taken over in 1958, was handed a new three-year contract but soon found himself speaking out about the lax attitude to training. After some disappointing results, including a 4-4 draw at struggling Batley, Traill blasted the 'shocking play' and 'lethargic approach' of certain players, complaining about some not even turning up for training. This surprising revelation, considering the relatively high pay Wakefield players received, was backed by a statement from Hadfield, who said that 'at Trinity there should be the rule, widely operated elsewhere, that a man who does not train does not play.'

After finishing seventh the previous season, Trinity should have been in a better position than mid-table in the newly reintroduced single division, but the team's unsatisfactory form continued with a 7-3 loss at Keighley, where Trinity 'nosedived to obscurity'.

The club was rocked during the following week when Stuart Hadfield, chairman since the 1959-60 season and a member of the committee for over twenty years, died suddenly of a heart attack. Managing director of a family-run fuel distribution company and a former Conservative councillor, Hadfield was, it was said, 'never afraid to speak his mind [and] might be regarded as one of the most controversial figures to have held a high position in rugby league... He always had a great interest in the well-being of the players and it was largely as a result of his striving that members of the team received remuneration on some occasions that staggered some of the less prosperous clubs.'

Vice-chairman Stan Milner stepped in and found immediate success in the final of the Yorkshire Cup when Trinity regained their old sparkle to give a 'masterly display' in defeating Leeds 18-2 at Fartown, watched by 13,754 spectators. Jones –who was soon to be called into the Great Britain team - had the crowd on their feet as he went in for two thrilling tries. Poynton launched the attacks, Vines led the pack in grand style and Fox crashed through tackles to score two tries as well as adding three goals.

As had happened so often in the club's history, Trinity rose to the big occasion only to plumb the depths against more moderate opposition. A miserable 3-0 defeat at Odsal against lowly, re-formed Bradford was followed by an inept performance resulting in a 20-6 defeat against Hunslet. But those two losses were preceded by a 16-10 win at Warrington, a match in which Brian Briggs made a comeback. The Boxing Day match at Headingley always provided an incentive for Trinity to show their best - and they did, winning 29-6 after leading 21-0 at half-time to give Leeds no hope. Fox kicked seven goals and scored a try, but there were strong performances also from scrum-half Terry Hopwood in only his second appearance, Tony Thomas and Don Metcalfe. 'This was rugby league at its best and provided an answer to those who say that the game is dying,' reported the *Wakefield Express*.

Fox and Jones were selected to play for Great Britain against France, and Vines was chosen for Other Nationalities, with Coetzer as reserve. But Trinity's finances were not in the best of health. At the half-yearly meeting it was revealed that the club had a bank overdraft of £5,500, with new chairman Milner reporting that it had been £8,000 when he had taken over. He hoped that the overdraft would be wiped out by the end of the season. 'Until then no silly money is going to be spent,' he stated.

The boom experienced by rugby league clubs in the fifties was over by the middle of the next decade, as Trinity officials often made clear. The high wages could not be sustained, and the club's bank statement showed why. The dilemma was alluded to in the *Wakefield Express*: 'As many rugby league players are quite willingly accepting cuts in their wages, and talk of club mergers to avoid "closing shop" have figured prominently in the news of late, it is interesting to learn of the attitude taken by the Wakefield Trinity management towards the widespread decline in support for the code…' The committee's plan was to offer a bonus if the team finished the season in the top eight, guaranteeing a money-spinning home tie in the play-offs which now involved the top sixteen clubs.

A good Challenge Cup run would also appease the bank manager. Trinity overcame Dewsbury at Crown Flatt in the first round, winning 11-2. The only try of the game came when Hopwood supported Holliday's thrust just after half-time, Fox kicking four goals. Trinity were on a winning streak in the league too. Their improved defence resulted in an eight-match unbeaten run with no try scored against. In the second round they accounted for Bradford at Odsal in a game not without controversy. Trinity took the lead when Fox dummied and sent Coetzer over but Bradford lost the chance to draw level when former Wakefield centre Ian Brooke, who had inexplicably been allowed to leave during the season before, was heading for the line but was tripped by Coetzer, who was sent off but no penalty try was given. Jones scored a fine try just before the hour to extend Trinity's lead but Brooke went over for a sparkling consolation try, giving a 10-7 result in Trinity's favour.

In the league Trinity maintained their winning run by breaking St Helens' unbeaten home record, winning 9-2 with Jones claiming the game's sole try and Fox contributing two goals and a drop goal. The third round of the Cup produced a home tie against Blackpool, who had caused a shock by winning at Belle Vue in the Cup in 1957. Trinity were fortunate to escape another upset and struggled to win by 4-0, with Fox kicking two goals.

Trinity extended their unbeaten run to seventeen matches with a dazzling display against leaders Castleford. All Trinity's seven tries were scored on the wing as the 15,000 crowd were thrilled to witness Coetzer's five tries and Jones's two. It was excellent preparation for Trinity's sixth post-war Challenge Cup semi-final, to be played at

Headingley, where they would meet Hunslet, their victors in the previous season's first round. The team went off to Harrogate for two days to prepare for the semi, but little good came of it. Up against a formidable Hunslet pack which gained the greater share of possession and gave nothing away, Trinity were unable to reproduce their usual winning style. For long spells they were forced to defend as Hunslet held on to the ball and took no risks even on a firm playing surface and in fine conditions. For the second season in a row the Parksiders put Trinity out of the Cup, this time winning 8-0 in front of 21,234 spectators. But they won no friends for rugby league. 'Few would disagree that a reproduction of the stuff supplied in this Headingley flop would do the code incalculable harm if put on before a crowd at the Empire Stadium,' the *Wakefield Express* reported. 'For one side to be deprived of possession to the extent Trinity were in this appalling travesty of a sport designed to appeal with its stirring movement is beyond description.' Fortunately for rugby league, in the middle of a crisis brought on by declining gates, the Wembley final, between Hunslet and Wigan, turned out to be a classic.

In the league, Trinity finished the season in much better shape than the early matches suggested and took fourth place, behind St Helens, Wigan and Castleford. In the last match of the regular part of the season, the 20-7 home win over Leeds, Neil Fox reached 1,000 goals for the club.

In the championship play-offs, Trinity beat Hull 15-9 and then fifth-placed Warrington 17-8 before meeting leaders St Helens at Knowsley Road in the semi-final. Without Poynton and Owen, Trinity nevertheless took the lead through a Rushton try and Fox conversion. Their early domination should have been sustained after Saints' second row Warlow was sent off after half an hour but once again they were hampered by lack of ball from the scrums as well as by the irrepressible Alex Murphy, who split the Wakefield defence to create St Helens' two tries in their 10-5 victory.

Reversing the general trend, Trinity's gate receipts over that 1964-65 season were up by a total of £4,500 to give a profit of over £500. With prudent management they had succeeded in turning round the previous season's loss of £3,748. Furthermore, the club announced ambitious new plans for a sports and social centre at Belle Vue.

Neil Fox was made captain for the second successive season at the start of the 1965-66 campaign, while 32-year old Derek Turner made an unexpected comeback to stiffen up the pack. Former favourite Ken Rollin was signed by Leeds for £1,000 to rejoin his team-mates from the 1960 Cup final, Albert Firth and Les Chamberlain, while hooker Geoff Oakes went to Warrington. Trinity persuaded ex-Wigan test centre Alan Davies, now at the end of his career, to join them for a transfer fee of £1,500 though his stay was a brief one. David Garthwaite, a 21-year old centre from Wakefield RU, also signed, making his debut in the 14-7 defeat by Halifax, a match in which Turner made his return. That was one of three losses in a row, to be followed by a quick exit from the Yorkshire Cup. Poor finishing was responsible for the home defeat by 8-4 at the hands of Hull, who had already got the better of Trinity in the league. Trinity's only points, in the absence of Fox, who had just undergone an appendix operation, came from two goals kicked by young full back Derek Woolley.

Trinity made a very significant signing when Neil Fox's 29-year old brother Don arrived from Featherstone for £3,000, which equalled Rovers' highest ever transfer fee. Originally a scrum-half, Featherstone's record points scorer had represented Great Britain two years earlier in the third test against Australia. He made his Trinity debut at loose forward in the otherwise disappointing 10-8 win over Doncaster. The club also signed 22-year old stand-off Ken Batty from West Park RU, Leeds.

Don Fox's old club Featherstone found him hard to handle in their 22-7 loss to Trinity, who recorded their sixth win in a row. Back-rower Bob Haigh was impressive too with his 'productive skill'. Derek Turner made only his second appearance of the season against one of his old clubs, Hull KR, but scored a try in an 'auspicious return'. By contrast, another former Belle Vue favourite, winger Fred Smith, made a comeback only to break a leg in the same match, which proved to be his last.

Trinity met the New Zealand tourists and beat them 16-4, prompting Kiwi skipper Billy Snowden to call Wakefield the best footballing side they had met so far on their tour. Neil Fox's try, to which he added five goals, gave him the club record of 189. The international centre already held the club points and goal-scoring records. Watched by a crowd of 7,484, Willis Rushton also gave a classy performance while try-scoring stand-off Batty earned praise. Loose forward Bob Haigh, with another telling display, was regarded as a strong candidate for the forthcoming tour of Australia and New Zealand.

Featherstone Intermediates captain and former Normanton Grammar School centre Mick Morgan, aged 17, was signed in the face of competition from Leeds, Wigan, Keighley and Featherstone. A month later Trinity signed the former QEGS and Wakefield RU forward Geoff Clarkson, aged 22.

In their first match of the season in Lancashire, Trinity, second in the table, lengthened their unbeaten record to twelve with a 7-7 draw at league leaders St Helens, who maintained their own undefeated sequence since the start of the season. Neil Fox kicked two goals, David Garthwaite registered Trinity's sole try, and the 'brilliant tactician' Don Fox dropped a goal and showed 'his tremendous value to the team with his judicious kicks, ball distribution and defensive work.' Trinity's 14-match unbeaten run was finally ended by Wigan, who, despite the efforts of forwards Ted Campbell, Derek Turner and John Bell, won 13-10 at Belle Vue thanks to a late, disputed try by Billy Boston.

At the turn of the year, Neil Fox was named captain of the Great Britain team to face France at Perpignan. But on the Monday after Christmas Trinity incurred their second defeat in a row by losing 11-9 at Leeds, where ex-Wakefield men Firth, Chamberlain and Rollin were to the fore. The 21,343 crowd, paying £3,373, gave the best figures for a league match at Headingley for four years. The following day Trinity unexpectedly switched their home match against Featherstone to Headingley in order to take advantage of the ground's undersoil heating. It didn't please all the fans but Metcalfe's masterly full-back display and Clarkson's promising debut helped Trinity to a 27-7 victory.

As a sign of things to come, albeit thirty years later, Bradford put forward the suggestion of a summer competition with midweek matches played in the evening during June and July, but Trinity did not lend their support to the idea. Doncaster, meanwhile, proposed a wholesale switch to summer, the season to run from April to September.

The screening of live rugby league matches was still relatively new and opinion was divided about its benefit. Wigan viewed television coverage as 'a creeping paralysis which in time will completely devour our game.' Television cameras were to be banned from Central Park the following season because of the perceived detrimental effect on attendances, though RFL secretary Bill Fallowfield pointed out that considerable income was derived from television compared to receipts from league matches. Wigan's stance was backed in principle by Trinity, who were concerned that the home match against St Helens, which was earmarked as Neil Fox's benefit game, had been listed by the BBC for televising. Sensing a potential loss for the Trinity captain, secretary-manager Eddie Thomas wrote to the RFL Management Committee asking them to find another match which could be broadcast instead.

In an attempt to solve Trinity's perennial hooking problem and lack of possession from scrums, the Blackpool and former St Helens hooker Eddie Bowden arrived on trial, as York's Laurie Milner had done earlier. The paucity of ball from the scrums was blamed for both Trinity's defeats at the hands of Wigan, as well as the loss at Leeds. As a letter-writer to the *Wakefield Express* put it, Trinity could 'carry the handicap against inferior teams but not against top-class sides. Oh for Len Marson!'

Neil Fox was granted a benefit at the age of 26, ten years after signing for Trinity. During that decade he had garnered most of the individual club records: the highest number of goals in a season; points in a season and points in a game; as well as equalling three times over the record for goals in a match. The benefit match against St Helens produced rugby league of 'breathtaking quality' despite the continuous rain. Turner was an inspiration as he had been so many times before and Poynton stood out in the backs. Trinity's front row of ex-Widnes prop Edgar Bate,

Eddie Bowden and Ted Campbell ensured an equal share of possession, while Neil Fox showed international form. Trinity took the honours by 20-12 and thus, with the earlier draw at Knowsley Road, took three league points out of four from Saints. It was a fine rehearsal for the first round of the Challenge Cup the following week. But that proved an entirely different matter. Beaten in the forwards and with wingers Jones and Coetzer starved of the ball, Trinity lost to Saints by 10-0.

When the selectors met to pick the Great Britain 1966 touring team, Trinity's only representative was Berwyn Jones. Neil Fox, though having recently captained the national side, was passed over, as was a legitimate contender in Bob Haigh. Bradford's ex-Trinity centre Ian Brooke was, however, a late selection, while Paddy Armour was appointed as team physio.

After a dip in form, Trinity ended the regular season on a stronger note. With Turner again showing his leadership qualities and winger Batty scoring three tries, Trinity defeated champions Halifax 18-0 at Thrum Hall despite having a number of star players missing. They followed it up with a 20-2 win at Odsal, where full back Geoff Wraith, deputising for Metcalfe, again showed his promise. Hooker George Shepherd, with recently signed open-side prop John Bath from Hull KR, got an even share of the ball from the scrums, and that after almost quitting the game following criticism from supporters.

Trinity finished in fourth place and won the Yorkshire League. In the top sixteen play-offs they beat Hull – who had three times beaten Trinity during the season – in the first round by 30-6. Haigh scored two of Trinity's eight tries and was the outstanding performer. In the following round, Hull KR, over whom Trinity had done the double, proved stiffer opponents. Trinity second row Derek Plumstead broke his jaw; Rovers' Cyril Kellett kicked a penalty which one touch judge thought had gone under the bar, but Trinity did not deserve to go through and lost by 10-9.

The annual general meeting was held at the new social club, a month before its official opening in August 1966. Built with sponsorship from the local brewer, Beverley Bros., the club's profits would go towards the running of the football club. Income from the pools had declined after ten years of providing valuable funding and aid from the Supporters' Club had also waned. Members learned once more that income from gates did not cover running costs.

Before the start of the 1966-67 season, Keith Holliday, Trinity's longest serving player with 438 matches to his credit, went to Bramley. Neil Fox was again made captain, with Derek Turner as vice-captain. Barbados-born winger Michael Hunte was signed from Lockwood (Huddersfield) amateurs. In the 28-15 victory over St Helens, Hunte scored two tries, showing 'fearlessness and skill'. Another relative newcomer, second row Geoff Clarkson, showed up well in the 19-7 win over Wigan, 'going through several times in a style to suggest that Belle Vue patrons have yet to see the best of this well-proportioned player's worth'. Despite these two fine wins, Trinity struggled to overcome lesser opposition in the Yorkshire Cup. In their first match under the new five-yard rule at the play-the-ball – previously the defence retired only three yards - Trinity drew 13-13 at Crown Flatt. In the week leading up to the game the Dewsbury players had reportedly been threatened with redundancy if they did not work harder. In an equally dour replay Trinity scraped through by 18-11 to face a second round trip to Fartown, where, though scoring two tries to one, they went out by 11-6.

In the same month of September, Gary Cooper, a Great Britain tourist of 1962, was signed from Featherstone for the very reasonable fee of £3,000. Though Cooper was selected for Great Britain as a centre, he was now more accustomed to the full-back role, a position which was already covered by Don Metcalfe and Geoff Wraith, not to mention Gerry Round, and where the former Wakefield RU back Richard Paley had recently made his debut. Peter Fox's arrival from Hull KR as an experienced forward whose presence would help to bring on younger players meant that all three Fox brothers were now at Belle Vue. Geoff Steel's return from York also strengthened the pack options. The state of flux in the side was shown by the fact that in the 27-13 defeat at Swinton, five players appeared in the Trinity ranks for the first time that season: Gary Cooper (centre), Tony Thomas (scrum-half) and an entire front row in Aussie prop Noel Dolton, Peter Fox and hooker Alwyn Hammond.

Though the introduction of the tap penalty at the start of the season had reduced the number of scrums, Trinity's search for a hooker went on. Bernard Prior, who had played for Great Britain against France in March, but had since announced his retirement, at the age of 31, laced his boots again when Trinity paid Hunslet £750 for his services.

A couple of months into his third season as captain, Neil Fox, whose form some believed had suffered, stepped down. 'Because of criticism by supporters who are used to a winning side, I am going to see if giving up the captaincy will improve my play,' he said. 'It will be nice to concentrate on my own game for a change instead of thinking about the other lads most of the time.'

In an attempt to make the game more attractive and to prevent one side from monopolising possession, a new rule was introduced. The forerunner of the present six-tackle rule was one which allowed a team to retain possession for four tackles and then a scrum would be formed – which had the unfortunate consequence of once more increasing the number of scrums, which were regarded as a blight. Trinity played for the first time under this rule against York on October 28, 1966 and won 17-10 but it was a dour affair.

Trinity's hooking problems looked to have been solved when, with a weakened team, they travelled to Wigan and came away with a 15-13 victory, Don Fox dropping a last-minute drop goal from 40 yards. Significantly Bernard Prior won the scrums 17-9. Though their form remained inconsistent, Trinity ended Hull KR's long unbeaten run by winning 22-14 in a match where full back Gary Cooper showed his attacking prowess, Neil Fox was back to his best with some powerful running, brother Don revealed all his guile and captain Harold Poynton was full of inspirational energy. Fox's seven goals made the difference in the 17-3 win at Halifax and the centre's 'robust tackling and spirited running' were a feature of the 13-0 victory over Swinton in which Poynton's 'non-stop industry' was also prominent. Over the Christmas period Trinity were humbled 28-6 at Headingley but destroyed Featherstone 27-0, a match in which Neil Fox reached 3,000 points for the club. Coetzer scored two tries in his usual thrilling, all-action style, while on the other wing Ken Hirst made a reappearance after two seasons' absence. Soon after, Trinity made big news by declaring their wish to sign Alex Murphy, who was coach at Leigh though still on St Helens' books as a player. A Trinity deputation including Derek Turner met up with Murphy, who, however, said that he was perfectly happy at Leigh, although that did not deter further attempts to bring the great half back to Wakefield.

Prop Noel Dolton returned to Australia after two years, but a more surprising return occurred when 23-year old Ian Brooke was re-signed from Bradford Northern for a fee of £8,000, made possible by a £6,000 loan from businessman Ronnie Fell and quickly repaid. Since the centre had joined the re-founded club two years earlier for £2,750, Bradford had profited handsomely from Trinity's poor judgement. Always a player of great promise, Brooke had been a big success on the tour of Australia and New Zealand, playing in all five tests.

At the end of Neil Fox's benefit year, a rugby league record cheque totalling £2,150 was handed over at a celebration evening at the new social club. Having recovered top form, Fox was also recalled to the Great Britain side to face France.

In the 18-5 win at Parkside, Gerry Round made a comeback, playing not at full back or centre but in the second row, where his partner Geoff Clarkson was the outstanding forward. Two weeks later the two sides met again in a first round cup-tie, with Trinity never having won a Challenge Cup match at Hunslet. In between the two matches, Bramley were beaten 21-11, almost half their players being ex-Trinity men: player-coach Keith Holliday, Gerry Mann, David Sampson, Malcolm Sampson, Terry Hopwood and Peter Barlow. Trinity duly beat a declining Hunslet side 28-2 in a one-sided game despite having Ray Owen sent off. In the second round they were drawn at Featherstone, where they had never lost a post-war cup-tie, of which there had been four Challenge Cup and four Yorkshire Cup matches. But in deep mud at Post Office Road, Rovers adapted better to the conditions. Trinity led following a Poynton try and Fox goal but Featherstone reversed the form and went on to win 11-7. Berwyn Jones, who had begun playing again but was left out of the side to face Featherstone, was contacted by Bradford and signed for £3,000.

Trinity now turned their attentions to the league championship. Third in the league behind Leeds and Hull KR, they strengthened their claim with a 21-7 victory at Hull, where Gert Coetzer scored three tries. An unusual feature of the match occurred when Neil Fox, who had dropped a first-minute goal, made another attempt which was disallowed because the ball had touched a defender on its way. As Hull re-started, the ball was fielded by Clarkson, who amazingly improved on Fox's second effort by sending the ball back over the crossbar for two points.

Over the Easter period, three wins out of three in games against Castleford, Leeds and Bramley and then a win at Batley – in which Mick Morgan made his debut - confirmed Trinity's third place in the table, as well as giving a sequence of fourteen consecutive wins, during which Gert Coetzer reached a hundred tries for the club.

Ronnie Fell, the businessman and leading racehorse owner whose generosity had already come to the club's aid, was invited most unusually by the Trinity committee, of which he was not a member, to take over as the Wakefield representative on the Rugby League Council. The RFL made a loan of £8,000 to the club for the installation of floodlights, an increasingly important asset to the top clubs, especially since the launch of BBC2's Floodlit Competition.

Trinity were once again looking to make their mark in the Championship play-offs. The League Championship was a trophy they had never won: they were defeated in the final in 1959-60 by Wigan and in 1961-62 by Huddersfield. The first stage held no fears as they knocked out Salford by 48-8, scoring forty points in the second half and ten tries in all, of which Ken Hirst claimed four. Workington were defeated 22-2 in the quarter-final, with Prior monopolising possession from the scrums and Hirst scoring two tries. Poynton was 'tireless in attack and on defence he caused smiles interspersed with gasps of astonishment at his cover work which on one occasion led him to stop three opponents in rapid succession.' The semi-final at Hull KR posed more of a problem. Hull KR were second in the table and had not lost at Craven Park since November 1965 when Trinity won there. In the current season Trinity were the only side to put more then twenty points past them but in the previous season Rovers had won 10-9 at Belle Vue in the quarter-final. This time Trinity's forwards led the way. Prior had the advantage from the scrums and Fox's four goals and Poynton's two drop goals made the difference. It was Poynton also who supplied the neat reverse pass for Hirst's try as Trinity won 18-6.

In the final at Headingley, Wakefield were therefore pitted against St Helens, who had finished the season in fourth position, one place lower than their opponents. Trinity and Saints were the only two teams never to have been outside the top ten in the last decade; in fact in the past nine seasons Trinity had never finished lower than seventh. But it was the weather which played the leading role. In a precursor of the 1968 Challenge Cup final, but arguably worse, sunshine was interspersed with hail, thunder and lightning to leave the pitch in a state of deluge. In the first period, a Neil Fox penalty gave Trinity the lead before a Cliff Watson try and two goals from Len Killeen gave Saints a 7-2 half-time lead. With Saints' tactics based around their forwards, Poynton and Fox both came in for rough treatment and all Trinity's attacking efforts came to nought. A Fox penalty brought Trinity within three points and then, seven minutes from full-time, Ray Owen seized a rare opportunity when Saints scrum-half Tommy Bishop lost control of the ball as it came out of a scrum. Owen tapped the ball over the Saints' line but was obstructed as he went to touch down and was awarded a debatable penalty try. Fox was unable to convert amid the hail and wind and also missed the chance to win the match from a last-minute penalty when Hirst was obstructed. With a 7-7 draw, the teams were set to meet in the replay at Swinton on the Wednesday.

Though the sides remained unchanged for the replay, the referee was replaced. George Philpott of Leeds, who had awarded Trinity a penalty try and disallowed a St Helens try for a forward pass, reported to the RFL that his wife had received an anonymous letter containing threats. His place at Swinton was taken by Joe Manley of Warrington.

With Don Fox looking on, Ian Brooke goes over for one of his two tries in the 1967 Championship final replay at Swinton, where Trinity beat St Helens 21-9 to win the title for the first time

RFL secretary Bill Fallowfield did not mince his words: 'Referees have to put up with plenty of abuse but it is taking things too far when one's family is brought into it. There is a small minority of so-called sportsmen who seem determined to upset everyone. Hanging is too good for such a dastardly act.'

A crowd of 33,537 saw Wakefield and St Helens clash again for the Championship title. Trinity began convincingly as Ray Owen dummied the defence and went over before Ian Brooke raced in from a Don Fox opening. Saints hit back when van Vollenhoven went in at the corner, which, with an earlier drop goal and a penalty, gave them the lead. But following a Hirst run, Owen's pass put Poynton in for a try converted by Neil Fox to give Trinity an 11-7 half-time advantage. Not only did Owen play a crucial role in attack but his cover defence proved vital when Bishop broke and kicked on, and the Trinity scrum-half sprinted back to touch the ball dead. Killeen added a second penalty to bring the score to 11-9 but from then on Trinity took command. Brooke went through after Owen had made the thrust, with Fox, who had had a pain-killing injection before the match, adding the conversion. Poynton's delayed pass sent Hirst in for the final try to which Fox could not add the conversion but kicked a penalty to give Trinity a decisive 21-9 victory and their first Championship title. Owen fully deserved the Harry Sunderland trophy, as well as making the committee forget about chasing after Alex Murphy. Poynton, with his fine passing and brave defence against the St Helens forwards, and Don Fox, whose touch-finding continually drove the opposition back, were equally prominent. Brooke's finishing and, in the forwards, Haigh and Clarkson's powerful foraging were also key factors in the victory.

The Championship-winning side received the same kind of reception on their return as the Cup-winning sides had had earlier in the decade. At the Town Hall dinner, chairman Stan Milner evoked the remarkable transformation which had come about during the course of the season. In November Trinity were 'down in the dumps. Things were not going at all well until along came their great friend Mr Ronnie Fell. He gave the club, the committee, the chairman and the team confidence from which their efforts had resulted in the League Championship trophy being brought to Wakefield for the first time.' Harold Poynton said that he thought the team bore comparison with the great side of the early sixties and paid tribute to the coaching and backroom staff of Ken Traill, Johnny Malpass (who had returned from Featherstone), Derek Turner, Paddy Armour and Jack Booth.

Ronnie Fell, whose business career was built on a successful construction company and who was described as one of the North's leading racehorse owners, decided to reward the Trinity players by chartering a plane to take fifteen of them on holiday to Spain. 'Mr Fell's limitless generosity has set more than rugby league circles talking,' said the *Wakefield Express*. His help was welcome. Despite increased gate receipts the club reported a loss of £2,960. Players' wages were up by over £4,000 but attendances were down and the bank overdraft stood at £9,769. But Fell's involvement was brief. In September, at the age of 50, he died, having built up his company into one of the biggest in the North.

Sixteen – A Second Wave of Success: 1967-70

The 1967-68 campaign got off to a record-breaking start. In their third game Trinity ran up their highest ever score when they hammered Batley 78-9, though the 71-0 against Leeds in 1945 remained their highest margin. Among the eighteen tries, Ken Batty scored a hat-trick, as did Richard Paley in only his third appearance for the club. Neil Fox broke the club goal-scoring record, and, with 33 points from twelve goals and three tries, broke his own points-scoring record, set a decade earlier.

During the close season long-serving full back Don Metcalfe, now 34, had been appointed coach of Keighley, and second rower Derek Plumstead had become yet another Trinity player to head for Bramley. David Jeanes, a 23-year old forward, was recruited from Wakefield rugby union. John Ridge, a local painter and decorator, was elected chairman.

In the Yorkshire Cup, Trinity beat Keighley 25-5 before meeting Hull KR three times, two of which ended in draws. In the league match the two sides drew 12-12 and in the Cup second round tie they again drew 13-13 after Cyril Kellett kicked a late, equalising penalty for Rovers. In the replay Rovers went through 14-5 after dominating for long periods. Three weeks later the sides met again, in the return league fixture at Craven Park, but for the fourth time Trinity failed to win as Rovers emerged victorious by 25-7.

Neil Fox was made captain of Yorkshire and Geoff Clarkson was also included in the team to face the Australians at Belle Vue. For this occasion the new floodlights, installed at a cost of £11,000, were switched on and a 20,000 crowd turned up to watch. Fox was in imperious form, initiating Roger Millward's late try which he converted with the last kick of the game to win it 15-14, after having scored the first try and played a big part in the two others. The centre was also selected to captain Great Britain in the first test but withdrew through injury, leaving co-centre Ian Brooke as Wakefield's sole representative.

Less than a month later Trinity themselves took on the Aussies at Belle Vue. In the past Trinity had always taken pride in matching the tourists, but the under-strength side they put out on this occasion was never going to halt the visitors' progress. Only four members of the Championship-winning side were on duty.

Forward Ray Spencer, just signed from Wakefield RU, was given a baptism of fire alongside Welsh wing recruit Mick Seator. Mick Morgan and Terry Crook made early appearances, Gerry Round was at loose forward and, although veteran half back Tommy Smales had come on loan from Bradford, David Hawley was pitched in to work the scrums. A crowd of over 10,000 was disappointed to see Trinity lose heavily by 33-7.

Front-rower John Bath had decided to retire, reducing the options among the forwards, but the signings which Trinity were now making tended to come from their own juniors or from local rugby union. If a bigger signing was envisaged, a cash-plus-player deal was often attempted. As the *Wakefield Express* pointed out, the heady days of the early sixties under the chairmanship of Stuart Hadfield owed a great deal to revenue produced by the pools. Then, the club drew a weekly income of £300 from that source, which now only provided half as much.

Though Geoff Oakes was finally re-signed from Warrington, the absence of the injured Fox brothers among others resulted in Trinity heading for mid-table obscurity. Neil Fox and Ian Brooke were both selected for the third test against the Australians but again Fox withdrew through injury. Trinity were interested in signing Featherstone scrum-half Carl Dooler, who had been on the tour to Australia, but the asking price of £15,000 was way beyond what Trinity and almost every other club could afford. By the beginning of December 1967, the heavy crop of injuries had resulted in no fewer than thirty-six players being used. In the league, nine matches had been won, six lost and one drawn, not unlike the season before, when they went on to win all but one of their remaining games and the Championship.

An appeal was made to supporters to take part in the weekly draw. Once more the comparison was made: at its height the so-called Trinity Development Fund produced an annual income of £15,000. Now that amount had dropped to below £7,000. 'What Trinity were able to do in those palmy days of the club when the best ever Belle Vue team was assembled in the early sixties is something that cannot be repeated,' said the *Express*.

However in the New Year a number of signings were made, principally from Whitehaven, of whom the most important were forward Matt McLeod and 19-year old scrum-half Joe Bonnar, who was signed for £3,250 as cover for Ray Owen, suffering recurrent knee problems. An 'unnamed benefactor' had made these recent signings possible after being introduced by Brian Briggs, now a member of the committee. It later transpired that a gift of £5,000 had been received from Colin Bartle, whose company was to take over the Trinity Social Club and transform it into the soon to be famous Wakefield Theatre Club. Briggs, previously landlord of the Fox and Grapes on Stanley Road before handing over to John Ridge, became bar manager of the club.

Though they had lost at Leeds on Boxing Day, Trinity went on record their fifth successive win when they defeated Huddersfield 17-7 a month later. Neil Fox, now fit again, captained Yorkshire against Lancashire. It was his final appearance for the county, for which he established records of 60 goals and 147 points. The following month he led Great Britain against France in Paris, with Ian Brooke as his centre partner.

In the first round of the Challenge Cup at Barrow, Trinity scored two tries to none in their 8-4 win, Bonnar sneaking an opportunist try and Don Fox, at prop, dummying his way through for the second. In the following round at Salford, before an attendance of 17,000, Trinity went through by an identical score despite being penalised to the tune of seventeen to two. Harold Poynton gave a masterly display, as the *Wakefield Express* recorded: 'Up against the former Welsh rugby union star, Watkins, the Trinity skipper gave a most entertaining demonstration of his craftiness and also his renowned ability as a tackler. Watkins was definitely second best and many times he sought relief by kicking in an effort to avoid being crowded out of the game by the Trinity skipper.' Trinity's two tries came when first Batty gathered Neil Fox's kick and supplied the pass which sent the centre crashing over. In the second half the provider turned scorer when Batty capitalised on good work by Don Fox and Gary Cooper.

Trinity's progress emulated their efforts of the previous season. After the Boxing Day defeat at Headingley they went on a nine-match unbeaten run and moved from mid-table to fourth by the beginning of March. But still, despite the quality of the football, the committee remained concerned about income through the gates, from which £1,000 per match was needed to break even. Revenue from games against teams in the lower part of the table often fell well below the target.

In the third round of the Challenge Cup at Belle Vue, Trinity beat Castleford 18-5 as the forwards proved more than a match for their opposite numbers, despite the fact that Don Fox had three teeth knocked out in the first minute. McLeod was in outstanding form, Batty scored two tries while Coetzer, at centre in place of the injured Brooke, and Haigh added one each.

The Cup semi-final draw put Trinity up against Huddersfield, the match to be played at Odsal, in spite of objections from both clubs, who preferred Headingley. Not without justification, for the Odsal pitch was deep in mud. In the lead-up, Trinity had beaten St Helens 23-3 without the services of Brooke, Poynton and Don Fox, and then Geoff Oakes, who broke his fibula in the match. Bernard Prior, who had retired four months before, offered to don his boots again, but the selectors opted to rely on George Shepherd. The Odsal pitch proved as bad as the clubs had feared. Described as 'a morass of mud sprinkled with sand', the ground conditions made 'a shabby burlesque' of rugby league. A crowd of 21,569 witnessed a scoreless draw. On much firmer ground at Headingley the following Wednesday, Huddersfield gave Trinity a scare by taking a 10-5 half-time lead, due partly to Valentine's first minute

Full back Gary Cooper, a Great Britain tourist of 1962, joined Trinity from Featherstone in 1966 and won the Harry Sunderland trophy for his display in the 1968 Championship final victory over Hull KR. Pictured here in a league match at Belle Vue, he gets the ball away to winger Ken Batty.

touchdown after charging down Don Fox's kick. But after the break Batty went over and Coetzer crossed for a second time, giving Trinity a 15-10 victory.

Trinity's sixteen-match unbeaten run came to an unexpected end when they lost 12-10 at home to Bramley, who were then in 23rd place, compared with Trinity's fifth. Bramley's tries were scored by ex-Trinitarians Dave Sampson and Terry Hopwood. It proved an unwelcome aberration as Wakefield went on to beat league leaders Leeds 10-5 and Castleford away 5-4, a Don Fox penalty seven minutes from full time winning the match at Wheldon Road. Fox also saved Trinity's embarrassment in the return match at Bramley by landing another late penalty to win 7-6.

His brother Neil, though still struggling with a groin injury, was chosen to captain the World Cup party bound for Australia and New Zealand, in which Ian Brooke and Bob Haigh were also named.

Trinity ended the season as runners-up in the league to Leeds and in the first round of the top 16 play-offs met Huddersfield for the fifth time that season. Gary Cooper's two first-half tries set Trinity on the path to a 20-11 victory over the fifteenth-placed club. In the second round they dispatched Castleford by 17-14, the tries coming from Batty, now fifth in the try-scoring list, Coetzer and Jeanes. In the Championship semi-final at Belle Vue, Trinity beat Wigan by the emphatic score of 26-9. In the continued absence of Neil Fox, brother Don again took responsibility for the goal-kicking, landing six from six, while hooker George Shepherd showed his increasing value to the side by winning the second-half scrums 13-3.

Hull KR, third in the table on points difference behind Wakefield, now stood in the way of bringing a second successive Championship title to Belle Vue. Six times the two finalists had clashed in the autumn, including BBC2 Floodlit Trophy matches, with Rovers winning three and drawing three. At Headingley, watched by 22,023 spectators, Trinity took the lead with a well-constructed try scored by Ray Owen and converted by Neil Fox but Hull KR refused to be dominated and hit back to level the scores at 5-5 at half-time. In the second period David Jeanes's powerful run brought the second try, again goaled by Fox, though Roger Millward dropped a goal to reduce the margin. The key moment came when Harold Poynton, Gary Cooper and Ray Owen combined to send Neil Fox over the line for the third try. With the centre troubled again by his groin injury, brother Don converted, before Poynton added a drop goal, giving a 17-7 lead which could not be overtaken. Rovers' late try produced a final score of 17-10 as Trinity retained the title. Gary Cooper took the Harry Sunderland trophy for an outstanding performance at full back.

In the *Yorkshire Evening Post*, Arthur Haddock wrote of Trinity's committed performance. 'Those who said Hull KR would take over as champions from Wakefield because Trinity would have their minds on Wembley under-rated the mettle of the men from Belle Vue. I doubt if anyone has seen better tackling than came from Hawley, Haigh, Poynton, Owen and Cooper as they snuffed out the best that Rovers could produce.'

The week after, champions Trinity turned their attention to the Challenge Cup final against Leeds, the league leaders, as they attempted to do the double for the first time in their history. Of the seven encounters between the two clubs in the Cup, Leeds had won four and Trinity three but they had never met in a final. There was experience in the Trinity camp: Neil Fox had played three times at Wembley; Harold Poynton twice; Ian Brooke, Gert Coetzer and Ken Hirst once; and Ray Owen once, with Widnes. Don Fox had appeared in four semi-finals with Featherstone and one with Wakefield, but never a final. Club president Frank West had the best record, having been a club official at five finals from 1946 to '68.

Harold Poynton receives the Championship trophy for the second time after Trinity's victory over Hull KR at Headingley, May 4, 1968.

But when the day arrived, Neil Fox's name was not on the team sheet. He had severely aggravated his groin injury in the Championship final. He later maintained that the Trinity committee had put pressure on him to play in that match or not be picked for the Cup final. Since – ludicrous as it now seems - the Great Britain selectors also wanted him to prove his fitness, he was selected against France the day before the Championship final and played the first half - without suffering ill effects. Had he not also played the day after he might have been fit to play in the Cup final, if the committee had allowed. He would then have played a fourth time at Wembley, where he might well have taken on the goal-kicking duties. In the event, torn groin muscles prevented him both from playing at Wembley and forced him to withdraw from the World Cup squad and the Great Britain captaincy. So many 'what ifs?' surrounded this Cup final.

Nothing could have prepared any of the players, officials or the 87,100 spectators for the most dramatic and most infamous of all Cup finals, the so-called 'Watersplash final'.

A violent storm hit Wembley just an hour before kick-off and would surely, in any other circumstances but a televised final, have forced a postponement. 'A background of torrential rain and thunder and lightning presented an awful scene never before paraded before a crowd at the stadium … [It] defied description … The heavy downpour of rain and hailstones [made it] utterly impossible for rugby league to be attempted. All three tries in the farcical show, labelled a cup final, were the outcome of mistakes due to the weather. The winners never crossed the Trinity line.'

Trinity had managed to establish a first half lead of 7-4, scoring the only try of the period. From his own half, Don Fox put in a searching kick downfield, where Leeds winger John Atkinson stopped the ball from slithering over the touchline. But as the ball skidded over the watery surface, Ken Hirst was up to take advantage, tapping the ball over the goal-line and touching down for Fox to convert from a position about eight yards in from touch.

The second half saw a further cloudburst and an already soaked Wembley turf was now under water in large areas. Amazingly both sides continued to play constructively, with Trinity equal to everything Leeds attempted and

Wakefield and Leeds players struggle in the freak conditions at the 1968 Wembley final

generally looking the more dangerous, although, as players slid about, the game became saturated with a never-ending stream of errors. Some ten minutes from the end, Barry Seaborne kicked ahead, the ball stopping in a pool of water and Hirst losing his footing as he tried to retrieve it. Atkinson kicked on, the ball slipped like a fish from Batty's attempt to cover it and the Leeds winger headed towards the line, vying with Coetzer to reach the ball first. Brooke finally made the ball safe, but Atkinson was judged to have been impeded, and referee John Hebblethwaite of York gave a hotly disputed penalty try. With the conversion to be taken in front of the posts, Bev Risman did not fail to add to his two first-half penalties and Leeds went 9-7 ahead amid mounting tension. Just over a minute from full time Risman kicked his fourth goal, but from the restart came the most frequently replayed and widely talked about sequence in Cup final history. At the restart Don Fox switched the direction of the kick, Hirst took the Leeds defence by surprise as he hacked on towards the Leeds goal-line where he touched down for a sensational try which took the score to 11-10 and would snatch victory for Trinity if Fox could convert from under the posts. Normally Fox could have back-heeled it over, but as he struck the ball the Lance Todd trophy winner slipped and, with some of the Leeds players not even daring to look, the ball went agonisingly wide. Fox sank to his knees and beat the sodden ground. The whistle went and Eddie Waring's commentary expressed what millions of television viewers felt. Never were the words 'poor lad' so heartfelt.

Leeds had not so much felt the joy of victory as the elation of being spared defeat. On their first Wembley loss, Wakefield's numbness turned into the inevitable questioning. Concerning the controversial penalty try, the referee was later quoted as saying, 'Atkinson was pushed and his shirt pulled. I have seen the incident re-run twice on television and it only confirms my decision.' It was pointed out that an earlier obstruction on Hirst was not penalised in the same way. Trinity chairman John Ridge commented: 'How could anyone award an obstruction try

The Championship-winning squad of 1968. *Back row*: M McLeod, G Steel, G Clarkson, G Shepherd, E Campbell, K Hirst, D Jeanes, R Haigh, D Fox. *Middle row*: R Paley, K Batty, I Brooke, H Poynton (capt.), G Coetzer, G Cooper, N Fox. *Kneeling*: D Garthwaite, J Bonnar, D Hawley, R Owen

in conditions like that when players were slipping and sliding? It was disgraceful.'

On the team's return home, thousands of fans were there to greet them, as for a Cup final victory. All the sympathy went to Don Fox, whose vision, out-of-hand kicking and tackling were a feature of the match. Banners were raised with messages such as 'Don Fox is the greatest'; 'Don't retire, Don, we think you are tops' and 'We were robbed by the ref'. Fox told the crowd that their wonderful welcome had indeed forced him to reconsider his retirement, though it was clear that nothing could erase the anguish of that failed conversion. The *Wakefield Express* commented: 'It is obvious that as long as rugby league football is played the controversial penalty try award to Leeds will be talked about in Wakefield. That – and not Fox's goal miss with the last kick of the game – is what supporters hold responsible for the defeat.'

At a more mundane level, Trinity's Cup and Championship runs had brought in considerable sums. From the Cup final, Trinity took just under £5,000 and from the two semi-finals against Huddersfield more than £5,000. The Championship final against Hull KR produced over £2,500 for the club and the semi against Wigan almost £1,300.

The period from 1958 to 1968 was Trinity's golden decade, during which they won twelve trophies and were four times runners-up. In the Challenge Cup, only Wigan made more appearances in the final, winning three out of six, as opposed to Wakefield's three from four. In the Championship, Trinity stood level with St Helens, with two titles from four finals. In all the previous 73 years of Trinity's rugby league history, their haul of trophies amounted to eleven; they were the beaten finalists on seven other occasions.

Before the start of the 1968-69 season, coach Ken Traill was given another three-year contract, but his former assistant, Derek Turner, now 36, was appointed as coach of Castleford from a list of eight applicants. On the committee, David Armitage, chairman from 1955-57, decided to retire after 21 years' continuous service, although he had first become involved with the club in 1929. Headmaster of St Catherine's School, he had also been secretary of Wakefield Schools Rugby League for over twenty years. His place was taken by former player John Leighton Davies. Shortly after, Stan Milner, who had been chairman until John Ridge took over and who had first joined

The Trinity squad of 1968-69. *Back row*: M McLeod, E Campbell, D Jeanes, T Ramshaw, D Hawley, R Haigh, T Hill, D Fox. *Middle row*: G Cooper, G Wraith, I Brooke, N Fox, R Paley, K Slater, K Hirst. *Front*: K Batty, J Bonnar

the committee in 1951, also announced his retirement, citing health reasons. In mid-season, one of the newest committee men, former second row forward Brian Briggs, left to take up a coaching post in Australia.

The players were to receive a pay rise in 1968-69. Winning pay away from home was increased from £16 to £18 and for home wins from £14 to £16. On the RFL's instructions, ground admission prices went up from four shillings to five (25 pence).

Inevitably the composition of the team began to change. Gary Cooper, recognised as the best attacking full back in the game, had signed from Featherstone two seasons before but was unsettled and was transfer-listed at £8,000. Following a third shoulder operation, Gert Coetzer was advised to stop playing and returned to South Africa in January 1969 amid many fond farewells. Since signing in 1963, the 28-year old winger had scored 122 tries with his powerful, tackle-breaking running.

Second rower Terry Ramshaw was signed from Bradford in a deal which took Geoff Clarkson and £2,000 in the opposite direction, but the league champions could not find their touch.

Five defeats in the first six league matches were followed by a Yorkshire Cup exit in the first round. Hull KR, by winning 30-18, scored more points in a match at Belle Vue than any other team in the previous decade. The final, as in the season 1963-64, took place at Belle Vue, where Leeds beat Castleford in front of a 12,573 crowd.

Derek Turner's Castleford knocked Trinity out of the BBC2 Floodlit Trophy in the first round, played over two legs. Among the few bright spots was the debut of 18-year old David Topliss, who took the right wing role in the 15-6 defeat at Halifax before impressing as a replacement for the suspended Poynton in the 22-3 away win at Batley. In the same match another Normanton youngster, Stuart Carlton, caught the eye with a strong display on the wing.

The problem of getting the ball from the scrums persisted. Geoff Oakes had decided to retire, George Shepherd was eventually transferred to Leeds for £750, and Tom Hill, the Cumberland hooker, made the familiar journey from Whitehaven to Belle Vue. At the same time, winger Keith Slater was signed from Headingley RU for £3,000. A Cambridge rugby union blue, Slater, who had been on the verge of England honours, was seen as a replacement for Coetzer and scored two fine tries on his debut in the 29-5 win over York. Within eight games he had scored ten tries, including two hat-tricks – an impressive record seeing that, by early October, Trinity had underachieved to the extent of being placed 21st in the table.

Gradually some of the established stars returned to the side. Gary Cooper came back after an absence of three months, though he had had able deputies in Richard Paley and Geoff Wraith. Similarly Joe Bonnar made up for the lack of Ray Owen, who was suffering the effects of a knee injury and constant travelling from his home town of Widnes, where, some years later, he would become club chairman. Neil Fox was back to form and was chosen to represent Great Britain against France, though there was some concern about another mainstay of the side and team captain, Harold Poynton, who, in his benefit year, had only played six matches owing to injuries. Trinity's interest in Featherstone scrum-half Carl Dooler was rekindled but in the end he went to Hull KR for £6,500, a much more modest sum than Featherstone had originally asked but still beyond Wakefield's means.

As at other clubs, the Trinity committee were continually concerned about lack of funds. As the *Wakefield Express* put it, every other club was facing bankruptcy, should the banks call in their loans. Live television broadcasts were often blamed for the game's financial woes, but, as RFL secretary Bill Fallowfield told the clubs, television fees more than made up for loss of supposed revenue through the gate. Players' wages, of course, accounted for the major share of a club's outgoings, and not just first-teamers. 'Well supported as many Trinity A-team matches are,' said the *Express*, 'it is not revealing any secret to say that the running of the reserve team is steadily driving Trinity and many other clubs to ruin.' The gloomy prediction of the Hunslet chairman was also quoted. Unless there was a big change, the days of several clubs were numbered, he believed, Trinity among them.

As the Challenge Cup came around, Trinity were given an easy draw against local side Ackworth, one of the two amateur clubs invited to take part in the competition. Trinity's passage was a formality and they won 50-7, Neil Fox kicking ten goals and Slater scoring four tries.

Then one Saturday morning in February, the club was shocked to learn of the death in a car crash of Gerry Round. The former international full back, who had been playing more recently in the back row, had made 241 appearances for Trinity in the past decade. Round was a player with flair, adept at running the ball out of defence and a more than useful kicker.

The Cup second round tie at Odsal, where the ground was deep in snow, was postponed three times before being played at Headingley on a Wednesday, the undersoil heating once more proving its value. Bradford's eleven-match winning run came to a halt with the 7-7 draw, which was only achieved when ex-Trinity winger Berwyn Jones scored the equalising try following a thrilling 75-yard sprint. Terry Price could not convert to win the match, in which the lead had changed hands three times. The very next evening the replay went ahead at Belle Vue, but after an hour's play neither side had scored. It took a thunderous Neil Fox charge from close range to give Trinity the lead and then Ken Batty profited from a loose ball to kick ahead and touch down, Fox converting both tries, the second from near touch. The score remained at 10-0 and Trinity were through to the third round after the two games had drawn a total of 26,000 fans.

The home tie against Rochdale was played two days later on the Saturday, which meant that Trinity played three Cup matches in four days. That was soon extended to four Cup-ties in eight days as the two sides fought out a 10-10 draw. There were echoes of the 1955 defeat against the same opposition after Trinity's ten point lead evaporated in the second period. Tries from Cooper and Hirst, with Fox's conversions, should have paved the way for victory but Rochdale proved tenacious and could have snatched a late win if a drop-goal attempt six minutes from full time had proved successful. In the replay at Rochdale, watched by 10,850 spectators – the Athletic Grounds' biggest attendance in almost a decade - Trinity were far more efficient. Hawley, Haigh and Batty stood out as a faster and cleverer Wakefield won 15-2.

One of the senior figures still to return to the side, Ray Owen, who had been out for a long time with a knee injury, was now ready to play again. Some asked whether there would be a repetition of the season before when Joe Bonnar had been the scrum-half in place in every Challenge Cup round before suffering a knee problem himself, which cleared the way for Owen to appear in the final.

More than just the usual local rivalry spiced up a thrilling Headingley semi-final against Castleford. Not only were Cas third in the league compared with Trinity's ninth place, but former Trinity skipper Derek Turner was making a big impression in his first season in charge. Turner's men had already beaten Trinity three times in the season, including the Floodlit Trophy win, and were seeking revenge for their Cup defeat by Trinity in the third round the year before. When Wakefield went 10-2 ahead after half an hour's play, Ken Hirst twice crossing the Cas line, victory seemed to beckon. Despite a Trevor Briggs try for Castleford, Wakefield held the lead until two minutes from the end, when second row Mick Redfearn, whose record as a kicker was not the best, booted a long-range penalty, adding to his previous three goals, to put Cas 11-10 up. A late try by Alan Hardisty and a fifth goal from Redfearn gave Castleford a 16-10 passage into the final, their first since 1935. It was Turner's first success as a coach, and it did not go unnoticed. At the end of the season he was poached by Leeds.

Trinity's end of season run-in was an up-and-down affair in which they were beaten on Good Friday yet again by Castleford as well as losing for the first time since the 1956-57 season at Post Office Road. In their last league game of the season, Trinity beat Hunslet 21-12 to finish in twelfth place, their worst for thirteen years. They travelled to fifth-placed Swinton in the first round of the play-offs and, lacking both Foxes, Brooke, Hirst and Jeanes, all injured, went down by 9-5, thus losing their chance of becoming the first club to win the Championship three years in a row.

Repeated warnings from the Trinity committee that the club could not survive on their gate receipts turned into a lengthy appeal by chairman John Ridge, who expounded the club's plight, which was, however, no different from that of many others. The committee were worried that the club's very survival was in question.

'Despite being one of the most successful clubs in Rugby League over the past decade,' said Ridge, 'our club has to find an average of £7,000 per annum from sources other than gate receipts to balance expenses. This is in spite of regular extra income from cup-ties and finals, and is quite apart from any extra finance necessary for ground improvements ... or for the signing of new players which is essential if the club's reputation for success is to be maintained.

'Like the majority of other sporting clubs in the country, our main source of additional revenue has come from the weekly development pools. In 1961 the annual income from these was £14,000 but despite conscientious efforts to maintain the figure, there has been a gradual decline until the present yearly income is below £6,000.'

'It would be easy to decide that it is not economically sound to maintain professional rugby in Wakefield when, along with so many other clubs, we cannot pay our way through turnstile receipts. It would be easy to relieve the regular financial pressure by selling some of our players. But the officials of Wakefield Trinity are determined that Rugby League football will survive its present troubles and that our club will remain amongst the leading exponents of the code.'

Summer rugby league became a subject for serious discussion in response to the crisis affecting many clubs. There was also a good deal of negative opinion regarding the screening of live matches, even though the BBC was handing a potential lifeline to ailing clubs by offering £600,000 over four years, which would give each club around £4,000 per season. One of the hostile clubs was Wakefield Trinity. Their view was echoed in the *Wakefield Express*, which asked pointedly; 'Surely there's a more honourable way of Rugby League clubs committing hara-kiri?'

Despite the gloom, Trinity actually announced a profit on the season amounting to £1,677, slightly down on the previous season's £2,238. The club's income had dropped from £51,000 to £40,000 but expenditure had also decreased by a similar amount as winning money has been paid out less often. However, at the July AGM members were informed that the club's bank overdraft stood at almost £11,000 compared to just over £4,400 the previous season. Les Pounder, who had been chairman from 1957 to 1959, succeeded John Ridge, who stepped down after completing the usual two-year period of office. It was a critical period that the club found itself in. There were questions about the fitness of the players, which had been nowhere more apparent than in the Challenge Cup semi-final against Castleford. Physio Paddy Armour responded by saying that the committee had asked him to discuss the team's fitness training. Armour thought that the team's fitness 'was not all it should be'. He added, 'Ideas have been introduced and discipline laid down which the players will be expected to follow.'

Certainly the quality of Trinity's play did not improve. In fact it simply got worse. In the Yorkshire Cup, which had been brought forward a month, a side lacking half a dozen first-teamers went out at the first attempt, losing 27-15 at Halifax. A fifth consecutive defeat came at the hands of York, who had not beaten Wakefield for fourteen years. Not only were Trinity short of experienced first-teamers for one reason or another, but the situation was made immeasurably worse when Neil Fox, the great points-scoring pillar of the side now in his fourteenth season, was transferred to Bradford for what seemed like the bargain price of £6,000, of which £3,000 was to be paid immediately and the remainder spread over the next fifteen months. Of course Fox's transfer was intended to ease the overdraft, but fans were outraged. The despondency at the club was reflected by letter-writers to the *Wakefield Express*, questioning team spirit and harmony in the committee room. 'Whatever it is, it requires sorting out,' wrote one supporter, 'before the Belle Vue ground becomes a development area for a housing estate or a supermarket.'

International second rower Bob Haigh, who established a new record for a forward when he scored forty tries in a season after moving to Leeds

The cornerstones of the old honours-laden team were gradually disappearing. Harold Poynton, after a twelve year career with the club, decided to retire, having played only sporadically over the past year. He had first started playing rugby league at Snapethorpe School and represented Wakefield City Schools.

'I used to watch Trinity train and went to a few matches,' he recalled. 'I played a bit of soccer and rugby union in the Army, which was easy. Then I signed for Trinity and although I had two chances to leave, to go to Leeds and then St Helens, I was happy to be at Wakefield.

'I got the nickname "Fishcake", because there was a fish and chip shop on Cross Lane, off Horbury Road, and I used to stop off there after training. Derek Turner pulled up once and said to me, "Nah then, Fishcake", and after that it stuck.

'I was only about ten stone two but it never bothered me to tackle big forwards. I got clattered plenty in return. Those Drake twins at Hull – I got an elbow from one of them, lost about four teeth and had cuts as well. I couldn't eat for a week. Mantle of St Helens was another one who hammered me, at Leeds [in the 1967 Championship final]. I didn't know where I was.'

After winning just one game out of ten at the start of the 1969-70 season, Trinity had hit rock bottom. 'The slump has reached a disastrous point from which there does not appear to be the slightest hope of the team ascending to a league position comparable with other seasons in the post-war period,' said the *Wakefield Express*. 'Belle Vue patrons are filled with anxiety as to the future existence of the club if things continue as they are.'

Nevertheless Bob Haigh's form in a losing side was considered bright enough to earn him selection for England against Wales and France, and, for the first time, for Yorkshire. Haigh, Joe Bonnar and David Hawley, the scorer of two tries, were the key figures in a surprising home victory by 28-13 over Bradford, a match in which prop Jim Mills was sent off, and a recent Trinity recruit, Frank Brown, a centre brought in from Leeds, kicked five goals from seven attempts.

Although Trinity had only had to hand out winning pay twice, the financial situation was becoming desperate. To save money, it was proposed to abandon A-team matches until later in the season, but the players rallied round and agreed to play for expenses only. Inevitably some fans looked back to the recent past when the club could look to benefactors for help, or so it was believed. Former chairman Stan Milner, now retired from the committee, explained that, during his long association with the club, only Ronnie Fell had given money to Trinity. Others might have loaned money, he said, but, in 1967, debts of £5,000 were personally cleared by Fell, who also acted as guarantor for an overdraft of £10,000 at the bank. Such was his generosity that when he went on an extended holiday to India, he left with the club a cheque for £20,000 (which was never cashed) to cover any expenses incurred in recruiting players.

By November Trinity were in the bottom four of the 30-club division, along with Doncaster, whom they defeated 32-3. This rare victory was followed by another – against Hull KR, who were beaten 28-13 by a Trinity side with a new half back pairing of Ian Brooke and youngster Kevin Harkin. Brooke, in the stand-off position in which he had been a junior international, scored three tries, Stuart Carlton kicked five goals and, as often happened, win or lose, hooker Tom Hill supplied ample possession from the scrums. Another player whose work rate could hardly be faulted, loose forward David Hawley, was wanted by Barrow but he declined to move.

At a meeting of clubs, it was decided to revert to the two-division system which had been rejected in 1963-64 after two seasons. Trinity had actually proposed three divisions and the disbanding of the County leagues. The RFL's decision meant that Trinity needed to finish in the top half of the table, which on current form seemed improbable. But, spurred on by that necessity, the team, now led by Bob Haigh, who had taken over from Ian Brooke, showed a sudden transformation, which started with a 27-5 defeat of Leigh. The pack was in much-improved form, with Ramshaw perhaps playing his best so far, Haigh and Jeanes also standing out and McLeod, Hill and Hawley in support. It was calculated that Trinity needed 25 league points from their remaining 14 games – a very tall order.

In another significant move, Trinity decided, along with other clubs but with 'considerable reluctance' and without unanimity, to introduce the playing of matches on Sundays. Trinity had once before played on a Sunday, when they visited Featherstone the previous season for a league game. Belle Vue had also been used for amateur matches on Sundays, but Trinity's match against Hull on December 21st 1969 was to be the first occasion when the club had played a match on that day of the week at home. The match was to be moved from the Saturday, traditionally the biggest shopping day before Christmas and therefore a poor one from the point of view of match attendances. The club's position arose from what the *Wakefield Express* starkly called 'an urgent necessity to meet their financial obligations or allow the club to perish.'

'It is an experiment,' said chairman Les Pounder. 'The decision was not arrived at very easily or without deep thought.' He added that the attraction of live matches on television on Saturdays created the need to seek other avenues. As it happened, the first Sunday match was delayed until the visit of Salford in the New Year, the postponement being forced by the arrival of snow. Such a profound change of habit was bound to upset some supporters, estimated to be in their hundreds, who were very much opposed to the idea.

As concern for the future of Wakefield Trinity, indeed the future of rugby league itself, was expressed, all aspects of the game were coming under scrutiny. In the light of the ascent of Leeds United, some questioned whether the historic preference for the oval ball in the local area was giving way to the round ball game. Figures tended to support the view according to the *Express*. It was reckoned that, in the Wakefield and District Amateur Rugby League, and counting the local clubs playing in the Leeds league, the number of sides turning out regularly was lower than in the Wakefield and District Football Association, in which 45 clubs competed. If the ten teams operating in the three local rugby union clubs were added, the two rugby codes equalled the soccer code. It was said that many young people, despite having played rugby of one code or the other at school, turned to soccer when they entered the workplace because works clubs tended to run soccer teams. The more glamorous image of soccer in the media was another draw. Recruitment to junior rugby league therefore demanded 'a tremendous concentration of effort at grass roots level'. As regards support for Trinity, 'there seems to be these days a hard core of around 3,000 supporters who grew up with a middle-of-the-table side of the 1940-50 era. The other 5,000 or so who jumped on the bandwagon for the bonanza of the 1960s appear to have found other Saturday afternoon pursuits.' The writer went on: 'The scramble for a limited spectator market is going to be such that many Rugby League clubs could find themselves in even more desperate financial straits than at present. There is no ready answer to the problem. A drive for development of the junior game, as suggested earlier, could help; and it may well be that, in the end, the Rugby League will have to forgo its annual financial boost from the BBC and scrap live televising of matches for a sink-or-swim policy. It could be added, of course, that something like 75 per cent of the English League soccer clubs fail to pay their way through the turnstiles. But they have not the problem of Rugby League caused by shrinking recruitment to the code.'

The new decade opened with Trinity in their lowest league position for a very long time. Though the revival continued with a 20-7 win over Batley, with Ian Brooke scoring two tries to take his total to ten in the last six matches, 23rd place was an unusually modest situation for Trinity to find themselves in. It was a matter of some alarm, as was made clear at the half-yearly meeting in January, when the season so far was described as one of 'contrastingly abysmal failure and striking recovery'. Secretary-manager Eddie Thomas summed up: 'To say we are turning the corner would be over-optimistic … Sunday matches are being gradually forced upon us, not with the unanimous approval of the committee but with the expectation of increased gate income and avoidance of competition with live television.' One member voiced the question to which everyone wanted an answer: where had all the money gone? Chairman Les Pounder responded by saying that gate money alone did not cover players' wages for every home and away game and the additional costs were 'tremendous'. He added that in one championship-winning year the club actually made a loss. When the club had been successful, money had been used to buy players, though, as an example, Pounder questioned whether, in hindsight, it had been prudent to pay £9,000 for Jan Prinsloo. Another burning issue was the transfer of Neil Fox. The club badly needed the money, came the answer from the stage, adding that every member of the committee would have been delighted if he had stayed but it was not to be. Another member commented that Fox's transfer was 'a tragedy' which had driven many supporters away.

Trinity's first-ever Sunday game at Belle Vue eventually took place on Sunday, January 11, 1970 against Salford. Trinity rose to the occasion and beat the visitors, who until then had only lost one match out of nineteen, but went down at Belle Vue by 7-5. In bad weather – mist followed by rain – 5,025 spectators turned up and the experiment was regarded as a success. A gate of 5,000 was the level of attendance needed to keep afloat but the average for the season so far had fallen nearly 1,000 short. It was not long before talks were being held with the players, who did not like their weekends being disrupted, about special Sunday payments. A bonus of £5 was agreed for the forthcoming Sunday match against Leeds, an arrangement regarded as 'outrageous' by some fans at a time when various appeals were being made to the public to relieve the club's plight. It was stated that the club's debts now stood at £25,000, of which £13,000 was owed to the bank, £6,000 to the RFL for the loan towards the floodlights cost and varying sums totalling several thousands owed to local traders as well as the council in unpaid rates.

The revival was short-lived. Trinity's sixteenth league defeat came with a 17-16 scoreline at Halifax and though they beat Keighley 29-2 with the help of Don Fox, making his first appearance of the season, they would soon lose an established member of the pack in Matt McLeod. The second rower or prop had arrived from Whitehaven two years ago at a fee of £1,750 but his family failed to settle and he returned to his former club, who paid Trinity £450. Soon after, another prop left when Ted Campbell announced his retirement at only 25, claiming that training was interfering with his work commitments.

In the first round of the Challenge Cup, Hull KR provided the opposition for the first time in the competition since 1907, when Trinity won 19-3. But in 1970 the Robins were the victors at Belle Vue by 16-9, thanks to a try from Roger Millward which turned the game, and an outstanding performance from second row Phil Lowe. The lure of the Cup was reflected in a 6,469 attendance – the best of the season – and much better than the league match between the two sides which was watched by only 2,958. Three weeks later Hull KR, on their own ground, sent Trinity to their seventeenth league defeat, winning 17-7.

But Trinity were still capable of springing an occasional surprise. Hunslet were hammered 59-3 at Belle Vue, a match in which scrum-half Bernard Ward, who had not been used regularly, kicked ten goals from thirteen attempts. Keith Slater scored a hat-trick and David Topliss went over for the try of the match – 'a brilliant 70 yard dash in which pace and swerve saw him tear through the Hunslet ranks'. George Ballantyne made a big impact in the second row while alongside him Terry Ramshaw, scorer of two tries, was named man of the match.

As the end of the season approached and second division football loomed, coach Ken Traill offered to quit a year before the end of his contract and the committee accepted his resignation. Traill, who had joined the club in 1957 and was Trinity's most successful coach with four Wembley visits and three Challenge Cups, plus two Championship titles, said that his decision had been influenced by strong criticism from within the committee. 'When a side suddenly starts slipping a coach must expect criticism,' he told the *Wakefield Express*, 'and I have had my share from supporters. They have a right to their opinions. But when you get a committee at sixes and sevens and interfering with team policy the time has come to call it a day. You can stand so much and I have been very tolerant in a situation which has been simmering for some time.' Traill added that he still believed Trinity could once more be a great team if money could be found to recruit two or three players in key positions.

Another surprise came in the form of a shock win over league leaders Leeds, who had lost just two league matches. 'Belle Vue erupts as Leeds are smashed' screamed the *Wakefield Express* headline. In their second Sunday outing, watched by 8,450 – 2,000 more than the previous best crowd of the season – Trinity won 30-23, with half backs Topliss and Ward outshining their more illustrious opposite numbers, Shoebottom and Seabourne. Ward kicked five goals and earned praise for his tactical kicking while man of the match Topliss scored two tries with his elusive running. Hill won the scrums and Haigh and Ramshaw were an inspiration.

But still Trinity were seventeenth in the league, just below the cut for the first division. Over Easter all hope of making the top flight was lost. A win at York was followed by defeat at the hands of second-placed Castleford and, frustratingly, at home to Dewsbury. It was Trinity's worst post-war season as they finished in 21st position, their lowest since 1935-36, when they finished 22nd. It was a dramatic decline from being champions two years before.

Don Fox, at 34, went to Batley for a nominal fee but worse for the future of the side was the transfer of captain and international second row Bob Haigh, aged 26, to Leeds for what looked like a bargain fee of £6,750. Trinity's debts forced the move. 'We obviously do not relish parting with a player of the calibre and personality of Bob Haigh, but what could we do?' asked chairman Les Pounder. The club was struck another blow when committee member and former chairman John Ridge died at the age of 45.

Centre John Hegarty was signed from Hawick Rugby Union club and was soon joined by Northampton and England forward Bryan West, a British Lion at the age of 21. Stuart Carlton went to Bradford in exchange for second row Bob Oswald.

Four candidates were short-listed for the post of coach in succession to Ken Traill – Peter Fox, A-team coach Don Froggett, Halifax's Jack Scroby and Featherstone loose forward Tommy Smales. In the end, none of them was appointed. Neil Fox, a late applicant, made a surprise comeback in the role of player-coach. Trinity waived the £3,000 still owed by Bradford for his transfer a year earlier and, at the age of 30, the record points-scorer was back at Belle Vue after gaining some coaching experience at Odsal. He had never wanted to leave Trinity, he said. 'My sole intention in coming back is to help re-establish Wakefield in the rugby world and I believe this can best be done in the role of player-coach. Young players look up to a fellow who can set an example in match play as well as in training.'

The appointment was a controversial one – at least among the committee. Four members were believed to have paved the way for the signing without the knowledge of the other four and then when it was finally put to the vote, the chairman's casting vote carried it. Fox arrived in a financial situation marginally less gloomy than when he left. Although gate receipts during the season just ended had seen a huge drop from £26,469 in the previous campaign to a mere £11,438, the club's overall liabilities had decreased from around £34,000 to £29,000. Chairman Les Pounder, who had recently been elected to the Rugby League Management Committee, said at the club's AGM that the great times could come round again but that it was essential to revive the membership. Trinity had just over 1,000 members – or season ticket-holders – compared to Leeds's 13,000.

Seventeen - Towards the Centenary and beyond: 1970-75

Of the many challenges Neil Fox had faced in a 14-year career to date, the position of captain-coach of a Trinity side which had just suffered one its worst seasons ever – when they had been without his services - was one of the most daunting. Some observers were quick to point out that he had asked to be relieved of the captaincy four years earlier because the responsibility had affected his play. But those reservations were set aside in a bright start to the 1970-71 season.

It was clear that Trinity were below strength in the forwards, particularly since Bob Haigh, with his constructive play and exemplary defence, had left for Leeds. Only four experienced forwards remained: Jeanes, Hill, Ramshaw and Hawley. Ballantyne was expected to continue to make an impression and new arrivals Oswald and West would soon get their chance.

So often slow off the mark in the past, Trinity made a fine start with a sparkling 35-9 triumph at Rochdale, who had finished above them in the league the previous season. Fox provided stirring inspiration, being involved in several tries and regularly mystifying the opposition defence. It was stand-off David Topliss, though, who earned the man of the match award with his three tries, all the result of his speed and elusiveness.

The reversion to two divisions had not materialised and was still three years away. Instead, the teams in the top half of the table in the previous season played each other home and away, plus three teams in the bottom half, and a similar arrangement applied to the teams in the bottom half. The Yorkshire and Lancashire leagues ceased to exist.

The club was saddened by the death of Frank West, who had recently been re-elected club president unopposed. A former mayor, he had served the club for three decades, was Trinity's representative on the Yorkshire County Rugby League and, among his many other duties, was an alderman and Conservative councillor. The managing director of EP Shaw Ltd, the soft drinks manufacturer, he was never seen at matches without a buttonhole. Ernest Corscadden, the club's honorary auditor for many years, succeeded him as president. Long-serving committee men were becoming rarer. Eddie Sugden, who had been a committee member for over twenty years, resigned following dissension in the board-room.

With a fixture list which produced games against only three top-class sides, Trinity's early-season form was perhaps flattering. When they came up against Leeds at Belle Vue in the first round of the Yorkshire Cup, they put up a good fight in an ill-tempered game but lost 20-10. It was followed by a surprise 10-7 home defeat at the hands of Dewsbury. For the first time, Fox made the switch from centre to loose forward – though he still wore the number four shirt – in the 22-12 win at Workington, a result which moved Trinity up to fourth in an illogical single-division table. Winger Keith Slater, who had ended the 1969-70 season with 23 tries, putting him eleventh in the try-scoring table, was selected for Yorkshire against Cumberland.

A 30-14 win at Barrow, where Topliss was again named man of the match, saw Trinity perched alongside St Helens at the top of the table, which would have been their rightful position a couple of seasons earlier, without the help of a considerably easier programme of matches. For the first time since changing their name from Liverpool City, Huyton came to Belle Vue and were hammered 63-0, Mick Morgan playing in the second row and scoring two tries and Slater three. For the time, it was an unusually high score, but fell short of the 78 points accumulated against Batley in 1967, the 73 against Broughton Moor in 1950, and the 73 inflicted on Bradford in 1961.

Once more Trinity fell victim to a leading side when Wigan visited Belle Vue in midweek. Bill Ashurst, playing at centre, scored fifteen points in Wigan's 18-5 win with a try, five goals and a drop goal. A fortnight later, Trinity slumped to their first away defeat in the league when they lost 25-10 at Salford – their fourth match in ten days.

The forward strength was bolstered by the signing of international second row Rob Valentine, brother of Great Britain's 1954 World Cup-winning captain Dave. In response to the question of where the money had come from, it was said that Trinity had just about paid their way through gate receipts and only a deposit had been paid for Valentine with the remainder staggered throughout the season. The former Huddersfield man, who had cost £4,500, made his debut in October in the 21-8 win against Rochdale. Topliss, meanwhile, continued to make a very favourable impression: joint leading tryscorer with Slater, he posted another hat-trick and man-of-the-match display in the 26-10 victory over Batley.

Utility back Ken Batty announced his intention to emigrate to Australia and two former Wakefield RU players, David Garthwaite and Richard Paley, decided to retire. A 22 year-old South African winger, David Barends, was signed on the recommendation of Ivor Dorrington. Barends was eased into the side in December and scored two tries in the 44-8 win over Blackpool, a match in which his centre, Neil Fox, also scored two tries as well as kicking seven goals. A week later Fox went on to equal his own goal-kicking record when he landed 12 goals, including two drop goals and a penalty kicked from half-way, in the 42-6 defeat of Workington at Belle Vue.

As Sunday games, which had generally proved popular, became more regular, it was agreed to pay players the same £5 bonus as in the previous season. But during the festive period, the usual Boxing Day fixture at Headingley could not take place, since Leeds were not one of Trinity's three designated 'first division' opponents. Instead Trinity travelled to Batley and won 12-4. Their fixture at Hull KR was played in snow and they could count themselves unfortunate to lose 12-10, a penalty goal well into injury time giving Rovers victory.

On a surprisingly sunny afternoon in January, a crowd of 10,606 turned up to watch Trinity beat Salford 14-7. Wakefield's first attendance above 10,000 since the 1969 cup-tie replay against Bradford (11,700), and the biggest crowd at Belle Vue for a league game since the Easter Monday fixture with Leeds in 1968 (13,760) was described as 'the most positive vote yet for Sunday football'. Though the committee were still not sold on the idea of playing on Sundays, the receipts of £2,243 presented a very persuasive argument. Against so-called 'first division' opposition in Salford, Topliss's break made the match-winning try for Slater, while full back Wraith saved what looked a certain try as he managed to cover both centre and winger in a two-on-one situation.

Trinity met the same opponents in the first round of the Challenge Cup a fortnight later and, as in the league game at Hull KR, fell foul of a disputed injury-time penalty. Without Neil Fox and several other first team figures, Trinity were leading Salford's expensively-assembled side by 6-4 when the penalty earned the home side a draw, watched by 14,276 spectators. Disappointingly Trinity lost the replay 15-8 at Belle Vue in front of the season's highest crowd of 11,733. They were consoled by gross receipts from the two ties of £7,703.

David Jeanes earned further representative honours when he was selected to play against France. Alongside him in the Great Britain pack was former Trinity second row Bob Haigh, who was to end the season as the league's top try-scorer with 40 – the first forward to do so. Trinity's Keith Slater was fourth with 33. Haigh put his success down to having a creative loose forward in the Leeds side, Ray Batten, and also expressed his admiration for coach Derek Turner and the pleasure of playing in such a well-drilled team. Haigh also gave his views on the direction he thought the game should take, in the light of the continuing dissatisfaction with one-division football. 'I believe the code's future lies in a highly competitive league composed of clubs with strong resources and a structure under which they would all play each other in a season. That would mean fewer fixtures but it would be a stronger competition,' he said. Haigh's argument would continue to be discussed in the coming decades.

The following week, Trinity routed Hunslet, bottom of the league and a shadow of their former selves, winning by the huge score of 72-8 without Fox and Brooke and with only one regular forward. Slater's seven tries equalled Fred Smith's 1959 record and the twelve goals kicked by scrum-half Bernard Ward equalled the record number kicked twice by Neil Fox, the most recent occasion being against Workington two months earlier. Topliss scored three tries before leaving the field injured and both hookers, Hill and Maskill, were sent off in the first half-hour for fighting. At 2,976 the attendance was Belle Vue's lowest of the season.

A solid performance at leaders Wigan, who had only lost one match all season, ended in an 11-5 defeat despite a 5-3 half-time lead. 'Trinity should certainly have had more than one try to show from the number of openings created by Topliss, whose mazy running earned the admiration of the Central Park crowd,' said the *Wakefield Express*. That display was in stark contrast to their next, in which second-placed Trinity were sent crashing to a humiliating defeat at third-from-bottom Huyton, who won 5-0. Though Wakefield's pack was almost an A-team six, there was no excuse for such a shocking performance, particularly since Huyton had been hammered 63-0 earlier in the season.

Just when they should have been consolidating their place towards the top of the table, Trinity went into a downward spiral, losing five matches out of six. Though Fox scored his 250th try for the club in the home defeat by mid-table Barrow, Trinity dropped to fifth place, earning them a tie at Belle Vue against Castleford in the first round of the top 16 play-offs.

International forward Mick Morgan, a member of England's 1975 World Cup squad, pictured here in action against Widnes

Trinity got the better of twelfth-placed Castleford by 10-4. Slater scored two fine tries; 'his first, which came after only two minutes, was sheer poetry, combining pace, sidestep and swerve in a 60-yard run which left four defenders helpless.' In the quarter-final at Leigh, in which Mick Morgan was as outstanding as Terry Ramshaw had been in the first round, Trinity gave another stern performance to win 8-5. In the semi-final at Central Park, however, they were totally outplayed. Wigan ran in eleven tries to win 49-15, Trinity's biggest defeat for 13 years.

It was clear that the Sunday experiment had been a success, producing most of the big gates. For the forthcoming 1971-72 season, half of the eighteen home games were to be played on a Sunday, five on a Friday evening, only three on what had been the traditional day, Saturday, and one on a Wednesday evening. The club even made a slight profit in the 1970-71 season of £1,652, thanks to a considerable rise in gate receipts of over £8,000, although match expenses, including players' wages, had also gone up by more than £6,000. The bank overdraft was not much changed but the outlook was different from a year ago. At the AGM a member asked why Bob Haigh had been transferred for the 'giveaway' price of £6,750, to which chairman Les Pounder replied that, at the time, Trinity had to make the most of their assets because their financial situation was so desperate. He went so far as to say that but for that deal, there might no longer be a Wakefield Trinity.

Former player John Leighton Davies took over as chairman as the new season got off to its earliest ever start on August 1st, when the Yorkshire Cup ties took place. But it looked as if kick-off had come too soon for some, Trinity's modest attendance of 3,415 for the 11-4 defeat of Huddersfield being easily the best of the round. Though Trinity were the most successful team in the competition in the post-war period, with seven trophies from eight finals, they had not figured in a final for seven years. Castleford saw to it that they would go no further than the second round as they knocked Trinity out by 13-10 in a highly controversial match. Referee Eric Lawrinson sent no fewer than six players off, three from each side, in a sixteen-minute spell midway through the first half. None of the sending-off offences was particularly serious and the Trinity trio who were dismissed – Jeanes, Wraith and Slater – had never been sent off before in a first-team match. Castleford went on to lose 11-7 to Hull KR in the televised final at Belle Vue.

Less than a month into the new season, Neil Fox was given a new three-year contract, although his present one had only run twelve months. He also became the first Trinity coach to have full control over team selection, with the chairman advising.

Winger David Smith, signed from Shaw Cross amateurs, made a two-try debut as York were beaten 32-3. The first defeat came in the sixth match of the season at Hull KR, which signalled some uneven form. The BBC2 Floodlit Trophy, in which Trinity had not won a single game since they had entered the competition, brought another defeat, this time by 23-16 at the hands of Hull.

David Jeanes was selected for the Great Britain team to face New Zealand in the first test and second rower Steve Lyons was signed from Featherstone for £3,000, with Terry Ramshaw leaving for Salford for £1,500. Trinity came back to hammer Workington 53-9, their twelfth consecutive victory against the Cumbrian side.

As at other clubs, attendances continued to give concern. Only 2,185 spectators saw Trinity beat Halifax on a Friday evening in mid-October, and just 2,100 were present at the Yorkshire v Cumberland match at Belle Vue, won 17-12 by Yorkshire.

For the eighth time in their history, Trinity played the touring New Zealanders, who had just won a test series against Great Britain for the first time in 63 years. Of the matches between Trinity and the Kiwis, the tourists had won four, Trinity had won the last two meetings in 1961 and 1965 and the first was drawn. The Kiwis added another victory to their tally as they defeated Trinity 23-12 in what was their first win over a Yorkshire side on the tour. Both sides had periods of dominance, with Geoff Wraith making four try-saving tackles in the first half alone. Winger Mick Major, recently signed from Huddersfield, scored a fine try over forty yards after centre Jack Marston had broken through.

Trinity's form up to the end of the year became much more consistent. Kevin Harkin's blind-side try and Neil Fox's conversion brought a 5-4 victory at Leigh before the new Player's No. 6 competition got under way. The first round tie at Widnes ended in a 10-10 draw and the replay at Belle Vue was heading for a similar finish until Harkin's injury-time drop goal secured Trinity's passage into the second round, where Bramley were beaten 10-5.

Between the second and third rounds, Trinity ran up their highest score of the season in beating Batley 59-9. From the thirteen tries the best was Topliss's 80-yard solo effort, while Terry Crook collected 23 points from ten goals and a try. With David Jeanes, who had been outstanding in the third test at Headingley, having taken over the captaincy, Trinity were on a winning run, which was extended by an 18-12 win over Blackpool in the third round of the Player's No. 6. Blackpool proved a tough nut to crack, but had two forwards sent off eight minutes from the end, when Trinity were leading by just three points. Once again Topliss was the star: 'Trinity would have been struggling without the genius of Topliss, who produced two flashes of brilliance to create tries for Marston and himself.'

The semi-final brought St Helens, unbeaten in their last eleven games, to Belle Vue. This time it was Neil Fox, at loose forward, who proved to be the man of the moment. Saints obviously thought so too. He went off with a broken nose, the result of an off-the-ball tackle as he chased his own kick, but by then, with an outstanding all-round display, he had put Trinity in a position to claim a 14-9 victory. From a scrum near the Saints' line he created a clear gap, using Topliss as a foil, and strolled through to touch down, as well as succeeding with two drop goals, the second from 45 yards, and two conversions.

As the New Year opened, Gary Cooper left the club after being appointed assistant coach at York, taking Dave Hawley and Bryan West with him in a move that proved unpopular with many Trinity supporters. A benefit was in full swing for Ian Brooke, whose retirement through injury was a huge blow to the club. Former Wakefield RU full back Les Sheard was signed from Castleford without a fee.

In the 22-4 victory over Huddersfield, Topliss gave another 'five star display', scoring three tries. 'Topliss's speed and eye for an opening made his display outstanding on a day when most players were struggling to cope with the greasy conditions. It would have been a very dull affair without his flair.'

The Player's No. 6 final, played at Odsal in front of an 8,295 crowd, proved entertaining despite the typically heavy conditions but ultimately disappointed the Trinity fans. With Mick Morgan acting as makeshift hooker, favourites Trinity enjoyed the majority of possession from the scrums and were 8-2 ahead after 18 minutes' play. But Halifax gradually took control and scored ten points in the last ten minutes to win the inaugural trophy by 22-11. In Trinity's worst performance for weeks, tries came from Topliss, Slater and Valentine, Fox kicking the only goal.

In the first round of the Challenge Cup, Trinity were matched against Doncaster, but only after a re-draw since, embarrassingly, a number of balls had slipped out of the famous bag. At a waterlogged Tatters Field, where an icy wind blew, Trinity struggled to make it to the next round, which they did by 5-3 when David Jeanes scored from Mick Morgan's break. There was a good performance too from hooker Tony Handforth, who won the scrums and kept the opposition defence guessing.

A tense Challenge Cup second round clash with Wigan ended in a thrilling 6-5 victory in front of 13,633 spectators - the biggest crowd of the season at Belle Vue. Against a background of his dispute with the committee over coaching policy, Fox provided the inspiration, crafting a superb try when he sold a dummy and crashed through two would-be tacklers to touch down. Hookers Handforth and Clarke were sent off after just 12 minutes for scrum offences, but Morgan stepped in and helped Trinity to a 23-7 scrum advantage. Wraith, who scored Trinity's second try, gave a faultless display at full back and Topliss was again singled out for praise for his piercing runs.

In the third round Trinity had to travel to Headingley. The omens were not good. Leeds were top of the table, Trinity were fourteenth and had not won there in a Challenge Cup tie for 48 years. The result went with form but Leeds had Terry Clawson to thank for his three penalties which gave them their ticket into the next round with an 11-5 win. Topliss scored a fine try, Fox kicked the goal and the 21,127 crowd showed that people appreciated Cup football between the two old adversaries.

In the league, Trinity were heading for a top eight place and a potential home tie in the play-offs. But tragedy struck in the last minute of the 12-9 victory over Castleford at Belle Vue. Trinity's 21-year old, highly promising second rower Peter Harrison fell awkwardly and broke his leg, necessitating an eight-hour operation, but the surgery was not successful and the leg had to be amputated. Ian Brooke, whose benefit season it was, very sportingly conceded the remaining events to his young team-mate, for whom fund-raising efforts were quickly put into place. Including £1,000 from a collection at Wembley, the fund eventually reached over £10,000. Brooke's generosity can be measured by the fact that his own benefit totalled just £225, a sum far lower than might otherwise have been expected.

As the regular part of the season neared its end, Jeanes was in fine form in the 20-8 victory over Hull KR, tearing through the defence from 35 yards out and shrugging off attempted tackles on the way to an inspirational try. Topliss scored four tries in the 44-14 defeat of Keighley, a match in which 18-year old debutant loose forward Ian Ellis kicked four goals and scored a try. But defeat in their remaining two games resulted in Trinity losing their grip on eighth place, which they surrendered to Rochdale. It was to the Athletic Grounds that they travelled in the first round of the play-offs and were knocked out by the score of 18-13.

New arrangements put in place by the RFL included the appointment of an official timekeeper at each club, the responsibility being removed from the referee. Peter Harrison accepted the duty at Belle Vue. The fixtures for the 1972-73 season reverted to a previous county-based formula, in which all clubs from the same county played each other home and away, plus three clubs from the other county, in Trinity's case Widnes, Swinton and Rochdale. The most important rule change amended the four-tackle rule to six, after the previous rule had failed to encourage open play.

Johnny Malpass, head remedial gymnast at Pinderfields, was relieved of his duties as trainer and believed that after a 36-year association with the club, he had been treated shabbily. His duties were taken over by Gary Cooper, who returned to the club from York to work alongside Fox as assistant coach. Don Froggett, after 24 years' service to the club, resigned as A team coach, citing conflict between work and training nights.

A profit of £769 was declared following a donation of £1,500 from the Supporters' Association which turned a potential deficit into a surplus. Gate receipts showed a rise of over £4,000 thanks to the club's progress in the Player's No. 6 Competition and the three Challenge Cup ties against Leeds, St Helens and Wigan. In elections to the committee, Ron Rylance and Eddie Sugden, both of whom had served before, were voted in, while the selection committee, having recently been the preserve of the coach and chairman, was again widened to five: Neil Fox, Gary Cooper, chairman John Leighton Davies, vice-chairman Jim Bowden and Les Pounder. The Trinity Players' Association, open to present and former players, was established, with Ron Rylance as chairman.

Trinity made a sparkling start to their centenary season of 1972-73, beating Castleford 35-10 at Belle Vue. David Topliss, last season's leading try-scorer, picked up where he had left off, scoring four, while Neil Fox showed his points-scoring talent had hardly dimmed as he accumulated two tries and six goals. In the first round of the Yorkshire Cup, Keighley were swept aside 38-17 before Featherstone were beaten in the league 35-11, a match in which Terry Crook ably deputised for the injured Fox, scoring a try and seven goals. But very soon the early-season pile-up of fixtures started to take its toll. League matches and the County Cups were staple autumn fare, but the RFL, in its desperation for cash, had since added the BBC2 Floodlit Trophy and Player's No. 6, making four competitions running almost simultaneously. It seemed to show that the game had lost a clear sense of direction. Not only did this surfeit affect performance, it also had a serious influence on attendances.

A preliminary round of the Floodlit Trophy, played over two legs, was an excess that the public evidently thought they could forgo. Trinity drew 7-7 with Hull, watched by a meagre crowd of 1,876. In the second round of the Yorkshire Cup at Belle Vue, Trinity inexplicably lost 11-9 to Halifax after winning comfortably at Thrum Hall in the league. In their fourth game in seven days Trinity beat Bramley 13-7 on the Saturday but a sign that fans were sated with what they perceived as second-rate fare appeared in the poor attendance of 1,351, which included a generous estimate of 750 members. In a mirror image of the two matches against Halifax, Trinity lost to Hull 18-10 in the league and four days later beat the same opposition at the Boulevard 11-3 in the preliminary round, second leg of the Floodlit Trophy.

Trinity's forward power was considerably weakened by the sale of international front-rower David Jeanes to Leeds, who paid £8,000. Chairman JL Davies said that Trinity were reluctant to let Jeanes go but wanted the money for essential team-strengthening. Needless to say, the transfer of Jeanes to Leeds was not popular with supporters, who had seen Bob Haigh leave for the same club only eighteen months before. Almost immediately it was announced that Trinity had signed 23-year old forward David Knowles from Upper Wharfedale RU club.

Trinity brought off a rare 34-10 win at Wigan, where both sides were below strength for the first round of the Player's No. 6 competition, in which Joe Bonnar, irrepressible, had one of his best games for the club. The Cumbrian scrum-half was also a livewire in both attack and defence in the 13-12 win over Leeds at Belle Vue, where the 8,041 attendance for this match, played on a Sunday, was bigger than any so far that season at Leeds, a traditional Saturday club.

The former Leeds, Bradford and Hull KR centre, 29-year old Geoff Wriglesworth, was signed from York for £1,400, while scrum-half Bernard Ward was transferred to Bramley for £1,000. Wriglesworth made his home debut in the 15-12 win over Huddersfield, when 'his determined running and inventive play made him a firm favourite.' David Topliss, who had twice been selected for Yorkshire, was called up into the Great Britain squad for the World Cup in France.

After defeating Swinton 18-6 away in the first round, Trinity beat Keighley 19-2 to progress to the semi-final of the Floodlit Trophy. In the same week they recorded a fine victory by 11-8 at Hull KR, where they had not won since 1965. Trinity registered their sixth win in a row with a 23-5 win over Widnes, Wraith scoring his eleventh try of the season, an outstanding solo effort. Widnes, fourth in the league, provided attractive opposition, but the crowd for this Saturday fixture numbered just 2,464. 'However loud the traditionalists shout, Trinity just dare not ignore the greater potential of Sunday afternoon football,' said the *Wakefield Express*.

In going out of the Player's No. 6 by 9-4 at Hull, Trinity failed to cross their opponents' line for the first time in 22 matches, and they fared no better in the semi-final of the Floodlit Trophy at Widnes, losing 16-9 after leading 9-3 at half-time. But in the league they went into fourth place as a result of doing the double over Hull KR when they scored ten tries in the 44-11 win at Belle Vue, 31 of their points coming in the second half. Joe Bonnar was once more in top form and David Topliss and Ray Layton each scored two tries.

It was at Headingley on Boxing Day that Trinity gave Leeds double satisfaction: first by losing 20-7 in a scrappy game in which Morgan was sent off; and second by allowing the home club to register their highest attendance of the season – 11,082 – which was also the best in the league on that day. But to put that into perspective: in 1960 the crowd for the equivalent fixture was 30,154. When Leeds played at Belle Vue earlier in the season, the crowd of 8,041 was twice as big as any attendance at the ground during the first half of the season.

Hooker Tony Handforth expressed his dissatisfaction at not being first choice in the position and, though Mick Morgan often switched successfully between the number 9 role and loose forward, two other hookers were signed in January 1973 – 18-year old Gary Hetherington from Castleford Under 19s and Eric Ingham from Oulton Welfare. Roy Bratt, a 19-year old forward from Allerton Bywater who had represented Yorkshire at Under 17 level, also arrived at the club.

The old-style fixture list was providing some uneven games, as when Trinity beat Doncaster 57-5, Morgan and Marston each scoring hat-tricks, and when they easily overcame Hunslet by 48-10, Topliss scoring three tries without exerting himself. At the half-yearly meeting, his last before retiring, secretary Eddie Thomas condemned the league programme as 'dismal' and claimed it was impossible to survive on income from gates alone, which was already modest and continued to decline. Chairman Davies said that the fall in attendances presented a sad outlook but that the new lottery which had been introduced was making slow but sure progress. Les Pounder, who was also a member of the Rugby League Council, again protested against the screening of live matches on television, which he held as the major reason for the drop in attendances. He said that he would vote against the renewal of the contract with the BBC, who were paying 'chickenfeed'.

Gary Cooper resigned as assistant coach, citing pressure of work and family, and Neil Fox took on sole responsibility for selection. Michael Bennett, who had responsibilities in the club's centenary celebrations, was appointed to take over as secretary from Eddie Thomas, who had long been a central figure at the club.

In the Challenge Cup, Trinity beat Huyton away by 18-6 and went on to defeat Leigh in the next round, again away from home, winning 5-0 in heavy conditions. In the third round Trinity were also drawn away and faced Dewsbury, eleventh in the league table. In the wind and rain at Crown Flatt and faced with a tenacious home defence, Trinity showed little penetration in the absence of the injured Topliss and were beaten 16-4 in front of a 14,000 crowd.

Prop Ted Campbell made a reappearance after being away for two years owing to work and was in the side which beat Rochdale 28-25. The week after, 19-year old winger Barry Lumb, signed from Stanley Rangers, kicked seven goals from eight attempts on his debut and prop Roy Bratt also scored a try on his first home appearance in the 29-16 victory over Batley.

Trinity slipped to seventh in the league but were back to their best form in the 28-12 victory at fourth-placed Featherstone. Fox, back in the centre alongside the excellent Wriglesworth, showed his immense value to the side by scoring a try and five goals and being involved in three other tries. In the 47-9 win over Hunslet, Topliss tore through the opposition to touch down four times. Keighley, however, proved a stumbling block as they won 15-14 at Lawkholme Lane thanks to six goals from full back Brian Jefferson, and did the double over Trinity for the first time in eighteen years. The absence of Fox and Topliss weighed heavily.

Trinity rounded off the regular part of the season with a 13-5 win at Castleford in which Morgan, who took over the hooking role after Handforth and his opposite number had been sent off, was a commanding figure. In the final match a sorry-looking Hull succumbed by 52-0 as Harkin scored three tries, Wriglesworth two and Crook two tries and eight goals.

Trinity finished fifth, entitling them to a home first round play-off against Widnes. Kevin Harkin again put in a fine performance behind the Trinity pack, who established early control to help set up a 20-0 half-time lead, which was extended to 33-6. But at St Helens in the quarter-final Trinity were outplayed and lost 28-0, their biggest defeat of the season. Topliss headed the club try-scoring list with 29 tries and Fox, now aged 34 and often playing in the back row, topped the points-scoring with 300. The Supporters' Club voted him their Player of the Year.

At the AGM, questions about Trinity's financial situation occupied members for over an hour, as the club had just posted a loss on the season of £4,765, with an overdraft at the bank of £18,272. Finance committee chairman Ron Rylance responded, saying, 'We realised at the outset of the year that economies would have to be made and this was not easy because there still exists the idea that Trinity are a comparatively wealthy club.' The deficit was due to three main factors: winning pay for much of the season; a rather poor fixture list and poor support.

Crowds would improve, the top clubs hoped, by reverting to two divisions. But when certain other clubs in the new First Division offered revised contracts, Trinity's players also demanded improved terms. The extra £5 payment to players for Sunday matches, which had been withdrawn midway through the season, was to be waived entirely. In the season just ended, terms had been £20 for an away win and £18 for a home win. The committee offered £25 and £20, which the players refused at first and then accepted. Separate terms would be negotiated for cup games.

Ex-Huddersfield player Jim Bowden was elected chairman and former Trinity loose forward Dave Lamming became the new A team coach. Signings were few: as winger Barry Parker joined from Leeds for £750, David Barends was sold to York at less than the £1,500 listing.

Trinity started 1973-74 almost where they had left off the previous season, except that they now figured in the new First Division. Following wins in the league at Castleford, Dewsbury and at home to Rochdale, Trinity had an easy passage into the second round of the Yorkshire Cup as they beat Doncaster 39-7. That victory gave entry to yet another new competition – the Captain Morgan Trophy, named after a brand of rum and open to the winners of the first round of the County Cups.

In the Yorkshire Cup second round, Trinity made the gulf in class obvious as they dispatched Keighley 39-4. In the proliferation of competitions, often necessitating two games a week, Trinity trounced Blackpool 47-13 in the first round of the Player's No. 6, a match in which Fox collected twenty points as well as a dislocated shoulder that kept him out of action for the best part of a month. After beating Oldham 22-0 in the league, Trinity faced Castleford in the semi-final of the Yorkshire Cup at Belle Vue. With two minutes of the match remaining, Trinity, seven points ahead, looked a safe bet for the final, having scored tries through Hegarty, Topliss and Wraith. Despite having had a man sent off midway through the second period, Castleford made a final effort which brought two tries, the second coming in the third minute of injury time to take them within one point of Trinity at 19-18. But Lloyd could not add the difficult conversion and Trinity were through to the final for the first time in nine years.

Before then the thirteenth meeting between Trinity and the Australian tourists took place, the home side having won four. Trailing 11-0 after 25 minutes, Trinity came back into the game with three penalties from Crook and, fifteen minutes from the end, a sensational try from Topliss, who 'beat several defenders with an electrifying diagonal burst from just inside the Australian 25.' Topliss's display put him into the reckoning for a test place, but Trinity went down 13-9, watched by a crowd of 5,863.

In their league programme, Trinity registered their first post-war victory at Warrington, where, in a fine performance, they won 13-10 and broke their hosts' unbeaten league record. Despite having Valentine sent off after 50 minutes, Trinity scored three tries to none, through Ballantyne, Lumb and Holmes. They defended resolutely, Wraith giving the lead and Topliss once more taunting the opposition with his weaving runs.

When the fourth competition of the season – the Floodlit Trophy - got under way in October, Trinity went out at the first stage, losing 10-9 at home to Bramley, who caused a major upset by going on to win the competition. But in a rehearsal for the Yorkshire Cup Final, a more focused Trinity beat Leeds 18-9 at Belle Vue, scoring two tries in the last five minutes. Topliss claimed the matchwinner, his hundredth try, with a fine individual effort.

There was some controversy about the venue for the final. Despite Leeds's participation, Headingley was chosen because the sponsors, Esso, wanted first-class facilities in which to entertain their guests and only the Leeds ground came up to the mark. 'It's not a healthy trend,' commented the *Wakefield Express*, 'when money can cause a century-old tradition to be dumped overboard.'

Wakefield had beaten Leeds in the final when they last won the Cup in the 1964-65 season. But having home advantage, and with Trinity lacking Fox, Wriglesworth and Lyons, all injured, Leeds were now clear favourites. Trinity led 2-0 from an early Crook penalty but had no more to show for their efforts. Leeds, well led by Hepworth, won 7-2, watched by a mere 7,535 spectators.

Player-coach Neil Fox found himself at the centre of a row which set the committee and a section of the membership at loggerheads. A group of A team players had reportedly approached the committee accusing Fox of favouritism in his team selection, for which he had had sole responsibility. As a result the committee decided that they would pick the team themselves. Fox, relieved of this duty, said that he would not look to have his contract renewed when the time came in August.

Two weeks later an extraordinary meeting was called following a petition by a member, seeking clarification of two issues: the reason why Derek Turner had been sounded out regarding the coaching position; and the committee's attitude towards the selling of key players. The meeting was described as 'stormy' and developed to the point where 'anger and bad manners were often demonstrated to an embarrassing degree.' Attended by some 300 members out of a total of 1,400, it was 'a sad night for a great club'. Calls were made for the committee to resign and the vote of confidence in Fox as a coach was taken as a vote of no confidence in the committee, who, however, said that key players – and Topliss in particular – were not for sale, adding that £8,500 had been wiped off the overdraft. The following day, club chairman Jim Bowden, vice-chairman Don Robinson, ex-chairman John Leighton Davies, committee member Ken Croft and secretary Michael Bennett all resigned. Bowden said that the behaviour of some of the members was 'deplorable' and Davies said he was not prepared to submit to mob rule. Secretary Bennett said he was prepared to stay on until the end of the year or until a replacement could be found. Trevor Woodward, elected as a new member at the previous annual meeting, had also threatened to resign if the present chairman were to remain, 'saying he could not serve under a chairman who, he claimed, had lost the confidence of the members.' Long-serving committee man Eddie Sugden also later resigned, leaving Les Pounder to take over as chairman, Ron Rylance as vice-chairman and two other committee men, Woodward and John Sellers. Pounder became the first committee member to serve as chairman three times, after stints in 1957-59 and 1969-71.

On the field, victory over Batley in the first round of the new Captain Morgan Trophy was followed by a 20-14 second round defeat at Featherstone. Those two matches represented the sum total of Trinity's involvement in the competition, which was withdrawn after only one season.

In the league an 18-12 win at Central Park over an under-strength Wigan was inspired by loose forward Mick

Morgan, who scored a try and made another. It was soon followed by Trinity's first league triumph at Widnes since 1946, though the two clubs had not met regularly in the intervening years. Trinity's 28-13 win included Crook's seven goals from nine attempts, two of which stemmed from the newly-introduced seven point try: Topliss had scored a brilliant try after jinking past a clutch of defenders inside the Widnes 25 and had scored under the posts, but had been fouled by Elwell after touching down. Crook converted and then added the penalty.

In the Player's No. 6 competition, second division Workington were beaten 10-7 before an exciting 18-all draw with St Helens ensued at Belle Vue. Trinity produced some impressive attacking play but in the end their defensive frailty allowed Saints to draw level and then win the replay at Knowsley Road by 16-10. In the league Trinity did the double over Warrington with a 26-15 home win in which scrum-half Terry Langton, signed six months earlier for £200 from Stanningley ARLFC, stole the show and scored a clever try from the blind-side of a scrum. Langton scored again when Trinity travelled to Leeds for the traditional Boxing Day fixture but after leading 12-7 at half-time they went down 19-14. Langton's brother, Barry, a stand-off, also signed from Leeds amateur rugby league, and, on occasion, proved a more than useful scrum-half.

At the half-yearly meeting in January, secretary Michael Bennett, who was to withdraw his resignation, announced that he felt that the club had turned the corner financially. But he added a comment which highlighted the tangled nature of the fixture list as semi-professional players were often having to cope with two matches a week – more towards the end of the season – as a result of the RFL running six different competitions – the League championship, the Challenge Cup, the County Cups, the Player's No. 6, the Floodlit and the Captain Morgan Trophy. 'I feel we have too many sponsored competitions,' said Bennett, 'and our experience has been that to make any money from these tournaments you have either to be beaten in the opening round or reach the final. It is a pity the sponsorship money cannot be directed towards our more established competitions and in this way we would avoid the fixture congestion we now have.' His views were echoed by chairman Les Pounder, who referred to the 'chaotic' fixture list. Pounder added that, in the aftermath of the resignations from the committee, he thought 'an unfortunate chapter in the club's history was now closed.' In this calmer atmosphere Neil Fox said he would be happy to stay as coach when his contract came up for renewal at the end of the season.

But Trinity's form dipped from that point on. They reserved their worst display of the season for the first round of the Challenge Cup. After losing the previous week at home to Widnes in the league, they went on to suffer a 27-7 reverse at Naughton Park in the Cup.

Steve Lyons, Kevin Harkin and Geoff Wraith were bound for Australia, which significantly weakened the squad, although their leaving did not satisfactorily explain the defeat upon defeat. Wigan's 21-0 victory at Belle Vue would not have been so bad if Trinity had not been in fifth place in the league and Wigan thirteenth and seeking to stave off relegation. The bottom four of the sixteen first division clubs were to go down. Trinity themselves were not yet clear of that threat. As the *Wakefield Express* said: 'Like a never-ending nightmare, the sad saga of Trinity's alarming decline goes on and on, this latest setback yielding a result which must have been greeted with sheer disbelief throughout the rugby league world.'

With a narrow home victory over Hull KR by 10-9, Trinity's relegation fears subsided, but coach Neil Fox dropped a bombshell when he suddenly announced his resignation. Ironically it was Fox who was largely responsible for the success against Hull KR, scoring the first try, kicking two goals, creating the second try and making numerous openings. 'It's been a very hard decision to make,' he said. 'I cannot say that anything specifically has made me make up my mind. I just feel I must make a clean break now that I consider the side to be free from relegation worries. It will be hard after nineteen years with Trinity but I imagine they will be able to get along without me.' It was with reluctance that the committee accepted Fox's resignation, which came after almost four years in charge of the side. At the end of the season and in recognition of his long service to the club, Fox was given a free transfer and was immediately signed by Hull KR, who beat three other clubs to his signature.

Neil Fox's career at Wakefield Trinity was both remarkable and unique. He had played 574 times for the club, second only to forward Harry Wilkinson's 618. His 4,488 points for the club far surpassed any other Trinity player's tally, while his first-class career total of 5,165 – up to that point – had been bettered in the game only by Jim Sullivan. As Robert Gate has pointed out, he had, at one time or another, held all the club records for tries, goals and points scored in a match, a season or a career.

At the same time, stand-off David Topliss, who became the new captain, voiced his disappointment at being left out of the Great Britain touring team to Australia. Believing that he could do better at another club, Topliss, whose form had declined in mid-season along with that of the team, promised to stay another year at Belle Vue after the committee told him that they were now in a position to make new signings, having received £10,000 for the Queensland-bound trio.

With Dave Lamming as caretaker coach, Trinity completed the double over Hull KR, winning 17-10 at Craven Park and went on to record their highest away victory in the league that season with a 35-5 win at Bramley, achieved with 'fast, flowing football'. The end of season run-in was less noteworthy as Trinity finished in seventh place.

In the first round of the championship play-offs, Trinity accounted for Dewsbury, winning 26-11 at Belle Vue. David Smith scored two tries to take his total for the season to 36 and full back Les Sheard also touched down twice in an immaculate display. In the quarter-final, also at Belle Vue, Trinity beat Featherstone 19-16 after trailing 16-4 on the hour. In a thrilling fightback, Topliss slipped the defence to score between the posts, Smith cut inside from the touchline to leave the cover defence in his wake and Bonnar scooted over the line from dummy-half. Stand-in coach Lamming, however, said that he would not apply for the permanent coaching position, saying he was not experienced enough at that level. In the championship semi-final at Warrington, Trinity's season ended as Alex Murphy created the two tries the home side needed to reach the final. Trinity went out by 12-7 but David Smith had the consolation of scoring Trinity's try and thus equalling Fred Smith's record of 38 in a season, making him a clear winner of the Player of the Year award. The attendance of 10,007 at Wilderspool was second only, among matches Trinity had been involved in, to the 10,390 recorded at Headingley on Boxing Day. The biggest at Belle Vue was the 7,834 crowd for the visit of Leeds. Trinity's average for the season, according to figures released by the RFL, was a meagre 2,197, but even that exceeded by 474 the figure for the previous season. Income from gate receipts was up by £4,000 and though the club made a loss of £1,400, it was significantly less than the £4,675 of the previous season.

In June, Peter Fox, who had guided Featherstone to Wembley in successive seasons and had briefly been on Trinity's books as a player, was appointed as successor to his younger brother and would have complete control of team selection. Among a host of signings of young players from the local area, the 17-year old twins Keith and Kevin Rayne, both second-rowers, were signed from Glasshoughton intermediates. At junior level Kevin had played for England and Keith for Yorkshire. Another forward, 20-year old Trevor Skerrett, was signed from Bison Sports while 32-year old Rob Valentine, who had spent three seasons at Belle Vue, was transferred to Keighley for £1,000.

At the annual general meeting, chairman Les Pounder, who was formally elected after becoming acting chairman following the resignations, appealed for solidarity, saying, 'A period of peace is urgently needed for us to regain the confidence of the rugby league world.' He paid tribute to the work of Neil Fox, who had left the club 'on a very friendly note'. Secretary-manager Michael Bennett and former player Bob Oliver were elected to the committee. Since they had functioned well with only four members since the upheaval, it was decided by a vote of club members to reduce the board from the traditional nine to six. Paddy Armour, who had been the club physio for 22 years, announced his resignation because of increasing professional commitments. His successor was Ben Qansah, of Ghanaian origin, who had previously been on the staff at Pinderfields and now worked at a Sheffield hospital.

In the first match of the 1974-75 season, when all league games would be played on Sundays, Trinity drew with

Peter Fox, who succeeded his brother Neil as coach in 1974, meets Les Sheard, Mick Morgan and David Topliss

Castleford 12-all, with Trevor Skerrett making his debut as a late substitute for David Knowles. In the first round of the Yorkshire Cup, Halifax were knocked out by 22-12. After that came the Floodlit Trophy and an absurd preliminary round with an even more ridiculous two legs involving Trinity and St Helens. Squeezed into the same week was a 27-13 defeat at Wigan in the league and a 24-14 win over Featherstone which put Trinity into the semi-final of the Yorkshire Cup. There were some outstanding performances in that victory over Peter Fox's old side. Topliss was 'his brilliant best, fast and elusive'. Sheard's coolness under pressure matched his attacking flair. Morgan 'played himself to a standstill' and Bratt was 'always in the thick of things', with Lumb landing six out of eight goal attempts. Sheard, though, turned down the chance to play for Yorkshire, which would have meant four games in six days, saying that he could not afford to take more time off teaching. As the *Wakefield Express* pointed out, Trinity had played nine matches in the opening month of the season; it would have been ten if Dewsbury's players had not gone on strike. 'Sheer madness for part-time professionals' the *Express* called it, 'and too costly for supporters.' This multiplicity of games inevitably brought its toll of injuries. Les Tonks, the 33-year old forward from Featherstone, was signed to ease Trinity's injury problems.

In the semi-final of the Yorkshire Cup, Trinity struggled to overcome second division Hull. The only try of the match came when full back Les Sheard put ex-Wakefield RU winger John Archer over with a fine, long pass. Topliss added a drop goal, now reduced to one point, to give Trinity an 8-6 victory. 'Trinity owed a tremendous debt to the skill and courage of Les Sheard, who twice saved his line and then returned after injury to set up the decisive score. This was poetic justice as Sheard had been the victim of a high tackle which kept him off the field for 20 minutes.'

Topliss and Sheard, who had withdrawn from a previous selection, represented Yorkshire against Lancashire, with Morgan as forward substitute. It was dual honours for Sheard, who had also played for the county at rugby union.

The Yorkshire Cup final at Headingley was declared to be the best seen in years, but that was little consolation for Trinity, as they lost 16-13 to second division Hull KR, who had Neil Fox in the pack facing his old team. Trinity got off to a promising start when Crook kicked a penalty and Hegarty scored the first try. Hull KR drew level and then took the lead before David Smith brought the teams to 10-all with the try of the match as he went past two defenders over 50 yards following Morgan's fine break from deep inside his own half. Rovers then took control, though Watson's crucial try was disputed. Bratt's late try for Trinity counted little. It was Trinity's fourth defeat in four consecutive finals following disappointments in the previous season's Yorkshire Cup, the 1971 Player's No. 6 and the 1968 Challenge Cup.

Injury-hit Trinity slumped to their heaviest defeat of the season at Widnes in the second round of the Player's No. 6, which they lost 35-13. Topliss asked to step down as captain and Morgan took on the role. Hegarty went to Dewsbury for £2,600, further weakening the squad. A 16-12 defeat at Bradford became Trinity's sixth loss in seven games. But, never failing to surprise, Trinity relieved St Helens of their hundred per cent record by winning 13-5 in heavy conditions at Belle Vue.

Malcolm Reilly led Castleford to an indisputable 35-8 win which made Trinity's side, as it was composed, look too weak for the top division. There was at least one bright spot: 'Topliss's class shone like a beacon on a night of despair for Trinity supporters.'

Gary Hetherington, the future founder of Sheffield Eagles and chief executive of Leeds, was transferred to York for £1,000 after making just five first team appearances in two years, and was soon followed by hooker Tony Handforth, who had played over a hundred first-team matches, for a similar fee.

When Sheard and Bratt returned to the side, they made an immediate impact as Trinity rediscovered their form to beat Leeds 23-15 at Belle Vue, in front of only 3,846 spectators, although that modest figure represented the highest attendance of the season so far. In the Boxing Day match at Headingley, Trinity again put up a stern display as they held third-placed Leeds to a 13-all draw thanks to a late drop goal from Ellis.

As the New Year of 1975 opened, the biggest crowd of the season so far – 4,213 – turned up at Belle Vue for the visit of Featherstone, a match which finished as a 12-all draw. David Topliss, who would be named in the England side to play France, withdrew his request for a move, and Trinity were successful in persuading a former Featherstone scrum-half, 23-year old Terry Hudson, to leave Hull KR, to whom they paid £3,500. Hull KR were reported to have paid £7,000 for Hudson two years earlier but the half back had now been out of the game for some time. His transfer to Wakefield was to have been partly financed by the sale of Joe Bonnar to York, but the Cumbrian refused to go, preferring to contest the scrum-half spot with Hudson and Barry Langton.

Trinity went on to cause a huge upset by beating Salford away by 16-6, a victory in which Henry Oulton's two superb goals played a significant part. That win was one of a six-match unbeaten run, including a 23-5 victory at Rochdale, where Topliss, forming a new half-back partnership with Hudson, scored a hat-trick. 'Three times Trinity's international stand-off left the Rochdale full back for dead, waltzing round him after mazy runs had cut a bewildered defence to shreds,' reported the *Wakefield Express*.

In the Challenge Cup, Trinity had a comfortable passage into the second round when they beat Huyton 33-5 at Belle Vue. The second round draw posed more of a problem, Trinity being pitted against favourites St Helens but with home advantage. With a big penalty count against them, Trinity trailed 9-7 going into the last quarter, much of which Saints spent camped in the Trinity 25 in an atmosphere of almost palpable tension. Earlier Smith had scored the opening try when he went past one defender and kicked infield, beating Saints full back Coslett to the ball and touching down. With Morgan, Skerrett and Bratt giving a big lead up front, Sheard went over from Morgan's pass with eight minutes remaining. It was left to Topliss to put the match beyond doubt when he made a half-break and then put in a well-judged kick to the corner for Archer to claim the final touchdown. Trinity went through 13-9, watched by a 6,315 crowd which would have been much bigger, the committee contended, if the match had not been shown live on BBC.

Before Trinity faced Neil Fox's Hull KR in the third round, Topliss contributed four tries to the 50-13 downfall of Bramley in a league match, in which Crook scored two tries and kicked ten goals from ten for a personal haul of 26 points. The home cup-tie against Hull KR attracted a crowd of 14,514 - the biggest of the season in Yorkshire and the highest at Belle Vue that decade. Receipts of £6,391 represented an all-time record for Belle Vue. The Robins were beaten 27-10, with Roy Bratt scoring two tries.

On the international front, Mick Morgan came on as a substitute for England against France at Headingley and scored a try. Les Sheard had earlier been selected for England against Wales and Morgan was to be called up into the England World Championship squad as a late replacement.

Hopes of going to Wembley for the first time since 1968 were dashed at Odsal, where Widnes, fifth in the league, overcame Trinity, eleventh, by 13-7, Trinity's sole try coming from Sheard. But Trinity fans comforted themselves in the knowledge that, only a few months earlier, a semi-final appearance seemed unthinkable.

A 10-10 draw with Bradford in the last match of the regular part of the season resulted in Trinity facing Castleford away in the championship play-offs, now known as the Premiership. With several first-teamers missing, Trinity went down 37-7.

Vice-chairman Ron Rylance resigned following differences on policy, which drew Peter Fox to say how much he regretted the resignation: 'He is so knowledgeable on the game that the club can ill afford to lose his services.' Chairman Les Pounder expressed a similar view and hoped he would reconsider, but he did not.

At the end of the season, a loss of £864 was announced, to which an unusually high figure of £7,500 for ground improvements contributed. Michael Bennett was succeeded as secretary by Alan Pearman, director of a Batley travel agents and a cousin of former Trinity loose forward Roger Pearman.

In the World Championship in Australia and New Zealand, Mick Morgan played in three matches in three different forward positions. On the home front, Andrew Fletcher, a 17-year old winger from Townville, and a nephew of Arthur Fletcher, the Trinity half back of the 1940s, was signed.

At the AGM, Trevor Woodward was elected chairman while Jim Walker, head of a Lofthouse Gate printing company, was voted president in succession to Ernest Corscadden, whose professional commitments compelled him to step down.

Eighteen – Back to Wembley: 1975-80

Coach Peter Fox was very optimistic about the side being put together for the 1975-76 season. County forward Graham Idle, aged 24, was the latest addition after signing from Bramley, with half back Barry Langton heading for the Barley Mow as part of the deal. The opening success at Castleford confirmed Fox's view, but there followed a string of five defeats - including a Yorkshire Cup exit at Hull KR and a Floodlit Trophy defeat by Dewsbury - which only ended with a double over Castleford.

Owen Stephens, a former New Zealand All Black and Australian Rugby Union winger, who had switched codes with Parramatta, began a short spell at Belle Vue. In his second match Stephens scored a hat-trick in the 30-13 win at Huddersfield, forming an effective partnership with centre John Sutcliffe. In the same match full back Henry Oulton kicked six goals for the third game in a row. But Stephens' stay did not last long - he returned home after two months following injury.

In the first round of the Player's No. 6 trophy, Trinity beat Bradford, the holders, by 32-12 at Odsal, Morgan setting a lead with his 'penetrative running and shrewd handling'. But in the second round they went down to Castleford at Belle Vue by 24-14. In a different vein altogether Trinity hammered a below-strength Warrington 47-4, David Smith claiming three tries. Smith scored a fine try on his county debut against Cumbria and kept his place, along with David Topliss, for the match against Lancashire in a side captained by Mick Morgan, who scored two tries as Yorkshire took the county championship title.

In the 35-5 win over bottom club Swinton, 19-year old full back Trevor Midgley made a sound debut, though Topliss was once more the star of the show as he touched down three times. The stand-off also picked up two tries when Trinity demolished Salford's hundred per cent home record in the league, winning 16-9.

The testimonial for Ted Campbell, who had played twelve seasons, realised £650. Campbell was given a free transfer to York, where he became the ninth former Trinity player, while scrum-half Joe Bonnar, who had made over 150 appearances for Trinity, went to Halifax in a player-exchange deal for Sammy Sanderson. As signings from Australia became more frequent, Australian centre Paul O'Brien, who had been named the best player in the Sydney Metropolitan league, arrived on a three-year contract.

Over the Christmas period, victories over Keighley and Huddersfield saw Trinity go fourth in the table. In the New Year's Day game, Mick Morgan's benefit match, Trinity beat third-placed Featherstone 13-5, the outcome settled by Smith's long-range interception try. With a 16-5 victory in mid-January at Odsal, where Les Sheard was in outstanding form, Trinity went clear at the top of the table, but lost their position when Salford gained revenge by winning 13-4 at Belle Vue, thus ending an eight-match winning streak.

This season of contrasts continued with a five-match losing run. In the first round of the Challenge Cup, Trinity met Featherstone at Post Office Road. Trinity sported a new shirt design, which incorporated a giant W instead of a V. It must surely rank, by some way, as their worst ever. The new kit certainly brought no luck as, lacking the injured Topliss and Sheard, as well as Hudson and Ray Handscombe, Trinity were ousted 23-9.

The slide down the league table was arrested by a 19-12 win at Oldham, inspired by Les Sheard's brilliant performance. 'Sheard has given many fine displays in the past,' said the *Wakefield Express*, 'but this must rank among his best. Rarely can a full back have dominated a game as he did with a succession of defence-splitting breaks which left Oldham gasping.' Henry Oulton, on the wing, also made a significant contribution, succeeding with five goal attempts from six. Oulton's outstanding goal-kicking was a major feature of a 10-7 win by a weakened side at

St Helens, the winger scoring all his side's points from penalties, most of them from difficult positions. It was only the second time Trinity had won at Knowsley Road since the war.

The Trinity committee gave permission to David Topliss to leave the club seven matches before the end of the campaign to spend the close season in Australia with Penrith, where former Dewsbury hooker Mike Stephenson and Wigan forward Bill Ashurst were also playing.

Leeds did the double over Trinity in the space of just over a week and compounded Wakefield's misery by making an approach for winger David Smith. As the 23-year old international became increasingly open to Leeds's interest, he declared that he wanted to leave and was listed at £12,000. He was critical of the committee, saying that 'he was not alone among the players in his disappointment over the manner in which the committee were operating the club.' He was also concerned that, in his opinion, there was no planning for the future and claimed that the pay scale was the lowest in the first division.

Winger David Smith scored 38 tries in 1973-74 to equal Fred Smith's record before moving to Leeds two seasons later

Two wins over the Easter period stopped the slide. An unexpected victory at third-placed Featherstone by 19-7 was built on Smith's three tries, the last coming from a fine break, from deep inside his own half, by Terry Crook, who also kicked five goals. A 14-7 win over Dewsbury was Trinity's first in the league since New Year's Day and condemned their opponents to the second division.

In the first round of the play-offs, Trinity, who finished seventh, were set to play second-placed Featherstone, in what would be the fourth match of the season between the two sides, Trinity having so far won two of them. They pulled off another surprise by winning 14-10 at Post Office Road. Sheard, voted Player of the Year, and Paul O'Brien scored superb solo tries, Crook kicked two fine goals and Trevor Skerrett gave a non-stop display, producing a 'phenomenal' tackle rate.

The committee had already decided, some weeks earlier, to part company with coach Peter Fox, who, however, wanted to carry on. They went ahead with their decision to axe Fox, citing 'a complete breakdown of liaison between the coach and committee and, in particular, club chairman Mr Trevor Woodward.' Trinity captain Mick Morgan told the committee that he and the players thought Peter Fox the best coach in the Rugby League and that any new coach would not be as able. 'This is not a players' revolt,' he told the *Wakefield Express*. 'It merely underlines the players' desire to get on with the job of playing football with the best possible advice at hand. We feel we should not be affected by any domestic differences – they should be settled in the boardroom.'

In the first leg of the Premiership semi-final, Trinity battled to hold league leaders Salford to 10-5, Skerrett scoring his side's only try from Sheard's pass. But in the second leg at Belle Vue Trinity failed to find inspiration and went down 14-5 in front of 7,048 spectators – the biggest home crowd of the season by some way.

Trinity's average attendance for the season was 3,364. The best supported clubs were Widnes, Leeds and Salford, but even they only averaged crowds of around 5,000. Trinity's loss on the year amounted to £11,474, a figure which was accounted for by the signing of Graham Idle and John 'Sammy' Sanderson, the contracts with Owen Stephens and O'Brien and fees for players who had come through the Colts. No income was received from the sale of players.

The AGM brought about what the *Wakefield Express* called a 'dramatic sequel to the Fox affair'. At the three-hour long meeting, chairman Trevor Woodward was sensationally voted off the committee by members, who clearly held him responsible for letting Peter Fox go when he wanted to stay. President Jim Walker said 'it was unfortunate that

[Woodward] could have been condemned for actions which were the collective decisions of the committee. The committee felt there was not sufficient variety in Trinity's play, that players were not improving and were lacking coaching in positional play. The decision was unanimous in the end.'

Consequently Les Pounder, who had served on the committee for 28 years and was Trinity's representative on the Rugby League Council, was elected chairman once again. The former Great Britain forward Geoff Gunney, aged 42, was appointed coach in place of Peter Fox. Gunney was known as a Hunslet man first and foremost, had made over 600 appearances for the club and played a major part in its rebirth as New Hunslet after the old Parkside club closed down. Gunney arrived saying that he would insist on physical fitness and getting the basics right. The players agreed new terms for the 1976-77 season, considering the pay scale 'a great improvement'. Centre Geoff Wriglesworth, after missing all the previous season with an ankle injury, was back in training, but David Smith, who had been the club's leading try-scorer since being signed from Shaw Cross, could not be persuaded to stay and was transferred to Leeds for £11,000.

As the 1976-77 season opened, Trinity's Yorkshire Cup campaign began with a 15-7 win over Bramley but ended with a 16-9 home reverse against Featherstone. Trinity's first league point came with a very creditable 7-all draw at St Helens, followed by another defeat of Bramley, this time by 20-5 in the preliminary round of the Floodlit Trophy, in front of a paltry 1,152 crowd at Belle Vue. Trinity soon went out of the competition, losing 5-2 to second division Huddersfield. When, at the end of October, Widnes put Trinity out of the Player's No. 6 by 10-8 at Belle Vue, the club had already made its exit from three competitions.

Gunney, in post for just three months, was made team manager and former Great Britain forward Brian Lockwood, who had been signed short-term until February, when he would return to Australia to play for Balmain, was given the job of coach. Second rower John Rangeley arrived from New Hunslet, Aussie centre Geoff Gerard was also signed until February, while goal-kicking full back or wing Henry Oulton was listed at £6,000. Centre David Noble went on loan to Doncaster, and Cumbrian forward Bill Kirkbride, after a three-year spell in Australia, was signed as a free agent.

Among the bright spots in an otherwise dismal first part of the season, a 16-6 home victory over Wigan was based on Eric Ingham's dominance in the scrums and another sparkling display by Topliss, the scorer of a 'stunning' try. 'After Crook made ground from his own 25, Topliss went through from acting half back on a long run which saw him weave his way past a bunch of defenders and eventually burst clear down the touchline, outpacing his final pursuer to touch down in the corner. It was the sort of try which only a player of exceptional ability could score and will long be remembered.' The match was also notable for the first-ever Aussie centre partnership in Trinity's ranks when Gerard came on to play alongside O'Brien. It was short-lived, however, as O'Brien returned home at the end of the year.

With three further defeats Trinity remained anchored in the relegation zone but then surprised everyone with their first win at Headingley for twelve years. Trinity did not look like a bottom-four side as, under Lockwood's astute guidance and with Morgan, Skerrett and young prop Nigel Murray in fine form, they outplayed Leeds by 18-8. Topliss was 'at his very best – razor-sharp, always looking for the opening and distributing cleverly, besides doing his share of tackling. Morgan's reverse pass sent Topliss streaking past a flat-footed defence to score by the posts.' Nevertheless Trinity were still struggling for their first division lives. The contrast with twelve months earlier, when they topped the league, spoke volumes.

The new year of 1977 started in hideous fashion. Trinity lost 52-0 at Featherstone on what was described as 'one of the blackest days in the history of the club'. With Morgan and Lockwood both sent off on the intervention of a touch judge, Trinity slumped to their biggest defeat in two decades. 'Some of us haven't forgotten,' wrote Frank Jeffrey in the *Wakefield Express*, "those terrible hidings at St Helens (69-17 in 1953 and 52-5 in 1957-8) and it will

County back row forward Graham Idle and stand-off David Topliss in action against Leigh, 1977

be a long time before Trinity's stunned supporters can erase the memory of the extraordinary happenings of this bitter afternoon.' Geoff Gunney was 'eased out' of his 'non-existent' role as team manager, while his predecessor Peter Fox had just been appointed England coach.

In the other code, the John Player Cup provided interest when Wakefield RUFC were drawn against one of the top clubs, Leicester. But College Grove was in no state for the match, snow and ice having thawed to leave the pitch unplayable. Club officials were delighted when the Trinity committee offered them the use of Belle Vue, where rugby union matches had occasionally been staged many years previously. In 1903 the Yorkshire Cup (RU) final replay took place there and five years later the match between Yorkshire and Australia. Unfortunately for Wakefield Rugby Union, the RFU refused permission for Belle Vue to be used. Professional grounds were regarded as beyond the pale. Instead Wakefield were ordered at 24 hours' notice to play at Kirkstall and so were deprived of home advantage. The RFU came in for strong criticism but to no avail.

Mick Morgan's benefit raised a record £3,600 and David Topliss was set to spend his second summer in Australia, this time at Balmain, at the suggestion of Brian Lockwood. The coach signed an agreement to return from Balmain to Trinity the following season on the promise of a three-year contract. In his absence, assistant coach Freddie Williamson would take charge.

At the half-yearly meeting, club president Jim Walker confirmed that £11,000 had been received from Leeds for David Smith and £14,000 had been spent on signing Lockwood and Kirkbride, plus seven others, including Rangeley and Riggs from Hunslet, though Rangeley did not appear after being dropped and Riggs was unavailable because of working away.

In February Trinity made what was heralded as rugby league's most spectacular signing of the season when 24-year old England Rugby Union scrum-half Mike Lampkowski arrived from Headingley RU club. Lampkowski had played four times for England the previous season and had impressed Trinity with his tough, muscular style. He received a signing-on fee of £4,000 with more promised for county and international selection, the money having been lent by committee members. With apparent weaknesses in the three-quarter line, however, the signing was criticised in some quarters when the club already had three scrum-halves on the books. President Jim Walker, who had adopted a higher profile than most of his predecessors in the post, stated that Hudson and Langton both had suffered long-term injury, while Sanderson could also operate at stand-off. It was no coincidence that Sanderson made an outstanding contribution to Trinity's next game – a 12-8 defeat of Widnes.

The biggest attendance of the season so far - 4,553 - was recorded for the first round Challenge Cup match against second division Halifax. Many of the crowd had no doubt turned up expecting to see Lampkowski's debut, which was however postponed, and fans had a double reason to be disappointed as Trinity laboured to overcome the visitors by 12-3. The new scrum-half made his first appearance off the bench in the 15-10 reverse at Wigan, playing impressively and scoring a try through sheer strength and determination close to the line.

In the second round Trinity faced a visit to Dewsbury, second in division two but boasting the best defensive record in the league. In a dull game played in a biting wind blowing across Crown Flatt, braved by 7,290 spectators, no tries were produced by either side and Dewsbury went through by 5-0.

Following a succession of poor results, Trinity headed out of the relegation zone with heartening wins against league leaders Featherstone and Challenge Cup finalists Leeds. Featherstone were beaten 12-7, which went some way to avenging the earlier 52-0 drubbing, Fletcher scoring two fine tries, one of them a length-of-the-field interception. Bratt's return bolstered the pack while Lampkowski gave an all-action display until he left the field with a broken nose after appearing to have been butted. The 19-18 victory over Leeds was earned by Henry Oulton's last-gasp penalty. Though his brother Willie, who had earlier been transferred to Leeds for £750, kicked three goals and another former Trinity player, David Smith, scored a try, Henry Oulton outshone both with a try and three goals. Trevor Skerrett, who powered through the Leeds defence for two tries, was named man of the match and hooker Ray Handscombe landed an uncommon drop goal.

Their chances of making the play-offs were improved by Topliss's decision to postpone his departure for Australia until the end of the season, while coach Brian Lockwood, also Australia-bound, left his assistant Freddie Williamson in charge. In the end Trinity avoided relegation but failed to make the play-offs, finishing eleventh out of sixteen. During the season, a total of 46 players were used, with Skerrett topping the appearances list with 35, closely followed by Idle on 34 and Topliss, the leading try-scorer and Player of the Year, with 32. Geoff Wriglesworth retired and Mick Morgan was transferred to York for £7,500. A profit of £1,067 was declared and president Jim Walker maintained that the players, with an average paypacket of £35, were among the best paid in the league, adding that committee members had contributed to bonus payments out of their own pockets. With an average crowd figure of 2,931, Trinity were fifth from bottom of the league in terms of attendances, Widnes coming out top with 6,129.

At the AGM, outgoing chairman Les Pounder said: 'You cannot go back to the sixties but our young players have a right to feel that the glorious eighties are just ahead.' Former player David Garthwaite and, in a curious twist, Trevor Woodward were voted on to the committee. Woodward, who had been ousted only a year earlier, was returned to the chairman's role by fellow committee members.

The first two rounds of the Yorkshire Cup opened the 1977-78 season. After beating Doncaster 23-10, Trinity were halted by Featherstone, the previous season's champions, who won 12-2 at Belle Vue, watched by 5,803 spectators. Scrum-half John Sanderson was signed by Leeds for £2,500, but David Topliss returned from Balmain to strike up what looked like being a formidable half-back partnership with Mike Lampkowski. Topliss had been offered 'a considerable sum' to stay with Balmain for two years but the stand-off said he preferred to re-establish himself in England and earn a Great Britain tour place.

In the Floodlit Trophy, Trinity overcame Bramley 14-4 in the preliminary round and beat Keighley 15-7 in the first round. But their league form promised little. They slumped to a fifth consecutive defeat against Workington before surprising everyone with a 15-0 victory at the Boulevard to earn their first league points. An 18-5 win against Bramley, in which ex-QEGS pupil Mark Endersby landed six goals from as many attempts, was followed by a 14-7 success against star-studded Salford.

Trevor Skerrett's impressive form was recognised in his selection for Great Britain Under 24s against France. Trinity once more looked to the ranks of England Rugby Union to make another important signing when 24-year old centre Keith Smith was signed from Roundhay RUFC. Smith had played four times for England and fourteen for Yorkshire but was well acquainted with rugby league, which he had played until the age of sixteen. His grandfather, who came from Wakefield, used to take him to watch Trinity and the youngster had played in the Leeds City schoolboys' team alongside John Holmes.

After beating Batley and then Cawood's, the amateur side from Hull, in the re-named John Player Trophy, Trinity defeated Leigh 12-9, a match in which Lockwood and Topliss played significant roles, Topliss going 40 yards for the match-clinching try. Lockwood's leadership and ball-playing skill was missed in the semi-final, however, when Trinity went down 15-5 to Warrington at Belle Vue.

The early part of 1978 saw upheaval at the club. Among the less dramatic events, long-serving centre Terry Crook was exchanged for Bramley's Geoff Clarkson, who returned to Belle Vue after spells with five other clubs. Nevertheless, it was uncommon to see a player leave in his benefit year, but Crook, now 30, said he wanted regular first-team football.

A rift developed between president Jim Walker and chairman Trevor Woodward which began when Walker distributed a document, at the ground and in the city, reviewing the events at the club since he became president. Woodward, for his part, challenged several points in the publication.

With Leeds doing the double over Trinity by winning 12-5 at Belle Vue despite a fine solo try from Topliss, relegation worries continued unabated. At the end of January, coach Brian Lockwood handed in his resignation, annoyed by what he saw as committee interference and certain officials 'who know little about the game' advising him about how to do his job. 'It's just like you telling your butcher how to cut his meat,' he said. Lockwood had particularly objected to a committee man going into the dressing-room after the defeat at Warrington and giving the players a roasting. 'We had a stand-up argument and since then the knives have been in my back,' he said.

The committee immediately arranged for Neil Fox to return from Huddersfield and a fee of £2,000 was agreed but Fox thought better of it and instead went to Bradford to join his brother Peter. Ian Brooke was then asked to combine his role of general manager with that of coach, while Freddie Williamson had charge of training, Bill Kirkbride looked after the A team and Dave Lamming the Colts. The team responded immediately by giving easily their best performance of the season when beating Wigan 22-6, giving unexpected pleasure to their incredulous fans. Topliss took over as captain, he and Lampkowski completely outplaying the opposing half backs. Ballantyne had a 'storming' game and the whole team was 'full of bold, imaginative running and eager support play'. Lampkowski scored two tries and Topliss, with an interception, and centre John Hughes the others, Smith kicking five goals. They followed up this exceptional display with a 16-8 win in the relegation four-pointer at Workington. It was no mean feat in Cumbria that the forwards – Ballantyne, Handscombe, Clarkson, Keith Rayne, Skerrett and Idle – dominated the opposing pack.

In the first round of the Challenge Cup at Whitehaven, scene of a famous Trinity victory in 1960, Topliss 'destroyed Whitehaven with a masterly display', despite being a marked man. The stand-off scored a try and kicked a drop goal and had a hand in the other three tries, claimed by Fletcher, Hughes and Sutcliffe, the latter making a reappearance after missing all the previous season with a broken leg. It was a different matter in the second round at Belle Vue, where a faster Leeds side won comfortably by 28-6. The 9,865 crowd paid a record sum of £7,140, beating Belle Vue's previous best receipts of £5,309 for the 1964 Castleford-Widnes Cup semi-final replay, which, however, drew a much bigger crowd of 28,736.

As a fear of relegation resurfaced, Trinity made a big splash when they made two forward signings which were the talk of Belle Vue and beyond. Though many observers thought that strengthening the three-quarter line was the priority, international second rower Bill Ashurst, 28, was signed from Wigan for £18,000, a club record fee, and front rower John Burke from Castleford for £3,000. Ashurst was a controversial signing because of his age relative to the fee and Burke, a Wakefield man, because of his disciplinary record which amounted to sixteen sendings-off, though he maintained that he had become something of a victim.

Ashurst made a sensational debut at Featherstone on Good Friday, exerting as much influence on a match as an individual can. If his late try had not been disallowed – for apparently having lost control of the ball over the line after beating two men with a chip ahead - it could have been claimed that he had won the match almost single-handedly. Featherstone won 19-16, leaving Ashurst to wonder what he had to do to finish on the winning side. He kicked two penalties and two drop goals, made a try for Midgley from a long pass and scored another himself when 'from just inside the Featherstone half he put in a shrewd kick, regathered under [full back] Box's nose and found Hudson in support. The scrum-half was stopped but Ashurst fooled the defence at the play-the-ball to crash over near the posts.' His distribution and tactical kicking also featured heavily in the game, so that 'the announcement that he had won the man-of-the-match award was a pure formality and it was a gross injustice that he should finish on the losing side.'

In a vital Easter Monday match, Trinity beat Warrington 15-11 with John Sutcliffe scoring a hat-trick, Ray Handscombe monopolising the scrums again and youngster Paul McDermott giving a fine display at full back in the absence of both Sheard and Midgley. Trinity moved out of the bottom four but soon plunged back into difficulty with their heaviest defeat of the season at leaders St Helens, who won 36-5. In another tense relegation clash, Trinity crucially beat Hull 9-7 at Belle Vue, Keith Smith steering them to victory from stand-off with three drop goals in the last twenty minutes and an individualist try to crown his best game for the club so far.

In the penultimate match of the season, Trinity finally erased all relegation worries with a superb 36-23 victory over St Helens at Belle Vue, making a mockery of their modest league position of twelfth. Leading 36-10 at one point before easing off, they avenged their earlier 36-5 hammering at Knowsley Road as Keith Smith scored two tries and kicked six goals, Ashurst again made a huge impact before going off injured at half-time and Burke also contributed a good deal, especially in defence.

The season ended with Bradford taking the Premiership with four ex-Wakefield men to the fore: coach Peter Fox, captain Bob Haigh, who had moved there from Leeds, Neil Fox and Dave Barends. Trinity, now with as good a team on paper as they had had for a while, reflected on what might have been if Topliss had not returned from Australia with a groin injury which caused him to miss half the games and if Lampkowski had not also been unavailable over the last two months with injury. Trevor Skerrett was named Player of the Season after making the second-highest number of appearances after Graham Idle and Keith Smith was the top points-scorer. Attendances had increased to an average of 3,808, which was 877 more than the previous season.

During the close season, the south stand was demolished without being replaced. The Council had had plans since the 1920s to widen Doncaster Road; the latest proposal was to make the road a dual carriageway, to which a shortage of cash brought a halt. There had been talk of moving the Trinity pitch further towards the Agbrigg Road end.

Yorkshire and England Schools forward Andrew Kelly, a 17-year old from the Trinity Supporters team was signed. Trinity were also on the look-out for established players, with winger Green Vigo, a close friend of Bill Ashurst, also in their sights but Wigan eventually persuaded the South African to stay at Central Park.

A surplus of £7,687 on the year's trading was announced, the balance achieved in no small measure by the £8,657 received from the club lottery, but liabilities stood at £58,520, an increase of £12,000 on the previous year. At the AGM, chairman Trevor Woodward said: 'I hope that at next year's meeting you won't be able to see me for trophies,' and stated that he thought relegation struggles were a thing of the past. He announced that discussions were taking place with the Council regarding plans to develop the ground, now that the stand and banking had been removed from the Agbrigg end. A further announcement was expected in September, when they 'would move as quickly as possible to provide covered accommodation at that end.' A proposal was later put forward to build a sports centre at the Doncaster Road end, with costs expected to be borne by a grant from the Sports Council to the local authority. Club president Jim Walker also told members that the total expenditure for the year was £115,000, going into six figures for the first time in the history of the club.

Trinity decided to look again at Welsh rugby union – an area that had barely been considered since just after the war, when John Leighton Davies was recruited. Brian Juliff, a 24-year old Wales B international winger from Pontypridd was the first to sign, having had a trial with Widnes six months before. Two months later came Steve Diamond, a 25-year old centre from Newbridge RU, and 26-year old winger Adrian Barwood, a former team-mate of Juliff at Pontypridd. Trinity's signing spree was not over. Cumberland county hooker Alan McCurrie was signed from Whitehaven for a fee of around £10,000. Trinity had also advertised in the national press asking rugby union players who thought themselves capable of switching codes to contact the club in confidence.

Among players who left, Henry Oulton and winger Keith Riggs were both transferred to Batley, for £1,000 and £2,000 respectively, and Terry Langton went to Halifax for £1,000. The much-travelled Geoff Clarkson, who had returned to Belle Vue from Bramley in exchange for Terry Crook, was transferred to Hull KR for £4,000.

One trophy which would not hide the chairman from view at the next AGM was the Yorkshire Cup. Without Ashurst and Burke (both suspended) and the injured Lampkowski, Trinity went out at the first hurdle, losing 16-11 to Hull KR.

Trinity had now assembled a stronger first-team squad which gave plenty of options as well as first-class cover for injured players. One of the most sickening injuries was suffered by Bill Ashurst in the match against his former team, Wigan. Trinity were 3-0 ahead when a Wigan forward was sent off for a foul on his ex-team-mate, who went straight to hospital with a fractured cheekbone and broken nose, an injury so serious that Trinity considered taking legal action against the Wigan player.

Former Trinity player Geoff Gerard returned to England as a member of the Australian tour party and Trevor Skerrett, qualifying through a grandmother born in North Wales, was selected for the Welsh to play against the tourists.

In the John Player competition, Trinity beat Batley 27-2 with newcomer McCurrie scoring a try, winning the scrums easily and being voted man of the match. In the Floodlit Trophy, though, Trinity went out in the first round, losing 20-11 at Castleford. Hooker Ray Handscombe, whose place McCurrie had taken, told the club he was not prepared to play for Trinity any more and was transfer-listed at £7,500. He eventually teamed up again at Featherstone with Mick Morgan, who had gone to Post Office Road from York.

Despite the new signings, a third consecutive defeat was recorded at Warrington, where Trinity lost 19-13 though Keith Smith scored a 'glittering' hat-trick and kicked two goals in what was described as one of the best centre displays seen in a Wakefield jersey for a long time, or at least since Neil Fox. Smith went on to score a second hat-trick in the 24-6 win at Huddersfield and then provided the touchline conversion, facing driving rain and strong wind, which ensured a 10-10 draw against Salford. In the 24-17 victory over Warrington at Belle Vue, Smith took over the captaincy in the absence of Topliss and Ashurst and 'completely dominated the first half in which Trinity ran in 18 points without reply in as many minutes.' The *Daily Express* made Smith their Player of the Month.

In the John Player competition, Trinity beat Halifax 15-10 in the second round, but went out at the quarter-final stage when they lost 16-13 at Bradford, whose winger Henderson Gill was awarded a controversial try with the scores at 13-all.

Prop Terry Clawson, signed for a nominal fee from Featherstone, went straight into the side for the Boxing Day match at Headingley, where Trinity suffered a 22-6 defeat. At the New Year 1979, Trinity were hardly in a better position than at the same time in 1978, despite the large amount of money spent on new players. Perhaps too much had been expected too soon but certainly Trinity had not yet had a return for their money on the signing of Bill Ashurst, their most expensive recruit by far, who, though capable of turning a match with his array of skills, had been sidelined through either suspension or injury.

Suddenly the committee announced, in early January, that coach Ian Brooke had been dismissed. The former international centre had succeeded Brian Lockwood towards the end of the previous season when Trinity were in danger of dropping into the second division. Announcing the decision, chairman Woodward said that 'the committee had agreed that the results were not in accordance with the undoubted talent which the club had on its register and were of the opinion that a change of coach hopefully would bring about an improvement.' The *Wakefield Express*, on the other hand, believed that the lack of improved results was 'no doubt due to the many injuries which have prevented a settled line-up, and lack of experience in defensive situations.'

Brooke believed that he had done 'a worthwhile job' during his short tenancy, which had lasted not quite a year. During that time Trinity had avoided relegation and were now occupying a position in mid-table, despite all the injuries and the problems they entailed. He maintained that he had not been consulted about any of the signings which the committee had made but had simply been left to work with the new players. The *Express* reported that 'his dismissal had come as a terrific shock.'

Brooke was succeeded by A-team coach Bill Kirkbride, who had arrived at Trinity after starting his career at Workington, followed by spells at Halifax, Castleford and Salford as well as three years in Australia. On being appointed first team coach, Kirkbride said that he would be 'putting a lot of emphasis on the fitness of the squad and the basics of rugby league', which was not very different from what Geoff Gunney had said when appointed two and a half years earlier. Les Sheard took over as A-team player-coach.

At the half-yearly meeting a fortnight later, Brooke's dismissal provoked a 'barrage of criticism'. One member pointed out that Trinity had had five coaches in three years. Woodward replied, 'I would rather change coaches every three months to get the right man,' which implied little faith in the committee's ability to select the right man or the patience to give the new incumbent time to make an impression. Another member alluded to the fact that Peter Fox had gone on to coach Great Britain and that if he was good enough to coach the national side, surely he was good enough for Wakefield. Woodward replied that Fox 'had not broken a lot of pots' with Great Britain, but admitted that he was doing well at Bradford. The chairman added: 'Unless you have worked with Peter Fox you don't know how hard he is to work with. I found it impossible to work with him.'

A league fixture backlog was compounded by the start of the Challenge Cup, which was sponsored for the first time in its 82-year history. The cigarette brand State Express was offering £55,000 in prize money in the first year of its sponsorship. In round one Trinity travelled the short distance to Post Office Road, where ex-Wakefield hooker Ray Handscombe, as if to prove a point, won an overwhelming number of scrums against the man who had replaced him in the Trinity side, Alan McCurrie, but the two sides could not be separated until three minutes from the end. With Idle outstanding and Smith having scored Trinity's sole try from his own kick ahead, Topliss and Smith combined to put Sheard in at the corner for the match-winner and Trinity went through by 10-7.

After eighteen months in professional rugby league, Keith Smith was selected for England to play against Wales,

The Trinity squad of 1978-79: *Back row*: Trevor Skerrett, Roy Bratt, Nigel Murray, Keith Rayne, Graham Brown, Dean Robinson, Graham Idle, Terry Clawson, Kevin Rayne, Brian Gregory, Bill Ashurst, Brian Juliff, John Burke, Bill Kirkbride (coach). *Middle row*: David Needham, Les Sheard, Chris Stringer, Steve Diamond, Mike Lampkowski, David Topliss (capt), Alan McCurrie, Paul McDermott, Adrian Barwood. *Front row*: Keith Smith, Trevor Midgley, John Thompson, Andy Fletcher, David Wandless, Stephen Reed, Stephen Tinker, Ben Qansah (physio).

facing Skerrett and Juliff. The centre played an important part in Trinity's 19-7 second round win at second division Oldham. Topliss, though, was out on his own, making a superb run which led to a try for Lampkowski. Diamond pounced on a loose ball for the first touchdown, Smith sent Juliff in for the second, Idle's inside pass opened the way for McDermott to score and finally Skerrett tore through the defence to create the last try of the game for Midgley. In the third round Trinity travelled to Barrow and were slightly fortunate to return with a win. The home side led 5-0 after 25 minutes before McCurrie, from a tap penalty, sent Skerrett ploughing over the line, Smith converting. But just after the half-time hooter sounded, McCurrie was sent off, apparently for kicking out at an opponent. With the two sides at stalemate, Smith attempted a drop goal three minutes from full time. The ball rebounded off a Barrow player and was snapped up by Topliss. The stand-off passed to Fletcher, who, in classic fashion, feinted to come inside and then left his opposite number on the outside to score the winner in the corner.

The need to clear outstanding league fixtures resulted in some mixed results. In what was billed as a Cup semi-final rehearsal, Trinity beat St Helens 23-3 at Belle Vue, Keith Rayne being named man of the match and McCurrie scoring two tries. But with nine first-teamers missing, Trinity lost to Workington by the astonishing score of 39-11, which was the highest recorded at Belle Vue since Leeds rattled up 45 points to 5 in 1953. Deputising hooker Chris Stringer was unfortunate to have to leave the field after half an hour with four broken teeth, a broken nose and a cut cheek.

In April, Neil Fox, after a career of 24 years, was officially recognised as the world record points-scorer. After Wakefield, Fox had played for Bradford, Hull KR, York, Bramley and Huddersfield, amassing 6,220 points – 4,488 of which were scored in Trinity's colours - beating Jim Sullivan's official figure of 6,022.

No one who saw it would disagree with the *Wakefield Express's* assessment of the Challenge Cup semi-final against St Helens at Headingley as one of the most dramatic in the history of the game. For the 11,871 fans at Headingley on that Saturday afternoon, April 7, 1979, and the millions who watched on television, it was indeed an 'emotionally draining' experience as Trinity fought back for a second time to go through to their first Challenge Cup final since

1968 by nine points to seven. Three minutes from the end, it appeared that Trinity's Wembley hopes had again been dashed as Saints moved the ball wide for winger Jones to beat the cover and touch down at the corner for what looked like a winning 7-6 lead. From the restart Saints again pressed the Trinity line, but David Topliss, ever alert to a final chance to turn the game, intercepted close to his own line. As Trinity drove downfield, Topliss, from inside his own half, dummied, made a sizzling break supported by Smith, who drew the defence for Fletcher to race over for the winning try. Smith could not convert but Trinity held out against the last waves of St Helens attacks in injury time and triumphed by 9-7. As Frank Jeffrey reported, that fabulous try 'turned Headingley into a near hysterical cauldron of joy and disbelief.'

If Topliss had been 'the game's supreme artist who threatened danger every time he touched the ball,' Trinity were well served across the field. Skerrett won the man of the match award for a rugged display among a set of forwards who tackled magnificently. Trinity had dominated for long periods but could find no reward for their pressure. Against the run of play Saints winger Mathias had touched down after half an hour's play. The scoreboard had remained motionless until Pinner dropped a goal on the hour, giving Saints a 4-0 lead. Trinity had finally opened their account when McCurrie put a kick towards the Saints' line and Fletcher profited from the full back's fumble to touch down, Smith adding a superb conversion, followed by a 35-yard drop goal to produce a 6-4 lead. The remaining few breathless minutes became part of Trinity folklore.

'I felt we were the better side and we seemed to be in front for most of the game,' recalled Topliss, 'and then St Helens scored with about five minutes to go and we were chasing the game. You learn from every coach you play for and Peter Fox was one who didn't like you going for interceptions, but he'd said to me when he was at the club, "If you think the game's gone, then you go for one", and I just saw Dave Chisnall passing the ball and I thought, "It's now or never" and I intercepted on my own line. I passed on to Keith Smith and then Andy Fletcher scored two plays later. That night the town went wild. Everybody was out, it was really buzzing. Nobody could believe it.'

Great Britain second rower Bill Ashurst was signed from Wigan for a club record fee of £18,000 in 1978

Trevor Skerrett, who had impressed on the 1979 tour of Australia and New Zealand, was transferred to Hull in 1980 for a world record fee of £40,000

Trinity's form in the lead-up to the final was, to say the least, patchy, but that was because in the five matches it was never possible to put out a full-strength team. The side which lost 32-10 at Castleford was composed mainly of A-teamers and Colts; another weakened team lost 38-3 at Featherstone, where Trinity had won in the second round of the Cup two months earlier; only seven of the probable Wembley side played in the 18-17 defeat at Leigh, at which point Trinity were fifth from bottom of the division. At Bradford they suffered a 50-5 thrashing – their heaviest defeat since the 52-0 whitewash at Featherstone on January 2, 1977; though with a stronger line-up they managed a home win against Rochdale 20-5 – a match which saw Bill Ashurst play his first game since December and in which victory had removed the threat of relegation.

It was not the best preparation for a Wembley final against a Widnes side which had already won the Lancashire Cup, the Floodlit Trophy and the John Player Trophy. The decision to play Bill Ashurst was a gamble. The match-winning flair of the second-rower was balanced by his lack of match fitness caused by a four-month lay-off. As he admitted afterwards, 'Probably I should have got involved a little more but I just didn't seem able to get into the game. The breaks went for Widnes.' Keith Smith simply thought that Widnes were too experienced for Trinity. Certainly the Chemics' well-organised defence was a major factor as they went about winning an unspectacular final by 12-3 in front of a 94,000 crowd. Though Widnes were favourites, the outcome was still hard to predict at the half-way stage, when the teams were locked on 0-0, Trinity rarely threatening the opposition line and their only scoring chances coming from McCurrie's failed drop goal attempt after 35 minutes and a missed penalty by Smith. It was not until the 50th minute that the first score materialised when Widnes's Mick Burke kicked a penalty, though Topliss was denied, moments later, when after cutting through he was stopped by Mick Adams's last-ditch tackle. When Stuart Wright won the race to touch down his kick ahead and Burke converted from touch, the match was as good as over, especially

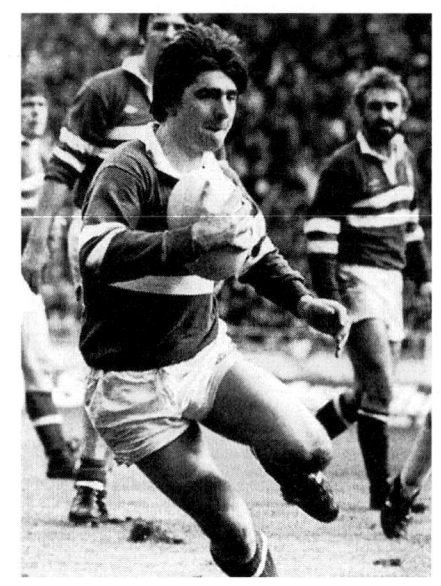

Stand-off David Topliss, a proven match-winner, captained the team from 1974 to 1981 and returned six years later as coach, maintaining Trinity's top-flight status with limited means

when Keith Elwell put a drop goal over to make it 8-0. Trinity's only score came when Andy Fletcher surprised the defence by collecting Keith Rayne's kick to the corner, but Smith could not convert. Eckersley added another drop goal and Eric Hughes went over for a late try. Trinity could have no complaints. There was no lack of effort, with Burke topping the tackle count among an industrious set of forwards. Topliss, always probing, was the game's best attacking player and won the Lance Todd Trophy, though he said, 'I would rather have been the worst man on the field and lifted the Cup instead.'

A former mayor of Wakefield, Leonard Boston, asked at Trinity's AGM if the club could afford to go to Wembley again, maintaining that they had received £52,000 from the Cup and £51,000 from the lottery, which, he said, represented a total increase of £86,000 on the previous year. He was disappointed therefore to see 'a miserable profit of £2,700'. Chairman Woodward said that they had spent a lot of money building the team, for whom winning pay was £60 a man, and that the season just ended – in which Trinity had finished tenth - had been 'exceptionally bad' for gates, although according to RFL figures, the average Belle Vue attendance was 4,068, an increase of 265. 'We have got to pay first class wages, stay at first class hotels and play on a first class ground,' he added, though only the first two points had been realised, since he freely admitted that the ground had been neglected 'for years'.

On the Great Britain tour, Trevor Skerrett played in two tests in Australia and two in New Zealand and was joined in the party by the uncapped John Burke, who was called up as a replacement for Jim Mills, and David Topliss, who replaced Roger Millward. Burke, who had been named Trinity's Player of the Year, decided, at 31, to go out on a high note and announced his retirement, as did fellow prop Terry Clawson.

Trinity started the 1979-80 season as they had ended the previous campaign – by beating champions Hull KR. Both sides had several players missing but Trinity went through to the second round of the Yorkshire Cup by 28-16, Lampkowski scoring three tries. In the next round they recorded a very impressive 30-5 win at Bradford, where they had so often failed in the past. The victory was plotted by Topliss, who gave another brilliant display.

It was Ashurst's turn to shine in the third successive win, achieved in the league at the expense of Wigan, who were defeated 22-6. Ashurst taunted his former club. Twice he created tries for Kevin Rayne, the second with a slick reverse pass, before kicking two drop goals inside ten minutes, and then, assisted by McDermott, making a try for McCurrie. In the Floodlit Trophy, though, with only four first-team regulars, Trinity lost at Castleford 22-12. Goal-kicking centre Steve Diamond was one of those missing after breaking his jaw against Wigan, and Terry Crook, who had joined the coaching staff after ending his playing career at Bramley, was pressed into service.

Perhaps prematurely, in view of the injury crisis which followed, scrum half Terry Hudson, who had been on loan at Batley, returned to his first club Featherstone. In the semi-final of the Yorkshire Cup, Trinity lost 12-7 to Leeds at Belle Vue, Ashurst and Leeds's Roy Dickinson both being dismissed and both being handed a two-match suspension.

In the John Player competition, Trinity beat Hull 25-18 at home and went on to knock out Featherstone by 21-12 in the second round. The quarter-final resulted in a 26-5 home win over Workington, who felt the force of Ashurst's return to action. The inspirational second rower set up the first try, kicked a drop goal and regularly had Workington back-pedalling with his touch-finding and intelligent distribution. Skerrett's performance was equally noteworthy as he put in some 'blockbusting runs and crunching tackling'. The semi-final ended in defeat by Bradford, who won 16-3 at Headingley. In a display described as 'feeble', as once more Ashurst's presence was missed, Trinity only managed to score in the dying seconds when McDermott touched down.

Lance Todd trophy winner David Topliss, followed by Graham Idle, Andy Fletcher, Mike Lampkowski and Steve Diamond, leads his defeated team from the Royal Box at Wembley 1979.

Trevor Skerrett shocked Belle Vue by putting in a transfer request and was listed at £50,000, which he called 'a bit embarrassing'. The 25-year old international forward, who had impressed on the tour of Australia and New Zealand, said he did not really want to leave, but had asked for a move because 'the team doesn't seem to be going anywhere and haven't won anything in the six years I've been with them.'

In mid-December Trinity suffered their first home defeat when they lost 15-4 to Hull and looked 'every inch a struggling team'. Coach Bill Kirkbride said that the retirement of John Burke and the injuries to Ashurst – who was due to enter hospital for his sixth operation, having played just 23 games since arriving from Wigan two years earlier – and Lampkowski had hit the team harder than many people realised. 'I need a leader on the field but I haven't got one,' he said. 'I had expected Bill Ashurst to be the leader but he has been very unlucky with injuries … When he is in the team he makes it easier for everyone. When he is out everybody suffers. We are a different side because there is no real link between forwards and backs.'

Over the Christmas period Trinity did themselves a lot of good with two victories despite some erratic play. Hull KR were defeated at Belle Vue 21-14 after Trinity had scored four tries in the opening sixteen minutes. Lampkowski returned to the side and McCurrie was prominent for consistently winning the scrums and for his smart play in the loose. On Boxing Day Trinity registered their first win at Castleford for four years, winning 26-13, again after setting up a big winning lead. Steve Diamond kicked seven goals from eight attempts and McCurrie was once more prominent, winning the scrums, scoring two tries and making the other two. 'The Cumbrian's kicks do not always come off and he is often criticised for giving possession away but he has certainly had the last laugh lately,' said the *Wakefield Express*.

Skerrett was taken off the transfer list and scrum-half Dale Fennell was signed from Featherstone in a deal involving Great Britain Colts player Stephen Reed. Ironically Fennell had lost his place in the Rovers side when Terry Hudson was signed from Wakefield.

In the first round of the Challenge Cup Trinity laboured to beat Hunslet, who had a man sent off after only eight minutes. Scoring four first-half tries, Trinity won 24-17. In the league an under-strength side travelled to Central Park and beat Wigan, fifth from bottom, by 23-16. The match-winner came three minutes from the end when Midgley fastened on to Sheard's inside pass to go over for a try converted by Diamond. Idle was outstanding in the forwards and Juliff claimed a hat-trick.

At this stage Trinity were eighth in the sixteen-team first division and faced second division Oldham in the second round of the Challenge Cup in a repeat of the previous year's tie. Trinity duly won by the narrow score of 10-5 though the result was hardly ever in doubt.

Keith Rayne was a try-scorer in England's 29-9 win over Wales, for whom Juliff posted their only try. The second-rower gave a fine display to win the man of the match award in Trinity's 18-15 win over Bradford, thus ending Northern's ten-match winning run. Johnny Thompson also gave a strong performance which was 'full of promise for the future.'

In the third round of the Challenge Cup, Trinity were drawn at Halifax, where they had won just six out of 22 league matches since the war. Second division Halifax also had the longest unbeaten run in the league with eleven wins and two draws and soon gave evidence of their tight defence as Trinity tried in vain to find a way through. The match became famous for an unusual tactic devised by coach Maurice Bamford which consisted in attempting drop goals whenever Halifax got near enough to the Trinity posts. Trinity had the major share of possession from the scrums but Halifax made theirs count. Stand-off Blair landed four drop goals and Birts one and a penalty as Halifax went through by 7-3. Not a single try had thrilled the 12,826 Thrum Hall crowd, Trinity's points coming from a Topliss drop goal and a Diamond penalty.

Coach Bill Kirkbride had set his team the target of maintaining their eighth place to make the play-offs but a 'nightmare' 27-5 defeat at Salford was followed by a 24-19 loss to St Helens at Belle Vue. Lampkowski and Diamond were in dispute over being relegated to the subs' bench, but the matter was resolved in time for Diamond to rescue Trinity from a humiliating defeat by third-from-bottom Hunslet when he kicked a penalty three minutes from the end to gain a 12-11 win. 'Rarely can a team have played so badly yet finished winners,' observed the *Wakefield Express*. 'Trinity sank to a new low with a succession of amazing blunders.'

Fortunately Keith Smith, operating at stand-off in place of the injured Topliss, inspired a 16-5 win at Workington. Smith's deceptive running, intelligent distribution and touch-finding were more than the Cumbrians could handle, while Lampkowski gave a powerful display in both attack and defence.

But that win was not sufficient to prevent Kirkbride's shock dismissal the following week, when Trinity slumped to a 35-12 home defeat – their biggest of the season - at the hands of Castleford. Trinity fielded a side lacking their three main attacking forces, Smith, Topliss and Ashurst. To make matters worse, two former Trinity players, Ballantyne and Wraith, scored two tries each. It was not chairman Woodward who instigated the sacking but a call for a special meeting by other committee members directly after the match.

'I was stunned after all the pressures we have had this season,' said Kirkbride. 'It has just left me speechless. To finish me like that when my contract was due to finish in two weeks' time is just not human. The committee don't know the first thing about rugby league and they don't know good players when they've got them. If they want to keep a coach in the future they'll have to give him support and encouragement rather than criticise him and his selection.'

As Salford became the fifth side to do the double over Trinity, with a 23-12 win at Belle Vue, the committee cast around for a new coach. Former Trinity back-rower Bob Haigh was approached but his current club Dewsbury would not release him. Trinity turned to the former Leeds international loose forward, Ray Batten, with former team-mate Alan Hardisty as A-team coach. Batten, grandson of the illustrious Billy, had retired from playing four years previously and had been coaching amateur side Heworth in York, where he lived. Ex-Great Britain stand-off Hardisty had been A-team coach at Leeds before returning to his first club Castleford as a scout. 'It is a calculated risk,' said Woodward. '[Batten] has no experience of coaching [a professional club] but has all the right credentials.'

On the playing roster, Trevor Skerrett was targeted by Bradford, who were told by Woodward, 'There is no way we will do a deal.' Topliss, in his benefit year, was wanted by Hull but said that he was happy to stay at Wakefield. Such news was unsettling but was as nothing compared to the fans' indignation at the prospect of the committee selling Belle Vue. In view of the diminishing prospect of the council building a sports centre at the Doncaster Road end, chairman Woodward said that a planning application would be submitted for the land there to be used for a supermarket instead. The club had already spent £18,000 demolishing the stand and levelling the banking at the Agbrigg end, which had resulted in a three-sided ground. Selling land at the opposite end would produce funds to develop the rest of the ground. An alternative was to sell the whole ground to a developer and ask the council for land to build a new stadium on another site, such as Pugneys. Woodward added, 'We are in the wrong place, with antiquated facilities in a built-up area.'

This front page news was greeted by outrage. In a letter to the *Wakefield Express*, a certain JE Richardson, described as a club patron, fumed: 'I would like to call for the resignation of the whole of the Wakefield Trinity committee at Belle Vue. After demolishing the end of the ground with no thought for the future, no assurances and guarantees … for development. Now to suggest selling the ground really does seem totally incompetent. The fact that £30,000 has been spent on doing it only highlights the mismanagement and the foolishness.'

Woodward responded by saying that the club had made no commitment to the unnamed development company, which was exploring the possibilities at its own cost, though a genuine offer had been made to lease part or all of the ground. The chairman added that he had been held up to personal ridicule and defended himself by saying, 'I freely give of my time, effort and money in a well-intentioned attempt to help Trinity and I do not think that my reward should be to sit in the stocks for people to hurl abuse.'

Referring to a letter in the *Wakefield Express*, he went on: 'Last week I was accused of dishonesty and lunacy … I am only human and it hurts … On May 8, I advised the committee that I was prepared to stand down as chairman. I trust that someone will come forward with limitless time and energy, a bottomless purse and a very thick skin.'

In the midst of this upheaval in the boardroom, faces would be missing in the dressing-room. Hull made an offer of £55,000 for Skerrett and Topliss, but Topliss turned down the move. Skerrett, who had signed for Trinity from amateur club Bison's in 1974, was sold for £40,000, a world record fee. Leeds made an unsuccessful bid of £25,000 for Great Britain Under 24 international Keith Rayne. Prop Colin Forsyth was signed from Bradford in exchange for Graham Idle, plus £2,500. The signing was made at the request of Ray Batten, who wanted more cover in the front row. Forsyth had cost Bradford £5,000 when he signed from York five years earlier, had played in Featherstone's Yorkshire Cup final side in 1967 and equalled the try-scoring record for a prop two seasons earlier.

In the close season of 1980 the knives were out. A 'Save Trinity Campaign' called for a vote of no confidence in the Wakefield Trinity committee. At a meeting of club members, the group failed by 148 votes to 140 to bring down the committee, but had an assurance from chairman Woodward that no decision would be made about selling the ground without the approval of members.

Concerning the club's financial situation, Woodward said that the bank required Trinity's overdraft to be reduced to £20,000, which necessitated the sale of players, and in particular Trevor Skerrett. When reference was made to a loan of £10,000 from outgoing president Jim Walker, Woodward claimed personally to have spent an even greater amount out of his own pocket 'without any strings', including inducements to players ('personal gifts') to sign for Trinity. Woodward quit as chairman following the AGM, saying that he was sick of all the abuse and innuendo.

An amendment to club rules protected the Belle Vue site. In future the committee would need a three-quarters majority vote of members in order to sell off any of the land or demolish any buildings standing on it, or indeed to carry out any development requiring money to be borrowed to finance it. President Jim Walker, soon to be succeeded by former Morley councillor Ted Hewitt, proposed by Woodward, had had the amendment drawn up, though admitted that the changes might have gone too far because they prevented the committee from taking initiatives. But he said that the amendment was aimed at taking the responsibility of ownership out of the hands of one man or a small minority to put it back into the hands of the members.

In fact, as Walker explained, the Belle Vue ground did not belong to the club, but to the Wakefield Trinity Athletic Co. Ltd, a company registered over a century ago [sic]. The majority of the shares in the company were owned by Wakefield Trinity RLFC, but minority shareholders could call for the liquidation of the company at any time, which would involve the sale of the ground and distribution of proceeds. Though unlikely, it had the potential to cause serious financial problems for the club. Walker therefore proposed to put complete control of the company into the hands of Wakefield Trinity by calling for a rights issue of new shares.

The need to safeguard the Belle Vue ground was set out in Walker's opening paragraph of a letter to the *Express*, in which he stated: 'To some people an offer of half a million pounds for a plot of land sounds attractive and very tempting, but when the land happens to be Trinity's ground at Belle Vue, then the only reply must be "not for sale". The ground is an integral part of the life, the traditions and history of Wakefield. It is the home of Wakefield Trinity.'

But, Walker admitted, the club's future was causing him concern from a financial point of view. Liabilities had increased by £20,000 over the past three years and if the trend continued the club would not be able to meet those debts, which stood at over £50,000. And still the problems in the boardroom carried on. Les Pounder, by the far the longest-serving member of the committee, who had taken over the chairmanship again at the age of 74, stormed out of a meeting following an argument and resigned.

Nineteen – A Second Descent into the Second Division: 1980-85

Within a month of the start of the 1980-81 season, Trinity's side had a different look. Trevor Skerrett and Graham Idle had left during the close season. In August and September, 31-year old scrum half Allan Agar, formerly with Featherstone, Dewsbury and New Hunslet, was signed from Hull KR, Mike Lampkowski moving up to loose forward. Terry Day, York's 27-year old centre and a former team-mate of Agar at Dewsbury, was signed in exchange for Paul McDermott and Graham Brown plus cash. Keith Rayne finally left for Leeds, who paid a club record fee of £35,000. Former Great Britain Under 24 full back Harold Box, 28, signed from Featherstone for an undisclosed sum, after a £15,000 bid had been rejected.

Added to that list, Bill Ashurst made his first appearance for ten months in the Yorkshire Cup first round clash at Hull KR. The second-rower gave 'a brilliant exhibition of touch-kicking and generalship' and helped Trinity to establish a 10-0 lead but when he left the field with a jaw injury Rovers took control and won 21-17. The team began to show its potential with a 16-14 victory at St Helens, scoring three tries to one in the process. Loose forward Lampkowski gave a typical non-stop display and scored the decisive try while Forsyth also made a big impression with his forceful running. At Halifax, who were beaten 22-11 to produce Trinity's third win in a row, Andy Fletcher, who had earlier played alongside Topliss and Kevin Rayne in the Yorkshire side beaten 17-9 by Lancashire, scored a hat-trick.

Trinity were given another test by Bradford at Belle Vue but emerged with a creditable 15-all draw. It was for a sublime moment conjured by Bill Ashurst that the match will be remembered. There are times when certain players stand head and shoulders above the rest and those occasions fell to Ashurst more often than most. Trinity were trailing in the first half when, out of nothing, the second rower cut inside and put a signature chip-kick over the defence. He regathered and drew full back Mumby, looked to pass to the supporting Topliss, but with a dummy 'fooled Mumby and everyone else' and raced 25 yards to score a brilliant individual try. Pure artistry, it lingered long in the memory.

Sadly the ex-Wigan star was to enter hospital for yet another knee operation, but, after a John Player Cup exit at the hands of Widnes, Trinity managed to maintain their generally good form. York prop Billy Harris, originally with Featherstone, was signed on an extended loan as Trinity moved in to the top four with a 24-15 win over Oldham, Barwood and Lampkowski scoring two tries each.

Topliss, man of the match and a try-scorer with his familiar ducking and weaving style, inspired Trinity to a 25-20 victory over Hull KR, a game in which forwards Bratt, Lampkowski, Forsyth and Thompson also stood out. With a 5-2 win at Hull, Trinity went top of the league on points difference from Castleford. The turning point of the match came when Hull, pressing the Trinity line, fanned the ball cross-field only for Fletcher to intercept and sprint 90 yards for the match-winner.

At the mid-point in the season, coach Batten admitted that Trinity's progress had exceeded his expectations and praised particularly Agar for making an effective link between forwards and backs. On Boxing Day, however, Castleford took over again at the top with a comfortable 23-8 win at Belle Vue against a Trinity side very much below par. On New Year's Day the side got back on track with a valuable 13-8 win at Featherstone and backed it up with a 19-14 home victory over Warrington, with Stephen Tinker, playing centre, registering a hat-trick.

Topliss received a record benefit of over £10,000, but was soon considering his future at Belle Vue as Hull made another move to lure him away. The stand-off said he was happy to stay at Wakefield, where he had played for 13 years, at least until the end of the season. Juliff and Diamond, as well as Box, who qualified through a Welsh grandmother, were selected for Wales, though the full back had not played for three months since breaking his arm.

At the half-yearly meeting, David Garthwaite, who had taken over as chairman, revealed that the club was losing £800 a week and that a writ had been served on the club by former president Jim Walker, who was pursuing repayment of his £10,000 loan. Garthwaite explained that the transfer fee received from Hull for Skerrett had been used to reduce the club's overdraft at the bank. The transfer of Keith Rayne to Leeds had helped to fund the purchase of Forsyth, Day, Agar and Box.

York refused to take Andy Fletcher, who wanted to leave for personal reasons, in a straight swap for Billy Harris, who was recalled and then sold to Oldham. York did however sign full back Trevor Midgley.

With an 18-8 win at Workington, where Alan McCurrie and young second row Andy Kelly gave eye-catching performances, Trinity went back to the top of the league. But at a price, as Harold Box broke his arm for a second time.

Centre or stand-off Keith Smith, a dual code international

After their first round victory over newcomers Fulham, Trinity drew their biggest crowd of the season - 9,604 - for their second round tie against Halifax, who had been their tormentors in the Challenge Cup the previous season. Trinity came back from 8-0 down, Smith, Juliff and Diamond all going over before McCurrie sealed the win when he surged forward from dummy-half, kicked ahead and touched down. The 'indestructible' Lampkowski took the man of the match award, but Fletcher sustained a broken knee-cap and was ruled out for the season. In the quarter-final at Warrington, who were second behind Trinity in the table, Batten's men started slowly and never recovered. Warrington's Courtney was sent off after just 17 minutes and Trinity's Agar just before half-time. After going out of the Cup by 13-9, Wakefield naturally switched their attention to securing a top four place.

Playing two matches a week in the run-up to the premiership play-offs, Trinity got themselves into the habit of winning one and losing one but retained fourth place. The heaviest defeat of the season was suffered, surprisingly, at Leigh by 36-10 but then Leeds were beaten 16-8 at Headingley – only the second time in a decade that Trinity had won there. As a below-strength Leeds side were beaten twice in five days – this time by 43-10 at Belle Vue - Smith scored a hat-trick, Diamond kicked eight goals and Topliss posted the 200th try of his career, but it was second rower Andy Kelly who took the man of the match award for his strong-running display and two tries.

Trinity finished the season behind Bradford, Warrington and Hull KR, and just above Castleford. Not for the first time a Wakefield official blamed the backlog of league fixtures for the side's injuries and indifferent form. As a result, said chairman Garthwaite, the build-up of matches had devalued the championship (league) and premiership (play-offs). For the third time in two weeks, Trinity met Castleford when they clashed in the play-offs at Belle Vue, but for the third time they were beaten, going down 25-8, and giving the impression they would be glad when the season was over. McCurrie was the only player to have figured in all the matches, while at the other end of the scale, injury had kept Smith and Box out for all but eleven games, with Ashurst playing just six times all season.

No sooner had the season ended than players were on the move. Topliss finally signed for Hull for £15,000, putting an end to months of speculation, after Castleford had also shown interest. The stand-off had made 406 appearances for the club after signing from Normanton ARLFC thirteen years earlier. He admitted he had had differences with certain members of the committee and said that he was leaving with deep regret, adding, 'My heart will always be at Belle Vue.' Allan Agar, who had been at Trinity for one season, left to become player-coach at new club Carlisle, where he would join forces with Mick Morgan. Fulham, who had won promotion to the first division in their first season, paid £10,000 for Steve Diamond, who led Trinity's point-scoring list and had appeared in all but two of their matches during the season. Chairman Garthwaite claimed, however, that the club would not sell star players and that those who had left had wanted to go.

The greatest surprise came when coach Ray Batten resigned following the dismissal of A-team coach Alan Hardisty, for which he roundly criticised the committee, saying that they should not get involved in the playing side. 'I'm sorry to be leaving Trinity but I am a man of strong principles and I am not prepared to be pushed around,' he told the *Wakefield Express*. 'I would have liked to stay on and help them win something. It was a difficult decision but I had no choice.'

Bill Ashurst, his playing career virtually at an end, was appointed first-team coach in succession to Batten. He called for an improvement in defence and a generally more professional and disciplined approach. Terry Crook was appointed assistant coach with responsibility for the A team.

In the face of competition from three other clubs, Trinity signed 20-year old stand-off John Lyons from Batley Victoria amateur club. The New Zealand Test forward Ray Baxendale, after protracted negotiations, arrived in October. Winger Adrian Barwood, who had started a new job back home in Wales, was transferred to new club Cardiff for £3,000.

Trinity's end-of-season accounts did not make for happy reading. The club made an overall loss of £3,405, but expenditure exceeded income by £35,750. Though gate receipts went up from £39,000 to £55,000, the increase was offset by the rise in wages paid to players and coaching staff – from £65,000 to £94,000. At the same time, income from the lottery decreased from £37,000 to £14,000. For these reasons, the sale of players was seen as a necessity. A total of £102,350 was taken from the transfer of Trevor Skerrett, Keith Rayne, David Topliss, Allan Agar and Steve Diamond. Almost exactly £70,000 was paid out in signing Harold Box, Terry Day, Colin Forsyth, Allan Agar and several junior players.

Garthwaite warned that more players might have to be sold if other ways of bringing in money could not be found. After producing valuable income over the past three years, Trinity's lottery, like many other such schemes across the country, was in decline as a result of the economic downturn. Sponsorship deals were still proving elusive. Garthwaite announced that, for business reasons, he was stepping down from the chairmanship and made a chilling prediction. 'If we sell star players,' he said, 'we are going to end up in five years' time with no players and wallowing in the second division.' Into the breach stepped John Scaife, a sales director who had joined the committee just one year earlier.

Trinity's progress in the Yorkshire Cup, at the start of the 1981-82 season, was brief. After a moderate performance in beating Dewsbury 18-6 at Belle Vue, they fell at Hull KR by 22-12.

Another poor display in their first league match at Hull, where they lost 20-7, made Trinity already look like relegation candidates to some observers. The presence of David Topliss in the Hull side only served to remind Trinity fans of what they were missing. In another moderate showing, Trinity managed to beat York 18-12, but that was overshadowed by the shock decision by Keith Smith to quit rugby league. A member of the team which had reached Wembley only two years earlier, Smith was one of the few class players now left and was expected to fulfil the key role of link man between forwards and backs. But the dual code international, who had joined Trinity in October 1977, had decided to retire for several reasons, including his struggle with injury and his recent promotion in his work as a brewery representative. Most of all, what he saw as an inability to reach his best form led him to believe that he was letting everyone down. Whatever Smith himself thought, there was no doubt that his departure was a huge blow.

A shortage of middle backs, now made worse, sent the committee searching for replacements. A deal was made with Barrow to take their former England Rugby Union man Nigel French on loan. The centre made his debut in a more encouraging team performance when Trinity lost 18-13 to Widnes at Belle Vue. But the team soon reverted to early-season form in a succession of heavier defeats. Hooker Alan McCurrie asked for a transfer after being substituted in the 32-6 fiasco at Hull KR. The Cumbrian felt he was being made the scapegoat for the side's failings and was listed at £40,000. Though he easily won the scrums in the home game against Leeds, which was lost 21-10, Trinity 'looked like a first division side in name only.' With the departure of Topliss and Agar and the retirement of Ashurst and Smith, with Lampkowski sidelined with injury, Trinity desperately needed a player with distribution skills and pursued Featherstone loose forward Keith Bell, Salford scrum-half Steve Nash, offering £35,000 each, and Wigan scrum-half Gary Stephens, but all the bids were declined. The squad was weakened further when Colin Forsyth, who joined Trinity from Bradford in a deal involving Graham Idle plus cash, decided that he too was finished with the game, after only 29 appearances in a Trinity jersey.

Further humiliation came when Trinity were ejected from the John Player Cup in the first round at Keighley, who won 27-22 after leading 26-9 midway through the second half. After Trinity recorded their seventh defeat in a row – by 17-12 at Warrington – there was a flurry of transfer activity, not all of it guaranteed to impress the fans. Centre Bryce Nicholson, a New Zealander, was drafted in following a trial period. More controversial was the move which took team captain Terry Day to Hull and brought scrum-half Clive Pickerill and Welsh international centre Graham Walters from the Boulevard to Belle Vue; not to mention the deal involving Alan McCurrie's transfer to second division leaders Oldham and prop Billy Harris, who had previously been at Belle Vue on loan from York, plus cash in exchange. McCurrie was replaced by Hull KR's reserve hooker Dave Heslop, who was signed for £4,000. Former Colts international prop Tony Rose had earlier been transferred to Huddersfield but Andy Kelly and Kevin Rayne were 'not for sale at any price', said chairman Scaife.

Five of the recent signings, including winger David Jones, who was soon to earn selection for Great Britain Colts, made their debut in a surprise 16-9 home win over St Helens, which put an end to the string of losses. It was decided not to retain the Barrow centre Nigel French, while scrum halves Dale Fennell and Barry Holliday also quit the club after the signing of Pickerill. They were followed by Andy Fletcher, who once more decided to leave after being picked for the A team.

In another transfer move which set tongues wagging, Trinity tried to sign their former second row Geoff Clarkson and team-mate Malcolm Swann from Leigh in a deal worth £11,000. Clarkson, 38, had first signed for Trinity in 1966 and was set to rejoin the club for a third time, the twelfth move of his career, but could not agree personal terms. Trinity enjoyed a second consecutive win - at the expense of Bradford, who went down 11-8 at Belle Vue - but the victory was marred by the injury to Andy Kelly, who broke his arm on his 21st birthday. Fellow second rower Baxendale also limped off, forcing full back Box into the pack. Trinity moved up to fourth from bottom, but then lost 16-5 at Wigan, who were having problems of their own.

The alarm on the terraces caused by the comings and goings of players was mirrored in the boardroom, or at least a corner of it. Former chairman and current committee member Trevor Woodward, claiming to be in 'a very small minority', broke rank and wrote to the *Wakefield Express* to express his concern about what was going on. He felt he must let Trinity members know how the club was being managed and gave details about the recent transfer deals, which, he claimed, resulted in a total net deficit of £15,750. 'The club has no money so that these deals can only be financed by the sale of players,' he wrote. 'The decisions have been taken to sell Rayne and/or Juliff subject to satisfactory offers.'

Widespread consternation among supporters was reflected by correspondence to the local newspaper. One writer asked the committee to explain their actions. 'If their policy is to bring a once great and respected club to its knees and ensure second division rugby for their supporters next season, they are doing a very good job,' wrote the supporter. 'If, on the other hand, as they claim, they are interested in building a team which will return to its former glories, they are going about it in a peculiar way. In the closed season, following a reasonably good season, they proceeded to demolish the nucleus of what had the makings of a good team … No team can be expected to survive when key players have been systematically frittered away.'

An entirely expected defeat at Widnes, who set a new first division record of twelve consecutive wins from the start of the season, was lightened by the performance of Lyons, who scored two tries and kicked three goals. Second from bottom, Trinity fell again at the hands of Leigh, who won 18-12 at Belle Vue, with Clarkson still in their ranks and despite having Martyn sent off just before half-time.

Trinity's recruitment had an air of desperation. Malcolm Swann was signed from Leigh though he had not played for a year owing to a back injury. Trinity sought medical advice and thought the signing worth the risk. Centre Derek Parker joined Trinity in a reported £20,000 deal with Bradford, with whom he had been in dispute and had not been in action since the previous season.

One boardroom drama succeeded another. At a specially convened meeting of the committee, former chairman Trevor Woodward was suspended until the end of the season as a result of the remarks he had made in the press in which he was said to have disclosed confidential information. Another committee member, Derrick Barras, resigned saying, 'The boardroom is shrouded in incompetence which I can no longer tolerate.' Barras, who had been on the committee for four years, claimed, 'We're in a whirlpool and going down. The assets are diminishing and liabilities are increasing. I can only see one end to it.' Another ex-chairman, David Garthwaite, managing director of Clark's Brewery, was next to quit, citing personal and business reasons.

Second rower Andy Kelly, who was transferred to Hull KR for £60,000 before making a return to Belle Vue as coach and guiding the club into Super League

Meanwhile Woodward's previous revelation about the committee's willingness to sell players was partly substantiated when Kevin Rayne joined his twin brother Keith at Leeds for £41,500.

The chairman at the centre of the current controversy, John Scaife, hit back and asked critics to look closely at events before he took over. 'I was not the man who took the decision to let Topliss, Agar and Diamond go and I could do nothing to keep Smith and Forsyth in the game. I did not ask Kelly to break his arm or Lampkowski to hurt his back.' While it was true that the transfer of those three players took place during Garthwaite's tenure as chairman, Scaife did play a part in the sale of club captain Terry Day to Hull and Alan McCurrie to Oldham. He justified those transfers by saying that the club wanted to bring in new blood, which took the form of Pickerill, Harris, Walters and Heslop.

After a five-week lay-off including the Christmas period and New Year, Trinity managed a 9-9 draw at bottom club Whitehaven, who took their first point after twelve consecutive defeats.

At the half-yearly meeting, a motion of no confidence in the committee was proposed by Derrick Barras.

The press were excluded 'for the good of the club' but were informed afterwards that the motion had been rejected by 'an overwhelming majority'.

Perhaps in an attempt to lighten the gloomy atmosphere and escape the freezing weather, the club announced that the team would be preparing for the Challenge Cup with a trip to Spain. Committee members would pay for themselves and players would contribute half their own costs.

Back-rower Graham Eccles, aged 32, was signed from Leeds, but Brian Juliff, dissatisfied with having to play second row instead of wing, asked for a transfer and was listed at £30,000.

Though it was only January, the match at Fulham was one of several relegation battles which would be fought up to the end of the season. Steve Diamond's two goals proved to be the difference in the London club's 13-12 win, though Lyons and Fletcher both scored two tries for Trinity in front of 3,948 spectators – Craven Cottage's lowest-ever crowd.

When the freezing weather finally relented and matches at Belle Vue were possible for the first time in two months, Trinity took two valuable championship points from Whitehaven, who had not won a match all season. Trinity owed their 15-12 win in large measure to Andy Fletcher's three tries, but the attendance of just 2,626, Wakefield's smallest crowd of the season, gave further cause for concern.

Despite their depleted side, Trinity fought hard to retain their first division status. In contrast to the previous week, the biggest crowd of the season turned up to watch Trinity's match with Hull, who brought a sizeable proportion of the 7,332 crowd, higher by 2,000 than the previous best. Hooker Colin Maskill, at 18, made his debut and memorable it was as he took the scrums and twice made breaks over half the length of the field. But with Topliss, Day and Skerrett in their side, Hull made their class tell in the end and won 14-10.

In preparation for their first round Challenge Cup tie at Bramley, the Trinity squad flew off to Majorca, where they trained for five days. Chairman Scaife insisted it cost 'no more than keeping them at home'. In any case, Bill Ashurst's men progressed to the second round after winning 16-4, their first away victory of the season. At the next stage Trinity met Oldham, against whom they had been drawn three times in the past four seasons in the same round. It was three out of three for Trinity as Harold Box kicked five goals, Clive Pickerill landed two drop goals, Andy Fletcher raced 50 yards for a thrilling try and Dave Heslop went over for Trinity's other try late in the game. In the third round Trinity clashed at Belle Vue with ambitious Leeds, whom they had not defeated in the Cup since 1937. The tie went with form as Leeds triumphed 20-2.

If Wakefield were responsible for Fulham's lowest crowd, so the London side attracted Belle Vue's smallest of 2,033, who watched Trinity beat their fellow-strugglers 18-13. Following a one-point defeat at home to Warrington, Bill Ashurst decided to make a comeback in the midweek match against mid-table Barrow. The ex-international second row lasted under an hour but made his presence felt as Trinity ran in five tries in their 23-20 win, to which Andy Kelly contributed a 40-yard solo effort to touch down late in the game. Trinity were now fourth from bottom, level on points with Castleford, and faced Wigan, sixth from bottom, at Belle Vue. Box proved the matchwinner with two vital penalties, one from 50 yards, and Trinity triumphed 17-14. But after winning four of their last five games, Trinity lost 14-3 at Featherstone. With a patched-up side, they managed an all-important victory by 14-5 over Castleford to move out of the bottom four, with Harris once more giving an exemplary performance. Trinity's third match in a week ended in a 28-7 defeat at Odsal, which meant that their next fixture – at the home of fellow relegation candidates Castleford – would determine their fate. As had been the case throughout much of the season, Trinity did not lack effort but badly missed a playmaker, with the result that they lost 15-7 and were condemned to life in the second division for the first time since 1904. Sunday, April 25, 1982 was recorded in the *Wakefield Express* as 'the blackest day in the club's history', which, though a little exaggerated, echoed their supporters' despair. In their remaining match, against Featherstone at Belle Vue, they went down 23-8 and suffered their seventh double of the season. Coach Ashurst counted 21 players unavailable that week. The number of players used in the first team over the season - 52 - told its own story. Not once did the same team appear in consecutive matches. Trinity finished third from bottom and were relegated along with Fulham, York and Whitehaven.

He was hardly to blame, but Ashurst was made to carry the can. Back came Ray Batten, having resigned at the end of the previous season, when Trinity had finished fourth. But two-thirds of his first-choice team had gone. 'I expect to go back up but we have to rebuild in between,' he said. 'There is no point in being promoted and coming straight back down again.' David Topliss, whose transfer was often blamed for the club's demise, was sounded out regarding a possible return to Belle Vue as Batten's assistant but he had just captained Hull to victory in the Challenge Cup, scoring two tries in the replay against Widnes, and had been named in the 31-man squad to prepare to meet the Kangaroos in the forthcoming test series. He was to captain Great Britain in the third test at Headingley. Not surprisingly Topliss wanted to play at least another season at the top level. In any case it was unlikely that Hull would have allowed him to leave, so popular was he on Humberside. Instead former Trinity second row Bob Haigh, who had formed such a formidable back row partnership with Batten at Leeds, was appointed assistant coach. Bill Ashurst, who would have been happy to stay at Belle Vue as a player even though his playing days were numbered, was appointed assistant coach to Alex Murphy at Wigan. Trinity's second-in-command before Haigh was appointed, Terry Crook, went to Batley as head coach.

Life in the second division imposed economies. The first essential was to reduce the playing register from 65 to around 40. The most significant departure was that of Andy Kelly. Hull KR, who had targeted the second row for some time, stepped in with an offer of £60,000, making the transfer the third most expensive ever. Trinity immediately signed forward Bryan Adams from York for £18,000 and then 31-year old stand-off Nigel Stephenson from Carlisle for a fee believed to be around £25,000. A year earlier Carlisle had paid £20,000 to Bradford for his transfer. Both deals made Topliss's £15,000 move to Hull look like a bargain buy. At the start of the season Brian Juliff signed for Wigan for around £25,000.

Before the 1982-83 season got under way, winger Lindsay Rotherforth, Yorkshire 200-metre sprint champion and a Great Britain Under 19 player, was signed from the Redhill amateur club. Further good news came when Mike Lampkowski resumed training after a long absence through injury and Colin Forsyth, who had not played for some time, returned to the club. Paul Gearey, a 20-year old back-rower, was signed from the Sandal amateur club, Castle.

Trinity got off to a good start in the league but slipped up badly in the first round of the Yorkshire Cup at Bramley, where they faded to a 15-13 defeat, for which they were accused of complacency by chairman Scaife.

At Colts level a new record was established in the 73-0 victory over Salford, when prop Brian Taylor scored two tries and kicked fourteen goals from fifteen attempts for a personal total of 34 points.

Plans were drawn up for a Sports and Social club, to be situated in the east corner at the Agbrigg end of the ground. It was to cost £250,000 and the development would be entirely funded by Mansfield Brewery. The ground floor would eventually be taken over by Trinity for offices and dressing-rooms to replace those in the old St Catherine's school building.

Trinity pulled off a valuable home win against leaders Salford, who were 5-2 ahead in the second half but were overhauled by a spirited Wakefield performance in the last quarter. The outstanding player was loose forward Mike Lampkowski, who, thought chairman Scaife, should have been in the Great Britain test team against Australia.

Trinity's need to strengthen the middle backs was hastened by the hip injury suffered by Derek Parker, who, at 30, was told he would not play again. After beginning his playing career with Leeds, he had arrived at Wakefield from Bradford for £18,000 during the previous season. Centre Paul Coventry, whose transfer Trinity had been chasing for some time, was signed from Featherstone for around £10,000.

Winger Andy Fletcher showed that his finishing was too good for most second division defences when he scored two fine tries in the 24-12 home win over Keighley, Trinity's fifth win in a row but one in which Johnny Thompson had the misfortune to break an arm. Trinity put up stout resistance at first division Widnes in the first round of the John Player Cup and led 10-7 at one stage before going out of the competition by 17-12. But then came a shock home defeat when mid-table Cardiff City beat third-placed Trinity 27-25 after trailing by fifteen points.

Since Trinity had finished in the top five at the end of 1982, the committee agreed that the first team squad of twenty would again be taken to Spain if the players paid half of their own costs.

Centre Phil Eden, originally signed from Redhill before playing in the Trinity Colts side, was promoted to the first team and made his debut at the age of 19 in the 16-8 win over Bramley – a victory which put Trinity just behind leaders Fulham in the table. Eden and loose forward Dean Williams were both selected in the Great Britain Colts side to face France. In a flurry of transfer activity, three players left the club: scrum half Dale Fennell went to Bradford for £4,000, winger Dennis Buckley to Rochdale for £3,000 and back rower Tim Slatter signed for Featherstone for £2,500. Trinity were glad to bank the transfer fees to stave off their rising running costs, but Dave Heslop, whose first team place had been taken over by 18-year old goal-kicking hooker Colin Maskill, was to retire at the end of the season with a serious neck injury.

As in the previous year, the players enjoyed training in the sun before their first round Challenge Cup tie, as coach Ray Batten put the players through their paces in Benidorm. Watched by the biggest crowd of the season so far - 3,451 - Trinity cruised through the home tie against Keighley, winning 27-5 after having the game wrapped up at half-time when they led 17-0. Malcolm Swann was named man of the match, which testified to the remarkable comeback he had made from a career-threatening back injury.

Trinity's nine-match winning streak came to a halt in the second round of the Cup at the Boulevard. Topliss gave a masterly demonstration of stand-off play by scoring a try and having a hand in four others, two of which were scored by another ex-Trinity man, Terry Day. Against Hull's star-studded side, Trinity stood little chance and lost 32-15 – but not before scoring three excellent tries of their own from Andy Fletcher, Lindsay Rotherforth and Bryan Adams. Rotherforth's effort was spectacular as he used his exceptional pace to go on a crossfield run and beat everyone on his way to the line.

Trinity failed for a second time against Fulham. In front of 3,983 supporters at Belle Vue, surprisingly the biggest crowd of the season, Fulham triumphed 25-15 to go five points clear at the top. The clash between the division's top two teams was eagerly anticipated but the visitors won more easily than the score suggested, despite a length of the field interception by Rotherforth. Ex-Trinity back Steve Diamond, the leading points-scorer in both divisions, added to his total with three tries. Batten criticised some players for not pulling their weight. 'It's alright players turning it on against clubs in the lower half of the second division but when it comes to the big matches they just don't seem able to make an impression,' he said. 'Some of them won't take on any responsibility and fall back and let others do the work.'

As predicted, Trinity clinched promotion at the first attempt after beating Huddersfield 36-11 at Belle Vue. Scaife praised Batten for transforming Trinity from a losing side to a winning one and for developing the club's youth policy. With Lampkowski back from injury, Trinity went on to record a notable double over Salford with a 19-10 away win over another promoted side. Box, from whom Nigel Stephenson had taken over the captaincy, made a quick return to form with two tries and three goals. 'He joined attacks at every opportunity and his bustling style invariably broke the tackle,' said the *Wakefield Express*.

But as Trinity looked towards life in the first division again, it was announced that the players had agreed to their wages being suspended for two months until the end of the season in order to ease the club's cash-flow problems. Winning wages, paid out 27 times, had drained the coffers. The financial position after a season in the second division was described as 'crippling'. With an average attendance of only 2,343, debts had mounted to over £200,000.

Batten admitted that to survive in the first division would be hard. The team needed to strengthen the back three forwards and required another centre, but no one could say where the money would come from. 'We haven't got a penny to spend on strengthening the team,' said Scaife, who also confirmed that the club had asked the local council for financial assistance.

During the close season, Scaife, Batten and committee man Duncan Farrar made a fact-finding trip to Australia at their own expense. It was now obvious that Britain, following the humiliation of the series whitewash by the Kangaroos, lagged behind Australia. On their return, Scaife said that they had all been impressed with the standard of play and the levels of fitness as well as players' individual commitment.

But no sooner had they got back home than, for the second time in two years, Ray Batten made the shock decision to resign. As part of a cost-cutting initiative, the committee had decided to dispense with the services of trainer Stan Timmins, who was responsible for preparing and conditioning the players. Batten objected and told the committee he was quitting on principle. Another significant cut announced by the committee was to suspend the A team for twelve months and to keep only a pool of 20 to 25 first team players, but the Colts would be retained.

A loss of £87,000 on the season was announced, putting the club into debt to the tune of £243,000 and bringing Wakefield Council to the rescue. 'Without the involvement of the council it would have been very difficult for Wakefield Trinity to continue trading,' said Scaife. Neither the club nor the council revealed the agreement that had been reached, but it was believed that the council was to take over the deeds – in effect the ownership of the Belle Vue ground – until the club moved to a new stadium at the proposed sports complex at Pugneys. This project had already faced objection in council meetings, notably from local councillor and future MP David Hinchliffe. Wakefield Council was to insist on a five-man finance committee being put in place to control spending and would nominate three members including the chairman of that committee. The club's wage bill for season 1982-83 had risen to £106,000 and showed a 'staggering' increase of £18,000 over the previous season, when they were in the first division. At the same time, gates for league matches were down by £18,000.

With Batten's departure, the club pulled off a significant coup in luring back former captain Derek Turner as coach. Out of the game for a decade, Turner had previously enjoyed success with Castleford and Leeds but had, until now, resisted all attempts to bring him back to Belle Vue.

The squad of 46 players was cut to 24, even though the number of players used during a season averaged over 40. Other players were to be loaned out. Chairman John Scaife and vice-chairman Les Eyre announced that they would relinquish their posts, citing business reasons, but remain as members of the committee. The new chairman was Jim Cranswick, a former mayor and British Rail driver, with ex-player Eric Ingham as his deputy, though the former Trinity hooker was to take over the chair when Cranswick resigned in September owing to ill health.

Wakefield Council agreed a rescue package involving a loan of £150,000 interest-free over five years, which was just as well because the bank refused to make further funds available. As part of the deal, the new five-man finance committee had to ensure that, henceforth, income exceeded expenditure.

As a result of their financial dilemma, Trinity missed out on signing the outstanding 18-year old scrum-half Deryck Fox from the Dewsbury amateur club, St John Fisher. The future Great Britain half back had already agreed to join the club but since Trinity could not now find the money to pay his signing-on fee, he went to Featherstone instead.

The 1983-84 season brought with it important rule changes. The value of a try increased from three to four points, while the handover (or turnover) rule was introduced to replace the scrum following the sixth consecutive tackle.

A week after the official opening of the Sports and Social Club, Trinity, now back in the first division, played Fulham in the opening match of the 1983-84 season at Belle Vue and won 18-14 thanks to two late penalties from Colin Maskill. They were not so fortunate against Wigan, who won 18-11, but there was much to commend in Trinity's performance. In his comeback game, Bill Ashurst showed against his old side what Trinity had been missing for so long. 'Ashurst came in for some heavy punishment but tormented his former team with his handling skills. He created the best try of the game when he swept through a gap and accelerated away before drawing the full back and sending the supporting Coventry over with a lovely reverse pass.' But sadly, as Ashurst went off midway through the second half, the comeback game only proved that his injured knees could no longer take the strain and he decided that his career was over. Mike Lampkowski was in a similar position, needing another knee operation, which was not career-threatening but would put him out for around two months just when he was needed most.

With nine changes from the previous week, Trinity suffered their heaviest defeat for four years as they crashed to a 38-0 loss at Hull KR. In the first round of the Yorkshire Cup, young forward Ian Hopkinson made a good showing with some powerful running though Trinity laboured to beat second division Halifax by 19-10.

A 27-26 defeat at Salford sparked a series of narrow losses which Trinity could ill afford, as coach Derek Turner constantly reminded his men. After beating Doncaster 32-14 in the second round of the County cup in midweek, Trinity just failed to beat Leeds in the league at Belle Vue, going down 20-19. The youthfulness of the forwards was shown by the fact that all but one were aged 21 or under.

In the semi-final of the Yorkshire Cup, Castleford put on a convincing display to beat their hosts by 34-12 at Belle Vue, before St Helens inflicted a humiliating 50-12 defeat – Trinity's fifth in a row in the league.

Kangaroo stand-off and captain Wally Lewis, widely regarded as the world's best player, arrived at Wakefield for a highly-paid ten-match spell in 1983-84

Trinity had ambitious plans to augment their squad with Australians as the international transfer ban was about to be lifted. They had aimed to recruit test centre Steve Rogers but the plan went awry when he broke his elbow in the final match of the Australian season. However, loose forward Alan Burns and centre or second row Glenn Worne, both aged 22 from North Sydney, were lined up to play at Belle Vue.

A disappointing 16-5 home defeat by Salford, second from bottom, watched by a crowd of only 2,163, brought a tongue-lashing from Ingham. 'The players were told in no uncertain terms that if there was any repeat of Sunday's performance they could all pack their bags and leave Belle Vue,' said the vice-chairman, who claimed to be 'disgusted' by the lack of effort.

Out of the blue, the startling news was revealed that Trinity had almost concluded negotiations with Australian test stand-off Wally Lewis, who had just been on tour with Queensland and who was widely regarded as the world's best player. Lewis was thinking over whether to return to England and to which club after Leeds had improved on Trinity's offer.

Two defeats in consecutive weeks by Warrington at Belle Vue – the first in the John Player Trophy, the second in the league – proved that Trinity were badly in need of inspiration. Supporters were not impressed by what they had seen, if an average attendance of 2,600 – scarcely better than the previous season in the second division – was anything to go by.

It was finally announced in late November that Wally Lewis, accompanied by his 18-year old brother Scott, would arrive in Wakefield in early December. He would be paid around £1,000 for each of ten games, an astronomical amount for the time, making him the highest-paid rugby league player in the world. Local building company N B Hough and London-based Overseas Bloodstock and Equine Investments put up the cash to beat off the attempts of Leeds, St Helens and Wigan to sign him. Tough-tackling prop Brad Waugh from Penrith would also arrive to shore up the front row. The Lewis brothers would be hosted by former player and committee member Brian Briggs at his pub, the British Oak, on Aberford Road.

A crowd of 8,179 – a record for a league game at Belle Vue since the reintroduction of two divisions in 1972-73 – turned up to see Wally Lewis make his debut against Hull, for whom Australian test scrum-half Peter Sterling was also appearing for the first time. Despite having arrived just 24 hours before, Lewis needed just seven minutes to open up the Hull defence and send brother Scott over the line. Lewis's breathtaking bullet passes – a rare skill at the time – earned the crowd's immediate admiration, not to mention his stern defence. Aussie front-rower Brad Waugh also put in a 'blockbusting' performance. 'Waugh spent much of the match locked together with Trevor Skerrett in a mighty contest which shook Belle Vue to its historic foundations.' The sides were level at 16-all at half-time, but it was Hull, master-minded by Sterling, who pulled away to win 32-16. Lewis, lacking match fitness and having suffered a hamstring injury after 20 minutes, rated himself as only 20 per cent fit, but the fans had seen enough to realise that greatness had descended on Belle Vue that day. Derek Turner, not a man to be easily impressed, said: 'I think he's got everything. He's not just a great player, he's got bags of guts and that's something I admire.' The committee were well pleased with receipts of £12,200 from an attendance which exceeded the season's previous best by more than 2,500.

A run of seven defeats was ended in style at Whitehaven, where Lewis, still lacking fitness and partnered by teenager Mick Norton at scrum-half, was a cut above and inspired a 38-10 win. The stand-off steered his new team to a second consecutive victory as Trinity defeated Oldham 28-22 at Belle Vue. Oldham, who saw themselves as championship contenders, were not fussy about how they stopped Lewis, who came in for some heavy treatment. At the very end of the first half Lewis cleverly kicked ahead and regathered before drawing the full back, New Zealander Nick Wright, and putting brother Scott in for a try. But in doing so he was flattened by Wright, who was sent off as Lewis himself was helped from the field. Trinity led 20-8 but the game threatened to get out of control as Waugh and Gearey, together with ex-Trinity hooker McCurrie, were sin-binned, reducing both sides to eleven players at one point. Lewis returned to the fray fifteen minutes after the restart to a roar of acclaim from the fans and Trinity held on for a crucial win.

At Castleford on Boxing Day, however, there were no festive celebrations for Wakefield supporters. Trinity badly missed Waugh's presence in the forwards and Castleford's young New Zealand scrum-half, Gary Freeman, a future international, took the honours in their 24-8 win.

The New Year began no better as Trinity's hopes of avoiding relegation were dealt a blow by the 14-12 defeat at Leigh after they had been 6-0 ahead. Nevertheless Waugh made some big tackles, Scott Lewis scored two tries and, most important for the future of the team, debutant scrum-half Nigel Bell was impressive. The new half-back pairing of Lewis and Bell scored all Trinity's five tries in the 31-22 demolition of St Helens at Belle Vue. Bell had been playing amateur rugby league at Eastmoor only a month before but was voted man of the match ahead of hat-trick hero Lewis, who used his skill and power to tremendous effect. The Aussie stand-off, after scoring two tries from close range, sliced between the opposing half backs and raced away from the full back to score his third. Bell, taking a pass from Lewis, broke the defensive line, raced 55 yards and crashed through the full back's attempted tackle to place the ball over the line. These were the sort of moments that the Belle Vue crowd, too often starved of such pleasures, had long waited to see.

At Warrington, Trinity again came close but not close enough as they went down 16-12. Lewis, hampered by a leg injury, struggled to impose himself on the game. Stephenson, Bell and Gearey were the pick of the team in a match which Trinity, still third from bottom, needed to win to keep alive their hopes of staying up. In the meantime, forward Lindsay Gill and Greg Gerard, brother of Geoff, were also recruited from Australia.

At Headingley, Trinity failed to halt Leeds's nine-match unbeaten run, as a series of unfortunate events played a big part in the 26-16 defeat. Props Waugh and Bratt both went off injured and second row Gill was sent off after clattering Leeds scrum-half Steve Martin. Referee Massey's decision was disputed by Lewis, who was also dismissed for allegedly using abusive language. Down to eleven men, Trinity conceded two more tries. The referee, who needed a police escort as he left the field, was pelted with snowballs by Wakefield fans. Lewis, in his penultimate league match, said he would not return to play in England as it was the worst refereeing he had seen.

After disputing the referee's decision in sending off fellow-Australian Lindsay Gill, Wally Lewis is sent off at Headingley, escorted by coach Derek Turner

Trinity made a better showing against Featherstone, winning 8-1. Loose forward Stephenson was Trinity's man of the match, marshalling the side in both attack and defence. Lewis suffered a head injury but played on and had a big role in the fourth win out of the nine league games he had played. His compatriot Gill headed the tackle count while Bell continued his astonishing start to his professional career, overshadowing his young opposite number, Deryck Fox.

The first round Challenge Cup tie at Halifax was Lewis's last match in Trinity colours. The Australian scored two tries, both from well-timed passes from Nigel Stephenson, whose guile unpicked the Halifax defence, but Gill was named Trinity's man of the match for his industry in both attack and defence.

Lewis scored six tries in his ten games, but injury, lack of full fitness and opposition thuggery only allowed fans glimpses of his ability. Five of those ten matches were won but he could not save Trinity from the descent into the second division. 'He carried us, there's no doubt about that,' said coach Turner. 'And don't forget he was playing with an injury most of the time. But he jibbed at nothing and gave total commitment, with or without the ball.'

Once Lewis had left, the team's limitations were exposed first at high-flying Widnes, who won 42-14. Burns and Waugh, injured, had already played their last match for Trinity. Pickerill replaced Lewis and Gill was sent off but Bell, whom Lewis had tried to persuade to follow him to Brisbane, was again Trinity's man of the match with two tries and highest tackle count.

Trinity's season finally fell apart when, without any Australian assistance to rely on, they collapsed to a 20-12 home defeat by York in the second round of the Challenge Cup – 'a display to rank alongside the worst ever at Belle Vue', said the *Wakefield Express*. Nigel Stephenson tried his hardest to bring some life to Trinity's performance but to no avail. Two days later coach Derek Turner handed in his resignation. He made no comment but chairman Ingham spoke for him when he said, 'Derek felt he was not getting anything like a hundred per cent from the players and this was something he could not accept. He was deeply upset by the performance [against York] and told me he could not see any point in carrying on … I can't blame him for resigning because the performance was dreadful. Pathetic is not a strong enough word to describe how we played and I was disgusted with the performances and attitude of some of our players.'

Assistant coach Bob Haigh stepped up. He promptly dropped Stephenson, Adams and Pickerill, since, with relegation now a certainty, the club intended to look to its players of the future.

Just when it appeared that Trinity's form could get no worse, it did. Bottom-of-the-table Whitehaven took Trinity apart at Belle Vue, winning 32-12 in front of a meagre crowd of 1,456, the smallest of the season. Once more a performance was described as Trinity's worst ever, with only Bell and Gearey rising above the modest form of the rest of the side.

A host of young players were brought in, including 17-year old Steve Rollin, winger Paul Hampson, stand-off Richard Kelly and loose forward George Oglethorpe. They helped to produce a much-improved display in the 12-0 defeat against Bradford. Hooker Colin Maskill, meanwhile, was off to Queensland to join Wally Lewis's old club, Valleys.

Inexperienced players cannot be expected to maintain a high level of form against top sides and the season ended with a series of four heavy defeats, the last of which, by 42-12 to Castleford at Belle Vue, was Trinity's ninth consecutive defeat since the Cup win at Halifax and since Lewis last played. It was a dismal end to the season, with Nigel Stephenson heading Trinity's try-scorers with just nine. Apart from the brief, sensational highlights provided by Wally Lewis, supported by the Australian contingent, and the heart-warming form of those two local products, Nigel Bell and Paul Gearey, there was nothing to cheer and plenty to decry. It was unfortunate too that Derek Turner, one of the greatest players ever to put on a Trinity jersey, and who had achieved almost everything the game had to offer, both as a player and as a coach with Leeds and Castleford, should, as the *Wakefield Express* put it, admit defeat for probably the first and only time in his career.

Former Trinity full back Geoff Wraith was appointed as the new coach, Trinity's sixth in five seasons. The former Castleford A team coach had been assistant to Malcolm Reilly and had brought an attacking style of rugby league to their second-string side. 'Wakefield Trinity don't belong in the second division and it is a sad sight to see them there because I have some great memories of this club as a player,' said Wraith. 'I'll be hoping to restore some of those former glory days but make no mistake, I am under no illusions about how difficult the job will be.' Former loose forward Dave Lamming was appointed as his assistant.

At the end of the season it was revealed that, although Trinity had slashed £71,000 from their outgoings, their total debts amounted to a quarter of a million pounds, including the £150,000 lifeline thrown to them by Wakefield Council. Chairman Eric Ingham, a self-employed plumber, said that the club's existence was still threatened and needed better support from the public. Despite the economies, the club still lost £16,000 during the year, though he believed that they would break even in the coming season. Trinity's relegation was blamed on a lack of professionalism on the part of senior players. If they had shown the same degree of commitment as Wally Lewis, said Ingham, Trinity would still be in the first division.

As Trinity prepared for life in the 1984-85 second division, their second spell there in three seasons, Ingham said it was his ambition to put Trinity straight back in the top flight and to make a small profit as well. Two years earlier, Trinity had signed a number of experienced players to help get them out of the lower division, but this time youth was to be the policy, although in truth, given the club's precarious financial position, there was no other option. The players would also have to take a drastic pay cut.

Trinity signed no fewer than seven of Sharlston's outstanding Under 17 side of the previous season, when they were coached by Trevor Bailey, now appointed Trinity Colts coach in place of Alan Box, who had enjoyed a successful five-year stint. Among the youngsters signed were hooker Billy Conway and full back Gary Spencer.

Early in the season Trinity travelled to newly-formed Mansfield, whose first home match this was. Before the game a number of former Trinity stars – Neil Fox, Derek Turner, Ron Rylance, Ian Brooke, Joby Shaw and Brian Briggs – were presented to the crowd. How coach Wraith must have wished he could have had players of their calibre, the *Wakefield Express* commented, instead of those giving a blundering performance against a Mansfield team of unproven ex-amateurs and written-off old pros. Trinity's ex-stars must have been 'cringing in agony and disbelief'.

In the first round of the Yorkshire Cup, Trinity went out at the hands of Bradford, or rather Ellery Hanley, who scored four tries, goaling the first two, in their 30-0 victory. When Trinity travelled to Essex to play new club Southend Invicta and duly won 22-13, only 385 members of the public turned up. In that game Nigel Stephenson kicked two drop goals to become the new record holder with 72, beating the tally of Whitehaven and Workington half back Arnold Walker.

By mid-October, Trinity had precious little experience in the side as Bell, Coventry, Fletcher, Stephenson, Tinker, Lampkowski, Gearey and Maskill were all injured, some of them long term. It was in this state of near-desperation that Geoff Wraith, at the age of 38, decided to return to action at full back against Whitehaven. Trinity's coach, who had signed for the club a decade earlier, made light of the years as he astounded the Belle Vue crowd with a first-minute break over 90 yards which dazzled the opposition defence until he faltered just short of the line. Brad Waugh also returned to the side and made an impact, which would have been greater if he had had better support. Neither of these efforts prevented Trinity from losing 16-8.

Probably the lowest point of the season arrived the week after in a debacle at Keighley. No fewer than six players were sent off by referee Mr Mean, four of them from Trinity – Box, Thompson, Jones and hooker Alan Shaw, newly signed from a local amateur side. Wraith selected himself again, this time at centre alongside 17-year old Mark Wild. It ended in a 46-10 rout which had consequences. Captain Nigel Stephenson announced his retirement from the game, saying he could no longer motivate himself. Wraith threw the towel in too, believing that Trinity's weak financial position prevented him from recruiting vital new players.

Assistant coach Dave Lamming was put in charge, while Trinity tried to arrange talks with Alex Murphy, who had been sacked by Wigan. The meeting never materialised and Lamming, together with Colts coach Trevor Bailey, remained at the helm. The squad was reinforced by temporary overseas recruits, who all featured in the 28-2 win over Doncaster. In addition to Waugh, centre Rod Snell and second row Darren Waters arrived from Perth, Western Australia. Centre Graham Gerard, younger brother of Geoff and Greg, came from Parramatta and forward Don Swanston from Christchurch, New Zealand. Seventeen-year old Colts hooker Billy Conway, a schoolboy boxing champion, made his debut and took the man of the match award. After nine matches, Trinity had used 35 players.

In the John Player Trophy, Trinity got no further than the preliminary round, losing 17-6 at Sheffield – a defeat which was thought to have cost the club around £5,000 since a lucrative first round tie at Leeds was in store.

Another talented Colt, full back Gary Spencer, not to be outdone by his team-mate Conway, took the man of the match award on his debut in the 12-8 home defeat by York, in which he impressed with his secure defence and intelligent running in attack.

Consecutive defeats at Fulham and Huddersfield dented Trinity's promotion hopes and led to the resignation of Eric Ingham as chairman after eighteen months in the post. Ted Hewitt, the club president for five years and the most experienced man in the boardroom, took over, combining the two roles.

Scrum-half Clive Pickerill, after three years at Belle Vue, was sold to Sheffield for an undisclosed fee and 20-year old hooker Colin Maskill, who wanted first division football, asked for a transfer and was listed at a world record fee of £75,000 before being sold to Leeds for £35,000 less. Nigel Stephenson, who had signed for £20,000 from Carlisle two and a half years earlier, came out of retirement and returned to his first club Dewsbury for a small fee.

In the preliminary round of the Challenge Cup at Doncaster, Harold Box inspired his men to a 25-6 win. In the first round proper, Trinity travelled to Whitehaven, once the scene of Wakefield heroics. Trinity triumphed again, winning 10-8 with full back Andy Sygrove collecting all his team's points with a try and three goals.

Mike Lampkowski made his first appearance for two years when he came off the bench. In the second round at Odsal on a Wednesday evening, Trinity went out of the Cup by 13-2 but did not disgrace themselves.

The 18-10 win over Mansfield on a Wednesday evening was witnessed by a mere 1,158 supporters, the lowest crowd of the season at Belle Vue. In the following match against Fulham, Lampkowski played his first full match since returning from his long lay-off and his explosive running, added to that of blockbusting Ian Hopkinson, paved the way for Trinity's 34-12 win.

After that, Trinity's season fell apart as they suffered a 50-10 reverse at promotion hopefuls Salford – the heaviest defeat of the campaign. Lampkowski suffered further damage to his troublesome knee and decided to call it a day. The big-hearted player, aged 32, had made 160 appearances after signing in February 1977. Worse than the defeat at Salford was the performance against Blackpool, who recorded their first ever victory at Belle Vue, winning 29-18 despite the fact that Trinity had led 14-0 at one stage.

Chairman Hewitt revealed that Peter Fox, who was set to leave Bradford at the end of the season, had been approached to return to Belle Vue, but had already agreed to join another club. Instead, Hull KR's former international forward Len Casey was signed as player-coach, for which the Robins were paid £3,000. It was intended that Lamming should be Casey's assistant but he resigned when he only found out about Casey's arrival from colleagues at work. Casey had not played for several weeks and admitted he knew very little about the Wakefield players. But he made an immediate impression in the return match at Blackpool on Easter Monday. The so-called iron man pulled the Blackpool defence apart with his deft ball-handling, strong running and crashing tackles. Centre Graham Gerard, in his last match before returning to Parramatta, was also outstanding, scoring the first try and making the second as Trinity got their revenge by 22-8 in only their second away win of the season.

The season petered out with Trinity ending up in eleventh place, which was only achieved by winning six out of the last nine games. Other statistics made grim reading. Only one league attendance – at the match against Huddersfield - rose above 2,000, while the Yorkshire Cup match against Bradford produced the biggest crowd – a paltry 2,303. Well over forty players had been used. Casey promised changes for the following season. As the *Express* commented: 'It would take a brave man to argue that Wakefield Trinity RLFC is not at an all-time low.'

The brightest aspect of the club was undoubtedly the form of the Colts side who, under Trevor Bailey, won their Challenge Cup and league title and finished runners-up to Hull KR in the premiership play-offs. Five members of the side had been selected for Yorkshire.

Casey made his first signing in stand-off Stuart Wainman, from West Hull amateurs, who had already appeared as a triallist for Trinity and twice for Hull. He was rated by Casey as better than Graham Steadman. Casey also brought in Tony Dean as A team coach and ex-Hull scrum half Kevin Harkin was signed on an indefinite loan.

At the end of the season Trinity declared a loss of £1,606, which represented substantial cost-cutting since the £86,000 of two years ago. But the club's liabilities remained stubbornly high at £223,772, which included the £150,000 Council loan. Compared to the previous season, playing expenses were reduced by a third, but gate receipts from league games fell dramatically from £47,000 in 1983-84 to £15,000. Chairman Hewitt said, 'We can't afford two more seasons of second division rugby. Promotion has got to be our number one priority next season. We must get back into the first division and if we don't the future doesn't really bear thinking about.'

Twenty – Out of the Gloom: 1985-90

Even before the 1985-86 season got under way, problems loomed in the form of the old West Stand, which had been inspected by officials from the County Council's fire and police departments in the wake of the Bradford City disaster. Even before the officials reported back, it was clear that the stand would not meet the new safety requirements and season ticket sales for that part of the ground were suspended.

Trinity badly needed to cut their cloth according to their diminished means. To strengthen their squad, prop John Millington was signed from Hull KR and Wakefield-based centre Graham Evans from Carlisle. Another local player, 34-year old scrum-half Kevin Harkin had already been signed from Hull on indefinite loan. Second rower Stuart Smith arrived from Hunslet and stand-off Andy Tosney, who had made almost twenty first-team appearances, signed professional forms. They failed to sign Bradford's Great Britain forward Dick Jasiewicz, who could not accept the terms offered and Aussie forwards Brad Waugh and Darren Waters did not return to Belle Vue because their clubs, Penrith and Canberra respectively, wanted them for pre-season training.

Just days before the start of the 1985-86 season, the RFL issued a new fixture list for the second division after both Bridgend and Southend Invicta had been suspended from the competition. Trinity made a decent start to their second consecutive season in the lower division, but the gulf in class was evident in the clash with Bradford in the first round of the Yorkshire Cup at Odsal. Trinity led 7-0 at half-time even after having Casey sent off in the 26th minute, though ultimately they were overwhelmed and lost 40-15. But in the lower tier, they continued to do well, beating Fulham 18-10 to go top.

They coped as expected with some none too demanding fixtures but pleased their fans when beating Workington, who were expected to push for promotion, by 25-4 in front of 2,161 spectators, Belle Vue's biggest crowd of the season so far. Among the star performers, John Lyons had scored six tries in five outings as he contested the stand-off spot with Stuart Wainman, while prop Ian Hopkinson was regarded by Casey as possibly the best forward in the second division and good enough to be considered for international honours.

Despite their progress, Casey was unhappy with his side's inability to score tries and lack of speed. Hull KR loose forward Tracey Lazenby, a former Colts international, who was on the transfer list at £10,000, was signed on loan and immediately impressed with his handling skills and vision.

But Trinity were missing the organisational ability of scrum-half Kevin Harkin, who was out of action for two months with a broken thumb. Looking anything but first division material they lost the league leadership with a 29-16 defeat at Whitehaven and a 15-12 loss at home to Barrow. They scraped through to the second round of the John Player Special Trophy by 24-22 at Blackpool and were rewarded with a home tie against first division Wigan. For this match only the West Stand was reopened as an unusually large crowd of 7,360 spectators turned up to see Wigan made to fight hard for their 30-21 win.

Casey urged the committee to 'move heaven and earth' to sign Lazenby, who, remarkably, had been made captain even while on loan. Although he had arrived at the club with a 'bad boy' reputation, Lazenby showed 'exemplary behaviour, both on and off the field.' But Trinity's finances could not even stretch to the bargain fee of £7,000 which Hull KR were asking. Once more the club was in a precarious position, so serious that Wakefield Council once more had to step in. At a members' meeting a proposal was put forward to save the club from bankruptcy. A second rescue package in just over two years was presented by committee member Stuart Farrar, who made it clear that a rejection of the plan would spell the end for the club. Farrar said that the previous loan of £150,000 had been utilised to pay pressing debts, but the club still had heavy liabilities. Over the intervening two years the committee had worked to a tight budget, but old debts, combined with interest payments, had taken Trinity 'to the brink of bankruptcy'. 'It soon became clear that, as soon as creditors closed in, the cash flow available to the club would be totally insufficient and that unless substantial amounts of money became available we would have had to fold,' said Farrar. 'I must stress the only option available in the event of this motion not being passed is simply the death of Wakefield Trinity.' Needless to say the members accepted the rescue plan, which involved the Council taking ownership of the ground and responsibility for the club's debts. The Council put forward five nominees, headed by local businessman Rodney Walker, to join four Trinity representatives on the new committee.

After that, Lazenby was signed as a key recruit to Trinity's promotion plans and in the New Year was joined by others from the Hull area. David Hall, a former international capable of playing in a variety of positions, was hailed as the answer to many of Trinity's attacking problems. Hall, at 31, had been a member of Hull KR's championship-winning side but had fallen out with the club and announced his retirement. In the event he played just three matches for Trinity, two of them off the bench. Another Hull KR player, prop Roy Holdstock, arrived on loan, taking the number of players signed from the area to seven. Another half back, Jimmy Green, was later signed from Blackpool in the hope that he would become Casey's sought-after playmaker.

The fixtures during the Christmas period were a far cry from the traditional battles of the past at Headingley. Trinity won 19-6 at Bramley on Boxing Day, watched by just 1,644 spectators, and on New Year's Day won 18-6 in the return match at Belle Vue, which was seen by just three people more. Fifth in the second division, Trinity entertained hopes of causing an upset against first division Bradford in the Challenge Cup. The televised first round tie was switched from Odsal to Headingley, where it was sure to go ahead. Trinity came close to overturning pre-match forecasts and in a tight, forward-dominated game were edged out of the competition by a slender 10-8 margin.

Three wins out of their last four games of the season, including a 44-14 romp at Carlisle, saw Trinity into the first division from the third and last promotion spot. Amid the relief of regaining their place at the top level, there was some concern about Trinity's ability to keep up with the pace. 'For the likes of Tracey Lazenby, Alan Shaw, Ian Hopkinson and Gary Cocks,' said Casey, 'the first division should see them shine ... [But] we are under no illusions there won't be any great fairytale next season.'

In June, Casey sprang a surprise. After just over a year at the club, he announced his decision to leave Trinity in order to take over at Hull, where he also ran a pub. His assistant Tony Dean, the former Hunslet and Hull scrum-half, stepped up to replace him. Dean announced that he wanted the team to play attractive, attacking football. Alan Rhodes, a former Castleford, Featherstone and York player, was appointed assistant coach. Ted Hewitt gave up the presidency for health reasons and was succeeded by former chairman Les Pounder.

Among the close season signings, Steve Evans, the former Featherstone and Great Britain back, arrived from Hull in a deal involving compensation for the loss of Casey. Warrington back row forward Tommy Gittins was brought to the club, along with the returning Steve Diamond, who had left five years earlier for Fulham, where he was leading points scorer in each of the three seasons he played there, after which he had spells at Warrington, Hunslet and Castleford. Four Australians - second row Rowan Brennan, winger Russell Klein, centre Glen Stanton and prop Robert Cowie - arrived at various stages of the early season.

Trinity's first five matches, including two Yorkshire Cup ties, were played away from home, so that work could be carried out in accordance with the new Safety at Sports Grounds Act. The most obvious result was the demolition of the old West Stand, which would have cost £150-200,000 to bring up to the new standards.

Trinity lost their opening eight league matches in the top flight. In between they scraped a first round Yorkshire Cup win by 14-12 at second division Batley, before going out of the competition by 21-12 at Hull. After a particularly disappointing 12-6 reverse at the hands of Leigh at Belle Vue, a match that was there for the taking, new chairman Rodney Walker said that there had been a problem of attitude and changes would be made if there was no improvement. Tracey Lazenby, who had been dropped and was selected in the A team, failed to turn up and was immediately transfer-listed at £40,000. Loose forward Dean Williams was also listed at £20,000.

Worse was to come. An appalling performance resulted in a 54-10 home defeat by Oldham, who had yet to win a game. 'I just can't put my finger on what went wrong,' said Dean.

Amid the gloom, Trinity pulled off an important signing when agreeing to a record £30,000 contract with Sharlston Under 17s loose forward Gary Price, who had been approached by seven other first division clubs, including Leeds and St Helens. Young full back Gary Spencer was included in the Great Britain 31-man squad to prepare to meet the Australian tourists.

As Trinity crashed to one of their heaviest defeats ever, losing 62-10 at Wigan, Penrith and future Australia coach Tim Sheens arrived on a seven-week stay as coaching consultant. The connection had been made when Sharlston U17s toured Australia two seasons earlier. Sheens would find plenty to occupy his thoughts.

One of Trinity's few playmakers, Tracey Lazenby, who had refused to accept playing in the A team, signed for Hull after making 34 appearances but left a lasting impression as a gifted footballer. Following yet another defeat, this time by 28-14 at the hands of Leeds at Belle Vue, Dean remarked: 'I am not concerned by our attacking displays. Those are things we can work on in training … but you can't coach players to tackle.'

In mid-November Trinity picked up their first league point of the season from a scrappy 14-all draw at home to Barrow. In the John Player Special Trophy, amateurs Millom were beaten 18-4 in an away preliminary round tie, but it was a laboured performance as Trinity struggled to overcome the 12-man Cumbrians, who had a player sent off as early as the 13th minute. In the first round proper, they went out by 36-22 at Halifax.

In the league Trinity found themselves adrift at the bottom and the home reverse to Featherstone by 29-2 in mid-December proved one too many. Tony Dean was sacked and Trevor Bailey was installed as caretaker coach till March when the situation would be re-assessed. At the same time Tim Sheens flew home, having presented his findings to the management committee.

At the half-yearly meeting, Walker and Bailey put forward their views on the way ahead. The chairman, who wanted the club to appoint a general manager to explore commercial opportunities, said: 'We have to run the club as a business. The future of the club is in the hands of local people both on and off the pitch.' He also stressed the need to continue to develop local players. Bailey, the first Trinity coach not to have been a professional player, said, 'With all my heart I can say that we want to keep our first division status but as a realist I know that will be hard to do. To come back we must develop a young side to win Division Two and then hope to buy two good players to keep us in Division One.' Among a number of comings and goings, Tommy Gittins was transferred to Barrow after just sixteen appearances and Dean Williams went to Rochdale. Bradford forward Dick Jasiewicz finally came to Belle Vue, in exchange for Steve Evans, who had played just fifteen times for Trinity. Forward Neil Kelly arrived from Featherstone in a straight swap for winger David Jones and prop Gary Van Bellen came from Bradford, initially on loan. Paul McDermott returned to Belle Vue for a third time, on loan from Whitehaven.

In the Challenge Cup, Trinity succeeded in beating second division Blackpool away, with Greg Stanton and Gary Cocks scoring the tries, Steve Diamond kicking three goals and John Lyons a drop goal. The Cup run ended in the most depressing fashion with a 25-2 home defeat by second division Whitehaven, who, with former Trinity hooker Alan McCurrie among the try-scorers, showed far more confidence than a feeble-looking Trinity. Bailey was moved to offer an apology to supporters, who, he said, deserved it 'after our diabolical second-half performance. The match exposed some of the limitations of our players.'

The signings went on. Kevin Harcombe, a goal-kicking full back or centre originally from amateur club Fryston and then Doncaster, arrived from Rochdale. Centre Steve Halliwell, an Australian with a British passport, was signed from St Helens, although he had established his record number of 49 tries (for a centre) with Leigh in Division Two. Both made their debut in the 36-12 defeat at Salford, where Harcombe was described as 'Wakefield's most dangerous and inventive player'. Of Halliwell, Bailey said, 'I believe that Steve can become another Wally Lewis for Wakefield and add an extra dimension to our game from stand-off half.'

By early March 1987 Trinity had played 21 matches and earned a single point. Their first league win came on March 15 when they beat mid-table Widnes by 38-20 at Belle Vue, Aussie winger Russell Klein scoring two tries in his final home appearance and Kevin Harcombe kicking seven goals. As the second division loomed, as it had for some months, players began to look to their immediate future. Gary Spencer felt that his future in representative rugby league would be hindered by staying at Wakefield and asked for a transfer, which was granted with a fee of £110,000, later reduced to £90,000. Scrum-half Jimmy Green, who had buzzed around the field in the eleven months since signing from Blackpool for £8,000, was transferred to Carlisle for an undisclosed fee.

Following the 15-12 loss at Odsal, Paul Mallinder became the fourth Bradford forward to be signed by Trinity, after Sheldon, Jasiewicz and Van Bellen. After a lengthy loan period, Paul Gearey was sold to Featherstone for £7,000. Just when it appeared that Trinity were making some headway, they collapsed in the face of a star-studded Wigan attack which ran in fourteen tries in Trinity's heaviest ever defeat. Henderson Gill and Ellery Hanley tormented an abject Trinity defence with three tries each, and Shaun Edwards and Steve Hampson both collected two tries in the 72-6 rout, of which 48 points came in the second half. Trinity's previous worst had come 66 years earlier in the 69-11 hammering by Hull in 1921, when a try was worth three points. What made matters worse was that the new record was witnessed by 5,400 spectators, Belle Vue's biggest crowd of the season. But Wakefield's lowest crowd of 1986-87 – 1,281 – saw a remarkable turnaround as Hull KR, who finished in sixth place, were beaten 19-4. John Lyons ran in two tries and kicked a drop goal and Paul Mallinder rallied the pack in Trinity's second league win of the season.

The brighter form continued with an end-of-season double over Cup finalists Halifax, who were beaten twice in the same week. In the match at Thrum Hall, won 19-10, Trinity even overcame the disadvantage of having eleven men at one point, as Mallinder was sent off and Lyons was sin-binned. Nevertheless they finished comfortably bottom of the heap, with four wins and a draw from 30 matches. The misery was temporarily dispelled by news of an apparently long-hatched plan to bring Wally Lewis and Gene Miles to Belle Vue on a 'self-financing' three-year contract, but the move was blocked in Australia. It was in any case hard to imagine two of Australia's brightest international stars – one arguably the world's best player, the other a future Test great - plying their trade in the English second division.

At the season's end, hooker Billy Conway had made the most appearances with 31 and John Lyons topped the try-scorers with fifteen, the only Trinity player in double figures. Attendances at league matches had shown an increase of more than a thousand over the previous season, when Trinity were in the second division. But the average of 2,636 was 850 down on their last season in the first division, in 1983-84 when Wally Lewis boosted fans' interest.

Pre-season ticket sales for 1987-88 were increased with the announcement of the return of David Topliss to Trinity as player-coach. Trevor Bailey, who had taken over in December as caretaker coach, was also considered, alongside twelve other candidates. Chairman Rodney Walker expressed the committee's 'respect and appreciation' for the work done by Bailey, who was asked to take responsibility once more for the Colts, as well as a new 'development unit', which would forge links with local schools and amateur clubs. Topliss's wish to come back to Belle Vue, after a gap of eight years, was irresistible. Walker said that the club was fortunate that the former test stand-off, who had received offers from first division clubs for his services as a player, wanted to return and play his part in reviving the club's fortunes.

The club's fifteenth coach in the eleven years since Peter Fox left, Topliss lost no time in appointing former Trinity players Tony Handforth and Ian Brooke, who had himself coached Trinity in 1978, as his assistants. In his very first move into the transfer market, Topliss pulled off a deal with Leeds which was to spark Trinity's revival. Young full back Gary Spencer and stand-off John Lyons, who had played 125 games for Trinity, scoring over 350 points, went to Headingley in exchange for centre Andy Mason, winger Phil Fox, half back Mark Conway and forward Keith Rayne, plus a substantial sum believed to be around £20,000. Yorkshire centre or winger Mason, aged 25, had been signed by Leeds from Bramley for £50,000 in October 1986, while 29-year old Fox, who had started his career at Widnes before moving to Leigh, went to Headingley just after Mason for £15,000. Conway, aged 23, a cousin of Trinity hooker Billy, was a former Leeds Colt who had represented Great Britain at both U21 and Colts level. The oldest of the quartet, 31-year old Keith Rayne, was returning to Trinity after playing at Belle Vue between 1974 and 1980. He had won representative honours with Great Britain, England and Yorkshire and had made over 160 appearances for Leeds. Topliss said he had been reluctant to see Spencer and Lyons leave but once it became known that Leeds were interested in them it would have been difficult to keep them happy. But the new coach was 'delighted' with the overall deal after a month of hard bargaining during which Leeds coach Maurice Bamford had offered 13 or 14 players to choose from. Topliss commented, 'I think this deal will see this club turn the corner.' He did not expect any other second division side to have as fast a set of backs and also talked about the possibility of adding a couple more players. But it was a sign of the standards that Topliss would set when he added, 'If I did bring players they would have to be able to make a difference to the side. In the past players that have come haven't actually gone out and won games for the club and I am not bothered about going out and getting just anybody if they are not good enough.'

Financially, the club was worse off than ever, despite the Council's imposition of a management committee. Trinity made a loss of almost £137,000 on the season, with net liabilities of £292,000. The loss was almost entirely accounted for by dealings in the transfer market. A total of £141,740 had been expended on new players and the recently-introduced contract payments, while only £11,000 had been recouped from the sale of Gittins and Gearey. Walker explained: 'We were permitted to spend £60,000 on team strengthening at the start of the season and we were given permission by the local authority to spend again later in the season when we signed such players as Kevin Harcombe, Gary Van Bellen and so on, plus money for Gary Price and the six Colts we took on. The original signings were made by Tony Dean and the second set, we, the committee, will have to stand up and be counted as we worked on advice given to us when we tried to strengthen the team.'

With Topliss back in Trinity's colours and Mark Conway playing alongside him, Trinity got their 1987-88 season off to an excellent start with a 56-8 win over Carlisle, who could not cope with their opponents' speed and power. 'Genuine pace has been lacking at Belle Vue for some time but Andy Mason's stunning second-half try brought the house down,' said the *Wakefield Express*. 'Not since the days of Andy Fletcher have we seen a Wakefield threequarter leave the defence for dead through sheer pace.' Dewsbury were defeated 25-14 in the preliminary round of the Yorkshire Cup and then again in the league by 22-0, to which Topliss, Wakefield's best player, contributed a try, taking him past 600 points for the club in 408 appearances. Coincidentally prop Gary Cocks was transferred to Crown Flatt for £5,000, following in the footsteps of Alan Shaw, who was sold for £3,000. Andy Mason, who had twice been selected for Yorkshire while with Bramley, won a third cap and became the first Trinity player to represent the county since Harold Box in 1981. He was to win another cap against Papua-New Guinea later in the year.

In the first round of the Yorkshire Cup, Sheffield, who were to prove difficult opponents during the season, were knocked out by 32-18, before Trinity themselves went out of the competition at Headingley by 36-8. In between the two rounds, winger Phil Fox became the first Trinity player since Wally Lewis - against St Helens in January 1984 - to score a hat-trick, when he crossed the Bramley line three times in the 62-10 win, to which Harcombe contributed nine goals. Trinity dropped their first league point in the 20-all draw with bottom club Mansfield despite Phil Eden emulating Fox by scoring three tries. Aussie winger Gregg Lennon added even more pace to the Trinity threequarter line when he arrived from North Sydney and scored twice in the 32-14 home defeat of Dewsbury but Trinity's creativity was hampered by a knee ligament injury to David Topliss, who would be out for five weeks. Gary Price, aged 17, made his debut in the 14-12 win at Sheffield and was involved in Trinity's first try, scored by Phil Fox, but it was a late penalty by Mark Conway which provided the league points from the top-of-the-table clash.

In early November Trinity tasted defeat for the first time when, in muddy conditions at Whitehaven, the home side triumphed 18-10. In the John Player Special Trophy, in which Topliss was the only player still active to have appeared in the 1971-72 final, Trinity now faced York. A surprising 22-all draw materialised at Belle Vue before Trinity went on to win the replay 30-6. In the second round, Springfield Borough, the old Blackpool club now playing at Wigan, with several old heads to direct them, put Trinity out by 14-8. At that point Springfield were fourth in the table, with Trinity just one place behind with three matches in hand.

Dick Jasiewicz, who wanted first division football, was placed on the transfer list at £40,000 and Stuart Wainman left the club, intending a return to amateur rugby league in West Hull. Gregg Lennon's stay at Belle Vue came to an abrupt end when he sustained a serious ankle injury. To replace him, Andy Fletcher was re-signed from Mansfield at the age of 30. In the New Year, Andy Kelly, who had left Trinity six years earlier for Hull KR, where he earned selection for England and Yorkshire, also returned for much less than the £40,000 asking price. He celebrated his homecoming with an excellent try in the 32-14 home win over Barrow.

Scrum half Nigel Bell went from playing amateur rugby league at Eastmoor to partnering Wally Lewis and became one of Trinity's core players over more than a decade

But during the festive season Trinity were twice disappointed as Featherstone, first on Boxing Day at Post Office Road, then at Belle Vue on New Year's Day, outclassed them by 17-14 and 21-16.

At the members' half-yearly meeting, Topliss reflected on his squad, saying, 'I am determined that Trinity will come back to strength. The season I left, six years ago, Trinity were third [actually fourth] in Division One. They went down the next and the committee at the time sold first division players and bought second division. The club is now trying to get good players to the club. I'm just hoping that when we go up the resources will be available to strengthen.'

Senior players like Nigel Bell and captain Keith Rayne continued to show the way. Both were prominent in the 28-10 win at Oldham, who were undefeated at the Watersheddings. In another tight tussle with Sheffield, Trinity went out of the Challenge Cup in the first round, losing 14-10 at Belle Vue, but turned the tables on Gary Hetherington's men with a 14-6 league win which sent them to the top of the league. Topliss singled out Bell for praise. 'He was absolutely phenomenal and made 45 tackles from scrum-half when a good forward performance usually averages around 30 to 35.'

Trinity made an ambitious attempt to sign Wigan's Ellery Hanley on loan when the Great Britain star was at loggerheads with coach Graham Lowe. Football committee chairman Stuart Farrar said that the move was not a gimmick. 'We will have to acquire players of this quality if we are to succeed in the first division,' he said.

Trinity's winning streak continued with an 18-8 win at Rochdale, which put them back at the top of the table. Andy Kelly was outstanding, making three breaks which led to two tries for Steve Halliwell and one for Billy Conway. Andy Mason posted a hat-trick in the 32-0 home win over Fulham, which extended the winning run to nine. It came to an end at Bramley, who pulled off a shock 12-10 win after Trinity had led 10-0 with seven minutes remaining.

The former Belle Vue Sports and Social club, which had closed its doors in January, reopened as the Wakefield Trinity Social Club for the benefit of season ticket holders. Supporters were able to celebrate there as, over the Easter period, Trinity beat York 34-11 at Belle Vue on Good Friday to gain promotion to the first division, though they lost the return fixture 17-8 on Easter Monday. Promotion rivals Oldham, in the penultimate match of the season, came to Belle Vue in a league leadership showdown. Watched by 6,522 spectators, Topliss played against his former club and made a classy break to send Mark Conway over, but Oldham snatched the second division title with a 23-22 win. After also losing by 32-16 in the last match of the season at Barrow, Trinity finished in third place. In the Division Two Premiership play-offs they beat York 44-23, with Eden, Bell and Halliwell scoring two tries each but lost 20-16 in the semi-final at Featherstone.

Centre Andy Mason, Trinity's top try-scorer between 1988 and 1994

Commenting on the way the 1987-88 campaign had gone, Topliss, who had been given a new two-year contract, said: 'The main aim this season was to gain promotion, though I was a little disappointed at the way we faded in the last two months… But last season was perhaps one of the hardest second division competitions to play in and I feel that next season will be one of the strongest first division competitions. At the moment we would appear to be the certainties to go down but we have five or six months to change that position.' Topliss praised Mark Conway, Keith Rayne and Nigel Bell as his men of the season, but added, 'We have not only to make signings but also to sign our own players again,' referring to the new contract system which had been introduced. Mark Conway ended the season as the club's leading try-scorer with 20, while Kevin Harcombe easily topped the points-scoring list with 244.

In June Trinity signed 31-year old Kiwi captain and second rower Mark Graham on a two-year contract from North Sydney, but Steve Halliwell returned to Australia to join the Gold Coast Giants, as they were then called. Topliss also headed off to Australia in search of new players. Football chairman Farrar said, 'For too long the Wakefield public have been forced to live on the memories of the 1960s. Now we are making a major effort to form a side that the city can be proud of.'

But once more the club made a significant loss on the season, announcing a deficit of £116,464 and net liabilities of £408,559, of which £218,280 represented the loan from Wakefield MDC. Among personnel changes, secretary Alan Pearman left the club for a Town Hall catering department post.

Once again the club tried to attract Wally Lewis back to Belle Vue. The Kangaroos' captain indicated his willingness to return, but his club Brisbane Broncos turned down his application to leave Australia, saying that he was needed for pre-season training. Lewis sent a message to Trinity, saying that he was 'most upset at not being allowed to join the club. I was looking forward to teaming up with Mark Graham at Belle Vue and I am sure he will prove to be a great asset to the club.' Trinity found an excellent replacement in Australian stand-off Steve Ella, who had played with Wigan three seasons earlier and had toured England as a 21-year old with the 1982 Kangaroos.

Forward John Glancy, who had made a strong impression against Trinity, was signed from Sheffield Eagles. Aussie prop Ian Roberts, who had also played for Wigan two seasons before, was recruited, as was New Zealand centre Mark Elia, formerly on St Helens' books. But neither signing materialised, as Roberts injured his foot and withdrew, and Elia joined Canterbury-Bankstown even though he had agreed to come to Wakefield. Trinity entered talks to sign the ex-Widnes Australian full back or winger Dale Shearer but the discussions proved fruitless. Kiwi prop Brent Todd, however, was brought over from Canberra. Rodney Walker, meanwhile, was elected to the RFL's six-man board of directors.

Victory over Warrington by 14-10 on the opening day of the 1988-89 season was followed by a sensational 25-20 win over glamorous Wigan. A near-capacity Belle Vue crowd of 8,114 watched with something approaching disbelief as Trinity racked up seventeen points in the opening twenty minutes' play. Steve Ella weaved his way through the defence to touch down, then Andy Mason sprinted 50 yards for Phil Fox to score at the posts, Ella converting both and adding a drop goal. Mark Conway intercepted a stray pass and sent Phil Eden charging 40 yards to the line despite a pulled hamstring. Inevitably Wigan came back and reduced the deficit to 17-16 before Mason's speed created another try for Ella. Wigan bombarded the Trinity line to score and reduce the margin again to a single point with ten minutes to go. Trinity repelled wave upon wave of Wigan attacks before Ian Sheldon, with a decisive pass, turned the ball inside for young full back Julian Russell to dive over the line.

A third win in a row came at Hull, where Trinity won 16-10 after trailing by nine points and having three men injured. Andy Kelly scored the matchwinner with a 30-yard interception, but before then Steve Ella showed his brilliance by piercing the defence and kicking ahead for Mason to touch down. The Aussie stand-off followed it up with a scintillating 70-yard run through the Hull defence before jinking over the line. Top of the table after three games, Trinity had made the best possible start to their return to the top flight.

After Sheffield had been beaten 28-8 in the preliminary round of the Yorkshire Cup, second division Dewsbury were Trinity's first round victims. Phil Fox scored three tries and Ella 18 points from a try and seven goals in the 46-20 victory. But Topliss was less than happy with the way his side conceded three late tries when they had led 40-2. It was ominous. A 36-18 home defeat at the hands of Salford was succeeded by a 15-10 defeat in the second round of the Yorkshire Cup at Headingley.

Without captain Mark Graham, who was on World Cup duty, Trinity suffered three defeats in eight days. A small consolation from the 34-12 defeat at Wigan which followed was that Trinity's newly-signed Kiwi, James Leuluai, scored a debut try from full back. He was later to be joined by a former Hull team-mate, veteran loose forward or second row Steve Norton. Mark Graham was then chosen to captain the Rest of the World against Great Britain and Steve Ella was selected at stand-off.

Three further defeats in the league were alleviated only by a 34-14 win against second division Carlisle in the first round of the JPS Trophy, in the second round of which Trinity knocked out Rochdale, also of the second division, by 38-12. But in the quarter-final at St Helens Trinity folded after leading 18-2 in the 23rd minute and were beaten 34-18. Graham, Ella and Leuluai were all prominent as Bell went over and Mason twice. Kevin Harcombe, back from injury and taking over the goal-kicking duties from Ella, even landed a penalty from the half-way line. But an ankle injury to Graham appeared to disrupt not only the captain's play but the performance of the whole side. Topliss had harsh words. 'There are not enough winners in the side,' he said. 'There is no way any side in a cup-tie, on a good winning bonus and with the chance of a semi-final place, should let that happen.'

Tracey Lazenby, who had made an unexpected return to the club, came on as sub in a 12-6 home defeat by Hull KR before showing his undoubted talent with a fine solo try in the otherwise unsatisfactory midweek performance at Widnes, where the champions won 40-12 and Trinity slipped to second from bottom in the table. The following week Mark Graham, the team captain, made the shock decision to retire immediately from the game. He had shown moments of real class but also carried the weight of responsibility and had played when not fully fit. His Kiwi team-mate Brent Todd, who had shown nothing like international form, also left the club after only nine appearances.

Keen to move on from the loss of the two Kiwis, Trinity carried off a cheering 15-14 victory at seventh-placed Featherstone on Boxing Day, their first league win since September and one which took them out of the relegation zone. Ella, the new captain, regained his best form, cutting through the defence to score a fine try, while Johnny Thompson led the forwards with a rousing display up front. On New Year's Day at Belle Vue, they carried on where they left off at Post Office Road to complete the double, winning 19-12. Trinity's fierce tackling won them the valuable championship points.

Former captain Mark Graham was the subject of questions at the half-yearly meeting. Football chairman Stuart Farrar said that since Graham's departure there was a different atmosphere at the club. Graham had had personal problems and injuries, and did not always agree with Topliss's coaching style. He could not be persuaded to stay, even until the start of the New Year. 'Ultimately I have got to say he let the club down,' Farrar said. As for Brent Todd, who was recommended both by Graham and Kiwi coach Tony Gordon, Farrar stated, 'He could not be faulted for effort or training even if his ability was disappointing.' Questioned about the club's finances, Farrar said that the situation was 'satisfactory', adding 'I am not convinced that if we were to go down [to the second division], [the Council] would close the doors. It is not the death knell it might have been.'

Australian test stand-off Steve Ella played 20 games for Trinity in 1988-89 and played a key part in the club's survival in the top division

Gary Price was selected for Great Britain Under 21s, while Under 19 international Alan Hunte, from the Eastmoor club, signed amateur forms with Trinity.

With a weakened side Trinity beat Bramley 18-10 in the preliminary round of the Challenge Cup, before Hunte made his debut at centre in the 38-14 home defeat by Castleford in the league and marked his home debut against Batley in the Challenge Cup first round with a try in the 34-4 victory. But in the second round Featherstone gained revenge for their two league defeats by triumphing 10-4 at Belle Vue in front of 7,695 fans.

In the 30-18 loss at Warrington, Ella dislocated his shoulder for the third time, which signalled his return to Australia after 20 appearances, in which he scored nine tries and kicked 34 goals, including two drop goals. Topliss paid tribute to Ella's efforts to keep the side in the first division. Trinity also lost the promising Hunte, who had just scored a hat-trick for Great Britain U19s in their narrow defeat by France. What was described as Trinity's best-ever offer to an amateur was bettered by St Helens.

Nevertheless Topliss's men battled on and sprang a major upset by beating leaders Castleford at Belle Vue. Unlike in previous matches, their finishing was decisive and Mason, Leuluai, Fletcher, Bell and Lazenby all touched down in the 26-8 win. They also showed their commitment by bouncing back from a 28-16 defeat at Headingley, where Billy Conway suffered a fractured cheekbone as a result of a late tackle, to stun Leeds in the return match the week after. Andy Wilson typified the side's dedication to the cause by returning to the fray after having fourteen stitches inserted in a genital injury and setting up the matchwinner, making a 60-yard break from which Mason went over.

In a fine all-round performance, Bell and Thompson were tireless and Leuluai gave confidence at the back with a finely-timed try-saving tackle on Carl Gibson as Trinity won 14-12.

Wakefield were now fourth from last, but, in a nerve-wracking end to the season, they lost a must-win game by 24-8 at fellow-strugglers Oldham, which plunged them back into the danger zone of the bottom three. The Easter period, as so often, proved crucial. A 27-10 home win over bottom club Halifax, to which stand-off Lazenby and centre Eden, with two second-half tries, made a strong contribution, was essential. Even more so was the fine 28-8 win at Odsal after Bradford had dominated the first period and led 8-6, Lazenby's try keeping Trinity in contention. In the second period Lazenby and Mark Conway, who scored two tries, dictated play as Trinity ran in two more tries from Leuluai and Eden. Injury struck again, however, when Paul Mallinder broke his ankle against his former club. Trinity moved ahead of fourth-from-bottom Bradford in the table and finally secured their first division status with an amazing 21-14 win over Cup finalists St Helens at Belle Vue after Saints had led 14-2 at half-time. For once, luck was on Trinity's side as the ball hit an upright to bounce back into the arms of Bell, who went over, and then a similar ricochet fell sweetly for Leuluai to pounce with the Saints defence caught out. Though it was no longer necessary for their survival, Trinity pulled off another win by coming from behind, this time at Halifax in the last game. After going 20-4 down, they recovered to win 22-20. Harcombe landed the decisive penalty goal seven minutes from full time after ex-Trinity man John Lyons was sanctioned for a late tackle on Billy Conway, who had sparked Trinity's revival when he came off the bench in the second half and scored almost immediately. 'Billy was in devastating form,' said Topliss, who also had charge of the Great Britain U21 side that season, 'I really think [GB coach] Mal Reilly has to look at him for an international jersey next season.'

After being in a precarious position for so long, Trinity won six out of their last eight games and finished the season in joint eighth place but missed out on a play-off spot on points difference. Tracey Lazenby, who had played an important part in Trinity's resurgence, headed off to Australia to spend the summer with Penrith. The A team captain, Johnny Thompson, who typified the resolve and determination of the side when brought back to first team duty against Featherstone at Christmas, received a benefit cheque of £9,000 and was named Players' Player of the Year. Topliss became the first coach since Peter Fox, thirteen years earlier, to last two seasons at Belle Vue.

The average gate of 4,680 was an improvement; although, to put matters into perspective, Wigan had nearly 15,000 per league match and Hull over 13,000. Gate receipts rose by almost £80,000 but that did not stop the club from making a loss of an equivalent amount, with liabilities now totalling close to £490,000. Income had risen by £190,000 on the previous year and included an £80,000 grant from Wakefield Council and £28,000 from sponsorship, mainly from British Coal. But expenditure had also increased dramatically, so that no money would be available to dip into the British transfer market. Chairman Rodney Walker put it into context by saying, 'Many other clubs that are perceived as successful are in a far worse state financially than Wakefield Trinity.' He added that the club had had to find £100,000 for player contracts which had not been necessary three years ago. 'We can't continue to lose money at the rate of £80,000 a year and I don't intend to preside over a club that continues to lose more money than it creates. I'm determined to see some progress and we hope to break even this [coming] year.'

In preparation for the 1989-90 season, Trinity intended making improvements to the ground by covering over the Doncaster Road end. It was planned to erect a stand taken from York's Clarence Street ground, which was soon to be demolished. But engineers advised that the project was not worthwhile because the structure would not have lasted long enough.

With no money available for British signings, Trinity again looked at making short-term overseas recruitments. They pulled off a coup by bringing the great ex-Kangaroo loose forward Ray Price out of retirement in the face of competition from five other clubs. Centre Brian Jackson was recruited from Price's former club Parramatta but Steve Norton, who played ten games for Trinity in 1988-89, would not reappear at Belle Vue, becoming a free agent.

The 1989-90 season got off to a poor start – 'a nightmare' Topliss called it - with an 18-17 defeat at second division Dewsbury in the Yorkshire Cup preliminary round. But in their first league game they were in much more serious mood and pulled off a fine win by 22-14 at Headingley, immediately followed by a 32-0 home victory over Leigh. With a much rearranged side they were taught a lesson by Wigan, who delivered a 38-10 defeat.

Ray Price and Brian Jackson made their first appearance in Trinity colours in the home fixture against Sheffield. Price, at 36, was playing his first match for three years and was understandably short of practice, but Jackson played well enough to be named man of the match. Trinity led 16-2 but collapsed alarmingly and went down 28-16. For a second time they built a good lead and were 21-10 ahead against St Helens at Belle Vue, but dropped their efforts and allowed local lad Alan Hunte to score the matchwinner.

Full back Andy Sygrove left for Doncaster for the £5,000 fee agreed by tribunal and at the same time Aussie utility back Chris Perry was signed from local amateur club Ackworth, coached by his cousin, and made his debut at full back in the 30-14 home win over Hull.

A quick exit from the Regal Trophy (formerly the John Player Special Trophy), in which Trinity were knocked out in the preliminary round by Hull, focused greater attention on the league. Over the Christmas period, they lost to Featherstone by 15-8 on Boxing Day, but gained revenge by 22-14 at Belle Vue on New Year's Eve. Phil Eden scored two tries and Tracey Lazenby produced another excellent performance at stand-off. An even better team display came at Castleford, where Andy Wilson and Billy Conway went off injured in the first half, then Phil Fox in the second, after 'swallowing his tongue'. Until the winger returned some fifteen minutes later, Trinity were a man short but fought out an impressive 18-16 win, with Phil Eden again touching down twice. 'It was my proudest moment as a coach,' said Topliss. 'We were down to twelve men and lacking protection from match officials.'

Consecutive home victories, against Salford and fifth-placed Warrington, saw Trinity maintain fourth place in the table. Ray Price, who again topped the tackle count against the Wire, came in for special praise from the coach. 'He is simply phenomenal,' said Topliss. 'He doesn't know the meaning of defeat. Having Ray and Keith Rayne in the same side is like having two captains on the field, both leading by example.' Topliss also praised the efforts of Nigel Bell, who, like Don Fox over two decades earlier, had moved up from scrum-half to the back three of the pack and then to prop, as necessity dictated.

In the Challenge Cup, Trinity were drawn at second division Swinton and toiled to earn a 10-all draw, allowing their hosts to claim a late equalising try after establishing an early lead. The midweek replay at Belle Vue, however, was dealt with more efficiently and Trinity went through to the second round by 32-4. But in the second round rehearsal Trinity lost 24-10 at Sheffield, for whom Daryl Powell scored two tries and kicked a drop goal and Mark Aston landed five goals and a drop goal. According to Topliss, it was Trinity's worst performance of the season.

In the Cup Trinity made no mistake with a 27-12 victory at Belle Vue, a match characterised by the astounding

Former Kangaroo loose forward Ray Price came out of retirement at the age of 36 to play with Trinity in 1989-90, where he led by example

work-rate of Ray Price. But his Parramatta team-mate Brian Jackson was to return home immediately with a knee injury. He was a very popular member of the side and played a vital role in his seventeen games, missing just one during his time at Wakefield.

In the quarter-final at Belle Vue, in front of the BBC's cameras and a capacity 8,100 crowd, Trinity could not quite match the international class of Wigan, the eventual Cup winners. Nevertheless they led 10-6 at half-time, from Andy Kelly's try and Mark Conway's three goals. But after the break, with the growing influence of scrum-half Andy Gregory, Wigan ran in tries from Shaun Edwards, twice, Kevin Iro and Ellery Hanley, Joe Lydon kicking five goals in the 26-14 victory. With Ray Price stretchered off with a back injury, Trinity could only muster a late try from namesake Gary.

In the league Trinity were disappointed with a 10-all home draw against Widnes, who owed their point to a late touchline conversion from Jonathan Davies. But it was a measure of their progress that Trinity should feel dismay at sharing the points with the World Club champions. A series of defeats, however, put their top eight place in jeopardy. As Phil Fox was transferred to Rochdale for £18,000 and young stand-off Tony Zelei went to Doncaster for £20,000, Topliss looked to put next season's squad together. Speaking of the financial restrictions, he commented that Wakefield Trinity were a first division side operating on a second division budget.

Ray Price decided not to take up an option on a second year at Belle Vue, but said he had been impressed by the 'guts' of his team-mates. He praised John Glancy and John Thompson and spoke of the potential of Gary Price, who was about to be called up into the Great Britain squad for the PNG and New Zealand tour as a replacement for Ellery Hanley. The former Kangaroo forward added that he thought Mark Conway had all the attributes to be a great footballer and only needed more self-confidence. As for the team's form, he said, 'When Brian Jackson was here and we were going well, it looked like we could finish in the top three but since he left we have hit a bit of a brick wall.' Like Wally Lewis before him, there was another aspect of the British game he would not miss. 'I used to bag Aussie refs but when I go home I will never do it again after what I've seen in England,' he concluded. Topliss said that Price had been an inspiration and would be a hard act to follow. 'He has been magnificent for us,' he said. 'It will take three men to replace him.'

As the season neared its close, an already relegated Salford were beaten 28-18 on their own ground, Eden scoring a hat-trick, but the Easter games brought disappointment. The Good Friday match at Bradford was lost 19-18 and the Easter Monday return game at Belle Vue by 36-12, which put an end to play-off hopes as well as Mark Conway's record of scoring in every game. He had the consolation of being named both Player of the Year and Players' Player of the Year.

Keith Rayne, at the age of 33, went to Batley as player-coach and James Leuluai to York. David Jones, a BARLA international winger, was signed from Wigan St Patrick's at the same time as the club also looked to firm up its Australian signings. Trinity had hoped once more to sign international centre Gene Miles, but his Brisbane Broncos club upped their offer in order to keep him. Penrith captain Chris Mortimer, able to play either stand-off or loose forward, was signed, leaving one more overseas quota spot, the first having been taken by Chris Perry.

Promising figures were published for the season just ended. The average league attendance had gone up to 5,428, but although gate receipts produced income of around £150,000, other commercial activity was becoming increasingly important. Sponsorship, ground advertising and hospitality now accounted for around £100,000. All of this went towards making a declared profit of £26,000, reversing the loss of £80,000 of the previous season. At the AGM, Rodney Walker saw a happier future for the club. 'Looking in the long term, say over five years, I would like to see a revitalised Wakefield Trinity, with a new stadium and improved facilities that perhaps could not be bettered anywhere else in rugby league … Assuming the facilities at present are unacceptable, there can be no point spending money there. The ground has outlived its time. People's expectations have changed and there have to be better facilities for parking, eating and so on.'

On the retirement of part-time secretary George Gledhill, Australian journalist Neil Cadigan, who had been the Sydney connection for Ray Price's signing, was appointed general manager responsible for marketing, development and media relations. Trinity were also in talks with Brisbane's Test prop Greg Dowling, but eventually Kiwi front rower Adrian Shelford, a Cup-winner with Wigan and then at Manly, was signed for two seasons. Closer to home, two sixteen-year olds, centre Richard Goddard and stand-off Nigel Wright, caught the eye in the pre-season Wigan seven-a-side tournament.

Twenty-one – Survival against the odds: 1990-95

The 1990-91 season began promisingly with Yorkshire Cup victories over second division sides Hunslet and Halifax. In their first County cup semi-final for seven years, Trinity, captained by Andy Kelly, faced Dewsbury, led by his brother Neil. Unlike the year before, Trinity made no mistake and won 25-2. For the first time since 1979 at Wembley, Trinity contested a final, in which they met Castleford at Elland Road, Leeds.

Watched by 12,362 spectators, Trinity drew first blood when, after only five minutes' play, stand-off Tracey Lazenby broke from a scrum on the half-way line and, reaching the 25, passed to Andy Mason, who went in at the corner for a fine try, Kevin Harcombe converting from the touchline to give a 6-0 lead. Castleford hit straight back when scrum-half Atkins touched down but a Harcombe penalty took the score to 8-4. Once more the combination of man-of-the-match Lazenby and Mason seemed certain to bring a try but the centre was brought down by winger David Plange's last-ditch tackle. A Lee Crooks penalty early in the second half reduced Trinity's lead to two points and it was wiped out altogether when, following a long break, Graham Southernwood's pass put Plange over for the decisive score despite a suspicion of double movement. As they had done for much of the game, Castleford pinned Trinity back with their deep kicking and gave them few chances. A late Roebuck drop goal made the final score 11-8. Trinity had failed to win their first trophy since 1968 but, said Topliss, 'We have overcome a big psychological barrier. We know we can compete in big games like this.'

Deflated, Trinity slumped to a 34-6 loss at the hands of Sheffield in their first match at the Don Valley Stadium. Topliss's selection options were increased, though, when utility back Ged Byrne was signed from Wigan together with South African forward Nick Du Toit, formerly with Wigan and Barrow. The two new signings, plus Chris Mortimer, who had just arrived from Australia, all figured in the 18-12 win at Hull KR, Trinity's first at Craven Park for seventeen years.

For the first time since 1973, Trinity were lined up to face a touring side and met the Kangaroos for the fourteenth time in their history when an estimated crowd of 8,000 plus fifty journalists turned up to witness the occasion. It was a furious game in more than one sense – fast and superbly entertaining despite the rainy conditions, with a sprinkling of old-fashioned biff. Three Aussies were sent off and two sin-binned, with one Trinity man dismissed and one yellow-carded. Trinity also had the advantage of a 24-7 penalty count. Kangaroo coach Bob Fulton was incandescent and made his feelings clear in a notorious interview with the BBC's Harry Gration. The Aussies – those who were left on the field - took it all in their stride and won 36-18. Nick Du Toit had the pleasure of scoring a close-range try, Andy Mason jinked his way over from 35 yards out and Andy Wilson went in at the corner direct from a scrum. Mark Conway kicked three goals, including a touchline conversion to Wilson's try.

In one of their best performances of the season, Trinity defeated previously unbeaten leaders Hull by 22-6 at Belle Vue. The scores were level at 6-6 at half-time but after the break Mason intercepted and raced 70 yards for a try and Wilson sprinted half the length of the field to touch down. Trinity more than matched Hull's big pack, with the front row of Adrian Shelford, John Thompson and John Glancy leading the way. In a fine run of form Trinity went on to secure their first league win at Warrington since 1976, winning 18-10 with another mighty display from Shelford.

In the preliminary round of the Regal Trophy at second division leaders Carlisle, Trinity romped home with a 28-10 win and in the league they accounted for current champions Wigan by 14-12 at Belle Vue, after trailing 12-2 at half-time. Price went over for a fine try and Byrne, against his former club, won a scramble to touch down behind the Wigan line. Once again, Trinity's tackling, led by Nigel Bell, was first class. Second division Hunslet were swept aside by 40-8 in the first round of the Regal Trophy but Trinity met their match, once more, when they faced Castleford in the second round at Belle Vue, losing 20-4. Their other local rivals, Featherstone, made it an unhappy Christmas for Wakefield by winning 14-8 at Post Office Road.

Nor did New Year 1991 begin any better. Featherstone did the double at Belle Vue, winning 16-8 and setting off a chain of defeats. Full back Gary Spencer, now 24, returned to the club from Leeds, having gone to Headingley in 1987 with John Lyons as part of the famous multi-player exchange deal. But the slide continued. Trinity lost at relegation-haunted Oldham by 26-22, only arresting the slump with a 12-all home draw with Warrington.

Even a first-round Challenge Cup win brought little cheer. Trinity made very hard work of beating second division Trafford Borough, the successor to Blackpool, Springfield and Chorley, by 18-7 at Belle Vue, a match closer than the score suggested. Topliss said it was the worst performance since he had been in charge. A 16-2 defeat at St Helens saw Trinity depart from the Cup, to be faced by the usual end-of-season backlog of fixtures, which amounted to five matches in fifteen days. A 16-8 defeat at Wigan put them in the relegation zone for the first time but they moved out of danger again with a much-needed 12-4 victory over fellow-strugglers Sheffield – Trinity's first league win since November. They pulled off an astounding 14-6 win at Hull, who had not lost at home for eighteen months and had been league leaders for much of the season. The young back three of Lynton Morris, Gary Price and Richard Slater tackled for all they were worth, while up front John Glancy, John Thompson and Nigel Bell revelled in the confrontation. But inconsistency dogged the side. The 16-6 home loss to Bradford caused Topliss to say he was ashamed.

Off the field, the club's future was also threatened. The Council announced its intention to stop Trinity's financial support – and Featherstone's, which it also supported - and to sell Belle Vue. Chairman Rodney Walker proposed forming a limited company to raise share capital, with a figure of £500,000 being mentioned. Generally clubs were reeling from the repercussions of the disasters at Bradford City and Hillsborough, as well as the new player contracts, both of which made unprecedented demands on finances. The Council had already spent £400,000 on repairs and renovation at Belle Vue and a further £100,000 of work was needed, the floodlights being the most urgent necessity.

Over Easter, Trinity faced Leeds twice, losing 7-0 at Headingley on Good Friday but drawing the return 14-all on Easter Monday. A 22-8 loss at St Helens left Trinity needing just one point from the match at long-doomed Rochdale. Once more fortune was on their side as Hornets had two men sent off in the first half and a third sin-binned in the second. Trinity managed a 25-6 win and maintained their first division status once more. Topliss commented: 'We've just kept our head above water in each of the past three seasons, but that isn't enough. We can't satisfy the fans by just finishing in mid-table [tenth out of fourteen]. We have to be seen to be attempting to match the others.' He added: 'In the last three years the top eight has been the same, barring one club. I can probably tell you the top eight for next season now, unless we do something to challenge that.' On the matter of relegation he said, 'Two very good sides have gone down [Oldham and Sheffield, plus Rochdale] when neither deserved to but we have survived because we have tackled better.'

At a meeting of Wakefield Council it was decided that the ground was to be transferred back to the club with the proviso that if Belle Vue was ever to be sold any profit would be due to the Council. The club would receive no further grant aid and would be responsible for maintenance. Walker estimated that £110,000 was needed for essential safety work before the start of the following season, with another £100,000 required for upkeep and running of the ground. He said that it was proving difficult to attract potential investors. 'The economic climate is bad,' he said. 'I have to say that at this point the future of the club is still on a knife edge.'

On July 5 at a meeting of members at the Town Hall, it was voted to make Wakefield Trinity a limited company, in line with the majority of clubs. Walker believed that the total amount raised, mainly from local businessmen, should prove sufficient to cope with urgent maintenance work on the ground and pay off outstanding debts and would give around £100,000 to spend on new signings.

On the playing front, Nick Du Toit and Chris Mortimer had both retired, but Canberra's international stand-off or centre Laurie Daley was reported to have agreed to join Trinity. Two home-grown players, Gary Price and Nigel Wright, the club's biggest-ever junior signings, were to become the first full-time professionals and would work in junior development.

In late August came the dramatic news that Trinity were set to fold 'in the absence of an eleventh-hour reprieve'. Nine days before the start of the 1991-92 season, cash-strapped Wakefield Council refused to loan £100,000 for essential maintenance work, which was required to replace the already condemned floodlights. The ground's safety certificate expired on August 31. However a last-minute deal pulled the club back from the abyss when four businessmen promised £200,000. A further £20,000 had been received in public subscriptions. A rent of £10,000 per year was due to be paid to the Council, who obligingly deferred the first payment for five years. As the new limited company came into being, Trinity had a new board, consisting of Rodney Walker, Stuart Farrar, Peter Robinson, Brian Eccles and Ted Richardson.

Stuart Farrar, who, with Rodney Walker, remained from the old regime, reflected that without the Council's intervention and aid over a five-year period Trinity would no longer be in existence. He commented, 'We're fortunate some local businessmen have given us the funds to stay alive and form the basis for a bright future… They know they will probably never get their money back. It will be like a donation. They just didn't want Wakefield to lose its world-famous rugby league club.'

Brian Eccles had been on Trinity's committee once before, in 1980, but resigned over the transfer of Topliss to Hull. He now reflected: 'I stood back in amazement as the committee did some of the daftest deals ever committed. So many people fell out with the club over that period.' Eccles was given responsibility for the ground, which he wanted to see redeveloped rather than move out of what he and many others thought of as the club's spiritual home. He expected the capacity of Belle Vue to be increased within two years from its present limit of just over 8,000 to 12-13,000. His business partner Ted Richardson was equally optimistic. 'Wakefield Trinity will be the best club in the Rugby League,' he told the *Wakefield Express*. 'We will compete with the likes of Wigan and be a well-organised club with excellent facilities and a very good team. That will happen within three years.'

The opening match of the 1991-92 season ended in a disappointing 17-8 defeat at promoted club Swinton, which Topliss described as 'a shambles'. He added: 'The players put in plenty of effort but we are still two men short of a winning team. We need the right men and they don't grow on trees.' But as the committee pointed out, without investment in the new club from the public there would be no cash available for new signings. They did, however, find the money to sign Great Britain Under 21 second rower Michael Jackson from Hunslet for £55,000 plus £15,000 after ten matches.

Laurie Daley, on whom Trinity had pinned hopes of making a star signing, withdrew from the arrangement owing to injury. The club switched their attentions back to Dale Shearer and then to Cliff Lyons, but ended up with neither. In the first home match of the season, Trinity snatched a late 22-18 win over Bradford. With the sides locked on 18-all close to the end of the game, Lazenby put up a steepling kick, Shelford collected the ball and transferred to Jones, who went over. The winger was selected for the first time for Lancashire and would oppose team-mate Andy Mason, who had been chosen again for Yorkshire.

In the first round of the Yorkshire Cup, Trinity won 24-18 at Halifax, with Jackson, the scorer of two tries, and Price making a promising combination in the second row. They easily accounted for Huddersfield, now in the third division, winning 52-9 at Fartown in the second round. Trinity went out of the Yorkshire Cup in the semi-final at Odsal, where Bradford player-coach David Hobbs was in top form with his kicking, landing five goals from all angles in their 14-10 victory.

Trinity provided another shock, though, when beating World Club champions Wigan 13-6 at Belle Vue. Michael Jackson was in dynamic form, scoring a try and making some devastating runs. But former Wigan player Ged Byrne, who had been listed at £70,000, went to Oldham in an exchange deal involving prop or second row Paul Round and Stanley-based winger or centre Paul Lord. Trinity's general manager Neil Cadigan also announced his resignation and returned to Australia in December.

The following week Trinity produced another surprise win at Belle Vue when they beat Leeds 22-10 after being 20-4 behind going into the last quarter of the game. Andy Wilson started the fightback with a typically mazy run out of his own 25 and Andy Mason finished off. Nigel Wright, the 17-year old of whom so much was expected, was brought on for the last fifteen minutes and produced a top-quality pass to Mason, who gave a superb ball out of the tackle for Phil Eden to score. Full back Gary Spencer, named man of the match, made another long run out of defence and passed to winger David Jones, who sprinted down the touchline and held off the pursuing Carl Gibson to touch down, bringing the score to 20-18. After more pressure on the Leeds's crumbling defence, Michael Jackson charged over the line for Trinity's fourth try in twenty minutes. 'For sheer drama this will take some beating,' said the *Wakefield Express*.

Supporters were thrilled with another victory against the odds when leaders St Helens were toppled 20-12 at Belle Vue. Michael Jackson again led the try-scoring as he went over twice, the second an exciting run from 40 yards. Jackson and his second row partner Gary Price were selected for Great Britain against Papua-New Guinea at Wigan, with Jackson going on to play for Britain against France. Richard Slater was chosen for GB Under 21s.

Trinity made victory over third division Nottingham City – who began life as Mansfield - a formality in the first round of the Regal Trophy as they won 42-11. But they were put out of the competition in the next round by Salford, who won 30-10 after Chris Perry had been sent off in the tenth minute for alleged tripping. A 12-8 home defeat by Warrington saw Trinity, despite their earlier heroics, pay the price for their inconsistency and slip to fourth from bottom of the table. Towards the end of a year which had seen the future of the club shrouded in uncertainty, the home match against Widnes was abandoned after 16 minutes due to the dense December fog which, rolling in from the Doncaster Road end, suddenly enveloped the ground with Widnes leading 8-0.

The Christmas period brought qualified success when Trinity beat Featherstone 18-10 away and then drew 14-all with Castleford on New Year's Day. Former Gold Coast Seagulls half back Geoff Bagnall arrived at Belle Vue in time to watch the draw with Castleford, making himself available for two and a half seasons. At the same time Trinity terminated the contract of Adrian Shelford, who had suffered recurring knee injuries. The Kiwi prop signed

International back row forward Gary Price was one of the club's first full-time professionals

Signed from Hunslet, second rower Michael Jackson quickly achieved international honours, touring Australia and New Zealand in 1992

Wakefield Trinity squad 1991: *Back row*: Tony Handforth (asst coach), Gary Spencer, John Glancy, Gary Price, Andy Kelly, Andy Wilson, David Jones, Darren Carter, David Topliss (coach). *Front row*: Craig McElhatton, Richard Slater, Adrian Shelford, Andy Mason, Mark Conway, John Thompson, Tracey Lazenby, Chris Perry, Michael Jackson

for Sheffield two months later. In need of another front-rower, Trinity tried to sign Widnes forward Joe Grima, but had to back out when it was decided that any cash the club had would have to go towards the installation of new floodlights, costing £140,000.

Bagnall made his debut off the bench at Wigan, though his appearance was overshadowed by the first match in Wigan colours of Martin Offiah, who had just been signed from Widnes for a world record £440,000 fee. Watched by 17,000 fans at Central Park, Offiah did not score but Wigan won 20-2, Bagnall having a useful game, though Wakefield's top performer was Nigel Bell at scrum-half. Bagnall made his home debut in the Challenge Cup preliminary round victory over Huddersfield and was sin-binned for retaliation, along with four others.

Trinity paid a record fee for a junior when they signed 17-year old English Schools centre James Mosley from the Huddersfield amateur club, Moldgreen. An outstanding prospect, Mosley was said to have been targeted by eight other clubs.

The widening gap between the top of the first division and the bottom half was illustrated when tenth-placed Trinity lost 40-12 at second-placed St Helens. They failed to redeem themselves in the Challenge Cup first round when they travelled to second division Workington and lost 13-8, a performance which Topliss called 'clueless'.

The new floodlights were switched on for the home game against Widnes which had been abandoned earlier in the season. With a superb defensive display, Trinity won 12-4, after Paul Lord touched down from Lazenby's angled grubber kick and Andy Wilson seized on a loose Widnes pass to race 35 yards to score.

A cheering 15-14 victory over Hull at the Boulevard was achieved when Tracey Lazenby, in his home city, booted the winning drop goal, before Trinity did the double over a fifth-placed Leeds side containing the likes of Garry Schofield and Ellery Hanley. In this 17-0 victory, Nigel Bell, now at loose forward, put in a typical blood and thunder performance and hounded Hanley wherever he went, well supported by sub Richard Slater. It was said of Bell: '[His] contribution was massive as he proved himself the master of Headingley, pushing Great Britain skipper Ellery Hanley deep into the shadows.' All three Trinity tries, scored by Perry, Spencer and Jackson, owed a lot to team effort as Trinity moved up to seventh. Geoff Bagnall was proving to be the leader Topliss had been looking for. 'Bagnall has certainly brought a new dimension to the Trinity game with his lightning speed off the mark and a refusal to accept defeat,' said the *Wakefield Express*.

Towards the end of the season thoughts turned to which players would be chosen for the Great Britain squad to tour Australia and New Zealand. As the *Express* pointed out, the name of Wakefield Trinity was unlikely to be bracketed alongside many of the selected squad, and yet 'what more could be asked of Bell, Glancy and Wilson this season?' In the event only Michael Jackson was named in the tour squad.

Trinity moved up to sixth in the table, a position which was unaltered by their remaining two results over Easter. A 28-4 defeat at Castleford on Good Friday was followed by a 28-10 success at home to Featherstone on the Monday, which sent Rovers into Division Two. It was in that match that Richard Goddard, at 17, scored his first try, which was, according to his coach, one of the best centre's tries seen at Belle Vue.

In the first round of the first division play-offs, in which they competed for the first time in eleven years, Trinity travelled to third-placed Castleford who, as they had done in 1981, went through, winning by 28-10. From a playing point of view, the season had proved the best in over a decade. Topliss, under whose guidance Trinity had gone, in five years, from relegation to play-offs – and on a shoestring budget - started talks regarding a new contract, which was soon extended by another two years.

The club's average attendance for the season increased slightly to just over 5,000, while neighbours Castleford registered 6,500 and Featherstone 4,000. Wigan again led the way with over 14,000.

On the other side of the world, Michael Jackson was named in the squad to face Australia in the first test, coming on as a second-half sub, and in the second test in New Zealand, also as sub. Having made a try-scoring debut for Great Britain against PNG at Wigan the year before, he had been named man of the match but also suffered an injury leading to a serious blood infection and a long absence, halting what had been a quick rise from relative obscurity at third division Hunslet.

Aussie utility back Chris Perry returned home, while prop Paul Mallinder started training again after being

Trinity celebrate winning the Yorkshire Cup by beating Sheffield 29-16 at Elland Road. *At back*: Martin Petfield (medic), Nigel Wright, Gary Spencer, Andy Wilson, Darren Fritz, Andy Mason, Peter Benson, Richard Goddard, Mark Webster, John Glancy. *In front*: Richard Slater, Billy Conway, Nigel Bell, Gary Price, Geoff Bagnall, David Jones, Lee Robinson (physio), Barry Smith (kit)

out of the game for a year following a bad ankle injury sustained at Bradford. Gary Price, who still had a year of his contract to run, asked to be put on the transfer list and a £160,000 price tag – later reduced to £120,000 - was placed on the 22-year old back-rower. Andy Mason, the side's leading try-scorer in four of the past five seasons, could not agree terms, at least initially, and was listed at £70,000. Mark Conway, who had been displaced at scrum-half by Geoff Bagnall, was also listed at his own request and was valued at £55,000. Trinity welcomed two new Australian recruits for the coming season in Queensland utility back Peter Benson and Canberra front rower Darren Fritz, who at 6 ft 5 and 17 stone was one of the biggest props in the game.

Trinity's 1992-93 season was slow to fire, beginning with six straight defeats in the league. But in the Yorkshire Cup, there were easier pickings. Trinity disposed of Doncaster in the first round, winning 54-14. Third division Keighley ran them close before Trinity, feeling the effects of their tussle with world champions Wigan in the league four days earlier, went into the semi-final by 22-16 following an injury-time try from Gary Spencer. In the semi at second division Featherstone, the home side had the misfortune to have Brendan Tuuta sent off just before the interval. With tries from Billy Conway, Mason and Benson, who kicked five goals, Trinity booked their place in the final at Elland Road by 22-8.

Despite a run of poor league form, Trinity produced perhaps their best performance of the season so far in the final against Sheffield Eagles. Stand-off Nigel Wright, at 18, gave a match-winning performance which earned him the White Rose trophy, as Tracey Lazenby had done two years earlier. Wright had a hand in three of Trinity's five tries and added a drop goal and a conversion. Together with scrum-half Geoff Bagnall, he master-minded Trinity's 29-16 victory which saw them take the Cup for the first time since 1964 and achieve their first victory in a final since the Championship of 1968. Trinity's scoring was opened after only five minutes by loose forward Richard Slater, who picked up a rebounding ball and went under the posts, Peter Benson converting. Wright landed a drop goal and quick-thinking by Bagnall from a tap penalty brought Trinity's second try, making the half-time score 11-0. After the break Wright slipped through the defence to create a try for Gary Spencer, which was soon followed by Andy Mason's dash over the line and a conversion by the stand-off. Sheffield, 21 points adrift, pulled twelve points back when Bruce McGuire touched down twice, but Benson kicked a penalty goal before Gary Price went over from a Billy Conway flicked pass, Benson adding the conversion before Sheffield ran in a late try through Mark Gamson. Seen by 7,690 fans, it was Trinity's tenth Yorkshire Cup win and the last ever, since the competition was disbanded at the end of the season. Trinity had appeared in twenty finals in all (including one wartime appearance), a record equalled by Huddersfield and bettered only by Leeds, with twenty-one.

On October 27, club records tumbled in the preliminary round of the Regal Trophy in which Trinity met Highfield at Belle Vue. Though not at full strength, and with three 18-year olds in the side – Wright, Goddard and second row Adrian Flynn - Trinity were far too powerful for the third division's bottom club, who were trounced 90-12. It was Trinity's highest-ever score, eclipsing the 78-9 registered against Batley on August 26, 1967. Andy Wilson contributed five tries, Darren Fritz four, Andy Mason three and Mark Conway two. Conway kicked thirteen goals

At the age of eighteen, stand-off Nigel Wright was named man of the match in Trinity's Yorkshire Cup final victory over Sheffield Eagles in 1992. He later signed for Wigan in a transfer which cost £145,000.

from seventeen attempts, breaking the record previously held jointly by Neil Fox and Bernard Ward, who both kicked twelve. Standing in for the rested Bagnall, Conway also broke the individual points-scoring record with 34, Fox having also held the previous record with 33 from twelve goals and three tries in that same match against Batley, though that was in the era of three-point tries.

As Trinity started to make progress in the league, they stumbled out of the Regal Trophy in the second round. Second division London Crusaders, formerly Fulham, sent Trinity reeling out of the competition with a 30-0 win, which made for a 'depressing' Sunday afternoon after it had taken around nine hours amid motorway traffic jams to get to the ground, where only around 500 fans witnessed the event, most of them from Wakefield. But elsewhere Trinity were finding their form, recording their biggest league win of the season with a 34-8 victory at Warrington. Andy Mason had a fine game, scoring two tries and tackling stoutly, and James Mosley, on the wing, became the fourth 18-year old to appear at senior level. Topliss considered the youngster's debut was one of the best he had ever seen. In the 20-16 win at the Boulevard, Mosley scored his first points at senior level with two well-taken tries, the first a 70-yard solo effort and the second the match-winner after Hull had drawn level. Nigel Wright also continued to show great promise, and was named as travelling reserve for England against Wales after just twelve full appearances at senior level.

Trinity entered negotiations to bring 30-year old Great Britain international Jonathan Davies to Belle Vue and, surprisingly, managed to raise the finance, through sponsorship, to secure a £200,000 deal over three years. The move only failed when Widnes, undergoing financial difficulties, insisted on a transfer fee to release the Welsh stand-off from his contract and Trinity decided that they could not meet their demands.

After a 34-14 home win over Salford pushed them up to ninth in the table, Trinity collapsed at home to relegation-threatened Leigh and suffered their heaviest defeat of the season, by 41-8, to the club with the worst record in the first division. They quickly made amends with victory in the first round of the Challenge Cup, in which, with a 'ferocious tackling display', they again beat Salford, this time by 20-12. Powerful prop Darren Fritz scored his ninth try of the season on his last appearance before returning to Australia. In the second round, however, it was Bradford who squeezed through by winning 20-18 at Belle Vue.

After seeing Jonathan Davies slip away from them, Trinity made tentative steps in the South African market, which had proved fruitful in the sixties. They had arranged trials for a goal-kicking rugby union three-quarter, Albertus Enslin, to come to Belle Vue for trials. A work permit and other necessary details were arranged but as Enslin was set to arrive he withdrew after he had been made a very well-paid job offer to remain in South Africa and continue to play rugby union. In addition Enslin had apparently been threatened with a life ban from rugby union simply for having rugby league trials. The apparent double standards applied by the South African authorities caused Wakefield MP David Hinchliffe to press the Rugby Football Union to clarify its policy of 'amateurism'.

Between January and mid-April, Trinity salvaged just one point - from a 26-all draw at Leeds. At least Nigel Wright and James Mosley had the satisfaction of being selected in the Great Britain Under 21 squad to face France, while Richard Goddard and Adrian Flynn were named in the GB Academy squad. The nine-match winless streak came to an end with a 20-6 home victory over Sheffield, Mason scoring two tries to take his tally to 22 for the season and Trinity raising themselves out of the bottom two. Not that relegation was a concern, since the first division was to be increased to sixteen teams as the RFL decided to move from a three-division system back to two.

Before the end of the season, a sponsorship deal with brewers McEwan's was agreed, guaranteeing a minimum of £129,000 over three years. As the club began to examine its finances before the new season, A-team coaches Ian Brooke and David Wandless were dropped as part of cost-cutting measures, despite the success they had had on the field.

Geoff Bagnall, who had become the first Trinity captain to lift a trophy for 24 years, signed a new one-year contract despite being chased by Hull and Salford. The half back he had displaced, Mark Conway, was transferred to Dewsbury for £17,500. Topliss had expected the combination of Bagnall and Nigel Wright to be one of the strongest in the first division but it caused a sensation – and uproar – when the 19-year old stand-off was signed by Wigan for £145,000, £5,000 more than Halifax had offered. Topliss was naturally disappointed at the departure of the youngster he regarded as 'the most talented player in recent years'. Fans were irate at the loss of another home-grown star after hearing so many promises that the club would not let its best young players go.

Rodney Walker, who had just stepped up to become chairman of the RFL, said that the club had been inundated with calls from angry fans asking for their season ticket money back. In turn he said that he and his fellow directors were 'devastated' by the reaction. 'The directors are as unhappy as anyone over the loss of talented young players of the calibre of Wright,' he told the *Wakefield Express*, 'but we have to accept that we cannot force players to remain at Belle Vue if they are determined to go to other clubs. The best we can do is to try to obtain the best price possible for the player to enable us to recruit replacements.' Walker reminded critics that two years earlier the Council announced without warning that there would be no further support for the club, whereupon a limited company was formed and the club was saved. Four directors each invested £50,000 and since then three others had put in £150,000. The Board was immediately faced with paying off £220,000 of old debts, plus £130,000 on replacing floodlights. During the present close season, more essential safety work would account for another £50,000. But, he claimed, evidence from the RFL showed that in terms of support from club lotteries and from the business community Trinity were at the bottom of the first division table. Consequently two people had been appointed to the club's commercial department in order to increase income. 'If the city and Trinity supporters want to see better players and the development of Belle Vue they must realise that that can only be achieved with the fullest support from them and the city of Wakefield,' he added.

Among new junior signings, 17-year old forward Francis Stephenson, son of former Trinity player Nigel, arrived from amateur club Dewsbury Moor. It was learned that Darren Fritz had signed a new contract with Canberra and would not be returning to Belle Vue, so the club turned its attention to another Canberra prop or second row, 27-year old Dave Woods, as well as 23-year old stand-off or loose forward Matthew Fuller from South Sydney, both of whom would arrive as soon as their Australian commitments were at an end. To cover the stand-off role, Batley and ex-Hull stand-off Lee Hanlan was signed for £17,000 and a four-player deal was fixed with Oldham. Gary Price and winger David Jones were to go to Watersheddings in exchange for Great Britain U21 centre Gary Christie and prop Mark Sheals. In the event Price pulled out of going to Oldham and opted for Featherstone instead, who agreed a transfer fee of £85,000, which went to Oldham for Christie. Sheals broke his leg in the pre-season friendly with Hunslet, and with Glancy and Mark Webster unable to agree new terms, Trinity signed 34-year old former Great Britain and Oldham prop Hugh Waddell from Sheffield on loan. Other new recruits included Wigan forward Mike Forshaw, Hull prop Ian Marlow, locally-based Hull forward Steve Durham and winger Lee Child from Leeds.

Before the start of the 1993-94 season, Trinity revealed ambitious plans for redeveloping Belle Vue. A new 4,000 capacity South Stand was envisaged to fit alongside the social club, now called the Coach House, and would have a sports hall underneath. Costed at half a million pounds, the plan was expected to raise Belle Vue's overall capacity to 20,000 and could be made possible with funding from the European Community and the Foundation for Sport and the Arts. It was also planned to use reclaimed land south of Agbrigg Road for car parking and a training pitch.

In the early season, Geoff Bagnall asked to be relieved of the captaincy, believing that the added responsibility was affecting his form and fellow-Aussie Dave Woods took over. The despondent mood which had set in continued with a 10-0 home defeat by struggling Widnes, despite a stunning fifty-tackle count from the ever-reliable Nigel Bell, whose benefit year it was. Trinity's already stretched squad was weakened further by the release of Bagnall, who had unexpectedly received an offer to join Darren Fritz at Canberra. However, Trinity moved quickly to sign up

19-year old Junior Kiwi captain Henry Paul, for whom Topliss forecast a bright future, saying, 'He has lots of class and ability and I think he will be one of the great players of the nineties.' Paul's debut for Trinity was delayed when he was called up to join the senior Kiwi team on their tour of Great Britain and France.

It was late October when Trinity recorded their first home win of the season, scraping a 22-21 win over Oldham and then putting up a fight at Hull before losing 16-8, a match in which Bell and Slater between them made a hundred tackles. The following month Rodney Walker resigned as club chairman and was made the club's first life president. A new member of the board, James Duncan, took over as chairman and gave Topliss 'a new mandate' to make additions to the squad. Duncan also promised a more modern management structure with a view to achieving more commercial revenue as well as investment. Less than a month later, Duncan saw his family property firm, hit by the recession in the construction industry, go into receivership.

After Andy Mason had reached a hundred tries for the club in the 34-10 loss at Castleford, Henry Paul made his debut in the 22-8 defeat at Salford, where he played stand-off alongside new scrum-half Billy Conway, and opposed Andy Gregory, whom Trinity had tried to sign from Leeds before Salford stepped in. 'Paul proved a revelation at stand-off,' said the *Wakefield Express*. 'With an injection of pace, a dummy here or a body swerve there he was able to open up the home side as and when it suited him.'

Inspired by Henry Paul's try and two goals, Trinity ended a five-match losing run with a 12-10 home win over Warrington, which took them out of the bottom two. Trinity's junior players continued to impress, running up a record score of 80-10 against Bradford Academy, in which Kieran Allen scored four tries and Matthew Rogers kicked twelve goals to set a new record for the Academy side, one short of Brian Taylor's record for the Colts, which the Academy had replaced.

But after the morale-boosting victory over title challengers Warrington and a close-run defeat by 20-16 at Leeds, Trinity disappointed their fans with a poor home performance as they lost 24-10 at New Year against Featherstone, who until then had recorded just one away win all season. 'It's the same old story,' said Topliss, as if weary of battling against the odds with slender means. 'Just when it looked as though we'd turned the corner we put in a totally inept performance against what really was a mediocre side. You have one result like that and everyone loses confidence – the players, the fans – and it's left to me to pick up the pieces.'

Club chairman James Duncan and another director resigned, leaving just three in charge of the club – football chairman Stuart Farrar and business partners Brian Eccles and Ted Richardson. One of the first moves of the three-man board was to ask the players and coaching staff to take a 20 per cent pay cut so as to balance expenditure and income for the rest of the season. Their cash flow problems were eased by the sale of 31-year old Paul Round, one of the club's most consistent forwards since his arrival from Oldham two years earlier, to Halifax for £25,000.

The Challenge Cup first round draw, which sent Trinity to Wigan, was greeted with some relief, at least from a money-spinning point of view. The match turned out to be more of a thriller than away fans had a right to expect. Andy Mason scored the first of his two tries after only four minutes as he picked off a Shaun Edwards pass and hared to the line with Martin Offiah in vain pursuit. Another dazzling try, the result of fine team work, came just after half-time when full back Henry Paul fielded a kick on his own line, evaded Offiah and set off downfield before giving the ball to Mason, who cut infield. On the half-way line the centre passed to Gary Christie, who returned the favour on the Wigan 22 before Mason gave Matthew Fuller what looked like a try-scoring chance. But as the cover defence reduced Fuller's chances, the Aussie off-loaded to Andy Wilson for what the *Express* thought must be the try of the season. To complete Trinity fans' delight, Paul converted from the touchline to level the scores. But it was former Trinity star Nigel Wright who produced the decisive score when he intercepted and ran half the length of the field to score. Trinity went out of the Cup by 24-16 but showed great character and resilience and, remarkably, voted to forgo their pay as a gesture towards helping the club out of its predicament.

Junior Kiwis captain Henry Paul, pictured here in action against Salford, made a big contribution to Trinity's 1993-94 season before signing for Wigan

For the second time, the club lost its Australian captain, when, after Geoff Bagnall, second rower Dave Woods was offered a two-year contract by Gold Coast Seagulls and left after just half a season. Trinity moved quickly to sign 35-year old prop David Hobbs from Bradford on a free transfer. His acquisition was aimed at giving the team more direction on the field of play.

Two weeks after their Cup defeat, Trinity were back at Central Park for the league match which marked the home debut of Wigan's giant winger Va'aiga Tuigamala. But it was Wakefield's Henry Paul who proved the star performer with a 40-metre try and goal in injury time, having also bundled Offiah into touch when a try loomed. Wigan were impressed for a second time and signed the Kiwi for the following season. Towards the end of the first half another spectacular try unfolded as Andy Wilson sprinted 60 metres before Lee Hanlan and Paul combined to put Mike Forshaw in for a try against his former club and Trinity won a headline-grabbing 20-13 victory.

At the first, long-awaited shareholders' meeting, details of recent transfers emerged. By far the largest fee was received from Wigan for Nigel Wright (£145,000). Michael Jackson and Gary Price had each been sold for £90,000 and Mark Conway had gone to Dewsbury for £17,500, making a total of £342,500. Not included in the accounts was the transfer of Paul Round to Halifax for £25,000. On the debit side, Lee Hanlan had cost £17,000 from Batley and Mike Forshaw £25,000 from Wigan. David Jones had gone to Oldham as part of a deal which saw Mark Sheals and Gary Christie arrive at Belle Vue, with Trinity paying an additional £90,000. The club also expected to have to pay Hull £15,000 for Ian Marlow and £5,000 for Steve Durham. The deal with Swinton involving Paul Lord and Simon Longstaff was a straight swap. Excluding contracts to overseas players, Trinity had laid out £168,000 in buying players, giving a decent return of £174,500, which went towards paying off some of the historic debt.

Director Stuart Farrar said the club expected to make a profit by the end of the year. Rodney Walker, who attended at the request of the current board since he had been chairman at the period under examination, paid tribute to the present directors and was greeted with 'supportive applause'. 'If not for the rearguard action of Ted Richardson, Brian Eccles and Stuart Farrar there would no longer be a Wakefield Trinity rugby club,' he said. 'We should support them for keeping this club going.'

In response to the question of why the residual debt of nearly half a million was taken on, the board replied that Wakefield Council, who owned the ground, would not have agreed to its transfer otherwise. According to RFL bye-laws, if a club stops trading, and has no other assets than its players, they become free agents. The board decided to take on the debt and protect their player assets.

Consecutive losses to St Helens and Widnes put Trinity deep in relegation trouble. A 20-all draw at Oldham secured a vital point though it was not enough. Even one point had seemed unlikely after Trinity went 20-4 behind but came back strongly in the last fifteen minutes. Andy Wilson brought off a scorching touchline run for the last-minute equalising try, after stand-off Henry Paul had scored two tries, kicked two goals and created a try for Bright Sodje, who had joined Trinity from Hull KR in a player exchange involving John Glancy. As for Paul, Topliss said, 'Henry Paul at 20 is an exceptional young player and is the best coup I have pulled off.'

A battling 10-8 home win over Hull put Trinity back on the road to first division survival. In the attritional forward exchanges, Nigel Bell led from the front, and Mark Webster and Lynton Morris also put in a huge tackling stint. Captain David Hobbs relieved the pressure with his tactical kicking, Academy prop Francis Stephenson made an encouraging debut off the bench and Bright Sodje scored his first try at Belle Vue. But with two disappointing defeats over Easter – by 29-20 at home to Leeds and by 42-22 at Featherstone – Trinity still had it all to do. A home victory over Salford eased their worries before Halifax gave Trinity a 54-16 thrashing at Thrum Hall. But no matter: fellow-strugglers Hull KR lost to Salford and would join Leigh in the second division the following season. After the Halifax game, which saw Henry Paul give away an interception leading to a match-turning try, Topliss rushed to the young Kiwi's defence, saying, 'Without him we wouldn't have stayed up. Wakefield Trinity owes him a lot.' Paul declared himself satisfied with what had been achieved. 'I set myself the goal of helping to keep Wakefield Trinity in the first division and I succeeded,' he said. 'Not even Wally Lewis could do that.'

Topliss himself signed off with a remarkable performance, at the age of 44, in Trinity's A team, which he guided to a 30-24 victory over Featherstone. He was joined off the bench by Academy coach Terry Crook, two years older than Topliss, who was playing his second game in five days owing to squad injuries. Topliss stole the show, playing the full 80 minutes, 'in patches showing nothing short of sheer brilliance laced with a hint of youthful ebullience', and putting Henry Paul, playing alongside him, over for two tries.

After twenty years at Trinity, thirteen as a player and seven as coach, Topliss severed his connection when he decided to take a break from coaching. He stated that he had probably stayed too long, the last two seasons being full of upheaval, and was disappointed that the club did not have the money or the backing to sign players he had identified as being essential to maintaining Trinity's sixth place and challenging for the top four. 'But I don't blame the board entirely,' he said. 'The Wakefield public has to shoulder some responsibility by its apathy. If it wasn't for the current board, the board at that time [two years earlier] and Wakefield Council, there wouldn't be a Wakefield Trinity today.' He named as the high spots of his seven-year stint the winning of the Yorkshire Cup and the famous player swap with Leeds. 'Those four players were the difference between first and second division football for Wakefield Trinity. That's another thing I'm proud of – stopping Trinity becoming a yo-yo side. Oldham and Featherstone came up with us that season and both went down again. Trinity didn't, though it's been a bit too close for comfort the last couple of seasons.' The high point of his last season was coaching the only side to beat Wigan at Central Park and coming within a whisker of dumping the champions out of the Cup.

The board lost no time in appointing David Hobbs, 35, as coach in succession to Topliss even though the former Bradford man had previously said he was not interested in the post. Hobbs was given a three-year contract and brought in ex-Bradford hooker Brian Noble, 33, as assistant coach in place of Tony Handforth. They were later joined by ex-Hull KR and Bradford scrum-half Paul Harkin.

Second row or centre Adrian Flynn was Trinity's only representative on the Great Britain Academy tour of Australia during the close season. The club's signings amounted to two Kiwi internationals – half back Aaron Whittaker and forward Robert Piva – and Wigan forward Ian Gildart. Great Britain U21 centre Richard Goddard, who had made fewer than ten first team appearances during the season, joined Castleford for a fee fixed by a tribunal at £75,000. But the team was suddenly short of centres as Andy Mason, at the age of 31 and after seven years at the club during which he had regularly led the try-scoring list, decided to retire.

Intimations of the upheaval that was soon to take place in rugby league came with discussions leading from an RFL-commissioned report called 'Framing the Future'. The notion of a super league, mergers between clubs and the setting of minimum standards suddenly came into focus and club chairmen would spend hours debating the way ahead. Rodney Walker, chairman of the RFL, was appointed chairman of the English Sports Council.

The early part of the 1994-95 season was not without its low points. The 44-12 rout by Bradford at Belle Vue was bad enough but worse was to come with the 22-10 reverse at newly-promoted Doncaster, at whose hands Trinity had not suffered defeat for over thirty years.

Wigan, against whom Trinity had done well the year before, inflicted a 46-0 hammering, causing coach Hobbs to blast his charges for lack of commitment. His troops rallied briefly with a 21-16 home win over Oldham, with Nigel Wright, back at Belle Vue on loan from Central Park until the end of the season, playing a major role by creating two tries and kicking two drop goals. Defeats at home to Hull and at Leeds saw Trinity drop to fourth from bottom, resulting in Hobbs again questioning the players' attitude.

A 48-8 defeat at third-from-bottom Salford resulted in a general outcry from fans, who started to question Hobbs's appointment. Hobbs had further dealings with his old club when centre Gary Christie went to Odsal in exchange for threequarters Daio Powell and Steve McGowan. Martyn Holland, a 17-year old junior who was Wakefield Schools 200-metre champion and who was also on Bradford City's books, signed for Trinity.

Two defeats at Workington, the first in the Regal Trophy, the second in the league in a much-criticised Boxing Day fixture, made Hobbs's position uncomfortable despite the board's declaration of faith in him. In between, Nigel Wright's try and six goals helped to see off Doncaster in a long-awaited 28-14 victory. A loss would have been unthinkable against a club who had not won at Belle Vue since their first visit in 1951.

In January, Hobbs left by mutual agreement. The A-team coaching pair of Paul Harkin and Andy Kelly were put in temporary charge and the team responded immediately with a 15-0 win over St Helens. Playing with rediscovered confidence, Trinity went on to record their first away win of 1994-95 when they beat Sheffield 41-14, which was also their highest score of the season.

Now in more upbeat mood, Trinity registered their first win at Widnes in nineteen years with a 20-4 score as Wright grabbed most of the points with a try, three goals and a drop goal. At this stage Trinity were tenth in the table out of sixteen but soon embarked on a second five-match losing run, including a 24-12 Challenge Cup first-round defeat at Whitehaven.

After representing England against France at Gateshead earlier in the season, Nigel Wright was whisked back, along with centre Adrian Flynn, from across the Channel, where both had been playing for GB U21s, to help Trinity win 12-10 at Oldham. Despite having played twice in 24 hours, Wright had a big role in the victory over mid-table Oldham, creating both tries and kicking two goals in a match which was also remembered for the fox which raced around the Watersheddings ground during the half-time interval.

But with defeats at bottom club Hull, by 11-10, and at Belle Vue by 14-10 to Sheffield, Trinity slumped to third from bottom. Kiwi forward Robert Piva was transfer-listed at £35,000, before he decided that he had had enough and returned home.

With Rodney Walker having vacated the office of club chairman, Ted Richardson took over. At the same time Wakefield Council agreed to sell the ground back to the club, for which £240,000 was needed.

With a makeshift side, captained by John Thompson, now almost 36, Trinity slumped to a heavy 56-14 defeat at St Helens, which led joint coaches Harkin and Kelly to ask that the RFL review the ten-metre rule at the play-the-ball, which had been extended from five metres almost three years before. Trinity's defeat was not the only one where a large score had been run up in the last quarter of the game. The coaches were prompted to write about the rule change in their match programme notes, where they highlighted what they saw as a big problem. 'We're all for cleaning up the play-the-ball but it has been speeded up to a point where neither players nor referees can stay on top of the game for the whole 80 minutes no matter how fit they are. And if a team has just one or two quality attacking players then the last quarter can produce disproportionate scores that do nothing for the credibility of the game or the entertainment of the paying public.'

At the same time as Trinity were keeping one eye on the relegation zone, the whole future of the divisional system was thrown into question. The players and coaching staff thought that with a 29-16 home win over Widnes, which moved them into fifth from bottom place, they would be safe. Nigel Wright – the subject of a campaign to raise £100,000 to keep him at Belle Vue – had once more made the difference, scoring 21 points from two tries, six goals and a drop goal. But there were rumblings going on in the background.

As the *Wakefield Express* reported, 'What should have been a tremendous relegation-saving victory for Wakefield Trinity over fellow division one strugglers Widnes was very much overshadowed by Super League merger proposals. Players, backroom staff and supporters were greeted by "No Merger" slogans daubed around the ground, while a half-time announcement by Wakefield Trinity chairman Ted Richardson over the public address system was drowned out by irate hecklers.'

The Super League idea had gained ground fast. On Saturday April 8, club chairmen had voted unanimously to introduce a new structure which was arguably the most revolutionary since the 1895 breakaway. The top tier of fourteen clubs would include a number of merged clubs, as well as two French clubs, Toulouse and Paris. It was envisaged that Wakefield Trinity would merge with Castleford and Featherstone to form a new entity provisionally called Calder. Other mergers would involve Hull and Hull KR; the so-called Manchester clubs of Oldham and Salford; the Cumbrian clubs of Workington, Whitehaven, Barrow and Carlisle; Widnes and Warrington, who would come under the banner of Cheshire; and the South Yorkshire outfits, Sheffield and Doncaster. The remaining clubs would form the 'first division', though actually it was the second division.

All this had come about as a result of a deal with Rupert Murdoch's Sky TV, which had been prompted to pay out £77 million – later upped to £87 million - over five years, with each Super League club receiving approximately one million per season and the other clubs a mere fraction of that amount. It was hardly surprising that clubs had voted in favour of accepting this manna, since 25 of the 32 were known to be in serious financial difficulty.

The mergers were not the only controversial innovation. In under one year's time professional clubs would play from March to October in the name of 'summer rugby'. The 1995-96 season would therefore be a shortened one, starting in August 1995 and ending in January 1996, two months before the start of the revolutionary switch to the new calendar.

RFL chief executive and former Wigan chairman Maurice Lindsay, who had negotiated with Sky and had driven the proposals forward, stated: 'The historic decision paves the way for the future of the sport, not only in Britain but across the globe.' Rodney Walker, as RFL chairman, said, 'Supporters will see a better game, in better surroundings and the deal will see their sport receive a greater profile nationally and internationally.'

Initial evidence, at least in the Wakefield area, suggested that fans did not want what they were being offered. Local councillor and editor of the Trinity fanzine, *Wally Lewis Is Coming*, Richard Clarkson, handed out impassioned leaflets at the Widnes game condemning the proposals.

Chairman Ted Richardson, who like other club chairmen supported the new scheme, said that he fully understood the fans' anger and frustration. What he said at half-time in the Widnes match was unheard by many, such was the vocal opposition, but he stated that no decision had been made about the merger with Featherstone and Castleford. Shareholders and supporters would be consulted.

In an interview with the *Wakefield Express,* Richardson said that fifty per cent of all income received from the deal would be pumped into stadium development. 'It will mean a better environment and amenities for everyone to appreciate,' he said. 'So long as we do not fritter away this opportunity in paying out more than we can afford this will go down as a milestone in history.'

Considering the possibility of a merger, Richardson added, 'The one thing we may lose if we go down the merger path is our name. Wakefield Trinity has been synonymous with the game of rugby league since we became a founder member 100 years ago and no one wants to see that disappear. Neither, I suppose, do Castleford and Featherstone. Maybe on a good day we could convince everyone that we are in the Metropolitan district of Wakefield and therefore it would be a good idea to keep Wakefield as our name. And since we would be three teams becoming one we could always opt for the one that means exactly that – Trinity! The name is going to be the main sticking point as far as I can see. If we could merge and keep our name would anyone complain?'

Richardson concluded, 'We are not burying our club, we are resurrecting it and moving forward to a new and brighter future. Some will never agree, others already agree that is the way forward. Like it or not, the Super League is the way forward for rugby league.'

It seemed that the discussions had an effect on the team's performance. With a 26-12 victory, Workington won at Belle Vue for the first time since 1979 and did the double over Trinity for the first time since the 1951-52 season. Worse was to come. A catastrophic performance at Castleford resulted in an 86-0 thrashing, which was Trinity's heaviest-ever defeat and widest losing margin, easily eclipsing the 72-6 loss against Wigan eight years earlier. As the *Wakefield Express* put it: 'What the anti-merger lobby has been trying to achieve for the best part of a fortnight with a hostile campaign was probably achieved in just 80 minutes at Wheldon Road, Castleford on Easter Monday. What club could possibly wish to merge with another that has a playing staff that lets in a staggering 86 points … without even looking like scoring a single point?'

Joint coach Paul Harkin said he was 'totally disgusted' with the display. It transpired that on the Sunday morning before the game five key players – Nigel Wright, Ian Gildart, Mike Forshaw, Adrian Flynn and Richard Slater - declared themselves unfit. Harkin also admitted that players had grumbled about not getting paid.

At the AGM it was claimed that well over 80 per cent of the 250 shareholders present supported the proposal for a merger. But in another twist to the tale of ground ownership, it emerged that Wakefield Council were 'dragging their heels' over Trinity's wish to buy it back. Richardson claimed that it had been agreed that Trinity should buy back 'its birthright'. It was explained that Wakefield MDC bought the ground for £165,000 and would sell it back to Wakefield Trinity RLFC Ltd for £700,000. 'That sum represented £240,000 and a further £460,000 over 20 years, plus covenants that would mean any money from a subsequent re-sale would be limited to usage by Wakefield Trinity or its successor for the benefit of rugby league in the borough area,' the *Express* reported. 'Shareholder Richard Clarkson said that Trinity had twice had chances to buy back the ground but only in the last two months had forced the issue.'

Wakefield MP David Hinchliffe said he thought the Council would be 'utterly stupid to sell the ground back to the club without actually knowing what is happening.'

At the end of the season, it was announced that Harkin and Kelly were to retain their position as joint coaches for the coming season. In a revised Super League plan, Castleford, who finished third in 1994-95, would have a place in the new elite division, but Trinity, thirteenth out of sixteen, would not. Some players began to look elsewhere. Nigel Wright returned to Wigan, saying he wanted to play in Super League. The campaign to raise £100,000 to bring him back permanently to Wakefield had brought in only £1,400. Mike Forshaw, who had had two excellent seasons at Trinity since arriving from Wigan, went to Leeds, and Gary Spencer, at 28, retired from the game to concentrate on his career in the fire service.

With two months to go to the start of the new, shortened season, the squad was far from fixed. Some players were being pursued by other clubs; most were in dispute over non-payment of wages and contract money. Richardson confirmed that one losing match payment and one month's contract money was still to be paid as the club was suffering an unexpected cash flow problem.

The first major signing since the Super League upheaval came when former favourite Darren Fritz agreed to return. Ex-Kiwi loose forward Mike Kuiti, 32, signed from Oldham in an exchange involving Ian Gildart. Former GB U21 centre or second row Adrian Flynn was transferred to Castleford for £70,000 in a deal which saw winger Jon Wray arrive at Belle Vue. Scrum-half Barry Eaton, a former Stanley Rangers and Trinity Academy player, also arrived for the start of the new season, which was both historic and transitional.

Twenty-two - Into the Super League Era: 1995-98

The Centenary season of 1995-96 held little promise for Wakefield Trinity and it was no surprise that it got off to an inauspicious start. A team particularly thin in the backs went down by 44-14 at home to Whitehaven in front of just 1,849 fans, most of whom could hardly believe what was happening. 'A wave of incredulity swamped the ground,' said the *Wakefield Express*. One disgruntled supporter wrote to the paper: 'I've seen all Trinity's Wembley finals since 1946, but this side would not win the Wakefield and District Amateur Cup.'

The air of unreality was prolonged by a 28-19 home defeat by Featherstone, which saw the home debut of 38-year old former Bradford full back Keith Mumby, playing at centre. With an 18-11 defeat at Batley, Trinity were well and truly stuck at the bottom of the so-called first (i.e. second) division. With the arrival of Aussie stand-off Steve Georgallis from Western Suburbs, Trinity managed their first win of the season at the fifth attempt, when Huddersfield were beaten 26-22. Another Aussie half back, Brad Davis, signed from York and, like Georgallis, scored a debut try when he helped Trinity beat Dewsbury 34-24.

As the club game took a month-long break in October to make way for the Centenary World Cup, Wakefield Council approved the re-sale of the Belle Vue ground to Wakefield Trinity, the terms including covenants on any future sale of the land. At the same time there appeared one of several schemes which were to be announced concerning a move to a new ground. Plans for an ambitious £300 million Sports City development were unveiled at the Town Hall. The scheme, which would cater for many different sports and would include a dedicated stadium for Wakefield Trinity, was earmarked for the former Sharlston Colliery site between Warmfield and New Sharlston. It was suggested that the scheme had the potential to offer the best Super League facilities in the country. The project had reportedly grown out of the plan for Pugneys Country Park, where a similar scheme had to be abandoned because of green belt restrictions. The former Wakefield power station site had also been considered but failed to fulfil the criteria.

As they looked towards being promoted to Super League at the earliest opportunity, Trinity appointed former Australian test forward and ex-Oldham coach Peter Tunks as chief executive. New signings were made: former Australia rugby union full back Andrew Leeds, who switched to league and had been playing most recently with Western Suburbs, joined Trinity, along with English-born centre Carl Grigg, who had been playing in Perth. Forwards Sonny Whakarau and Darren Summerill were signed from Sheffield, from where French international back Freddy Banquet, who was due to play for Paris St Germain in Super League, also arrived.

After a shock exit from the Regal Trophy at Batley, by 21-14, Trinity managed to end Widnes's eight-match unbeaten run by winning 12-10 at Belle Vue. It was at Huddersfield that they secured their first away win of the season, with Freddy Banquet, in his first full match for the club, contributing two tries to the 22-14 victory. The Frenchman also touched down twice when Trinity toppled leaders Keighley by 16-4 at Belle Vue. Banquet increased his haul to eight tries in three games with four in the 30-16 win at Rochdale, from which Trinity went on to record their fifth win in five matches with a 34-4 win over Hull – revenge for the earlier 56-8 hammering. The team's much improved performance coincided with the arrival of Tunks, who was already casting an eye over the squad and coaching staff in preparation for the coming 'summer' season.

The traditional festive period fixtures, which were to be played for the final time as part of the regular season, were called off. The matches at both Christmas and New Year fell victim to the weather; the first, at Featherstone, owing to the frozen ground, the second, at Belle Vue, because of fog.

Early in the New Year of 1996 it was announced that Mitch Brennan, a former Queensland State of Origin player and marketing executive at Canberra Raiders, was to join Trinity and would be in charge of first team coaching, although Harkin and Kelly would remain part of the coaching team. Brennan's appointment was inspired by the plan to get Trinity into Super League as soon as possible.

As the Centenary season fizzled out in January, giving the distinct impression that it was less of a celebration of a glorious hundred years than a curtain-raiser to an already glorified new era, Trinity completed their season with four matches in ten days, the last a 28-6 home defeat to Salford. In the three-division system, they finished seventh out of eleven in the second tier, known confusingly as the first division. Wayne Flynn, the younger brother of Adrian who had played in a variety of back positions in the first team, maintained the family tradition by being chosen for Great Britain Academy.

Though the league season had finished, the Challenge Cup carried on. Trinity were drawn at Carlisle, the club of Steve Georgallis three seasons earlier, although the Aussie was unable to return there, having already departed for his homeland. With the powerful back three of Wayne McDonald, Sonny Whakarau and Mike Kuiti having a big role, Trinity went through by 34-18. In the next round Trinity met West Hull at the Boulevard, the amateurs having already knocked out professional opposition in the previous two rounds. Freddy Banquet, who had flown in from France the night before, scored a hat-trick as Trinity went through to the quarter-finals by 40-8.

In the quarter-finals they travelled to Odsal, rarely a favourable venue for Trinity, and so it proved again as Bradford made it to the semi-final by 30-18. But the future Super League side were pushed hard by Trinity, for whom second row Whakarau was in top form with three tries, two of them created by Brad Davis, who scored the other himself.

New signings were unveiled a fortnight before the first 'summer season' of rugby league, which began in March 1996. Trinity's overseas contingent rose to eight, with the likes of wingers Lino Foai, a Samoan, and Lamond Copestake, a Fijian playing in New Zealand. From Australia came centre James Corcoran, back row forward Jamie Kelso, hooker Adam Nable and experienced prop Dennis Beecraft.

Chief executive Peter Tunks had been largely responsible for bringing these players in. His right-hand man Mitch Brennan was handed a multiple role at Belle Vue, being head of the commercial team as well as having overall responsibility for coaching. Team selection, as in the old days, was made by a team of four – Tunks, Brennan, Harkin and Kelly.

Two important facts emerged from the AGM. First, the club had shown a small profit in the half-year up to the end of January 1996. Second – and very significant in the future - the agreement with Wakefield Council over the selling-back of Belle Vue was not now 'encumbered' by covenants restricting the resale of the ground by Wakefield Trinity. That would be of importance when using the value of the ground as collateral at the bank or selling it to a developer as part of a move to a new stadium.

In the new first division in a new season, Trinity made a familiar start as they lost heavily by 52-2 at Hull. Meanwhile in the top tier, former Wakefield favourite Freddy Banquet scored the first-ever try in Super League when he touched down for Paris Saint-Germain against Sheffield Eagles.

A new four-substitute, six-interchange ruling came into force, requiring all teams to work with a 17-man matchday squad. Another innovation widespread in Super League was the bolting-on of new nicknames, usually alliterative, such as Wigan Warriors or animal-based, like Leeds Rhinos, or both, like Warrington Wolves. The idea had originally come from America and was believed to assist with marketing the game to a new audience. As far as a new Trinity nickname was concerned, chairman Richardson said it was premature to suggest a replacement for 'Dreadnoughts' – a name which had long since ceased to be used and in any case was never appended to the club name as was now intended. 'Wakefield Warriors' and 'Trinity Tornadoes' had been bandied about. 'I'm not saying we won't consider changing the nickname,' said Richardson, 'But I do believe we mustn't change it simply for the sake of it.'

Former Great Britain scrum-half Mike Ford was signed from Warrington and Richard Pearson arrived from Huddersfield in exchange for James Mosley. Martin Law, the older brother of Trinity Academy player Graham Law, was signed from Leeds. Winger Lino Foai scored a hat-trick in the 32-26 home defeat by Salford; a loss at Huddersfield was followed by a 30-10 home reverse at the hands of Keighley, who had not won at Belle Vue since 1973 and who now had Sonny Whakarau in their ranks.

After two months of the season had passed, Brennan wrote in his regular *Wakefield Express* column called 'Mitch's Pitch': 'Our efforts to date are not reflected in our results on the pitch.' And then, in capitals: 'It is our policy to fix the problem – not the blame.' Just a couple of months into the season, Brennan was already saying that Super League in 1998 – rather than 1997 - was the club's objective.

A letter to the *Wakefield Express*, from Councillor Norman Hazell, echoed what many supporters of long standing must have been thinking. 'Reflecting on the great Trinity team of the early 1960s,' he wrote, 'I cannot help contrasting its make-up with that of today which is not exactly enjoying the same amount of success in spite of recruiting players from Australia, Fiji, Western Samoa and goodness knows where else, and at some cost, I suppose.

'The great Trinity team of 1960 had Keith Holliday (Eastmoor), Ken Rollin (Sharlston) and Harold Poynton (Lupset) at half back, Don Metcalfe (Primrose Hill) at full back, Neil Fox (Sharlston) and Alan Skene (South Africa) centres to Fred Smith (Eastmoor) and John Etty (Batley). In the forwards, Derek Turner (Plumpton), Brian Briggs and Albert Firth (both Stanley) played behind Jack Wilkinson (Halifax), Geoff Oakes (Belle Vue), Malcolm Sampson (Stanley) and Les Chamberlain (Leeds). The coach, Ken Traill, came all the way from Hunslet and helped the team to become one of the truly great sides in the history of the game – and how proud we were of the success of our largely homespun team.'

Trinity were set to transfer Carl Grigg and Mike Kuiti to Batley in a £50,000 deal, but when the centre scored four tries in the 50-14 rout of Dewsbury, both Trinity and the player changed their minds and Kuiti, aged 33, went to Mount Pleasant alone. Ford took his place as captain for the first time in the 24-17 home defeat by Hull. Forty-point losses at leaders Salford and second-placed Keighley showed the gulf between the top teams, even in this division, and mid-table Trinity.

It was at this stage that half back Brad Davis began to emphasise his value to the side. Entrusted with the goal-kicking and showing marked improvement as the season progressed, Davis scored 103 points in the final seven matches of the season. The victory by 31-4 over Widnes was described as a virtual one-man show as the Aussie racked up 23 points from four tries, three goals and a drop goal. In the 30-22 home win over Whitehaven he scored three tries and landed five goals. Against Dewsbury, who took a 50-point beating for the second time, he scored two tries and kicked seven goals, but took second place in the try-scoring to rampaging forward Wayne McDonald, who scored three. Centre Daio Powell also scored a try on his return to first team duty after being cleared of serious criminal charges in Australia.

At the end of the first summer season, Trinity finished in sixth position in the eleven-team first division, one place higher than the previous campaign. Chief executive Peter Tunks, who had a one-year contract with the club, informed the board that, as a result of funding from the RFL to the lower divisions being less than anticipated, his salary could not reasonably be met. The RFL had revised the amount of News Corporation funds it was granting – in Trinity's case by around £100,000 less per season over the next five years. The club and Tunks, who was responsible for an unprecedented number of signings, therefore agreed a parting of the ways. Mitch Brennan would add the role of chief executive to his impressive list of responsibilities. Paul Harkin also left after two years at the club.

'Internally we have achieved our objectives though the public perhaps doesn't see it,' said Brennan, summarising the season and referring to players' increased fitness and training programmes.

Nigel Bell, now 34, returned to the Eastmoor club as an amateur player after impressive service over twelve years. Wayne Flynn, after being listed at £125,000, went to Sheffield in exchange for second row Ian Hughes. Daio Powell was transferred to Halifax, from where utility back Craig Rika, loose forward Mick Martindale and hooker Roy Southernwood arrived. Prop Richie McKell and half back Jason Twist were signed from Australia. As the club looked towards the start of the 1997 season, only prop Dennis Beecraft remained of the six who had been recruited from overseas, none of them, for a variety of reasons, having proved their value. Terry Crook, the first coach of the Academy five years earlier, left his position, which was to be made full-time, choosing to stay in post as a local government officer. Billy Conway, who had had his testimonial season the year before and who had been at the club for 13 years, the last one spent mainly in the A team, was not offered a new contract and was listed at £30,000. Two more Australians were signed: wing or centre Roger Kenworthy from Canberra and half back Ron Trautman from Brisbane. Former Scottish rugby union player Jim McLaren also arrived via Canberra.

There were new moves affecting the ground. Outline planning consent was sought to build houses on the land. The intention was to improve the valuation of the ground, which could then be used as collateral at the bank for further loans, or to sell the land for housing to help finance a possible move to a new stadium. 'We have no plans to move,' said Ted Richardson. 'We've already spent money improving the ground since the end of last season. But that's not to say we are not prepared to move at some point in the future if that course of action is for the good of the club.' At the same time Richardson also said he intended putting it to shareholders to close the share issue 'in order to safeguard rugby league in Wakefield.' At the same time fresh investment from the current major shareholders might be possible ahead of 'a major season and a tremendous year for Wakefield Trinity.' He believed that the club should be protected from a possible 'unscrupulous takeover'. Another venue for a new ground was suggested: at a purpose-built stadium, shared with Wakefield Rugby Union at Durkar.

After the traditional calendar had been stood on its head, the 1997 season started with the Challenge Cup in January. Amateur side Ovenden were beaten 52-0, while in the next round (the fourth) Trinity beat Swinton 9-4, a generally unconvincing display brightened by man of the match Martyn Holland. But in the fifth round, Trinity went down to Super League side Oldham, who won 22-14 at Belle Vue in a match in which scrum-half Paul March made his debut. In the opening league game, Brad Davis immediately made his mark with two tries and five goals in the 23-10 home win over Dewsbury and was given a new three-year contract, even though his present deal had a year to run. Following wins over promoted side Hull KR and Whitehaven, and a 15-all draw at Featherstone, Trinity suffered two 40-point defeats at the hands of front-runners Hull and Huddersfield, which showed there was some way to go to catch up with the division's best.

After it was announced that Freddy Banquet, the club's top scorer in the centenary season with nine tries from seven outings, was to return to Belle Vue, Mike Ford was transferred to Super League neighbours Castleford and was soon to be followed by two others. Brad Davis's try and five goals in the 31-10 win over Workington put him at the top of the division's points-scoring table and brought him wider attention. After two defeats, one by 42-22 at the hands of Keighley, who had gone into receivership, the other by 30-10 at Whitehaven, it became clear that Trinity would not be taking up the single promotion place for Super League. Davis, keen to play at that level, asked for a transfer and was listed at £200,000.

Coach Mitch Brennan, after 16 months at the helm, decided that it was time for him to go too. He bade farewell after the home match against Featherstone in the first week of June and handed over to his assistant Andy Kelly. Brennan said he thought he had taken the club as far as he could with the resources available. It had always been his intention, he said, to leave at the end of the season, but decided to leave earlier when it became obvious that Trinity were not going to be promoted. He said, handing over to Kelly, 'This is as much Andy's team as it is mine … Promotion from within is the key to success.'

At the same time, it was revealed at the AGM that Trinity's debts had risen to £742,000. Life in the new first division had brought its own problems. The difference between the old first division and the new first (i.e. second) division amounted to a drop of £108,000 in gate receipts. Sponsorship and advertising had more than halved, as had the lottery, and shop sales were running at a loss. Ted Richardson explained that Paul Caddick, who was to become chairman of Leeds, had shown an interest in taking over the club, but the Trinity board had turned him down, wanting to avoid the 'danger of people becoming too powerful at the club'. Caddick had allegedly wanted Trinity to play at Glasshoughton and the board felt that that was 'a step too far'.

Sonny Whakarau arrived from Keighley for a second spell at Trinity and prop Dale Laughton was brought in from Sheffield as a replacement for Aussie Richie McKell, who joined Castleford after only four games for Trinity. But his departure was not so keenly felt as that of Brad Davis, who also headed for Wheldon Road in a £100,000 deal, to the disappointment of fans, some of whom believed that Trinity were becoming little more than a nursery for Super League clubs. Director Stuart Farrar pointed out that, though the club did not want him to leave, Davis had cost just £15,000 from York so that the transfer made 'useful profit'.

Andy Kelly's first game in charge resulted in a 30-16 defeat at Huddersfield, at which point Trinity were lying in fifth place. Billy Conway was brought back into first-team action and former Great Britain loose forward Gary Divorty, whom David Topliss had wanted to sign several years earlier, came from Hull on a free transfer. Five games into his stewardship, Kelly was still looking for his first win, after suffering two-point defeats by Widnes and Keighley. The losing sequence was the worst since the 1994-95 season, when twice Trinity had a run of five defeats. The run was broken in the last match of the regular part of the season as Swinton were beaten 29-10, resulting in fifth place in the league table. In the long-winded premiership play-offs, Trinity found themselves in a so-called East Yorkshire pool with Hull, Hull KR, Featherstone and York, against whom they would play on a home and away basis in order to determine which teams would go forward to the quarter-finals. Trinity made a poor showing, scrambling a 34-26 home win against second division York in front of a record low attendance at Belle Vue of 838, besides beating Hull KR 23-16 – the only victories in eight matches. The squad was ravaged by injury but the 13-10 defeat at York, amid thunder, lightning and a downpour, and before just 633 supporters, was particularly grim. Kelly nevertheless pointed to encouraging performances from youngsters Martyn Holland, David and Paul March and Ryan Horsley, and was optimistic about the coming season.

Jim McLaren returned to rugby union in Scotland and Banquet, less successful in his second stint at the club, to France. Banquet claimed that he had only been paid three weeks' wages in three months at Belle Vue and a £3,000 cheque handed over to him when he left bounced. The directors admitted that the cheque had not been honoured at the bank and agreed to pay him in instalments what he was owed. Ted Richardson said that the financial position of the club was 'no secret' and that some players were owed money. Wayne McDonald, Micky Clarkson and Ian Hughes went to an RFL tribunal claiming non-payment of contract money and wanting to be made free agents as a consequence, but their application failed. Clarkson claimed he was owed £4,000. Players' union representative Nic Grimoldby, who put their case to the tribunal, said, 'They have lost faith in Trinity – and who can blame them after the problems they have faced getting their wages?' Eventually all three overcame their grievances and returned to the club.

As he sought to bolster the squad for the coming 1998 season, Kelly lined up 23-year old goal-kicking centre or stand-off Garen Casey, a former Australian Schools player who had over fifty first-grade games under his belt with Parramatta and then Penrith. He came with a recommendation from Sheffield Eagles coach John Kear. Sheffield utility back David Mycoe, originally from Wakefield, was also signed. Aussie forward Matt Fuller, who was at Belle Vue for the 1993-94 season, returned to the club from Perth Western Reds and Wakefield-born Gary Lord arrived as a free agent.

In another episode in the story concerning the proposed move to a new stadium, the Council backed a consortium's plans for a sports village situated off M1 junction 40, between Lupset and Queen's Drive, Ossett. The stadium was to be shared by Trinity, Wakefield RU and Ossett Town FC among others.

The 1998 season opened with a straightforward 44-6 Challenge Cup third round win over amateurs BRK. But in the fourth round, Trinity came up against Warrington, who triumphed 42-6 at Belle Vue. The match was evenly contested for the first hour, after which the Super League side ran in five tries.

When Trinity beat pre-season title favourites Whitehaven by 38-22, with Casey and McDonald both scoring hat-tricks, they stretched their winning league run to four and went equal on points with Hull KR at the top. It was in east Hull that Trinity suffered their first reverse of the season when they went down by 36-6, leaving Rovers as the only unbeaten side in the division.

In Super League, meanwhile, Nigel Wright, who had been on loan at Wakefield in 1994-95 after signing for Wigan in 1993, had his contract terminated by the Central Park club. At the age of 24, Wright had been troubled by an ankle injury for the past three years, which effectively ended a highly promising career.

Trinity continued to score freely, beating Rochdale 38-0 at home, with Martyn Holland scoring three tries and Casey a try and five goals. In the Good Friday home victory over Featherstone, centre Adam Hughes, on loan from Leeds, and Casey each touched down twice. Hughes, brother of second row Ian, added two more in the Easter Monday 15-4 win at Hunslet. Trinity did well to come away with a 26-all draw from Dewsbury, where the Kelly brothers were once more in opposition as coaches. Trinity were reduced to twelve men when forward Andy Fisher, on loan and making his debut, was sent off, though an RFL disciplinary later found that he had no case to answer. Captain Roy Southernwood touched down twice and Adam Hughes scored a try and kicked five goals.

In May, former Hunslet and Huddersfield coach Steve Ferres was appointed as chief executive. Ferres had taken Huddersfield into Super League, but he insisted that he had not come to Belle Vue to coach, although his talent-spotting might prove useful should Trinity move into the transfer market. He claimed that the club was examining no fewer than three alternatives for stadium sites and reiterated the need to bring back supporters to the club, particularly 'former fans who think the club has slipped back into the Dark Ages.' Commenting on Ferres's appointment, chairman Richardson said, 'If we are to go for Super League then we need to have the right personnel in key positions. Steve's undoubted ability as a businessman and his vast experience in the game should start to drive us to Super League.' But Maurice Lindsay, now Super League managing director, was reported in the press as saying that Wakefield's entry to Super League was unlikely. He further stated that he would be against a team such as Trinity joining unless they were able to prove that they could invest in a better team and facilities.

With a 60-14 home win over Leigh, Trinity extended their unbeaten league run to seven. Casey scored a try and kicked eight goals, while Wray, Rika and Paul March scored two tries each. Unfortunately only 1,400 fans turned up to watch the eleven-try feast. With a 30-16 win at Whitehaven, not the easiest ground to take two points from, Trinity went six points clear at the top of the table before the eight-match unbeaten run came to an end at Swinton.

Coach Andy Kelly, though, had proved his worth and was given a two-year extension to his contract. With prop Dennis Beecraft about to return to Australia, Trinity filled the vacant quota space by signing centre Josh Bostock from the Balmain club. Bostock made an immediate impression by scoring three tries in the 46-28 win at Rochdale. Trinity added another important recruit when 17-year old centre Ben Westwood signed from the Academy, the first to do so for eighteen months.

At the AGM, Rodney Walker, who still held a significant shareholding in the club, gave the meeting the benefit of his experience as chairman of the RFL. In the light of recent comments by Maurice Lindsay, he told the assembly that the RFL Council had already agreed that the first division winners, now defined as the first division grand final winners, would be promoted to Super League. Though that club still had to meet certain criteria for admission, Sir

Rodney told the audience that at present only half the Super League clubs met the standards set for stadium and average attendance.

David Hinchliffe MP had written to Lindsay stating concerns about what the Super League boss was reported to have said. Lindsay replied that the criteria regarding financial stability, minimum stadium standards, existing or potential spectator base and available investment capital would apply. He repeated what he had said to the *Yorkshire Post*: that nothing would give him greater pleasure if Wakefield were able to satisfy all the criteria and therefore be an asset to Super League.

A surprise 21-0 loss at Featherstone saw Trinity's lead over Hull KR at the top of the table cut to just two points. But possibly their best display of the season so far, when ending Dewsbury's six-match unbeaten run with a 25-18 win at Owl Lane, followed by victory over Hunslet, saw their lead restored to four points. Even more impressive was the 64-8 demolition of Widnes, although the Chemics, now the Vikings, were a shadow of their former selves. It was Trinity's highest score of the season, to which Bostock contributed three tries, Southernwood and man of the match Fisher two each, and Casey scored a try and kicked eight goals. Casey later signed for Salford, who would have his services from January 1999 after offering a much higher contract than Trinity thought he was worth or could match.

But Trinity stumbled for a second time at Featherstone, as the home side, after being 18-0 down, mounted a second-half fightback to win 29-18. They faltered again, going down 38-12 at home to Hull KR, who recorded their third win of the season over Trinity and inflicted their heaviest home league defeat, and in doing so took over the leadership of the division on points difference.

The run-in to the end of the season went exactly to plan, except that the RFL handed Andy Kelly a record fine of £7,500, of which £5,000 was suspended, as a result of a dispute with two Featherstone officials after the defeat there. Kelly was also banned from the dug-out.

Roger Kenworthy, in his new position of scrum-half, scored four tries in a brilliant display in the 56-16 win over Keighley, to which Casey added ten goals from eleven attempts. Adam Hughes scored three tries in the 28-12 win over Rochdale, helping to confirm Kelly's boast that this Trinity side was capable of scoring tries from a variety of positions, which had not always been true in the recent past.

With a 15-2 win at Whitehaven, the penultimate game of the season, Trinity wrapped up the first division title. Before the game they held a four-point lead over second-placed Hull KR, who lost at Hunslet by virtue of ex-Wakefield man Richard Goddard's late drop goal. Trinity's fifth consecutive win was inspired by Kenworthy's fifty-metre try, and Casey's try under the posts, three goals and a drop goal. It gave them their only divisional title since the Yorkshire League of 1966, but all was still to play for as far as promotion to Super League was concerned. Trinity received the League Leaders trophy before an anti-climactic final match at home to Dewsbury, who showed greater enthusiasm and won 16-12.

Having beaten Hull KR 19-16 in the qualifying semi-final, Trinity met Featherstone in the Grand Final at the McAlpine Stadium, Huddersfield. Such was the nature of the play-offs that Rovers, who had finished fourth in the table, had also triumphed over Hull KR, winning by the handsome score of 54-6 in the final eliminator at Craven Park.

Wakefield chairman Ted Richardson was perhaps over-egging it in saying that never before in the history of modern rugby league had so much hinged on one game. But certainly the outcome of the clash between two sides who, under the original Super League proposals, would have merged, sent the finalists on very different paths well into the next century.

Watched by a crowd of 8,224 and seen live on Sky television, the First Division Grand Final was an exciting match played at a fierce pace, set initially by Trinity. Only two minutes into the game, hooker Roy Southernwood

Australian stand-off Garen Casey lands the touchline conversion which decided the first-ever First Division Grand Final. Trinity beat Featherstone 24-22 and earned a place in Super League in 1999.

The Trinity players celebrate their First Division Grand Final win over Featherstone at McAlpine Stadium, Huddersfield, on 26 September 1998

burrowed over from acting half back before captain for the day Matt Fuller put winger Josh Bostock over at the corner, Garen Casey failing with both conversion attempts. Featherstone hit back with a converted try but Ian Hughes's lobbed pass created the chance for Bostock to touch down in the same spot to give Trinity a 12-6 half-time lead. Early in the second half, a fired-up Featherstone hit back and went 18-12 ahead with two converted tries, but in this tense contest Trinity drew level when Sonny Whakarau and Roger Kenworthy combined to send Casey through a gap for a try which the stand-off converted. Drop-outs at both ends were a sign of the mounting pressure and with just ten minutes remaining Featherstone regained the lead. At 22-18 they appeared to have done enough to take the trophy and earn a possible place in Super League. That confidence was justified when sub Asa Amone released Karl Pratt, who sprinted along the touchline for what looked like the 73rd minute match-winner, only for referee Nick Oddy to call the winger back for Amone's knock-on – a huge psychological blow to Featherstone and the late turning-point of the game. Trinity swept upfield, and McDonald off-loaded to Stephenson, who put the ball down over the line to level the scores at 22-all. All depended on the touchline conversion attempted by Casey, who had missed three earlier efforts. The Aussie stand-off made no mistake this time, sending the ball between the posts for a 24-22 victory in the first-ever First Division Grand Final as Super League beckoned.

The season was not quite over. A new competition, the Treize Tournoi, contested by French and English first and second division clubs, took place over four weeks in October. Trinity, without three of their Aussies and drained after the play-offs, lost 34-12 at Villeneuve, the French champions, for whom Freddy Banquet kicked five goals. In the next match, at Belle Vue, they narrowly beat Limoux 38-36. Bostock touched down three times but was outscored by Limoux centre Lawrence Raleigh, who claimed four. After beating Limoux on their own ground by 24-10, Trinity lost 25-22 at Belle Vue to Villeneuve, who beat second division champions Lancashire Lynx in Toulouse to win the competition.

Trinity had quickly put together their dossier of application to Super League. Their initial bid was knocked back for further clarification in five out of six areas before a re-submitted application was finally accepted. The club had now provided the information necessary to satisfy the majority of requirements, reported the independent franchise panel. So began the work of preparing the club's entry to the top tier. For one thing, ground work needed to be done at Belle Vue, though Richardson stated that the club hoped to move to the proposed new Queen's Drive site in time for the start of the millennium.

Critics were silenced and Trinity prepared for Super League IV, a rather pompous renaming of rugby league history which had echoes of the French Revolution. But Trinity got a shock when it transpired that, even after getting the go-ahead from the franchise panel, they would not be given the same share of central hand-outs as other clubs and would receive nothing at all in their second year, should they stay up. 'We gained promotion firmly believing that we'd get the same as the other Super League clubs,' said Richardson. The club was left in the tricky position of needing quickly to put together a squad capable of competing at the higher level but not knowing what cash was available.

Twenty-three – Big Ambitions: 1999-2003

For their first season in Super League, it became clear that Trinity would have £225,000 less from the share-out of funding than the other clubs. Whether they were relegated or not at the end of the coming 1999 season, they would receive no funding from Rupert Murdoch's News Corporation at all. Ted Richardson said that the board of directors had invested nearly £750,000 to meet Super League criteria and would need to find more money yet. 'I think it is an understatement to say that we have our backs to the wall,' he stated.

Despite the constraints, Trinity set about building their Super League squad and signed Aussie half back Glen Tomlinson, who had previously been at Batley, Bradford and Hull, loose forward Willie Poching, ex-St George and Hunter Mariners and a Samoan international who had also played a couple of games with Hunslet the season before; stand-off Shane Kenward from St George and prop Frank Watene from Auckland Warriors reserve grade. Queensland State of Origin winger Adrian Brunker was also recruited, Gary Price returned to the club from Featherstone, for whom he had played against Trinity in the Grand Final, and Ian Talbot, Wigan and Great Britain Academy hooker, arrived. But there was to be no return for Nigel Wright, who, after being released by Wigan, signed for Huddersfield. In a second flurry of signings, Vince Fawcett joined from Warrington, utility back Lynton Stott and winger Neil Law from Sheffield, and forward Paul Jackson from Huddersfield.

Young half back Paul Handforth, son of ex-Trinity hooker Tony, signed professional forms, before the biggest pre-season signing was announced. Former New Zealand international Tony Kemp, 31-year old loose forward or stand-off, formerly with Leeds and Castleford, was recruited and was immediately made captain. Centre Adam Hughes, who had been the club's top try-scorer with 20 the previous season, was signed permanently from Leeds.

Former Featherstone and Hull player Jon Sharp arrived as assistant coach to Andy Kelly, and John Harbin was appointed to head youth development and also act as conditioner.

Chief executive Steve Ferres announced that the club would finally receive £575,000 from central funds and although that was almost a third less than other clubs, he boasted that Trinity would be in the top five within three years.

The Challenge Cup came first and Trinity scraped an unimpressive 12-2 win over first division Batley at Belle Vue. In the following round a much stiffer test awaited and though they gave Bradford a good run for their money the more experienced side won by 26-8.

Before Wakefield Trinity's first-ever Super League match came two important announcements: first that the club had managed to secure the biggest-ever shirt sponsorship deal in Super League as Sainsbury's prepared to part with £600,000 over two years, which compensated somewhat for the miserly deal Trinity had got from the RFL. The second was that, following the Super League fashion for nicknames hitherto not associated with the club, Wakefield decided to append, after over 125 years' existence, the rather infantile moniker of Wildcats.

On March 7, 1999 Wakefield Trinity competed in their first Super League match, which took place at Castleford. Trinity's first try in the competition was scored by Willie Poching and though his team registered two tries to one they went down to a last-minute penalty goal, losing 12-10. Watched by a crowd of 4,004, Trinity recorded their first Super League win when they beat Salford 22-10 at Belle Vue in the second match of the season, with David March scoring two tries. In the same week, second row forward Jamie Field was signed from Leeds.

Victories proved scarce. Trinity's first visit to new club Gateshead brought only a 24-6 defeat on Good Friday before Wigan delivered a 52-22 lesson at Belle Vue on Easter Monday. They came good in the home match against

London Broncos, when Adam Hughes scored three first-half tries and kicked six goals in a 24-point haul as part of Trinity's 40-8 triumph over the Wembley finalists.

As they hovered just above the bottom three teams, Trinity learned that their fellow Super League clubs were not in favour of abandoning relegation, so that one club, other than Gateshead who were protected from the drop, would go down, provided the top first division club fulfilled the criteria to be promoted.

It had been tough going so far, but in their first Sky-televised 'home' game, switched to Barnsley FC, which was considered more suitable for the cameras, Trinity created a sensation. Without Kemp and Poching, they achieved what Sheffield coach and Sky pundit John Kear called 'the result of Super League so far', by defeating St Helens, who had not lost a match since the start of the season. Clearly the underdogs, Trinity had been given 24 points on the coupon, but in the end, as St Helens coach Ellery Hanley admitted, they 'out-enthused' the leaders in an exhilarating game played in an electric atmosphere. When Saints scored first through Keiron Cunningham in only the sixth minute, few would have guessed what was to follow. Centre Adrian Brunker, Neil Law and Paul March, the latter audaciously stealing the ball from Chris Joynt, scored first-half tries and Adam Hughes kicked four goals to put Trinity 20-6 ahead. But that incredible start was soon eclipsed as Saints pulled back to 20-18 and then overtook Trinity early in the second half when Sean Long touched down. What had promised so much seemed to have been dashed away but a Hughes penalty put Trinity level at 22-all. Paul Newlove and Joynt both went close but the Trinity defence held firm. Tommy Martyn tried and failed with a drop-goal attempt. Newlove was again heading for the line but Lynton Stott rescued the situation. Once more the saviour, Stott drifted infield and produced what he had practised in training – a successful drop goal from 25 metres as the clock ticked down. Martyn had one last desperate attempt to kick a penalty from inside his own half but the ball drifted wide and Trinity, to the acclaim of ecstatic fans, had done what many had thought impossible.

That victory set others in train. Away wins at Huddersfield and Warrington were followed by an 11-10 triumph over Castleford to which David March contributed two first-half tries and Tony Kemp the winning 76th minute drop goal. In midweek the fifth win in a row came at Halifax by 36-16 and Trinity moved up to eighth in the fourteen-team table.

The winning streak was ended at Salford, where, playing their third match in a week, Trinity lost 28-14. At least they had the consolation of knowing that the Rugby League Council had rubber-stamped funding to the tune of £550,000 before they became eligible to draw on Super League money in 2001. The amount agreed was made up of £300,000 for finishing as first division champions the season before, with £250,000 to come if they avoided relegation.

Another key recruit from the Academy joined when 17-year old former Lock Lane centre or second row Gareth Ellis signed. But a string of defeats put a different aspect on the season. After the seventh loss in a row – by 24-6 at home to Sheffield – a damning verdict appeared in the *Wakefield Express*: 'Gone is the passion and positive aggression. Gone is the kicking game. Gone is the ball retention. Gone is the wonderful passing that tore so many sides apart during that blissful five-match winning sequence.' Worse was to come when bottom club Hull completed the double by winning 23-18, condemning their visitors to an eighth successive defeat. The losing run was brought to an end with a 26-20 home win over Halifax, in which the redoubtable Andy Fisher touched down twice before breaking an arm.

After the stunning victory over St Helens earlier in the season, Trinity went some way towards recording what would have been an astonishing double. Saints, second to Bradford in the table, were leading Trinity 28-4 after 33 minutes but were only 34-32 ahead going into the last quarter. Wakefield had scored five tries in fifteen minutes after half-time as McDonald, Songoro, Kemp, Poching and Kenward all found their way to the line before Saints pulled away to earn a face-saving 42-34 victory. Generously, coach Ellery Hanley went so far as to say he thought

Wakefield deserved to win. Trinity boss Andy Kelly praised Tony Kemp, saying that the loose forward had had a superb game but bemoaned the fact that he had not been match fit for much of the season, owing to injury and suspension.

Trinity's 36-10 defeat of Salford at Belle Vue enabled them to realise their pre-season target of ten wins, but having achieved that goal they fell to their heaviest defeat of the season, when they suffered their third loss against newcomers Gateshead, where, with several first-teamers missing, they were hammered 66-6. In a match which also saw Ben Westwood make his debut off the bench, Andy Kelly witnessed his men crash to the biggest defeat of his tenure, which had started over two years earlier. Apologising to fans he said he was 'absolutely ashamed' of the performance. But rival coach Shaun McRae mitigated the disaster when he said, 'Wakefield were unlucky to catch us on a day when we were red hot.' Trinity would quickly discover that, in Super League, what would once have been regarded as huge scores were relatively common, even between teams of similar competence.

In the final match of the season, Trinity took another drubbing when Wigan won 60-24 at Belle Vue. Wakefield had led 24-22 at half-time but when Wigan cranked up the pressure they collapsed to concede 38 second-half points. Trinity finished eleventh out of the fourteen Super League clubs after putting together a competitive squad with relatively little money. Willie Poching had an outstanding season, taking three player of the year awards at the club, but was pushed hard by second rowers Gary Price and Andy Fisher.

After playing an important role in the club's first season back among the elite, chief executive Steve Ferres decided to step down. He thanked the fans, saying: 'Wakefield Trinity must have the best away support in rugby league. The home support is not always what it should be, but away from home it's something very special.'

Following Ferres's departure, Academy coach and development manager John Harbin was made general manager and former Wakefield Council leader John Pearman became the new chief executive. Pearman, brother of former Trinity secretary Alan, had left the Council in the early nineties to 'pursue his own business interests' and had been apparently working with Richardson and Eccles on their ventures.

A host of player signings followed. Tongan forward Martin Masella from Leeds, centre Tony Tatupu from Auckland Warriors and Castleford stand-off or centre Francis Maloney were among the first wave. Winger Bright Sodje, who had been at Belle Vue five years earlier, signed from Sheffield, whose on-loan winger Neil Law became a permanent Wakefield player. Bradford loose forward Steve McNamara came on a three-year contract; hooker Ryan Hudson, a local amateur product, signed from Huddersfield; and full back Steve Prescott, formerly with St Helens, arrived from Hull.

The biggest attempted coup was to bring New Zealand rugby union winger Jonah Lomu to Belle Vue. The All Black was reputedly offered a £1 million two-year contract. Said Pearman: 'We believe we can match any offers that may be on the table and present this highly gifted and talented individual with the opportunity and incentive to build a new career in rugby league in the company of the league's most ambitious club.' But Lomu turned the offer down, saying that he did not wish to switch to rugby league. Pearman denied that the attempted signing had been a publicity stunt.

The signings made so far had reportedly cost more than £1 million and in another seven-figure deal the board drew up plans for improvements at Belle Vue involving the erection of a stand at the Agbrigg Road end which would include corporate hospitality as well as offices.

As Shane Kenward and Adrian Brunker were released, full back Martyn Holland, who had missed all the previous season after knee surgery, re-signed. Winger Paul Sampson, nephew of ex-Trinity players Malcolm and Dave Sampson, and a former English Schools 100-metre champion, signed from Wasps rugby union club.

At the AGM, debts of just over £1 million up to the end of 1998 were revealed. The same amount was to be spent on improving facilities at Belle Vue, since the public inquiry into the Queen's Drive proposal had delayed progress on the new stadium. In response to repeated questions about where all the money was coming from to fund both the stadium improvements and the plethora of new players, no specific answer was given.

In January former Great Britain international half back Bobbie Goulding, released by Huddersfield, became Trinity's tenth major signing in the close season. He was offered a 12-month contract to play for his sixth club.

As the portentous year 2000 began, the Challenge Cup provided the first matches, just as in previous Super League seasons. Trinity entered the competition at the fourth round stage, when they travelled to Leigh of the Northern Ford Premiership, formerly the first division. With Steve McNamara kicking eight goals from eight attempts and Adam Hughes scoring two tries off the bench, Trinity went through by 40-28. It was a different story in the fifth round as Trinity met Bradford at Belle Vue and were humiliated by 46-0. Kelly criticised his team's lack of application. They compensated by winning 22-18 at Headingley in the first league match of Super League V, as it was referred to. Trinity owed the win to a final effort by McNamara, who touched down from a miscued Francis Maloney drop-goal attempt.

Trinity might have splashed out on new signings, but the season was less than two months old when certain players discovered that cheques they had been handed bounced. The club apologised, saying that cash flow problems had arisen when money which had been promised had not yet been received.

The 14-10 home defeat to London Broncos was followed by a reshuffle among the coaching staff. Tony Kemp, who was unlikely to figure in many more matches as a player, was made assistant coach and John Harbin was given the task of tightening up on discipline and training.

There was no immediate sign of improvement. Trinity embarked on a seven-match losing run, in the middle of which they went down by 34-6 at home to Hull with a display described as 'pitiful'. 'One struggles to come up with a value-for-money performance from any of the home games played this season,' said the *Wakefield Express*. Harbin said he was appalled by the manner of the defeat and reported what one supporter had said to him after the 'pathetic' display. 'He told me he plays for an amateur side for nothing. In fact he pays subs for the privilege. Then he told me that if he played like our players played on Sunday he'd be dropped. It's a fair point.'

Off the field, Trinity were fined £5,000 by Super League for making a headline-grabbing but illegal approach to Wigan's Jason Robinson. Prospects of a new stadium at Queen's Drive were fading, as Trinity needed to raise £6-7 million as their share of the funding, which was an impossible target unless the Council stepped in. Instead, attentions were turned to a site near Stanley close by the M62. Ted Richardson would neither confirm or deny that he owned the land.

Trinity suffered their fifth consecutive defeat when they lost 36-10 at Halifax. Without Goulding and Tatupu again, as well as McNamara, the team was given a lead by Poching and Stephenson but too many players were found inadequate. 'I for one am totally committed and honest about wanting what's best for Wakefield Trinity,' said Andy Kelly. 'Unfortunately there are a lot of people at the club who don't feel the same way.' But within days Kelly, who had led Trinity to promotion in his first full season and to survival in the club's first Super League season, and his assistant Jon Sharp – who was to join Batley - were on their way out of the club. Tony Kemp stepped up as head coach until the end of the season.

Kemp's first match in charge, against his former club Leeds, ended in a 30-24 loss, although his side rallied from 26-6 down and could have drawn the game if Jamie Field's last-minute effort had not been ruled out.

As far as anyone outside the boardroom could tell, former Wakefield Council leader John Pearman, the Trinity chief executive, was now the majority shareholder in the club, after having reportedly paid £300,000 for approximately 75 per cent of the shares, 'following a revaluation with a new company called Wakefield Sporting Ltd.' Chairman Ted Richardson denied that he had sold his shares to Pearman and was said to retain a 20 per cent stake. It was also reported that contracts had been drawn up for the sale of the Belle Vue ground to the value of £1.2 million.

Pearman, who had run a business consultancy since stepping down as Council leader in 1992, was to provide land to the value of £1.6 million, situated between Stanley and Whitwood, for the benefit of the club. The land, he said, would produce income of £1.9 million (also reported as £1.3 million) over three years. He said: 'Wakefield Trinity is my chosen charity and I believe we can grow and develop opportunities we have never had before. I want Trinity to be the best in the country.' The land apparently owned by Pearman consisted of eight acres near the M62, for which planning permission for commercial use had been given. Pearman had also been involved in rescuing Trinity in the mid-1980s, when the Council bought the Belle Vue ground, which was later allowed to be bought back by the club.

A loss of £61,000 was announced for the year ending 1999. Though turnover had increased by £700,000, players' wages had almost doubled from £510,000 to £977,000, which drew the following comment from Pearman. 'We currently have a £1 million salary bill for players – double what it was 18 months ago and yet we are not achieving the level of success that is needed ... We have made mistakes. We thought that buying players would transform our position overnight.' Kemp commented, referring to the need for another centre, 'We don't need big signings. We need young players with the heart and courage to give a full 80 minutes.'

Back on the field of play, where matters at least seemed more straightforward, Trinity gave an improved display in losing 30-22 at home to St Helens. Kemp's first win in charge came at Warrington with a 32-16 triumph to which Goulding, back after a six-week absence, contributed two tries, five goals and two drop goals. Then it was back to square one. The merged club, Huddersfield-Sheffield, ended their own ten-match losing streak with a 27-20 victory at Belle Vue as Trinity gave a performance described as 'unacceptable' by a 'devastated' Kemp.

But with a 36-10 victory over Salford, Trinity registered their first home win for over two months. A 27-22 win at London Broncos was followed by a comparatively acceptable 30-20 home defeat by Bradford, in which Paul Sampson scored a fine 70 metre try to add to the two he had scored against London. Kemp said the team spirit was excellent. 'I think the penny has finally dropped and there have been big changes in relation to attitude,' he said.

But Kemp's upbeat comments were almost immediately called into question by a 56-6 hammering at Hull, where the home side had lost four of their last five games. A defeat by the same score at the hands of second-placed Wigan gave no reason for confidence, either. Recently displaced coach Andy Kelly was quoted as saying, 'The club has lost credibility and hard work has been destroyed. I still have a tremendous affinity for Wakefield ... I certainly don't get any pleasure from seeing what is going on there.'

Kemp, who was eventually to become assistant coach at New Zealand Warriors, made his mind up to return home at the end of the season in the absence of any firm offer from the club.

In mid-August it was revealed that chief executive Pearman 'had been forced to stand down after allegedly failing to bring much-needed investment to the club, now £1.5 million in debt.' Richardson had reportedly delivered an ultimatum to either come up with the money or leave. A meeting with Pearman, his solicitor and accountant, and Richardson and new chief executive Stuart Farrar had been called off because Pearman was in hospital in Amsterdam, where he had been staying. Meanwhile the company who built the hospitality stand at the Agbrigg end had issued a writ for £850,000.

Despite the unsettled background, and to everyone's surprise, Trinity managed to bring off a 32-16 win over St Helens - only their third home win of the season. Ten changes had been made from the Wigan game and the refreshing attitude was typified by the energy and fervour of the March twins and Martyn Holland, in his first Super League appearance of the season. 'Enthusiasm won us the game,' said Kemp. It was followed up by a 22-0 defeat of London Broncos, albeit in front of just 2,370 supporters – the lowest attendance of the season. Willie Poching and Tony Tatupu were selected for the Samoan World Cup squad – the first time any Wakefield Trinity player had had that distinction.

After Trinity had lost for the third time in the season to bottom club Huddersfield-Sheffield, Kemp said that

Samoan international loose forward Willie Poching was one of Trinity's first signings as they entered Super League in 1999

preparation during the week had been hindered by the uncertain situation regarding players' pay. 'It's a day-to-day thing at the moment for players,' he said. 'We have two weeks to get through and then we can walk off and say we managed to keep our heads together and performed creditably on and off the pitch.'

The club issued a statement saying: 'We have announced proposals for the lodging of a creditors' voluntary arrangement in the light of the continuing failure of ex-chief executive John Pearman to fulfil promises to provide substantial financial support and valuable land assets for use by the club. Club officials are working around the clock with their professional advisors, in liaison with the Super League and Rugby Football League authorities to map out a future for the club.' Chairman Richardson said he believed that, with the club having around £1.5 million debt needing to be cleared, a CVA was the best way to ensure that it could continue. They had taken out a bank loan to pay players' wages. Richardson insisted that, before entering into any agreement with Pearman, the board had spoken to Pearman's accountant and solicitors and had been assured that what was promised could be delivered.

The players, not knowing quite what the future held, began to examine their options. McNamara, Sodje, Tatupu and Tomlinson were all released. Maloney had agreed to go to Salford and Prescott to return to Hull, while Sampson headed back to rugby union. The contracts of all players over the age of 24 were cancelled. Wigan signed Francis Stephenson, one of the club's brightest prospects, though he did not want to leave. Andy Fisher, coming to the end of his playing career, signed for Dewsbury and Adam Hughes for Halifax. Masella and Jowitt also left.

Two matches remained to be played. Fans could be forgiven for expecting a whitewash but on the contrary Trinity battled hard before losing 26-18 at home to Warrington after being 20-6 down at half-time. Willie Poching led the fightback, 'at the hub of everything with a magnificent skipper's display' and scored a key try when going over from close range, shaking off the attempted tackles of three defenders. Poching was one of those who had decided to go ahead and play after being offered only match payments. 'In the end I decided that I had enjoyed my time here and I thought I owed the club something,' he said.

Pearman denied the allegations made against him. He told the *Wakefield Express* that he rebutted the 'outrageous and unworthy' allegations and had consulted his solicitor. He insisted on his allegiance to the club and recalled that, as leader of the Council, he met a delegation from the club in November 1985 after a winding-up petition had been made and 'authorised' the Council to buy Belle Vue from the club to enable it to pay debts and to survive. He said: 'I cannot recognise the same person who took such risks to help the club with the criticisms that have been heaped on me in the past few weeks.' Believing that he had been made a scapegoat, he added: 'I cannot pretend that some of the events of the past few weeks are other than testimony to a certain naivety and foolishness on my part. That is very different, however, from the impression the club seeks to project of my role in all these events.'

To bring a sense of realism back to the club, at least in terms of player transactions, Steve Ferres was brought back as recruitment director. He said that he would not overspend and wanted to build a team around Willie Poching. 'There won't be any superstars but there will be thirteen blokes who will wear their hearts on their sleeves for Wakefield Trinity,' he said. John Harbin took over as caretaker coach.

In the last match of a season many were glad to see the back of, Trinity again played with more like their old passion at fifth-placed Castleford despite losing 20-8. All seventeen of the squad that day were British, including British passport-holder Frank Watene. Among the young players of the future who made up this side of an average age of 23 were Gareth Ellis, Ben Westwood, Ryan Hudson, Keith Mason, Paul Jackson and David and Paul March. Trinity ended the season tenth out of the twelve clubs.

But there was a question of whether Wakefield would be allowed to remain in Super League, given the financial problems and indebtedness to players and other staff. The Super League clubs voted unanimously that Wakefield Trinity be allowed to remain in Super League if the CVA was accepted, but on stringent terms. They insisted on two new directors being appointed, one of whom should be a suitably qualified finance director. Super League chairman Chris Caisley said: 'It is generally the case that those clubs who find themselves in such dire circumstances are the clubs who make poor decisions and the stringent conditions which we have imposed are designed to try to ensure … that the Wakefield club does not make the same mistakes in the future.'

The CVA was accepted by creditors and the club could breathe again. Willie Poching and Gary Price were the first to re-sign and Brad Davis, aged 32, was lined up to make a return to Belle Vue from Castleford. Fijian winger Waisale Sovatabua was signed from Huddersfield-Sheffield.

John Harbin, the English-born Australian who had joined the club in a development role, was given the coaching job on a permanent basis, with Gary Price his assistant and John Thompson and Mick Hughes in charge of the A team and Academy as before. Steve Ferres stepped up the signings: Aussie Justin Brooker arrived from Bradford and New Zealander Julian O'Neill from St Helens. Stand-off Martin Pearson, originally with Featherstone, then Sheffield and Halifax, before playing rugby union in France, was brought in and Tony Tatupu re-signed. Back-rower Ben Rauter was recruited from North Queensland Cowboys and Dane Dorahy, son of ex-Hull KR stand-off and Wigan coach John, came back to the club after his previous stint was cut short by injury. Keighley centre Richard Smith was signed on loan for the season.

Harbin said that he was not prepared to tolerate anyone who was likely to disrupt team spirit. 'The problem for Andy Kelly last year was that he had six or seven wanting to rock the boat. The squad won't be big enough for that to happen this time around and that's why it is being chosen so precisely.' Willie Poching, who led Samoa in the World Cup in the autumn, was made team captain.

The club was once again desperate for money and the various schemes advertised had brought in just £22,000 when £350,000 was needed to pay for the hospitality stand. One speaker at a poorly-attended supporters' meeting rightly referred to 'an element of disillusionment over the last few years.' In fact many would have grounds for thinking that the year 2000, with the sorry entanglement behind the scenes, was the club's worst ever in terms of public perception.

The 2001 season began with a potentially tricky fourth-round Challenge Cup tie at Northern Ford Premiership club Workington, but in reality there was not a hint of an upset as Trinity ran in ten tries in their 56-6 win. They also faced NFP opposition in the fifth round when they travelled to Oldham, where they won 26-6, with Sovatabua scoring two tries, as at Workington. But relative to other Super League teams the Trinity squad was a small one and a young one. Harbin made an important comparison between the Wakefield side of the previous season and the present one. 'Last year's players with a slight injury would declare themselves unfit for a month. This year players are masking injury to play. It speaks volumes for the spirit at the club.'

Trinity came up against Bradford in the Challenge Cup for the third year in a row. In the previous two years they had lost in the fourth round, and in the quarter-final of 2001 they did not fare any better, losing 38-0 to the Challenge Cup-holders at Belle Vue.

Keen to maintain a positive outlook, John Harbin had something to say about the league defeat at Headingley, where the hosts were flattered by the 42-14 score. 'Leeds had their signings from Canberra and Brisbane,' he said, 'and we had guys from Methley Monarchs, Normanton Knights, Keighley Albion and Dewsbury Moor – and we were level with them at half-time. That says a lot about the amateur game in this country.'

Trinity achieved their first league victory of the 2001 season in their third game when they defeated Halifax 30-14 at Belle Vue, with Martin Pearson kicking seven goals against his former club. The defeat caused Halifax coach Gary Mercer to resign two days later, saying that if his team had had Wakefield's 'passion and enthusiasm' they could have won.

On the Thursday evening before Easter, Trinity overcame a 10-0 deficit to beat Bradford 16-12. It was a stunning performance in which Neil Law, Trinity's top-scorer in the previous two seasons, crossed for two tries before half back David March came off the bench and went over from dummy-half with his first touch to score the decider. On Easter Monday two more league points accrued with a 24-16 win at Huddersfield.

Three successive defeats saw Trinity go next to bottom, where they would stay a long time against another background of controversy. A prospect of a league points deduction and fine loomed as the club was alleged by Super League to be in breach of salary cap rules during the previous calamitous season of 2000. After the 36-26 loss at St Helens, Harbin commented: 'We get on with business to show other people they'd better start getting their act together, just like we are on the field.' Without specifically mentioning the possibility of a points deduction, he went on, in sabre-rattling mode: 'They can take away our status in Super League, they can do what the hell they like – but they can't take away our spirit. I've never known anything like it in all my 35 years of being connected with sporting teams and there's been some world champion athletes among them.'

Comments like those fuelled the widespread perception among Trinity fans that 'they don't want us in Super League', which first came about, justifiably, when other clubs refused promoted club Trinity the same share of Sky money as the rest. On the other hand, it was true that both the state of the Belle Vue ground and the mismanagement which had gone on during the previous season had given Super League serious grounds for complaint.

This second crisis – or rather the second phase of the same one – seemed to be having its effect on the players, in spite of Harbin's brave face. A 62-10 drubbing at Bradford was followed by a 38-22 loss at Belle Vue to bottom club Huddersfield, whose first win of the entire season it was, coming after seventeen games. Super League announced that, according to their figures, Trinity's spending on players was 74 per cent as opposed to the allowed limit of 50 per cent. The club insisted that the true figure was 49 per cent because money owed to players would never be paid under the terms of the CVA. As it stood, Trinity risked losing six league points, which would put them into a neck and neck race for survival with Huddersfield.

The defeats continued. A narrow 19-18 loss at the hands of Warrington in an ill-tempered game at Belle Vue was played amidst a deduction of four league points and a £30,000 fine, both suspended as Trinity appealed against the ruling.

The eleventh consecutive defeat - by 26-16 at Salford - came as Ted Richardson said that he wanted to step down as chairman after six years in charge. Twelve losses in a row, the most recent suffered at London Broncos, who won 44-18, was believed to be the worst in Trinity's history, easily beating the nine consecutive league and cup defeats in 1983-84, and clearly their worst in Super League. But Harbin reiterated his confidence in his players and their ability to avoid relegation. The outcome of the enquiry into Trinity's alleged salary cap breach was that the club would be docked two league points, which put bottom club Huddersfield within one league point of Trinity. The three month- long losing run finally came to an end on August 19 with a 23-20 home win over Salford.

In the run-in to the end of the season, and with Trinity's future in Super League far from clear, John Harbin pointed out that the club had nevertheless created one of the best development set-ups in the game. The Alliance team had reached the play-offs for the second year in a row, following on from the Academy's Grand Final appearance the year before. 'We have established a real solid structure with a feeder chain to the first team,' said Harbin.

Trinity had three games left to ensure their survival. They did themselves a big favour by winning 23-10 at Halifax against a side two places above them in the table. Leading 16-2 at half-time they absorbed all the pressure Halifax could exert and picked up two precious points. Martin Pearson kicked five goals and a drop goal in a fine display against his former club.

That victory meant that Trinity needed just one point from their home match against their relegation rivals. But Huddersfield, one point below Trinity, had gained a reputation as Wakefield's bogey team and so it proved. In the dogfight at Belle Vue, Trinity went ahead for the first time when, after an hour's play, Ryan Hudson put a drop goal over. But Huddersfield lost no time in regaining the lead and took the score to 21-13. David March scored a late try for Trinity but Huddersfield defied the odds to win 21-19 and take the relegation battle to the final day of the Super League season.

For Trinity everything hinged on the match at Salford. It did not help that, off the field, all was far from calm. Chief executive Tony Docherty, who had joined the club only four months earlier as commercial director, resigned and Ted Richardson, who said that he would stand down as chairman, announced that he was to give his majority share-holding to the club in the form of a trust.

On the field, however, there could be no dithering. Trinity had to win against a Salford side which was one place above them in the table. Salford were safe from relegation and had nothing to play for, though they had no intention of giving their opponents an easy ride. The Reds had lost their previous five matches but played as they had not played for weeks. As the *Wakefield Express* said, fans would probably never see a match like it again. Referee Russell Smith sent four off and sin-binned two in a match in which tempers ran high. First to go were Martin Pearson and Malcolm Alker, who were yellow-carded for fighting in the first half. After 50 minutes' play, Salford centre Stuart Littler was dismissed for tripping – though later found not guilty. Five minutes later, ex-Wakefield half back Bobbie Goulding was shown the yellow card for deliberate offside but as he was leaving the field became involved in fighting with Trinity centre Justin Brooker and both were red-carded. Salford's Graham Holroyd was later sent off, also for alleged tripping, and Salford ended with ten men and Wakefield twelve.

As the game unfolded, Pearson had landed two penalties to give Trinity an early lead. But Salford's Aussie winger Michael Hancock went over for a converted try, and though Gareth Ellis hit back for Trinity, the home side took a grip on the game. The Reds added a penalty and two tries, the second scored by ex-Trinity centre Francis Maloney to take a ten-point lead with Trinity back-pedalling. But Willie Poching went over for a crucial try just before half-time, spotting a gap and wrong-footing Goulding. Davis converted and Trinity were back in contention at 18-14. After the break however, Littler intercepted and went 90 metres for a try converted by Holroyd and Trinity looked doomed again. They battled on and were rewarded when Neil Law twice showed his finishing power, Pearson converting both tries for a two-point lead, to which he then added a penalty goal. Salford missed a golden opportunity to draw level but March made no mistake when he skipped over to make certain of the 32-24 victory by which, since Huddersfield also won, Trinity stayed in Super League.

Or had they? Rumours were rife that Super League was about to be reduced to ten teams, to which Harbin alluded after the thrilling win. 'People underestimate us and think we're propping up the table,' he said. 'The big clubs wouldn't survive without us. They would play four or five games against each other and people would be bored and wouldn't watch it. You wouldn't get better entertainment than that today. Nobody left, did they?'

Centre Justin Brooker, disappointed to have been sent off in his last game in Trinity colours before returning to Sydney, summed up the team spirit that had seen the team through. 'I don't think I will ever play with a better bunch of blokes than the ones at Wakefield,' he said.

With various uncertainties in the air, Trinity needed to get down to the business of offering new contracts for the next season. But they could not do that and, crucially, could not even agree new terms with their coach until a new executive board was in place. Keith Mason, Trinity's 19-year old prop, went off to Melbourne Storm and, equally galling to fans, their captain and hero Willie Poching, like many before him, was snared by Leeds. It was decided, surprisingly in view of their future value to the club, not to offer contracts to Paul March and Danny Brough.

Second rower Gareth Ellis became Trinity's captain in the 2003 season, when he was also selected for Great Britain. He went on to win honours with Leeds before joining Wests Tigers in Australia

At board level, Ted Richardson repeated his wish to vacate his position as chairman. But a group which was keen to take control wanted clarification of Richardson's position as well as further financial information, while Richardson, the majority shareholder, wanted guarantees from the consortium as to how they would be able to satisfy the banks and Super League. 'I feel I have always acted with the club's best interest at heart,' wrote Richardson. 'I did not want to be the guarantor to Super League but no one else came forward and without it in place we would be in the first division. I do want to step aside. I don't think it can be made any clearer. Take on the guarantee with SLE, convince the bank you are worthy of their support and … I will be delighted to resign knowing people are working for the good of the club.'

In turn, Super League Europe wrote to the Trinity board to say that the club would be readmitted in 2002 though they had failed the Points Assessment programme and therefore forfeited membership. Stringent conditions were again attached to Trinity's re-entry. Apart from Richardson's personal guarantee, the club would have to present a new business plan and would have to achieve a 50 per cent pass mark in the Points Assessment process or it would be relegated at the end of the 2002 season. The hospitality stand, which had been the cause of wrangling between the club and the construction company, would have to be retained or replaced by a similar structure. SLE would also reserve the right to send an observer to board meetings.

To the disappointment of players and fans, John Harbin announced from Australia that he would not be returning to the club, saying that he had not been offered a contract and needed to secure his future. Harbin said that he was disappointed that, after all the team spirit that had been built up and the euphoria of the Salford game, Keith Mason, captain Willie Poching and Supporters' Player of the Year Ryan Hudson were all leaving. 'I found it very difficult to come to grips with all that has happened in the space of time it took to fly to Australia from England,' he said. Mason and Hudson, along with Ben Westwood, were also set to tour South Africa with Great Britain U21s.

Peter Fox, who had left the club 25 years earlier and who had not coached since leaving Bradford in 1995, was appointed as director of rugby. Peter Roe, who had led Halifax to promotion a decade earlier and most recently had coached Featherstone, was appointed to succeed Harbin. The former Trinity coach, meanwhile, took up Dewsbury's offer to become their chief executive and mentor to their new player-coach Andy Fisher, who was joined by numerous other ex-Wakefield players, including future Trinity chief executive James Elston.

Going back to a previous boardroom crisis, it was decided to take no further action against former chief executive John Pearman. The insolvency company dealing with Trinity's CVA said that there was 'no prospect of a return from Mr Pearman'. Diane Rogerson, the daughter of Ted Richardson, became the new chief executive.

Key signings for the coming 2002 season included back-row forward Ian Knott from Warrington, ex-GB prop Paul Broadbent from Hull, who was also added to the coaching team, alongside Brad Davis and Shane McNally, a member of the Queensland team which toured Great Britain in 1983. Australian forward Troy Slattery, who had played for Huddersfield three seasons earlier, and half back Nathan Wood from New Zealand Warriors were recruited. Aussie centre Kris Tassell arrived via Salford and forward David Wrench was signed from Leeds, initially on trial. Front-rower Julian O'Neill left for Widnes and Gary Price decided to retire at the age of 32.

The hospitality stand at the Agbrigg Road end was finally paid for when Trinity handed over a sum of around £150,000 to the construction company, much less than had originally been required.

In their first match of the 2002 season, Trinity ran in six tries to defeat Sheffield in the fourth round of the Challenge Cup, and in the fifth round were drawn at Widnes, coached by Neil Kelly. Second-rower Ian Knott was already proving his value to the side by scoring the try which sealed the match and converting as Trinity went through by 12-4. But that was as far as they would get. Leeds dished out a 46-10 beating at Headingley in the quarter-final.

Trinity's first league win of the season came in their third game when they beat Salford 32-18 at Belle Vue, with Knott scoring a try and kicking six goals, but in the following match Widnes gained quick revenge for their Cup exit by beating Trinity 43-10 on Good Friday. Ex-Trinity men Adam Hughes, with three tries, and Barry Eaton, who landed eight goals from nine attempts, played a big part in Widnes's victory. From then on, Trinity, pre-season favourites for relegation, would spend the rest of the season in the bottom three.

To boost the depleted squad, loose forward Martin Moana was signed from Doncaster and former Leeds winger Phil Hassan from rugby union. Full back or winger Andrew Frew, Super League's second top try-scorer with Huddersfield the previous season, was brought back from Australia. With the exception of a 30-18 away win at Castleford, where centre Kris Tassell scored three tries, the following twelve games were all lost.

There was, however, some honour in the home 30-14 loss to Challenge Cup winners Wigan. Centre Gareth Ellis scored two tries in six minutes to give Trinity the lead on the hour but then Wigan claimed three tries in the last quarter. 'Wigan have been very complimentary and said we gave them a hell of a game,' said Roe. 'Great plaudits, but once again not the two points we needed.' By contrast the 26-25 home defeat at the hands of sixth-placed London Broncos was a match which, said Roe, was one Wakefield should have won, particularly after establishing a thirteen-point lead. To make matters worse, the squad was weakened when Nathan Wood, who had played so impressively against Warrington, was enticed away to Wilderspool despite Trinity's improved contract offer. Ben

Westwood was targeted by the same club and left soon after. Trinity were paid around £90,000 in compensation.

Wakefield were given a 42-18 drubbing at bottom club Salford, which pitched Peter Roe's side into last place. The coach was so unhappy with his players' performance that he cancelled their day off and brought them in for training at 6.30 on the Monday morning. He reiterated that he personally would not 'walk away'.

But, with just one win from the last twelve games, Roe was dismissed, despite the fact that his predecessor John Harbin had had much the same record the season before. Ten matches remained when assistant coach Shane McNally was handed temporary control of the side.

The former Queensland development officer had immediate success as Trinity drew 22-22 at home to Widnes, their first point from the last seven matches. In his second match in charge, Trinity did even better, winning 31-24 at London Broncos after trailing 18-0 at half-time. Trinity's revival started with an interception try scored over 80 metres by Moana before David March sent man of the match Brad Davis over. Even when London took the lead again, Trinity came back at them, French international Julien Rinaldi pouncing on a Broncos error to go over and Martyn Holland rounding off the victory with a solo effort. Now one point ahead of bottom club Salford, Trinity strengthened their squad – and coaching staff – by signing Leeds centre or loose forward Adrian Vowles, elected Man of Steel three years earlier when with Castleford.

After defeats at the hands of Hull and St Helens, Trinity took a point from another 22-all draw, this time on the ground of relegation rivals Salford. In a see-sawing game, Trinity lost a ten-point lead, which would have repercussions until the end of the season. The one point gained from the draw put Wakefield into third from bottom place, with Warrington and Salford below them, but after four further defeats they slipped right down to twelfth. Not for the first time – nor the last – all hinged on the last game of the season, as Trinity faced Warrington at Belle Vue and Salford clashed with top six hopefuls Castleford at the Willows. Trinity raced to an 18-0 lead after only a quarter of an hour and there was no holding back against a Warrington side who offered little resistance. Davis and Vowles both scored hat-tricks as McNally's men ran up their highest score of the season, winning 50-10. But Trinity fans were in no hurry to leave Belle Vue. They faced an agonising eight-minute wait until the result of the Salford game came through. When the 20-10 result in favour of Cas was finally announced, the Trinity faithful were overcome with a mixture of relief and joy. With the worst defensive record in Super League, Trinity had finished one point above the Reds. 'We want to get away from this end of the table. It's not pleasant,' said McNally.

No sooner had the 2002 season ended than team-building for the 2003 campaign began. Brad Davis, ever popular at the age of 34, was given a new one-year contract. Wakefield-born winger Jon Wells signed from Castleford, as did young French forward Olivier Elima, with hard-working prop Paul Jackson going in the opposite direction.

Trinity delved deep into the Australian market. Prop Dallas Hood had already been signed up, stand-off Ben Jeffries and utility back Matt Seers, a former State of Origin star, both arrived from Wests, while props Clinton O'Brien, an NRL Grand Finalist, and 21 year-old Michael Korkidas were recruited from Newcastle and Sydney City Roosters respectively. Korkidas was to make an immediate impression on the fans in the pre-season friendly win at Featherstone, despite being sin-binned.

Promising 21-year old forward Chris Feather signed for Leeds for around £45,000 and Martin Moana returned for a second spell with Halifax. Kris Tassell, who was due to play for Wales against the Kiwis, alongside ex-Trinity players Keith Mason and Adam Hughes, was released and later signed for Swinton in National League Two, where Peter Roe was now coaching.

As the club aimed to get away from merely ensuring survival and become play-off contenders, centre Richard Newlove, younger brother of Paul, and stand-off Jamie Rooney, whose transfer fee had been whittled down from £40,000 to around £10,000, were both recruited from Featherstone. Trinity's tenth signing was 23-year old Australian utility back Colum Halpenny, who came from Halifax bearing an Irish passport.

Homegrown players were also achieving recognition. Gareth Ellis, a star of the England A tour to Fiji and Tonga, signed a new three-year contract despite attention from St Helens, Leeds, Wigan and Brisbane Broncos. Academy winger Matty Wray had the distinction, alongside Bradford's Normanton-born back-rower Jamie Langley, of helping England Academy inflict a first defeat on the Australian Schoolboys after thirty years, as they won 28-22 at St Helens.

As the 2003 Super League season started in early February with the fourth round Challenge Cup ties, Trinity faced Castleford at Belle Vue in a game that proved a typical derby. Fortune was not on Cas's side. Former Trinity player Ryan Hudson was sent off in the first quarter following a scuffle with Matt Seers, who was only sin-binned. Nevertheless Graham Steadman's men led 18-14 and had a try contentiously disallowed by the video referee. The decisive score came when, with six minutes remaining, Paul Handforth broke clear and handed on to Ben Jeffries, whose inside pass sent Waisale Sovatabua over. Ian Knott converted to give Trinity victory by 20-18.

Two weeks later Trinity lost their opening league match by 28-14 at home to Hull, before meeting Widnes in another home Cup tie. Neil Kelly's men had another former Trinity player to thank as centre Adam Hughes scored two tries and kicked three goals in their 22-12 win.

Despite a now more competitive-looking squad, it took Trinity a while to get off the mark in the league, losing next to Bradford by 22-10 before a 20,000 crowd at Odsal and then by 34-29 at home to Wigan, watched by 4,500. In a thrilling match in which the lead changed hands several times, Trinity were 29-22 ahead at one point. Brad Davis was involved in all three of Trinity's tries in the opening half. The Aussie half back fired out a fine pass to winger Jon Wells, who sold his opposite number a brilliant dummy before going away on the outside to score a wonderful try and then Davis himself went over from Jeffries' inside pass.

Davis and Ellis, both try-scorers, were outstanding in the 20-14 win over Castleford, Trinity's second win over their neighbours in less than two months and their first league victory, which came at the fifth attempt. At Headingley the league leaders and Challenge Cup finalists came under a heavy barrage and only a last-minute drop goal gave the home side victory by 13-12. Jamie Rooney, in his first start for Trinity, landed four goals from four attempts. That performance was the prelude to one of those shocks Trinity always seemed capable of springing, especially against St Helens, who were beaten 16-10 at Knowsley Road. Trinity put up excellent defence against free-scoring Saints, while the forwards, with Korkidas and Hood giving a lead, made the platform for half backs Davis and Rooney to control play and end a four-match losing sequence. Rooney contributed three goals and two drop goals, while Newlove and Sovatabua scored the tries.

The 22-18 home defeat of Halifax gave Trinity back-to-back wins for the first time for over two years but hopes of producing three on the run were dashed by a 36-12 reverse at home to London Broncos. A familiar mid-season slump, resulting in a string of seven defeats, meant that only Halifax, who had had two points docked for a salary cap breach, stood between Wakefield and the foot of the table. On a brighter note, Gareth Ellis featured in the Yorkshire side which beat Lancashire 56-6.

Once again plans for Belle Vue were announced. Instead of a new stadium, this time it was a £400,000 'first-phase redevelopment programme' at Belle Vue, which would become possible mainly through grants, including one from the Football Foundation, since Wakefield & Emley FC were now partners of Trinity. A more ambitious second phase would return the ground to being a four-sided stadium with covered north and west terraces.

The losing streak came to an end with the 30-18 win over doomed Halifax, followed by a 26-all draw at home to London Broncos, in which Jamie Rooney kept Trinity in the game with a try and five goals. Rooney was also in prolific form in the narrow 30-28 defeat at Widnes as Trinity hit back to reduce a 20-point deficit. Playing alongside Brad Davis, back to his best after a lay-off through injury, the stand-off scored three tries and kicked six goals from six attempts.

With four matches remaining, 32-year old Adrian Vowles was released from his contract after struggling with injury. Matt Seers and Waisale Sovatabua were also allowed to leave at the end of the season, while Jon Wells was set to join London Broncos and Brad Davis was bound for Villeneuve. French international centre Sylvain Houlès, with Super League experience at Huddersfield and London, was brought in from Dewsbury and made an immediate impact in the 35-28 win over Hull. It was Trinity's first win over Hull in twelve Super League clashes and their highest score of the season. The victory was set up by a three-try blitz in six minutes of the first half when first Korkidas went over and then debutant Houlès produced the pass which put Dave Wrench over for his first try of the season. Paul Handforth, in outstanding form, made the break for Houlès' spectacular long-range try.

Trinity went on to inflict Halifax's record 26th straight defeat by winning 68-6 at Belle Vue. Rooney scored three tries and, for the second time in three weeks, kicked seven goals, which gave him a personal tally of 26 points. Colum Halpenny, an ever-present in the side, also scored three tries against his former club and Steve Snitch scored an interception try almost from his own line.

At the end of the season, in which Trinity finished eleventh, coach Shane McNally was given a two-year contract and former Castleford, Wigan and Hull scrum-half Tony Smith was appointed assistant coach. The club made important signings in New Zealand international second row David Solomona, from Parramatta, Aussie centre Sid Domic from Warrington and compatriot Jason Demetriou, who had spent the last three years at Widnes, after spells at Rochdale and Lancashire Lynx.

Wingers Semi Tadulala, from Melbourne Storm, and Newcastle's Justin Ryder were also brought in, as well as hooker or half back Albert Talapeau, who had played alongside Solomona for Samoa in the World Cup. Sylvain Houlès, however, had just signed a contract only for it to be revoked when he injured his knee playing for France.

Top points-scorer Jamie Rooney, who had represented England in the European Nations tournament, was given a new three-year contract after revitalising Trinity's attack. Gareth Ellis, made club captain in mid-season, was selected for the full Great Britain team which lost 18-12 to Australia in the third test, becoming the first Wakefield player to represent Great Britain since Michael Jackson eleven years earlier. Hooker David March, who had been tipped for representative honours, exemplified Trinity's best fighting spirit and carried off four awards at the club's end of season ceremony.

Twenty-four – The Great Escape: 2004-07

After a week's training camp in Portugal, Trinity embarked on the 2004 season with renewed confidence and as strong a squad as they had fielded in Super League. Though an opening day defeat by 34-20 came at Warrington's new Halliwell Jones stadium, a record-breaking performance followed in the fourth round of the Challenge Cup. Trinity ran riot at Chorley Lynx, a National League Two side, amassing 88 points to six. Jamie Rooney created a new club record for points in a game with 36 from three tries and twelve goals, but fell just one goal short of equalling Mark Conway's total of thirteen, set in 1992 against Highfield. Ben Jeffries scored five tries, as the half backs claimed a 56-point haul between them. Rooney continued scoring prolifically with two tries, four goals and a drop goal in the fifth round tie at London Broncos, where Trinity went through by 29-10, although they got no further than the quarter-final, when they were defeated 20-4 at Wigan.

In the league, Trinity got off the mark with a 27-20 victory at Salford in which Sid Domic scored two tries, the second coming from a brilliant Solomona pass, giving a taste of what was to come. A satisfying 42-10 victory at Castleford was Wakefield's highest win at Wheldon Road since 1961 and was achieved after the sides had been level at 10-10 at half-time, after which Trinity scored 32 unanswered points, with Ellis, Jeffries and Tadulala all touching down twice. It was all the more remarkable for the fact that Wrench suffered a broken leg and Rooney fractured an ankle.

The 36-12 home defeat by Leeds meant that Trinity were still without a win at Belle Vue after four matches but they were consoled by the crowd figure of 7,680, the highest there since the club joined Super League in 1999. The first home victory of the season finally came when Widnes, unbeaten by Trinity in seven matches since their promotion to the top flight, came unstuck by 40-10. David March, who had the goal-kicking duties in the absence of the injured Rooney, landed six goals and scored a try.

A close-run game at home to Wigan, which was lost by 20-14, frustrated coach McNally, who pointed out that it was the fourth defeat by seven points or fewer. 'We have got to show more belief,' he said. 'Maybe it's something to do with the club's past history that they are not used to winning regularly, but that is where that attitude belongs – in the past. We have got to look to the future now.'

Trinity finally laid the Huddersfield bogey, ending a nine-match losing run against them with a convincing 38-6 win at the McAlpine Stadium. Ellis and Solomona were in superb form, with Ellis drawing particular commendation from McNally. The coach reckoned that his 23-year old captain, the youngest in Super League, was the best player he had ever coached.

The growing potency of the Solomona-Domic combination was apparent in the 48-18 win over London Broncos. The pair, operating on the left side, shredded the London defence, with Solomona, normally the provider, touching down no fewer than four times.

In June the club came out of the CVA which had been in force since September 2000, although it was not expected that there would be a rush to make any more new signings. 'We try to get good value for money,' said McNally, 'and this year I think we have done that. There will be a heavy reliance on developing our own players, as this season's squad shows.' A six-figure sponsorship deal led to the ground being named the Atlantic Solutions Stadium. In the 1990s Belle Vue had also been known as the McEwan's Stadium after the principal sponsor.

Trinity put on a fine all-round display to overcome St Helens at Belle Vue and were not at all flattered by the 41-22 score. David March, with seven goals from seven attempts, and Ben Jeffries, who scored two tries, were particularly impressive and so were young back-rowers Mark Applegarth and Rob Spicer, whom McNally called 'sensational'. The victory over the Challenge Cup holders was, said the coach, 'one of the most satisfying performances of my career'.

Trinity moved into the top six for the first time and recorded their sixth home win in a row with a 46-18 triumph over Salford, with Domic, Tadulala and Demetriou each scoring two tries. Solomona again proved what a fine signing Trinity had made when, at London Broncos, he scored two tries, made one for Domic and another for Jeffries via Domic. Trinity were running into their best form at the right time. Widnes were hammered 40-6 at Belle Vue as Trinity piled up 28 second-half points, and Huddersfield, mathematically rivals for the last play-off spot, were edged out thanks to Jeffries' late drop goal, which produced their eighth successive home win.

Trinity had developed ruthlessness. In the last match of the season they consigned neighbours Castleford to National League One with a 32-28 triumph. Cas had led 18-10 but Solomona touched down either side of half-time to swing the game in Trinity's favour and then made the opening for Handforth to make the decisive score.

Finishing sixth in the table, Trinity reached the play-offs for the first time in Super League and had to face third-placed Hull away. The odds were against them in the first half as first Ben Jeffries was dispatched to the sin-bin for lying on after making a try-saving tackle, then Gareth Ellis was also yellow-carded for alleged interference at the play-the-ball, leaving Trinity with eleven men at one point and on the end of an 8-1 penalty count. Despite David March's self-converted try from dummy-half, Hull went ahead by 14-6. Wakefield hit back as Halpenny touched down from Jeffries' kick, the video referee granting the try after disallowing two others. Feather, on loan from Leeds, used his strength to force his way over, Tadulala rose above the opposition to take Jeffries' well-judged kick and place the ball over the line, and Demetriou showed great skill and composure to claim Trinity's final try, to the acclaim of the vociferous band of travelling supporters. Hull were defeated 28-18 – Trinity's sixth win in a row, another Super League record for them – and a visit to Wigan for the elimination semi-final beckoned.

Wigan were unbeaten at home for over a year, but Trinity went 14-0 up after 17 minutes as Colum Halpenny, Duncan MacGillivray (who had arrived in mid-season to replace Dallas Hood) and Solomona crossed. Wigan came back but the video referee's doubtful decision to refuse Jeffries' 60th minute try for a knock-on was probably the turning point. A try would have put Trinity eight points ahead but it was Wigan who ended as 18-14 winners. Though clearly disappointed, Shane McNally, named Super League Coach of the Year, paid tribute

Australian stand-off Ben Jeffries, Trinity's top try-scorer in 2005

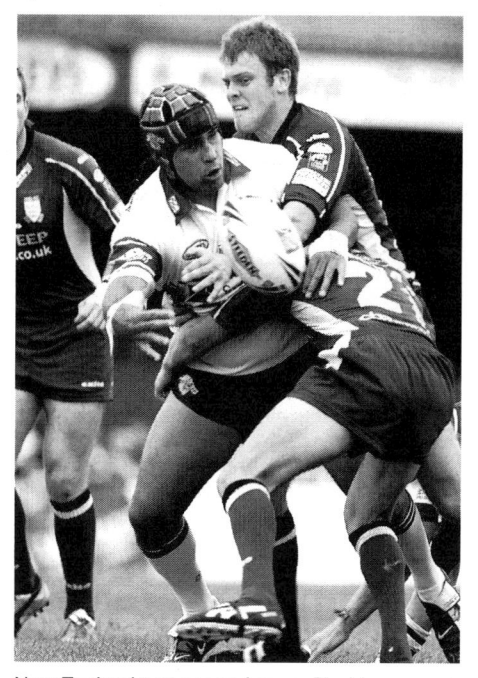

New Zealand test second rower David Solomona joined Trinity from Parramatta and impressed with his handling skills

to his men. 'The season has been fantastic,' he said. 'The guys showed their fighting spirit tonight, though their performance was not the best. But their bravery, spirit, courage and desire cannot be questioned and I am extremely proud of what they have achieved.'

The Opta-produced statistics for the season showed Michael Korkidas to be the game's top metre-maker, with Sid Domic also figuring in the list. David Solomona was ranked the top off-loader; Domic - whose 25 tries was the highest total scored for Trinity since David Smith's haul of 38 thirty years earlier - and Ben Jeffries featured in the top ten try-scorers and David March among the top five tacklers and goal-kickers. Gareth Ellis was named in the Great Britain squad and Duncan MacGillivray in Scotland's.

When Paul Handforth decided to join Castleford, Trinity brought in Aussie scrum-half Sam Obst from Whitehaven. Obst, the National League One player of the year, was signed as cover for half back and hooker. Geoff Evans, Trinity's first full-time conditioner, left the club but his work in improving fitness levels had paid off, McNally stressing that the appointment a year earlier was one of the keys to the club's success. For the first time Trinity had players selected in the Super League Dream Team when Sid Domic and David Solomona were both picked for the hypothetical side.

Trinity's captain and young Great Britain star Gareth Ellis left for Leeds for a fee believed to be around £200,000, after protracted negotiations with other clubs, including Bradford, Hull and Warrington. He was succeeded as captain by Jason Demetriou. Former Australia and Queensland star Julian O'Neill, not to be confused with the prop of the same name, signed for Trinity as a loose forward. Formerly with Brisbane Broncos, London Broncos, Wigan and Widnes, the 32-year old had more recently been playing rugby union in France.

On the opening day of the 2005 season, Trinity gained their first win at Bradford in Super League as they defeated the previous season's runners-up by 28-16. It was also their first opening day win since joining the competition in 1999. Trinity went one further by also beating Wigan for the first time in Super League, winning 18-16 at Belle Vue. The three Wakefield tries came when Demetriou finished off a passing movement in which he was involved three times, before Rooney raced 80 metres to score after intercepting. The third, decisive try came when O'Neill, Korkidas and Solomona combined to put Tadulala over, Rooney kicking his third goal. Under mounting Wigan pressure, Trinity held out for a deserved victory which made many people take note.

But it was a different matter altogether when they travelled to snow-covered Brentford to face London Broncos. Trinity were hammered 72-8, their heaviest defeat in Super League. Demetriou called it a freak performance, but not unknown in modern-day rugby league. McNally admitted: 'We were very poor but London were fantastic ... If we played every week like we did at Bradford we'd win Super League. We just had a bad day at the office. Worse things happen. No one's immune to it.'

A succession of three defeats, including a spectacular 64-16 drubbing at St Helens, was ended in style with a shock result at Headingley on Easter Monday. Playing against the current champions, who included Gareth Ellis and Willie Poching in their pack, Trinity won handsomely by 44-28, with David March and Jason Demetriou each scoring two tries and Jamie Rooney kicking six goals. David Solomona played for much of the game with a broken hand as Leeds lost at home for the first time in the league since August 2003.

What was equally surprising was that Trinity's form slumped immediately afterwards as first they lost at home in the Cup to Hull, who won 36-12, and then suffered a series of league defeats, including a 48-20 home loss to Warrington, which was their fifth in six games. A 40-18 defeat at bottom club Leigh resulted from another familiar collapse after Trinity had built up what should have been a winning lead. Just as embarrassingly, Trinity went on to lose 47-34 at home to Widnes, who had taken over at the bottom of the table from Leigh. David Wrench sustained a severely bloodied nose after a clash of heads with Darrell Griffin, but returned to the field from hospital.

Significantly, conditioner Adam Trypas returned immediately to Australia for personal and family reasons.

Centre Sid Domic and second rower David Solomona were selected in the hypothetical Dream Team in 2004. A future Wakefield player, Ali Lauitiiti, then with Leeds, is on the extreme left.

Questions would be raised about the team's fitness. Jules O'Neill, who was named man of the match in the 35-28 home defeat by Hull, took his team-mates by surprise when he quit to join his former club Widnes, causing captain Jason Demetriou to say that he felt that O'Neill had let the club down. Trinity stopped the slide temporarily with a 36-24 win over Salford, scoring four tries in the last quarter. Solomona, back in action after a two-month lay-off, soon made his presence felt by scoring the game's opening try, carrying a bunch of defenders with him over the line. Rooney kicked six goals from eight attempts.

But the home match against Leeds turned into a wipe-out. A crowd of 9,457 – a Belle Vue record in the Super League era, beating the previous best of 7,680 the season before and the 8,500 who had watched Leeds United reserves play Liverpool reserves over two years earlier – watched as Leeds destroyed Trinity by 70-6. Second rower Ali Lauitiiti ran in five tries, a record for a forward in Super League. Leeds coach Tony Smith said: 'That can happen to any Super League team. We have seen that throughout the season.' But the *Wakefield Express* was unimpressed, saying: 'With the exception of Gareth Ellis [now with Leeds] and Paul Handforth [who had gone to Castleford], this was pretty much the side that saw Wakefield through to the play-offs last season. It would have been unthinkable in 2004 for that Wakefield side to lose so heavily. In 2005 heavy defeats are becoming the norm.'

A better display against Huddersfield, where Trinity clawed back from 28-0 down to lose 40-22, nevertheless ended in a loss, their sixth in seven games. It earned McNally the sack – and after the 2004 Coach of the Year had only signed a new contract four months earlier. Chairman Ted Richardson said: 'We're damned if we do and damned if we don't. If we'd continued with how things were going in the hope that Shane would turn things around and been relegated, people would have pointed the finger and said why didn't we do something sooner. And if we'd done it earlier in the season people would have said we hadn't given Shane and the players enough time. It's been a very tough decision.' McNally's assistant, the relatively inexperienced Tony Smith, was given temporary charge of the team, but the sacking was not popular, as letters from many fans to the local paper testified.

Smith's first game in charge, with ten matches left, resulted in a 38-26 home defeat by St Helens and though the new coach was disappointed, he believed the performance was 'excellent'. He dubbed the team's display 'magnificent' after his second game, which brought a 44-34 defeat of Bradford at Belle Vue. Jeffries and Rooney each scored two tries as Trinity did the double over Bradford for the first time in their Super League history.

They went on to win 44-18 at Widnes in a match the home side needed to win to avoid relegation. As Tadulala, outstanding all season, confirmed his fine form with a hat-trick, and Solomona celebrated a renewed contract with an outstanding display of handling skills, Trinity controlled the game throughout, speeding to a 24-0 lead. David March kicked seven goals despite being sin-binned twice.

Even better, Trinity did the double over Wigan with their first win there in a decade as they triumphed 34-28, thanks to a controversial late try by Solomona, awarded by the video referee after it had been thought that the referee had called 'held'. Ben Jeffries, who had also signed a new contract, scored an outstanding try in the 50th minute when he slipped through the defence and outpaced the cover from inside his own half. Halpenny scored two early tries and the excellent Obst, replacing Rooney, who was out with knee ligament damage, scored another. Smith said, 'Solomona came off really badly winded and I passed the message down that I needed him to go back on and win us the game. He set up one try and scored the last one. That's what kind of a player he is. It took somebody of his class to unlock the Wigan defence.'

Smith was handed a two-year contract after that match, but his next in charge produced a far different outcome as Trinity were humbled 44-12 at home to Huddersfield, who moved to eighth in the table, one place above their opponents. Nor did Trinity do themselves justice in the next two games, losing heavily at St Helens and Salford.

Off the field, there was good news as the club announced a profit for the third year in a row, on a turnover approaching £2 million. It was also revealed that in the previous season, when the team reached the top six for the first time, the budget had been half that of other teams which qualified for the play-offs.

Trinity completed the 2005 season in tenth place out of twelve, though Jason Demetriou, looking back on the season, thought the squad had been good enough to make the top six again. Trinity conceded almost 1,000 points, however, for an average of almost 36 points per match.

In the autumn David Solomona figured in the victorious New Zealand team which beat Australia 24-0 in the Tri-Nations final at Elland Road. Darrell Griffin was selected for England against France in the international friendly, while Michael Korkidas captained Greece against Malta in Sydney.

New signings included ex-Sydney Roosters front rower Ned Catic and New Zealander Monty Betham, who succeeded Jason Demetriou as team captain. Coach Tony Smith promised to improve the team's fitness levels. 'Last season we weren't as fit as we should have been,' he said. 'We changed conditioner midway through the close season and that sort of thing affects you.' Smith also added that he had no plans to bring in an assistant coach.

Trinity had a tough start to the 2006 campaign with a fixture against Grand Final winners and World Club champions Bradford at Belle Vue. Despite losing 20-14, they showed plenty of determination and were pounding the Bradford line in search of the equalising score when the final hooter went.

In Trinity's first win of the season – by 26-6 at Harlequins, as London Broncos were now known – Semi Tadulala scored a hat-trick and had Solomona to thank as the Kiwi second rower provided two try-making passes and a deft grubber kick. With two tries of his own, Solomona almost made the difference as Trinity lost by just two points to Huddersfield at Belle Vue. But a miserable display at Salford, where a 48-10 defeat reflected a leaking defence which had let in 36 unanswered points by half-time, saw Trinity drop to next to bottom of the table. 'I couldn't believe it was the same team that's played in the last four weeks,' said Smith. 'There's only one word to describe them and that's "pathetic". I gave them a right roasting at half-time.' Smith added that the first half of the match was the worst performance he had experienced since becoming coach.

Though Smith had so far refused to have an assistant, former Huddersfield player Lee St Hilaire arrived as his

Stand-off Jamie Rooney, shown here sprinting through the Leeds defence, lies third in the all-time list of Trinity's points scorers

second-in-command. In the same week, Steve Ferres returned to the club whose promotion he had overseen as football manager in 1998. Ferres was appointed as chief executive, a position he had held at York, and replaced Diane Rogerson as she became executive director. 'I've got a great affinity with Wakefield Trinity,' said the former Bradford player. 'It never left even when I left the club. There's something special about the people involved with the club and the supporters. There's a real passion for the game around Wakefield.'

After an eight-month absence through injury, Jamie Rooney made his presence felt when, in the single-point defeat at home to Warrington, he scored two tries, kicked four goals from four attempts and a drop goal as Trinity went 21-0 up at half-time but ended up losing 22-21. It was a similar scenario to the Huddersfield game. The same pattern emerged in the home Challenge Cup tie against Wigan when Trinity led 22-6 in the 39th minute only to surrender their advantage and lose 32-22.

Wigan, struggling at the wrong end of the table, set their sights on Solomona but he turned down their offer. Bradford Academy centre Ryan Atkins arrived at Belle Vue and was followed, a month later, by front-rower Adam Watene, cousin of former Trinity player Frank.

John Kear, who had been sacked as coach of Hull, was reported to be wanted by Trinity, but Ferres dismissed the rumours, saying that Wakefield were not seeking a new coach at the moment. 'Tony Smith is committed to the job he's doing and we're confident he can get it right,' said Ferres.

The stadium question loomed yet again. Club officials were well aware that Wakefield Trinity would not be likely to survive as a Super League club when the new franchising system was put into place for 2009, even if they managed to avoid being relegated. It had been decided that to revamp Belle Vue was inappropriate because of inadequate seating, as well as poor access and limited parking. The club said that money was in place to fund a new stadium but were asking Wakefield Council to find a site.

In the home league match against Wigan, the week after the Cup tie, Trinity built up a substantial 32-6 half-time lead, with Solomona showing the visitors what they lacked by making three of the five first-half tries. For once Trinity safeguarded their advantage and went on to win 40-14, with top performances from Michael Korkidas, Olivier Elima and hooker Sam Obst, as well as half backs Jeffries and Rooney, who scored a try and kicked eight goals. Wigan coach Ian Millward was sacked two days later. The 42-22 mid-season win over Harlequins saw Trinity climb to seventh in the table, while Wigan were bottom.

A 34-8 defeat at St Helens was Saints' twelfth win in a row, watched by a crowd of over 10,000 – the biggest at Knowsley Road for a Trinity visit since 1967. But the result went Trinity's way when they faced troubled Wigan for a third time at Belle Vue. Atkins scored the first try and Demetriou went over for what proved the matchwinner, beating three or four Wigan defenders on his way to the line. A controversial incident could have robbed Trinity of victory, but instead it was Wigan's new coach Brian Noble who was left disappointed. With two minutes remaining, Colum Halpenny's tackle on Pat Richards saved the day as the video referee ruled that the Wigan player had lost the ball in the tackle as he went over the line and that Halpenny had not dislodged the ball, resulting in a 'no try' verdict and a 10-8 win for Trinity.

Trinity's first visit to Perpignan resulted in a 28-20 win for the Catalan Dragons, masterminded by Stacey Jones, returning to action after breaking his arm in only the Dragons' second Super League match. At Belle Vue, in weather more like the south of France, Trinity lost for the third time in a season to Salford, who won 36-18 – a defeat which began to inflame the team's many critics. Their riposte was a 17-16 victory at Warrington

In a relegation battle at Wigan, Trinity went down 42-24, allowing their opponents to move off the bottom of the table, to be replaced by the Catalans, who, however, had a three-year Super League licence and could not therefore be demoted during that time. Trinity were third from last with twelve league points – the same as Wigan.

The season reached crisis point at Huddersfield. Trinity swept to an 18-0 half-time lead, as the home side were booed off the field by their fans. A Rooney penalty extended Trinity's lead soon after the restart and it looked as if they would overcome the hoodoo of Huddersfield, who had won nine out of ten previous Super League meetings with Trinity. But everything fell apart as Trinity suffered yet another second-half collapse and let in five tries in under twenty minutes. Huddersfield's stars had looked anonymous in the first half but suddenly Brad Drew, Robbie Paul and Kevin Brown sprang into action as Wakefield visibly wilted. To make matters worse, it was ex-Trinity forward Steve Snitch who claimed Huddersfield's fifth and decisive try to give an improbable 26-20 victory. It was the fifth time that Trinity had seen a half-time lead overhauled in the second period. Said coach Tony Smith: 'It's absolutely unbelievable. I'm sick to the back teeth of it. How can the coach be blamed for that? We started off so well and looked a class above in the first half in every department. After ten minutes of the second half we folded like a pack of cards and looked absolutely knackered. I think it's obvious it's a fitness problem with us.' Senior player Jason Demetriou, however, thought that the problem was more of a psychological one. 'Anyone watching the game would have seen fitness as an issue, from the amount of times we couldn't get back onside in the second half when the likes of Robbie Paul were running through. It was very difficult in the heat, which played a big part, but a lot of what has been happening is a mental thing when we've been getting in front. We've been losing winning leads in our heads and everyone is guilty of it.'

Under Tony Smith, ten wins had been garnered from 31 games, with just one from the last seven. Ferres said that both he and Smith had come to the conclusion that it was time for a change and the coach, who was contracted until the end of the next season, parted company. His assistant Lee St Hilaire also resigned.

In the absence of a coach, Solomona, Betham and Demetriou took charge of the side as they prepared to face Bradford at Belle Vue. But Trinity were well beaten, losing 42-20, which put them two league points adrift of Wigan and the Catalans at the foot of the table.

After Salford assistant coach James Lowes turned down the opportunity to take over at Belle Vue, John Kear was appointed, a move which received general acclaim from fans and players alike. 'John was someone the players were looking forward to getting,' said Demetriou. 'I think it was important the club appointed someone with a lot of experience because the situation we are in is going to require that.' Kear had been out of the game since losing his job at Hull three months earlier, but had famously guided that club the year before, and Sheffield in 1998, to victory in the Challenge Cup. With six games left to play, it was often repeated that the end of season run-in would be like playing six Challenge Cup finals. Many were those who thought that saving Trinity's Super League future would be an even greater achievement than winning the Cup.

Kear, who had earlier offered to help out Tony Smith in an advisory capacity, held the view that his successor had been given the job of head coach too early. His assessment of the squad he inherited was that 'Wakefield have got some very good players. They've got one world-class player in David Solomona and other really good Super League players.' Kear brought in Paul Broadbent, the former Wakefield and Hull player and Sheffield's Cup-winning captain, as his assistant. 'Paul epitomises the qualities I wanted to bring to the club,' he said. 'He's got a good work ethic, never gives up and is tough.' However, Broadbent said he was not prepared to give up his commitment, in the middle of the season, to York, where he was also assistant coach, and would do both jobs at the same time.

The first stage on Trinity's road to Super League salvation was the match at Castleford, where Kear had once played as a winger. The two clubs were set to meet twice in these last six games. Trinity played all the second half with twelve men after Betham had been sent off for punching. Catic was also dismissed towards the very end of the game for a head butt. But, with aggressive defence, they knocked Castleford off their stride, preventing them from scoring a single point, and won 18-0. Kear called the performance 'absolutely magnificent'. He added: 'I don't think any team I have coached has given as much as that … I think throughout the season Wakefield have put in the odd good performance and got a result only to suffer a backlash afterwards where they've let themselves down with their mental preparation. The performance at Cas was basically the response to two weeks of training where we worked really hard.'

While Wigan were docked two points for breach of the salary cap, Trinity followed up their success at Wheldon Road with a 34-14 home victory over the Catalans. Jamie Rooney scored three tries and kicked seven goals for a total of 26 points, which equalled his own club record in Super League.

The match against Leeds would prove a stern test, even though the Headingley club had suffered five defeats in a row. But they had never lost at Belle Vue since Trinity entered Super League and maintained their record with a 14-12 victory, with which Kear said he was 'bitterly disappointed', but thought the game had all the intensity and quality of a play-off rather than a relegation battle. The *Wakefield Express* reported: 'After so much mediocrity this season, it was such a breath of fresh air to see so much passion, commitment and no little skill from revitalised Trinity.' Nevertheless, Wakefield and Catalans were bracketed alongside each other at the foot of the table, with one point fewer than Castleford and two fewer than Wigan and Huddersfield.

With the following weekend given over to the Challenge Cup final, Kear's charges had a weekend off to brace themselves for the remaining three matches of the season. Regardless of the outcome, Kear was offered, and accepted, a one-year contract. It was a tall order to go to St Helens, Challenge Cup winners and league leaders, and come away with two points. Trinity battled bravely against Saints' superb defence but went down 34-12, with new signing Tevita Leo-Latu making his debut off the bench. Kear thought that Trinity's display was strong enough to have earned victory against most other clubs. Undeterred, he commented: 'I always felt four [wins] would be enough. We're down to the wire now, so … we've got to win these next two.'

With Castleford one point ahead in the table, Trinity needed to win at Bradford and beat Cas at Belle Vue in the last game, in the meantime hoping that Salford would beat the Wheldon Road outfit.

As Trinity prepared to travel to Odsal to face fourth-placed Bradford, who had won thirteen of the sixteen previous meetings between the two clubs, Kear said, 'It's as big as any game I've been involved in and I include internationals and Cup finals in that. Should we remain in Super League, I think for me it will be comparable to getting into the semi-final of a World Cup or winning two Challenge Cups. It would be a massive achievement.'

Watched by 11,451 fans, Trinity beat the Bulls 20-12 after leading 18-6 at half-time. Solomona proved inspirational, providing the pass for Tadulala's try after Bradford had gone 6-0 ahead. Latu, Jeffries and Rooney combined to send Halpenny over for the second, before Solomona went blindside from dummy half and supplied Catic with the pass for Trinity's third. A Rooney penalty was Trinity's only second-half score, but great defensive work denied any hope of a Bradford comeback. Meanwhile Salford beat Castleford 26-16 at the Willows to set up a sensational last game of the season.

A capacity crowd of 11,000 piled into Belle Vue on the Saturday evening for the local derby to end all local derbies. Trinity did not get off to the best start as Castleford took an 11-2 lead and Jeffries had a try disallowed for obstruction. But James Evans, signed on loan from Huddersfield two months earlier, profited from Betham's kick ahead, then Demetriou forced his way through to give Trinity a 14-11 half-time advantage. In this mesmerising, heart-stopping game, Cas regained the lead soon after the restart but Betham went over to snatch back the initiative. Kevin Henderson touched down. Rooney landed a drop goal. Cas had a try disallowed by the video referee, and then the crowning moment came when Rooney's high kick was misjudged by the Cas defence and Evans touched down for the second time. Trinity won 29-17 and Kear, who some people had said was crazy to take on the job eight weeks earlier, declared, 'Mission impossible has been done.'

For the second time in three seasons Trinity had sent Castleford down, this time with the highest number of points in Super League history. Cas's Australian coach Terry Matterson, commenting on an uncertain future for himself and his players, said: 'That's the tragedy of promotion and relegation. But you love this relegation thing over here, for some bloody reason.' Solomona, who had played with an injury, agreed, and confessed to having had sleepless nights. 'I can't say enough about how I hate relegation,' he said. As one of fourteen overseas players in the 17-man squad, he paid tribute to the team's remarkable commitment to the club, adding: 'I've played with a lot of good, close teams and this is about as close as you can get.'

Steve Ferres pointed out that eleven of the squad had played for the club in 2004 when they reached the play-offs. 'It's fair to say they underperformed till the last six games and credit to John – he got the best out of the team and the players responded.'

The euphoria took a long time to die down, but once it had, thoughts turned to preparation for the following season. Semi Tadulala, wanting to play for Fiji in the next rugby union World Cup, signed for Gloucester RU, but later came straight back to Belle Vue after his work permit application failed, and Darrell Griffin signed for Huddersfield, but the biggest surprise came when the inspirational David Solomona, who had turned down the idea of moving to Wigan and insisted he wanted to stay at Wakefield, changed his mind and signed for Bradford in a £200,000 plus deal which brought 20-year old Brett Ferres, nephew of Steve, to Belle Vue. Solomona said he was 'gutted' to leave Wakefield but the offer was too good to turn down. Among others to arrive at Belle Vue were Castleford winger Waine Pryce and Danny Sculthorpe, the Wigan forward who had been on loan at Wheldon Road. Kear said his most important signing of the season was conditioner Colin Sanctuary.

During the international season, Rooney, Atkins and Ferres all represented England and Elima played for France in the Federation Shield tournament which also involved Tonga and Samoa.

Coach John Kear celebrates Super League survival after Trinity beat Castleford 29-17 in the final match of the 2006 season

In the ongoing quest for a new ground, the latest, albeit fanciful, plans to be unveiled concerned a state-of-the-art stadium in Thornes Park. It was to have a 14,000 capacity and would cost £15 million. A feasibility study was to be undertaken by the Council, although a casual observer could probably have saved the time and expense: access by road would be difficult; the Council did not own the property which would have to be demolished to make way for the new structure; and siting a stadium in the middle of a public amenity would be bound to bring protests.

Though Trinity lost the opening match of 2007 against promoted side Hull KR, they pulled off another coup at St Helens' expense at Belle Vue. The champions led 18-6 but Trinity had plenty in reserve and posted a surprise result by winning 29-22. Trinity backed up with a 36-24 home win against Salford, who had won five of the previous six meetings between the two clubs, and then brought off a fine 19-6 win at Kear's former club Hull to go top of Super League – on points difference from four other clubs - for the first time. Jamie Rooney and Ben Jeffries were influential figures, and Jason Demetriou, Paul March and Brett Ferres the try-scorers, in Trinity's first Super League win at Hull apart from the 2004 play-off. But Kear refused to get carried away, saying, 'We're fully aware there's a lot more hard work to be done. We won't believe any of the publicity that we don't get anyway.' With a 40-20 home win against the Catalans, Trinity recorded four successive wins for the first time in three years. Rooney masterminded the victory as he created three tries with his kicking, put in two 40/20s, raced ninety metres for an interception try and kicked six goals from seven attempts.

In the Challenge Cup, Trinity had no difficulty disposing of National League Two side London Skolars in a match switched to Belle Vue, but the 52-4 victory was a hollow one built on a patchy team performance. It was Huddersfield, once again, who exposed those failings as they picked up their twelfth win out of thirteen meetings with Trinity, cruising to a 56-12 victory on Good Friday before Trinity completed an unhappy Easter programme by losing 36-24 at home to Bradford.

After such a promising start to the season, Trinity fell into an habitual mid-season slump, losing narrowly at home to Hull and then yet again to Huddersfield, this time at the Millennium Stadium in Cardiff on the Magic Weekend. Bradford put Trinity out of the Challenge Cup in the fifth round as they won 14-4 at Belle Vue. A 34-14 defeat at St Helens was Trinity's fifth in a row and their eighth match without a win, putting them eleventh in the twelve-team league. The slide was finally arrested by an 18-12 home win over the Catalans amid a deluge.

Looking to the future, chief executive Steve Ferres reiterated the need for a new stadium, saying that a new location was vital to Trinity's continued existence in Super League, for which licences would be awarded in 2009 with automatic promotion and relegation coming to an end. 'If you look at the statistics over the last twenty years,' he said, 'Wakefield lie in eleventh position for their crowds. For league position over that same period we are actually eleventh as well. If you take that as a barometer, the top twelve teams would be in Super League and we'd be eleventh and scraping in.' Ferres was said to be fully confident that the proposed state-of-the-art venue at Thornes Park would go ahead. He added: 'The only way that I think the RFL could refuse us admission would be on the basis that the ground does not meet requirements … Feasibility studies are under way … and then hopefully it goes straight to planning.'

Trinity suddenly found their best form as they overturned Wigan, winning convincingly by 32-6 at Belle Vue to go back into the top six. It was no coincidence that Ben Jeffries rediscovered his old form, which also coincided with French international half back Maxime Grésèque, outstanding for France against Great Britain at Headingley, being brought in for a short spell and being introduced to the crowd. Jeffries silenced his critics with an outstanding display, scoring a try in each half and laying on others. Captain Jason Demetriou gave a fine lead, playing 'like a man possessed' and shrugging off would-be tacklers on his cross-field run to the line. Prop Richard Moore brought a huge cheer when, unstoppable, he charged fifty metres for a memorable try.

Jeffries was again in top form and Ryan Atkins scored two tries as bottom club Salford were beaten 35-18 at The Willows. But then Huddersfield again. Just when Trinity had opened up a 13-0 lead, Huddersfield came back into the game and scored four tries in fifteen minutes early in the second half to win 24-23. Kear, who had been in charge for just a year, said it was his most disappointing day since being at the club.

It was followed by what he called 'one of our very best performances over eighty minutes' as his charges dismantled Leeds at Headingley, winning 23-16 – probably the highlight of the season. The scoreboard showed 16-16 with five minutes remaining when Rooney slipped a drop goal over and centre Luke George scored his first Super League try to clinch the victory. Trinity moved up to fifth as Wigan were docked points for a salary cap breach.

Having signed former Great Britain Academy centre Sean Gleeson from Wigan in mid-season, Trinity captured ex-London Broncos and New Zealand Warriors centre Tony Martin to add stability to the back line. But it was front-rowers Adam Watene, Richard Moore and Ricky Bibey who were laying the foundations for the team's current success. All were making the most of a second chance. Watene had been discarded by Bradford, while Bibey, who had been at St Helens and Wigan and Moore, who had also been at Bradford, both arrived from Leigh and were putting their Super League careers back on the rails.

A series of defeats in the last four matches of the season, including the seemingly inevitable loss at Huddersfield – the fourth time in the season that the men in claret and gold had triumphed over Trinity – resulted in Trinity just failing to make the play-offs. Captain Jason Demetriou, scorer of two tries in the defeat at Huddersfield, was rewarded for an inspiring season by being named in the 2007 Dream Team. The season ended on a low note with a 46-4 loss at Leeds, watched by almost 20,000 spectators, with Trinity finishing eighth.

The signings for the 2008 season included two from the Huddersfield side which had so tormented Trinity:

hooker Brad Drew, who, at 32, was still regarded as a top playmaker, and full back or winger Paul Reilly. But the key signing, made all the more necessary with the departure of Ben Jeffries to Bradford, was former Wakefield Academy half back Danny Brough, who came to Belle Vue from Castleford after having played under John Kear at Hull and indeed kicked the winning goal in the 2005 Challenge Cup final. Winger Peter Fox went to Hull KR and Olivier Elima returned to France to join the Catalan Dragons. Paul March became the youngest coach in the National Leagues when he joined York and was soon to be reunited there with his brother David. Forward Oliver Wilkes, utility back Scott Grix and Aussie winger Damien Blanch all arrived from Widnes.

Matt Blaymire, Jamie Rooney and Richard Moore were selected for the train-on squad which was preparing for the series against New Zealand and although none made the final selection, Rooney and Moore appeared in the Northern Union team which played the New Zealand All Golds in the centenary international at Warrington.

Nigel Wright and Francis Stephenson both returned to the club; Wright as assistant coach with responsibility for the Under 21 Academy and Stephenson as the club's general manager. Former Academy player James Elston was appointed marketing and community director, but Steve Ferres bowed out for a second time after apparently being thwarted in his wish to bring in an investor who would buy the club from Ted Richardson. Trinity had just revealed a loss of almost £250,000 for the period up to the end of 2006, but Richardson claimed that the club was in a 'comfortable' position.

Twenty-five – On the Brink: 2008-13

For the 2008 season, Trinity had lined up an array of play-makers at half back and hooker in Brad Drew, Jamie Rooney, Danny Brough, Sam Obst and Tevita Leo-Latu. Drew and Rooney had already proved their value in Super League, but ex-Wakefield Academy player Brough admitted that he had made a 'make or break' move back to Belle Vue. Trinity also had an abundance of goal-kickers in Brough, Rooney, Drew, Martin and Obst.

Brough made an impressive debut and, with Demetriou switching to loose forward, Trinity got off to a fine start with a 26-24 win at Bradford. Qualifying through a Glaswegian grandfather, Brough was named Scotland's World Cup captain. But there was bad news for Jason Demetriou, who suffered the blow of being told that he had a potentially serious neck injury which would keep him out for the season. It said much for the Australian's mental attitude that, after undergoing surgery, he was back playing within two months.

In April Trinity embarked on a rare sequence of six consecutive wins, including two cup-ties. First Warrington were beaten 16-2 at Belle Vue in sleet and snow before Huddersfield were defeated 18-16 on their own ground as Trinity ended a run of nine consecutive losses against the claret and golds. In the Challenge Cup fourth round against Salford, now the National League One front-runners, Trinity went through comfortably by 38-8 with Moore and Bibey outstanding up front and Obst named man of the match. In the fifth round, National League Two side Barrow were routed 58-6 at Craven Park, Brough again kicking nine goals from ten – as he had done against Castleford in the league - as well as scoring two tries. Another NL2 side, Oldham, proved stubborn opposition in the quarter-final before being knocked out 46-4 as Trinity advanced to the semis for the first time in 29 years.

Castleford were beaten 32-16 away, as Trinity pulled off their third win of the season and ninth in a row over their neighbours and Huddersfield were beaten again as Demetriou signalled his return with a try in the 28-26 home win. Trinity moved up to fourth in the table, but at home to the Catalans, many of whose players had turned out for France in the 56-8 defeat by England four days earlier, Trinity threw away a 10-0 lead, did not score a try after the thirteenth minute and lost 30-14. The pattern continued with a heavy defeat at Warrington and in the game against Cup semi-final opponents Hull at Belle Vue, Trinity again crashed in the second half to lose 26-18. The last three matches had produced second-half sequences of 20-0, 20-6 and 20-0.

But there was relief all round at the news that Wakefield had been granted a Super League franchise – or licence, as it was now known - for 2009 to 2011. The decision had been expected as the division expanded from twelve to fourteen clubs with the addition of Salford and Welsh outfit Crusaders. Trinity were graded, along with seven other clubs, at grade C, the lowest band. The RFL's assessment report stated: 'Whilst well maintained the ground is limited and old-fashioned. However the club recognise this and have plans for a new stadium. These are not as far advanced as might be the case despite projected occupation by 2010 and evidence of a Plan B would have been beneficial. There is good progress within community development and attendances are improving … There has been a recent improvement on the pitch and increased investment in the playing department. Youth development works reasonably well and pre-16 players are attracting national honours but the club has not always been able to retain the best local talent.' RFL executive chairman Richard Lewis added a general warning. 'For clubs who have ambitions for new stadiums,' he said, 'they need to ensure by 2010 when the next licence application process starts, that they are more than just plans.'

Much had been made of Trinity's aim of getting to Wembley for the first time since 1979. John Kear's previous success with Sheffield and Hull was taken as a good omen for Wakefield in 2008. In the league, Trinity were seventh and Hull tenth. But within the first ten minutes of the clash at Doncaster's Keepmoat Stadium, watched by 14,716 spectators, Trinity trailed 18-0 and struggled in vain to catch up despite some valiant efforts. Hull's early lead was reduced when recent signing Matt Petersen, the Australian of American origin who had finally arrived at Belle Vue after a long process, went over from Atkins's pass. Blanch touched down from Brough's kick but Hull scored a fourth try before sub Leo-Latu crossed and Atkins grounded the ball over the line after Petersen knocked back Brough's kick. At half-time Hull's lead of 24-20 was far from impregnable. Hull scored first after the break but Blanch crossed for a second time from Drew's kick and the outcome was still uncertain, though Tickle, who kicked six goals from six compared to Brough's unusually inconsistent two from six, added a crucial penalty. Trinity's hopes evaporated when the video referee denied Blanch a hat-trick as he ruled that the winger's leg was in touch as he went over. Both sides had scored five tries but Trinity had perhaps put themselves under too much pressure from the start. 'I thought the occasion got the better of us,' said captain Demetriou.

If their form had suffered before the semi-final, the team seemed unable to get over the disappointment after it, losing twice at home, both by over forty points, first to leaders and Cup finalists St Helens and then to bottom club Castleford. The first win in nine matches came at Perpignan, where the Catalans had only lost once in eleven games before this 38-32 defeat. As Trinity finished in eighth place, John Kear summed up the season: 'We were in with a shout of the top six because of an excellent first two-thirds [of the season] and we got to the semi-final of the Challenge Cup … In two years we've gone from perennial relegation strugglers to challengers for the top six and a Challenge Cup semi-final,' he said, although the club had reached the play-offs four years earlier.

The departing Nigel Wright, who had been in charge of the Academy Under 21 team, but had taken up a post as assistant coach at Warrington, gave another slant on Trinity's situation: 'It is very frustrating because the club can't afford to give players more money to keep them and young lads are being pinched by bigger clubs who can offer them more … It's the same for John Kear … If he had the money to work with then Wakefield could consistently compete in the top six of Super League.'

As players prepared themselves for the World Cup in Australia, Scott Grix was named captain of Ireland, with Damien Blanch and Sean Gleeson alongside him in the squad. Scotland, with Danny Brough as their captain, called on Oliver Wilkes, Kevin Henderson and Duncan MacGillivray, while Tonga selected Tevita Leo-Latu. But there was no Wakefield representative in England's squad after Ryan Atkins was not included in the final group.

The club suffered a huge setback when popular front-rower Adam Watene collapsed and died during a training session. 'Everyone is stunned, shocked and devastated,' said Kear. 'We have not only lost a very good rugby league player but we have also lost a champion of a man and a true gentleman. His contribution to Wakefield was more than just to the club. He was a respected member of the community as a whole. He was one of our true leaders.' Watene, aged just 31, was captain of the Cook Islands and had played for New Zealand Warriors in the NRL before coming to England to play for Castleford and then Bradford before making his mark at Wakefield.

The club was forced, eventually, to review its squad of players. Duncan MacGillivray decided to retire and return to Australia, after drawing praise from Kear for his 'immense' contribution to the club since 2004. Prop James Stosic, a New Zealander of Macedonian parentage, was signed from Gold Coast Titans and Steve Snitch re-signed after two years at Huddersfield. Brett Ferres, however, left for Castleford.

The 2009 season got off to the best possible start with a 12-6 win at Wigan despite the fact that eight first-team regulars were missing. Winger Dave Halley, on loan from Bradford, showed his pace to good effect to score twice on his debut, his first try coming in the first minute of play. The two other debutants, Snitch and Stosic, also put in strong performances, but it was Brad Drew who carved out the openings, helped by Sam Obst, in the absence of Brough and Rooney. Almost inevitably, captain Jason Demetriou set the tone.

A comprehensive dismantling of Warrington by 48-22 at Belle Vue was assisted by three tries from full back Matt

Blaymire and two each from Halley, including one over 80 metres, and Dale Ferguson, with seven goals from seven attempts landed by stand-in kicker Tony Martin. The performance, against a team with more stars in it than Wakefield's, drew a telling comment from John Kear. 'It's part of my philosophy of coaching that a champion team will always beat a team of champions,' he said, 'because a champion team is together, is united and is working towards a common goal and my players are demonstrating that in bucketsful at the minute.' So much so that, after four matches, Trinity moved up to second place in the table.

The club suffered a second blow, however, just six months after the death of Adam Watene, when 20-year old forward Leon Walker collapsed and died while playing in a reserve game at Celtic Crusaders. Walker, originally from Morley, had played for Yorkshire and England Under 18s and had just joined Trinity from Salford. Not surprisingly, the performance against St Helens at Belle Vue the following weekend was a subdued one and resulted in a 42-18 defeat which also sent Wakefield down to eighth in the league.

In the Challenge Cup, Trinity easily disposed of Leigh, who were operating in the Championship, as the division below Super League was now known. Neil Kelly's men were beaten 54-0 at Belle Vue, with Blaymire, Blanch and Obst each scoring two tries, and Brough contributing a try and seven goals.

Scrum half Danny Brough, a former Wakefield Academy player, returned to Belle Vue from Castleford and became a key player with both out-of-hand and place kicking

The Easter period proved productive as Castleford were beaten 35-6 on their own ground on Good Friday and Bradford were defeated 24-22 at home so that Trinity took over the fourth spot previously occupied by Cas. The third win in eight days came at Hull, where Trinity triumphed 21-14.

But through May Trinity's form dived in familiar fashion. A 40-26 home defeat by Wigan was succeeded by a 32-16 loss to Bradford during the Magic Weekend held at Edinburgh's Murrayfield. In the fifth round of the Challenge Cup, Trinity lost for the second time at home to Wigan as they went out by 28-17, leaving John Kear a very disappointed man, not to mention the fans. At the same time, the first rumours were surfacing regarding Danny Brough's possible move to Huddersfield. Brough and team-mate Danny Sculthorpe were both disciplined by the club for their part in an alleged drinking incident which apparently took place on the return from London following Trinity's 24-17 defeat by Harlequins. In the meantime chairman Ted Richardson denied that the club needed to sell players in order to cut the wages bill.

Their fifth consecutive reverse, this time at the hands of Huddersfield, who hammered Trinity 54-6, was the club's biggest since the 60-4 loss at St Helens almost four years earlier. Trinity conceded forty points in the second half. Sculthorpe was allowed to leave on loan for Huddersfield, from where Michael Korkidas, after spells at Salford and Castleford, returned to Belle Vue in a reciprocal deal.

The 37-22 home win over Hull was due in no small measure to an exceptional performance by Danny Brough, whose out-of-hand kicking constantly had his former team back-tracking. The half back landed five goals from six attempts, kicked a drop goal and scored an 80-metre interception try as well as firing a long cut-out pass from which Matt Petersen went over. Centre Ryan Atkins, meanwhile, scored England's opening try in the 66-12 demolition of France in Paris.

Brough's half-back partner, Jamie Rooney, however, went to ambitious Championship club Barrow. It was a tribute to his ability that, in six seasons at Wakefield, Rooney had risen to third in the list of Trinity's all-time top points-scorers, though it should be remembered that he was operating in an era when teams scored much more liberally than in the eras of Neil Fox and Charlie Pollard, the only two players above Rooney in the table.

As transfer activity increased, Bradford's former international hooker or prop Terry Newton was signed on a two-year contract, while Trinity's promising young forward Jay Pitts was signed by Leeds. Shane Tronc, a 27-year-old front rower from North Queensland Cowboys, was signed at the same time as Glenn Morrison, Bradford's 33-year old former State of Origin second rower. Ricky Bibey was set to return to one of his former clubs, Leigh.

At St Helens, Brough's tactical kicking, well supported by Obst, the tackling of Snitch and Ferguson, and the leadership of Demetriou contributed to a satisfying 22-20 win. The captain always led the way and was to end the season not only as Trinity's top tackler but also top tackle-breaker, according to Opta statistics.

Despite defeat at Castleford, Trinity went on to finish the season in storming fashion, winning their last five matches as Salford, Celtic Crusaders, Warrington, the Catalan Dragons and Hull KR all succumbed.

The RFL sent out a warning to five clubs, including Wakefield, reminding them that their place in Super League would be in jeopardy if plans for either a new or improved stadium were not significantly advanced. Trinity's Thornes Park project, such as it was, had fallen through nine months earlier, as many had forecast, although it was said that new plans had been formulated for a 12,000 capacity venue near Stanley.

Their fifth place in the league – Trinity's highest ever in Super League – earned them a place in the play-offs (now expanded to eight teams) for only the second time. But they were not at their best and the season ended with a disappointing 25-16 home defeat to eighth-placed Catalans in the first round. The Academy did better. The youngsters beat Wigan 30-4 in the Academy Championship Grand Final.

Among the leavers, the highest profile belonged to Ryan Atkins, who said he did not want to leave Wakefield, but when Warrington stepped in with a £150,000 transfer fee, the club found it hard to refuse. Steve Snitch signed for Castleford, Brad Drew returned to Huddersfield, taking Scott Grix with him, and Oliver Wilkes went to Harlequins. Tony Martin and Frank Winterstein signed for Crusaders and James Stosic, unable to procure the Macedonian passport which would have taken him off the quota, left the club.

Ben Jeffries returned to Belle Vue after two years at Bradford and 24-year old Fijian international centre Daryl Millard was signed from Canterbury Bulldogs. Prop Paul King arrived from Hull and utility player Paul Johnson, a former international, came from Warrington.

Before the 2010 season started, Trinity were forced to settle a debt of £194,000 to avoid a winding-up petition by Her Majesty's Revenue and Customs. At the end of the season, a repetition of the same scenario occurred, but this time it was former chairman Sir Rodney Walker who took charge of the £164,000 bill.

In between, the season got off to a good start with an 18-10 win at Harlequins, where five players made their debut, including Millard, who scored the opening try. A home victory over the Catalans by 28-20 saw Trinity go to the top of Super League, albeit after only two matches. With the third win on the run, Trinity's fans were overjoyed, since the victim was Leeds, who had not lost at Belle Vue for eighteen years but who were soundly beaten by 28-18. Sean Gleeson started the scoring following a Shane Tronc offload before Ben Jeffries scooted over for the second. Trinity also put in some fine defence, with superb last-ditch tackles from Demetriou and Brough. Man of the match Brough, who landed six goals from eight attempts, intercepted a pass close to his own line and sprinted the length of the field to score Trinity's third. The half back again showed his value when Daryl Millard touched down from his fine crossfield kick. Leeds came back towards the end of the game with two Scott Donald tries in six minutes, but Trinity held firm for an outstanding win.

The season was only three weeks old when hooker Terry Newton, who had signed from Bradford during the close season and had not yet played for Trinity, was suspended from playing after failing a drugs test. The former international became the first sportsman to be found guilty of taking human growth hormone. His contract was terminated by the club.

Trinity's first defeat of the season came at St Helens in the fourth match. Millard scored two tries and Morrison was outstanding but Kear was disappointed with the result, which was in itself a sign of Trinity's progress and ambition. But it was the same old story against Huddersfield, who put fifty points past Trinity for the second time in two seasons when they won 52-0 at Belle Vue. 'It would have been hard to predict that result,' said Kear, calling his side's display 'very inept.' They found their form again at Hull KR, winning 31-18. Shane Tronc powered over for two tries but was to stay at Belle Vue only a month longer. He returned to Australia after his wife had failed to settle.

Even more important, Danny Brough ended months of speculation by signing for Huddersfield despite Wakefield's efforts to keep their star half back. 'We offered Danny a first-class contract,' said Kear, 'certainly the best I have seen since I have been at the club.' Trinity received an undisclosed fee for Brough, whose contract with Trinity had six months left to run. Kear paid tribute to Brough's importance to the side, saying, 'He helped us go from survivors to genuine Super League competitors.' At the same time, second row Danny Kirmond, a former Stanley Rangers player, arrived on loan from Huddersfield and stand-off Paul Cooke was brought in from Hull KR. No transfer fee was paid for Cooke, who was attempting to resurrect a once highly promising career and who had formerly played under Kear at Hull before his much-publicised move across the city. He made his debut off the bench in the 36-6 home win over Salford.

With Brough, Rooney and Drew all gone, Sam Obst became an increasingly important member of the side. 'He typifies the spirit and commitment that the players have for the club,' said Kear. But endeavour was not quite enough. Trinity lost 54-14 at Wigan on Easter Monday, and with a 20-10 home defeat by Crusaders – a display described as 'unacceptable' by the coach – Trinity slipped to eighth in the league. As the Challenge Cup came around, Trinity made a quick exit when they went down 23-16 at Harlequins. It was clear that the team had struggled since Brough's departure, as well as the unforeseen loss of Newton and Tronc, and Morrison's long lay-off through injury.

A run of defeats – the 29-10 home loss to Bradford was the sixth – was interrupted by a 54-12 win over next-to-bottom club Harlequins, but was followed by four more losses. Trinity got back on track with a surprise 41-0 trouncing of Brian Noble's Crusaders. It was unexpected because Trinity had been held up on the road to Wrexham, the journey taking almost six hours, and the kick-off was delayed by a further two hours. John Kear, in the meantime, had pledged his future to Wakefield after the Catalans had wanted him to replace Kevin Walters at the end of the season. But Trinity had insisted on compensation for losing their coach, who had a year left to run on his contract, and the Catalans refused to pay. Though he put a very positive spin on it, how Kear must have wished for a new start. Following the embarrassing 46-14 home defeat by Hull KR, he fumed, 'Is that as bad as it gets? I'll let you decide', before going on to class the display as the worst of the season. 'Unfortunately all our shoddy performances have been at home,' he reflected.

After a brief respite with a 29-6 home victory over Hull, Trinity lost all their remaining six fixtures. 'We fell away very worryingly,' said Kear after the 50-6 home defeat by St Helens. 'This is the biggest hole we've been in since I've been here … The results over the last couple of months are either a resounding win or an absolute hiding and Super League isn't supposed to be like that – it's about working hard and winning competitive games … We haven't got pivotal players who organise as well as others … We're missing players who've left the club …'

As if to confirm what Kear had just stated, Trinity found themselves on the end of another thrashing at Huddersfield, losing 58-6. To make matters worse, Brough and Drew, two of the pivotal players Kear was referring to, were in top form, with Brough bagging 22 points.

Before his final game at Belle Vue, Jason Demetriou, who, at the age of 34, had not been offered a new contract, looked back over the seven seasons he had spent at Wakefield. 'From the end of 2006 we have been moving forward,'

Jason Demetriou, team captain over five seasons up to 2010, typified Trinity's fighting spirit

he said. 'We just missed out on the play-offs in 2008 and recorded our highest finish last year, but I think we have hit a brick wall. With players like Danny Brough and Shane Tronc leaving, the quality we had at the start of the season has gone and that makes it tough … My first season in 2004 was memorable because I had never played in a team where everyone was so together. At the time I took it for granted but I realise now how special that team was …' The Trinity captain believed that Trinity's best team performance during his time at the club came at Wigan in the opening game of 2009, which was won 12-6 – the first match after Adam Watene's death in October 2008.

But there was no happy ending on Demetriou's last home appearance. Trinity were beaten 36-18 by Warrington, which virtually put an end to their play-off hopes. It was followed by a 38-28 defeat at Bradford, ending the home side's record twelve-match losing run. Trinity's own losing streak continued right up to the end of the season when they went down by 16-10 at Salford, who finished in twelfth place out of fourteen, one below Trinity.

It said something of the ability and similar commitment of another Australian, Glenn Morrison – and, for that matter, of the rest of the team - that, at the age of 34, he should be named Players' Player of the Year and the club's Man of Steel in his first season at Belle Vue.

As the club looked ahead to the next round of Super League licences, to be made known in 2011, a statement was put out to the effect that they were 'delighted' with the progress of the proposed new stadium at Newmarket, though planning permission was still a long way off. It was also stated that the new stadium had 'created a unique opportunity for growth and new investment in the club.' Not for the first time, the board declared themselves willing to work with new investors or even to step aside 'in order to take the club to the next level and further enhance its licence application.' Among changes in the club's administration, James Elston had returned to the club as chief executive after a spell at Hull KR as operations manager.

As he looked to building the squad for 2011, John Kear promised a 'complete makeover'. He said: 'Last season we were too accepting when things went against us. Wakefield have always been a team that fought against adversity and last year we capitulated too easily.' Kear looked to recruit young British players 'with the hunger to do well and perhaps a point to prove.' It also looked as though Kear was operating within tight budget restraints as he set about combing Super League Academy sides such as St Helens and Wigan and hunting down players with potential but who might have lost their way at other clubs. After all, he had a strong record in this area, as the likes of Richard Moore, Ricky Bibey and Danny Brough had proved.

Among the leavers, Gleeson and Leo-Latu went to Salford and Blanch to the Catalans. Cooke and Johnson were released. New Zealand Test half back Jeremy Smith was signed after spending two years at Salford, second row Frankie Mariano joined from Hull KR, former Hull half back or hooker Tommy Lee arrived from Crusaders, winger Kevin Penny from Warrington and another ex-Kiwi, full back Motu Tony, formerly with Hull, was also recruited. Ten new signings were announced.

The new playing strip for the coming season was modelled on that worn by Harper Oliver Hamshaw in the 1880s which was kept in Wakefield Museum. The nod to the past came about as Trinity prepared to move out of their home since 1879, and into the new stadium at Newmarket, with the 2011 season being billed as their last at Belle Vue. But ominously the stadium plans were referred to the Secretary of State, since the new venue fell partly within green belt.

Wakefield Trinity began the year 2011 on the edge of collapse. Chairman Ted Richardson launched an appeal asking for 500 supporters to buy £1,000 worth of shares so that the club would not go bankrupt as a result of another demand for non-payment of taxes. Richardson blamed the crisis on the delay in getting planning application for the new stadium at Newmarket, stating that the developers were due to hand over £350,000 to the club once planning approval had been given. But Richardson's pleas fell on deaf ears. After the sale of new shares had realised only £31,000, Trinity were duly issued with the winding-up order initiated by the Inland Revenue, the third such order in twelve months. As a consequence the club applied to go into administration in order to avoid being bankrupted.

The crisis, which arrived right at the start of the season, could hardly have come at a worse time. Doubts surrounded the club's future, at least in Super League. But in mid-February the club was bought from the administrators by Andrew Glover, a local businessman and owner of a double-glazing company, whose familiarity with rugby league up to that point was quite limited. James Elston remained as chief executive, with Davide Longo, formerly community trust manager, replacing Francis Stephenson as general manager.

At one point it had been uncertain whether Trinity would even be able to raise a team to compete in the Magic Weekend opener in Cardiff. But compete they did, losing to Castleford by 40-20 in the most difficult circumstances. The administrators had been bound, they said, to realise what assets they could, and sold Sam Obst to Hull and Dale Ferguson to Huddersfield for undisclosed fees, before Daryl Millard signed for the Catalans. For having gone into administration, Wakefield were docked four points by the RFL, which at least made them no worse off than the Welsh side, Crusaders, who had earlier lost the same number of points for the same reason.

It said something for the spirit which John Kear managed to rekindle in the team – and a makeshift-looking one, as well – that they travelled to Perpignan and rattled the Catalans with an emphatic 38-14 win. Second rower Frankie Mariano and centre Chris Dean each scored two tries as Trinity unexpectedly dominated the game.

Further uncertainty hung over the club as it looked towards the awarding of franchises – to take place in mid-season - with the stadium once more proving the biggest stumbling-block. New chairman Andrew Glover, while expecting the Newmarket development to go ahead, had drawn up contingency plans of redeveloping Belle Vue, although the idea of ground-sharing with Barnsley FC was abandoned. Major signings were ruled out, but a number of minor moves took place, including former Whitehaven prop Kyle Amor arriving on loan from Leeds and threequarter Josh Griffin from Huddersfield.

To say the least, victories were not expected to be plentiful, but following losses to Salford and Bradford, Trinity achieved an encouraging 20-6 win at Hull, where Glenn Morrison gave an inspiring lead and full back Aaron Murphy made try-saving tackles. Throughout April and into May, Trinity picked up valuable league points as they tried to hoist themselves up the table ahead of the RFL's licensing decision. In a high-scoring game at Belle Vue, Harlequins were beaten 52-32, Griffin proving his value with a try and eight goals. On Good Friday, Trinity again showed their resolve by wiping out Castleford's 20-point lead with four tries in eighteen minutes to win by 28-24 at Wheldon Road. Half back Kieran Hyde scored the first of those four and had a hand in the next two. Another dramatic win, this time by 26-24 over Hull KR at Belle Vue, came when Hyde kicked the match-winning penalty after the hooter had sounded.

In the Challenge Cup, Trinity went through to the fifth round after their 50-10 win at Doncaster, where they scored six tries in the last half-hour. But the team's half back options were further weakened when Ben Jeffries decided to return to Bradford.

The bottom-of-the-table clash at Crusaders ended in a 23-10 win for the home side, compounding Trinity's problems. Nor was there any satisfaction to be gained from the fifth round Cup tie at home to Castleford. As the teams were locked on 18-all at the final hooter, extra time and the golden point system came into play, resulting in no fewer than six drop goal attempts, most of them farcical and all unsuccessful. The match was finally decided when Trinity conceded a penalty for ball-stealing and Castleford winger Kirk Dixon sent the ball between the posts and Cas into the next round.

As the RFL's licensing decision came ever closer, the club called a public meeting at the Cedar Court Hotel, attended by 1,000 fans. All were asked to join a new membership scheme to boost the club's support, and heard rallying cries and a statement of the new owner's plans for the future.

After a relatively rare victory over Huddersfield, Trinity did not win a single game for almost three months, suffering a string of nine consecutive defeats and conceding an average of over fifty points a match. In the middle of it all, the club and supporters anxiously awaited the outcome of the RFL's licensing process which would give places in Super League for the next three years. With a final push, the membership target of 5,000 was reached, though what bearing it would have on the RFL's decision was unknown. With Widnes certain to be promoted, Wakefield was the club heavily tipped to be left out.

At the eleventh hour, as the media were all assembled to hear the pronouncement, Crusaders, to the amazement of everyone outside the RFL, dropped their application. The result was that Wakefield, who had never been relegated in their thirteen-year Super League history, were reprieved by what must surely rank as one of the greatest pieces of good fortune that has ever come their way.

RFL chief executive Nigel Wood, however, added a note of caution. 'The facility [stadium] is something that needs significant attention,' he said, 'and probably, because of the chequered financial performance in the recent past, Wakefield need to demonstrate some stability in that area.

'They have always had a reputation of producing players but I think they should concentrate on [improving] the facility, the financial [performance] and no doubt they want a few more spectators as well.'

RFL chairman Richard Lewis added: 'What we are saying is that they are worthy of the licence providing they deliver on their promises and their plans.'

Wakefield chief executive James Elston vowed: 'The job now is never to put the club in this situation again.'

Things started to change rapidly. After more than five years at the club, John Kear, whose contract was about to expire, saw his position come under review. It was soon announced that Trinity's longest-serving coach in the Super League era would leave at the end of the season, since all had agreed that it was time for a change.

The first match after the awarding of the licence should have been an opportunity for celebration and a performance from the team that showed they were worthy of the trust placed in them. It was not to be. Ironically, Trinity crashed at home to Crusaders, whose players faced an uncertain future but lashed their hosts to the tune of 40-6. Kear confessed that his players looked as if they didn't care.

With no new coach yet announced, Trinity went ahead with recruitment for the following season and quickly signed up Kiwi and Samoan international second row Ali Lauitiiti, 32, from Leeds, New Zealand centre Vince Mellars from Crusaders and prop Steve Southern from Newcastle Knights. England winger Peter Fox was to return to Belle Vue from Hull KR and forward Oliver Wilkes from Harlequins.

Among the leavers, Julien Rinaldi, who had given much-needed direction, returned to Harlequins, Luke George went back to his first club Huddersfield, and ever dependable full back Matt Blaymire, who had given excellent service over five years, decided to retire at the age of 29 following injury problems.

The RFL eventually stated that Wakefield Trinity had again been awarded a grade C licence, the lowest. Those responsible for the appraisal said that they recognised that 'new ownership had injected enthusiasm, capital and business acumen into the club… Wakefield's performance on the field and across the current licence period [2009-11] has been acceptable and their community programme is excellent. However commercial, financial and governance performance in this licence period has been poor, with the club entering administration in February 2011.' The RFL added that the club faced a number of challenges and referred once again to the stadium, to commercial and supporter growth and the need to be more competitive on the pitch.

The final match of the season, in which once more Trinity avoided bottom place, was a much more fitting end to Kear's period in charge. The nine-match losing run came to an end at Belle Vue with a 26-14 victory over Bradford, giving supporters the chance to rejoice that they had been waiting for. The genial Kear spoke of his sadness at leaving but pride in what had been achieved, with, at the top of the list, the monumental four wins out of six to ensure survival when he first arrived in 2006, the best-ever Super League finish of fifth in 2009 and the Challenge Cup semi-final.

As Kear took up the offer of the head coach position at Batley, Trinity replaced him with another coach locally bred but arriving from Hull, Richard Agar, whose father Allan had been Wakefield's scrum half in the early eighties. Although some signings for the forthcoming 2012 season had been made before he was appointed, Agar quickly added others as he set about transforming Trinity's playing roster. After bringing his Australian assistant coach James Webster and loose forward Danny Washbrook with him from Hull, Agar made a dozen other signings including centre Dean Collis and PNG hooker Paul Aiton from Cronulla, forwards Danny Kirmond and Andy Raleigh and half back Kyle Wood from Huddersfield, with Aaron Murphy and Tommy Lee going in the opposite direction. A new half back partnership was lined up in the form of Tim Smith, who had played for Wigan in 2008-9 and was another to be released by Cronulla, and Isaac John from New Zealand Warriors. Full back Richie Mathers came on a year's loan from Castleford and 29-year old Southern, who had led Newcastle Knights' reserve grade in 2011, was made captain. Glenn Morrison, though, was to limit his activities to coaching after sustaining a career-ending shoulder injury in training.

In all seventeen new players were recruited for 2012, which was believed to be a club record. James Elston revealed that the previous season's squad had cost £1.2 million to put together, with a number of players being signed with one eye on descent into the Championship. The 2012 squad, though he judged it 'far superior' had cost only £70,000 more. Richard Agar also disclosed that no player earned more than £100,000 although two were being paid between £75,000 and £100,000. The amount Trinity were spending was around half a million pounds below the salary cap and, said Agar, 'way behind a lot of other clubs.'

With so many players new to the club, it naturally took some time to make them into a team. Though the opening game resulted in a 32-14 victory for Wakefield at promoted side Widnes, the next did not come until six matches later when the Catalans were beaten 32-20 at Belle Vue. In that game, half back Isaac John, who had taken on the goal-kicking duties, landed six from six, but he was replaced by the experienced Paul Sykes, who arrived on loan from Bradford. None of the losses endured so far were on the scale of those suffered in the latter part of the previous season.

Wakefield did not linger long in the Challenge Cup, going out at the first attempt at Headingley, where Leeds won 38-18. Trinity's third league victory, which came at the end of the third month of the season, was gained at the expense of Salford, who went down 26-22 at Belle Vue. Signs of better things to come were also evident in the 32-26 win over Castleford during the Magic Weekend at Manchester, which was seen by over 30,000 fans. Danny Kirmond, from Sharlston, took over the captaincy from Steve Southern and, in Agar's words, made 'a big impact'. The team was beginning to weld together, which was seen in the 32-30 home win over Agar's former club, Hull, who took a 30-10 lead only to be overhauled as Ali Lauitiiti went over for the decisive try late in the game. Paul Sykes, playing at stand-off, was also having a growing influence on the team. 'He has put in some outstanding field kicks and towering bombs and done some real damage,' said Agar.

A defeat at Headingley by four points out of 84, preceded a run of three more losses, but after the last of those, by 52-10 to rampant league leaders Wigan, Trinity turned a corner. In August they made a push for the play-offs, first by beating Huddersfield 35-14, and then Leeds by 38-18 – only the second time in Super League that Trinity had beaten them at Belle Vue. Half back Tim Smith again showed his class by creating five tries and scoring one in the 40-12 win over Castleford, before Sykes won two matches in succession with last-minute drop goals. After Kirmond had scored two tries in three minutes and Lee Smith, on loan from Leeds, has also touched down twice, Sykes landed the drop in the dying seconds to condemn St Helens to a 33-32 defeat. In the very next game and again in the very last minute, the ex-Bradford man sent the ball between the posts for a second dramatic win, this time by 31-30 over Hull KR.

With victories in the last two games of the season – against Widnes and Salford – Trinity created a new club record of seven successive wins in Super League, which was a triumph for the new coach and the newly-assembled team. Finishing eighth in the table, they qualified for the play-offs and faced fifth-placed Leeds at Headingley. Trinity lost 42-20 to the eventual champions, but a satisfied chairman, Andrew Glover, announced, 'We've far surpassed our expectations.' With a large membership increase, crowds averaged 8,172, up by 1,620 on 2011.

Among individual statistics, loose forward Danny Washbrook made the highest number of tackles in all Super League, with Paul Aiton also figuring in the top ten. Tim Smith figured second in the list of 'try assists', Ali Lauitiiti fourth in the offloads table and Ben Cockayne was Super League's fourth highest metre-maker, according to Opta statistics.

The comings and goings were fewer than at the end of the previous season, but Steve Southern, who failed to settle, returned to Australia after just one year of a three-year contract and another forward, Paul Johnson, who, after arriving from St Helens, was named Players' Player and Coaches' Player of the Season in 2011, went to Hull. As a replacement, former State of Origin prop Justin Poore signed from Parramatta, while Paul Sykes was handed a permanent one-year contract.

Another 12-month lease on Belle Vue was signed, as had happened for the past two years, since the ground no longer belonged to the club but to the Bank of Ireland. In December, at long last, final approval was given by the Secretary of State for the £19 million stadium development at Newmarket to go ahead. The plans had first been passed by Wakefield Council, but the government had stepped in because the land fell within green belt. A public enquiry twelve months earlier had heard objections from Leeds City Council and local residents. In June the Secretary of State, Eric Pickles, had announced that he was 'minded to approve' the plans provided that certain conditions were met. By the end of the year, developers Yorkcourt were set to go ahead with the business park and stadium, which was to be leased to Wakefield and District Community Trust, headed by Sir Rodney Walker, and with Wakefield Trinity as the anchor tenant. 'We're now well placed,' said chief executive James Elston, 'to create a really secure future for this club.'

It was not long, though, before financial worries reappeared. In the first month of the 2013 season, the main sponsor, scrap metal merchants Eric France, went into liquidation, leaving a hole in the club's funds. Those concerns did not go away, despite the fact that Trinity were operating on one of Super League's smallest budgets, as they continued to spend only two-thirds of the maximum permitted under salary cap rules.

In the first home game of the 2013 campaign, a 36-20 victory over Hull KR was aided by a hat-trick

Wakefield captain Danny Kirkmond, supported by Danny Washbrook and Ben Cockayne.

from winger Ben Cockayne against his former club. The ex-Normanton amateur had, said coach Agar, once been 'cast aside but fought his way back and into the England squad.' He added, as his predecessor John Kear might also have done, 'We've provided an environment for players like these to kick on and improve as individuals and players.' Agar himself was appointed head coach of France's national team to lead them into the autumn's World Cup.

Front-rower Kyle Amor was another to show obvious development, while centre Lee Smith became an increasingly important member of the team, especially during Paul Sykes's absence through injury. Smith ended the season as the club's top goal-kicker and included in his tally a drop goal which, coming two minutes from full time, gave Trinity a 27-26 win at Hull in July. Sykes, as in the previous season, had shown the same skill in producing the one point which earned a 23-all draw at home to Salford in March, as well as in the 37-16 win at Castleford, in a match which ended seven minutes early because of a fire scare.

Entering the Challenge Cup at the fourth round stage and fielding several reserves, Trinity made light work of an enthusiastic but outclassed Hemel Stags of Championship One. Lee Smith scored two of his team's eleven tries and kicked nine goals. But in the next round at Hull, Trinity went out of the competition by 24-6 at the hands of the eventual finalists.

A 46-10 victory at Salford on a Monday evening in front of the television cameras started a four-match winning run in June and July, during which London Broncos, Hull – thanks to Smith's drop goal – and Widnes were beaten.

Trinity came within two points of defeating Leeds in the following game, which was watched by 18,387 spectators, Headingley's highest Super League crowd of the season – proving that old rivalries were still a big draw. A week later Trinity had their chance for revenge, in a match which had been rearranged after snow in March had covered Belle Vue. Wakefield's best attendance of the season and their second highest in Super League – 10,031 – witnessed an enthralling struggle. After a 12-all stalemate up to the hour, in which hooker Paul Aiton scored both Trinity's tries, Leeds went 19-12 ahead. But prop Justin Poore crashed through the visitors' defence for a try converted by Lee Smith, second rower Frankie Mariano went over, and Wakefield were in the ascendancy by 24-19 with eight minutes left. But the reigning champions came back, scoring from a deflected kick-through to take a one-point lead, which they extended to produce a final score of 31-24.

Those two defeats preceded a downward spiral that would last until the end of the season. Play-off hopes faded with a 26-24 home loss to Bradford and were extinguished by further defeats at Warrington and at home to St Helens. In the penultimate match of the season, a 40-0 crash against Huddersfield, who took the League Leaders trophy, lengthened the losing run to six. But in a rousing finale, Trinity beat Castleford by 36-32 to finish in eleventh place. Ali Lauitiiti swung the game, powering over the line before sending young winger Liam Kay away for his hat-trick with just twenty seconds remaining.

Agar maintained that the squad had 'come a long way' since the start of 2012. 'Though we didn't make the play-offs, the general feeling within the group was that we had been consistent over a longer period this year, but we've fallen on the wrong side of the ledger in the close games.'

Among players who stood out, PNG World Cup hooker Paul Aiton proved 'a tough competitor, week in, week out', Ali Lauitiiti figured among the league's top offloaders, while winger Peter Fox headed the club try-scoring list, followed by Danny Kirmond, Ben Cockayne and centre Dean Collis. Kirmond, said Agar, 'evolved as a person and a player, with a level of performance that got him talked about as an England player.' Scrum-half Tim Smith, the hub of the attacking play, left a gap when Salford signed him for a substantial sum just before the season's end.

After the club was forced to stave off a winding-up petition from HMRC, the scrum half's transfer fee temporarily eased concerns. But a £400,000 shortfall over the season was announced. Chairman Andrew Glover, in post for two and a half years since buying the club out of administration, stepped down to head the newly-established Sport and Education Academy. One of Glover's achievements had been the erection of a roof at the Doncaster Road end of the ground for the first time in the club's history and he now expected to oversee the move to Newmarket. He was replaced by Michael Carter, a self-confessed fan, a club shareholder and former deputy managing director of Yorkshire Traction, who, along with fellow-director Chris Brereton, was to play an active role in the running of the club and 'ensure we are a Super League club when we become the anchor tenants at Newmarket.' With promotion and relegation about to be reintroduced in the coming season, Carter revealed that a six-figure sum had been turned down for Danny Kirmond, around whom Trinity intended to build their future team, in which it was hoped that local talent would play a leading role.

Towards the end of a hard season, second rower Kirmond, selected in the 2013 Dream Team, nevertheless repeated what a privilege it was to lead the team and showed a sense of Trinity's history. 'When you look at the people who've captained the club, it's an honour to have your name up there,' he said. 'Coming from the local area, from Sharlston, it means even more. I watched quite a few Featherstone games when I was younger, but Wakefield is always where I've lived and to captain my home town club is a massive privilege and a real honour.

'A lot of the legends of the club still come to matches, and it inspires you. People like that inspired me as a youngster as well, watching great captains leading the team out. It's something I never really imagined I'd do, but it brings the best out of me. Everyone is quite honest here and the first thing anyone mentions is the team spirit we have, which is the most important thing. When you're in difficulty, that's what gets you out of it.'

Afterword

Few are the professional clubs, in rugby league or in other sports, which have not known hard times. Wakefield Trinity is clearly no exception. The twenty-first century has seen rugby league at the top level dominated by a handful of clubs who have found a means of accruing high levels of income, based on their population or a wealthy benefactor or both. Wakefield has never been in this fortunate position. The club's greatest days have been enacted, to a large extent, by players which the club has found on its own doorstep. Those players are now both harder to find and harder to keep, as the top professional sportsmen naturally gravitate towards the top clubs. To an extent, that has always been true. The difference is that club loyalty, as shown throughout the decades by innumerable Trinity players, from Bill Horton to Harry Wilkinson to Nigel Bell, is an increasingly rare commodity. But somehow the spirit of the team survives, and many an outsider has borne testament to that. Honours are more scarce, even in simple numerical terms. But it is to Trinity's great credit that they compete at the highest level. At the present time, Wakefield is one of only eight clubs from the 1895 split still operating in what used to be called the first division, and of those only Huddersfield and Hull can point to an earlier foundation date. Leaving aside the five Challenge Cups, the two Championships, the ten Yorkshire Cups (fourteen including the pre-NU years) and seven Yorkshire Leagues which have been won along the way, Wakefield Trinity's position at the heart of the community and the core of rugby league is perhaps its greatest triumph of all.

Sources

Reports provided in the *Wakefield Express* have proved indispensable, as have others published in the *Yorkshire Post* and *Yorkshire Evening Post*, while the specialist publications, *League Express*, *Open Rugby* and *Rugby League World* have also been consulted.

Robert Gate's books, *Rugby League Lions*, *The Struggle for the Ashes*, *The Rugby League Fact Book* and his biography of Neil Fox have been repeatedly referred to, as have Tony Collins's two histories of the game, *Rugby's Great Split* and *Rugby League in Twentieth Century Britain*. Trevor Delaney's *The Roots of Rugby League* and *Rugby Disunion* have also been used. John Lindley's two books on Trinity, *Dreadnoughts* and *100 Years of Rugby* have been extensively consulted; no less so the Rothmans Yearbooks and League Publications Yearbooks.

Notes

Since many quotations have been taken from the *Wakefield Express*, as is made clear in the main text, I have kept notes to a minimum. However, because of their special historical relevance with regard to the early days of the club, I have retained those which follow.

Chapter 1
1 Wakefield Express, 26 Nov. 1949.
2 According to notes made by the late local historian, Peter Wood, a Sunday School class at Holy Trinity, run by a Mr Dunhill, formed a football team in 1871. Wood does not state his source and no other information has been found about what must have been, at best, an informal arrangement to play the game.
3 Wakefield Free Press and West Riding Advertiser, 28 June, 1873.
4 Wakefield Express, 23 Nov. 1872.
5 Yorkshire Evening Post, 1 Nov. 1902.
6 Wakefield and West Riding Herald, 28 Dec. 1872.
7 Wakefield Express, 14 Dec. 1872.
8 Trinity team: H Stones (capt), TO Bennett, J Verity, J McConnell, T Wilkinson, T Whitehead, - Powell, JW Whitehead, EC Whitehead, A Saville, C Wraith, T Perfect and three members of the Wakefield club.
9 Trinity team: H Stones (capt), TO Bennett, TB Waite, J Verity, J McConnell, JA Grace, TS Whitehead, JW Whitehead, T Best, J Langton, E Atkinson, E Spink, J Wood, A Hayley, EG Whitehead.
10 Wakefield Free Press and West Riding Advertiser, 28 June, 1873.
11 Yorkshire Evening Post, 1 Nov. 1902.
12 Wakefield and West Riding Herald, 29 Jan. 1876.
13 Yorkshire Evening Post, 16 Nov. 1901.
14 Yorkshire Post, 29 Dec. 1874.
15 Yorkshire Evening Post, 1 Nov. 1902.
16 Yorkshire Evening Post, ibid. The photograph as described does not appear to have survived. It is possible that the interviewees are referring to the one of 1875, in which players seem to be wearing what is thought to be the club's first strip of black and blue horizontal stripes.
17 Athletic News, 23 March 1877.

18 Wakefield Express, 27 April 1878.
19 Information provided by Mr Joe Haigh of Tavora Street, Wakefield Express, 13 April 1979.
20 Athletic News, ibid.
21 Athletic World, quoted in Wakefield and West Riding Herald, 16 Nov. 1878.
22 Wakefield Express, 22 Dec. 1877.
23 Wakefield and West Riding Herald, 4 Jan. 1879.
24 Wakefield Express, 19 April 1879.
25 Ernest Parker, a Trinity member and later official, witnessed the event. Wakefield Express, 6 July 1929, and elsewhere.
26 Wakefield Express, 8 Nov. 1952
27 Wakefield Express, 6 July 1929
28 Wakefield Express, ibid.
29 Wakefield and West Riding Herald, 15 and 22 Nov. 1879.
30 Wakefield Express, 20 Sept. 1879.

Chapter 2
1 Wakefield and West Riding Herald, 15 Nov. 1879.
2 Yorkshire Post, 2 Dec. 1879.
3 Yorkshire Evening Post, 16 Nov. 1901.
4 Yorkshire Evening Post, 1 Nov. 1902.
5 Quoted in YEP article.
6 Yorkshire Evening Post, 16 Nov. 1901.
7 The Yorkshireman, Oct-Nov 1890.
8 YEP, 8 Nov. 1902.
9 Wakefield Express, 27 March 1880.
10 Wakefield Express, 3 April 1880.
11 Wakefield Express, 13 Nov. 1880.
12 Yorkshire Post, 11 April 1881.
13 Wakefield Express 7 Jan. 1882.
14 Yorkshire Evening Post, 1 Nov. 1902.
15 Wakefield Express, 7 Jan. 1882.
16 Wakefield Express, 28 Jan. 1882.
17 Ibid.
18 Wakefield Express, 25 March 1882.
19 Wakefield Express, 8 April 1882.
20 Wakefield Express, 18 Nov. 1882.
21 Wakefield Express, 10 Feb. 1883.
22 Wakefield Express, 2 Dec. 1882.
23 Wakefield Express, 10 March 1883.
24 Wakefield Express, 3 Nov. 1883.
25 Wakefield Express, 6 Oct. 1883.
26 Wakefield Express, 1 Dec. 1883.
27 Wakefield Express, 9 Feb. 1884.
28 Wakefield Express, 16 Feb. 1884.
29 Wakefield Express, 15 March 1884.
30 Wakefield Express, 29 March 1884.
31 Wakefield Express, 27 Sept. 1884.
32 Wakefield Express, 4 Oct. 1884
33 Ibid.
34 Wakefield Express, 31 Jan. 1885.
35 Wakefield Express, 29 Nov. 1884.
36 JC Lindley, 100 Years of Rugby, p. 34.

Chapter 3
1 Evidence from TO Bennett to YEP, 1 Nov 1902.
2 The Yorkshireman, April 1890.

Chapter 4
1 Yorkshire Post, 23 Sept. 1983, quoted in Delaney, Rugby Disunion, pp 149-150.
2 Leeds Mercury, quoted in WE, 14 Oct, 1893.

Chapter 5
1 Athletic News Football Annual, 1897.
2 Collins, Rugby's Great Split, p. 162

Chapter 6
1 Yorkshire Post, 5 Dec. 1910

Chapter 8
1 Lindley, 100 Years of Rugby, p. 60.
2 Ibid, p. 162

Acknowledgements

I am indebted to those reporters who captured all the triumphs and tribulations associated with Wakefield Trinity Rugby League Football Club, and recorded as well all the more mundane, but essential details which can often prove enlightening. I have never been more conscious of the value and importance of the *Wakefield Express* and of the skill and enthusiasm of its rugby league men.

No one acquainted with the history of Wakefield Trinity can be unaware of John Lindley's two pioneering works, *Dreadnoughts* and *100 Years of Rugby*. My already well-thumbed copies were even more battered by the time I had completed my own research.

I have been glad of the assistance offered by two senior historians of the game, Robert Gate and Tony Collins, both of whom have produced essential works on the history of rugby league. Similarly, Harry Edgar, whom I have known since the great days of *Open Rugby*, has been very helpful in providing elusive pictures, reading the typescript and offering advice. Lee Robinson, the former Trinity physio who has taken on the much-needed role of official club historian, has given welcome assistance. The records which follow have been taken from information he has provided. I am grateful for the help given by the late Peter Wood and the eminent local historian, John Goodchild. I am also thankful for the wise background information liberally given by my former colleague Neal Rigby. Danny Spencer, Andy Morgan and Andy Young also responded to my various enquiries.

From past players, I have gleaned insights and sometimes photographs from Jack Perry, Don Robinson, the late Don Froggett, the late Joby Shaw, Neil Fox, John Etty, Harold Poynton and Ian Brooke. Daryl Topliss and Molly Smith have also kindly supplied photographs from their husbands' era.

Among the many people who have helped obtain photographs, I should particularly like to thank Norman Hazell, Jimmy Metcalfe, Terry Kelly, Michael Spink and Richard Fairclough. Equally I thank Kenny Smith of Photomakeovers for his work.

I am very grateful to the staff of Wakefield Libraries, who were never less than helpful during the many hours I spent there; and to the Wakefield Express for permission to quote extensively from their newspaper and to reproduce archive pictures. Unfortunately it is not always possible to know the provenance of articles and photographs. Any infringement of copyright is unintentional and will be corrected in a future edition.

My colleagues at League Publications, in particular Tim Butcher, who also read the typescript, and designer Paul Rohan, have worked unstintingly to bring this work to fruition and to them also I am grateful.

Finally I wish to thank my daughter Laura for her interest and help, and above all my wife Judy for her encouragement, support and productive dialogue throughout this long project.

Records

Historic matches

The first recorded team of Holy Trinity Young Men's Society which played against Wakefield on Boxing Day, 1872 at Mount Pleasant, Eastmoor and lost by three goals and four touchdowns to nil:
H Stones (capt.), TO Bennett, J Verity, J McConnell, T Wilkinson, T Whitehead, Powell, JW Whitehead, EC Whitehead, A Saville, C Wraith, T Perfect, plus three members of the Wakefield club.

The first full team of Holy Trinity Young Men's Society members which played against Wakefield on February 8, 1873 at Mount Pleasant and lost by three touchdowns to one:
H Stones (capt.), TO Bennett, TB Waite, J Verity, J McConnell, JA Grace, TS Whitehead, JW Whitehead, T Best, J Langton, E Atkinson, E Spink, J Wood, A Hayley, EG Whitehead.

YORKSHIRE CHALLENGE CUP FINALS (RFU)

April 12, 1879: Wakefield Trinity beat Kirkstall by two goals, one try and six touchdowns to nil (at Halifax).
Trinity: A Hayley (capt.), B Longbottom; CE Bartram, H Hayley; CT Baldwin, JW Whitehead; TO Bennett, A Hirst, W Ellis, W Jackson, B Kilner, JW Kilner, TB Parry, J Longbottom, G Steele.

April 3, 1880: Wakefield Trinity beat Heckmondwike by three goals, six tries and seven touchdowns to a try and two touchdowns (at Cardigan Fields, Leeds).
Trinity: A Hayley; CE Bartram, H Hayley; CT Baldwin (capt.), H Hutchinson; B Kilner, JW Kilner, B Longbottom, G Steele, W Ellis, TO Bennett, HB Pickersgill, W Jackson, A Shires, EJ Spink.

April 9, 1881: Wakefield Trinity lost to Dewsbury by one goal to four touchdowns (at Cardigan Fields, Leeds).
Trinity: A Hayley; CE Bartram, H Hayley; H Hutchinson, JH Cuthbert; B Kilner (capt.), JW Kilner, B Longbottom, G Steele, W Ellis, A Shires, G Logan, EJ Spink, J Jubb, W Jackson.

April 1, 1882: Wakefield Trinity lost to Thornes by a goal and five minor points to a try and five minor points (at Cardigan Fields, Leeds).
Trinity: A Hayley; CE Bartram, H Hayley, G Jubb; JH Cuthbert, H Hutchinson; B Kilner (capt.), G Steele, W Ellis, WG Thompson, W Jackson, F Mawer, J Jubb, JW Kilner, EJ Spink.

April 21, 1883: Wakefield Trinity beat Halifax by one goal, two tries and eleven minor points to nil (at Cardigan Fields, Leeds).
Trinity: HO Hamshaw; WE Hartley, CE Bartram, H Fallas; H Hutchinson, A Fisher; G Steele (capt.), W Ellis, JH Fallas, G Jubb, MB Oldroyd, T Shires, H Dawson, W Jackson, J Latham.

April 2, 1887: Wakefield Trinity beat Leeds St John's by two goals and two minor points to two minor points (at Halifax).
Trinity: HO Hamshaw; CE Bartram, H Fallas, F Ash; H Dawson (capt.), H Hutchinson; H Ward, J Latham, G Jubb, FW Lowrie, T Harrison, H Whiteley, A Thompson, P Booth, F Ross.

April 7, 1888: Wakefield Trinity lost to Halifax by two tries and two minor points to one try and one minor point (at Cardigan Fields, Leeds).
Trinity: JH Fotherby; F Ash, H Hayley, H Fallas; H Hutchinson (capt.), H Dawson; H Whiteley, JH Jones, W Binks, P Booth, T Harrison, A Thompson, TH Wordsworth, J Latham, FW Lowrie.

April 5, 1890: Wakefield Trinity lost to Huddersfield by one goal and one minor point to three minor points (at Halifax).
Trinity: H Stafford; H Fallas (capt.), JH Fotherby, M Varley; H Dawson, JH Thompson; P Booth, W Binks, R Dawson, J Latham, H Whiteley, A Garforth, JH Jones, A Thompson, JE Gomersall.

April 11, 1891: Wakefield Trinity lost to Pontefract by one goal, one try and three minor points to one goal and three minor points (at Headingley).
Trinity: T Collin; JH Fotherby, C Overton, H Fallas; J Bedford, R Hudson; JH Jones (capt.), W Binks, R Dawson, H Whiteley, J Dawson, W Smith, J Harnell, P Booth, R Pickering.

WAKEFIELD TRINITY'S FIRST MATCH UNDER NORTHERN UNION RULES

September 7, 1895: Wakefield Trinity lost at Bradford by 11-0.
Trinity: Harry Kershaw; RB Wood, T Howell, W Gameson, J Goldthorpe; J Anderton, E Milsom; J Allchurch, J Eyre, J Day, JT Ducker, W Binns, W Crossland, W Varley, T Westerby.

MATCHES AGAINST TOURING TEAMS (RFU)

October 31, 1888: Wakefield Trinity beat Maoris by one try and seven minor points to three minor points.
Trinity: HO Hamshaw; F Hulme, JH Fotherby, P Brannan; H Hutchinson, R Dunn; J Latham (capt.), A Thompson, W Binks, P Booth, F Ross, JH Jones, R Dawson, F Lowrie, JE Gomersall.

MATCHES AGAINST TOURING TEAMS (NU AND RFL)

October 23, 1907: Wakefield Trinity drew with New Zealand Professional All Blacks 5-5.
WT scorers: try – Lynch; goal – Metcalfe.
Trinity: Metcalfe; Booth, Lynch, Ward, McPhail; Slater, Newbould; J Taylor, G Taylor, Auton, Riley, Beaumont, Parkes

December 19, 1908: Wakefield Trinity beat Australians 20-13.
WT scorers: tries – Newbould 2, Bennett, Sidwell; goals Metcalfe 4.
Trinity: JD Metcalfe; EW Bennett, W Lynch, E Sidwell, WG Simpson; TH Newbould, H Slater; J Walton, G Taylor, R Beaumont, S Parkes, AK Crosland, H Kershaw

November 18, 1911: Wakefield Trinity lost to Australians 24-10. Attendance: 5,000.
WT scorers: tries – Bennett, Newbould; goals – Smith 2.
Trinity: C Smith; EW Bennett, J Garrity, TW Poynton, WG Simpson; H Slater, T Newbould; G Taylor, AK Crosland, J Walton, A Burton, J Taylor, H Kershaw

October 22, 1921: Wakefield Trinity lost to Australians 29-3. Attendance: 6,000.
WT scorer: try – Pickup.
Trinity: C Pollard; AA Rosenfeld, T Pickup, A Siswick, D Brannan; JB Paterson, J Parkin; H Armstrong, H Booth, J Wild, T Durkin, H Rafter, C Agar

December 28, 1926: Wakefield Trinity lost to New Zealanders 29-24. Attendance: 6,000.
WT scorers: tries – Davies 2, Waters, Parkin; goals – Pollard 6.
Trinity: R Ward; C Pollard, T Davies, A Siswick, T Pickup; J Parkin, J Pearce; J Kendall, J Waters, W Howell, D Maidment, T Coles, C Glossop

September 28, 1929: Wakefield Trinity beat Australians 14-3. Attendance: 9,796.
WT scorers: tries – Parkin, Ray; goals – C Pollard 4.
Trinity: C Pollard; S Ray, J Jones, E Pollard, S Smith; T Davies, J Parkin; H Hewitt, R White, L Higson, W Horton, D Maidment, C Glossop

October 28, 1933: Wakefield Trinity lost to Australians 17-6. Attendance: 5,596.
WT scorers: goals – Bonner 2 drop goals, Thompson penalty goal.
Trinity: WG Bonner; E Batten, R Moore, W Holt, J Pearce; E Thompson, S Herbert; L Higson, H Field, J Hobson, W Horton, GH Exley, H Wilkinson

October 9, 1937: Wakefield Trinity lost to Australians 17-10. Attendance: 8,696.
WT scorers: tries – Whitworth, Watson; goals – Teall 2.
Trinity: W Teall; R Appleyard, W Whitworth, H Turner, T Ryan; S Herbert, W Ball; H Wilkinson, C Carter, W Eddom, GH Exley, C Flowers, A Watson

December 6, 1947: Wakefield Trinity lost to New Zealanders 30-3. Attendance: 12,000.
WT scorer: try – Bratley.
Trinity: R Rylance; J Perry, W Stott, D Boocker, D Baddeley; A Fletcher, H Goodfellow; J Booth, L Marson, J Higgins, F Moore, WJD Howes, L Bratley

September 25, 1948: Wakefield Trinity lost to Australians 26-19. Attendance: 20,000.
WT scorers: tries – Fletcher 2, Booth, Bratley, H Jones; goals – Murphy, Rylance
Trinity: R Rylance; D Boocker, H Jones, R Jenkinson, J Duggan; A Fletcher, H Goodfellow; J Booth, L Marson, J Higgins, H Murphy, R Hughes, L Bratley

November 14, 1951: Wakefield Trinity lost to New Zealanders 26-18. Attendance: 9,800.
WT scorers: tries – Boocker, Mortimer, Froggett, Fletcher; goals – Mortimer 3
Trinity: E Luckman; J Duggan, D Froggett, F Mortimer, D Boocker; G Meredith, A Fletcher; J Booth, SJ Shaw, W Hudson (capt.), D Robinson, WJD Howes, R Hughes

November 12, 1952: Wakefield Trinity lost to Australians 58-8. Attendance: 6,074.
WT scorers: tries – Evans 2; goal – Burton.
Trinity: E Luckman; F Reynolds, H Burton, D Froggett, D Boocker; L Constance, R Evans; J Booth, D Horner, D Robinson, A Storey, R Kelly, WJD Howes.

December 3, 1955: Wakefield Trinity lost to New Zealanders 27-16. Attendance: 4,838.
WT scorers: tries – Bell, Bridges, Jaques, Fletcher; goals – Ripley 2.
Trinity: D Ripley; E Cooper, E Lockwood, K Holliday, C Bell; K Rollin, A Fletcher; J Booth, K Bridges, R Kelly, P Armstead, R Jaques, C Clifft

December 10, 1956: Wakefield Trinity beat Australians 17-12. Attendance: 3,381.
WT scorers: tries – Hirst, Rollin, Bullock; goals – Fox 4.
Trinity: E Wilkins; F Smith, N Fox, K Holliday, K Hirst; K Rollin, J Bullock; D Harrison, J Shaw, F Haigh, R Kelly, P Armstead, L Chamberlain

November 28, 1959: Wakefield Trinity beat Australians 20-10. Attendance: 17,615.
WT scorers: tries – Firth 2, Vines, Fox; goals – Fox 4.
Trinity: GV Round; F Smith, J Etty, N Fox, S Smith; H Poynton, K Holliday; J Wilkinson, G Oakes, DG Vines, M Sampson, A Firth, D Lamming

October 28, 1961: Wakefield Trinity beat New Zealanders 20-7. Attendance: 16,528.
WT scorers: Fox, Prinsloo, Skene, Holliday; goals – Fox 3, Round.
Trinity: GV Round; F Smith, A Skene, N Fox, J Prinsloo; C Greenwood, K Holliday; J Wilkinson, M Kosanovic, A Firth, DG Vines, B Briggs, D Turner

October 26, 1963: Wakefield Trinity lost to Australians 29-14. Attendance: 15,821.
WT scorers: goals – Fox 7.
Trinity: D Metcalfe; F Smith, K Hirst, N Fox, G Coetzer; H Poynton, K Holliday; J Wilkinson (R Haigh), M Kosanovic, M Sampson, DG Vines, B Briggs, D Turner

October 30, 1965: Wakefield Trinity beat New Zealanders 16-4. Attendance: 7,484.
WT scorers: tries – N Fox, Batty; goals – N Fox 5.
Trinity: D Metcalfe; A Thomas, W Rushton, N Fox, D Garthwaite; K Batty, K Holliday; E Bate, G Shepherd, E Campbell, D Turner, R Haigh, D Fox

October 28, 1967: Wakefield Trinity lost to Australians 33-7. Attendance: 10,256.
WT scorers: try – Batty; goals – N Fox 2.
Trinity: G Cooper; M Seator (M Morgan), I Brooke, N Fox, T Crook; K Batty, D Hawley; N Vaughan, G Shepherd, E Campbell, G Steel, R Spencer (D Fox), GV Round.

October 24, 1971: Wakefield Trinity lost to New Zealanders 23-12. Attendance: 5,367.
WT scorers: tries – Major, Morgan; goals – Fox 3.
Trinity: G Wraith; M Major (R Valentine), J Marston, J Hegarty, D Barends; J Bonnar, B Ward; D Jeanes, A Handforth, S Lyons, P Harrison, N Fox, M Morgan.

October 3, 1973: Wakefield Trinity lost to Australians 13-9. Attendance: 5,863.
WT scorers: try – Topliss; goals – Crook 3.
Trinity: G Wraith (L Sheard); D Smith, T Crook, J Hegarty, B Lumb; D Topliss, J Bonnar; G Ballantyne, M Morgan, R Bratt (N Cooper), R Valentine, K Endersby, E Holmes.

October 9, 1990: Wakefield Trinity lost to Australians 36-18. Attendance: 8,000.
WT scorers: tries – Du Toit, Mason, Wilson; goals – M Conway 3.
Trinity: C Perry; D Jones, G Byrne, P Eden, A Mason; T Lazenby, M Conway; A Shelford, J Thompson, N Bell, A Kelly, N Du Toit, G Price. Subs: R Slater, A Wilson, B Conway, L Morris.

CHALLENGE CUP FINALS

April 24, 1909: Wakefield Trinity beat Hull 17-0 at Headingley. Attendance: 23,587.
WT scorers: tries – Bennett 2, Newbould, Crosland, Simpson; goal – Metcalfe.
Trinity: JD Metcalfe; EW Bennett, W Lynch, E Sidwell, WG Simpson; H Slater (capt.), T Newbould; J Walton, AK Crosland, R Beaumont, J Auton, G Taylor, Herbert Kershaw

April 18, 1914: Wakefield Trinity lost to Hull 6-0 at Halifax. Attendance: 19,000.
Trinity: L Land; B Johnson, W Lynch, TW Poynton, BA Howarth; J Parkin, W Millican; A Dixon, AK Crosland, WL Beattie, E Parkin, A Burton, H Kershaw (capt)

May 4, 1946: Wakefield Trinity beat Wigan 13-12 at Wembley. Attendance: 54,730.
WT scorers: tries – Stott 2, Croston; goals – Stott 2.
Trinity: W Teall; R Rylance, W Stott (capt.), J Croston, D Baddeley; J Jones, H Goodfellow; H Wilkinson, L Marson, J Higgins, GH Exley, WJD Howes, L Bratley

May 14, 1960: Wakefield Trinity beat Hull 38-5 at Wembley. Attendance: 79,773.
WT scorers: tries – Fox 2, Skene 2, Holliday 2, Rollin, Smith; goals – Fox 7
Trinity: GV Round; F Smith, A Skene, N Fox, J Etty; K Rollin, K Holliday; J Wilkinson, G Oakes, DG Vines, A Firth, L Chamberlain, D Turner (capt.)

May 12, 1962: Wakefield Trinity beat Huddersfield 12-6 at Wembley. Attendance: 81,263.
WT scorers: tries – Fox, Hirst; drop goals – Fox 3.
Trinity: GV Round; F Smith, A Skene, N Fox, K Hirst; H Poynton, K Holliday; J Wilkinson, G Oakes, A Firth, B Briggs, D Williamson, D Turner (capt.)

May 11, 1963: Wakefield Trinity beat Wigan 25-10 at Wembley. Attendance: 84,492.
WT scorers: tries – Coetzer 2, Sampson, Poynton, Brooke; goals – Fox 5.
Trinity: GV Round; C Greenwood, I Brooke, N Fox, G Coetzer; H Poynton, K Holliday; J Wilkinson, M Kosanovic, M Sampson, DG Vines, D Turner (capt.), R Pearman

May 11, 1968: Wakefield Trinity lost to Leeds 11-10 at Wembley. Attendance: 87,100.
WT scorers: tries – Hirst 2; goals – D Fox 2
Trinity: G Cooper; K Hirst, I Brooke, G Coetzer, K Batty; H Poynton (capt.), R Owen; D Jeanes, G Shepherd, D Fox, M McLeod, R Haigh, D Hawley

May, 1979: Wakefield Trinity lost to Widnes 12-3 at Wembley. Attendance: 94,218.
WT scorer: try – Fletcher.
Trinity: L Sheard; A Fletcher, K Smith, S Diamond, B Juliff; D Topliss (capt.), M Lampkowski; J Burke, A McCurrie, T Skerrett, W Ashurst, Keith Rayne, G Idle

YORKSHIRE CUP FINALS (NU AND RFL)

December 3, 1910: Wakefield Trinity beat Huddersfield 8-2 at Headingley. Attendance: 19,000.
WT scorers: tries – G Taylor, Simpson; goal – Metcalfe.
Trinity: JD Metcalfe; EW Bennett, W Lynch, TW Poynton, WG Simpson; TH Newbould, E Sidwell; H Kershaw, AK Crosland, J Walton, J Auton (capt.), G Taylor, J Taylor

November 22, 1924: Wakefield Trinity beat Batley 9-8 at Headingley. Attendance: 25,546.
WT scorers: try – Parkin; goals – Pollard 2, Parkin.
Trinity: L Abrahams; C Pollard, W Batten, P Reid, E Thomas; J Parkin (capt.), T Pickup; B Gould, R White, W Blower, F Gibson, W Horton, C Glossop

December 1, 1926: Wakefield Trinity lost to Huddersfield 10-3 at Headingley. Attendance: 11,300.
WT scorer: try - Bateson
Trinity: R Ward; E Bateson, W Batten, T Pickup, C Pollard; J Pearce, J Parkin (capt.); JW Higson, R White, W Howell, T Coles, W Horton, C Glossop.

November 19, 1932: Wakefield Trinity lost to Leeds 8-0 at Fartown. Attendance: 17,685.
Trinity: G Robinson; E Brogden, F Lingard, E Pollard, F Smart; J Pearce, S Herbert; L Higson, S Gee, J Hobson, W Horton, H Wilkinson, GH Exley

October 27, 1934: Wakefield Trinity drew with Leeds 5-5 at Dewsbury. Attendance: 22,598.
WT scorers: try – Burrows; goal – Pollard.
Trinity: G Bonner; W Farrar, F Smith, E Pollard, F Smart; C Pickard, A Burrows; H Wilkinson, H Field, J Hobson, W Horton (capt.), GH Exley, D Rowan.

October 31, 1934 (First replay): Wakefield Trinity drew with Leeds 2-2 at Fartown. Attendance: 10,300.
WT scorer: goal – Pollard.
Trinity: G Bonner; W Farrar, F Smith, R Moore, F Smart; A Burrows, E Pollard; H Wilkinson, H Field, J Hobson, W Horton (capt.), GH Exley, D Rowan

November 7, 1934 (Second replay): Wakefield Trinity lost to Leeds 13-0 at Hunslet. Attendance: 19,304.
Trinity: G Bonner; R Moore, F Smith, E Pollard, F Smart; C Pickard, A Burrows; H Wilkinson, H Field, J Hobson, W Horton (capt.), GH Exley, D Rowan

October 31, 1936: Wakefield Trinity lost to York 9-2 at Headingley. Attendance: 19,000.
WT scorer: goal – Oliver.
Trinity: R Oliver; T Ryan, J Malpass, J Pearman, F Smart; S Herbert, H Goodfellow; H Wilkinson, C Carter, J Hobson, W Horton (capt.), GH Exley, A Watson

June 22, 1940: Wakefield Trinity lost to Featherstone 12-9 at Bradford. Attendance; 7,077.
WT scorers: try – Turner; goals – Teall 3.
Trinity: W Teall; R Jenkinson, H Turner, R Oliver, GH Exley; S Herbert, H Goodfellow; H Wilkinson, V Darlison, H Nicholson, A Flowers, S Orford, L Marson.

November 3, 1945: Wakefield Trinity lost 5-2 to Bradford N at Halifax. Attendance: 24,292.
WT scorer: goal - Stott
Trinity: W Teall; R Copley, W Stott (capt.), J Jones, D Baddeley; R Rylance, H Goodfellow; H Wilkinson, L Marson, J Higgins, H Murphy, F Moore, L Bratley.

November 2, 1946: Wakefield Trinity beat Hull 10-0 at Headingley. Attendance: 29,000.
WT scorers: tries – Fletcher, Rylance; goals – Perry 2.
Trinity: W Teall; J Perry, J Jones, J Croston, D Baddeley; R Rylance, A Fletcher; H Wilkinson (capt.), L Marson, J Higgins, GH Exley, H Murphy, L Bratley

November 1, 1947: Wakefield Trinity drew with Leeds 7-7 at Fartown. Attendance: 24,334.
WT scorers: try – Goodfellow; goals – Stott 2.
Trinity: W Teall; J Perry, W Stott (capt.), D Boocker, R Jenkinson; A Fletcher, H Goodfellow; H Wilkinson, L Marson, J Higgins, H Murphy, J Booth, L Bratley

November 5, 1947 (replay): Wakefield Trinity beat Leeds 8-7 at Odsal. Attendance: 32,500.
WT scorers: tries – Wilkinson, Bratley; goal – Perry.
Trinity: W Teall; J Perry, R Jenkinson, D Boocker, R Rylance (capt.); A Fletcher, H Goodfellow; H Wilkinson, L Marson, J Higgins, H Murphy, J Booth, L Bratley.

November 3, 1951: Wakefield Trinity beat Keighley 17-3 at Fartown. Attendance: 25,495.
WT scorers: tries – Hughes, Robinson, Boocker; goals – Hirst 4.
Trinity: E Luckman; J Duggan, L Hirst, D Froggett, D Boocker; G Meredith, A Fletcher; J Booth, D Horner, W Hudson, WJD Howes, D Robinson, R Hughes.

October 20, 1956: Wakefield Trinity beat Hunslet 23-5 at Headingley. Attendance: 31,147.
WT scorers: tries – Smith 2, Cooper 2, A Mortimer; goals – F Mortimer 4.
Trinity: F Mortimer; F Smith, A Mortimer, C Bell, E Cooper; K Holliday, K Rollin; D Harrison, K Bridges, F Haigh, R Kelly (capt.), P Armstead, L Chamberlain

October 18, 1958: Wakefield Trinity lost to Leeds 24-20 at Odsal. Attendance: 26,927.
WT scorers: tries – Metcalfe 3, Rollin; goals – Fox 2, Mortimer 2.
Trinity: F Mortimer; F Smith, D Metcalfe, N Fox, S Smith; K Holliday, K Rollin; W Adams, J Shaw, S Evans, R Kelly, L Chamberlain, K Traill (capt.)

October 29, 1960: Wakefield Trinity beat Huddersfield 16-10 at Headingley. Attendance: 17,629.
WT scorers: tries – Fox 2, Etty, Smith; goals – Fox 2.
Trinity: D Metcalfe; F Smith, A Skene, N Fox, J Etty; H Poynton, K Rollin; J Wilkinson, G Oakes, L Chamberlain, B Briggs, A Firth, D Turner (capt.).

November 11, 1961: Wakefield Trinity beat Leeds 19-9 at Odsal. Attendance: 16,429.
WT scorers: tries – Turner, Skene, Smith; goals – Fox 5.
Trinity: GV Round; F Smith, A Skene, N Fox, C Greenwood; H Poynton, K Holliday; J Wilkinson, M Kosanovic, A Firth, B Briggs, DG Vines, D Turner (capt.)

October 31, 1964: Wakefield Trinity beat Leeds 18-2 at Fartown. Attendance: 13,527.
WT scorers: tries – Jones 2, Fox 2; goals – Fox 3.
Trinity: D Metcalfe; B Jones, A Thomas, N Fox (capt.), G Coetzer; H Poynton, R Owen; E Campbell, G Shepherd, DG Vines, D Plumstead, R Haigh, K Holliday.

October 20, 1973: Wakefield Trinity lost 7-2 to Leeds at Headingley. Attendance: 7,535.
WT scorer: goal – Crook.
Trinity: G Wraith (L Sheard); D Smith, T Crook, J Hegarty, B Parker; D Topliss, J Bonnar; R Valentine, M Morgan, R Bratt, D Knowles (G Ballantyne), K Endersby, E Holmes.

October 26, 1974: Wakefield Trinity lost to Hull KR 16-13 at Headingley. Attendance: 5,639.
WT scorers: tries – Hegarty, Smith, Bratt; goals – Crook 2.
Trinity: L Sheard; D Smith, T Crook, J Hegarty (E Holmes), J Archer; D Topliss (capt), J Bonnar; G Ballantyne, R Handscombe, R Bratt, T Skerrett, A Tonks (N Goodwin), M Morgan.

September 23, 1990: Wakefield Trinity lost to Castleford 11-8 at Elland Road. Attendance: 12,362.
WT scorers: try – Mason; goals – Harcombe 2.
Trinity: K Harcombe; D Jones, A Mason, P Eden, A Wilson; T Lazenby, M Conway; A Shelford, B Conway, J Thompson, A Kelly (capt.), G Price, N Bell. Subs (both used): R Slater, C Perry.

October 18, 1992: Wakefield Trinity beat Sheffield Eagles 29-16 at Elland Road. Attendance: 7,690.
WT scorers: tries – Slater, Bagnall, Spencer, Mason, Price; goals – Benson 3, Wright; drop goal - Wright
Trinity: G Spencer; D Jones, A Mason, P Benson, A Wilson; N Wright, G Bagnall (capt.); M Webster, N Bell, J Glancy, G Price, D Fritz, R Slater. Subs: R Goddard, B Conway.

CHAMPIONSHIP FINALS

May 21, 1960: Wakefield Trinity lost to Wigan 27-3 at Odsal. Attendance: 82,087.
WT scorer: try – Fox
Trinity: GV Round; F Smith, A Skene, N Fox, J Etty; K Rollin, K Holliday; J Wilkinson, G Oakes, DG Vines, A Firth, L Chamberlain, D Turner (capt)

May 19, 1962: Wakefield Trinity lost to Huddersfield 14-5 at Odsal. Attendance: 37,451.
WT scorer: try Fox; goal – Fox.
Trinity: GV Round; F Smith, A Skene, N Fox, K Hirst; H Poynton, K Holliday; J Wilkinson, M Kosanovic, DG Vines, A Firth, B Briggs, D Turner (capt.).

May 6, 1967: Wakefield Trinity drew with St Helens 7-7 at Headingley. Attendance: 20,161.
WT scorers: penalty try – Owen; goals - N Fox 2
Trinity: G Cooper; K Hirst, I Brooke, N Fox, G Coetzer; H Poynton (capt.), R Owen; J Bath, B Prior, E Campbell, G Clarkson, R Haigh, D Fox.

May 10, 1967 (replay): Wakefield Trinity beat St Helens 21-9 at Swinton. Attendance: 33,537.
WT scorers: tries – Owen, Brooke 2, Poynton, Hirst; goals – Fox 3.
Team as above.

May 4, 1968: Wakefield Trinity beat Hull KR 17-10 at Headingley. Attendance: 22,023.
WT scorers: tries – Owen, Jeanes, N Fox; goals – N Fox 2, D Fox; drop goal – Poynton.
Trinity: G Cooper; G Coetzer, I Brooke, N Fox, K Batty; H Poynton (capt.), R Owen; D Jeanes, G Shepherd, D Fox, M McLeod, R Haigh, D Hawley.

PLAYER'S No. 6 TROPHY

January 22, 1972: Wakefield Trinity lost to Halifax 22-11 at Odsal. Attendance: 8,295.
WT scorers: tries – Topliss, Slater, Valentine; goal – Fox.
Trinity: G Wraith (B Ward); K Slater, J Marston, J Hegarty, M Major; D Topliss, K Harkin; D Jeanes (capt.), M Morgan, S Lyons, P Harrison (R Spencer), R Valentine, N Fox.

FIRST DIVISION GRAND FINAL
September 26, 1998: Wakefield Trinity beat Featherstone 24-22 at McAlpine Stadium, Huddersfield. Attendance: 8,224.
WT scorers: tries – Bostock 2, Southernwood, Casey, Stephenson; goals – Casey 2.
Trinity: M Holland; K Gray, A Hughes, M Law, J Bostock; G Casey, R Kenworthy; F Stephenson, R Southernwood, G Lord, I Hughes, S Whakarau, M Fuller (capt). Subs: A Fisher, S Richardson, W McDonald, D Mycoe (not used).

Player records

Compiled from information provided by Lee Robinson

MOST APPEARANCES FOR WAKEFIELD TRINITY

Harry Wilkinson	618	1929-49
Neil Fox	574	1956-69, 1970-74
AK 'Nealy' Crosland	533	1900-22
GH 'Mick' Exley	449	1928-47
Bill Horton	441	1924-38
Keith Holliday	438	1952-66
Herbert Goodfellow	434	1933-51
David Topliss	417	1968-81, 1987-88
Ernest Bennett	386	1898-1914
Charlie Pollard	385	1919-32
Jimmy Metcalfe	375	1897-1911
Tommy Newbould	365	1902-19
Nigel Bell	358	1983-96
Jonathan Parkin	342	1912-30
Billy Teall	325	1936-48
Harold Poynton	319	1957-70
Jack Walton	317	1902-13
Archie Siswick	317	1919-30
Len Marson	305	1939-53
Arthur Fletcher	303	1943-57
John Thompson	302	1978-97
Harry Murphy	290	1940-52
Herbert Kershaw	288	1906-22
Charlie Glossop	287	1923-31
Billy Conway	276	1984-97
Mick Morgan	270	1967-77
Joe Pearce	269	1924-33
Fred Smith	267	1956-65
Ernest Pollard	260	1926-35
Billy Lynch	258	1904-19
Jack Booth	257	1946-55
Tommy Pickup	257	1920-28
Harry Field	255	1927-36
Bill Walton	251	1895-1901, 1904-07
Bob Haigh	250	1962-70
Phil Eden	250	1982-93

TOP TRY-SCORERS

Neil Fox	272	1956-69, 1970-74
David Topliss	195	1968-81, 1987-88
Fred Smith	188	1955-65
Ernest Bennett	184	1899-1914
Dennis Boocker	127	1947-54
Gert Coetzer	122	1962-68
David Smith	115	1971-76
Herbert Goodfellow	114	1933-51
Arthur Fletcher	114	1943-57
Ted Bateson	113	1925-33
Tommy Poynton	111	1906-15
Andy Mason	111	1987-93
Ken Hirst	100	1955-68

TOP FORWARD

Len Bratley	94	1937-49

MOST TRIES IN A SEASON

Fred Smith	38	1959-60
David Smith	38	1973-74
Fred Smith	37	1958-59
Alan Skene	35	1959-60
Billy Simpson	34	1910-11
Dennis Boocker	32	1953-54
Neil Fox	32	1957-58
Keith Slater	31	1970-71
Fred Smith	30	1956-57
Neil Fox	30	1959-60
Jan Prinsloo	30	1961-62
Freddie Smart	29	1931-32
Gert Coetzer	29	1963-64
David Topliss	29	1972-73

TOP FORWARD

Len Bratley	25	1945-46

MOST TRIES IN A MATCH

Fred Smith	7 v Keighley, 25 April 1959	
Keith Slater	7 v Hunslet, 6 February 1971	

TOP GOAL-KICKERS

Neil Fox	1,836	1956-69, 1970-74
Charlie Pollard	654	1919-32
Jimmy Metcalfe	387	1897-1911
Frank Mortimer	378	1951-59
Jamie Rooney	359	2003-08
Terry Crook	325	1968-81
Mark Conway	320	1989-92
Ernest Pollard	319	1926-36
Steve Diamond	264	1978-87
Leslie Hirst	239	1949-55
Kevin Harcombe	228	1987-90
Danny Brough	209	2008-10
Ron Rylance	204	1941-50
Billy Stott	199	1944-48
Sam Lee	188	1937-39
Colin Maskill	165	1982-84
David March	157	1997-2007
Brad Davis	151	1996-97, 2001-03
Tommy Newbould	150	1902-15

316

MOST GOALS IN A SEASON

Neil Fox	163	1961-62
Neil Fox	146	1958-59
Neil Fox	140	1959-60
Neil Fox	138	1972-73
Neil Fox	132	1966-67
Neil Fox	124	1957-58
Garen Casey	119	1998
Kevin Harcombe	116	1987-88
Steve Diamond	115	1979-80
Neil Fox	113	1964-65

MOST GOALS IN A MATCH
Mark Conway   13 v Highfield, 27 October 1992

TOP POINTS SCORERS

Neil Fox	4,488	1956-69, 70-74
Charlie Pollard	1,425	1919-32
Jamie Rooney	968	2003-09
Mark Conway	865	1989-92
Frank Mortimer	855	1951-59
Ernest Pollard	800	1926-36
Jimmy Metcalfe	783	1897-1911
Terry Crook	782	1968-81
Ernest Bennett	679	1898-1914
Ron Rylance	669	1941-50
David Topliss	602	1968-81, 87-88
Steve Diamond	593	1978-81, 86-87
Fred Smith	564	1955-65
Leslie Hirst	499	1949-55
Brad Davis	495	1996-97, 2001-03
Danny Brough	489	2008-10
Billy Stott	488	1944-48
Kevin Harcombe	481	1987-90
David March	478	1997-2007
Jack Perry	469	1943-49

MOST POINTS IN A SEASON
Neil Fox   407   1961-62

MOST POINTS IN A MATCH
Jamie Rooney   36 v Chorley, 27 February 2004

HIGHEST SCORE
90-12 v Highfield, Regal Trophy prelim round, 27 October 1992

HIGHEST LEAGUE SCORE
78-9 v Batley, 26 August 1967

HIGHEST SUPER LEAGUE SCORE
68-6 v Halifax, 14 September 2003

HEAVIEST DEFEAT
Castleford 86 Trinity 0, 17 April 1995

HIGHEST ATTENDANCE
37,906, Huddersfield v Leeds, RL Challenge Cup semi-final, 21 March 1936

HIGHEST ATTENDANCE AT TRINITY MATCH
30,676, v Huddersfield, RL Challenge Cup, 26 February 1921

HIGHEST ATTENDANCE POST-WAR
28,524, v Wigan, RL Challenge Cup third round, 24 March 1962

HIGHEST ATTENDANCE SUPER LEAGUE
11,000, v Castleford, 16 September 2006

Mike Rylance has written extensively on rugby league, from national newspapers to magazines and yearbooks, both in Britain and France. The founding editor of *League Express*, he continues to contribute to that newspaper, as well as to *Rugby League World* magazine. He taught modern languages at Queen Elizabeth Grammar School, Wakefield for over thirty years and has an even longer association with the Trinity club. His previous book, *The Forbidden Game*, an investigation into the fate of rugby league under the war-time Vichy government, received considerable acclaim.